Sociology

Making Sense of the Social World

BARBARA MARLIENE SCOTT
Northeastern Illinois University

MARY ANN SCHWARTZ
Northeastern Illinois University

Allyn and Bacon

BOSTON   LONDON   TORONTO   SYDNEY   TOKYO   SINGAPORE

We dedicate this book to our marital partners, Roger Scott, Sr., and Richard Brewer, our families, friends, teachers, students, and especially to all the social change agents mentioned in this textbook. We also dedicate this book to the untold number of agents of change whose individual and collective efforts have made this a better world.

Editor-in-Chief, Social Sciences: Karen Hanson
Senior Editor: Jeff Lasser
Editorial Assistant: Susan Hutchinson
Developmental Editor: Sylvia Shepard
Marketing Manager: Brooke Stoner
Cover Administrator: Linda Knowles
Composition Buyer: Linda Cox

Manufacturing Buyer: Megan Cochran
Production Coordinator: Deborah Brown
Editorial-Production Service: Anne Rebecca Starr
Text Designer: Melinda Grosser for *silk*
Photo Researcher: Laurie Frankenthaler
Electronic Composition: Omegatype Typography, Inc.

Copyright © 2000 by Allyn and Bacon
A Pearson Education Company
160 Gould Street
Needham Heights, Massachusetts 02494

Internet: www.abacon.com

Between the time Web site information is gathered and then published, it is not unusual for some sites to have closed. Also, the transcription of URLs can result in unintended typographical errors. The publisher would appreciate notification where these occur so that they may be corrected in subsequent editions.

Library of Congress Cataloging-in-Publication Data
Scott, BarBara Marliene.
    Sociology : making sense of the social world / BarBara Marliene
Scott, Mary Ann Schwartz.
      p.   cm.
    Includes bibliographical references and index.
    ISBN 0-205-26780-7
    1. Sociology. 2. Social action.   I. Schwartz, Mary Ann.
  II. Title.
HM586.S36   1999
301—dc21   99–32261
                                 CIP

Printed in the United States of America
10 9 8 7 6 5 4 3 2   04 03 02 01 00

Photo Credits
p. 2, Richard Emblin/Black Star; p. 10, North Wind Picture Archives; p. 19, Library of Congress; p. 20, AP/Wide World Photos; p. 30, Courtesy of Robert D. Bullard; p. 33, Alan Carey/The Image Works;

Photo credits continue on page 526, which is considered an extension of the copyright page.

Contents

3 ⊚ Social Change, Collective Behavior, and Social Action   60

4 ⊚ The Dynamics of Social Behavior: Human Cultures   88

5 ⊚ Social Structure, Groups, and Organizations   112

6 ☉ Socialization: The Process of Becoming Human   138

7 ☉ Societies and Human Sexualities   166

10 ☯ Race, Ethnicity, and Structured Inequalities 262

11 ☯ Inequalities of Gender and Age 302

12 ☉ Marriages and Families: Intimacy in Social Life   334

13 ☉ Religion and Education   368

14 ☉ The Economy, Work, and Politics   404

15 ☉ Health, Illness, and the Delivery of Health Care   436

Epilogue ☯ Social Action: By Whom? Social Change: For Whom?   472

Preface

The idea for this book crystallized several years ago when we compared our growing dissatisfaction with introductory textbooks on the market because they did not facilitate or enhance our particular approach to introducing students to sociology. We wanted a textbook that had an accessible, reader-friendly writing style, that was engaging and student-oriented, that paid more than cursory attention to inclusiveness of diversity both in terms of the issues covered and in terms of the theory and research used, that encouraged critical thinking and student involvement in the social worlds in which students live, that integrated a cross-cultural perspective and, very important, that had a <u>feminist</u> perspective. In addition, we were also concerned that students in introductory sociology courses often expressed feelings of powerlessness and pessimism due to the nature of much of the subject matter (e.g., racism, inequality, poverty, crime, violence). We believe it is essential for us as educators and as sociologists to challenge these attitudes. Our focus on social change and social activism over the years as a primary method of teaching sociology has proven to be effective in challenging students' notions that "You can't fight City Hall." This focus is also empowering in that it enables students to move beyond a "victim analysis" view of the world and social experiences, to instead emphasize human agency and the power of individuals and groups to create/initiate and/or resist social change.

Our commitment to and excitement about educating students about sociology spans a combined sixty-plus years. During this time, we have focused not only on what sociologists do, but also on how sociology and sociological knowledge can be used in our everyday lives. Thus, we wrote this book not only as a means of addressing certain pedagogical issues, but also because we believe that the introductory course is, by far, the most important point at which to excite students about sociology. As students first encounter key sociological concepts, principles, theories, and contributions as well as its promise, sociology facilitates their abilities to view the world, their individual lives, as well as the challenges of the new millennium through its lens. In addition, we have collaborated for a long time in the courses we teach and the pedagogical strategies that we use, we share a common philosophical view of the teaching/learning process, and we have collaborated on another textbook, now in its third edition. Therefore, we bring to this textbook not only strong experience in classroom teaching, but also in writing for learning.

We believe that *Sociology: Making Sense of the Social World* offers a unique, creative, and timely approach to introducing students to sociology. Our approach is inclusive, theoretical, and student-oriented: (1) This text is *inclusive* of issues of race, class, gender, sexual orientation, and age—themes that are woven into every chapter of the book. We emphasize that these issues are central to sociology and integrate them throughout the textbook. In this regard, we focus on the link between social structure and people's own personal experiences to present material that is interesting and, more important, relevant to students' lives, thus encouraging stimulating and challenging classroom discussions. We have included the research of a wide variety of scholars who have had limited exposure in most introductory textbooks. (2) This text is *theoretical* in that it is rooted in social change theory. Throughout the textbook, beginning with chapter openers profiling an agent(s) of change, we explain sociology through the processes of individual (agency), collective (social movements), structural, historical, and global change. We emphasize that change is a two-way process—that students can initiate and influence the worlds in which they live in addition to being influenced by them. We also very consciously utilize a feminist approach, but not to the exclusion of other approaches. In this context, we introduce the dominant theoretical sociological and feminist paradigms in the beginning chapters of the book. We carry these theories throughout the book and critically evaluate them to help students see the strengths and weaknesses of each when applied to various topics. This approach helps students to gain a balanced view of the diversity within the discipline of sociology, and it enhances their ability to compare and contrast different explanatory systems. (3) This text is *student-oriented* in that it both consciously engages students as active agents in the teaching/learning process and challenges them to examine their personal belief systems and experiences as well as societal and theoretical views of the diverse experiences and lifestyles of all human beings.

Pedagogy

We have used several pedagogical strategies to facilitate student involvement in understanding the structures and functions of diverse social systems. Our chapter openers, Applying the Sociological Imagination exercises, boxes, and end-of-chapter study questions are all aimed at developing critical thinking skills. These features examine timely and often controversial aspects of social life and encourage students to reflect on and evaluate their knowledge of the social order.

Chapter Openers

Each chapter begins with a profile of an agent(s) of change that teachers can use to reinforce im-

portant chapter/course concepts and topics. These compelling real-life narratives about people from different walks of life invite readers to think sociologically about the issues covered in the chapter within the context of their own values, expectations, and experiences relevant to that topic. For example, in Chapter 1, we introduce Craig Keilburger, a young man whose interest in the murder of a Pakistani child his age led him to form an organization to fight the abuses of child labor. The experiences of Craig Keilburger and other agents of change illustrate the intimate connection between personal behavior and larger sociohistorical and structural features of social life. In addition, the chapter openers provide a historical context for social action and social change. Without this historical perspective, students often have difficulty interpreting the changes that are occurring around them and throughout the world.

Feature Boxes

Each chapter includes boxed features that add insight to and information about various concepts, themes, or theories presented in the chapter in which they appear. These boxes are designed to expand the reader's depth of knowledge as they enhance her or his encounter with the study of sociology.

Data Box   These boxes provide extended information on a topic covered in a given chapter. For example, in Chapter 5 we present extended information about human rights defenders and in Chapter 6 we present key statistics about the views and behaviors of today's adolescents. In addition to showing data from the Census Bureau and empirical studies, these boxes reflect important demographic and social trends. The data support the discussion of key concepts and patterns discussed in the textbook and they do so in a way that will not leave students overwhelmed by "sheer numbers."

Sociological Reflections   These boxes are designed to engage students in critical reflection and encourage critical thinking through the exploration of controversial issues or contemporary events and themes. For example, in Chapter 10 students are encouraged to think critically about the social construction of race and the role of government agencies in constructing race and ethnicity. In Chapter 12 they are invited to critically examine polygamy as a rising trend in suburban America. As others have pointed out, there is a reciprocal relationship between active learning and critical thinking. Therefore, the Sociological Reflections boxes facilitate the development or enhancement of critical thinking skills within a framework of active learning. At the end of each box, questions challenge students to critically analyze and/or evaluate a particular issue or topic, to apply various concepts and theories they have learned to that issue or topic or to think about and formulate solutions to particular issues or problems.

Cultural Snapshot   These boxes illustrate the interconnectedness of the world. They demonstrate similarities and differences across cultures, demonstrate how the sociological imagination helps us to understand social worlds beyond our national borders, and emphasize the importance of a global perspective. They also emphasize cultural diversity within the United States. Each Cultural Snapshot box focuses on a thought-provoking issue or topic such as cannibalism, gangsta rap, widowhood in India, and the Taliban of Afghanistan.

Sociology through Literature   These boxes use fiction to enrich the study of sociology and provide yet another springboard from which students can develop a more in-depth understanding of various sociological concepts. Almost forty years ago, sociologist Lewis Coser called attention to the wealth of sociologically relevant material available in literature, and we have increasingly used literature in our teaching to provide concrete examples of ongoing social processes and social behavior in our effort to illuminate abstract sociological theories and research. For example, in Chapter 10 we present an excerpt from the novel *Amistad* that combines historical scholarship with the art of literature to chronicle the real revolt by African slaves aboard a Spanish slave ship. The literary account presented in each box brings sociological concepts alive and provides the instructor with a creative way to present social issues (such as human beings as chattel property) and important sociological con-

cepts (such as social inequality) as well as to develop interesting classroom assignments.

Applying the Sociological Imagination

These in-chapter exercises enable students to become active participants in the teaching and learning process. These exercises are designed to help them learn to apply sociology to their everyday lives by *doing* sociology. Each exercise challenges students to think critically about some aspect of social life and to see the relationship between personal behavior and how society is organized and structured. For example, in Chapter 7, we challenge students to think critically about female genital mutilation and its relationship to female powerlessness and inequality. Other Applying the Sociological Imagination exercises examine contemporary as well as historical issues relative to topics covered in the chapters.

End-of-Chapter Material

At the end of each chapter, students will find a summary of the chapter's key points, a list of key terms and key people, a set of questions for discussion and review, suggestions for further reading that include both fiction and non-fiction sources, and a list of Internet resources. These aids are designed to facilitate a quick review of the material in the chapter and to encourage students to explore a variety of resources to expand their knowledge beyond the contents of this textbook.

Key Points to Remember   These lists provide a quick review for students by presenting a brief, concise reexamination of main chapter topics, points, and/or themes in an easy-to-read format. These summaries highlight and reinforce the most important concepts and issues presented in the chapter and allow the reader to review the chapter material in a systematic way.

For Further Reading, Sociology through Literature, and Internet Resources   At the end of each chapter, we have provided lists of additional resources that students can use to expand their knowledge of key topics and issues. These lists contain a variety of resources aimed at encouraging students to dig a bit deeper into the exciting world of sociology. The "For Further Reading" lists add depth to the material discussed in each chapter, while the suggested novels provide students with another arena in which to apply their sociological imaginations. The Internet resources provide Web sites ranging from governmental agencies to activist organizations, allowing students to gain technological skills as well as to explore ideas and issues on their own.

Key Terms and Key People   Important terms and concepts that help students understand and analyze issues and topics from a sociological perspective are boldfaced and defined in the text. These key terms are listed at the end of each chapter and defined in the glossary at the end of the book to facilitate the study and review process. The names of various people whose work is critical to understanding particular topics or issues and/or who have made outstanding contributions within particular topical areas are also listed at the end of each chapter.

Questions for Review and Discussion   Every chapter includes a set of questions that promote critical thinking skills. As we have already indicated, we think it is imperative to give students every possible opportunity to develop and/or enhance their critical thinking skills. These end-of-chapter questions are thought-provoking and require the reader to do more than simply memorize and regurgitate information they have learned in a particular chapter.

Epilogue

We end this book with the same personal touch we began it with. In the epilogue, we tie together its emphasis on social activism and social change to provide students with a practical framework and examples of how to become active agents of change if they so choose. We welcome any reader of this textbook to share her or his experiences of social activism and social change with us by contacting us at Northeastern Illinois University, 5500 North St. Louis Avenue, Chicago, IL 60625, or by e-mail at: b-scott1@neiu.edu or m-schwartz@neiu.edu. We believe, after all, that each of us has the power and potential to change some aspect of society, no matter how big or small.

Supplements

The following supplements are available for instructors:

- **Instructor's Resource Manual/Test Bank.** Written by Jackie Fellows of Riverland Community College, the *Instructor's Resource Manual/Test Bank* provides an overview and summary, teaching objectives, outlines, key terms and people, lecture and discussion ideas, and a variety of test questions (multiple choice, fill-in-the-blank, true-false, and essay) for every chapter in the text.
- **Computerized Testing.** Allyn and Bacon Test Manager (for DOS, Windows, and Macintosh) is an integrated suite of testing and assessment tools. Professors can create professional-looking exams in just minutes by building tests from the existing database of questions, by editing questions, or by writing your own. Course management features include a class roster, gradebook, and item analysis. Test Manager also has everything you need to create and administer online tests.
- **Allyn and Bacon Transparencies for Introductory Sociology II.** This set of one hundred color acetates illustrates key sociology concepts through graphs, tables, charts, and lecture outlines.
- **PowerPoint Presentation.** This software for Windows contains ready-to-use text and graphic images designed specifically for this book, enabling a professor to create complete multimedia presentations in the classroom. PowerPoint software is not required; a PowerPoint Viewer is included to access the images.
- **Sociology Digital Media Archive.** This CD-ROM for Windows and Macintosh contains hundreds of resources to incorporate into multimedia presentations: lecture outlines, graphs, tables, charts, maps, video clips, and Web links.
- **Allyn and Bacon Interactive Video for Introductory Sociology, © 2000.** This custom video features both national and global topics. The up-to-the-minute video segments are great for launching lectures, sparking

classroom discussion, and encouraging critical thinking. The accompanying video user's guide provides detailed descriptions of each video segment, specific tie-ins to the text, and suggested discussion questions and projects.

- **A&B Video Library.** Qualified adopters may select from a wide variety of high-quality videos from such sources as Films for the Humanities and Sciences and Annenberg/CPB.
- *Learning by Doing Sociology: In-Class Experiential Exercises.* Written by Linda Stoneall of University of Wisconsin at Whitewater, this manual offers step-by-step procedures for numerous in-class activities, general suggestions for managing experiential learning, and trouble-shooting tips. It contains twenty-two exercises on a broad range of topics covered in introductory sociology courses.
- *The Blockbuster Approach: A Guide to Teaching Sociology with Video.* Written by Casey Jordan of Western Connecticut State University, this manual provides extensive lists and descriptions of hundreds of commercially available videos, and shows how they can be incorporated into the classroom.

The following supplements are available for students:

- **Study Guide.** Written by Jackie Fellows of Riverland Community College, the study guide provides summaries, learning objectives, outlines, key terms and people, and self-test questions with answers for every chapter in the text.
- **Allyn & Bacon Quick Guide to the Internet for Sociology.** This handy reference provides a general overview of using the Internet, plus information about sociology on the Internet, lists of useful URLs, and ideas for research.
- **Web Site.** Both professors and students can access the specific site to accompany this book at <www.abacon.com/scott>.
- *The Essential Sociology Reader.* Edited by Professor Robert Thompson of Minot State University, this "essential" anthology consists of sixteen readings in sociol-ogy. An introduction to each reading provides a context for the selection, and discussion questions appear at the end of each article.

- *Careers in Sociology,* **Second Edition.** Written by Professor W. Richard Stephens, Jr., of Greenville College, this supplement goes beyond the academic career path to explore careers in applied sociology. It examines how people currently working as sociologists entered the field, and how a degree in sociology can be a preparation for careers in areas such as law, gerontology, social work, and the computer industry.
- *Breaking the Ice: A Guide to Understanding People from Other Cultures,* **Second Edition.** This guide helps students better understand and interact with people from other cultures, encouraging them to react and draw upon their experiences. Drawing upon her own personal experience as a Ugandan-born woman living in the United States, Professor Daisy Kabagarama of Wichita State University uses examples to illustrate behavior in different cultures. Numerous exercises are included to help the reader discover and deal with her or his own biases.
- *Thinking Sociologically: A Critical Thinking Activities Manual,* **Second Edition.** Written by Professor Josephine Ruggiero of Providence College, this book contains a series of twelve related exercises that focus on helping students to improve their critical thinking skills. Through these exercises, they will learn how to identify and challenge commonly held assumptions, and how to better understand and use the sociological perspective. The exercises are arranged to allow students to build increasingly more complex skills to help them think sociologically.
- *Doing Sociology with Student CHIP: Data Happy!,* **Second Edition,** and *Analyzing Social Issues: A Workbook with Student CHIP Software.* Written by Gregg Lee Carter of Bryant College, these workbooks provide students with the opportunity to explore sociological issues using real data.

- ***Hands On Sociology,*** **Revised and Expanded Edition.** Written by William Feigelman of Nassau Community College, this workbook shows students how to use STATA statistical software to analyze actual social data drawn from various archival sociological data sources.

Acknowledgments

Although our names appear on the cover of this textbook, its publication would not have been possible without the commitment of time and energy and the collaboration of many people. First and foremost, we thank our families for their patience, loyalty, good humor, understanding, and encouragement that kept us centered and allowed us the space to complete this project. They were angelic in their understanding of our sometimes short tempers, the long days away from them as we collaborated on various aspects of this book, the many nights we burned the midnight oil while they tried to sleep, and the frantic pace of our lives as we struggled to meet our deadlines. In a very real sense, our students are co-authors in this enterprise. Their many questions, responses, and classroom presentations challenged us to find more meaningful ways to introduce them to the fascinating study of sociology.

We would also like to thank the skilled librarians at Northeastern Illinois University for their invaluable assistance. We are especially indebted to librarians Richard Higginbotham and Patrice Stearley who, like modern-day sleuths, tracked down numerous references and uncovered useful and new resources for us. No matter when we called upon them or what we requested of them, they came through for us. We also wish to acknowledge the significant contribution to our research provided by Misty Sienkowski, the graduate assistant in the Sociology department at Northeastern Illinois University. Misty's skills on the Internet rarely failed to turn up interesting and relevant information for our research. A special thanks, too, to Arlene Benzinger, Administrative Aide and Office Manager in the Sociology department at Northeastern Illinois University, who provided us with unwavering support and important help in ways too numerous to list here. One million thanks to you, Arlene. Words cannot express how grateful we are, but each time you see us, just check out our faces. And thanks to the Sociology department's student workers, Rania Azroui and Erica Yanez, who, despite the demands of office work and a full load of classes each semester, always made themselves available to help us in any way we needed and did so cheerfully. We are indeed grateful for their assistance and support.

Moreover, the support of many talented people at Allyn and Bacon is reflected in the pages of this textbook. In particular, we owe a huge debt of gratitude to Karen Hanson, Editor-in-Chief, Social Sciences, for her extraordinary patience and long-standing support, as well as her unwavering commitment (through thick and thin) to seeing that this book became a reality. Karen's sometimes firm, sometimes gentle, prodding, her wise and thoughtful insights and advice, and her sheer will and perseverance kept us on track (although not always on deadline). We are grateful to Sylvia Shepard, our developmental editor, who provided wise counsel and many helpful suggestions as this textbook unfolded. Our thanks also to Anne Starr, production editor, who set our priorities and kept us organized, and who, along with Leslie Brunetta, copyeditor, challenged us on many occasions to sharpen our thoughts, rethink an issue or topic, reconceptualize or rearticulate a point to provide further clarity, or to simply discard what we came to agree was less meaningful narrative. Clearly, we feel their skills, creativity, and wide-ranging knowledge have made this a better book. Jo-Anne Naples, permissions editor, as well as a host of others (for example, photo researcher, illustrator, designer, and so on) have also contributed significantly to the successful completion of this book. To them we are also grateful.

Finally, we extend our thanks to all of our colleagues who devoted time, energy, and effort to reviewing some portion of this book. We are grateful for their timely, thoughtful, and often extensive comments and suggestions. We took them very seriously and they certainly helped us avoid major mistakes and weaknesses while enhancing our ability to draw upon the strengths of the manuscript. We hope they will see the fruits of their labor throughout the pages of this book. They are Matilda Barker, Cerritos College;

Clifford Broman, Michigan State University; Carol D. Chenault, Calhoun Community College; Michael Fraleigh, Bryant College; Lisa M. Frehill, New Mexico State University; Michael Kimmel, State University of New York at Stony Brook; Patricia A. Larson, Cleveland State University; Judith K. Luebke, Mankato State University; Thomas H. Shey, Chapman University; Kathleen A. Tiemann, University of North Dakota; Pelgy Vaz, Fort Hays State University; Theodore C. Wagenaar, Miami University.

Last, but certainly not least, as always we wish to acknowledge and thank each other for a spirited and always enlightening collaboration. Although each of us individually could have written an introductory sociology textbook, neither of us could have written *this* book alone. As with all of our work together, this truly has been a collaborative effort in every sense of the term. We have spent numerous hours together discussing, writing, rewriting, and yes, sometimes arguing about, key issues and ideas. Our differ-

ent racial backgrounds have helped us to be more sensitive to issues of diversity, racial/ethnic myths, and styles of expression. In all these interactions, we have grown tremendously as sociologists, teachers, and most important, as friends. This collaboration has and continues to be intellectually stimulating and fun.

Keeping in Touch

It is our hope to have a second edition of this textbook. With that in mind, we invite you to share your suggestions, questions, and comments with us as you use this book. We welcome your reactions and constructive advice. You can contact us by e-mail at b-scott1@neiu. and m-schwartz@neiu.edu.

BarBara Marliene Scott
Mary Ann Schwartz

About the Authors

BarBara Marliene Scott earned a B.A. in Sociology and two masters degrees: a Master's of Arts in Sociology and a Master's of Philosophy from Roosevelt University, Chicago. She earned a Ph.D. in Sociology from Northwestern University, Evanston, Illinois. Professor Scott is Chairperson of the Department of Sociology, Criminal Justice, Social Work, and Women's Studies at Northeastern Illinois University. She also served as the Acting Coordinator of Northeastern's Women's Studies Program and Coordinator of the General Education Program. She is a long-time union activist and a former union chapter vice president. She is actively involved in the movement aimed at integrating race, class, gender, and sexual orientation into the college curriculum. She often gives lectures with a slide presentation examining the intersection of race, class, and gender in print advertising.

Her teaching and research interests include marriage and family, introductory sociology, sociological and feminist theory, and sociology of racism, Africana women, gender, and media; racial identity and the politics of inclusion; African American women's activism, including agency, identification, and oppositional consciousness; mass media and popular culture, and the migration patterns of African Americans in the United States.

Dr. Mary Ann Schwartz is a Professor of Sociology and Women's Studies at Northeastern Illinois University. She earned a B.A. in Sociology and History from Alverno College, Milwaukee, Wisconsin; a Masters of Science in Sociology from the Illinois Institute of Technology, Chicago, and a Ph.D. in Sociology from Northwestern University, Evanston, Illinois. Professor Schwartz has been actively involved in improving the academic climate for women; she was a co-founder of the Women's Studies Program at Northeastern, where she also served as department chairperson. A long-time union activist, she served as union president at Northeastern and later as legislative director for her union's Local. She is currently the editor of *Universities 21,* a newsletter devoted to sharing ideas on academic issues. She also serves as a faculty consultant to the Network for Curriculum Infusion, an organization that presents workshops across the country on how to integrate substance abuse prevention strategies into the college curriculum.

Her research and teaching interests are marriage and family, socialization, nonmarital lifestyles, work, aging, and the structured relationships of race, class, and gender.

Sociology

Making Sense of
the Social World

An Introduction to Sociology

AGENT OF CHANGE: CRAIG KEILBURGER

In 1995, although they never met one another, the life histories of two young boys, one from Pakistan, the other from Canada, crossed. Iqbal Masih, a twelve-year-old, was gunned down while visiting relatives in a rural village. When Iqbal was four years old, his parents sold him into bondage to a village carpet maker for about sixteen dollars. For six years, he worked fourteen hours a day, six days a week, living on an inadequate diet and subject to frequent beatings. At the age of ten, he managed to escape. Befriended by members of a human-rights organization, the Bonded Labor Liberation Front, Iqbal gained his freedom and started school. For the next two years, until he was murdered, he spoke out against the abuses of child labor. Many believe he was killed to silence his criticisms.

Halfway around the world, Craig Keilburger, a grade-school student in Toronto, Ontario, read about Iqbal Masih's death. He saw that he and Iqbal were the same age, and he was shocked by the differences in their lives. Sensing the injustice done to Iqbal and millions of other children like him, Craig talked to his teachers and classmates. With their help, he founded an organization of children aged ten to sixteen, called Free the Children, to advocate for children's rights. Craig convinced his parents to let him take a seven-week trip to India and Pakistan, where he met and talked with child laborers his age and younger. Among the child laborers he met were:

- an eight-year-old girl who worked in a recycling plant separating used syringes and needles for their plastics. She wore no shoes or gloves, and no one had told her of the dangers of her work.

- two brothers, one seven and one fourteen, who worked in a carpet factory and were paid the equivalent of twenty cents a day, which they were forced to exchange for food. In effect, they earned no money.

- a seven-year-old boy who worked in the hot sun making clay bricks from sunup to sundown.

Source: Most of the information is from two sources: S. Greenhouse. 1996. "Child-Labor Abuses Draw Youthful Protest." *New York Times* (December 25): B1, B4; "A Children's Crusade." 1996. In M. Reecer, "Children without Childhoods." *American Educator* (Summer): 23.

The Sociological Imagination

Although Craig Keilburger was probably unaware of it at the time he founded Free the Children, his actions reflect what sociologist C. Wright Mills (1959) called the **sociological imagination,** the ability to see how individual experiences are connected to the larger society. It is tempting to see child labor in other countries simply as a necessity, as a way to help families survive. However, the fact is that children are being hired rather than adults, denied an education, and forced to live in conditions that threaten their health and well-being. According to Kailash Satyarthis, a human rights activist, "In India there are 50 million child laborers, but there are 55 million adults unemployed" (quoted in Ryan, 1993, p. 62). Factory owners hire children because they are a cheaper source of labor and are easier to intimidate and control than adults.

The sociological imagination allows us to distinguish between what Mills calls "personal troubles of milieu" and the "public issues of social structure." According to Mills, a "trouble" is a private matter, occurring within the character of the individual and within the range of his or her immediate relationship with others. So for Iqbal, his personal troubles meant being separated from those he loved, being unable to attend school, and having to work under harsh and even life-threatening conditions with little hope of relief from these surroundings. An "issue," however, is a public matter that transcends the individual's local environment. Craig Keilburger and his classmates did further research and found that Iqbal's situation was not unique. Rather, they found that Iqbal's situation is far too

common. According to the International Labor Organization, between 100 million and 250 million children under the age of fifteen work. More than 95 percent of these children live in the developing world, many of them making minimum wages as bonded laborers working under life-threatening conditions. They are denied an education and even a childhood. These can be seen as structural problems caused by the ways in which economic and social opportunities are organized in an increasingly global economy.

According to Mills, many of the conditions individuals experience today, such as child labor, poverty, divorce, and unemployment, are due to structural arrangements in a society. Thus, to understand the changes that affect our personal lives requires us to look beyond our private experiences to the larger political, social, and economic issues that affect our lives and the lives of others in our society and around the globe. Mills believed that in order to understand our own life chances and those of others, we had to become aware of the broad social events and trends surrounding us. This means becoming aware of history and biography (people's location in the social structure of their society) as well as the relations between the two. To do this requires asking three questions: (1) What is the structure of a particular society, and how does it differ from other varieties of social order? (2) Where does this society stand in human history, and what are its essential features? (3) What varieties of women and men live in this society and in this period, and what is happening to them?

These three questions constitute the core of the sociological imagination. Such a perspective can help us to understand the social forces that shape people's lives and why, for example, a Craig Keilburger is attending school while an Iqbal Masih is a bonded laborer. On a personal level, using the sociological imagination can help us to understand much of what occurs in our daily lives, for example, patterns of dating, marriage, divorce, or employment opportunities. On a societal level, the sociological imagination can also help us to perceive ways in which we as individuals and as members of social groups can act to change the social world in which we live. After learning Iqbal Masih's story and that of millions of others like him, fourteen-year-old Dianna English was moved to take action. She collected $180 in a bake sale and 400 signatures on a petition calling for a ban on importing products made by child labor. Her explanation for her actions reflects a sociological imagination:

> It's something that is affecting children my age, who, except for being from a different family and country, are no different from me. I could have easily been in their position. As a person who has a house and goes to school and is not working 16 hours a day, I have a responsibility to help them. (Greenhouse, 1996, p. A10).

Dianna English's insight reflects what sociologist Peter Berger described as a process of critical thinking, or *debunking*—asking questions, evaluating evidence, and checking for biases (our own and others). He points out, however, that not everyone is comfortable doing this. Questioning taken-for-granted assumptions can be threatening or unsettling to some people. Berger warns that "people who prefer to believe that society is just what they were taught in Sunday school, who like the safety of what Alfred Schuetz has called the 'world-taken-for-granted,' should stay away from sociology" (1963, p. 24). In his book *An Invitation to Sociology,* Berger suggested, "It can be said that the first wisdom of sociology is this— things are not what they seem. Social reality turns out to have many different layers of meaning. The discovery of each new layer changes the perception of the whole" (1963, p. 23).

Berger compares thinking sociologically to entering a new and unfamiliar society in which there is the "sudden illumination of new and unsuspected facets of human existence in society" (1963, p. 23). If you are curious about human beings, if you are willing to look behind the scenes

to discover the different levels of meaning that human behavior often has, Berger and we invite you to join the sociological enterprise.

Applying the Sociological Imagination

The study of sociology requires us to learn a new way of thinking about the world in which we live. Here are five erroneous but commonly held beliefs: (1) Most sexual assaults and rapes are committed by strangers. (2) Distributing contraceptives to teenagers through school clinics will push them to be more sexually active. (3) Older workers are less productive than younger workers. (4) The incidence of homosexuality in the United States is higher today than it was fifty years ago. (5) The high divorce rate in the United States shows that marriage is no longer popular.

Pick any one of these false beliefs and find a research study dealing with that topic. What are the results of the study? Why do you think people continue to hold this false belief even in the face of contradictory evidence?

Defining Sociology

One of the defining features of sociology is its focus on people living in a social context rather than as isolated individuals. In a society like the United States, where individualism is highly valued, we tend to see ourselves as unique individuals making free and independent choices and having distinct personal experiences. Although this is true to some degree, we must also understand that our lives are intimately connected with others, that our choices are often constrained, and that our experiences are part of the larger **social structure,** relatively permanent patterns of interaction and relationships found within a society. For example, your choice to attend this school was affected by a number of social factors—income, previous educational experiences, family background, and geographical location. **Sociology,** then, is the systematic study of human social behavior, groups, and societies and how these change over time. Let's examine the elements of this definition more fully.

The term *systematic study* refers to the way sociologists collect, analyze, and explain data (information) about human social behavior. For example, Mitchell Duneier (1992) spent several years observing and talking to a small group of African American men who met regularly at the Valois Cafeteria in Chicago's Hyde Park neighborhood. The analysis of his data, published as *Slim's Table,* challenged commonly accepted stereotypes of working-class men and analyzed the crucial interplay between standards of moral worth and feelings of self-esteem.

A *group* consists of two or more people who interact frequently within a structured situation and who share a common purpose and identity. Much of what we do, feel, and think centers around the groups to which we belong—families, friends, gangs, political parties, labor unions, and sports teams, to name a few.

The concept of *society* refers to people who live in a specific geographic territory, interact together, and share a common culture and identity. Societies vary across time and place and along a number of different economic, political, cultural, and social dimensions. For example, much of Africa is agricultural, while Germany is highly industrialized. Saudi Arabia is extremely wealthy, while Nicaragua is quite poor. Some societies are homogeneous like Japan, where the vast majority of the population shares the same ethnic traditions, while others are more heterogeneous, or diverse, like the United States, which is composed of people from a wide variety of racial and ethnic backgrounds.

The last element of our definition, *social change,* is probably no stranger to you. Think for a moment of how computers have altered our lives. They have opened up vast new opportunities to communicate with people around the globe and created new recreational and job opportunities. At the same time, however, they have also created new divisions in society between those who have access to them and those who do not. Human behavior, groups, and societies are never completely static, yet the rate at which and the ways in which they are altered over time vary tremendously.

In sum, sociology seeks to understand how patterns of behavior are established, maintained, and changed over time. Thus, the scope of sociology is extremely broad, ranging from the study of dyads (two-person groups) to the study of to-tal societies. However, sociology is not the only social science interested in the study of human behavior. As we can see in the Sociological Reflections Box, although they share the same basic subject matter, each of the social sciences has a distinct focus and concentrates on different aspects of human behavior.

Pre- and Nonscientific Ways of Looking at the World

We pointed out earlier that having a sociological imagination requires a distinct way of looking at the world. For many of you, this way of thinking about human behavior will be new and challenging. We think it is worth the effort. With Mills, we believe that for people to understand the world around them and to have more control over their lives, they need to develop and to be able to apply the sociological imagination. The benefits of this approach will become clearer when we compare it to other ways of looking at the world.

Imagine the uncertainty and challenges faced by the first humans. Like us, they must have questioned the world around them and worried about coping with unfamiliar situations. No doubt, they, too, constructed theories to explain why some people sickened and died while others lived, why vegetation and small game were sometimes plentiful and other times scarce. Like many of us, they relied on their own experiences, common sense, and religious beliefs to answer their questions and to provide guidelines for organizing their lives. These ways of knowing can be useful and can provide comfort. However, as the following discussion illustrates, knowledge gained in these ways is often inaccurate or unreliable.

Common Sense Throughout the ages, people have relied on knowledge gained from personal experience to help them understand human behavior. Common sense, or what we often think of as the obvious, can be very useful in our everyday lives. You know not to touch something hot. This commonsense notion probably arose after someone shared the painful learning experience of getting burned. Unfortunately, commonsense notions are not always true.

Sociological Reflections

Sociology and the Other Social Sciences

Sociology does not have a monopoly on the study of human behavior. Other disciplines are equally interested in studying how human beings behave. All of the social sciences, including sociology, share two common assumptions: (1) human behavior is patterned, and (2) these patterns can be discovered and understood through the use of the scientific method. Although there is some overlap in what is studied, each discipline has its own distinct focus.

Sociology is the broadest of the social sciences in that it focuses on the totality of group life rather than on specific segments of social life. Walter Gove (1995) believes that this fact places sociology in a unique position vis-à-vis the other social sciences in that sociology can be an integrative discipline, drawing together the knowledge gained by all of the other social sciences into a more comprehensive explanation of human behavior. Insights into human behavior are enriched by taking an interdisciplinary approach to understanding it. Sociology also has the unique advantage of being able to take itself as an object of study.

Social Science	Focus
Psychology	Individuals, including their thoughts, emotions, perceptions, and behaviors
Economics	Human behavior in relationship to the production, exchange, distribution, and consumption of goods and services
Political Science	Power, government, voting behavior, and public administration
Anthropology	Culture, for example, the way of life of a people, most typically less technologically developed societies or subgroups within modern societies
History	Past events, either of a unique and singular nature or in comparison to other similar events

In this chapter and throughout this textbook, we will examine some of the social forces that have influenced various sociologists and, in turn, how they themselves influenced the way in which knowledge was constructed.

Throughout this textbook, we will identify a considerable number of commonsense ideas people currently hold about our social world that, under examination, turn out to be false. For example, many people believe that the majority of welfare recipients are African Americans. The reality is that the majority of people receiving welfare are white. College students often express the view that living together before marriage increases the likelihood of having a stable marriage. To the contrary, however, some researchers have found that cohabitation prior to marriage actually increases the probability of divorce (Hall & Zhao, 1995).

In addition, commonsense notions can be contradictory. Think about the advice you might receive if a significant person in your life had to relocate. Some will say, "Absence makes the heart grow fonder," while others will say, "Out of sight, out of mind." Which advice is closest to the truth? The answer is, "It depends." Alfie Kohn's (1988) research suggests an answer. People who are deeply involved with one another tend to weather separations, but those whose romantic relationships are not as deep or serious do not. Of course, not all commonsense ideas are inaccurate. Most people probably wonder why researchers bother to study the relationship between social class and rates of prison incarceration. "Doesn't everyone know that there are more poor than rich people in jail?" Although the answer to this question is yes, sociological analysis not only enables us to check commonsense notions like this against social reality but also provides us with a framework for understanding the causes of such relationships.

Religion Throughout history, many ideas about human social existence were based on a belief in supernatural beings and unchanging natural laws. When someone died or when crops failed, early humans were likely to see it as a result of some supernatural force. Although these beliefs were not scientific, they often had beneficial effects. One current example concerns the role of faith in the healing process. Initial research findings indicate that severely ill patients who identify themselves as religious do better on average than patients who do not see themselves as very religious (Idler & Kasl, 1992). On the other hand, adherence to a religious belief system can have negative effects as well. Today, as in the past, most religious people do not question or challenge the reality, truth, or authenticity of the teachings of their particular religion. In fact, challenging existing beliefs may lead to severe punishment and even death. For example, in the early seventeenth century, the Italian astronomer Galileo supported the views of the Polish mathematician Copernicus that the earth and all the other planets revolved around the sun. This view was contrary to Church teachings that the earth was the center of the universe. Threatening to brand him a heretic, Church authorities forced Galileo to retract his heliocentric view. A more recent example occurred in 1989 after writer Salman Rushdie published *The Satanic Verses,* a book that fundamentalist Muslim leaders in Iran felt was blasphemous. Rushdie lived the next nine years in hiding because of a death threat imposed by the Ayatollah Khomeini, then Iran's supreme religious leader. It was only in 1998 that the Iranian government dissociated itself from this fatwa (or religious edict).

Philosophy and Rational Proof Early Greek philosophers, such as Socrates, Plato, and Aristotle, recognized that the truth or falsehood of an idea could not be determined based solely on common sense or religious beliefs. The truth of an idea does not depend on whose idea it is or on the position that person holds or on what a culture teaches its members. Rather, they argued, truth can be arrived at only through rational proof, a careful evaluation of the quality of reasoning that led to an idea.

This evaluation is conducted using the rules of logic in a process that questions our preconceived assumptions, sees if they contain any contradictions, compares them to other evidence, and evaluates whether our conclusions make sense in this light. If an idea cannot withstand this scrutiny, it probably is not true and should be rejected or at least viewed with skepticism until new supporting evidence can be found. If, however, the idea survives this process, we can have some confidence that there is some truth to it. As we shall see shortly, this emphasis on proof became a powerful tool in Western thought and contributed to the development of both the natural and the social sciences.

The rational proof process is not as easy as it sounds. From birth on, we are taught the "truth" as seen by our parents, peers, and religious, political, and cultural leaders. As we will see in Chapter 6, these socialization experiences become deeply embedded in our views of ourselves and of the world. When we encounter a new idea—for example, concerning the origin of homosexuality—or someone challenges our existing beliefs—for example, on welfare—we typically demand proof of the new idea or of the challenges. But we rarely demand proof of the beliefs we already hold (Charon, 1995).

Just as we question some of the ways of looking at the world, we also need to be open to the possibility of using alternative ways in order to enhance our knowledge. A good example of this latter principle is the working together of Western-trained scientists and the Shamans of the Amazon rain forest. Ethnobotanist Mark Plotkin (1994) routinely travels to South America to learn about plants known to native healers. He believes that the traditional healing methods that rely on nature and tribal spirits can be effective in treating a variety of ailments. In fact, Plotkin tells the story of how Western medical specialists tried unsuccessfully for years to cure his chronic elbow tendinitis with a variety of techniques but to no avail. After he allowed an Amazon tribal healer to treat it with plants and chants, the pain stopped and has not returned.

Sociology through Literature   There is yet another way of knowing that can enrich our study of social life. Lewis Coser (1963) called attention to the wealth of sociologically relevant material available in literature. Although he cautioned that creative writing is not a substitute for scientific and analytic knowledge, he recognized that literature can provide concrete examples of ongoing social processes that can help to illuminate abstract sociological theory and research. A little later in this chapter, we will see how the discipline of sociology emerged in response to major social upheavals brought on by the social processes of industrialization and urbanization. By reading Herman Melville's descriptions of the extreme poverty existing in nineteenth-century Liverpool, we can gain a more vivid understanding of the social dislocation that accompanied the transition to an urban industrial society and that informed the theoretical perspectives of the early founders of sociology (see Sociology through Literature box). Throughout this

Sociology through Literature

The Shame of Liverpool

In the following excerpt from his book *Redburn* (1849), Herman Melville describes some of the wretched conditions endured by many of the urban poor in the nineteenth century. When we consider the millions of homeless people in cities around the world today, Melville's description of Liverpool has a distinctly modern ring.

> In going to our boarding-house, the Sign of the Baltimore Clipper, I generally passed through a narrow street called "Launcelott's-Hey," lined with dingy, prison-like cotton warehouses. In this street, or rather alley, you seldom see any one but a truck-man, or some solitary old warehouse-keeper, haunting his smoky den like a ghost.
>
> Once, passing through this place, I heard a feeble wail, which seemed to come out of the earth. It was but a strip of crooked side-walk where I stood; the dingy wall was on every side, converting the mid-day into twilight; and not a soul was in sight. I started, and could almost have run when I heard that dismal sound. At last I advanced to an opening which communicated downward with deep tiers of cellars beneath a crumbling old warehouse; and there, some fifteen feet below the walk, crouching in nameless squalor, with her head bowed over, was the figure of what had been a woman. Her blue arms folded to her livid bosom two shrunken things like children, that leaned toward her, one at each side. At first, I knew not whether they were alive or dead. They made no sign; they did not move or stir: but from the vault came that soul-sickening wail.

> I made a noise with my foot, which in the silence, echoed far and near; but there was no response. Louder still; when one of the children lifted its head, and cast upward a faint glance; then closed its eyes, and lay motionless. The woman also, now gazed up, and perceived me; but let fall her eye again. They were dumb and next to dead with want. How they had crawled into that den, I could not tell; but there they had crawled to die. At that moment I never thought of relieving them; for death was so stamped in their glazed and imploring eyes, that I almost regarded them as already no more. I stood looking down on them, while my whole soul swelled within me; and I asked myself, What right had any body in the wide world to smile and be glad, when sights like this were to be seen: It was enough to turn the heart to gall; and make a man-hater of Howard. For who were these ghosts that I saw? Were they not human beings? A woman and two girls? With eyes, and lips, and ears like any queen? with hearts which, though they did not pound with blood, yet beat with a dull, dead ache that was their life.

How might you explain Launcelott's-Hey using the sociological imagination? In your opinion, who suffered the most from industrialization? Who benefited? Compare and contrast life in nineteenth-century Liverpool and urban inner cities today.

Source: H. Melville. 1849. *Redburn: His First Voyage.* Republished by Doubleday Anchor Books, Garden City, NY, 1957, pp. 173–174.

textbook, whenever appropriate, we will use excerpts from literature to provide concrete examples of complex and abstract sociological concepts.

The Development of Sociology

Although there continued to be many ways of viewing the social world, major societal changes and trends in the eighteenth and early nineteenth centuries gave way to a new scientific way of explaining social phenomena. Three of these historic trends are especially notable: (1) industrialization and urbanization, (2) European imperialism, and (3) the influence of the natural sciences, especially biology. Although some of the tenets of sociological thought have always been with us, it was not until the nineteenth century that sociology emerged as a formal discipline.

Industrialization refers to the process by which whole societies were transformed from reliance on human and animal power and handmade products to reliance upon machines and other advanced technology. **Urbanization,** on the other hand, refers both to the process by which masses of people moved from rural to urban areas and to the increase in urban influence over all areas of culture and society (see the Data Box). Changes brought about by these social revolutions had a profound effect on the living and working conditions of individuals and families. For example, with the rise of industrial factories, masses of individuals and whole families moved from rural areas to cities to work in them, breaking their traditional ties to the land, their ancestors, and their traditional ways of life. This led to many other changes, both in individual family life and in as society as a whole.

Although the positive aspects of industrialization and urbanization are many, these processes also led to the emergence of many new

In the 1870s, both women and men were employed in factories where they worked long hours in closely supervised, often airless, unhealthy conditions. In textile mills such as this, accidents were frequent, but workers were afforded no compensation when they couldn't work because of injuries.

" WARRANTED 200 YARDS."

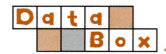

The Growth of Urbanization and Industrialization

- In 1800, 97 percent of the world's population lived in rural areas. The remaining 3 percent lived in communities of 5,000 or more (Hauser & Schnore, 1965). Today, 50 percent lives in urban areas.
- In 1800, 94 percent of the U.S. population lived in rural areas; 6 percent lived in towns of 2,500 or more. By 1920, the population was equally divided between rural and urban areas. Today, 75 percent of the U.S. population lives in cities (U.S. Bureau of the Census, 1994).
- In 1820, approximately 80 percent of U.S. workers were employed in agriculture; by 1990, fewer than 3 percent were employed in agriculture (U.S. Bureau of the Census, 1975; 1992).

social problems, for example anonymity, inadequate housing, crowded cities, unsanitary and unhealthy work and living conditions, and high rates of poverty, pollution, and criminal behavior. In rural areas, family members had worked together to produce what they needed to survive. In cities, because of low wages, even very young children had to work long hours in often unfriendly, unsanitary, and hazardous factories with no job security or protection from workplace accidents or other illnesses caused by the work environment. In some factories, children were chained to the machines to prevent them from running away. (As you learned in the opening section of this chapter, child labor continues to be a problem in many countries around the world.) As a number of European scholars and social thinkers observed these emerging social ills, they set the framework for the early development of sociology.

European imperialism, the policy of extending a nation's territory and power through conquest, colonization, and domination of other nations, exposed Europeans to an array of cultures very different from their own. This exposure led some scholars to ask questions and develop theories about how cultures evolved and what caused them to differ. At the same time, use of the scientific method—objective, systematic observations used to test theories—in the natural sciences was transforming knowledge and the world. People began to question the rele-vancy of various philosophical, theological, and lay explanations of social life. They asked: What is the nature of human beings? Under what conditions do people live? What or how do people think? What is the nature of human societies? What causes society to change and how can we account for periods of relative stability? What is the relationship between the individual and society? These questions not only encouraged but also required thoughtful explanations of what was going on in the world. Thus, as these scholars pondered the changing social scene, their primary concern was to explain how and why societies change and what social forces hold societies together to create order and stability over time. With the emergence of sociology as a science, the idea of applying the scientific method to the study of the social world dominated social thinking. The foundational categories used in early social theory were an attempt to account for what was then a striking difference between modern societies and the preceding traditional ones. This dichotomy of modern versus traditional became the hallmark of sociological thinking with innumerable variations (Lemert, 1993).

Early Social Thinkers and Contributors to Sociological Knowledge

Sociology is rooted in the actions and activism of individual women and men. As we will see, many of the early sociological thinkers, such as

Karl Marx, Max Weber, Émile Durkheim, Harriet Martineau, and W.E.B. Du Bois, spoke and wrote on a number of controversial public and political topics and the Chicago School of Sociology consisted of reformers, journalists, settlement house workers, and clergy members. In this sense, sociology began as a public activity—as provocateur of social conscience, as object of controversy (and sometimes ridicule), and as a source of new thinking about the social world (Lemert, 1993). In general, the classical theories of many of the early contributors to the discipline of sociology were grand theories of society; they were preeminently attempts to explain the nature of modern societies, of which the capitalist economy is a central feature. Each theorist, however, approached the explanation of capitalist society differently; each had profoundly different presuppositions and assumptions about the nature of modern society.

Auguste Comte (1798–1857) Generally considered to be the founding father of sociology, Auguste Comte was the first person to use the term *sociology,* describing it as the scientific study of society. Comte provided the first systematic sociological analysis of society, which reflected his concern about the "deplorable state of anarchy" that pervaded society following the French Revolution. He felt strongly that sociology, with its focus on "principal needs and grievances of society," would bring order out of chaos (Zeitlin, 1994, p. 81). Comte's positive philosophy, or **positivism**—the belief that knowledge should be guided by facts rather than by imagination, intuition, speculation, or purely logical analysis; the use of observation, comparison, experimentation, and the historical method to gain the facts needed to analyze society—was intended as an ideological tool to control social life. Some sociologists continue to find Comte's positivist, "natural science model" appropriate for their work. Others suggest that sociologists have overemphasized the positivist approach to the point of detriment to the discipline. Still others suggest that sociological knowledge has never been completely objective and value-free. Rather, historically, it has focused on the experiences of a few, excluding the influence of the race, class, gender, and age of the masses of people in society (see for example Andersen, 1997; Andersen & Collins, 1995; Collins, 1991).

Comte's own work is a case in point. Although Comte argued that through science, not religion, we could gain objective, value-free knowledge, his own work was less than value-free. For example, when Comte wrote of "the whole of the human species," he was essentially speaking of the "whole of the white race." As to class, Comte believed that the class structure should not be tampered with and that a scientific elite should have moral authority over the lower and working classes. Further, Comte described the subordination of women as natural given that, according to him, the female sex was in a state of perpetual infancy. In this context, he claimed that sociology would prove that the equality of the sexes was incompatible with all social existence. In short, Comte argued the organic inferiority of women and attempted to provide a scientific rationale for his viewpoint (Zeitlin, 1994). Thus, despite his claims about a "value-free" science, almost everything he wrote was based not on observation and reasoning (the scientific method) but on his own personal values and sentiments. This latter point calls attention to the voices missing historically within the discipline of sociology and what that has meant in terms of the shaping of the discipline.

Herbert Spencer (1820–1903) Herbert Spencer is best known for his view that society is analogous to the human organism—he believed that it is made up of a number of interrelated parts (social institutions such as the family, religion, the economy, education, and government) that work together to ensure stability, order, and the survival of the various parts as well as the society as a whole. Spencer is often referred to as an *evolutionist,* because he applied the principle of biological evolution to society. His primary concern was with explaining social change, and he used the term *survival of the fittest* to describe the process of evolutionary changes in social structures and social institutions. Although Spencer claimed to have developed this concept, it is most often attributed to the 1859 work, *The Origin of Species,* by Charles Darwin. As a result, Spencer's view of society became known as *Social Darwinism*—the idea that human societies that are best adapted to their environments will survive and prosper while those that are poorly adapted will die out.

Although Spencer is remembered as one of the founding architects of the discipline of sociology, much of his work not only reflected a strong bias but also was seriously flawed. We can see, for example, how Spencer's belief in survival of the fittest supports the position of those who have an interest in keeping the masses poor and working for low wages. It is also highly supportive of racist ideologies and discrimination because, he explained that the failure of people to be "equal" is the result of the operation of the natural laws of evolution and that any intervention (attempts to equalize people and conditions) would violate these laws. Spencer's ideas and concepts relating to the survival of the fittest can still be found in some sociological thinking as well as in some U.S. social and political policies. For example, although slavery predates Darwin's formal statement of survival of the fittest, it was this type of thinking that provided the rationale for the enslavement of people of African descent as well as the extermination of Native Americans. In our more recent history, Social Darwinism, in conjunction with various other belief systems such as religion, has formed the basis for a range of behaviors and practices, including U.S. imperialism around the world and continuing racist policies and practices at home. Even today, vestiges of Spencer's Social Darwinism can be found operating in various social and political policies in countries around the world, for example, Bosnia's recent program of "ethnic cleansing."

Karl Marx (1818–1883) Perhaps more than any other social thinker, Karl Marx has had the most profound impact on the development and shaping of sociological thought. A nineteenth-century economist, philosopher, social theorist, and political activist, he has been described by some as an erratic genius who wrote brilliantly on a wide range of topics. Although most of Marx's writings were directed toward political activist audiences and although he did not consider himself to be a sociologist, several of his ideas contain such profound sociological insights that he is generally regarded as one of the founders of the discipline.

As a social activist, Marx was involved in some of the most politically and intellectually controversial movements of his day. Marx's ideas and viewpoints are more than simply academic theories because the notion that theory must be connected to social and political practice (the melding of theory and praxis) is paramount in all of his work. That is, he strongly believed that social scientists should not only study and interpret society but also be instrumental in changing it. Because of his active role and particularly his leadership in the revolutionary labor movement, Marx was never able to secure a university career. Because of political and economic repression in Germany and the French government's objection to his presence in Paris, he and his family settled permanently in political and philosophical exile in England.

Observing the growing industrialism of his day, Marx saw, firsthand, the resulting oppression and exploitation of workers: their long work hours, meager food supplies, and low wages contrasting with the vast profits enjoyed by the owners of production. The conditions of work in industrial factories during his lifetime were deplorable, and in *Das Kapital* (1867/1967) (his three-volume work on capitalism, inequality, class, and social change), he cites many examples of the exploitation of labor, including child labor. Perhaps more than anything else, Marx's work is a scathing critique of **capitalism**—a privately owned system of production of goods and services that are sold to a wide range of consumers in which the owners try to maximize profits. Marx believed that the problem of inequality between classes lay in the social organization of capitalist production that was characteristic of industrial society. Fundamental to Marxian thought is *economic determinism,* the notion that every aspect of social life is based on economic relationships. Based on his historical analyses of various societies, Marx believed that, at any given time in human history, those who own or control the *means of production,* the instruments people use to produce their livings (for example, tools, land, factories, capital), form the dominant group in society and are able to control and coerce the less powerful and thereby to maintain their positions of power.

Marx believed that all industrial societies are characterized by competition and conflict between two main classes: the **capitalists,** owners of the factories and other scarce goods and services in society that produce wealth, and **the proletariat**—workers whose labor produces the products of capitalism. These two groups have fundamentally opposing interests as well as unequal power. Conflict between the two groups is inevitable because the capitalists can only maximize their profits by exploiting the workers. At the same time, Marx argued that it is in the workers' interests to resist exploitation by revolting and overthrowing capitalist oppression and establishing in its place **communism,** a classless system in which the means of economic production are collectively owned and wealth and power are evenly distributed.

With the failure of communism, some Marxist scholars have had to concede that much of Marx is outdated. However, in a very general sense, Marxian views and analysis still carry considerable weight. Within the discipline of sociology, Marx's ideas and viewpoints form the basis of the contemporary theoretical paradigm we call the *conflict paradigm* (see Chapter 2). In addition, his genuine concern for workers and his belief that the government should look after them will continue to be a centerpiece of economic and political debate for some time to come. Few people want to see a return to unbridled capitalism; even the most ardent economic conservative concedes that some government intervention into economic affairs is necessary. Thus, the debate now and into the next century is not whether the government should intervene but rather about what kind and how much intervention is necessary (Meyers, 1991).

Émile Durkheim (1858–1917)   More than anyone else, Émile Durkheim helped to make sociology a "respectable" academic discipline. Like Marx's, many of Durkheim's ideas and theories have become benchmarks within the discipline of sociology. For example, his theories about social solidarity or cohesion are the basis for the contemporary sociological paradigm we call *functionalism* (see Chapter 2). His fundamental

premise in this regard was that society is more than simply the sum of its parts. It has a unique character all its own and is not reducible to the actions or behavior of any one individual; it transcends the individual because it does not depend on any particular individual for its existence. Like several other nineteenth-century social thinkers, Durkheim was concerned about the impact of the rapid social changes brought about by rising industrialization and urbanization. In opposition to a Marxian conception of society and social change based on classes and class conflict, Durkheim formulated a theory based on social solidarity which arose from his concern about social order and cohesion in a society.

Although Durkheim disagreed with some aspects of the sociological writings of Comte and Spencer, he was nonetheless influenced by both men. Durkheim developed a view of society that focused on social institutions, the individual's need for social support and social control, and the superior moral influence of society in shaping the nature of the individual. For Durkheim, moral ideas are the real glue of a society. Society is, after all, nothing more than a community of ideas, and Durkheim firmly believed that it is the similarity of positive moral ideas that is the single bond that can unite human beings into society. Thus, Durkheim proposed that various moral ideas or **social facts**—norms or collective practices that include all of the ways of acting, thinking, and feeling that exist outside of individuals but exercise control over their behavior—contribute to order and cohesion in society. Durkheim believed that Marx gave too much importance to economic factors and class struggle and not nearly enough to social cohesion and social solidarity.

Durkheim wrote on a wide variety of subjects: education, religion, order and justice, deviance, crime and punishment, the division of labor, and, in his classic study, *Suicide* (1897), he introduced statistical analysis to sociology as a method of studying social phenomena. He suggested that in modern society, suicide is the result primarily of the state of society rather than of a psychological state. Severe strain that can lead to suicide is caused by **anomie,** a condition of society in which the normative standards of conduct are weak or absent and social control becomes ineffective as a result of the loss of shared values and a sense of purpose in society. A century later, his work on suicide is still quoted.

Max Weber (1864–1920)   Like Marx and Durkheim, Max Weber (pronounced VAY-ber) had a tremendous impact on the development of sociology. Like others of his time, he was deeply concerned and occupied with the vast and rapid changes brought about by the industrial revolution. However, unlike the macro theoretical approaches of Marx and Durkheim, Weber's central approach in his analyses of society was to focus on what he termed **meaningful social action,** the motives that underlie human behavior, the ways in which people interpret and explain their own behavior and that of others, and the way that these actions and meanings affect the social order. Weber believed that an understanding of the meaning of social action requires being able to understand social action from the point of view of the actor. Thus, he developed a special methodology—which he termed *verstehen,* a German word that literally translated means "empathetic or interpretive understanding"—in order to understand how people think and feel about their behavior. As a method of analysis, *verstehen* refers to the subjective, empathetic, or introspective analysis of social action.

Although Marx saw the economic mode of production (the organization of work and its activities) as giving rise to capitalism, Weber saw ideas, values, and the thought system as giving rise to capitalism. For Weber, it is not only economic systems but also belief systems or systems of ideas (especially religious ideas) that are central forces in social change. In perhaps his most famous work, *The Protestant Ethic and the Spirit of Capitalism* (1905/1976), Weber stresses the important role of ideas in historical change. Weber's primary focus is on the economic relevance of a specific religious ethic (the Protestant ethic or, more specifically, Calvinism, a precursor to Presbyterianism), that is, on the impact of religious values on economic conduct. Although Marx contended that the Protestant Reformation was a by-product of the rise of capitalism, Weber concluded that it was no accident that Protestantism and capitalism developed during roughly the same period in Europe. Weber's central thesis is that the Protestant Reformation promoted a mentality and produced a social climate in which capitalism could develop and persist. To test this thesis, Weber compared several countries in which Protestantism or Catholicism was the dominant religious system. Comparing significant cultural differences between Protestants and Catholics, he noted that Catholicism as a belief system encouraged a traditional way of life among its adherents. On the other hand, under Protestantism, members were expected to lead exemplary lives, devote themselves to work, live simply, and not accumulate an undue amount of material goods. Perceiving economic success as a sign of salvation and unable to use the money they accumulated for personal adornment, they saved their money and reinvested it in their expanding businesses.

Weber was also a political activist who frequently sought to influence government officials and policies. Unlike Marx, however, who advocated the melding of theory and praxis, Weber drew clear lines between his academic work and his political activities and strongly criticized those who did not. In this context, Weber purported an objective or *value-free sociology,* in short, that personal convictions or biases should not be a part of sociological research or its conclusions. In contemporary sociology, this emphasis on objectivity has enabled the discipline to adopt scientific models that establish positivist methods of scientific observation. However, this focus on objectivity and the certification of white males as the sole experts in conducting scientific research often excludes the subjective experiences of people of color and women, making them either "invisible" or "nonscientific."

Georg Simmel (1858–1918)   Georg Simmel (pronounced ZIM-mel) was one of the least recognized of the early contributors to the field of sociology. Born in Germany and completing his studies at the University of Berlin, he was a contemporary of Weber and Durkheim. However, unlike these two, Simmel, a Jew in anti-Semitic Germany, occupied a marginal status in academia. He never obtained a full-time academic position in spite of the support of such scholars as Weber. Despite this, he wrote many articles and books, was a cofounder, with Weber, of the German Society for Sociology, and became well known nationally and internationally.

Simmel believed that society consists of an intricate web of multiple relations between individuals who are in constant interaction with one another. It is the task of sociology to study the forms of these interactions as they occur and reoccur in diverse historical periods and cultural settings. *Society,* he argued, is just a name for a number of individuals connected by social interaction. There is no society outside or in addition to the individuals who compose it. Sociologists, therefore, should concern themselves with the particular patterns and forms in which humans associate and interact with one another and with the crystallization of those interactions into group characteristics.

Although there are some similarities between Simmel's approach to sociology and those of sociology's other pioneers, there are some important differences. For example, in contrast to Marx's revolutionary optimism, Simmel held a view of the future that was more consistent with Weber's view of modern society as an "iron cage" from which there is no escape. According to Simmel, social life both impresses itself upon the individual—allowing her or him to become specifically human—and imprisons the human personality by repressing the free play of spontaneity. Thus, on the one hand, it is only through institutional life that humans attain freedom, while on the other hand, their freedom is forever endangered by these same institutional forms. Further, whereas Marx stressed the importance of conflict in social change and suggested that there could eventually be an egalitarian society devoid of social conflict, Simmel argued that conflict, like social harmony, was a necessary and often useful element of social life. Although harmony is necessary for stability and the development of society, a totally harmonious society would be incapable of development or change. At the same time, the good society is not conflict-free. Conflict can and often does strengthen the existing bonds of society or establish new ones. Thus, peace and feud, conflict and order are correlative and necessary for progress and change. In contrast to other sociologists discussed so far, Simmel's interest in and activism relative to current affairs and social and political issues were minimal.

A Sociology of Sociology: Missing and Invisible Scholars

What does the picture we have presented of the early contributors to sociology tell us about the production and reproduction of knowledge and who controls and defines that which passes as knowledge? Is there something missing in this brief description of the early contributors to the discipline of sociology? We think yes. Until very recent times, most recognized contributors to the early development of sociology were European or Euro-American males "who took for granted the parochial notion that the culture of a relatively small number of white people in the north explained the 'is and ought' of the world" (Lemert, 1993, p. 9). Because those who typically have had the power to validate that which passes as knowledge (historical or otherwise) have primarily been white and male, the works and contributions of many early scholars and social thinkers have gone virtually unnoticed and unreported simply due to their race or gender. This fact, it seems to us, attests to the racism and sexism existing in the male-dominated intellectual community generally and in the discipline of sociology particularly.

On the one hand, it might be argued that few people of color and women were writing as sociologists during the early years of sociology, thus accounting for their invisibility. However, on the other hand, raising questions about what sociological theory is and the extent to which there is a consensus behind the answers to these questions when people other than white males are part of the group reaching the consensus, makes it apparent that race, class, and gender are important factors to consider in any discussion of either the historical or the contemporary development of sociology. It thus becomes apparent that we must look beyond the so-called classical sociologists to writings from outside the academy in order to give a more accurate history of the development of sociology (see, for example, Lemert, 1993).

Until recently, few people of color or women have been recognized for their sociological writings or contributions to the early development of the discipline. This is a function of several factors, including the facts that in Europe and the United States, (1) women and people of color were by and large excluded from academia, the home of sociology; (2) their writings were seldom taken seriously and, in order to get published, women often had to use male pseudonyms; and (3) race and gender issues were not central sociological concerns. These factors reflect the generally subordinate position of most people of color and women as well as the control wielded by males of the intellectual and economic elite.

Although people of color and women were excluded from academia and the discipline of sociology during its emergence and formative years, they were, nonetheless, writing social theory. Many of these writers wrote from the standpoints of their personal experiences of the brutalities of racism and sexism. Their names include many we have only recently learned to associate with a sociological imagination (see Table 1.1).

Although there have been many missing voices, two examples can help to put the contributions of people of color and women scholars in proper perspective. One was a prominent British sociologist and political activist, and the other was the first African American sociologist and a social activist. Throughout this textbook, we will bring the works of people of color and women from the margin to the center of theoretical discussions and analyses, emphasizing the importance of their contributions to the sociological study of society and human behavior and pointing out their exclusion wherever necessary. By giving voice to those who have been historically silenced in the discipline and by combining their work with the theories and research of recognized sociologists, we hope to provide students with sound theoretical frameworks for understanding and utilizing the sociological imagination.

Harriet Martineau (1802–1876)   In every respect, Harriet Martineau was an important cofounder of the discipline of sociology. Born into a British upper-class family, Martineau lived when women were not expected to work outside the home, to be activists, or to be scholars. Rather, they were expected to get married, bear children, and fulfill a domestic role. Moreover, during this time period, women were viewed as appendages to the men in their lives: fathers, brothers, husbands, or other "responsible" men. Thus, Martineau's achievements as a scholar, traveler, and activist occurred against great odds. Although she is best known for her translation of Comte's *Positive Philosophy,* her own book *How to Observe Manners and Morals,* written in 1838, was one of the earliest works on social research methodology. Added to this, Martineau's sociological analysis of inequality in the U.S. social system as compared to that in Europe, published in her book *Theory and Practice of Society in America* (1837), was one of the first and most thorough sociological treatises on U.S. social life. In this work, she noted a deep division between the *aristocratic class,* consisting of the wealthy and highly educated segment of the population, and the *democratic class,* consisting of artisans, craftsmen, unskilled workers, and poor farmers.

Like many early sociologists, Martineau was a political activist as well as a scholar. She was an ardent abolitionist well before her arrival in the United States. Recognizing the growth of and injustice inherent in the slave system and in the political and social condition of women in the United States, she argued that there could be no real justice in a society that was divided into those who command and those who serve. She identified economic dependency as the primary determinant of women's oppression but also recognized that the lack of voting rights excluded women from political power as well. Particularly disturbing to Martineau was the advocation of despotic rule over women by many distinguished liberal-democratic writers such as Thomas Jefferson and James Mill. For example, in his writings, Thomas Jefferson excluded women, infants, and slaves from full citizenship, and James Mill excluded women based on the premise that their interests were adequately represented by their fathers and husbands. Their subordinate position notwithstanding, Martineau believed that American women had many more advantages than women in traditional societies. She anticipated women's liberation would come about as

TABLE 1.1 ☉ People of Color, Women, and the Development of Sociology, 1792–1948

Year	Author	Publication
1792	Mary Wollstonecraft	*A Vindication of the Rights of Women*
1818	Francis Wright	*Views of Society and Manners in America*
1844	Margaret Fuller	*Women in the Twentieth Century*
1856	Antoinette Blackwell	*Shadows of Our Social Systems*
1883	Helen Campbell	*Prisoners of Poverty*
1892	Ida B. Wells-Barnett	*Southern Horrors*
1892	Anna Julia Cooper	*The Colored Woman's Office*
1892	Charlotte Perkins Gilman	*The Yellow Wallpaper*
1893	Ida B. Wells-Barnett	*Lynch Law in All Its Phases*
1893	Aline Valette	*Socialism and Sexism*
1896	Mary Smith	*Alms House Women*
1898	W.E.B. Du Bois	*The Study of the Negro Problem*
1898	Charlotte Perkins Gilman	*Women and Economics*
1902	Jane Addams	*Democracy and Social Ethics*
1903	W.E.B. Du Bois	*The Souls of Black Folk*
1906	Elsie Crews Parsons	*The Family*
1907	Marianne Weber	*Marriage, Motherhood, and the Law*
1916	Annie M. MacLean	*Women Workers and Society*
1925	Dorothy Swaine Thomas	*Social Aspects of the Business Cycle*
1939	E. Franklin Frazier	*The Negro Family in the United States*
1941	Charles S. Johnson	*Growing Up in the Black Belt*
1945	St. Clair Drake & Horace Cayton	*Black Metropolis*
1948	Oliver C. Cox	*Caste, Class, and Race: A Study in Social Dynamics*

Source: This list draws upon the work of Shulamit Reinharz (1993) and the preliminary research in this area by the authors of this textbook and represents a sample of sociological or sociologically relevant publications and/or contributions of African American and women's studies. This is a selected, thus necessarily limited, list.

a result of a sexual revolution. That is, when women as a class of people became conscious of how they were subordinated, they would exert a moral and political power strong enough to break the bonds of their oppression and subordination. Recognition of Martineau's contributions to sociology, long overdue, includes the recent establishment of a chair in sociology in her name at the University of Massachusetts.

William Edward Burghardt Du Bois (1868–1963)

Although he was both a sociologist and a social activist, W.E.B. Du Bois's work and contributions to the field of sociology went largely unrecognized for many years. Du Bois earned an undergraduate degree from Fisk University and in 1895 became the first African American to earn a doctorate from Harvard University. Du Bois went on to read sociology, economics, and history in postgraduate study at the University of Berlin under Max Weber and other prominent German scholars. From the time of his return to the United States until shortly before World War I, he was responsible for impressive pioneering research on African Americans. His work *The Philadelphia Negro* (1899) was the first scientific study of African American life and the first important sociological study of an African American community in the United States and the problems its members confronted.

Like his European counterparts, Du Bois was influenced by rapid turn-of-the-century industrialization and urbanization, but he was particularly concerned about racism in the United States. During his early career, Du Bois believed that careful empirical research could supply the basis for achieving a racially egalitarian society. He contended that race prejudice was caused by

Sociologist and social activist W.E.B. Du Bois, largely unrecognized by sociologists until recent times, conducted the first important study of an African American community in the United States. His pioneering work provided a rich legacy for numerous scholars of race relations across a variety of academic disciplines.

ignorance and that social science would provide the knowledge needed to defeat injustice. Du Bois rejected justifications of racism based on supposed biological differences or inherent inferiority, emphasizing instead the critical importance of historical and environmental factors. He believed in sociology but believed that it had to move from broad abstractions and unsystematic fact gathering to an empiricism whereby observation and accurate measurement would produce real knowledge (Rudwick, 1974).

The real significance of Du Bois's early work to the discipline of sociology lies in the fact that he single-handedly initiated serious empirical research on African Americans in the United States. His generalizations about social problems later became standard in sociology. But in 1899, when *The Philadelphia Negro* was published, it was ignored by the elite in the profession. Not one of his many articles on African Americans was ever published by the prestigious *American Journal of Sociology*. Despite the lack of support for his work, Du Bois amassed a body of data that not only compared quite favorably with the social survey research being done at the time but also provided a valuable storehouse of information to his successors and contributed greatly to the development and use of the social survey methodology.

As we have seen, many early scholars were interested in using social science and scientific explanations of social phenomena to improve human society. Thus, much of their work was imbued with a reformist spirit. In this tradition, Du Bois occupied a dual role of scholar and activist-reformer. As a social activist-reformer, Du Bois is perhaps best known as the most prominent articulator of African American protest during the first half of the twentieth century, primarily because he was one of the principal founders of the *National Association for the Advancement of Colored People (NAACP)* and for almost twenty-five years editor of the NAACP's official publication, *The Crisis*. But even in his sociological research, he accomplished much more than simple description and analysis. Du Bois's role as a social reformer, for example, is evident in his research, which called for and recommended solutions to the problems faced by African Americans.

Beginning right after the Civil War, Du Bois's life spanned ninety-five years, stretching from Reconstruction, through Jim Crow, the lives of Booker T. Washington and Marcus Garvey, and the founding of the NAACP to the civil rights movement and ending in 1963 just as Dr. Martin Luther King, Jr., prepared to deliver his now famous "I Have a Dream" speech in Washington, D.C. In some respects, it can be said that Du Bois's life embodied, even acted out, a large portion of the social history of race in the modern United States (Lemert, 1993, p. 12–13).

American Sociology

From its beginnings in Europe, sociology spread to the United States in the late nineteenth century amid rapid and sweeping social change. A need to analyze the growth of cities, the rise of factories, the organization of and strikes by labor, European immigration, African American migration to cities, the growth of city slums, and crime contributed to the nature and development of sociology in the United States. Lester Frank Ward (1814–1913) is considered to be the founder of American sociology. He believed that the growing industrial society could be best studied using sociological analysis. The first departments of sociology in the United States opened in 1889 at the University of Kansas, in 1892 at the University of Chicago, in 1894 at Columbia University, and in 1897 at Atlanta University (an African American university) under the direction of W.E.B. Du Bois.

The Chicago School Robert Ezra Park (1864–1944) and Ernest Burgess (1886–1966) founded what came to be known as the *Chicago School of Sociology*, which conducted a wide range of studies of social life in urban America. Under their leadership and the direction of Albion Small (1854–1926), the department's first direc-

Perhaps more than most people, Jane Addams (1860–1935) had her hand on the pulse of the pressing social issues of her day. Founder of Hull House, a refuge for immigrants, the sick, and the poor, Addams, pictured speaking with some of her many youthful visitors, strove relentlessly to bridge the gap between the powerful and the powerless. She is the only sociologist to be awarded the Nobel Peace Prize.

tor, the University of Chicago became the center for teaching and training sociologists and dominated the discipline for most of the first half of the twentieth century. As in Europe, the majority of early American sociologists were white males. Several of these men had ministerial backgrounds and were social reformers whose broad sociological concern was with social problems and their amelioration. They used the city of Chicago as a kind of social laboratory to study the pervasive social problems that came in the wake of industrialization and urbanization: crime, delinquency, poverty, slums, and gangs. Although many of these sociologists championed the cause of the exploited and oppressed masses in society, most of them were not immune to the prevailing racial and sexual prejudices of the day.

Although the sociology department at Chicago did not discriminate against women or people of color, the department's female faculty members never achieved full-time status and were eventually set apart from the male sociologists into a newly developed school of social work. Women writing sociology, such as the preeminent Jane Addams (1860–1935), were never able to penetrate the male-dominated sociology department at the University of Chicago even though they were sometimes more prolific writers and had their hands, like Addams, on the pulse of the pressing social problems of their day. As a consequence, they were forced to turn to practical work or applied sociology such as working with the poor.

Although Jane Addams wrote eleven books, published numerous articles (some in the *American Journal of Sociology*), and pioneered studies of social problems in Chicago, she is still not recognized fully for her sociological insights and writings. A political activist, social reformer, and feminist, she was a recipient of the Nobel Peace Prize in 1931, but she is perhaps best known as the founder of the settlement house movement and Chicago's Hull House, a settlement house for poor people and recent immigrants to the city. Unwelcome in academia, Addams worked tirelessly on behalf of poor people, especially poor immigrants, focusing on housing, working conditions, and education. At Hull House, immigrants, intellectuals, feminists, social reformers, and political activists alike engaged in discussions of various urban problems. Much of Addams's work on these problems influenced some of the very same men who denied her access to a regular position in the Sociology Department at Chicago. Sociologists from the Chicago School often came to Hull House to gain some of the insights that Addams had concerning class issues, the adjustment of newly arrived immigrants to cities, and the exploitation of them as workers.

Post–World War II   After World War II, the center of sociological training and study shifted from the University of Chicago to eastern Ivy League universities such as Harvard and Columbia, Midwestern universities such as the University of Wisconsin and the University of Michigan, and West Coast universities such as the University of California at Berkeley. The newer breed of sociologist was less concerned with the study of social problems and social reform and more concerned with positivist research methods, statistical modeling of social processes, and the development of general sociological theories. Scholars such as the Harvard sociologist Talcott Parsons introduced the grand theories of Durkheim and Weber to U.S. sociologists and both Parsons and Columbia University sociologist Robert Merton successfully advanced the functional paradigm in sociology. Functionalism is a conservative perspective that tends to rationalize the status quo and to minimize important processes of social change (see Chapter 2).

The functionalist paradigm dominated sociological thinking and research until the 1960s, when Marxian theory, which provided a critical perspective to U.S. sociologists and their students, became more widely accepted. A leading voice in this regard was C. Wright Mills, who was openly critical of American injustices and inequalities. He was particularly critical of the U.S. class system and the dominance of economic elites—a small group of politicians, businessmen, and military leaders—who ran the country in terms of their own interests (see his *The Power Elite,* [1956]). After Mills's death in 1962 and with the rise of social movements such as the civil rights movement, the black nationalist movement, the peace movement, and the women's movement, many U.S. sociologists returned to a social activist role. The critical perspective as well as an interest in social activism remain important aspects of sociology today.

The Present Although many contemporary sociologists continue to use these earlier theoretical perspectives as frameworks for developing concepts and theories relevant to contemporary social life, others call for an antiracist approach to the study of social life, which would include a complete critique and transformation of the old sociological canon. Today, sociology as a discipline can be found in most societies around the world. It has a particularly strong presence in the Western world, especially in the United States, France, England, and Germany. However, with the wide-ranging and sweeping reforms that occurred in Eastern Europe in the 1980s, sociology and sociological research rose to prominence as a method of addressing important social problems in these countries, such as the breakup of the family, suicide, and crime. Contemporary sociology consists of a wide range of theoretical perspectives and paradigms. Few sociologists today attempt to develop broad, all-inclusive theories of society and human behavior. Rather, most choose to develop theories of the *middle range*. Robert Merton suggested that sociologists should take a middle road between the grand theories of the early thinkers and narrow specialized theories to develop theories of the middle range—explanations of specific issues or aspects of society. For example, a middle-range theory might be one that explains dating and mate selection patterns or patterns of upward mobility and success among working-class families.

The majority of contemporary sociologists work in or are connected to academic institutions. However, many others are employed in federal, state, and local government agencies or private corporations in a variety of positions ranging from research analyst to director of human resources to consulting. Sociologists can also be found applying sociological analysis and skills in the criminal justice and health care systems as well as in social service agencies and the military. Although there is often disagreement within the discipline as to the shape of society, past, present, and future, there is some consensus that as we move into the twenty-first century, sociologists will be studying a vastly different world from that of our predecessors. With increased geographic mobility, sophisticated technology, the increasing power of the mass media, increasing multiculturalism and diversity, and increased globalization, sociologists today are faced with new and interesting challenges that will allow them to demonstrate the utility of possessing a sociological imagination.

Social Action, Social Policy, and Social Change

Now that you have a feeling for what sociology is and how it developed over time, a logical question to ask is, What can we do with this knowledge? Earlier, we noted that the sociological imagination can be empowering in that it can help individuals understand their places in the social world and that it can be a basis for promoting social action. In addition, we are seeing more sociologists play a role in the development of **social policy,** a plan or course of action adopted by a political body, business, or other organization designed to influence and determine decisions, actions, or other matters of concern. However, it is important to recognize that a policy role, like any other social role, does not exist in a vacuum. Rather, it exists in a social context which is often highly political and partisan. Indeed, we live in a time when many issues affecting social life are debated in public arenas, ranging from newspaper editorials to the U.S. Supreme Court. Many issues, such as abortion, prayer in public schools, the divorce rate, welfare, and sex education, have become politicized and even polarized, with people arguing heatedly over how to deal with them. For example, over the last decade, we have seen voter initiatives in many states on issues as diverse as proposals to deny welfare benefits to undocumented immigrants, to end affirmative action, and to permit the use of marijuana for medical purposes.

In the United States, as in other countries, competing political parties have emerged with distinct philosophical orientations. The party that is in power generally supports funding for research and employs individuals who will support its goals. Thus, who and what gets studied and reported upon frequently depends on the political climate of the day. Although sociologists may agree on the empirical facts regarding a specific social issue, such as who is on welfare, for how long, and at what cost, they may have different views on how to solve the "problem." After all, in their private lives, sociologists represent a wide range of political perspectives, ranging from conservative to radical. Public officials are prone to listen to those whose viewpoints correspond most closely to their own. Thus, throughout this textbook, as we examine a number of policy initiatives that attempt to address today's social issues, we will raise questions such as, What assumptions underlie these policies? and Who benefits from these policies?

As we saw earlier, sociology, by definition, includes the study of the processes and consequences of social change. Four aspects of social change will concern us throughout the remainder of this textbook:

1. Social change is ubiquitous, that is, it occurs everywhere.
2. Although some change is unplanned and unanticipated, other change is carried out through purposive social action.
3. Social change can have both positive and negative outcomes.
4. Social change is often resisted by people for a variety of reasons—fear of the unknown, vested interests in existing social arrangements, ideological opposition, inertia, and the force of tradition.

The sources of social change are many. They can be external events, such as war and conquest and cultural contact and diffusion, or environmental factors or internal events, such as innovations, invention, and population shifts. We will discuss each of these more fully in Chapter 3.

Frequently, people feel powerless to control their lives, especially in periods of rapid social change. There is a fairly widespread assumption among many people that "you can't fight city hall." Indeed, purposive social change is often difficult. Nevertheless, as we saw at the beginning of this chapter, people can be agents of social change through social action. Social researchers Kent Schwirian and Gustavo Mesch (1993) have identified eight stages in the process of social action:

1. People have shared interests, ideologies, and concerns about the existing situation.
2. A change trigger (a significant event or experience) emerges from either within or without the social system that motivates individuals to collective action.
3. People undertake a process of planning their activities in response to the change trigger.
4. People mobilize their resources to support their planned action.
5. People engage in activities they think will accomplish their goals.
6. People observe the effect of their action on the situation that prompted them to action in the first place.
7. People evaluate their success or lack thereof.
8. People reformulate their strategy and action plans and undertake new or repeated actions until they achieve their goals, expend all of their resources, see only futility in continued action, or unalterably fail.

In the chapters that follow, we will provide examples of individuals and groups who have experienced one or more of the outcomes of this process.

Sociology for the Twenty-First Century

At the dawn of the twenty-first century, the diversity of human life, not only within the United States but also around the world, is a reality finally acknowledged. Many people today, scholars and the public alike, encapsulate the notion of diversity in the concept of **multiculturalism**—the notion that society is a combination of many different subcultures or groups, that each of these groups retains some of its customs and traditions, that these should be accepted as valid and valuable, and that all of these groups should coexist (Cyrus, 1997, p. 4).

Multiculturalism

Look around you. Who are the people you see? Can you identify all of the many cultural, racial, and ethnic groups that live, work, and play around you? The society in which we live today is very different in terms of the racial and ethnic makeup of its members from the society into which our parents and grandparents were born and raised. Although U.S. society has always been diverse, during much of U.S. history, the majority of the population has been made up of white English speakers who have dominated all social institutions and positions of power and authority. Today, we can witness considerable change in the racial and ethnic makeup of this society. For example, one of every four people in this country now defines her- or himself as Hispanic or *nonwhite*. Some demographers predict that by the mid-twenty-first century, the *average* American may well be a person of color. Figures compiled by the United States Census Bureau make this trend apparent (see Table 1.2).

Using the categories employed by the Census Bureau gives us only a limited picture of the true racial and ethnic diversity of U.S. society. Within each racial and ethnic category are often many different cultural groups. For example, the category Asian Americans includes peoples from over nineteen distinct cultures, such as those found in Sri Lanka, Japan, China, India, Pakistan, Mongolia, Korea, and the Philippines, to name a few. Likewise, the category of Native Americans conceals numerous distinct Native American nations, such as the Cherokee, Chickasaw, Navajo, Apache, Seminole, Shoshone, and Sioux nations, among many others. Among Hispanics or Latinos, there are a number of distinct cultural groups, such as Puerto Ricans, Mexican

TABLE 1.2 ☉ Race/Ethnic Composition of U.S. Population, 1995, and Projections, 2050

Race, Ethnic Group	1995	2050
Hispanic Origin	10.2%	22.5%
White	73.6	52.5
Black	12.0	14.4
Am. Indian/Eskimo/Aleut	0.7	0.9
Asian/Pacific Islander	3.5	9.7

Source: Adapted from *Statistical Abstract of the United States,* 1995 (p. 19) by U.S. Bureau of the Census, 1995, Washington, D.C.: U.S. Government Printing Office.

Americans, Cubans, and Panamanians. The same holds true for the category black. All people of African descent, whether or not they were born in the United States and whether or not they are of mixed descent (for example, biracial people), are lumped together as black. Thus, Jamaicans, Haitians, and people from the continent of Africa are all labeled and categorized as black within the United States. These misrepresentations of the diversity within cultural categories of race and ethnicity also occur for whites. The term *white* is used to describe any person of European descent, yet Europe includes a wide variety of peoples and cultures. Even when a person is of mixed cultures, she or he is defined as white so long as the mixture does not include people of African descent.[1] Added to the diversity of any specific geographic area is the global reality of diversity. Today, people of color constitute the majority of the world's population.

The concept of multiculturalism is not accepted by everyone. Some people believe that

---

[1]This practice is rooted in the U.S. policy known as the "one-drop rule." The one-drop rule describes the set of social practices whereby someone with any traceable African heritage is defined as "black." This rule is applied only to blacks—no other category of people is defined by only "one drop." (See Chapter 10 for a more detailed discussion.)

the recognition of diversity or multicultures in U.S. society devalues and does away with what are referred to as *traditional American values.* They argue that perspectives given from the standpoints of race, ethnicity, class, and gender distort the true cultural and intellectual traditions in U.S. society and that such perspectives of culture force us to very radical extremes of political correctness. On the other hand, those who support a multicultural perspective believe that an examination and understanding of society from these diverse perspectives, including a traditional and white middle-class perspective, gives us a much more accurate picture of U.S. society and the world; it enhances our understanding of the society in which we live and those in which others live around the world, and it enriches our lives and our society (Cyrus, 1997).

Sociology will go a long way in helping us understand multiculturalism and the implications of the "coloring" of U.S. society in the twenty-first century. Since the days of the founding of the discipline, sociology has examined how social forces and social structures influence human behavior and society and has helped us understand the process of social change both on an individual and societal level. Particularly under the influence of feminist sociologists, questions of how and under what conditions power and authority are related to issues such as race, class, gender, sexual orientation, and age have been some of the most important sociological questions of the second half of the twentieth century.

Globalization

You do not have to be a seasoned global traveler to know that forces that shape our lives are increasingly global in nature. Today, the mass media make most of us increasingly aware of the rapid social changes that are unfolding around the world. For example, countries in Europe and Asia have been transformed almost overnight. Countries that were once poverty-stricken now pose considerable economic challenges to the United States and Europe. For example, poverty and homelessness have in-creased in the United States while Hong Kong and Singapore have emerged as two of the most modern metropolitan areas in the world. The pace of social change is tied to the processes of globalization and has an impact on all of us. Globalization is not new. It began centuries ago when explorers such as Christopher Columbus left their own countries in pursuit of new sources of wealth and power. These early international contacts produced new economic and political structures that are still evident today. What is different today, however, is the depth and breadth of this process (Schwartz & Scott, 1997, p. 278).

Rapid changes in the U.S. and global economies, increasing movement of people both within and outside of countries, and political and social upheavals around the world have necessitated a more systematic and global approach for students studying society and human behavior. In the past, most of us lived out our lives without much awareness of and largely unaffected by global events. Today, however, our global interdependence with people around the world is increasingly visible and felt by all of us as new technological developments provide easier, cheaper, and faster means of communication and transportation. Joan Ferrante (1992) defines **global interdependence** as a state in which the lives of people around the world are intertwined closely and in which any one nation's problems—substance abuse, environmental pollution, unemployment, inequality, racism, sexism, disease, inadequate resources, terrorism, and war—increasingly cut across cultural and geographic boundaries. Recognizing local, national, and international forces that shape our lives and connect us to others in our neighborhood, our country, and in various regions of the world enables us, as C. Wright Mills (1959) suggested, to grasp history and biography and the connections between the two. Armed with such an understanding, we will be better able to respond in ways that improve our own lives and those of the larger communities in which we live. Throughout this textbook, we will emphasize global connections as they relate to the various topics we discuss. Whenever possible, we will make reference to both the international and the local aspects of globalization.

Applying the Sociological Imagination

Try to identify an example of global interdependence by using a contemporary social problem in the United States, such as substance abuse, terrorism, or AIDS. Can you identify ways in which the lives of people in the United States are linked by or through this problem with the lives of people outside of the United States?

Key Points to Remember

1. C. Wright Mills developed the concept of the sociological imagination, the ability to see how individual experiences are connected to the larger society. The sociological imagination allows us to distinguish between "personal troubles" experienced by individuals, such as the bonded labor of Iqbal Masih, and public issues that transcend the local environment of the individual, such as the worldwide problem of child labor.

2. Sociology is the systematic study of human social behavior, groups, and societies and how these change over time. Sociology shares two basic assumptions with the other social sciences: human behavior is patterned and these patterns can be discovered and understood through the use of the scientific method. Sociology is the broadest of the social sciences in that it focuses on the totality of group life rather than on a particular area of social life. Sociology provides an understanding of how human behavior is influenced by people's membership in groups and how individuals affect the groups to which they belong.

3. Sociology is a distinct way of looking at the world. It involves a process of critical thinking or debunking—asking questions, evaluating evidence, checking for biases (our own and others').

4. Major societal changes and trends in the eighteenth and early nineteenth centuries gave way to a new scientific way of explaining social phenomena. Sociology, as an academic discipline, emerged in the wake of two major changes and trends: industrialization and urbanization.

5. Sociology is rooted in the actions and activism of individual women and men. Many of the early social thinkers and contributors to the development and expansion of sociological knowledge spoke and wrote on a number of controversial public and political topics. These early thinkers included Auguste Comte, Herbert Spencer, Karl Marx, Émile Durkheim, Max Weber, Georg Simmel, Harriet Martineau, W.E.B. Du Bois, and Jane Addams.

6. Until recent times, few people of color or women have been recognized for their sociological writings and contributions to the early development of sociology. Among the missing voices is Harriet Martineau, a British sociologist and political activist who, in every respect, is a cofounder (with Auguste Comte) of the discipline of sociology, and W.E.B. Du Bois, the first African American sociologist and a political activist who was one of the first American sociologists to publish a systematic and objective study of life in U.S. cities.

7. Sociology spread to the United States in the late nineteenth century. The first departments of sociology in the United States included the University of Kansas, 1889; the University of Chicago, 1892; Columbia University, 1894; and Atlanta University—an African American university—in 1897.

8. The University of Chicago became the center for teaching and training sociologists and dominated the discipline for most of the first half of the twentieth century. Known as the *Chicago School,* its professors and graduates had as their major concern the pressing social problems of the day and social reform.

9. Although the sociology department at the University of Chicago did not deny people of color and women access, white male sociologists' writings by and large advanced the prevailing beliefs about the proper place of people of color and women.

10. After World War II, the center of sociological training shifted to eastern Ivy League universi-

ties such as Harvard and Columbia; Midwestern universities such as the Universities of Wisconsin and Michigan; and West Coast universities such as the University of California at Berkeley. The focus of sociology also shifted from social reform to an emphasis on positivist research and general sociological theories. Sociologists Talcott Parsons and Robert Merton are notable during this era.

11. Students today, as at no other time in our history, live, work, go to school, and recreate in environments that are increasingly multicultural and global. The possession of a sociological imagination offers students an opportunity to explore the complexities of multiculturalism and diversity in various forms and offers concrete understandings of how race, class, and gender impact and shape human experience.

12. The forces that shape our lives are increasingly global in nature. Recognizing the global connection to our individual and group experiences, like recognizing multiculturalism and the diversity of the world, stimulates the sociological imagination. By understanding the forces that shape our lives and by being able to see and understand the local, national, and international processes that connect our lives to people living on our block, in our neighborhood, in our country, or in various regions of the world, we are better able to respond in ways that improve our own lives and those of the larger communities in which we live.

Key Terms

sociological imagination	capitalism	anomie
social structure	capitalists	meaningful social action
sociology	proletariat	social policy
industrialization	communism	multiculturalism
urbanization	social facts	global interdependence
positivism		

Key People

Craig Keilburger	Émile Durkheim	W.E.B. Du Bois
Peter Berger	Max Weber	Lester Frank Ward
Auguste Comte	Georg Simmel	Robert Ezra Park
Herbert Spencer	Harriet Martineau	Ernest Burgess
C. Wright Mills	Karl Marx	Jane Addams

Questions for Review and Discussion

1. How can the sociological imagination contribute to our understanding of child labor and other behaviors? Using the examples of Iqbal Masih and Craig Keilburger, explain what C. Wright Mills meant when he talked about the need "to grasp history and biography and the relations between the two within society"?

2. Some critics of classical sociological theory argue that it is largely an unreformed bastion of racism, sexism, class elitism, and Eurocentrism.

Do you agree? Why or why not? Give examples to support your position. How might a focus on the intersections of race, class, and gender lead to a transformation of the entire body of classical sociological theory?

3. Why are global issues sociologically relevant? In your opinion, what are the three most important global issues today? For each issue, explain the global interconnections and the local consequences. How does the sociological imagination help with an understanding of these connections and consequences?

4. Think of some aspect of social life today that you would like to see changed. Using the stages of social action outlined by Schwirian and Mesch, draw up a plan for purposive social change. How can the sociological imagination help you in this process?

For Further Reading

Baca Zinn, Maxine, and Bonnie Thornton Dill. 1994. *Women of Color in U.S. Society*. Philadelphia: Temple University Press. A comprehensive anthology of articles that explores various aspects of the lived experiences of women of color in the United States, placing race, class, and gender at the center of analysis.

Blackwell, James E., and Morris Janowitz. (Eds.). 1974. *Black Sociologists: Historical and Contemporary Perspectives*. Chicago: University of Chicago Press. This book is an extension of the 1972 National Conference on Black Sociologist held at the University of Chicago. It is the first work to assess and interpret the contributions of black sociologists to the development of the discipline.

Deegan, Mary Jo. 1988. *Jane Addams and the Men of the Chicago School, 1892–1918*. New Brunswick, NJ: Transaction. An excellent discussion of the sociological insights and contributions of Jane Addams and insights into the male-dominated Chicago School of sociology.

Goetting, Ann, and Sarah Fenstermaker. 1985. *Individual Voices, Collective Visions: Fifty Years of Women in Sociology*. Philadelphia: Temple University Press. A collection of biographical essays by women sociologists that shows how individuals' experiences have led to sociological perspectives on women and society.

Henslin, James M. (Ed.). 1995. *Down to Earth Sociology*. (8th ed.). New York: Free Press. This collection of readings shows how the sociological perspective can be applied to everyday life.

Johnson, Allan G. 1991. *The Forest for the Trees: An Introduction to Sociological Thinking*. San Diego: Harcourt Brace Jovanovich. A good introduction to core concepts and theoretical frameworks in sociology, illustrating why a sociological perspective is worthwhile.

Ladner, Joyce A. (Ed.). 1973. *The Death of White Sociology*. New York: Vintage Books. A classic anthology of the works of a group of African American writers and scholars, who critique mainstream sociology for accepting white bourgeois standards as the norm and consistently treating all other social patterns—especially those found in African American culture—as "deviant."

Sociology through Literature

Morrison, Toni. 1987. *Beloved: A Novel*. New York: Alfred A. Knopf. A classic example of fiction as living text. Set in post–Civil War Ohio, *Beloved* is a story about the impact of slavery as told through the "memory" and "remembering" of an escaped African American female slave.

Internet Resources

http://www.asanet.org/ This is the homepage of the American Sociological Association. It provides information about the association and provides links to meetings, conferences, and publications.

http://www.ucm.es/OTROS/isa/ This is the homepage of the International Sociological Association. It provides information on its activities and publications and links to other sociological associations.

http://www.lib.berkeley.edu/GSSI/sociolog.html The University of California at Berkeley Library Sociology homepage provides links to its collections and resources as well as to other related sites.

http://www.freethechildren.org/ This Web site provides a mission statement, data on child labor, and information on how people can join the Free the Children campaign against child labor.

2

Thinking and Working Sociologically

AGENT OF CHANGE: ROBERT D. BULLARD

Robert D. Bullard, Professor of Sociology and Director of the Environmental Justice Resource Center at Clark Atlanta University, has been a key activist in the grassroots environmental movement. This movement has greatly impacted public thought about environmental issues and has shaped national environmental policy. One example of Bullard's activism and the melding of theory and practice (and of the linking of university and community) occurred in 1979 in Houston, Texas, where a group of African American residents were embroiled in a bitter fight to keep a garbage dump out of their suburban, middle-class community (Bullard, 1997). The group went to court to challenge the siting of the waste facility under the civil rights law. Working with the group, Bullard and a group of his graduate students (at Texas Southern University) conducted a research study that found a clear pattern of discriminatory treatment in the siting of waste facilities in Houston, a pattern consistent with other forms of racial discrimination perpetrated throughout the country. They found, for example, that from the early 1920s to 1978, all city-owned landfills (five sites) and most city-owned incinerators (six of eight facilities) were located in African American neighborhoods. This was clearly unequal treatment given that African Americans represented only one-fourth of the city's population. In addition, this same pattern was evident after waste disposal was taken over by private industry in 1978. Three of the four privately owned landfills used to dispose of household garbage were located in African American communities. According to Bullard and his collaborators, these actions amounted to *environmental racism*—any policy, practice, or directive that differentially affects (whether intended or unintended) individuals, groups, or communities based on race.

Although the Houston residents were unsuccessful in blocking the building of the landfill, they did impact local environmental policies and regulations, including by convincing the city council to adopt an ordinance restricting the location of waste facilities. More important, since the group's 1979 lawsuit, no other municipal solid waste facilities have been built in a community of color in Houston.

Bullard's and his students' research was pivotal to these policy changes. The community-based research of these sociologists is an excellent example of how theory, research, and social action combine to build relationships, strengthen communities, and affect positive social change. As we discuss later in this chapter, theory and research go hand in hand. Theory provides insights into the nature of individual attitudes and behavior as well as that of whole societies, and research provides the objective observations upon which theories are based. Furthermore, as in the case of Bullard and his students, successful social and political activism is most often tied to systematic research and careful interpretations of research findings. Although we treat these issues separately throughout this textbook, we emphasize their interrelatedness.

Source: Bullard, R. D. 1997. "Dismantling Environmental Racism in the Policy Arena: The Role of Collaborative Social Research." In P. Nyden, A. Figert, M. Shibley, and D. Burrows, *Building Community: Social Science in Action.* Thousand Oaks, CA: Pine Forge Press, pp. 67–73.

The Link between Theory and Research

For some people, the terms *theory* and *research* imply highly abstract and complex thinking and esoteric procedures for collecting data. Although many may be intimidated by the terms, all of us, in fact, engage in theorizing and research in our daily lives. We theorize whenever we attempt to explain some phenomenon. In order to expand this point, let's consider a very contemporary and trendy behavior: body piercing. Once a backroom ritual, body piercing has become a fashionable and profitable industry embraced by a wide variety of people. For example, one twenty-three-year-old college dropout, with holes drilled in her ears, brow, nose, tongue, and breast, estimates that she has spent well over $5,000 on body piercing. Asked if it hurt, she said, "It's like I was dying." *Another* devotee of piercing had needles driven through his scrotum and the shaft of his penis.

Who are these people, and why do they puncture their bodies, particularly in areas as sensitive as the genitals? We typically wonder why people act and think the way they do, especially if their perspectives and behaviors are outside what we consider to be the *norm.* In our everyday theorizing, most of us would likely explain this phenomenon in terms of the personal characteristics of the people who pierce their bodies: they are weird, seeking attention, or sadomasochists predisposed to harming themselves. In contrast, sociologists would look beyond the individual behavior and personalities of body piercers to the social and historical context or environment in which this behavior occurs.

The sociological perspective and various theories within the discipline provide unique organizing frameworks for understanding human behavior. For example, a sociological perspective might direct us to examine body piercing within the framework of collective behavior, as part of a larger "body modification" social movement, as an expression of independence within a society that often attempts to homogenize people, as an act of rebellion against American cultural ideals of beauty, as a conscious repudiation of Western norms and values, or as behavior that is related to a wider dissatisfaction with traditional Western rationality, logic, and sexual norms and to

Much to the consternation of many parents, body piercing, once the backroom ritual of a few, has become a fashionable and profitable industry embraced by young people across race, gender, and class.

anger directed at the impact of Western technology on the natural environment and at the state of American political and social life (Leo, 1995). Other sociologists might view body piercing as a *rite of passage,* a spiritual outlet in a society that long ago lost its taste for dramatic rituals to mark the passage from childhood to adulthood (Rogers, 1993, p. 65). Although not all sociologists would explain body piercing in the same way, in general, their theories are more systematic, more comprehensive, more guided and constrained by rules, and more self-conscious than our everyday theorizing.

Applying the Sociological Imagination

What do you know about body piercing? Are any parts of your body pierced? If yes, why did you pierce your body? Do you know anyone with pierced body parts? How do they explain this behavior? Conduct a literature search to determine what types of sociological research has been conducted on body piercing. What insights can we gain from this research about who pierces various parts of their bodies and why?

We have seen how scientific theories differ from everyday theorizing, but what, exactly is theory? A **theory** is a statement (or set of statements) that explains how or why facts are related. The task of bringing together isolated observations or facts into an understanding of human society and behavior is captured in sociological theory. For example, by carefully recording and documenting the historical locations of city- and privately owned waste facilities and garbage incinerators, Robert Bullard and his students constructed a theory about environmental injustice in African American communities. Theories contain certain assumptions about the world—about the nature of society and human behavior. Different assumptions lead to different questions and, potentially, to different answers or explanations about society and human behavior. In addition, most theories include stated or unstated value judgments concerning the topic or issues related to the topic. For example, if we use a theory that assumes that culture is an integrated system, held together through a basic harmony and consensus of values and interests, then in looking at behavior such as body piercing, we are likely to ask questions about value consensus or the functions or dysfunctions of such behavior for individuals, groups, and society. And we are less likely to raise questions about conflicting values and interests held by diverse groups in society. Although social scientific theories are ideally expected to be objective and value-neutral, *all* such theories include value judgments and tend to support a specific position or viewpoint. Because they contain assumptions about the nature of human beings and their societies, all theories implicitly or explicitly suggest that certain arrangements are desirable, good, or better than others. Given this fact, some sociologists advocate value specification, that is, specifying or stating one's values and biases at the outset so that the reader knows exactly where the writer is coming from.

So, how do we know if a particular theory provides a viable explanation of its subject matter? The answer to this question lies in an understanding of the relationship between theory and scientific research. Theories provide insights, often in the form of abstract ideas, into the nature of individuals and society, and scientific research provides the objective observations that verify theories. Theories that cannot be verified by **empirical evidence**—data that can be confirmed by using one or more of the human senses—mean nothing in and of themselves. Likewise, facts have meaning only when we interpret them based on some theoretical framework or perspective. Contrary to popular belief, facts do not speak for themselves. In addition, as we saw in the opening section of this chapter, theory and research can combine in such a way as to create a venue for meaningful social activism. Although all research is political in some sense, when used collaboratively, it can increase an individual's or group's capacity to address, shape, and influence important social issues and policies. Figure 2.1 depicts the relationship between theory, research, and social action that will help guide our discussion.

As we have seen, sociologists can provide answers to our questions about how and why humans behave the way they do. These how/why questions can be answered in a variety of ways, determined by the perspectives or theoretical paradigm(s) used by the sociologist. A **theoretical paradigm** is a "definition of reality" (Kuhn, 1962); it is an abstract model for selecting crucial concepts and forms of evidence. Each paradigm

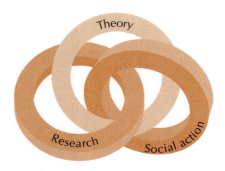

FIGURE 2.1 ◐ **The Relationship between Theory, Research, and Social Action**

provides us with a guide to doing research; each directs our attention to what to study, what questions to ask and how we should ask them, and what research methods are most appropriate for gathering our research data; and each provides a framework for interpreting and explaining the data we collect. Therefore, as will become evident, by providing a distinct framework in which to fit our observations, each paradigm interprets reality and explains data in a different way.

In the next section, we examine and critique some of the major theoretical perspectives that have impacted scientific research in the field of sociology. As you encounter each perspective, think about how the choice of a particular theoretical perspective will influence not only the way data are interpreted but also the very nature of the questions asked and thus the theories we develop to explain the phenomena.

Thinking Sociologically: Theoretical Paradigms

Traditionally, three major theoretical paradigms have shaped how mainstream sociologists view the world: structural functionalism, conflict theory, and social interactionism. In the next section, we will examine these as well as two other paradigms that have taken on greater and greater significance as social researchers have highlighted issues of inequality, powerlessness, and diversity in their work: feminist paradigms and multiculturalism.

Structural Functionalism

Structural functionalism, most often referred to simply as functionalism, is rooted in the ideas and works of early sociologists such as Auguste Comte, Herbert Spencer, and Émile Durkheim. *Structural functionalism* centers on the premise that society operates as a system (much like the human body or system) made up of a variety of interrelated parts or structures, each of which performs one or several important social functions or meets vital social needs of the society. The terms *system* and *function* are key terms in functional analysis. The term *system* refers to the interrelatedness and interaction of the parts and *function* refers to the consequences or outcomes any given structural element or part has in relation to itself, other parts of the system, and the system as a whole. Working together as a system, these parts contribute to the functioning and stability of the entire society. These parts, sometimes referred to as *subsystems,* are the various social institutions in society, such as the economy, family, education, religion, and the government. Each of these parts has a function for maintaining society. The educational system, for example, functions to teach citizens literacy and other skills that are essential if both the individual and society are to survive.

In functional analysis, it is assumed that society is an organized, stable, well-integrated system of interrelated institutions, all of which work together in harmony for the good of the whole. These institutions provide the rules governing behaviors that serve to maintain a kind of equilibrium or balance and a set of common values that bind people together. Therefore, a key question of functional analysis is, Why does a societal part or element exist, and what social function does it serve? That is, how does it contribute to the order and stability of the whole? Some key assumptions of this perspective are:

- The social world is organized into systems of interrelated parts.
- The overall system is bound together by consensus, with all parts of the system stemming from the same widely shared values and by functional integration.
- Society, as well as its subsystems, has certain basic needs that must be fulfilled. The interrelatedness of society's subsystems can be viewed as meeting certain "survival needs" of society.
- Change occurs through evolution—the adaptation of social structures to new individual and societal needs and demands and the elimination of outmoded or unnecessary structures.

Modern functionalism continues to view society as a system of interrelated, interdependent parts. Society is therefore seen to have an underlying tendency to be in equilibrium or a state of balance; it is orderly and stable because these parts have built-in mechanisms of social control. Social change is, therefore, viewed as disruptive to this equilibrium unless it takes place relatively slowly. The primary emphasis on consensus, harmony, order, and stability implies that a system is always moving toward greater progress and equilibrium. Tensions and conflicts may arise in the system, but they are temporary in nature. In the event of social disruption or change, built-in social mechanisms restore societal order and equilibrium. Thus, from this perspective, change is slow and gradual. Over time, the system accommodates itself to this evolutionary or gradual change and what was once disruptive to the system now becomes institutionalized. Social integration and stability is based upon and maintained through the consensus among a society's members of a certain set of values and norms.

Talcott Parsons (1902–1979), an American functionalist, expanded the ideas of sociologists like Herbert Spencer and Émile Durkheim identifying the basic tasks that all societies must perform in order to survive and the ways in which these tasks are performed in society. According to Parsons, the major tasks of society include the achievement of goals, an incentive to work and cooperate, adjustment to the environment, and the integration of the various parts of society into a whole. Furthermore, the successful performance of these tasks is facilitated by exchanges that link parts of society (Parsons, 1951; Parsons & Shils, 1951). Each part of the overall system maintains and supports the others through value consensus, an underlying agreement among members of a group about what the goals of the group should be and how they might be achieved. For example, the gendered division of labor defined women's roles in the home and men's in the workplace. These social arrangements were supported and reinforced in the 1950s by various social institutions, such as the government, religion, and education.

Robert Merton (b. 1910), another contemporary structural functionalist, focused his attention on the differential impact of social structure on human behavior (Merton, 1968). For example, American industry may be critical to the survival of both the individual and society through its provision of goods and services on which our way of life depends, but it also pollutes the environment and does so differentially in communities depending on the race, ethnicity, and social class of the residents (recall Bullard's research findings, recounted at the beginning of the chapter). Further, Merton pointed out that every social pattern or human action has more than one outcome or function, which can be either positive or negative. Although many of these functions are not obvious and may be unintended, they are often very significant to the overall maintenance of society. In this context, Merton distinguished between **manifest functions,** social patterns that are overt or obvious and intended, and **latent functions,** which are hidden or unrecognized, unexpected, and unintended. For example, the manifest function of schools in society is to teach literacy and other skills that are essential if a modern industrial society is to survive. However, the school system has several latent functions as well. Schools keep children in an industrial society occupied until they are old enough to work; elementary and secondary schools serve a child-care function by freeing parents for several hours each day; and schools provide opportunities for high social position for some students while channeling others into lesser roles, for example, as do college preparatory and vocational education programs.

Merton also recognized that not all social patterns are **functional,** that is, have positive effects which may help to maintain the system in a balanced state and/or promote the achievement of group goals. Sometimes, some parts or social patterns within the system may actually be disruptive of social equilibrium and therefore be dysfunctional. **Dysfunctional** social patterns have negative effects which may hamper the achievement of group goals or reduce the capacity of the system to adapt and survive. Thus, a person using a functional analysis would determine functionality by asking questions such as, Does the behavior or social pattern promote or constrain the achievement of individual and/or group goals? Does it promote stability and order in the system as a whole?

As you have probably realized, implicit, if not explicit, in this view of functionality and dysfunctionality is a value judgment: that some social patterns are more desirable and others less so. However, in reality, not all goals can be achieved. When some goals are achieved, they benefit some individuals while placing others at a disadvantage, and there is often disagreement not only about which should be a group's goals but also about what is a negative or positive outcome. For example, although the presence of a pool of people who can be exploited in terms of low wages and poor working conditions might be functional for a capitalist economy, it is dysfunctional for the goals of individuals and groups who make up the pool of exploited labor. On the other hand, various alternatives to the exploitation of labor and poverty would be dysfunctional for the affluent because they would require a redistribution of power, wealth, and prestige. Thus, the evaluation of whether a social pattern is functional or dysfunctional depends both on one's own values and on where one is located in the social structure. Sociologists using functional analysis must therefore identify for whom or for what social patterns or behaviors are functional.

Critique Although functional analysis fell out of favor somewhat during the 1960s and 1970s, its overall impact can still be detected as we move into the twenty-first century, and there is a resurgence of interest in functional analyses by some who refer to themselves as neofunctionalists. A functional analysis offers a reasonably sound explanation for the origins of social elements and social systems and demonstrates their functional utility. Modern functional analyses account for the multiple levels of human behavior—biological, social, cultural, and psychological.

However, although functionalism may be a useful framework for identifying a society's structural parts and the alleged functions of these parts, critics contend that what function a particular structure serves and why is not always clear. At the heart of most critiques of functionalism is the charge that it tends to be inherently conservative in its orientation and that it does not adequately account for diversity, conflict, and change, which are obvious characteristics of contemporary society. Critics argue that functionalism's stress on consensus and integration in fact conceals them. With its view that society is characterized by consensus, stability, and integration, functionalism considers conflict as destructive and as occurring outside the system rather than as indicative of problems within the system itself. Furthermore, it doesn't necessarily elucidate the experiences of women, poor people, and people of color. It therefore tends to promote and rationalize the status quo as social reality when it may be better viewed as the ideological and normative system constructed by and existing for the elite white male members of society (Ritzer, 1996). In this context, some critics of modern functionalism charge that it has not kept pace with the rapid social changes impacting societies and that its explanations of contemporary societal patterns are accordingly weak (Lindsey, 1997).

Conflict Theory

Like functionalism, the *conflict paradigm* focuses on the macro level of society (see Table 2.1). Emanating from the writings of Karl Marx,

TABLE 2.1 ◑ Comparing Theoretical Perspectives

Theoretical Perspectives	Level of Analysis	Focus	View of Society	Basic Questions	Critique
Functionalist perspective	Macro	Social order and consensus	A system of interrelated parts that interact and function for the maintenance of society as a whole	What are the major parts of society? What social function do they perform?	Has a conservative bias; tends to rationalize the status quo
Conflict perspective	Macro	Competition, conflict, and change	A system characterized by conflict, tension, competition, and inequality	How is inequality built into the social system? Who benefits and who is systematically deprived by a social pattern?	Overemphasis on conflict and the conspiracy of the elite
Interactionist perspective	Micro	Symbolic communication between individuals	A dynamic and ongoing system of actions and symbolic interactions	How do people understand and interpret symbols and social situations, and how do these, in turn, influence their behavior?	Ignores larger social institutions and structural realities such as inequality, racism, and sexism
Feminist perspectives	Macro/micro	Gender inequality	A system characterized by status quo relations that are unequal and oppressive	Where are women? Why is the situation as it is?	Woman-centered; explicitly ideological

it directs our attention to large social structures and societal institutions and is based on the notion that conflict is natural and inevitable in all human interaction. Thus, the conflict paradigm directs us to examine the ever-present facts of competition, coercion, inequality, oppression, and conflict in society and particularly those processes that lead some people to have greater power and control and others to have little or none. It also directs us to examine techniques of conflict control and the ways in which those in power maintain and perpetuate their influence and privilege. For example, in his classic study of wealth and power in the United States, C. Wright Mills (1956) identified a power elite consisting of a small group of businessmen, politicians, and military leaders who, according to Mills, rule U.S. society in their own interests. A key premise in conflict theory is that disorder, disagreement, and open hostility among individuals and groups is normal rather than abnormal, as the functionalist would contend.

Contemporary conflict theorists have refined traditional Marxian conflict theory to reflect contemporary patterns of behavior and social structure. Thus, conflict is not viewed simply as a clash between class groups or owners and nonowners of the means of production. Rather, these conflicts occur within and across a wide variety of groups. For the purposes of our discussion here, contemporary conflict theory can be understood in terms of some of the following key themes or assumptions:

- Society is characterized by change, conflict, and coercion.
- Humans have basic interests, or things they want and attempt to acquire.
- Each group in a society has a set of common interests, whether or not its members are aware of this. When people develop a consciousness of their common interests, they may became a social class.
- Power is always at the base of social relationships and it is always scarce, unequally distributed, and coercive.
- Social structure is based on the ability of some groups to dominate or impose their wills on others.
- The intensity of class conflict depends on the presence or absence of certain political

and social conditions; on the distribution of power, authority, and rewards; and on the openness of the class system. (Wallace & Wolf, 1991; Smelser, 1981)

Given these assumptions, when using this theoretical paradigm, we are led to ask questions about power and about how those who have it benefit from the existing social arrangements in society. Specifically, we might ask: Which individuals and groups are more powerful and which are less powerful or powerless? Who benefits from and who is systematically deprived by particular social arrangements? Who dominates and at the expense of whom? Sociologists using a conflict paradigm are thus interested not in how various institutions in society, such as the family, are integrated and function for the whole of society but rather in how institutions create, maintain, and perpetuate privilege and power for some individuals and groups and keep others in a subordinate and oppressive position. While a functional analysis would rationalize the status quo, a conflict analysis would critique or challenge the status quo.

Although functionalism dominated U.S. sociology for more than half a century, the conflict paradigm became increasingly important and acceptable due to focused attention on widespread racism, sexism, and other inequalities as well as on abuses of political power and authority during the 1960s and 1970s. In fact, for those who experience oppression, the conflict paradigm provides an ideological rationale for challenging the status quo as well as a voice. It offers a concrete set of propositions that explain unequal access to resources in terms of institutional structure rather than personal deficiencies and failures; it relates social and organizational structure to group interests and the distribution of resources. As we learned from Bullard's research, power, high social position, and decision-making authority, such as the authority to decide where landfills and waste dumps will be placed, are not equally distributed throughout society. Thus, unlike functionalism, the conflict paradigm does not view norms, values, and ideas as external to and placing constraints on individual behavior. Rather, it views people as being as much involved in using the system of norms, values, and ideas as in being used by it (Schwartz & Scott, 1997).

Critique In contemporary society, the conflict paradigm provides one of the most useful frameworks for analyzing how factors such as race, class, gender, age, ethnicity, and sexual orientation are connected to the unequal distribution of scarce goods and resources, such as wealth, property, education, and prestige. A major strength of this paradigm is that it provides a historical framework within which to identify social change, for example, the major shifts in the distribution of societal resources and social and political power. However, like functionalism, it is not without faults. The conflict paradigm, particularly those aspects of it that are tied to traditional Marxism, is often criticized for its overemphasis on class or economic inequality and the allegedly inevitable conflict between classes. In so emphasizing tensions, conflict, and struggle, it de-emphasizes consensus and shared values and norms across classes and other groups. In addition, because of its emphasis on social change, conflict theory is considered by some critics to be "radical" and "activist," suffering from a strong ideological bias. It should be noted, however, that although the conflict paradigm may seem explicitly value-laden, as we have pointed out, all theories contain ideological components.

Another important criticism of the conflict paradigm is leveled at the implied conspiratorial element that is associated with its charge that a ruling economic elite is consciously organized to rule and deny others power and privilege. Although the organized power and privilege of a small group, whether consciously organized or not, is an important element for explaining social inequality, critics suggest that there are a host of other factors that equally explain inequality (Lindsey, 1997). Some critics, such as George Ritzer (1996), argue that a major problem with conflict theory is that it is not sufficiently different from structural functionalism; it is more a kind of structural functionalism turned on its head, they believe, than a truly critical theory of society. One criticism aimed at both the conflict and structural functional paradigms is that both focus an analysis of human behavior and society almost entirely on a macro level, offering very little to our understanding of individual thought and action. In the next section, we consider some micro-level perspectives and approaches to the study of society and social behavior.

Interactionist Paradigm

Whereas the functionalist and conflict paradigms are concerned with macro patterns (large-scale patterns) that characterize society or groups, the *interactionist paradigm* focuses on micro patterns (small-scale patterns) of face-to-face interactions between individuals in specific settings. It is based on two key assumptions: (1) humans do not respond directly to the physical world but to our subjective interpretations of the physical world, and (2) humans are constantly engaged in interpreting the worlds in which they live and acting accordingly. Still, human behavior is fluid. Society is a dynamic process that is continuously being created and recreated as humans interact, negotiate, and define social reality. This process of constructing and negotiating social reality by means of definitions is embodied in the classic statement of William I. Thomas, which has come to be called the **Thomas Theorem:** "If [humans] define situations as real, they are real in their consequences."

To illustrate this theorem, let's look again at the issue of environmental racism in terms of race relations in the United States. For example, if we define African Americans as inferior, such definitions will shape our behavior with and toward them. Because whites control most major centers of institutional power, some whites are not only in positions to determine the ecological fate of various African American (and other) communities but also, more important, they are major players in shaping environmental regulations and laws governing environmental pollution. By acting upon their racialized and often racist definitions of African Americans (whether consciously or not), those whites who have the power to make environmental decisions often do so in ways that are discriminatory, as Bullard and his students found, and that have adverse effects, according to Bullard's and other research, in many African American neighborhoods across the country. So, in this instance, whites have defined a situation as real and thus, it is real in its consequences for African Americans. The interaction paradigm is a broad perspective that includes a number of specific and interesting viewpoints: symbolic interactionism, dramaturgical perspective, and ethnomethodology.

Symbolic Interactionism *Symbolic interactionism,* which is the most developed and utilized of the interactionist theories, focuses on the use of shared symbols—objects, words, sounds, and events that are given meaning by members of a society. As you will learn in Chapter 4, language is the most important set of symbols that humans use. Human beings interact with one another based on their shared understandings of the meanings of words and other cultural symbols and on their understandings of social situations as well as their perceptions of what others expect of them within those situations. Thus, a major emphasis is on the subjective meanings that people attach to their own and other peoples' behavior as well as on the various processes through which people come to construct and agree on various definitions of reality.

Charles Horton Cooley (1864–1929), a social psychologist, was the first to emphasize the link between the individual and society, developing the idea that social interactions with other people had a profound impact on personality development (Cooley, 1964). Building on Cooley's work, George Herbert Mead (1863–1931) introduced the concept of symbolic interaction, suggesting that interaction between people largely takes place in terms of symbols, particularly language. Essentially, Mead (1962) saw society as a dynamic system of socialization within which the social self develops through interaction, language, and socialization. As a result of socialization, we can anticipate what other people expect of us and modify our behavior accordingly. Interaction occurs in a patterned and structured way because people can and do agree upon the meanings of shared symbols, such as language, signs, and gestures. Group members respond to each other on the basis of these shared meanings and expectations for behavior. In this sense, we do not react automatically to one another. Rather, we carefully choose from among a number of alternatives, depending on the specific situation.

Given these principles of symbolic interactionism, it is understandable why a major concern is with process—the process through which people learn the symbolic frameworks of their cultures. For example, by what process do some children in the United States learn that some groups are superior to others? How do some children learn to accept gang or other nonnormative behavior and others do not? Thus, symbolic interactionism directs our attention to the socialization process, or social learning, a topic we will elaborate upon in Chapter 6.

Like the other paradigms we have discussed, the symbolic interactionist paradigm invites us to ask specific kinds of questions. For example, what kind of interactions are taking place between people? How do people understand and interpret symbols and social situations, and how do these, in turn, influence the course of their interaction with others? How do people come to agree about what should be done and how people should behave in particular situations? Looking at the environmental research of Bullard and his students, questions shaped from an interactionist paradigm might have asked, Why do people of different racial, ethnic, and social class groups act the way they do, and why do they often act towards each other in discriminatory ways? Or, what processes are involved when a loose network of people (for example, academics, community people, lawyers) come together to challenge the status quo (environmental decision makers)?

Dramaturgical Perspective The *dramaturgical perspective,* which makes analogies to the theater and drama, was developed by Erving Goffman (1959). In general terms, this perspective supports the Shakespearian notion that "all the world's a stage, and all the women and men merely players." According to Goffman, when people interact, they want to present a certain sense of self that will be accepted by others and viewed positively as well. Thus, in their role performances, people attempt to create and maintain certain impressions which others evaluate. As in the theater, roles can be constructed and acted out to convey the best possible impressions or the impressions that we want to give. Goffman called this process *impression management.* Think about it: you are probably engaging in impression management when you respond to a professors' questions, dress for school, interview for a job, or talk to a stranger.

Keeping with the analogy of the theater, Goffman distinguishes between our front-stage performances (our public behaviors, those that we want the audience to see and believe) and back-stage performances (our private behaviors, those that we do not want the audience to see). In the front-stage region, we often use props, including mannerisms, clothing, and other possessions, such as pipes, jewelry, and cars, to help us manage an impression. On the other hand, in the back-stage region, we engage in behaviors that often contradict the impression we are attempting to manage in the front-stage region. Presenting a nice clean and tidy living room when a guest arrives while our bedroom is untidy with old newspapers, books, clothes, and other items strewn about is an example of the difference between front- and back-stage behavior. The condition of our bedroom contradicts the impression of the good housekeeper role we are attempting to manage in the front-stage region. A key point of dramaturgical analysis is that one's personal identity shifts as the roles one plays shift, daily and over the course of one's life.

In addition, Goffman examined, in detail, various unspoken rules that govern our behavior. In devising our role performances, we take into account the expectations that others have for us. These shared expectations provide countless little rules and assumptions that we hardly think about but that are essential to effective interaction. According to Goffman, these unspoken rules include *studied nonobservance* and *civil inattention.* By *studied nonobservance,* Goffman meant that people participate in a common, unspoken agreement to maintain one another's face. Even though our audiences may assess the performances we are attempting to manage as false, they will rarely challenge us. The interaction and the performer's embarrassment would probably be highly uncomfortable for everyone involved. So we participate in a studied nonobservance of potentially embarrassing situations. For example, we pretend that we do not hear the growling of someone's stomach or we pretend to believe the obviously fictitious excuse of the student who attempts to hand in a late assignment. Much of what Goffman refers to as "polite behavior" consists of this kind of implicit bargain among people to

help one another keep face by not questioning the impressions they are attempting to manage.

Additionally, in our interactions with strangers, we must display appropriate levels of civil inattention. That is, we behave in ways that show that we are aware of their presence yet we avoid eye or other contact with them; we politely ignore them. For example, when walking down the street or standing in an elevator, our eyes may meet but no recognition is typically allowed. Civil inattention represents a very delicate balance between the recognition of those around us and a studied deference to them. In other words, we respect their right to unaccosted anonymity (Manning, 1992). Goffman is considered to be a key figure in the development not only of the dramaturgical perspective but also of the ethnomethodological perspective.

Applying the Sociological Imagination

Can you readily think of examples of when you or people you know have engaged in studied nonobservance? How essential was the studied nonobservance to the effectiveness of the interaction? Have there been times when this kind of "polite" behavior has broken down? What happened on these occasions?

Ethnomethodology A relatively new perspective in sociology, *ethnomethodology* can be defined as the study of the organization of everyday life. It examines the written and unwritten rules and procedures that people use to carry out their daily routines and the ways in which they construct, interpret, reconstruct, and use these rules of conduct to make sense out of their worlds and to interact effectively with others. Founded by Harold Garfinkel (1967; 1988), its major focus is on the taken-for-granted shared understandings and agreements of everyday life.

As we go about our everyday lives, we engage in a variety of behaviors without thinking much about why. We abide by rules of conduct even though they are not written down, and these rules govern much of our daily lives. We are usually unaware of these unwritten rules until they are violated. Garfinkel has used a number of experiments whereby unwritten rules are violated in order to uncover the unspoken, unwritten expectations that people in various roles and situations have of one another. In one such experiment, Garfinkel had his students behave at home as though their role was that of a house guest, not a daughter or son. The students called their parents Mrs. or Mr., displayed courteous table manners at dinner, politely asked permission to do such things as use the refrigerator, bathroom, and telephone. The result of this unexpected behavior was a disruption of the normal family routines and interactions, so much so that many of the students could not keep up the role for very long. According to Garfinkel, the students' parents interpreted their behavior as signs of arrogance, rudeness, and even emotional instability and it took a while to soothe their anger and anxieties and restore normalcy to their interactions. Such experiments have provided important information about the set of agreements that we typically take for granted but that are important foundations for our daily interactions.

Critique   A major strength of the interactionist paradigm is that it brings the individual back into our analyses. Rather than viewing individuals as passive beings who simply respond to society's rules, interactionists view humans as actively engaged in constructing, shaping, sustaining, and changing the social worlds in which they live. It is a quite useful framework for examining the complexities of relationships and the daily workings of social life. It helps us understand how the roles that humans play are key in their social constructions of reality.

Conversely, a major criticism of the interactionist paradigm is that its narrow focus on the subjective aspects of human behavior and the social situations in which they occur forces one to ignore the objective and structural realities of everyday life, such as inequality, racism, sexism, and the unequal distribution of wealth, status, and power among various groups. In this context, the interactionist paradigm is often criticized for ignoring larger social institutions and structures and societal processes of stability and change, all of which have a significant impact on social interaction and on our individual/personal experiences. Another criticism is that

many of the concepts used in this perspective are imprecise and confusing and therefore incapable of providing a firm basis for theory and research.

Feminist Paradigms

As you found in Chapter 1, the sociological imagination provides a compelling way in which to make sense of the experiences of women and men as they exist in contemporary society. In many ways, the sociological imagination parallels *feminist paradigms* in that a basic tenet of feminist paradigms is that women can see how their private experiences are rooted in social conditions by discovering their shared experience with other women (Andersen, 1997). As you probably noticed, we refer to feminist paradigms in the plural. This is because feminist theory is not a single unified perspective. Rather, just as there is more than one sociological perspective, there are multiple feminist perspectives, reflecting the heterogeneity of feminist thought. However, although they are diverse, they are not mutually exclusive perspectives; they contain certain common characteristics or principles.

The major sociological paradigms discussed thus far are rooted primarily in men's experiences and render women and their experiences invisible, as if they didn't exist. As a result, whether intended or not, these perspectives present a skewed view of the social worlds in which both sexes participate. Even when women are accounted for in these paradigms, their experiences are often analyzed in terms of male or masculine models. Although such models are valid for examining male experiences, they are inadequate for understanding women's different experiences. Feminist paradigms offer powerful new perspectives in sociology by focusing on and examining social life and human behavior from the standpoint of women and with women at the center of the analysis.

According to Patricia Madoo Lengermann and Jill Brantly (1988), feminist paradigms are woman-centered in three ways: (1) the starting point of their investigations is the situations and experiences of women, (2) they treat women as the main subjects in the research process and view the world from the distinctive vantage points of women, and (3) they are critical and activist on behalf of women. It should be noted that simply because a theory deals with women or gender issues does not automatically make it a feminist theory or perspective. One way to test whether a theory is feminist is to determine if it reflects a *feminist consciousness,* an awareness rooted in a commitment to activist goals. In addition, Janet Chafetz (1988) suggests that to be considered a feminist theory or perspective, it should incorporate three basic principles: (1) gender is the central focus, (2) status quo gender relations are viewed as problematic, in that they are tied to inequality and oppression, and (3) gender relations are viewed as the result of social, not natural, factors. In general, all feminist paradigms address two fundamental questions: Where are women? and Why is the situation as it is? By focusing our attention on these two questions, feminist paradigms direct us to examine the ways in which specific definitions of gender affect the organization of social institutions and patterns of gender inequality. Moreover, feminist paradigms provide an ideological framework for addressing issues of women's inequality, oppression, and inferior social status. At some time, you have probably heard the feminist dictum "the personal is political." By this, feminist theorists mean to focus our attention on the connections between our personal lives; larger social, political, and historical factors; and our individual consciousnesses.

Although feminist theories cross disciplinary boundaries, they are compatible with the sociological imagination because they link individual experiences to social organization. Like other major sociological constructs such as race and class, gender is an important category of experience which influences who gets what in society. In this context, feminist paradigms suggest the following about women vis-á-vis men: (1) women's experiences are different from those of men, (2) women's status in most instances is unequal to that of men, and (3) women are oppressed, constrained, subordinated, controlled, or abused by men (Lengermann and Niebrugge-Brantley, 1996). In so distinguishing women's lives from men's and placing their experiences at the center of analysis, feminist paradigms underscore the inadequacy or limitations of the major sociological paradigms and other male-centered theories in accounting for the social worlds in which both women and men live.

Feminist paradigms often point out the diversity in women's and men's statuses, roles, and experiences by examining the experiences of groups of women who heretofore have been rendered invisible in mainstream sociological paradigms and analyses. Such feminist paradigms use the conceptualization of the intersections of race, class, gender, and sexuality as a major analytic tool. A feminist analysis of environmental racism and injustice, for example, would direct our attention to the fact that gender is clearly an important factor, along with race and class, in explaining the impact of environmental injustice. For example, major decision making in the United States, such as concerning where and when landfills and incinerators will be located, is controlled primarily by men who, along with often racist attitudes, hold sexist attitudes as well. Thus, to ignore the inextricable link between these various social locations is to present only part of the environmental picture.

Critique   As with conflict paradigms, a major strength of feminist paradigms is that they relate social and organizational structure to group interests and the distribution of resources. They offer viable frameworks for analyzing how various social locations, particularly gender, are connected to the unequal distribution of scarce resources or the things that count in society. Although woman-centered, feminist paradigms enable us to view both women and men in new and different ways. In this respect, feminist analyses of men's lives point out that although men benefit from institutionalized power and privilege, they too are subjected to sexist cultural expectations of gender (masculinity) that impact their identities, emotions, social status, and roles. In this sense, feminist paradigms can be viewed as modifications and extensions of the major sociological paradigms, especially the conflict paradigm (Andersen, 1997).

Perhaps the foremost criticism of feminist paradigms is leveled at the fact that they are woman-centered. They are criticized, particularly by mainstream sociologists, as being biased and explicitly ideological. Feminist theorists respond to this charge by affirming the woman-centeredness of their frameworks and directing attention to the historically value-laden androcentric, or male-centered, nature of most mainstream sociological theories and paradigms. Another criticism of feminist paradigms is that they tend to exaggerate male power and imply (consciously or not) that *all* men exercise the same degree of power and authority vis-á-vis women. Although this criticism has some merit, it cannot be generalized to critique all feminist paradigms. To the extent that a feminist theory or paradigm is grounded in an analysis of the intersections of gender, race, class, and sexuality (a paradigm long absent in mainstream sociology), it enables us to understand that men, no less than women, are racialized, belong to different classes, and are gendered. Thus, like women, their experiences in a society (for example, gender privilege) will vary according to where they are located within these social hierarchies.

Multiculturalism

A *multicultural paradigm* explicitly acknowledges the impact of the intersection of race/ethnicity, class, gender, and issues of colonization and exploitation and links these structured experiences to social behavior. The usefulness as a theoretical construct, of linking the distinct but interlocking categories of race, class, and gender, was first pointed out in the 1960s in the writings of African American feminists who were critical of mainstream feminist paradigms that either ignored or inadequately dealt with issues of race, class, and heterosexuality in their analyses. Since that time, it has been incorporated into the discourse of all of the social sciences and offers an interdisciplinary framework for theory construction (Lindsey, 1997). Certainly, the issue of diversity will be an important theme that is carried over well into the next century.

The sociological insight in this perspective is the idea that these categories are socially constructed. A multicultural framework helps us understand how these social categories simultaneously work together; how they are experienced simultaneously by individuals, and how they are combined with other categories of experience, such as age, sexual orientation, and religion, to structure our lives. Such perspectives allow for a broader-based sociological perspective.

Critique   Because multiculturalism is not yet widely recognized as a distinct perspective,

there is little formal critique of it. However, because it is most closely associated with feminist perspectives, it is subject to the same or similar criticisms.

Linking Theory and Research

As you become more familiar with sociology and the sociological perspective and as you encounter the various theoretical paradigms discussed in this and other chapters in this textbook, the details of each paradigm will become clearer. As you will see, each perspective represents a particular view of social reality and directs our attention to a set of questions unique to that view of reality. Each paradigm has advantages and limitations and none of them precludes others in explaining social reality. Although these paradigms provide important insight into the nature of human behavior and society, they are merely speculative ideas about social life by themselves. To test their validity or to confirm them, we must engage in the scientific enterprise known as scientific research.

Doing Sociology: The Research Process

Sociologists do not pursue knowledge in a haphazard or random fashion. All scientific research (regardless of one's theoretical orientation) is guided by the **scientific method,** a systematic, organized set of procedures that ensure accuracy, honesty, and consistency throughout the research process and, when taken together, produce the best possible results for the creation of empirical knowledge. In general, scientists use these procedures (1) to select and formulate a research question and operationalize major concepts, (2) to review relevant literature, (3) to select an appropriate research design, (4) to collect data, and (5) to analyze the data, draw conclusions, and report the findings (see Figure 2.2).

How these steps are actually carried out is influenced by a number of issues, including the particular research question under study. The research process is sometimes influenced by practical matters such as the availability and source

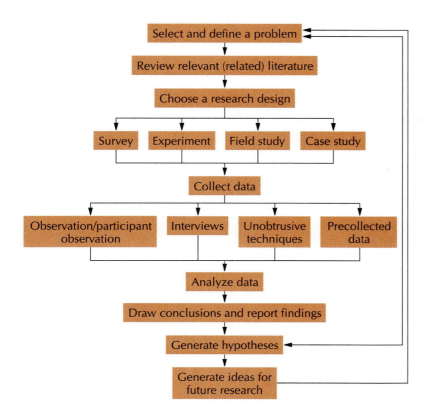

FIGURE 2.2 ☉ Steps in the Scientific Method

of funding, access to subjects, characteristics of subjects, and time constraints. As a consequence, biases, compromises, selectivity, and other nonscientific issues often creep into scientific research and can have an effect from the beginning to the end of the process. The research process may also be influenced by the perspective taken by the researcher. For example, many feminist researchers hold the perspective that research should be inclusive, collaborative, and empowering and that their task should be to document the lives of people (particularly women) whose experiences have been either ignored or distorted by mainstream researchers. To this end, they typically use research methods such as ethnographies and case studies and collect their data through in-depth face-to-face interviews and participant observation, research methodologies most conducive to the achievement of these ends. In this section, we elaborate the steps in the research process.

Applying the Sociological Imagination

As we briefly explore each step in the research process, use your sociological imagination to think of a topic or issue that you might want to explore or investigate using the scientific method. Develop a research project, following each of the steps outlined below.

Defining the Problem

The first thing you do in conducting scientific research is to decide what you want to study. The range of possible topics is very broad. For example, in her seminal work on the *Social Construction of Whiteness,* Ruth Frankenberg (1993) studied the manner in which white women in the United States experience, reproduce, and challenge the racial order in which they live.

Once you have decided on a research problem, as Frankenberg did, you should make a careful statement of the problem to be studied and, if applicable, form a **hypothesis**—a statement about the relationship between two or more events or phenomena that can be tested to determine its validity. Hypotheses are stated in terms of some relationship between **variables**—traits, qualities, or characteristics that can take on different values in different individual cases. An **independent variable** is thought be the cause of changes in other variables, while a **dependent variable** is thought to be influenced or affected by (that is, dependent on) the independent variable. In the case of Frankenberg's research, one of her hypotheses is that there is a relationship between social geography (social contexts and social settings within which people live and interact with others) and the construction of the concept of race or of racial thinking.

Very often, sociologists use concepts that are vague or abstract, which must therefore be operationalized. **Operationalize** means simply to restate concepts in concrete, measurable terms. For example, Frankenberg operationalized social geography so that it could be measured in terms of where white women lived: their homes, their streets, their neighborhoods, their schools, and where they vacationed. As you recall, one of the criticisms of symbolic interactionism is that many of its concepts are imprecise or vague. Because they are imprecise, it is difficult, if not impossible, to operationalize them. The result is that testable propositions cannot be generated (Ritzer, 1996).

Sociologists, like other scientists, have two major concerns about the measuring devices they develop and use: reliability and validity. **Reliability** refers to the ability of a measure to meet the test of replication, that is, repeated applications should produce the same results. **Validity** refers to the extent to which an instrument accurately measures the variable it claims to measure.

Reviewing the Literature

A review of the literature, a survey of the existing theory and research on a particular subject, provides background information that can stimulate new ideas about your research, suggest a variety of leads in terms of how you should proceed with your own research, suggest theoretical approaches and questions you might ask, and generally save you a tremendous amount of time that might be spent duplicating what has already been done. If little or no research has been done in the subject area, you become the expert on the topic. For example, when Frankenberg conducted her research, there was little research on the topic to draw from. That has, of course, changed since 1993.

Choosing a Research Design and Collecting Data

Once you have specified the purpose of your research, you must devise a plan of action or research design that will guide your research. Among the many alternative research designs available to sociologists are four types that they typically use: the survey, the experiment, the field study, and the case study. Likewise, researchers most often use one or more of the following methods of collecting their data: interviews, observation, unobtrusive techniques, and precollected data. The research design that you choose will, in large part, determine which method(s) you will use to collect your data, analyze and evaluate it, and draw conclusions.

The Survey   A *survey,* the most common research design used by sociologists, involves gathering information by asking people a number of questions about their behaviors or attitudes. These questions may be asked in a face-to-face interview, in a telephone interview, or with a paper-and-pencil questionnaire. Interviews can range from the use of highly structured questionnaires using fixed responses and precoded questions to the use of highly informal open-ended questions that allow subjects to give essay-like answers in their own words. The interviewer may be detached (as when questionnaires are mailed out anonymously) or very involved (as when the interviewer lives with the research subjects over a period of time). Personal interviews can last anywhere from a few minutes to several hours and can probe the innermost secrets and details of a person's whole life or focus on just one aspect of it. Interviews are one of the best known ways of discovering the meanings that people attach to events, objects, and their own and other people's behavior. For example, Ruth Frankenberg conducted thirty in-depth, face-to-face interviews, which enabled her to gain considerable insight into the meaning of whiteness for the women she studied and into the social contexts and settings within which "articulations of whiteness" take place.

Large-scale surveys select a sizeable number of people and collect a great deal of information from them. Survey research can be used to study a wide range of human behavior as well as variables that are not directly observable, such as attitudes, values, opinions, and beliefs. For example, university research centers such as the National Opinion Research Center (NORC) at the University of Chicago routinely conduct large national and local surveys of U.S. public attitudes, values, opinions, and behavior relative to a wide range of topics using samples representative of the noninstitutionalized adult population.

Because it is usually impossible to survey every single person in the populations they want to study, sociologists use a **sample,** the selection of a number of individuals in such a way that they are representative of the larger group. In order to ensure that the sample is representative, researchers use a *random sample* technique—the research subjects are selected in a manner so that every person in the population under study has an equal chance of being selected. Some researchers using a survey research design use a *stratified random sample,* a grouping of the population under study according to the characteristics they believe to be important to their study, for example, age, race, sex, class, sexual orientation, and religion. Researchers sometimes use what is called a *cross-sectional design,* a sample or cross section of the population they are studying at a particular point in time. In this sense, surveys are somewhat like still photographs because they show the subjects at only one point in time. Survey data become the foundation for the work of many social scientists.

Survey research is extremely common in our society. For example, the Harris and Gallup polls, the Nielsen ratings, and the U.S. census are just a few of the instruments that, whether they are completely accurate or not, constitute the basis for much of our knowledge about ourselves and other people. You or someone you know has probably been surveyed by some researcher or group of researchers about subjects ranging from political attitudes and behavior to consumption patterns to attitudes and opinions about such emotionally charged subjects as abortion, physician assisted suicide, racism, and homophobia.

Surveys have both advantages and limitations. They are useful for many research purposes because they allow researchers to describe, classify, measure, compare, and find relationships among a number of variables. In addition, the survey design is perhaps the least expensive way to gather large amounts of data quickly (it is not necessary to question each individual person in the population under study). However, because they portray only one point in time, they are not very useful either for making cause-and-effect statements about social phenomena or for studying social change. Additionally, a limitation of the survey design is that researchers must rely on people to answer survey questions honestly and accurately. Because the survey is generally designed to elicit standard answers to standard questions, people are often forced to respond in terms of categories that may not truly apply to them. Further, because people sometimes disguise their real feelings and behaviors when they feel that they are private or unacceptable to others, the survey may not be the best strategy for studying attitudes and behaviors that are sensitive, such as sexual behaviors, prejudices, drug use and abuse, or prostitution. Because the survey generally focuses on the individual rather than on the context—the social situation in which people find themselves—we know little about the social setting within which attitudes are formed and behavior takes place.

The Experiment   The *experimental design* consists of a controlled method of observing behavior in which the researcher manipulates independent variables in order to assess their effects on dependent variables. Because people observing the same phenomena may see and hear things differently, social scientists have developed standardized ways of observing behavior, including the use of predetermined categories of behavior to direct observations. The observational technique the researcher uses will vary from one research situation to another, depending on whether the subjects know that they are being observed and on how much the observer wants to be involved with or detached from the people she or he is studying. Although observational techniques can be used with most research designs, they are especially appropriate for the experimental design.

The experimental design is used to study cause-and-effect relationships between variables as well as social change. Most often, this design is used to test a theory or a hypothesis derived from a theory. Experiments are sometimes conducted under controlled conditions in a laboratory setting. However, they do not have to be conducted in a laboratory. In the classical experimental design, the researcher randomly assigns research subjects to one of two groups: an *experimental group,* the group that experiences the independent variable, or a *control group,* the group that does not experience the independent variable. The researcher attempts to match the two groups on everything except experience of the independent variable and then compares the two groups to determine whether the experience with the independent variable caused any unique change in the dependent variable.

A classic example of an experimental design used in social science research is that conducted by Phillip Zimbardo (1972) and his associates. These researchers wanted to study the impact of prison structure on human behavior. In the classical experimental design tradition, they attempted to replicate the real world of prisons by setting up a mock prison in a laboratory. They randomly divided a group of college students into two groups: guards and prisoners. So thoroughly did the students in both groups internalize and act out their make-believe roles that the experiment had to be stopped shortly after it had begun. This research has long been used as an example of some of the critical ethical issues that emerge in the conduct of social science research generally and the experiment specifically. Later in this chapter, we discuss more fully some of the ethical issues involved in doing scientific research.

Like surveys, experiments have advantages and limitations. In general, the advantages of the experiment include control over the environment, the ability to isolate an experimental variable, and the fact that many experiments require relatively small amounts of time and money and a small sample size. These features make it possible to replicate an experiment many times using different subjects; if the results remain the same, this strengthens a researcher's claim that the findings are valid and means that the findings can probably be generalized to a larger population (Babbie, 1992).

The major limitations of the experimental design include:

1. A limitation of areas of study of interest to sociologists. For example, it would be unethical to study behaviors such as sexual intercourse, drug abuse, suicide, or child abuse in a controlled laboratory setting.
2. Research subjects often behave differently in controlled environments than in their natural settings. This research effect—subjects performing behaviors or answering questions in an untypical way because they want to be viewed in a favorable light—has been labeled the **Hawthorne Effect.**
3. A laboratory setting is often artificial. Setting up a social situation for investigation in a laboratory setting requires that researchers try to eliminate, as much as possible, all variables, other than the independent variable, that might influence the dependent variable. This means that they must often eliminate factors that would exist in real-life situations and contribute to the effects of both the independent and the dependent variables. The findings from experimental studies may therefore not be generalizable to the "real worlds" in which we live.

Field Research   When researchers want to study social life in its natural setting, they typically choose the field research design. In fact, most sociological behavior is best studied where people are more likely to behave naturally and less likely to try to behave in expected ways. Although this research design takes researchers to the natural setting and is flexible and less structured than other research methods, it is nonetheless rigorous research, using observation, interviews, and ethnographies. An *ethnography* is a systematic description of a culture and activities of a group of people from the group's point of view. The ethnographer typically focuses on a particular culture or subculture in an attempt to understand what its members do, how they do what they do, and the meanings they attach to their behaviors. Therefore, by necessity, ethnographers use data collection methods that allow them to study conditions or processes that are hard to measure numerically. Ethnographic research is particularly useful and relevant in areas of study in which researchers have historically studied and measured groups from the perspective of the researchers' own cultural, racial, or class biases (Schwartz & Scott, 1997). In this context, ethnography has special relevance as a research technique for studying groups of color that heretofore have been studied primarily from the cultural perspective of white middle-class researchers.

A popular way of collecting data in field research is to participate in the activities of the group that is being studied. This method of collecting data is referred to as *participant observation*. It requires researchers to develop self-discipline, emotional neutrality, and rapport with the research subjects and to observe behavior systematically. As participant observers, researchers have a unique vantage point as members of the group from which to observe events as they are experienced by the group. Because the researchers share experiences with the group members, they are able to assess the social situation from the perspective of the people involved.

A good example of a participant observation study is Kathleen Ferraro's (1989) investigation of whether Phoenix, Arizona, police officers arrested men who battered women after the city's police department instituted a strong arrest policy for domestic violence calls. Because she thought police officers might not be truthful in interviews, she decided to observe, firsthand, the interaction between the officers, the alleged abusers, and the abused women. Ferraro and five associates rode with Phoenix police officers throughout their ten-hour shifts, accompanying them on every aspect of their jobs, including talking with crime victims. They found that, despite police department policy, the officers by and large did not arrest men who battered women. Through their participant observation, these researchers found that police officers typically did not arrest abusers among groups of color, such as Mexican, Native, and African Americans, because they believed that violence was a way of

Ethnographic research provides valuable information about people from their own point of view. Sociologist Mitchell Duneier's ethnographic study of the African American men who hung out in a Chicago restaurant, Slim's Table, provides important cultural knowledge about a group that had been studied primarily from the cultural perspective of white, middle-class, male researchers.

life among these groups and arrests would be ineffective (reported in Sullivan, 1992).

Unobtrusive techniques, which allow researchers to collect data without disturbing the social situation or the actors within it, provide yet another way in which researchers can collect data in a field setting. For example, a researcher decided to observe the water level at a local water reclamation plant as a measure of the popularity of television programs. He reasoned that if a show was popular, few people would use the bathroom during the time that the program was on; they would wait until the commercial. In short, the water level would be high when the program was on and low during the commercials, when a large number of people would be using the bathroom. On the other hand, if the program was unpopular, there would not be a significant difference in water level between when the program was on and when there was a commercial. As this example illustrates, unobtrusive techniques do not disturb the natural setting in which behavior occurs. In addition, data collected this way incurs relatively little cost and can be useful as a supplement to other research methods.

Like other research designs, field research has certain advantages and limitations. The advantages center on the fact that field research generally, and field methods such as participant observation and unobtrusive techniques specifically, allow the researcher to study subjects in their natural settings. Many people may be unwilling or unable to give researchers insight into certain aspects of their behavior. However, observations of their behavior is independent of their willingness or ability to report on their behavior.

A limitation of field research is that not all behavior can be studied in its natural setting or participated in by "outsiders." A good example is sexual behavior. Another limitation of this design is that the researcher's presence often creates a new social situation. This problem was described earlier in terms of the Hawthorne Effect. Unobtrusive techniques have an additional set of limitations. An obvious limitation has to do with the interpretation of data collected in this manner. First, very often such measures provide only part of the picture—they are incomplete. Second, a major problem with unobtrusive techniques has to do with questions of ethics. People are free to accept or reject researchers' observations of their behaviors and to refuse to answer questions if researchers inform them that they are being studied. They have no such freedom when researchers use unobtrusive methods. The ethical question here is, Does the researcher have the right to *take* information about her or his subjects without their permission?

The Case Study   Primarily used in descriptive and exploratory studies, the *case study* design concentrates on one instance of the event/subject being studied. Researchers choosing this research design can use one or more of a variety of data collection methods. For example, in her book *Men and Women of the Corporation,* sociologist Rosabeth Moss Kanter (1977) observed and interviewed women and men in a large industrial supply company over a five-year period. She found that everyone in the corporation is bound and limited by organizational systems that exist in the corporation because of the way such organizations are structured: they are too large, too hierarchical, not democratic enough, and inequitable in their distribution of rewards and opportunities. Although women and men differed in their experiences, work, and careers within the corporation, and although the inequities women experienced were evident, women and men had in common the fact of being limited by their organizational circumstance.

A major advantage of the case study lies in the richness of its descriptive examples, which results from the intensive study of one or a few units. The results of case studies often suggest innovative hypotheses that can subsequently be tested utilizing some other research design, such as the experiment or survey design. On the other hand, although case studies furnish clues about behavior, they cannot test hypotheses because they are about isolated cases. Further, it is difficult to differentiate cause from effect in case studies and generalizing from the case study involves a high and generally unknown amount of risk. These limitations notwithstanding, case studies have played an important role in the development of the social sciences, and studies such as Kanter's have provided a significant source of insights, understandings, and hypotheses later applied to larger populations.

Using Precollected Data   Not all research requires the collection of original data. *Secondary analysis,* the utilization of publicly accessible information or data, is also an effective research method. Precollected data include newspapers, books, magazines, government-generated documents and statistics (such as the Uniform Crime Reports and the U.S. Census), survey results obtained by research centers (such as NORC), radio and television broadcasts, songs, diaries, records kept by groups and organizations, historical records, sales records, court records, and letters. All of these sources of data provide information that can be obtained at minimal or no cost to the researcher. The systematic examination of precollected data guided by some rationale in order to extract thematic patterns and draw conclusions about social life is called **content analysis.**

The content analysis technique is commonly used by researchers to analyze the various media. For example, researchers Victoria Holden, William Holden, and Gary Davis (1997) examined the growing controversy about the racial imaging of indigenous peoples symbolized in sports-team nicknames such as "Braves," "Redskins," and "Indians." Native Americans across the country are challenging such sports-team names and accompanying team mascots as racist portrayals of their people as uncivilized savages. Holden and her colleagues wanted to gain insight into the role that mass media play in conflicts such as this. Analyzing primarily newspapers, they found a new sensitivity to the concerns of Native Americans reflected, in part, by the heavy news coverage of the nickname controversy and by policies announced by at least three major daily newspapers that abandoned the use of "Redskins" and various other controversial nicknames in their pages.

One advantage of using precollected data is that the researcher does not have to be concerned with the Hawthorne Effect. It also takes less time and money than other research designs. However, a major limitation of this method is that, because they were collected by someone else, the data may not specifically address the issues that the researcher is studying. There may also be questions about what the data mean. For example, using census data to research the meaning and extent of interracial marriage in the United States causes problems because the Census Bureau regards Latinas/os as an ethnic rather than a racial group; it therefore does not identify interracial marriages among Latinas/os. Some of the major strengths and weaknesses of the research designs and data collection techniques presented in this section are summarized in Table 2.2.

Analyzing the Data and Drawing Conclusions

Data analysis involves searching for meaningful links between the facts that have emerged during the course of research and organizing the data so that comparisons can be made and conclusions drawn. For example, Ruth Frankenberg (1993) meticulously analyzed the narratives of the women she interviewed and concluded that their "material and conceptual environments were shaped in complex ways by long histories of racism" (p. 45). Although the women lived in many different ways, certain patterns emerged in the interview data which Frankenberg clustered around four types of childhood experience: (1) "apparently" all white, (2) racially conflictual, (3) race difference present but unremarked, and (4) quasi-integrated. Frankenberg's work is representative of what sociologists call **qualitative analysis,** analysis that focuses on specific or distinct qualities within the data that show patterns of similarity or difference among the research subjects. These similarities and differences are distinguishable in terms of quality and kind but not in terms of magnitude or numbers. In contrast, analysis of survey data, such as that contained in the Gallup polls, is referred to as **quantitative analysis,** a process in which the data can be analyzed using numerical categories and statistical techniques (for example, determining the percentage of respondents who report particular attitudes or behaviors).

The process by which we find links between the facts is subjective: it is guided by the researcher's theoretical perspective. For example, through a process of careful documentation and analysis, Frankenberg interpreted her data within a social constructionist theoretical framework in which she emphasized the social, political, and historical rather than "essential," or natural, character of whiteness. Among her conclusions is the

TABLE 2.2 ⊘ **Research Designs and Methods: A Summary**

Research Design or Method of Data Collection	Application	Advantages	Limitations
Survey	For collecting information on numerous subjects of research	Can sample the attitudes and behaviors of large populations at relatively low cost	Not useful for studying cause and effect; must rely on people giving accurate information
Experiment	For explaining relationships between variables	Allows researcher to test hypotheses derived from theory; can be used to study cause and effect	Laboratory setting is often artificial; limits the range of topics that can be studied
Field research	For investigating firsthand how people live, talk, and behave	Because it is carried out in the natural setting, yields richer and more comprehensive data	Limits the size of the sample
Case study	For exploratory or descriptive research	Allows for intensive or in-depth analysis of a specific group or setting	Limited in scope; can't generalize results to a larger population
Precollected data		Researcher does not have to be concerned with the Hawthorne Effect; saves both time and money	Because it was collected by someone else data may not specifically address the researcher's issues
Observation		Its directness; behavior is studied as it occurs	Not all behavior can be observed
Interview		Enables researcher to gather fuller information, including the subjects' spontaneous reactions	Lack of anonymity; Hawthorne Effect
Unobtrusive techniques		Enables researcher to study behavior without disturbing the natural setting in which behavior occurs; is relatively inexpensive	Provides only a partial picture; getting data without the permission of subjects raises some ethical issues

premise that racism is a "white issue," that is, an issue that shapes white experience as well as the experience of communities of color, and that social relations in the United States, no matter how neutral they may appear, are, in fact, racialized.

Ethical Issues in the Conduct of Scientific Research

Central to a discussion of scientific research, particularly when human subjects are involved, is the issue of *ethics,* which deals with what behav-

ior is proper or improper with respect to moral duty and obligation (Sullivan, 1992, p. 168). Recognizing the importance of providing researchers with ethical guidelines, the American Sociological Association (ASA) developed and published (in 1971, last revised in 1995) a comprehensive Code of Ethics for sociologists to follow. It set out some of the following codes of conduct:

1. Researchers should maintain objectivity and integrity in their research.
2. Researchers should respect their subjects' rights to privacy and dignity.
3. Research subjects must be protected from personal harm.

4. Researchers should preserve confidentiality.
5. Researchers should disclose all sources of assistance and financial support.
6. Researchers should not misuse or abuse their role as researcher.

In addition, federal legislation requires that researchers allow subjects to decide whether their thoughts, feelings, or actions will be used in a research project by securing (in verbal or written form) their *informed consent,* consent based upon knowledge of the purpose of the study and all possible consequences for one participating in the study that might reasonably influence one's decision to participate.

Many ethical questions can arise that are not as easily formulated as those put forth by the ASA. Most sociologists agree that we should be open and honest; we should not falsify our results or plagiarize (steal someone else's work). Most also agree that we should not subject our research subjects to harm, invade their privacy, or deceive them in order to study their behavior. These ethical norms are as relevant for other sciences and their research as it is for the social sciences. Tess Gerritsen's novel *Harvest,* for example, illustrates the ethical issues that have emerged in medicine in response to the growing practice of providing organ transplants to the seriously ill (see the Sociology through Literature box). Similarly, social science researchers' techniques in gathering their data sometimes call into serious question the extent to which their methods and research threaten their subjects' privacy, anonymity, and sometimes even their lives. One of the most fascinating, provocative, and controversial studies illustrating these other ethical issues has been conducted by sociologist Laud Humphreys (1970a, 1970b, 1975) (see the Sociological Reflections box).

In recent years, several sociologists have gone to extreme measures to protect their research subjects, even facing threats of jail sentences or threats upon their lives. For example, in 1993, after a group of animal rights activists broke into a research facility at Washington State University, released the animals, and destroyed computers and files, a graduate student named Rik Scarce, who was conducting research on radical environmental groups, was called before a grand jury investigating the incident. Although otherwise cooperative, he refused to answer questions that might violate the anonymity and the confidentiality of his research subjects. As a result, he spent 159 days in jail for contempt of court (Scarce, 1993, 1994).

The Politics of Doing Sociology

Sociology, like all other sciences, makes a distinction between pure and applied science. **Pure sociology** refers to the notion that sociological research should be value neutral and that the motivation for research should be the desire for basic knowledge that will advance understanding of human society and behavior, not the values of a particular researcher. Because there will always be disagreements about values, value choices can never be included in the process of scientific inquiry. **Applied sociology** consists of research designed to focus our knowledge on a particular issue or concern with some practical outcome in mind. A primary focus of applied research is social policy or reform and behavioral changes. That is, an intended outcome is the recommendation of some social policy that can be implemented or some social intervention that will help reform society, for example, to alleviate poverty, racism, or sexism. The Bullard study of environmental racism (which opened this chapter) is a good example of applied sociology in which the research had the intended impact on both local and national environmental policies.

Given the goals of applied research, then, it has a political aspect that is worth noting. By the term *political,* we refer to processes that affect the distribution of power and resources in society (Nyden et al., 1997). For example, social betterment is not an objective condition but rather a value judgment; it involves conflicting values and interests and opposition between groups having varying amounts of power (Sullivan, 1992). The question is always, Social betterment for whom? Applied researchers are drawn into this conflict of values and interest; thus, their relationship to the power structure becomes a very important issue to consider.

Sociology through Literature

Hearts for Sale

The following passage is from *Harvest,* a novel by Tess Gerritsen that tells the story of an "organs for cash" ring, run by an elite cardiac transplant team of doctors operating out of a prestigious New England hospital. After a series of puzzling events surrounding the unexplained appearance of a heart harvested for a wealthy, middle-aged woman, a young female doctor, Abby DiMatteo, begins to unravel the transplant team's lethal conspiracy of organ selling, which includes buying young Russian boys under the pretext of bringing them to the United States to be adopted and then killing them for their organs. Dr. DiMatteo is beginning to pull some of the pieces of her investigation together, and she and the chief resident, Vivian, report their suspicions to the head of the transplant team, unaware that he is the leader of the conspiracy.

"Cash for organs. Is it possible?"

In the midst of stirring cream into his coffee, Dr. Ivan Tarasoff stopped and glanced at Vivian. "Do you have any proof this is going on?"

"Not yet. We're just asking you if it's possible. And if so, how could it be done?"

Dr. Tarasoff sank back on the couch and sipped his coffee as he thought it over. It was four forty-five, and except for the occasional scrub-suited resident passing through to the adjoining locker room, the Mass Gen surgeons' lounge was quiet. Tarasoff, who'd come out of the OR only twenty minutes ago, still had a dusting of glove talc on his hands and a surgical mask dangling around his neck. Watching him, Abby was comforted, once again, by the image of her grandfather. The gentle blue eyes, the silver hair. The quiet voice. *The voice of ultimate authority,* she thought, *belongs to the man who never has to raise it.*

"There have been rumors, of course," said Tarasoff. "Every time a celebrity gets and organ, people wonder if money was involved. But there's never been any proof. Only suspicions."

"What rumors have you heard?"

"That one can buy a higher place on the waiting list. I myself have never seen it happen."

"I have," said Abby.

Tarasoff looked at her. "When?"

"Two weeks ago. Mrs. Victor Voss. She was third on the waiting list and she got a heart. The two people at the top of the list later died."

"UNOS wouldn't allow that. Or NEOB. they have strict guidelines."

"NEOB didn't know about it. In fact, they have no record of the donor in their system."

Tarasoff shook his head, "This is hard to believe. If the heart didn't come through UNOS or NEOB, where did it come from?"

"We think Voss paid to keep it out of the system. So it could go to his wife," said Vivian.

"This is what we know so far," said Abby. . . .

Later, as Dr. DiMatteo continues her investigation, she finds herself framed for drunk driving, shot at and almost killed by members of the organ-selling team, one of whom is her lover. Finally, after uncovering the fact that the team is killing Russian boys for their hearts, she herself is slated to be the next harvest victim.

Although this novel does not pertain to sociological research specifically, it nevertheless raises many important ethical as well as legal issues that researchers and other professionals responsible for the well-being of human subjects must adhere to. Gerritsen's fiction is painfully reminiscent of the real-life, infamous Tuskegee Syphilis Study (upon which the movie *Ms. Evers' Boys* was based), a study of untreated syphilis conducted by medical doctors and U.S. public health officials over a forty-year period (1932–1972) that used 430 African American sharecroppers in Alabama as the subjects of what the researchers claimed to be a "scientific experiment." Read the Gerritsen novel in its entirety and look up the Tuskegee study. The best general accounts of this study are "The 40-Year Death Watch," *Medical World News* (August 18, 1972), pp. 15–17, and Dolores Katz, "Why 430 Blacks with Syphilis Went Uncured for 40 Years," *Detroit Free Press* (November 5, 1972).

What are the similarities between *Harvest* and the Tuskegee study? What are some of the social values and attitudes that affect the professionals' behaviors in each case? What role does race, age, and gender play in each case? Explain your reasoning.

Source: Reprinted with the permission of Simon & Schuster, Inc., from *Harvest* by Tess Gerritsen (Pocket Books, pp. 222–223). Copyright © 1996 by Tess Gerritsen.

Ethical Dilemmas in Scientific Research

While a sociology graduate student, Laud Humphreys (1970a) undertook research in an area of behavior into which there had been virtually no previous sociological research: the casual sexual encounters between male strangers in public washrooms, known to them as tearooms. Humphreys was interested in how these encounters were initiated, the roles performed by different men in the act of fellatio, and the family lives and other social background characteristics of the participants. Only a small percentage of people with homosexual inclinations participate in this type of impersonal sexual activity, and Humphreys wanted to find out more about the particular characteristics of those who did. Acting as the "watch queen," or lookout, he was able to observe hundreds of sexual encounters without his identity as a researcher and outsider becoming known to the other participants.

In order to secure background information on each of the men he observed, Humphreys quietly took down their car license plate numbers and then traced their names and addresses through public motor vehicle records. After waiting one year to ensure that he would not be recognized, Humphreys changed his appearance and went to the homes of these men in yet another disguise: as a survey researcher looking for information on quite a different topic. Through personal interviews with the men, Humphreys was able to obtain some rather interesting details about their personal lives without letting them know he was studying their sexual behavior. For example, Humphreys found the following:

1. Most of the tearoom clients were married men in their middle thirties, living with their wives and having otherwise fairly exemplary lives. They had an average of two children, most had at least at-tended college, and their families appeared to be unaware of their tearoom activities.
2. The men worked in occupations ranging from truck drivers and machine operators to clerical workers, managers, teachers, and postmen.
3. A large number of the men identified themselves as heterosexual; others self-identified as gay, ambisexual, or bisexual.
4. A number of the men were practicing Roman Catholics.
5. The majority of the men were white.

Although Humphreys's study won an award for outstanding research, it was strongly criticized by many sociologists and in the popular press. The most serious criticism lodged against Humphreys was that he used systematic deception, both initially to observe the men's sexual encounters and later to gain entry to the men's homes to get detailed information about their lives. His critics argued that Humphreys unjustly intruded in these encounters and that he should have identified himself as a researcher, even at the cost of losing some sources of information. In the second edition of his book (1975), Humphreys acknowledged the seriousness of the ethical questions his critics had raised. Although he took great care to maintain the confidentiality and anonymity of his research subjects, he agreed that he should have identified himself as a researcher.

Suppose you wanted to replicate/update Laud Humphreys's research on homosexual sexual behavior in public washrooms. How would you go about it? Where, if anywhere, would you draw the line between your quest for knowledge about this behavior and the subjects' rights to privacy? How would you avoid the ethical issues raised in the Humphreys study?

A number of issues are involved in the politics of scientific research. First, although making a conscious decision about what is a better society is not, in and of itself, a problem, it can raise some ethical issues related to the research process. Sociologists deal with some of these issues through adherence to a professional code of ethics. Second, funding is based on a researcher's ability and willingness to study the topic from the particular perspective of the funding agency. Thus, although not explicitly stated, funding sources typically expect findings that will support their philosophical or political perspectives or positions. Finally, how research findings are used is also a political issue. When applied researchers conduct research for a particular group, they must consider whether their research will be used to help maintain or extend oppressive and exploitative patterns of dominance and subordination in society (Sullivan, 1992). They must also consider how the mass media might present, use, interpret, or distort their findings (Thompson & Hickey, 1996). As major television networks move increasingly into the realm of defining, studying, analyzing, and explaining major social problems, they often call on sociologists to provide expert commentary. Unfortunately, the media increasingly define what is appropriate research and, by handpicking the experts, they also define who and what is worthy of public attention.

Scientific Research in the Twenty-First Century

Researchers utilizing the research designs and data collection methods outlined in this chapter as well as new and advancing technology will continue, for better or worse, to shape social and political debates, issues, programs, and outcomes well into the next century. Some issues of concern and their implications for social policy and social change in the future include (1) research and advancing technology, (2) research and issues of diversity, and (3) the trend toward activist research.

Research and Technology

New information technology has improved our ability not only to communicate with one another but also to access data. The Internet (the electronic superhighway), for example, enables us to access a wide variety of census data, international and national statistics, public and private library holdings, and articles and other resources we need for our research, and we can talk and collaborate with and share our research with colleagues around the world. The research uses of the new technology are vast. A colleague

of ours recently used the Internet (via e-mail) to conduct interviews with people all over the United States. These and other technological advances will surely continue to transform sociological research, but they will also raise additional ethical issues. For example, technological advances have made it much easier to collect data about people and to study them without their knowledge or consent. Today, as well as in the future, research ethics must encompass the privacy, dignity, safety, and confidentiality issues raised by the new information technology.

Research and Diversity

In a multiethnic and racially and religiously diverse world, sociologists and other social researchers will be faced with researching issues about individuals, groups, cultures, and subcultures that will require a knowledge of and sensitivity to a myriad of issues related to diversity. Researchers must know the populations they study. This requires an awareness of diversity within a general group. Consider Latinas/os. Although people having roots in several different Spanish-speaking countries make up this population, most survey researchers refer to it as if it constituted a single ethnic community. There is very little data about Latinas/os that distinguishes characteristics such as national origin (e.g., Mexico versus Cuba) and nativity (e.g., U.S.- versus foreign-born), characteristics that are essential to defining ethnicity and determining its effects. R.O. de la Garza (1993) argues that survey researchers have shown little interest in collecting this kind of data. As a result, there is no reliable basis for evaluating Latinas/os' attitudes about issues, such as immigration and language policies, that will continue to be key in political campaigns and elections well into the next century. At the very least, a lack of accurate data about the views of the diverse population of Latinas/os perpetuates negative stereotypes and makes debates about their views meaningless. Lumping all Latinas/os into a single category distorts reality and makes ethnicity a one-dimensional and immutable phenomenon (de la Garza, 1993). This observation could also be made for several other populations that researchers typically know little about but about whom they make broad and sweeping generalizations. In the twenty-first century, attention to these and other cultural dynamics in a multicultural and diverse world will be a must.

The Trend toward Activist Research

If sociology is to continue to be a viable and useful discipline, sociologists will have to continue and expand their long tradition of sound scientific research and careful but spirited critique of dominant paradigms and the status quo. Sociological research will become increasingly more action oriented, aiming to shape or formulate social policies that improve the quality of human life for *all* people. We are already seeing this trend as more and more sociology departments focus on applied sociology and as sociologists both inside and outside the university collaborate with community organizations and activists, social service practitioners, and political leaders to use their research to help find solutions to societal problems and to initiate positive social change. Whether or not you choose to major in sociology, we encourage you to apply the sociological imagination not only while reading this textbook but also in your ongoing social interactions and in ways that you deem useful for the betterment of all people.

Key Points to Remember

1. Sociological theory and research go hand in hand. Theories provide us with basic insights into the nature of individuals and society and research provides us with the objective observations by which theories are verified.
2. A theoretical paradigm is a broad explanation of social reality from a particular point of view. The three theoretical paradigms most used by sociologists are structural functionalism, conflict theory, and social interactionism. Some sociologists also use feminist and multicultural paradigms.
3. The work of sociologists is guided by the rules and principles of the scientific method. Its guidelines include defining the problem, reviewing the literature, choosing a research design, collecting data, analyzing the data, drawing conclusions, and reporting the findings.
4. Central to the conduct of scientific research, particularly when human subjects are involved, is the issue of ethics. A researcher should not expose subjects to physical or mental danger, no matter how important the resulting knowledge would be. The American Sociological Association developed a comprehensive Code of Ethics which includes among its basic principles objectivity, respect for subjects' right to privacy and dignity, confidentiality, and honesty.
5. *Pure sociology* refers to the notion that sociological research should be value neutral and advance our understanding of society and human behavior. *Applied sociology* refers to research designed to be used for social betterment, that is, to change or improve society.
6. Research is never completely objective. A number of issues are involved in the politics of scientific research including (1) the imposition of the personal values of the researcher, (2) the source of funding, and (3) the use to which research findings are put.
7. Some of the issues pertaining to scientific research in the twenty-first century will include (1) research and advancing technology, (2) research and issues of diversity, and (3) the trend toward activist research.

Key Terms

theory

empirical evidence

theoretical paradigm

manifest functions

latent functions

functional social patterns

dysfunctional social patterns	dependent variable	unobtrusive technique
Thomas Theorem	operationalize	content analysis
scientific method	reliability	qualitative analysis
hypothesis	validity	quantitative analysis
variable	sample	pure sociology
independent variable	Hawthorne Effect	applied sociology

Key People

Robert Bullard	William I. Thomas	Erving Goffman
Talcott Parsons	Charles Horton Cooley	Harold Garfinkel
Robert Merton	George Herbert Mead	Ruth Frankenberg

Questions for Review and Discussion

1. Pick three of the following topics and indicate why the particular social pattern has occurred and continues to occur using functionalist, conflict, interactionist, feminist, and multicultural perspectives: poverty, wealth, racism, rap music, the glass ceiling, domestic violence, unemployment, affirmative action. Is any theoretical perspective more or less effective than the others for explaining the topics you chose? Which theories, if any, suggest social actions that might help resolve the issue? What social actions do they suggest?

2. The local chapter of Mothers Against Drunk Driving has asked your sociology class to conduct a study of student drinking and driving patterns. What variables would you include in your study? What measurement concerns would you need to address? What political and ethical issues might arise in carrying out such research? How would you resolve such issues?

3. Some sociologists take the position that only theories and knowledge that can be applied to resolving problems in the real world are worth anything. What do you think? Do you agree that only that knowledge which helps to solve problems should be considered valuable? Why? Why not? Can you think of particular bodies of knowledge that are considered valuable but do not help to solve social problems?

4. In several high schools, there are clinics that, among other services, provide students with birth control pills if they request them. By making birth control pills available to teenagers, the clinics hope to reduce the teenage pregnancy rate among their student populations. You have been given the challenging task of designing a study that shows whether or not the clinics are meeting their stated objective. How would you design such a study?

For Further Reading

Bart, Pauline, and Linda Frankel. 1986. *The Student Sociologist's Handbook.* (4th ed.). New York: Random House. A valuable resource for sociology students. It provides a step-by-step outline for writing field reports and research papers and includes a large bibliography for those interested in conducting sociological research.

Kohn, Melvin. 1989. *Cross-National Research in Sociology.* Newbury Park, CA: Sage. A valuable paperback that includes seventeen essays on global research.

Nyden, Phillip, Figert, Anne, Shibley, Mark, and Darryl Burrows. 1997. *Building Community: Social Science in Action.* Thousand Oaks, CA: Pine Forge Press. This book, containing twenty-seven case studies, provides a good discussion of how social science research techniques can be used in a multitude of settings to effect meaningful social change.

Reinharz, Schulamit. 1992. *Feminist Methods in Social Research.* New York: Oxford University Press. A good review of the relationship between the research methods that feminists typically use and conventional research designs and methods.

Sociology through Literature

Bannister, Robert C. 1991. *Jessie Bernard: The Making of a Feminist.* New Brunswick, NJ: Rutgers University Press. An interesting biography of a woman who became a sociologist when few women did so.

Internet Resources

http://diogenes.baylor.edu/WWWproviders/Larry_Ridener/INDEX.HTML. This Web site provides information on the contributions of some of the early sociologists, such as Comte, Marx, Spencer, Durkheim, Weber, Cooley, and Mead.

http://www.luc.edu/depts/curl and http://www.luc.edu/depts/curl/prag The Loyola University Chicago Center for Urban Research and Learning and the Policy Research Action Group World Wide Web Home Page respectively. Through these home pages, you can explore recent developments in collaborative research and action networks.

http://www.indiana.edu/~appsoc/job.html A checklist for those considering a career as an applied sociologist.

http://www.census.gov/ The statistical results of the censuses, surveys, and other Census Bureau programs are available through this Web site.

3

Social Change, Collective Behavior, and Social Action

AGENT OF CHANGE: AUNG SAN SUU KYI

In 1991, Aung San Suu Kyi was awarded the Nobel Peace Prize for her efforts to bring democracy to her country of Myanmar, also known as Burma, in Southeast Asia. For most of the 1990s, she has been under house arrest for speaking out against the country's repressive military dictatorship, known as the State Law and Order Restoration Council (SLORC). Under the terms of her arrest, she is allowed to see only her husband and children, and only on rare occasions.

Suu Kyi had been living in England with her family when her mother became seriously ill. In 1988, she returned to the capital city of Rangoon to care for her. At that time, protestors, most of them university students, were demonstrating against the repressive policies of the government preceding the military dictatorship and demanding free, multiparty elections. Between August 8 and 13 of that year, riot police killed nearly 3,000 demonstrators. In 1989, the military seized control. Suu Kyi, whose father had negotiated with the British for Burma's independence and been assassinated by political rivals when she was two, joined with other antigovernment leaders to form the National League for Democracy (NLD).

On April 5, 1989, as she and other NLD organizers were returning home, they were stopped and ordered off the road by government troops. Waving her companions away, she continued walking toward the soldiers even after being threatened with being shot. As she advanced, the order to shoot was overruled. After that incident, she continued to give prodemocracy speeches. Her growing popularity created fear among the military rulers and they placed her under house arrest. In 1990, the SLORC agreed to hold an election but refused to allow Suu Kyi to run for office. The NLD won the vast majority of contested seats, but the SLORC refused to recognize the election results. Although still under house arrest, Suu Kyi continues to work for nonviolent political change (Wallechinsky, 1997).

Clearly Myanmar, as the SLORC prefers to call the country, or Burma, as the followers of Suu Kyi prefer to call it, is a society beset with great conflict. On the one side, there are social actors who want to resist change and to maintain their power; on the other side, there are social activists who are promoting change in the direction of a democracy. The stakes are high. Activists on both sides face the possibility of arrest and even the possibility of loss of life. What type of society will emerge from this conflict is unknown. Myanmar, like any other society, must adapt to changing conditions. However, as we will see in this chapter, how quickly a society responds to changing conditions depends on many factors.

Source: Information from Wallechinsky, D. 1997. "How One Woman Became the Voice of Her People." *Parade* (January 19), pp. 4–6.

Understanding Social Change

Sociologists define **social change** as a process through which patterns of social behavior, social relationships, social institutions, and systems of stratification are altered, modified, or transformed over time. As we discussed in Chapter 1, social change is ubiquitous, that is, it occurs everywhere and at all levels. However, the rate of social change can vary dramatically from one society to the next. In some societies, like the United States, the pace of change is quite rapid. When we purchase a computer today, we joke that it will be outdated before we get it out of the box. In other societies, the pace of change is quite slow. In some parts of Asia, Africa, Australia, and the Middle East, indigenous people still hunt, fish, plant, and enact traditions similar to the way their ancestors did centuries ago. To the outside observer as well as to the individuals within those societies, change may go on almost undetected. However, indigenous populations everywhere, whether they want to or not, are increasingly being drawn into the changes taking place in the world around them. For example, as the Amazon rain forests in Brazil are cleared for development, the native Indians of the region die or are pushed into villages where it is almost impossible to sustain their traditional ways of life. Change often breeds conflict and affects people in different ways. In this case, the land developers of the Amazon view the supplanting of the rain forest as beneficial to their own interests and to the economic future of Brazil. Conversely, indigenous peoples, environmentalists, and anthropologists see this same behavior as harmful to the world's ecosystem as well as to a society's culture.

Theories of Social Change

Social change is not a simple matter to explain. Part of the difficulty stems from the assumptions, often unrecognized, that people make about the value of social change. Various explanations of social change equate change with progress. One theorist after another has suggested that societies evolve toward greater and greater progress or perfection. However, the notion that change means progress is a value-laden assumption that implies that change desirable for one group or society is desirable for all other groups and societies. The fact is that social change can be progressive for some at the same time that it can be extremely difficult and disruptive for others. For example, the development of nuclear weaponry is progressive from a military standpoint but it led to a destructive Cold War between the United States and the former Soviet Union. Moreover, ongoing nuclear development and testing in countries around the world has increased the risk of a nuclear war and exposed thousands to varying degrees of radioactive fallout. Countries as varied as Britain, France, China, and, most recently, India and Pakistan have all conducted nuclear tests. These tests have affected an untold number of human lives and destinies and, according to some experts on the topic, they will continue to do so for as long as 300,000 years. The use of nuclear power stands now as one of the greatest threats to the survival of civilization (Zastrow, 1995).

From these examples, we can see that the value of change is relative. Thus, we will use a *cultural relativist perspective* to examine explanations of social change. Cultural relativism is the idea that all cultures and groups develop their own ways of dealing with the specific demands of their environments. This perspective allows us to raise important questions about how and why social change occurs, why some societies change more rapidly than others, whether social change must follow the Western model, whether social change is progressive or regressive, and who benefits from and who is systematically constrained by social change.

Evolutionary Theories   Evolutionary theories of social change suggest that social change occurs naturally, constantly, and continuously and is both necessary and inevitable. It occurs through relatively fixed stages, moving toward greater progress and better conditions of life. Most sociologists classify evolutionary theory in terms of the following scheme: unilinear, multilinear, and cyclical. *Unilinear evolution theory* assumes that societal change follows a predetermined and uniform path, evolving from simple to complex. For example, in the nineteenth century, Herbert Spencer contended that all societies followed uniform, natural laws of evolution which decreed "survival of the fittest"; those aspects of society most fit would survive and those that were not would die out or disappear. In this manner, society naturally evolved to greater progress and improvement. Subsequently, Lewis Morgan (1877) developed a unilinear theory of social change that justified colonialization and exploitation of "inferior" indigenous peoples. He proposed a three-stage sequence: savagery, barbarism, and civilization, with English society

as the epitome of the third and final stage of societal development. Today, Morgan's views have been discredited as highly ethnocentric, and unilinear theory in general is considered unreliable and flawed. Indeed, the growing recognition and appreciation of the rich diversity of human cultures has all but discredited these types of evolutionary theories.

Multilinear evolution theory replaced unilinear explanations of social change. This theory suggests that instead of a single path, there are multiple routes leading to similar stages of social development. A central tenet in evolutionary theory of either type is the notion of progress, that societies evolve toward greater and greater progress and toward a higher state of perfection. But, as the example of nuclear weapons demonstrates, *development, progress, improvement,* and *perfection* are not synonymous terms.

Cyclical evolution theories suggest that change occurs as societies move forward, backward, up, and down through an endless series of cycles. Proponents of cyclical theories liken the development and change of societies to the life stages of the human organism: birth, infancy, youth, adulthood, old age and decline, and, finally, death. In his controversial book, *The Decline of the West,* German social critic, Oswald Spengler (1926) employed such a model to suggest the decline of Western society. He argued that the West had passed through adulthood in the eighteenth century and by the early twentieth century was in old age and a deep spiral of decline. According to Spengler, this process was inevitable and there was therefore nothing we could do about it.

Historian Arnold Toynbee (1946) explained these cycles with his challenge and response theory of change, in which he claimed that the fate of a given society depends on the challenges presented by the environment and the manner in which its people respond to those challenges. Toynbee essentially concurred with Spengler's fatalistic view that although societies may endure for hundreds of years, they are doomed to die.

What we are witnessing in Western societies today—the increasing challenges and crises of poverty, war, racism, violence, terrorism, fear, sexism, sexual assault, serial murder, children killing children, crime, gangs, child abandonment and abuse, and alienation—may well be indicative of the decline that Spengler wrote of leading to the death of Western civilization. However, most modern sociologists reject the biological analogy inherent in evolutionary theories of social change such as Spengler's as well as the notion that progress means improvement. Toynbee's theory helps us understand social change in historical context but it does not allow us to predict social change. Although the theories of these men have limitations for explaining social change, they do help us understand some of the changes in human societies that have occurred over time.

Applying the Sociological Imagination

Do you agree or disagree with Toynbee and Spengler? Do the challenges and crises of Western society signal the decay and the impending death of Western civilization? Can rich nations such as the United States prevent such decline?

Functionalist Theory   As you learned in Chapter 2, the functionalist perspective views society as a system of interrelated parts, each contributing to the stability, equilibrium, and maintenance of the overall system. A functional theory of social change focuses on the potential disruptions caused by change rather than on its benefits for social systems. Functionalists are cautious about social change because it may provoke a radical restructuring of a social system. In this context, change is seen as a threat to system stability or equilibrium.

Noted functionalist Talcott Parsons (1964) developed an *equilibrium theory* of social change in which he contended that all parts of a system are interdependent. Thus, change in one part of a social system requires compensatory change in other parts of the system. As long as the changes in one part of the system are counterbalanced by changes elsewhere in the system, without disruption of important social functions, equilibrium is maintained and the system is not harmed

by social change. For example, advances in computer technology have changed the face of many work places and increasingly necessitate a computer-literate work force. U.S. society has responded to this need with an increased emphasis on and availability of computer training beginning sometimes as early as pre-school and kindergarten. More public and private dollars and resources are spent to train people to use computers, colleges and universities give priority to computer science programs, and an increasing number of elementary and high school teachers and college professors, across disciplines, are emphasizing computer literacy in their classes. Changes such as these help to keep the various parts of society in balance and ensure equilibrium, social order, and stability. For Parsons, societal change represents an integration of new and old elements within society through what he called a "moving equilibrium," or a movement toward a new and harmonious system.

Change in the various parts of society sometimes proceeds at different rates. William Ogburn (1922) referred to this unequal rate of change as **cultural lag,** which in some cases may be benign but in others threaten the smooth functioning of the overall society. Cultural lag that can threaten the smooth functioning of the overall society can be seen in the way that medical advances have outpaced the development of ethical and legal norms that usually govern such advances. Cloning is one example. The cloning of a sheep not only made news in 1997 but also sparked debate around the world about this new technology and the ethical issues it raises. Among the questions raised were, how will it be regulated and by whom? Some people fear that human cloning is next and have been outspoken in their view that it is morally unacceptable. As Table 3.1 shows, the vast majority of the American public seems to agree. In 1997, President Clinton charged a federal commission with the task of investigating the legal and ethical implications of this new technology. In the same year, the House subcommittee on basic research scheduled a meeting to address some of the same ethical issues raised by the prospect of cloning human beings. Some scientists say that human cloning could happen by 2004. If they are right, the continuing

TABLE 3.1 ⊘ **Should We Clone Humans?**

	Yes	No
If you had the chance, would you clone yourself?	7%	91%
Is it against God's will to clone human beings?	74%	19%
Should the Federal Government regulate the cloning of animals?	65%	29%

Source: Kluger, J. 1997. "Will We Follow the Sheep?" *Time* (March 10), p. 71. © 1997 Time Inc. Reprinted by permission. From a telephone poll of 1,005 adult Americans taken for Time/CNN on Feb. 26–27, 1997 by Yankelovich Partners Inc. Sampling error is ±3.1%. "Not sures" omitted.

lag between biotechnology and bioethics has the potential to be highly disruptive of the smooth functioning of our society.

Functional theories of social change also address **differentiation,** a pattern of social change whereby one part of society splits into two or more new parts. For example, family differentiation has led to social institutions such as the schools, day care centers, businesses, and churches taking over functions once performed by the family. Society must then adapt to the creation of these new parts, integrating them so that there is a new equilibrium. According to the functionalist view, societies are constantly adapting and evolving as new forms of differentiation take place, and this pattern of evolution is generally toward more complex and differentiated social structures. An implication of this viewpoint is that slow, integrative, incremental, and orderly change is a constant in society. Nonetheless, the functionalist perspective on social change is most often criticized for ignoring social change, especially that change that is rapid and substantial.

Conflict Theories   None of the theories of social change discussed thus far deal adequately with the issue of conflict as a significant mechanism of social change. In contrast to such theories, as we saw in Chapter 2, a conflict theory of social change focuses on how constant tension and struggle between competing groups in an unequal society lead to social change. German philosopher Georg Hegel's dialectical approach provided the basis for much of this thinking. Utilizing this approach, Karl Marx described social change as a *dialectical process* characterized by three stages of development and change. The *thesis* represents the status quo and contains within it the seeds of its own destruction, or the *antithesis* (opposition). The conflict and struggle between the thesis and the antithesis leads to a compromise, or *synthesis.* This synthesis becomes, in time, the new social order or new thesis that will be challenged by its own antithesis, resulting in another synthesis—and the process continues. In this Marxian scheme, capitalism is the thesis and the capitalists' oppressive and exploitative treatment of workers, used in order to maximize their profits, leads workers to resist, which is the antithesis. Clashes with the capitalists ultimately lead to a synthesis, a dictatorship of the proletariat. This synthesis becomes the new thesis, containing the seeds of its own destruction as the dialectic process continues.

Modern conflict theorists such as Ralf Dahrendorf (1959) suggest that conflict occurs in every social institution and among many different groups, not just the two basic classes identified by Marx. This conflict always produces social change but, contrary to Marx's view, that change is not always revolutionary. Although the revolutionary change that Marx predicted has not occurred, others of his predictions of change have borne fruit. For example, Marx suggested that early capitalism would spawn the rise of large-scale industry, the emergence of multinational corporations, and the concentration of capital in a few giant corporations. These predictions are everywhere evident today.

Forces of Social Change

The forces of social change are many and varied; some forces are external to a society and others come from within a society. Among the major forces of social change are cultural contact and diffusion, revolution and warfare, alterations in the physical environment, invention and technology, and demographic trends.

Cultural Contact and Diffusion   Today, when North Americans travel to distant places, they often feel somewhat at home when they recognize such symbols as McDonald's golden arches or the Coca-Cola logo. At home, few Americans stop to think that the clock they refer to was a medieval European invention, that the bathroom and toilet they use are but modified copies of Roman originals, or that the umbrellas they carry were invented in India (Linton, 1937). Yet this **diffusion,** the spread of culture traits from one society to another, is the inevitable result of contact between cultures. With modern communication technology reaching into the most remote corners of the globe, the rate of diffusion has accelerated dramatically over the past century. Diffusion has been a mixed blessing for many societies. For example, developing societies often welcome the medical and technological skills of industrialized societies but regret the spread in their cultures of elements of Western culture such as rock music, fashions, and films which they view as undermining their own culture's attitudes and values, especially among their youth.

Revolution and Warfare   Two common sources of social change are revolution and war. Michael Kimmel (1990, p. 6) defines revolutions as "attempts by subordinate groups to transform the social foundations of political power." War or armed conflict, whether internal (as, for example, the U.S. Civil War) or external (as, for example, World War II), obviously produces major changes. On a micro level, families are disrupted by the temporary or permanent loss of both combatants and noncombatants. As a result, many children grow up without one or both of their parents. On the macro level, whole physical infrastructures may be destroyed, seriously damaging economic and other social institutions. Just the financial costs of war are enormous (see the Data Box). Further, after a war is over, millions of people may be left homeless. Territorial boundaries may be changed. New nations and new forms of government may be created. Although new political alignments may be forged, animosities engendered during the conflict may continue to simmer and break out anew, as recently occurred among the Serbs, Croats, and Muslims living in Yugoslavia.

The Physical Environment   Changes in the physical environment caused by natural disasters, climatic changes, or industrial activities can have enormous impact on people's lives and foster numerous other changes. The physical destruction caused by natural disasters such as earthquakes disrupt local economies and result in many changes as communities are rebuilt. In many parts of the world, land has been overgrazed, forests have been denuded, and major waterways have been polluted by oil spills, thus threatening many species of plant, bird, and marine life. These activities not only alter the ecological balance of nature but they have con-

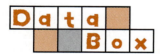

Financial Costs of Various Wars in 1990 Dollars

The American Revolution	$1.2 billion	Korean War	$263.9 billion
The Civil War	$4.4 billion	Vietnam War	$346.7 billion
World War I	$196.5 billion	Gulf War	$61.1 billion
World War II	$2,091.3 billion		

Source: The U.S. War Center: Louisiana State University, http://www.cwc.lsu.edu/index.htm (March 23, 1997).

sequences for the social order. On the one hand, traditional ways of earning a living may be damaged or disappear completely. The younger generation may be forced to leave home in search of new work, thus disrupting family life and the future viability of a community. On the other hand, people may respond to these events by establishing new codes of conduct or developing new technology in an attempt to control future events.

Invention and Technology   Societies also change as a result of **invention**, the creation of new things, whether material, such as the telephone and the computer, or nonmaterial, such as women's suffrage and the theory of relativity. Some societies are more inventive than others. The rate of invention in any society depends primarily on two critical factors. First, the existing cultural base of a society must have a level of knowledge, skills, and resources needed to make the invention possible. Second, societies differ in their degree of receptivity to inventions and the resulting changes they bring. Highly industrialized societies like the United States and its Asian and European counterparts encourage new inventions and invest significant amounts of resources in their development. Currently, the United States and its allies are putting billions of dollars into an effort to build an international space station. In contrast, more traditionally oriented societies often resist inventions in an attempt to maintain the stability of their way of life. For example, the Amish, an orthodox Anabaptist sect that separated from the Swiss-German Mennonite church in the late 1600s and eventually settled in what is now southeastern Pennsylvania, forgo many of the inventions that characterize modern life—including electricity, automobiles, and telephones—in an effort to remain constant to their values and customs. To the degree that it is possible, "the Amish maintain customs of dress, music, transportation, and morality from the 1600s and continue to reject 'worldly ways' " (Savells, 1997, p. 474).

Like invention, **technology,** the application of knowledge for practical ends, is another major source of change. New technology frequently develops in response to a perceived or real need, but it also may create new problems. For example, car phones allow us to remain in contact with homes or offices while on the road, but they also have made driving more hazardous. Canadian researchers report that talking on a cellular phone while driving is as dangerous as driving while intoxicated ("Car phone," 1997).

When sociologists examine technology, they are not concerned with the technology itself but rather with its social significance, that is, its ability to influence the way people think and how they relate to one another. For example, in recent years, some sociologists have raised a concern that the increasing amount of time people spend engaging in non-face-to-face interaction with relative strangers on the Internet is eroding their personal relationships at home. Others see today's communication technologies as contributing to *cultural leveling,* a process in which diverse cultures become homogenized, that is, looking much alike.

Demographic Trends   Changes in birth, death, and migration rates are **demographic trends** that affect the size and composition of a population, which, in turn, can have major impact on a society. If a society's resources are scarce, increases in births can push a population toward starvation and chaos. On the other hand, if a society fails to reproduce itself in sufficient numbers, it may suffer from a labor shortage or even face eventual extinction. **Migration** refers to the movement of people into or out of a geographic area. Today, upwards of 100 million people live outside their place of birth or citizenship. Michael Teitelbaum and Sharon Russell (1994) analyzed how mass migrations, often sparked by famine and warfare, affect both the sending and receiving societies. Throughout the world, refugees from poorer countries are struggling to enter wealthier countries. Fearing that their economies can no longer support an influx of poor immigrants, the wealthy countries are limiting the number and length of stay of immigrants. Such fears have engendered intense emotional debate, especially when immigrants are primarily people of color and the receiving nations are predominately white. For example, one of the most controversial issues in the 1996 national elections in the United States concerned proposed policy changes that would end welfare assistance to many immigrants and their families.

Today upwards of 100 million people live outside their country of birth, moving from poorer countries to wealthier ones in the hope of starting a new life, like these newly naturalized American citizens. Patterns of mass migration have resulted in significant political and social change.

Collective Behavior, Social Action, and Social Change

When we consider the forces of social change, it is easy to slip into thinking along deterministic lines, that is, thinking that social change is something that is imposed on us by amorphous forces and that does not involve our active involvement. The reality is quite the opposite; change happens largely as a result of human social action. As we have seen at the openings of these first three chapters, an individual, regardless of her or his position in society, can become a significant agent of social change by recognizing a problem or a need and then becoming personally involved in seeking a solution. Another important mechanism for producing social change emerges when individuals join together to act collectively to forestall or to bring about social change. For example, in the late nineteenth century, U.S. workers grew increasingly frustrated by their long work week, low pay, and unhealthy working conditions. They joined together in what has become known as the union or labor movement. Although labor's struggle was long and difficult and is by no means over today, it made possible the eight-hour day, paid holidays and vacations, and safer working conditions for generations of workers. Those of us who are prone to think, "You can't fight city hall," can learn a great deal by examining collective behavior and social change.

Think back to the start of your day. If you are like most of us, you woke up at a regular time; had breakfast; dressed in clothes suitable for your day's activities; walked, waited patiently in line for a bus, or drove your car; arrived at school or work at an agreed upon time; and probably greeted numerous people en route to your destination—all the time performing these activities without much conscious thought. As we will see in Chapters 4 and 5, much of our daily behavior is structured and predictable because we have learned the cultural expectations of our society. However, we may at times find ourselves in situations that are relatively unorganized and somewhat unpredictable in which expectations of appropriate behavior are either unclear or unknown. The behavior that is likely to emerge in such situations is called **collective behavior,** the relatively spontaneous and unstructured behavior engaged in by large numbers of people who are reacting to a common stimulus.

Explaining Collective Behavior

Sociologists have long been interested in what causes people to act collectively. Because much of collective behavior is relatively spontaneous and unstructured, generalizing about how people will react in many situations is difficult. Nevertheless, a cumulative body of research has led to the development of three explanatory models of collective behavior: contagion theory, emergent norm theory, and value-added theory.

Contagion Theory   The French scholar Gustave Le Bon (1841–1931) was one of the first writers to call attention to the social-psychological aspects of collective behavior, especially that exhibited in crowds and mobs. Le Bon (1960/1895) emphasized the emotional contagion that often occurs within large gatherings of people who are in close proximity to each other, which makes possible the rapid communication of attitudes, moods, and behaviors. Le Bon argued that the anonymity of such settings could easily give rise to a "collective mind," thereby releasing people from their sense of personal responsibility and allowing them to engage in irrational or antisocial behavior. Although few sociologists today subscribe to the notion of a collective mind, they do take note of the imitative nature of collective behavior and recognize how quickly some forms of collective behavior can escalate out of control (Blumer, 1951; McPhail, 1991). For example, initially peaceful demonstrations can turn into rock-throwing melees if some participants become excited, agitated, angry, or fearful and communicate that to others.

Emergent Norm Theory   As we have seen, contagion theory emphasizes behavior that, at least on the surface, appears irrational. Despite this appearance, sociologists Ralph Turner and Lewis Killian (1993), drawing on the tenets of symbolic interactionism, argue that collective behavior, although never entirely predictable, is still governed by norms or standards of behavior. However, unlike other forms of social interaction, these norms emerge in the context of the unfolding behavior as participants attempt to give meaning to what is happening at the moment. This, however, does not mean that behavior will not get out of control. For example, if people

waiting to attend a rock concert define the admission process as fair, they are likely to wait patiently in line for their turns. But, if they perceive that some people are getting preferential treatment, they may define the situation as unjust and believe that they have a right to storm the barricade, even though their behavior becomes unruly. This example shows how a collective definition of appropriate and inappropriate behavior emerged in the concert-going crowd.

Value-Added Theory   Neil Smelser (1963) sought to explain in yet another way how existing social conditions give rise to the development of collective behavior. His value-added theory identifies six conditions that have to combine in order for collective behavior to develop. Examining these factors can help us see how and why different forms of collective behavior emerge where they do and why some societies are more susceptible to episodes of collective behavior than are others.

1. *Structural conduciveness* refers to pre-existing social conditions that enable collective behavior to develop. For example, in societies that, like the United States, have long traditions of freedom of association, large gatherings in public places are commonplace. In contrast, totalitarian societies often forbid such gatherings, thus inhibiting the probability of collective behavior from developing. Prior to the student protest gatherings in Tiananmen Square in Beijing in 1989, such collective action was rarely possible in China.
2. *Structural strain* refers to the feelings of anxiousness, frustration, or deprivation that result from patterns of behavior such as discrimination, poverty, economic or political uncertainty, and persecution and harassment. For many African Americans, the 1996 criminal trial of O. J. Simpson exacerbated the already tense relations between whites and blacks in the United States and confirmed blacks' distrust of the white-controlled criminal justice system and of the behavior of many white police officers.
3. Growth and spread of a *generalized belief* occurs when the potential participants in

collective behavior form a belief about the strained situation and initiate a response. For example, rioters in many urban centers have shared the belief that local authorities have often brutalized and mistreated the citizens under their control.

4. A *precipitating event* or *factor* is an incident that triggers collective behavior. For example, the arrests and beating of gay men in the Stonewall Bar in New York's Greenwich Village in 1969 is said to be the precipitating factor that launched the lesbian and gay liberation movement.

5. *Mobilization of participation* for action occurs when a leader emerges and urges people to do something about the situation. For example, after Rosa Parks, an African American woman, was arrested for refusing to move to the back of a bus, the young Martin Luther King, Jr., grassroots organizer Ella Baker, and a number of other people came forward to lead the Montgomery bus boycott of 1955.

6. *Breakdown* in the traditional mechanisms of social control refers to the indecisiveness, inaction, delay, or incompetence of the police, the military, or community and public officials when attempting to handle a potentially explosive situation. Maintaining order in tense situations is a daunting task. On the one hand, the absence of a police presence seemingly encourages mob behavior such as vandalism and looting. On the other hand, a strong show of force too early can inflame an angry mood and itself ignite violent mob behavior.

Forms of Collective Behavior

Collective behavior takes many forms. Some forms are short-lived, spontaneous, and unstructured, whereas others are more structured, formalized, and long-lasting. Some collective behavior, such as fads, are fun, for the most part harmless, and generally leave no lasting change on society. Other collective behavior, such as panics and out-of-control crowds, can result in destruction and death, with the result that new norms and controls are established to prevent recurrences of such behavior. Still other collective behavior, such as social movements, tend to be long-lasting because they have a specific goal of changing the social order in some fundamental way. As shown in Table 3.2, John Lofland (1985) categorized these collective behaviors in terms of the dominant emotions expressed. Although only social movements are intended to produce social change, all of these forms of collective behavior emerge in response to changing social conditions, especially in periods of political and economic uncertainty. Some collective behaviors develop when people who are geographically dispersed but who have access to the same stimulus act in similar ways and influence one another indirectly; this is called **mass behavior** (Turner & Killian, 1987).

Mass Behavior   The most common forms of mass behavior are fashions, fads, crazes, rumors, urban legends, and mass hysteria. An interesting, quick, and fun way to gauge how some aspects of society change is to examine clothing and hair style changes in family photo albums.

Fashions, the styles of appearance or behavior that are favored by a large number of people for a limited period of time, cover a wide range of phenomena. Two examples are styles of homes and household decor (the ranch home of the 1960s with its yellow or green kitchen ap-

TABLE 3.2 ☉ Elementary Forms of Collective Behavior

Organizational Form	Dominant Emotion		
	Fear	Hostility	Joy
Mass (geographically dispersed)	Mass hysteria	Mass rioting	Fashions, fads, crazes
Crowd (in proximity)	Panics	Mobs, riots, protests	Expressive crowds

Source: Based on "Collective Behavior." 1981. In M. Rosenberg and R. Turner (eds.), *Social Psychology.* New York: Basic Books, pp. 411–466. Reprinted in Lofland, J. 1985. *Protests: Studies of Collective Behavior and Social Movements.* New Brunswick, NJ: Transaction Books, p. 42.

pliances versus the contemporary townhouse with its white appliances) and styles of cars (the fins of the 1950s versus the aerodynamic cars of the 1990s). Language, too, becomes fashionable or unfashionable. For example, each new generation of young people expresses approval in its own way, the fashion moving from *swell* to *neat* to *right on* to *really* to *awesome* (Lofland, 1985).

Fashions both contribute to and reflect social change. They also function to convey information about a person's social position (Rubinstein, 1994). For example, those who wear expensive clothes and jewelry or drive luxury cars do so, in part, to distance themselves from the general population. Although modern tools of communication, such as beepers and cellular phones, are deemed necessary in some lines of work, many of these items are purchased primarily as status symbols. The desire to belong or to have the latest fashion has created some serious social problems. Parents often feel pressured to buy expensive clothing and other items for their children that they can't afford. Young people have been robbed and even killed for their fashionable jackets or running shoes and gangs have adopted certain colors and styles of dress as their trademarks.

Other forms of mass behavior are more transitory and often more frivolous. **Fads,** for instance, are short-lived patterns of unexpected behavior, engaged in by only a segment of the population, most often adolescents and young adults. Can you imagine yourself eating gold fish or streaking naked across campus? These behaviors might intrigue or appall us today, but in the 1920s and in the 1970s, your college counterparts across the country engaged in these activities. More recent fads include break dancing, bungee jumping, and body piercing. People engage in such behaviors for a variety of reasons—to shock the public, to create a distinct identity, or simply for fun. How public and widespread they become depends a great deal on interpersonal communication and the media's response to them (Aguirre et al., 1988).

Generally speaking, fads play only a small part in the lives of participants. At times, however, people can become so preoccupied with an activity that it dominates their lives. Sociologists refer to such mass behavior as a **craze,** exciting mass involvement that lasts for a relatively long period of time (Lofland, 1985). Jean Chatzky (1992) called attention to the economic nature of many crazes. Two examples, both involving financial speculation, will serve to illustrate this process. In seventeenth-century Holland, people speculated fiercely in the buying and selling of tulip bulbs. The value of some bulbs exceeded their weight in gold; each bulb cost more than a house. Unfortunately for the Dutch, other countries did not attach the same value to the bulbs. When the price of bulbs fell dramatically, thousands of people lost their life savings.

More recently, riots erupted in Albania after the government cracked down on operators of pyramid schemes who promised investors high rates of return over short periods of time. Cash from new investors is used to pay dividends to earlier investors with the results that all the investors believe that they are making or soon will make money. When the supply of new investors is exhausted, the pyramid collapses and people lose their initial investment. Many Albanians who sold their homes and their livestock in order to invest were devastated by the collapse of these pyramids. Approximately $1 billion, or 43 percent of the nation's gross domestic product, was invested in numerous get-rich-quick pyramid schemes involving at least 800,000 people in a population of less than 4 million (Hundley, 1997).

Rumors are another common form of mass behavior. The term refers to unverified forms of information transmitted informally from one person to another in a relatively rapid fashion. A popular party game known as "pass it on" or "telephone" illustrates the workings of rumors. In this game, one person tells another person a story, that person in turn whispers the story to another, and so on until the last person tells the story out loud. In most cases, the initial story changes significantly. In party situations, the changes are amusing and generally quite harmless. However, a classic research study on rumors, using a similar procedure, revealed more disturbing aspects of this behavior (Allport & Postman, 1947). We have used a version of this research in our classes over the years. Student volunteers are asked to leave the room while one student studies a picture depicting passengers on a bus or subway. Two men are standing in the aisle, one appearing to threaten the other.

The student is then asked to describe this scene to a second volunteer, who has not seen the picture and who, in turn, tells it to a third. The last volunteer then tells what she or he has heard while the class again views the picture. It frequently happens that after a certain point in the retelling, the scene changes and the person being threatened is described as white and the person doing the threatening as black even though just the opposite is depicted in the picture.

Why does this happen? Several factors are involved in this social process. First, when people receive information and then pass it along, some important details are ignored or forgotten in the telling. Others then reorganize the information to fit into frameworks that are already familiar to them. Rumors often reflect people's deep-seated fears, hopes, anxieties, preconceptions, and prejudices. If the rumor relates to information that people have especially strong feelings about, the degree of change in the retelling is likely to be high. Given the state of race relations in the United States, it is not surprising that many white people are quick to associate threatening behavior with black people, especially in anonymous or ambiguous climates in which rumors circulate.

Although some rumors are started with malicious intent, it is more typical that rumors are not premeditated (Kapferer, 1992). Rumors may even begin with a factual basis, but if there is little substantial information forthcoming, people tend to fill in the gaps with speculation. Once rumors get started, they are difficult to stop unless compelling data is presented in rapid fashion to prove the rumor false or out of date. In 1996, TWA Flight 800 exploded in the air shortly after takeoff from New York City; rumors of bombs and missiles spread quickly. The FBI and the National Transportation Safety Board were quick to react, holding numerous briefings to provide updates on the results of their investigation into the causes of the crash in order to prevent inaccurate information or rumors from spreading.

Rumors originate and circulate for a number of reasons. They provide a way for people to make sense out of a confusing or ambiguous situation. They provide information concerning topics of critical interest to people in situations in which reliable sources of information aren't forthcoming or when official sources are no longer trusted. Finally, rumors can provide relief from boring jobs or humdrum lives and give attention and status, however fleeting, to the storyteller.

Although some rumors capture the popular imagination and are entertaining (for example, the sightings of Elvis Presley in all manner of places) others can have significant and damaging consequences. Over the years, major U.S. businesses have been the subject of rumors about alleged product contamination practices (P. A. Turner, 1993). McDonald's had to contend with the unsubstantiated rumor that the company used red worms in its hamburgers. Other companies have found themselves accused of evil deeds. During the 1980s, Procter & Gamble, manufacturer of such products as Tide, Folger's coffee, and Ivory soap, was confronted with rumors that it engaged in satanic activities and that its corporate trademark (adopted in the late 1800s) was a symbol of satanism. Procter & Gamble spent millions of dollars in an attempt to dispel these rumors. Despite the fact that no evidence was ever presented to support them, the rumors persisted and, in 1991, the company felt it necessary to change its corporate logo.

Another form of mass behavior that has become highly visible in the latter half of the twentieth century is the **urban legend,** a contemporary, orally transmitted, unsubstantiated story that is widely circulated and believed. It is similar to rumors in that it is based on fears, anxieties, and deep-seated concerns, but it also involves more complex factors, often focusing on the hazards of modern life and the threat it presents to the innocent or ignorant (Best & Horiuchi, 1996).

Folklorist Jan Brunvand (1981, 1989), who has made extensive studies of urban legends, analyzed the strong appeal of these stories. First, the stories are told and repeated as if they happened in close proximity, that is, to "a friend of a friend." Second, urban legends are transmitted by people who believe in their authenticity. Third, the main character(s) and/or locales are readily identifiable. Many urban legends have a factual basis in actual events but evolve into something more as the stories are repeated. Finally, people abstract moral lessons about modern life from these stories which "often depict a clash between modern conditions and some aspect of a traditional life-style" (Brunvand, 1981, p. 189), clashes that are keenly felt by many of today's harried citizens. Some of the more widely disseminated urban legends include:

- the tragic tale of the young woman who went to a tanning salon and was broiled (Brunvand, 1989).
- the revenge story of the cement truck driver who poured concrete through the sun roof of his friend's car after he discovered his friend was having an affair with his wife (Brunvand, 1981).
- the oft-repeated stories of rats found in soft drink bottles, pets exploding in microwave ovens, and razor blades found in Halloween treats (Best & Horiuchi, 1996).

Sociologists studying this type of mass behavior have identified common elements running throughout such stories. For example, all of them express fear and anxiety about the dangers of living in an impersonal, modern, technological society, and they all relate to issues or concerns that are current and over which people often feel they have little or no control.

Fear is also an element in **mass hysteria,** a form of dispersed collective behavior by which people react emotionally to a real or perceived threat or danger. A classic example of mass hysteria occurred on Halloween eve in 1938 when the Mercury Theatre of the Air broadcast a dramatization of H.G. Wells's novel *The War of the Worlds* (see the Sociology through Literature box). When the music they were listening to was

Sociology through Literature

The War of the Worlds

Imagine that you are living in the New Jersey area and that you have just turned your radio dial to a station with a program in progress. What you hear coming over the airwaves is this excerpt from the Mercury Theatre of the Air's broadcast of H.G. Wells' novel, *The War of the Worlds*.

Announcer Two: Ladies and gentlemen, I have a grave announcement to make. Incredible as it may seem, both the observations of science and the evidence of our eyes lead to the inescapable assumption that those strange beings who landed in the Jersey farmlands tonight are the vanguard of an invading army from the planet Mars. The battle which took place tonight at Grovers Mill has ended in one of the most startling defeats ever suffered by an army in modern times; seven thousand men armed with rifles and machine guns pitted against a single fighting machine of the invaders from Mars. One hundred and twenty known survivors. The rest strewn over the battle area from Grovers Mill to Plainsboro crushed and trampled to death under the metal feet of the monster, or burned to cinders by its heat-ray. The monster is now in control of the middle section of New Jersey and has effectively cut the state through the center. Communication lines are down from Pennsylvania to the Atlantic Ocean.

Railroad tracks are torn and service from New York to Philadelphia discontinued except routing some of the trains through Allentown and Phoenixville. Highways to the north, south, and west are clogged with frantic human traffic. Police and army reserves are unable to control the mad flight. By morning the fugitives will have swelled Philadelphia, Camden, and Trenton, it is estimated to twice their normal population.

At this time martial law prevails throughout New Jersey and eastern Pennsylvania. We take you now to Washington for a special broadcast on the National Emergency . . . the Secretary of the Interior . . .

What was it about this radio broadcast that made it so frightening to so many people? Do you think that there could be a reoccurrence of the mass hysteria that followed the broadcast of *The War of the Worlds* in 1938? Why or why not?

Source: Excerpted from the script of the 1938 Orson Welles Broadcast of H.G. Wells's *The War of the Worlds,* adapted by Howard Koch. In Cantril, H. 1940. *The Invasion from Mars: A Study in the Psychology of Panic.* Princeton, NJ: Princeton University Press, 22–23.

interrupted, many listeners thought they were hearing an authentic news bulletin about a Martian invasion. Those people who were frightened by the broadcast reacted in several ways: some hid; some cried; some prayed; some called the police; some telephoned family and friends to warn them of the danger or to say goodbye. Others attempted to flee the danger in their cars. Estimates are that approximately 6 million people listened to that broadcast and that about 1 million of them manifested mass hysteria.

Several factors contributed to this behavior. Many people were anxious concerning world events; the economic strains of the depression were still evident and World War II loomed on the horizon. Station interruptions to bring late-breaking news were increasingly common. Familiar geographical locations were used in the dramatization. Researchers also found that many other people were not emotionally affected by the broadcast. In general, they were people who had higher levels of education than those who were frightened and they were more likely to use critical thinking to evaluate the situation; for instance, they turned the radio dial to see if other stations were carrying this "news" or checked their radio program guides to confirm what was being aired (Cantril, 1982).

Episodes of mass hysteria pop up periodically and take various forms, such as perceiving an illness. Occasionally, groups of employees or students complain of dizziness, nausea, and fainting, yet health authorities and building inspectors can find no reason for the complaints (Stahl & Lebedun, 1974; Small et al., 1991).

Crowd Behavior   A **crowd** is a temporary gathering of individuals in close physical proximity who share a common focus or interest. We spend much of our time in crowd situations—waiting in long lines to buy tickets to an event, cheering the hometown sports team, enjoying a rock concert, or watching a Fourth of July fireworks display. In these cases, regardless of whether we are alone or with friends, the gathering of people is relatively unstructured and short-lived. We are unlikely to be well acquainted with most of the people there or to share a sense of belonging with them as we do when we belong to a group (see Chapter 5). Rather, what we have in common with the others who are present is that we share a space and a common focus of interest.

Types of Crowds   Many crowds are orderly, disperse after the focus of attention is over, and do not exhibit collective behavior; however, others do. Sociologists have constructed categories to distinguish the different types of crowds and their characteristic behaviors (Blumer, 1969). *Casual crowds* form mostly by accident or happenstance; people's attention is attracted to some point of interest, such as a construction site, an accident, or a display in a store window. They stop only briefly, and then move on, and others take their place until the focus of attention is gone. With the possible exception of temporarily blocking or slowing traffic, casual crowds have little impact on social life and occur with little or no notice given to them. Similarly, *conventional crowds,* as a rule, do not produce collective behavior, albeit for different reasons. People in these crowds gather for a specific purpose and at predetermined times, for example, to listen to a concert, to watch a sporting event, or to attend a play. These events are commonplace in our lives and behavior in such crowds is governed by generally agreed upon conventions about what is appropriate. If individuals deviate too much from these conventions, for example, by becoming too rowdy or by disturbing others' enjoyment of the event, they may be asked to leave or may even be forcibly removed from the premises. Under certain conditions, however, even casual and conventional crowds can produce collective behavior.

Other types of crowds serve different purposes. *Expressive crowds* provide a way for people to give vent to their feelings in ways that would be unacceptable in other settings. Celebrants at Carnival in Rio de Janeiro, Mardi Gras in New Orleans, New Year's Eve in Times Square, sporting championships, religious revivals, rock concerts, and the always popular college spring break feel free to dance in the streets, gesture wildly, sing or shout in boisterous ways, dress in rather outlandish ways, or even take off their clothes altogether.

Participating in expressive crowds can be fun and exciting, but there is always the possibility that an expressive crowd can evolve into an acting crowd. This is especially the case when alcohol and other drugs are involved. Whereas the dominant emotional tone in an expressive crowd is joy, hostility is the dominant emotional tone in *acting crowds,* emotionally charged collectivities that focus their attention and activity toward some goal. Crowds are fluid; under certain conditions, any large gathering of people can become emotionally aroused and quickly change from one form of crowd to another. For example, in recent years, some members of expressive crowds celebrating World Series victories in the United States or soccer World Cups in Europe have turned into *mobs,* a type of acting crowd that threatens to or engages in destructive or violent acts, such as overturning cars, breaking widows, setting fires, and attacking people on the street. If the violence becomes widespread, with large numbers of people joining in, it is called a *riot.*

The stimulus for a riot can take many forms, and riots are likely to occur when tensions have been simmering for some time. The uncertainty accompanying the processes of urbanization and industrialization led to riots in Europe in the eighteenth and nineteenth centuries. During the French Revolution, rioters stormed the infamous Bastille prison. Between 1811 and 1816, angry British craftsmen (known as Luddites) rioted and destroyed textile machinery which they believed would put them out of work. Other riots have developed out of deeply embedded religious or racial/ethnic animosities. In Northern Ireland, violence periodically breaks out between Catholics and Protestants; in the Middle East, numerous clashes have occurred between Muslims and Christians. In the United States, major race riots occurred in Chicago in 1919, in Detroit in 1943, in several urban areas in the wake of the 1968 assassination of Martin Luther King, Jr., and in Los Angeles in 1992 in the aftermath of the acquittal of four white police officers videotaped in the act of beating black motorist Rodney King (R. H. Turner, 1994). A lack of basic necessities can also set off a riot. For example, food shortages and starvation triggered food riots in Somalia in the early 1990s.

When we consider how fluid crowds can be and how quickly their emotional moods can shift, it is not surprising that some communities take strong measures when crowds are expected to form. Many communities and event organizers try to prevent trouble from occurring by employing extra security personnel, providing additional public facilities, and utilizing other forms of crowd control, often at considerable expense to taxpayers.

Sociologists have identified and studied yet another crowd form. *Protest crowds* are gatherings of people whose behavior is directed toward achieving a political goal (Lofland, 1985). Common strategies of protest include mass rallies, marches, demonstrations, sit-ins, boycotts, and strikes. Many of these activities take the form of *civil disobedience*—nonviolent action that seeks to change a law or social policy by refusing to comply with it. India's Hindu nationalist and spiritual leader Mahatma Gandhi (1869–1948) and U.S. civil rights leader Martin Luther King, Jr. (1929–1968) advocated civil disobedience and nonviolence as a strategy to protest their countries' discriminatory policies and practices. Tragically, both leaders died violent deaths, victims of their assassins' futile attempts to resist change. Sidney Tarrow (1994) believes that cycles or waves of protest are likely to occur when a society experiences major social shocks such as an international economic recession, a period of warfare, and hasty or ill-conceived government action.

Protest activity is quite commonplace in modern society. Throughout the late 1960s and early 1970s, student protests against the Vietnam War erupted on college campuses all across the United States. With the collapse of communism in Eastern Europe, protest crowds have taken to the streets to protest economic hardships brought about by the transition from socialism to market economies. Technology's ability to provide instant and global coverage of a protest almost anywhere in the world helps to fuel cycles of protest. With the media's presence, protesters are able to get their messages out quickly, thus often enabling them to win national and international support for their causes. In late 1996 and early 1997, thousands of students in Belgrade, the capital of the Federal Republic of Yugoslavia, held daily demonstrations demanding that the government reinstate opposition election victories in fourteen cities. Encouraged by these events, student protesters in Sofia, Bulgaria, worried about their country's deteriorating economy, demanded that their government hold legislative elections two years earlier than the scheduled end of the term. Feeling pressured by the public nature of these demonstrations, both governments acted to meet these demands (Woodard, 1997). Although the majority of protests are nonviolent, they can quickly escalate into violent confrontations. Two circumstances that commonly trigger aggression among initially peaceful protesters are excessive efforts at crowd control on the part of public officials and the appearance of counter demonstrations.

Mass hysteria can sometimes trigger a form of collective behavior referred to as **panic,** an irrational, collective flight from some real or perceived danger. People panic when there is a generalized belief that they must get out of a perceived dangerous situation immediately, for example, a burning or collapsing building. Panic behavior is especially likely when escape routes are limited or closing or where there is a belief that only some people will be able to escape the danger. Panics are often deadly, leaving behind people who were crushed in others' rush to escape. Such was the case in the 1942 Coconut Grove fire in which 500 patrons were killed and 200 more were injured. The December 7, 1942, issue of *Newsweek* described the tragedy:

> Every available table was taken. . . . [A] girl, her hair ablaze, hurtled across the floor screaming, "Fire!" That shriek heralded catastrophe. Some 800 guests, insane with panic, lunged in a wild scramble to get out the only way they knew—the revolving-door exit. Flames flashed with incredible swiftness. . . . Smoke swirled in choking masses through hallways. The revolving doors jammed as the terror-stricken mob pushed them in both directions at the same time. Blazing draperies fell, setting women's evening gowns and hair on fire. Patrons were hurled under tables and trampled to death. Others tripped and choked the six-foot wide stairway up from the Melody Lounge. Those behind swarmed over them and piled up in layers—layers of corpses. . . . (quoted in Schultz, 1964, p. 10)

The fire was quickly extinguished; the majority of deaths and injuries were attributed to the resulting panic, not to the fire itself. Of the 100 people who escaped unhurt, half were employees who were familiar with alternative exits.

Applying the Sociological Imagination

Identify the types of crowds you have been in. Did your behavior vary by the type of crowd you were in? What emotions were connected with the types of crowds? Did any or could any of those crowds have evolved into another form? Why or why not?

Social Movements

As you have learned, collective behavior is usually relatively unorganized and of short duration. On the other hand, when individuals organize their activism with specific goals in mind, make a deliberate and concerted effort to realize those goals by the mobilizing of people, organizations, and other resources, and maintain their activities over a long period of time, they form what sociologists refer to as social movements. A **social movement** is any collection of people who organize together to achieve or prevent some social or political change. In looking at social movements, our focus shifts from explaining how and why society and social relationships are the way they are to explaining how and why societies are always changing. In addition, the study of social movements allows us to see that sociology is not just about the constraints and negative impact of society on individual behavior and actions. It is also about what ordinary as well as notable people do to change the social worlds that they inhabit.

Some of the most significant efforts to promote or resist social change in societies have been those aimed at correcting what the individuals involved perceived to be a moral or social wrong. Despite the enormous power of societal institutions and other social forces beyond the control of individuals, formal organizations of individual activism (whether based on racial, ethnic, national, religious, political, class, or other interests) are often crucial to social change and can sometimes shake the foundations of a society. Such has been the case with various social movements in the United States, including the abolitionist, labor, civil rights, women's, student's, ecology, black nationalist, peace, fundamentalist, and lesbian and gay liberation movements.

Social movements develop rather easily in democratic societies in which people have the freedom to organize and protest against what they perceive to be a problem in society. They are less likely to develop in more traditional societies in which there is widespread acceptance of cultural values, beliefs, and norms. Most scholars of social movements note that diversity and a lack of consensus about cultural norms, values, and beliefs contribute to collective demands for social change. In many industrialized societies, such as the United States, many people believe that they have not only the right but also the obligation to protest and to act individually and collectively when they believe that injustice is being practiced by the government, societal institutions, or their fellow citizens. Those people most likely to participate in such self-conscious change are usually those who perceive or experience a sense of injustice in society but whose only means to bring about change is collective action. They are often people who are marginalized by the normal operation of their society's political and social systems.

Although social movements are similar to the various collective behaviors we have discussed, they are nonetheless distinguishable from them in the following ways:

1. Social movements are longer-lasting than collective behavior.
2. Social movements are goal oriented, whereas collective behavior is spontaneous and unplanned.
3. Social movements are structured, whereas collective behavior is generally free-form.
4. Social movements involve large numbers of people, whereas collective behavior may involve relatively small numbers.

In social movements, there is generally a sense of group identity and camaraderie; the participants agree, with varying degrees of conviction and urgency, that some set of norms, values, beliefs, or practices are constraining or unjust and must be changed, and they agree, more or less, about how to promote the change.

Social movements vary considerably in terms of structure, ideology, goals, and methods. Some social movements are centrally organized and have a strong and effective hierarchial structure which may be secretive, democratic, or authoritarian. For example, social movement organizations such as the Ku Klux Klan often have a centralized and secretive hierarchy of positions. The environmental movement, on the other hand, consists of a wide variety of dispersed groups and organizations that embrace a variety of environmental issues, goals, and movement strategies as well as leadership styles and structures.

The ideological bases of social movements range from liberal to conservative. Likewise, their goals and the ideas for or against which they choose to act collectively are extremely diverse. Some social movements seek large-scale social change in all or a significant portion of societal institutions, whereas others seek to change individual consciousness. Some social movements seek only superficial change, while others seek to remake society completely. After its initial goals have been realized, a movement may have to switch goals because a countermovement acts to forestall or reverse the resulting changes. For example, after the 1973 Supreme Court *Roe v. Wade* decision, which legalized abortions in the United States, the pro-choice movement's goal changed from effecting legislative and legal change to opposing legislative and legal change that would reverse or overturn the court's decision. This switch in goals was instigated in large part by an effective countermovement which denies women's right to choose abortion and works tirelessly to change or overturn *Roe v. Wade*.

Letter-writing campaigns, nationwide strikes, voter registration drives, and nonviolent protest and civil disobedience (such as protest marches and "sit-ins") as well as coercion and overt violence are among the various methods used by social movements to achieve their goals. A social movement may employ any one or several of these tactics to realize its goals, but one method generally becomes the overriding means to the movement's end. For example, although the civil rights movement employed any number of tactics, such as letter writing and voter registration drives, its main tactic was nonviolent protest and civil disobedience. Many resistance movements also use civil disobedience as a major tactic to realize their goals. For example, a major tactic used by Operation Rescue, a movement aimed at closing abortion clinics and outlawing abortion, is to block the entrance of clients seeking the services of the clinic.

Explaining Social Movements

Sociologists have developed a number of theories to explain why social movements arise and how they are consciously and deliberately organized to effect social change. Two of these are resource mobilization theory and relative deprivation theory.

Resource Mobilization Theory   There is general agreement among sociologists that Smelser's value-added approach, discussed earlier in this chapter, provides a useful tool for understanding some episodes of collective behavior. However, there is some disagreement as to whether all six conditions he listed as necessary for collective behavior to develop must in fact be present or be present in the order he gave in all instances of such behavior. Some sociologists especially doubt the applicability of Smelser's theory to well-organized efforts to produce or resist change. They see such activities as part of an ongoing process, and they explain the degree of success of different social movements by using a *resource mobilization model (RM),* which looks at the capacity of social movements to attract resources, mobilize people, and build crucial alliances (Gamson, 1990; Oberschall, 1973).

An underlying assumption of the RM model is that modern society inherently produces anxieties, frustrations, grievances, conflicts, and the desire for social change among differing segments of the population. Yet, according to Charles Tilly (1978), individuals' responses in any given society are significantly constrained by large-scale social and political processes. Although no social movement can emerge and grow without a committed group of individuals, the development of social movements depends, in large part, on the ability of social actors to acquire money, membership, and political support for their cause as well as on the ability to overcome the efforts of control agents who resist the protesters' demands (Valocchi, 1993). When these resources are minimal or absent, as is the current case in the struggle to bring democracy to Myanmar, a successful outcome is only a remote possibility.

Relative Deprivation Theory   An important question raised in resource mobilization theory centers on the motivations and types of people who become involved in collective action. One answer to this question comes in the form of *relative deprivation theory.* According to this theory, social movements are likely to develop when people perceive a gap between the reality of their situation and what they think their situation should be (Marx & McAdam, 1994). When people compare themselves with others in society who have more wealth, power, prestige, leisure, and other scarce goods and resources, they are likely to feel relatively deprived and are often motivated to form or join a social movement as a way to close the gap between what *is* and what they think *should be.* In fact, researchers have found that social movements are more common in relatively affluent societies than in poorer ones; social movements often arise when conditions are improving but have not been experienced to the degree that people expect and desire (McAdam et al., 1988). Critics of the *relative deprivation theory* contend that it does not go far enough in explaining collective social action. They argue that although relative deprivation is a feature of all industrialized societies, social movements do not always emerge in them.

Interestingly, some social scientists have suggested that both the relative deprivation and the resource mobilization theories imply that individuals are more likely to engage in collective social activism when their situation is getting better than when it is getting worse. When things are very bad and repressive in a society, people tend to have little faith that they will be able to do anything to change their situation. However, when times begin to get better, these sociologists argue, people begin to feel optimistic about political and social freedom—they begin to believe that their situation can change and that the gap between themselves and the haves can be narrowed. Moreover, when the economy is bad, people have few resources to use to support a social movement, no matter how motivated they might be to join it. When the economy improves, more people have resources that they can afford to use to support collective social action. This phenomenon of *rising expectations,* a situation in which people experience some improvements in their lives and come to expect further improvements, is embodied in James C. Davies's (1962) J-curve theory of social movements and social revolutions (see Figure 3.1). Essentially, Davies suggests that as long as what people hope to get is relatively close to what they actually get, there is little likelihood of the emergence of a social movement or revolution. However, the likelihood of a social movement arising or of a revolution occurring is greatest when a long period of improving conditions, accompanied by rising expectations that improvements will continue, is followed by a reversal or halt in improvements. The resulting gap gives people cause to be angry and creates a crisis.

Types of Social Movements

Sociologists and other social scientists have identified at least five types of social movements which are differentiated on the basis of their goals and the type and amount of change they seek to produce. These five are reform, revolutionary, resistance, alternative, and religious social movements.

Reform Movements *Reform movements* attempt to improve society by changing some specific aspect of the social structure. Reformists' goals are generally limited, and they tend to work within the system to change existing public policy and laws so that they are consistent with their own values. Although reform movements are often ignored or actually repressed, many bring about legislation that addresses their goals. For example, as a result of the actions of members of the lesbian and gay movement and other concerned citizens, the Chicago City Council voted in early 1997 to extend health benefits to domestic partners of lesbian and gay city workers.

The disabilities rights movement is another example of a reform movement that has resulted in important social change. Since the 1970s, advocates for persons having physical and mental

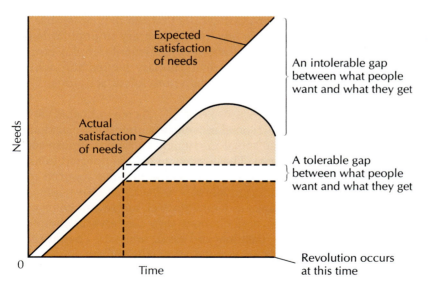

FIGURE 3.1 ☉ **The J-Curve Theory of Revolutions** *Source:* Davies, James C. 1961. "Toward a Theory of Revolution," *American Sociological Review, 27* (February): 6.

disabilities have been organized and deliberate in their efforts to gain equal rights. Using lawsuits and political lobbying, disabilities rights advocates have been instrumental in the passage of legislation that has significantly changed the accessibility of public facilities to those who are physically challenged. The 1973 *Vocational Rehabilitation Act* prohibits discrimination by any program or organization receiving federal funds against persons having a disability. The 1990 *Americans with Disabilities Act* makes employers and providers of public transportation, telecommunications, and public services responsible for providing reasonable accommodations for individuals who have disabilities.

A classic example of a U.S. reform movement is the civil rights movement. This movement sought fundamental reform in societal institutions, social and political policies, and laws in order to enforce the civil rights constitutionally mandated for all Americans. The goal was for African Americans and other marginalized citizens to have full and equal participation in society. As with many reform movements, a major tactic of the civil rights movement was civil disobedience as a way of calling attention to unjust laws. However, not all members of the movement agreed that civil disobedience was the best method of achieving the movement's objectives. Some factions, such as the Black Panther Party, argued that freedom and equality for African Americans should be gained "by any means necessary." For the Panthers, the tactics used to achieve this goal ranged from reform activities such as establishing community centers and free breakfast programs for African American children to arming against the brutality and excesses of an oppressive police state and presence in the African American community.

Other recent examples of reform movements include Mothers Against Drunk Driving (MADD), a movement that seeks effective solutions to the drunk driving and underage drinking problem in this country; various environmental movements, such as Greenpeace, the Sierra Club, and Friends of the Earth, that seek to reform the ways in which society treats the environment; animal rights movements, such as Friends of the Sea Otter and the Farm Animal Reform Movement (FARM), that seek to impact legislation about the treatment of animals; and labor movements, such as the Mexican American Farm Worker's Movement, that seek to improve working conditions for laborers.

Revolutionary Movements   Unlike reform movements, *revolutionary movements* work outside the system, seeking to bring about total or radical change in society. Most revolutionary movements fail to achieve their goals of completely restructuring society, eliminating old institutions, and replacing them with new ones. Still, a number of revolutionary movements have had a phenomenal impact on history. The United States was founded based on the revolutionary activities of English colonists who struggled against perceived injustices imposed under the rule of the British monarchy. They saw simply reforming the monarchy as an insufficient way to address these injustices. Rather, they sought a completely new form of government. In other parts of the world, revolutionary movements have successfully ended apartheid in South Africa and led to the collapse of communist regimes in Eastern Europe. Most students of revolutionary movements believe that people who are dissatisfied with society or some aspect of it will generally attempt a reformative effort if the system allows it. They suggest that revolutionary movements only develop when reform tactics are severely suppressed and all avenues to reform are closed off or when people believe that reform will not significantly address the social or political ills that the movement has targeted. In any event, contrary to popular belief, many revolutionary movements employ both reformist and revolutionary tactics and achieve their goals through nonviolent activities.

Resistance Movements   As we indicated earlier, not all social movements promote social change. Some social movements actively oppose social change. These movements are referred to as *resistance movements*. Sometimes referred to as countermovements or backlash movements, resistance movements seek to prevent changes or to reverse changes they perceive as threats to their personal and social interests. They are most likely to emerge when the reform movements whose goals they oppose are strong and effective. The goal of resistance movements is often to return to a past or traditional way of life that they believe has been undermined.

Contemporary examples of resistance movements in the United States include Operation Rescue and the conservative New Christian Right, which actively opposes feminism, homosexual rights, abortion, and many progressive issues and policies related to racial equity. The New Christian Right emerged in the mid-1970s as a response to the successes of social movements such as the civil rights, women's, lesbian and gay rights, and antiwar movements of the 1960s and 1970s. People in the new Christian Right believed that social changes brought about by these reform movements threatened traditional values and social roles and the survival of major societal institutions such as the family. The New Christian Right consists of a number of social movement organizations, including the Heritage Foundation, the Moral Majority, and the Eagle Forum. All of these groups seek to restore society to a time they believe was characterized by decency, religious and spiritual faith, and morality. Phyllis Schlafly's conservative Eagle Forum, for example, is a countermovement organization that opposes the goals of the women's movement. The successes of this and other resistance movements can be seen in the shift from a more liberal to a more conservative mood in the United States since the 1980s. Their influence has been especially strong in state and local political elections and in the writing of public and social policies.

Another important resistance or countermovement today is the *anti-affirmative action movement,* consisting primarily of whites who strongly oppose legislation and government programs designed to address historical discrimination against categories of people, such as various groups of color and women, in hiring and admissions processes. This movement has been increasingly successful in reversing affirmative action legislation. Not only whites belong to this movement. For example, when Supreme Court Justice Clarence Thomas, a political conservative and an African American, was head of the Economic Employment Opportunity Commission (EEOC) during the 1980s, he presided over a significant curtailment of federal enforcement of affirmative action policies. Meanwhile, judges appointed by the conservative Reagan and Bush administrations handed down court rulings that further weakened affirmative action. And in 1996, the California Board of Regents voted to end affirmative action programs in its public university system, the largest in the nation.

Alternative Movements   Social movements that seek limited change in some specific aspect of people's behavior are known as *alternative movements.* Their goal is self-improvement. For example, Planned Parenthood can be considered an alternative movement because its focus is changing a specific behavior of individuals of childbearing age by educating them about the consequences of sexual activity. Another example of an alternative movement is the Women's Christian Temperance Union, a movement that emerged in the late 1800s with the goal of getting people to stop drinking alcohol.

Religious Movements   Sometimes referred to as redemptive or expressive movements, *religious movements* are not interested in changing society or the political structure. Rather, they attempt to radically change individual spiritual consciousness by converting people to their particular religious belief system. They seek to bring about an inward personal transformation in the individual by providing gratification through self-expression. Such movements are successful to the extent that they are able to appeal to the psychological and social needs of people who believe that traditional religions have failed them or who are looking for "meaning" in their lives. Evangelical religious groups are examples of this type of social movement. Others include the Hare Krishna and the Unification Church. However, not all religious groups fit this category. For example, some fundamentalist religious groups, like the Taliban (see the Cultural Snapshot box), become politicized and take on characteristics of a revolutionary or counterrevolutionary movement. Further, not all expressive or redemptive movements are religious in nature. For example, several expressive movement groups within the larger men's movement have emerged with the goal of changing men's consciousness so that

Cultural Snapshot

The Taliban of Afghanistan

In the fall of 1996, the Taliban, a group of religious warriors, seized control of Kabul, the capital of Afghanistan, and imposed the same harsh rule they had already established in other parts of the country. *Taliban* means "student" in Islam. The Taliban's goal is to create a pure Islamic state based on the teachings of the Koran and a strict interpretation of Sharia, or Islamic holy law (Sciolino, 1996). Immediately after taking control of the government, it closed girls' schools, forced women to stay home from work, banned music, shuttered movie theaters, forbade surgeons from operating on members of the opposite sex, and reintroduced stoning as the penalty for adultery and amputation of hands as the penalty for theft. Women were ordered to wear the burqa, the head-to-toe garment fitted with a slit for the eyes, whenever they appeared in public. Men were ordered to grow full beards and dragged off the streets for prayer. These actions have created serious problems for the population, especially for children because prior to the Taliban takeover of Kabul, 85 percent of the staff of orphanages and 70 percent of the teachers were women (Faruqi, 1996). There is considerable controversy in the Muslim world about the harsh, and some would say distorted, interpretation of Islamlic law imposed by the Taliban.

Which theory of social movements do you think best explains the actions and success of the Taliban? What problems, if any, do you see emerging from the success of resistance movements like the Taliban?

they feel free to express whatever thoughts, fears, and anxieties they may have.

Resistance to Social Change

As you have seen, change is not a simple matter. Individuals and groups working for social change are often confronted by other individuals and groups who resist them. Why do people resist change even when the change is just? One reason is vested interests in the status quo and another is a fear of losing something that they value. For example, the protests, marches, sit-ins, and other individual and collective actions in the 1950s and 1960s in the United States were important revolutionary mechanisms for reducing overt racism and racial segregation. However, not everyone agreed that racial equality and social justice were desirable objectives. Some individuals and groups actively resisted this kind of social change. For example, in 1957, Governor Orval Faubus of Arkansas called out the National Guard to prevent African American students from attending Central High School in Little Rock, Arkansas. Likewise noted for his staunch resistance to the integration of African Americans into the institutional life of the South, Alabama Governor George Wallace blocked the doorway of the University of Alabama, in 1963, denying entry to two African American students. These men and others valued a way of life that they saw as stable and religiously ordained and that, by the way, granted them a privileged position.

People also resist change because of their romanticized notion of traditional values and "the good old days." For example, various white supremacist groups, such as the Skin Heads, the White Aryan Resistance, and the Ku Klux Klan, view various legal reforms that have attempted to equalize the status of marginalized groups such as African Americans as a serious threat to whites. Members of these organizations seek to return to a time when white Protestants held all political, economic, and social power and something called "traditional values" prevailed. Their sometimes violent tactics are often cowardly and conducted in secret. Such movements have spawned politicians who have successfully won public office and who have sparked a political movement to restore "traditional values" and "traditional society."

Still other people resist change simply because of inertia; they have become complacent, even if their lives are far less than ideal. Any change would perhaps require them to do something different, which can be frightening (Lauer, 1991). Often, people who accept the legitimacy of the status quo resist change because embracing it would force them to rethink the legitimacy of societal institutions that have previously defined their entire existence.

Still other people resist change due to misinformation. For example, in 1996, the Oakland, California, Board of Education decided to recognize Ebonics (a pattern of communication characteristic of some West Africans, people of the Caribbean, and African Americans) as a legitimate linguistic system which teachers could use to teach standard English in much the same way they use other languages. This decision fueled debate, resistance, and cruel and crude jokes about African American culture and the patterns of speech used among many of its members. Misinformation and lack of knowledge about African American culture, linguistics in general, and the proposed methods of instruction and their goals led to a major backlash.

Attempts to promote social change inevitably provoke some form of resistance because there will always be someone who will stand to lose in the process of change. As we have learned in this chapter, social change has both positive and negative consequences. How social change is perceived depends, to a great extent, on one's position in the social and political hierarchy. Social change that brings about equality and access to the opportunity structure is beneficial for those who have been locked out but is viewed as negative by those whose traditional power base will be eroded. The benefits of social change are complicated by the fact that a by-product of social change is often personal injury and even death. History is replete with examples of the brutalization, imprisonment, and murder of untold numbers of people around the world who have struggled to win or to maintain basic human rights.

Predicting Social Change in the Twenty-First Century

It is virtually impossible to predict social change with any significant degree of accuracy. As late as the end of the 1970s, few people foresaw the end of South African apartheid. Nor were scholars and public officials any better at predicting the collapse of socialism in Eastern Europe, the dismantling of the Berlin Wall, and the rapid globalization of society.

However, some general predictions seem likely to come true. Issues of gender and racial and ethnic divisions and violence are deeply embedded in cultures around the world and will likely continue to demand fundamental changes in social structures throughout the world. The increasing globalization of labor and capital suggests to some social researchers, such as Gary Marx and Douglas McAdam (1994), that social movements will become increasingly internationalized or global in the twenty-first century. New technological developments will continue to tie human beings together in a world community. As a result, some sociologists believe that movements aimed at reducing inequalities will continue well into the next century. Conversely, others predict a rise in conservatism which will find expression in changes in the way society treats such groups as the poor, the homeless, and criminals as well as in increased resistance to the social and collective actions of people of color and women to achieve parity.

Of course, although opposites of one another, these two predictions are related; progressivism and conservatism exist in reaction to one another as each tries to undermine the gains of the other. In addition, it seems safe to predict that technology will continue to stimulate social change as industries and the jobs available within them change. In particular, the accelerating development of medical technology and of sophisticated weaponry will probably pose problems that will stimulate social change.

A sociological perspective on social change and the social forces that shape such change will enable people to act more consciously, deliberately, and effectively to shape the world into a place where people can live harmoniously and equally. Undoubtedly, as societies change, so, too, will sociology and the methods by which we study and understand social change. Recall that this is how sociology developed as a discipline as social activists, scholars, and others grappled with a changing world in the mid-nineteenth century. As issues of diversity and social inequality continue to loom large on the global horizon, sociologists will need to pay more attention to the study of freedom and equality and the various obstacles that must be overcome in order to ensure this freedom and equality. Indeed, a growing number of sociologists around the world are moving back to the sociologist-as-activist role in which they are engaged in activities and/or scientific research that serves to improve people's lives.

Key Points to Remember

1. Social change is a process through which patterns of social behavior, social relationships, social institutions, and systems of stratification are altered, modified, or transformed over time.

2. Sociologists have developed a number of theories to help explain social change. These theories include evolutionary theories, which can be unilinear or multilinear, both of which assume that societies progress toward a higher state; functionalist theories, including cyclical theories that assume that societies are similar to the human organism in that they are born, reach adolescence, mature, grow old, and die; and conflict theories, which view social change as a dialectical process.

3. The sources of change are many and varied. Some sources of change are external to a society; others are internal. Common forces of social change are cultural contact and diffusion, revolution and warfare, the physical environment, invention and technology, and demographic trends.

4. Much of social change is brought about by human action. An individual, regardless of her or his position in society, can be an agent of change. Another important mechanism for producing social change emerges when individuals join together to act collectively to forestall or to bring about social change.

5. Collective behavior is the relatively spontaneous and unstructured behavior engaged in by large numbers of people who are reacting to a common stimulus. Collective behavior is likely to emerge in response to changing social conditions, especially in periods of political and economic uncertainty.

6. *Mass behavior* refers to people who are geographically dispersed but who have access to the same stimulus and who act in similar ways and influence one another indirectly. Common forms of mass behavior are fashions, fads, crazes, rumors, urban legends, and mass hysteria.

7. A crowd is a temporary gathering of individuals in close physical proximity who share a common focus or interest. Sociologists have identified five types of crowds: casual crowds, conventional crowds, expressive crowds, acting crowds, and protest crowds. Crowds are fluid; under certain circumstances, any crowd can be emotionally aroused and quickly move from being one type to being another.

8. Social movements consist of large numbers of people who organize together to achieve or resist some social or political change. Although social movements are similar to other forms of collective behavior, they are distinguishable from them because they: (1) are longer-lasting, (2) are goal oriented, (3) are structured, and (4) involve large numbers of people. The resource mobilization and relative deprivation theories are commonly used to explain social movements.

9. Social movements vary considerably in terms of a number of characteristics, including structure, ideology, goals, and methods. Sociologists

have identified at least five types of social movements: reform, revolutionary, resistance, alternative, and religious.

10. Individuals and groups working for social change are often confronted by other individuals or groups that resist particular types of social change. People resist social change for a number of reasons including vested interest in the status quo, fear of losing something that they value, romantic ideas about traditional values, inertia, and misinformation about change.

11. Social change has both positive and negative consequences. Although change can bring about parity and greater access to the opportunity structure, it can also lead to unbridled exploitation and oppression.

12. Predictions about the future of social change are difficult to make with any degree of accuracy. Some experts predict that social change in the twenty-first century will continue to be tied to globalization; others predict a rise in conservatism and increased resistance to social and collective actions taken to achieve parity.

Key Terms

social change
cultural lag
differentiation
diffusion
invention
technology
demographic trends

migration
collective behavior
mass behavior
fashions
fads
craze

rumors
urban legend
mass hysteria
crowd
panic
social movement

Key People

Aung San Suu Kyi
Herbert Spencer
Oswald Spengler
Arnold Toynbee

Talcott Parsons
William Ogburn
Neil Smelser

Mahatma Gandhi
Martin Luther King, Jr.
James Davies

Questions for Review and Discussion

1. Assume that you are involved in a discussion with friends over a problem that occurred on campus. One friend says, "Something should be done about the matter." Another friend chimes in, saying, "Forget it, you can't fight city hall." How would you respond to these

two comments? Identify a problem on your campus and plan a strategy to deal with that problem.

2. Consider some of the major technological changes that have taken place in the United States in the twentieth century, for example, air conditioning, transportation, and communications. Discuss the way in which patterns of social behavior, social relationships, social institutions, and inequality have been altered or transformed as a result of these new technologies. Were there winners and losers in these changes? Explain.

3. In this chapter, we indicated that cultural diffusion is not just a one-way street. Develop a list of U.S. cultural practices and artifacts that have been diffused to other countries. In your opinion, what are the implications of the diffusion of U.S. culture worldwide?

4. Have any forms of collective behavior occurred in your community in the last year or two? What changes, if any, came about as a result of this behavior? Were these changes positive or negative? Can you identify any situations in your community in which there is a potential for collective behavior to develop? What factors are involved in these situations? Does your analysis support Smelser's value-added theory, the contagion theory, or the emergent norm theory of collective behavior? What steps, if any, do you think should be taken now to minimize the likelihood of this behavior developing?

For Further Reading

Davis, Fred. 1992. *Fashions, Culture, and Identity.* Chicago: University of Chicago Press. This work provides clear insights into the functions of fashions.

Lin, Nan. 1992. *The Struggle for Tienanmen: Anatomy of the 1989 Mass Movement.* Westport, CT: Praeger. The author provides a detailed examination of the spontaneous and crafted elements of the Chinese students' antigovernment demonstrations.

McAdam, Douglas. 1990. *Freedom Summer.* New York: Oxford University Press. An interesting book about youth who traveled to the South in the 1960s to join protest movements against racial discrimination and segregation and how this experience affected the rest of their lives.

Morris, Aldon. 1984. *The Origins of the Civil Rights Movement.* New York: Free Press. This work has become one of the classic statements on the U.S. civil rights movement. Morris emphasizes the fact that the civil rights movement grew out of a long and protracted struggle on the part of the African American community to gain equality and social justice.

West, Guida, and Blumberg, Rhonda. (Eds.). 1990. *Women and Social Protest.* New York: Oxford University Press. An excellent investigation of women's involvement in collective behavior and social movements in various countries around the world.

Sociology through Literature

Zola, Emile. 1885. *Germinal.* This novel depicts a crowd of striking French miners whose emotions are aroused by their desperate situation; they turn into a mob and engage in horrible acts of violence.

Internet Resources

http://www.cdt.org/index.html   The Center for Democratic Technology examines the impact of policy decisions regarding technology.

http://weber.u.washington.edu/-jamesher/ index.html   A homepage of the new Social Movements Network.

http://www.ssc.wisc.edu/-myers/cbsm/   A homepage for the American Sociological Association's section on collective behavior and social movements.

4

The Dynamics of Social Behavior: Human Cultures

AGENT OF CHANGE: C. DELORES TUCKER

C. DeLores Tucker, chair of the National Political Congress of Black Women in Washington, D.C., launched a passionate and personal crusade against the style of popular music known as gangsta rap in 1992. Tucker, a long-time civil rights and political activist, described the music as morally bankrupt, and, joined by her organization of African American women, she began a battle with companies that sell rap albums that extol sexual violence against women. Tucker and her group said that gangsta rap was violent, sexually explicit, and demeaning and threatening to women; that it celebrated the rape, torture, and murder of women; and that it generally dehumanized black people. They argued that black children were being exposed to music and videos that offered only negative images of human relationships. Companies that peddle such music for profit were damaging children and should be stopped, they said ("Women Politicos," 1993).

In 1994, Tucker's activism sparked Senate hearings on the effects of hardcore, or gangsta rap, on America's youth. The hearings were only part of a growing movement against gangsta rap. In 1995, Tucker's campaign was joined by the conservative Republican former education secretary William Bennett, the Republican Senate majority leader Bob Dole, and two Democratic senators, Joseph Lieberman of Connecticut and Sam Nunn of Georgia. With Tucker in the lead, the group launched a radio ad campaign targeting Time Warner, BMG, PolyGram, Thorn-EMI, and Sony Music. The ads asked listeners to write letters to these companies demanding that they control the sale to children of rap and rock music containing obscene lyrics (Holland, 1996).

The individual and collective actions of Tucker, her allies, and others resulted in an announcement by Time Warner, the world's largest media and entertainment conglomerate, that it would sell its 50-percent share in Interscope Records, one of the biggest gangsta rap labels in the country, and an announcement by Wal-Mart, the largest retailer in the United States, that it would not stock CDs having lyrics or cover art that the retailer found objectionable.

Why would such unlikely collaborators as Democrats and conservative Republicans work together? They agreed that there is some standard of decency that the music industry should adhere to and that the lyrics of gangsta rap were indecent and detrimental to young people. And they are not alone in their thinking. A 1996 survey showed that 75 percent of Americans were convinced that films, television, and music provoke violence in young people (Davidson, 1996). Some observers of American culture view vio-lence, rape, misogyny, and sexism as being deeply embedded in the cultural fabric of the society.

The debate about gangsta rap and the media's responsibility to filter out materials that fail to meet some standard of moral decency illustrates some of the components of *culture.* For example, ideas about morality and proper codes of conduct are embedded in a group's belief system, its moral and value systems, and its normative systems, as well as its *popular culture*—everything people do during their leisure time. Most debates about gangsta rap music center on whether or not it promotes antisocial behavior such as hatred and violence through misogynous and violent lyrics and images. Examining the popular culture of a society gives us informed insight into the ways in which popular culture can be commercialized to provide considerable wealth to those who produce and market it, as in the case of gangsta rap. It also helps us understand products, services, and leisure activities that appeal to and entertain various segments of the society, as well as how these elements relate to or are counter to core cultural values in the society.

What Is Culture?

Culture is all of the ways of knowing, acting, thinking, and feeling that humans acquire as members of societies; when taken together, these ways compose the total way of life of a particular group. It is a blueprint for living within a particular society and consists of the knowledge, values, beliefs, ideas, art, laws, customs, language, behavior, material objects, and every other or related capability and habit members of that society acquire. Culture is a human construction and is therefore flexible and diverse. In this sense, there are no *uncultured* people or societies. Furthermore, there is no logical way to decide that one culture is better than another. Culture is learned, shared, and transmitted from person to person and from generation to generation, and, as we will see later in this chapter, it is relative to particular times, places, and circumstances.

Applying the Sociological Imagination

Take a moment and reflect on the following questions: What might life have been like for you had you been born into a group that had no prior knowledge, customs, language, or material objects to help it meet the needs of individual members and conquer the problems of survival? How would you have communicated with members of the group? How would you have protected yourself from the environment and predators? Who would decide what work was important for the survival of individuals and society, and how would that work have been divided? Who would keep order in the group, and how would that have been done?

The questions in the Applying the Sociological Imagination box address only a few of the problems of survival that human beings encounter in their various social environments. However, if you are like most people today, these are not easy questions to answer because we are so accustomed to the ready-made prescriptions for survival that our cultures provide us. Fortunately for us, our ancestors figured out answers to many of the questions of human survival in the United States. And, in fact, most members of U.S. society (regardless of race, class, gender, ethnicity, or sexual orientation) tend to respond to these questions similarly. From a sociological perspective, members of a particular society view the world and respond to it in similar ways because they share the same culture. People differ in the ways they view and respond to the world because their cultures differ.

Unlike other animal species, human beings are not born with **instincts**—unlearned, biologically predetermined behavior patterns common to a particular species that occur whenever certain environmental conditions exist. Thus, we have to learn and create ways of responding and adapting to our environments. When we are born, we do not know how to walk, talk, feed ourselves, or dress ourselves. We must learn these things; they must be taught by one generation to the next and used every day in deciding how to act. Further, although each of us is a unique human being, our culture shapes our identities—our sense of who we are—and it provides us with a framework for viewing and understanding the world. Culture provides a storehouse of the pooled learning of a people; it provides meaning to the physical world and to our thoughts and emotions (Kluckholm, 1999); it guides us as we solve the problems of everyday living and allows us to live in a fairly predictable and orderly world. According to Clyde Kluckholm (1999), culture is like a map: with it you can navigate a society; without it you will be barely human.

Components of Culture

Culture consists of a number of components: the language we speak, the rules we make and follow, the rewards or sanctions we develop for conformity and nonconformity, the values and customary habits that we share with others in so-

ciety, our sense of morality, and the artifacts, tools, and technology we develop and use. We will now discuss each of the components of culture: the symbolic, the normative, the cognitive, and the material. Even though the specifics of each may vary from one culture to another, all cultures have these components.

The Symbolic Component

An important characteristic feature of culture is that it is symbolic. Many of the aspects of our ordinary, everyday lives have important symbolic content. Culture could not exist without symbols because people would have no shared meanings and understandings to help them make sense out of their lives and no way to communicate with others.

Symbols   A **symbol** is simply anything that meaningfully represents something to human beings; it is an arbitrary sign that can be used in an abstract way and whose meaning is shared by people. Gestures, facial expressions, words, numbers, and pictures are all symbols. When there is consensus about what an object, behavior, or event means, it makes living in the culture in which it occurs far more predictable and stable. The American flag is an important symbol for many people living in the United States. For some, it is such an important symbol that it has taken on a kind of sacredness. For these people, any desecration of the flag (for example, burning or stepping on it) is tantamount to attacking the United States itself. For others, the flag is offensive; it symbolizes exclusion, oppression, racism, discrimination, and hatred. For still others, the American flag is a symbol of the political power structure. Thus, in the 1960s, when college students burned the American flag or wore it stitched to their clothes, they were protesting the American political power system. As these examples suggest, symbols are important and powerful sources of communication; they transmit a wide variety of ideas and values, and they can generate feelings of love and animosity, patriotism and exclusion simultaneously. For each group, the American flag is a meaningful symbol of some set of beliefs or values.

Our lives and our culture are full of symbols. A whistle blown by a traffic policeman, a whistle from a young woman directed at a young man (or vice versa), a clenched fist, a siren, a crucifix, a chair, a bell, a swastika, and a burning cross are but a few of the many symbols in our culture. Further, symbols shape how we think about such categories as female and male. Traditionally in our culture, colors connote different symbolic meanings for females and males. We associate pink and soft pastel colors with females and blue and other darker colors with males. Thus, if we encounter a male dressed in pink, we think he is odd (how many males do you know who wear pink suits, pants, or socks?). The symbolic meaning of these colors for the genders go beyond clothing. For example, in the world of work, we refer to work that is predominantly female as *pink-collar* work and that which is predominantly male (mechanic, electrician, plumber) as *blue-collar* work. Such symbolic meanings are not trivial or unimportant. The messages that they transmit about gender are long-lasting and affect how people are treated.

Another example of the ways in which symbols affect how we view and define ourselves and others in our culture is the symbolic meanings we attach to colors used to define race and ethnicity. The predominant and most familiar in this respect is the use of the terms *black* and *white* to define people racially. In this context, black symbolizes a wide variety of people ranging in color from pinkish white to blue black, as long as their heritage includes ancestors from Africa. On the other hand, white symbolizes people of European descent, regardless of their actual skin color. Furthermore, the term *white* symbolizes Arab Americans, Asian Tatars, Kurds, and Iranians, people who range in color from yellowish tan to very dark brown. These color symbols used to define race greatly impact not only our views and beliefs about people and how we relate to them but also who gets what in this society (see discussion in Chapter 10).

Language   One of the most important characteristics distinguishing humans from other animal forms is our capacity to communicate with one another through the use of **language,** a system of symbols learned within a particular culture that convey ideas and enable people to think and communicate with one another. Language is perhaps the most important set of symbols that hu-

mans use. While some animals, such as chimpanzees, have been taught a limited "vocabulary" of physical objects, only humans have spoken language and an ability to manipulate these symbols to express abstract ideas and views about themselves and the worlds they live in. This is the keystone of culture. Culture could not exist without language because, by definition, culture is the shared knowledge, thoughts, beliefs, values, and ideas of a people. And, without language of some sort, we could not share and pass on our culture and history to future generations. Like humans, animals can respond to their environments, but only in terms dictated by their physiology. Almost everything we learn in our culture is learned through language in the course of social interactions with other human beings. It is through language that we become cultured and thus fully social human beings. Language can be verbal (spoken words) or nonverbal (gestures, written, images, facial expressions), written or unwritten. Each is an important way in which we express ourselves and share our histories, experiences, ideas, and beliefs with others. Equally important is the fact that language allows us to interpret reality. Remember, as we have already pointed out, events in and of themselves mean nothing. We have to give them meaning. We create a reality of meaning through language and other symbolic systems.

Language and the Social Construction of Reality   Language not only facilitates communication but also unlocks the human imagination and shapes and structures our reality. Sociologists Peter Berger and Thomas Luckmann (1963) refer to this important role of language in their classic work *The Social Construction of Reality.* Language allows us simultaneously to confer meaning on the world and to derive meaning from the world.

People who share a culture share common definitions of social reality, but not all individuals or groups within a particular culture construct identical versions of reality. The existence of different social realities of the American flag for different individuals and groups within U.S. society is an example of this point. Furthermore, contrary to popular thought, not all languages reflect the same basic reality in the same basic way. For example, words and concepts cannot always be freely and accurately translated from one language to another. Some languages have words that cannot be translated into another language, and others have words for objects, events, and concepts for which other languages have no word at all. An accumulation of research on languages around the world indicates that languages often interpret the same phenomena in very different ways. Additionally, some researchers have suggested that language does not so much mirror social reality as structure it for us in a wide variety of ways. A classic statement in this regard is embodied in the **linguistic-relativity hypothesis,** which holds that people who speak a particular language must necessarily interpret the world through the unique grammatical forms and categories that their language supplies.

The Sapir-Whorf Hypothesis The insight provided in the linguistic-relativity hypothesis originated in the works of anthropologist Edward Sapir (1929) and his student Benjamin Whorf (1956). Both men strongly advocated the linguistic-relativity hypothesis, arguing that the worlds that different people live in are distinct worlds, not simply the same worlds having different symbols and labels attached. Thus, different languages give rise to different social realities. In other words, we know the world only in terms of the languages we speak. Their point of view—not only that thinking and perception are expressed through language but also that language actually shapes how we perceive and thus experience the world—is also sometimes referred to as the *Sapir-Whorf hypothesis.*

One of the easiest ways to illustrate this notion is to look at the vocabularies of various languages. Sapir and Whorf noted that the vocabularies of various groups reflect their physical and social environments. Thus, for example, Eskimos have many different words to represent various kinds of snow, while non-Eskimo North Americans have only one word for snow. Eskimos can make distinctions between different types of snowfall that English speakers cannot generally perceive, for example, falling snow, drifting snow, fine snow, granule snow, powdery snow, dry-wind-driven snow, ice-crust-surface snow. When English speakers say it is snowing outside, it could be falling, drifting, fine, granule,

powdery, dry-wind driven, or ice-crust surface, the one word covers it all. While these distinctions are of considerable importance in Eskimo culture, they have little utility or meaning in our culture unless, of course, you are an avid skier. Similarly, Filipinos have ninety-two different words to distinguish kinds of rice, a staple in their diet, while we have but a few. The language of Indians living in the highlands of Guatemala contains over one hundred words for different kinds of corn, distinctions that are very important to them but that most of us would not likely notice. And gauchos, horsemen of the Argentine prairies, distinguish 200 different colors of horses; the Dugum Dani of New Guinea have seventy different words for sweet potato, their staple crop; and the Arabic language is said to contain a thousand different expressions for sword (Lenski, Nolan, & Lenski, 1995).

This discussion of language may lead you to see language as restrictive and limiting. But the fact is that language and culture give rise to each other. They are in constant interaction: culture influences the structure of language and the ways in which we use it and, at the same time, language influences and shapes cultural content and our cultural interpretations of reality. By this we mean that language reflects a people's cultural concerns, and it may therefore help or hinder certain kinds of thinking. However, it does not determine *what* we think. When we view language in this way we can see how it reflects the various distinctions that are important to the way of life of particular communities.

The Normative Component

A second important component of culture is the normative component. **Norms** are simply the rules or standards and expectations that guide the behavior of members of a society. They are the ready-made definitions of situations, the blueprints for our expectations about appropriate and inappropriate behavior. Sociologists have recognized at least three major categories of norms: folkways, mores, and laws. Norms are both *prescriptive*—those that tell us what we should, ought, and must do—and *proscriptive*—those that tell us what we shouldn't, oughtn't, or mustn't do. An example of a prescriptive norm in our culture is the expectation that people will knock on a closed door before entering. On the other hand, rules of etiquette that forbid you to speak with your mouth full of food and laws that prohibit us from appearing in public nude are examples of proscriptive norms.

Some norms are *explicit;* they are out in the open and most everyone is aware of them. For example, most of us are aware that it is inappropriate as well as a violation of a legal norm to appear nude in public. Explicit norms are learned and transmitted from generation to generation through such formal means as the family—for example, when we tell our children not to speak with food in their mouths. Other norms are *implicit;* they lie hidden beneath the surface and are not easily stated. They are passed on from one generation to the next, but mostly informally through observation and modeling. For example, what do you typically do when you enter an elevator? If you are like most Americans, you generally get over to one corner, try to avoid touching other passengers, have minimal eye contact with riders, and intently watch the little light as it flickers on each number indicating the floor. Do you remember being explicitly taught that this is the appropriate or normative behavior in our culture? Most of us were not. But we learned this behavior in interaction with family and other members of our culture.

Folkways and Mores   William Graham Sumner (1960), an early sociologist, first classified norms as either folkways or mores (pronounced MORE-ays) based on their importance to the well-being of society. Both types of norms apply to many of the same areas of behavior, and both types are largely survivals from some earlier time. The most important distinction between these two types of norms lies not in their content but in the degree to which people in a society feel compelled to conform to them, the intensity of feeling associated with adherence to them, and the strength of reactions to their violation.

Folkways are synonymous with customs and are the norms that specify the ways things are or are not typically done. People do not feel a really strong need to conform to folkways. They are not associated with strong moral feelings, and they are not considered to be essential to the survival of the society. Therefore, when

people violate folkways, it usually provokes only mild feelings and raised eyebrows. In fact, most of us are unaware of folkways most of the time as we go about our daily activities of sleeping in a bed rather than on the floor, taking a bath or shower, eating with a knife and fork rather than our hands, saying "excuse me" or "thank you," drinking coffee from a cup rather than a glass, and crossing the street on the green light.

Many folkways have been handed down to us from the past and their original functions have been blurred over time. For example, the custom that when a man walks with a woman he should walk between her and the street seems to have originated in medieval Europe when buildings were built such that the second story jutted out over the sidewalk. It was customary for people to empty their chamber pots into the streets from the overhanging windows. Men were to walk on the outside to protect women from the splash of slop. Sociologists refer to a custom or folkway that has survived like this even though its original function is no longer applicable as a *cultural survival.* Although it was functional at one time, it is a meaningless but harmless practice that many people continue to engage in.

Mores, on the other hand, are rules for behavior that are embedded in our morality. They are deemed so important that adherence to them is considered essential for preserving morality, peace, and stability in a society. Like folkways, mores are often passed down from some earlier time; however, mores involve much more clear-cut distinctions between what a culture defines as right and wrong and are associated with values that a society holds very dear. The violation of mores provokes intense feelings and strong reactions and is considered important enough to be punished severely. Punishment for such violations ranges from ostracism to death. Examples of mores include the principle of monogamy and the prohibition against killing people (except in war).

Mores are considered to be so important a guide for behavior that they are often codified into **laws,** legally enacted norms, in which case their violation is formally punished. Laws lay out the punishment for mores ranging from traffic rules to rules of respect for property to rules of respect for human life. As with other kinds of norms, the intensity of feeling connected to laws varies with the particular law. For example, some laws, while important, are not considered vital to the general maintenance of society. Violations of these laws are referred to as misdemeanors and include acts such as petty theft. Other laws are considered to be absolutely essential to the well-being of the society, and violations of them are referred to as felonies and include acts such as sexual assault. Because laws tend to be the result of conscious and deliberate thought, planning, and legislative action, they can be changed more readily than folkways and mores.

Mores that provoke some of the strongest and most intense feelings and reactions are taboos. **Taboos** are norms that are considered so basic to a society that to violate them would be to weaken the moral fiber and integrity of the society. Tabooed behavior is considered terrible and loathsome. All cultures contain taboos, and they are often of the "thou shalt not" type. The most familiar in U.S. culture are the taboos against having sexual relations with close blood relatives (incest) or with corpses (necrophilia) and against eating human beings (cannibalism).

Social Control   All societies have norms that govern acceptable and unacceptable behavior. But how do they enforce these norms? As active participants in our culture, we learn to accept folkways, mores, and laws as the basic rules of living in our society and we reinforce them in others through **sanctions,** which are a form of control in which rewards and punishments are meted out to ensure the proper functioning of society. Sanctions can be positive or negative, formal or informal. *Positive sanctions* are the rewards we receive when we adhere to the normative guidelines. For example, positive sanctions include recognition, status elevation, promotions, and awards. *Negative sanctions* are the punishments applied by others when we violate normative guidelines. This type of sanction includes fines, imprisonment, ridicule, ostracism, and beatings. Sanctions are referred to as *formal sanctions* when they are applied by or enforced through legal authorities such as the police and the judicial system. However, most sanctions, whether positive or negative, are *informal sanctions* that are informally applied in the course of our day-to-day interactions with other people. Examples of informal sanctions include not leaving a tip because of poor service; booing our favorite or the rival basketball team; giving or receiving a kiss, hug, or praise for a job well done; shame; avoidance; and raised eyebrows. Taken together, sanctions of all kinds form the basis of a culture's system of **social control,** systematic practices developed within a culture to encourage conforming to norms and to discourage deviation. The normative structure of society is extremely important because without rules to guide behavior and interaction, society would not be possible.

The Cognitive Component

The cognitive component of culture includes ideas, attitudes, values, beliefs, and knowledge; it provides us with a framework for constructing and understanding reality. The cognitive component of culture has a strong influence on and can be used to analyze individual behavior. For example, many people are desperately afraid of flying yet continue to do so. Even after many airplane crashes and increasing discussion and concern about the safety of air travel, millions of people continue to fly. What ideas, values, and beliefs are so important in our society that millions of people will sacrifice their comfort and put their fears aside in order to engage in a behavior that is obviously problematic for them? An important part of our idea and belief systems is the notion that "time is money," "time is of the essence," and "time flies" (so we fly with it).

All cultures have a set of values, beliefs, ideas, and attitudes that is unique to them. With amazing force, these values and beliefs shape our lives and determine, in large part, how we will behave and live out our lives. The veil and purdah used in some Middle Eastern societies is a case in point. The veil and the all-enveloping garments that often accompany it are only the outward manifestations of a cultural pattern and set of ideas about women and men that are deeply rooted in the cognitive component of Mediterranean society. A basic belief in many Middle Eastern cultures is that women should be placed in a special category of honor and protection. This view is bound up with the belief that, because of their sexuality, women present a danger to society. Women are in need of protection because they are unable to control their sexuality, are tempting to men, and hence are a danger to the social order. In sum, they need to be controlled so that society may function in an orderly way. The seclusion of women through veiling is seen as protecting their sexual chastity and thereby not only their individual honor but also the honor of the male members of their families. The power of cultural values and beliefs can be seen in the fact that many Middle Eastern women agree that seclusion is a practical protection, and they continue to wear the veil voluntarily even though social reformers, both inside and outside their culture, have pointed out that this behavior is symbolic of men's higher status, power, and wealth and helps to preserve male domination. For most of these women, their sense of personal identity is tied to the use of the veil. For example, many women who previously wore veils say that they felt self-conscious, vulnerable, and even naked when they first walked on a public street without the veil. The veil is not just a garment but instead the outward sign of a complex cultural reality. Recognizing this fact, Middle East feminists and reformists opposed to veiling do not demand just an end to the veil but rather an end to the various ideas, values, and principles that the veil symbolizes and that govern patrilineal society (Fernea, 1997).

Knowledge   *Knowledge* is simply the ideas and information in a culture for which there is empirical support. As part of our knowledge system, we know things such as that the earth is round and not flat, how to repair automobiles, how to prepare food, and how to cope with the common cold. We also know things such as that the higher the level of education one attains, the greater one's chances of acquiring a high-paying job.

Knowledge affects behavior and changes over time. The discovery of effective polio vaccines has meant that most people no longer place severe limits on where they and/or their children go during the summer months. Forty years ago, children were kept away from crowds all summer for fear that they might contract polio. Clearly, knowledge is not static. It can be disproved or replaced. Thus, what is knowledge today may not be knowledge tomorrow.

Beliefs   *Beliefs* refer to the ideas and hypotheses that a culture holds about the nature of society, its organization, the nature of human beings, and their relationship to their society. Beliefs are the mental convictions we hold about the truth or falsity of certain things. They are social constructions that are typically accepted as *truths* based not on objective evidence but on social agreement, as in the belief in Muslim cultures about the sexual danger of women.

Generally, beliefs can be distinguished from knowledge in that beliefs cannot necessarily be demonstrated by empirical evidence. If they are so demonstrated, they are no longer beliefs but knowledge. An example of a belief is that dancing in a circle and chanting to the gods will cause rainfall. An example of knowledge, on the other hand, is the body of empirical data that describes the meteorological factors involved in rainfall. Beliefs can be based on tradition, experience, faith, scientific research, or some combination of all of these. For example, religion is a classic example of a belief system based on tradition and faith. It is a system that includes innumerable beliefs that are not based on scientific knowledge or fact and cannot be empirically verified. For example, how do we verify the belief that there is a God? That there is a heaven and a hell? A devil?

Cultural beliefs are reflected in the way we interpret other people's behavior as well as in the way we react to them. If, for example, we think that all men are strong and fearless and all women are weak and need protecting, women may feel "safe" when they are with men because they believe men can protect them better than they can themselves. The belief that women need protecting underlies many U.S. cultural practices, such as men opening the door for women and walking between women and the street. Although these may, at first glance, seem trivial practices, they are powerful ways of maintaining subordinate/superordinate relationships.

Values   What accounts for the popularity of U.S. television programs, such as *Lifestyles of the Rich and Famous,* that promote the desirability of wealth, high status, and social mobility? Our interest in such programs generally signals an endorsement of certain U.S. **values,** collective ideas and criteria used by members of a society to evaluate objects, ideas, acts, feelings, or events concerning their relative desirability, merit, correctness, and appropriateness. Although norms are the more concrete rules and guidelines of behavior, values are the abstract ideas that are used to *judge* what behavior is good, right, and desirable. Our values not only affect how we view our social environment but also are tied to our sense of self, our sense of who we are.

As we will discuss in Chapter 6, we learn the values of our culture from family, friends, school, and religious organizations. Certain values and beliefs serve as a form of *cultural capital* that can be used by some groups to gain and maintain high status and social advantage in society while others are left at a disadvantage. For example, elite education and wealth are forms of cultural capital in that they are often prerequisites for access to the elite and upper classes and the things that count in U.S. society. Members of the poor and working classes typically do not acquire this type of cultural capital. According to French sociologist Pierre Bourdieu (1984), members of the upper classes are trained to use this type of cultural capital to deny access to poor and working-class group members, thus maintaining their positions of high status and power and preserving the class structure.

Some people believe that the norms of a society are simply a reflection of societal values. Thus, they believe, if we value success and achievement, our norms will call for behaviors that reflect these values. Others hold the opposite belief that norms are simply habitual behavior that we have developed over a long time and that, once they have developed, we invent abstract justifications, or values, for the continuation of these habits.

Before we discuss some of the core U.S. values, can you list some of them? In fact, are there such things as core U.S. values? Most sociologists think that there are and, depending on their theoretical perspective, they see these core values as either essential or detrimental to individuals and society. Conflict theorists, for example, view values as the social construction and political tools of those in power. They suggest that the core values are those of the ruling class and that they are used to oppress and ex-

ploit other people. Functionalists, on the other hand, view values as shared sentiments that are widely held in a culture and that are essential for a functioning society. Conflict theorists emphasize the degree to which values vary from one group to another within a culture, while functionalists emphasize consensus and the sharing of common values within a society.

American Values   Since the 1970s, most sociologists (regardless of their theoretical perspectives) generally cite the research of Robin M. Williams, Jr., on core U.S. values. In his research, Williams (1970) identified ten core values in the United States:

1. **Individualism.** Americans believe that individuals are responsible for their successes and failures. Success is viewed as the result of individual stamina and hard

One of the most visible symbols of success in the United States today and increasingly around the world is the ubiquitous "Golden Arches" of McDonald's, founded by Ray Kroc, pictured here.

work. Conversely, those who fail do so because of some one or more negative individual traits, such as laziness, stupidity, immorality, and ignorance.

2. **Achievement and success.** Americans are encouraged to compete with and to do better than others. Achievement and success are often measured in terms of quantity and types of possessions.

3. **Activity and work.** By and large, Americans are judged on the basis of the kinds of activities and work they do. People who work are praised for their industriousness, conscientiousness, and achievement, while those who do not, for whatever reason, are derided as lazy, no-account, ne'er-do-wells. Further complicating this value of activity and work is the fact that not all activity and work is culturally defined as good, useful, or acceptable.

4. **Science and technology.** Americans depend on science and technology for our very way of life. We believe—sometimes blindly—in science and technology, even when they are proven to have detrimental effects on our lives. Our belief in science forces us to value rationality over other emotions, such as intuition.

5. **Efficiency and practicality.** Americans judge the value of activities and objects on the basis of efficiency and practicality and whether they produce material results. Activities or objects that are sheer fun are therefore sometimes tossed aside simply because of their "impracticality" or "inefficiency."

6. **Progress and material comfort.** No idea has influenced U.S. life and lifestyles more than the notion of progress. We are constantly seeking new and improved ways of doing things, especially those things that give us material comfort and pleasure. The value of progress is the basis for Americans' belief in their superiority and the idea of progress is central to the works of some of the early social thinkers discussed in Chapter 1.

7. **Equality/equal opportunity.** U.S. society was founded on the principle of equality. For most Americans, this means not equality of condition and outcome but equality of opportunity. This also implies that those who have superior talent or who make a supreme effort to get ahead will be more successful than others, deservedly so.

8. **Freedom and liberty.** The United States was supposedly built upon the ideals of freedom, liberty, and equality for all people. However, this has usually meant individual freedom and liberty rather than rights for all citizens. Moreover, freedom and liberty have never been extended to all people in the United States. Our notion of freedom is generally that individuals ought to be free to pursue their personal goals with little or no interference from other individuals or the state.

9. **Racism and group superiority.** Despite the fact that we say that we believe in freedom, equality, and liberty, most people in this society judge others according to race, ethnicity, national origin, and/or other personal characteristics such as gender, age, social class, and sexual orientation. Attitudes of superiority are pervasive, with each group judging itself to be superior to other groups. These attitudes of superiority can be seen in historical practices such as slavery and the slaughter and displacement of Native Americans as well as in ongoing discriminatory practices, segregation, and hate crimes. Although most Americans claim not to be prejudiced, U.S. society as a whole values men over women, whites over people of color, able-bodied people over the physically challenged, and the young over the old.

10. **Morality and humanitarianism.** The importance of the value of *morality,* the notion of right or wrong, is often used by politicians seeking our votes by emphasizing the lack of morality among those of the opposite political party and in society generally. Essentially, we value doing the "right" thing. Our view of morality is tied into our notions of humanitarianism. We believe that we should aid others in times of need. Unfortunately, the U.S. value of humanitarianism linked with its value of morality has sometimes led the United States to impose its will or to define what is good and right for others to the exclusion

or suppression of their will. Meanwhile, this humanitarianism is not always evident at home, where people often decry the welfare system and view the homeless with derision. According to Robert Pear (1995), after the 1995 earthquake in Kobe, Japan, some Americans felt far more comfortable giving aid and assistance to Japan than they did giving welfare assistance to unmarried teenage mothers in the United States.

Value Contradictions   As we can see, U.S. values are not always consistent and can sometimes even contradict each other. *Value contradictions* occur when values conflict with one another or when the achievement of one makes it difficult, if not impossible, to achieve another. For example, we value equality of opportunity, yet we oppose gays and women being ordained as priests. Similarly, we value good health and spend millions of dollars each year attempting to maintain a healthy lifestyle. Yet we also spend millions of dollars on things that are counter to a healthy lifestyle such as drugs, alcohol, cigarettes, and junk food. It should also be evident from this discussion that not all Americans share core or common values. The United States is not alone in holding contradictory or inconsistent values; all societies have value contradictions.

Although we provide a separate discussion of various elements of culture, remember that these elements do not occur individually or in a vacuum. Rather, they are linked together to form a whole culture; it is often impossible to separate them one from another when analyzing people's behavior. For example, how people think and behave around the issues of welfare dependency and welfare reform reflects a combination of their values, knowledge, and beliefs in certain cultural norms and practices.

"Ideal" versus "Real" Culture   In no society does every single person conform to every single norm all of the time or hold all of the exact same values all of the time. Sociologists describe this phenomenon as ideal versus real culture. *Ideal culture* refers to the norms and values that a people claim to hold. *Real culture,* on the other hand, refers to the norms and values that people actually adhere to in practice. Comparing ideal and real culture often reveals contradictions. For example, we say that we are honest and value honesty and integrity, yet many of us take (steal) items from places of work all the time. Or we view ourselves as law abiding, yet we will run a stop sign or drive above the speed limit if a police officer is not visible. This is why sociologists usually distinguish between ideal and real culture when they study a culture; they need to know not only what people in a culture believe and value but also how they actually behave.

The Material Component

The *material component* of culture consists of all the artifacts (physical objects) that humans create, use, and share with one another. Examples abound: this textbook that you are reading, paper, pencils, computers, telephones, chairs, microwave ovens, stereos. All of these artifacts are the results of our application of technology to the physical environment and the types of artifacts cultures produce reflect their levels of technological advance. For example, the proliferation of shopping malls, mass-produced housing, and skyscrapers are all reflective of the sophistication of U.S. technology. They also reflect our beliefs, values, understandings, expectations, and desires.

The mass production of every conceivable item, gadget, and trinket reflects our value of progress and material comfort. However, not only do values influence our material culture but also the reverse is true. The invention of the automobile and the jet airplane have led us to place a high value on speedy and efficient modes of transportation. We can often see evidence of cultural lag when material culture changes faster than nonmaterial culture. For example, rapidly changing technology has led to the ability to prolong life. However, there is a lack of consensus regarding whether or not we should prolong a person's life under certain conditions.

Understanding Other Cultures

Culture is not a fixed phenomenon, nor is it the same in all places or to all people. It is relative to time, place, and particular people. Learning about other people can help us to understand ourselves and to be better world citizens.

Cultural Unity and Diversity

One of the most common ways of studying cultures is to focus on the differences within and across cultures. These differences are infinite. However, there are some general practices that seem to occur in all known cultures. Although their specifics may vary from one culture to another, sociologists refer to those elements or characteristics that can be found in every known culture as **cultural universals**. George Murdock (1949) classified eighty-eight general categories of behavior that can be found in all known cultures, including travel and transport, kinship, political behavior, and death. For example, in all societies, funeral rites include expressions of grief, disposing of the dead, and rituals that define the relations of the dead with the living.

Anthropologists have suggested that biologically based cultural universals include a long period of infant dependency, year-round (rather than seasonal) sexuality, and a complex brain that enables humans to use symbols, languages, and tools (Kottak, 1994). Sociobiologists often use the existence of these universals as evidence that many cultural patterns have an underlying biological basis. They point out that there are certain problems posed by the environment and certain conditions of human biological existence that all cultures must confront.

Whether the ultimate explanations for them are biological or not, certain cultural universals have biological aspects. For instance, all cultures have norms that regulate the sexual behavior of their members. The specific norms and practices associated with this regulation may vary enormously; in some cultures, homosexual behavior is prohibited, for example, while in others it is required, as in a group in New Guinea that requires teenage boys to engage in homosexual relations as preparation for heterosexual marriage. And one of the most significant cultural universals is the **incest taboo,** a cultural norm prohibiting marriage or sexual relations between certain kin. Humans everywhere consider certain people too closely related to mate with or to marry, although they may differ about which people these are. An-

other cultural universal that has a biological aspect concerns work: all cultures either currently assign or in the recent past have assigned economic activities to individuals on the basis of age or sex.

Whether the underlying basis of human behavior is biological or purely learned, how we channel that behavior is an important aspect of culture. For example, in some cultures boys are taught not to cry even when they would like to or when they are in pain. Our reaction to physical pain is tempered by our culture. According to Mark Zborowski (1952), human beings react to pain differently, depending on their cultural experiences. In his study of contrasting expressions of pain, for example, he found that Jews and Italians felt free to talk, complain, moan, groan, and cry about their pain and openly sought the sympathy of family members and medical personnel whereas "old Americans" reserved crying, moaning, and groaning to times when they were alone. We can see from his observations that various aspects of our biology and physiology are often directed into culturally prescribed channels. Although sociobiologists have put forth some interesting theories about the biological roots of human culture, research to date does not show that our biology determines our behavior in any rigid sense. Rather, there is a preponderance of research that shows that the vast majority of human behavior is learned within a cultural context.

Although human cultures are more similar than different, the differences are more noticeable. The concept of **cultural diversity**—the wide range of differences across cultures—forces us to recognize the fallacy of the notion of a common culture and it highlights the importance of climate and geography as well as of other social circumstances (such as the level of technology) in shaping culture. For instance, if a woman gives birth to twins in a certain Australian tribe, she will kill one of them because to have more than one baby makes her feel like an animal having a litter. However, a tribe living along the Niger Delta kills both the twins and their mother, but the Bankundo of the Congo valley holds twins and their mothers in high esteem and honor (Robbins, 1993). Food habits provide interesting insights into cultural diversity (see the Cultural Snapshot box).

Cultural Snapshot

Food for Thought: Eating Habits Cross-Culturally

All human beings experience hunger and need nourishment to sustain life. However, what humans eat depends on their culture. Most Westerners are repelled by the thought of eating lizards, grasshoppers, locusts, ants, or termites. However, in some societies, these are eaten with gusto. In Korea, dog meat is defined as edible, while people in the United States think of dogs as their best friends and can't fathom eating them. In the early 1990s, some restaurants in China experienced a shortage of dog meat, so they advertised for people to bring in their dogs for slaughter. Those who responded were offered a handsome reward. In India, despite hunger and undernourishment, devout Muslims will not eat pork, but in New Guinea and Melanesia, pigs are considered holy and are eaten on all important occasions. And most people in India regard cows as sacred and will not kill or eat them, while in the United States, we eat almost all parts of the cow including the cow's tongue.

Even within cultures, there are vast diversities in terms of food habits. In the United States, for example, there are those who eat chocolate-covered roaches, while others consider roaches disgusting vermin. Some groups eat hog testicles (more commonly called hog nuts or mountain oysters), some eat pig intestines (chitterlings), some eat linings of cows' stomachs (tripe), and still others eat cow brains; some who eat one of these wouldn't dream of touching the others; many Americans find all of these foods repulsive. One of the more intriguing food habits in the United States was reported by Karen Janszen (1981). According to Janszen, *placentophagia*—the act of eating the placenta, or afterbirth, following the birth of a baby—started sometime in the 1970s with the American home-birth movement and may be more commonplace than we know. By having babies at home, many parents end up holding the placenta, and what some hospitals sell to drug and cosmetic companies, some of these parents plant, dump in the garbage, flush down the toilet—or eat. Those who eat placenta believe that the practice is natural and take it very seriously; they describe it as mind blowing, radical, and spiritual. Placenta eaters tend to be young, white, middle class, and college educated. Some estimates are that placenta eating occurs following approximately 1 to 2 percent of home births in East Coast states and after about 5 percent in West Coast states.

The placenta is human flesh, and most Americans consider eating human flesh cannibalism. However, placenta eaters do not consider themselves cannibals. They note that humans are perhaps the only animals that do not routinely eat their placenta. Most terrestrial mammals eat the afterbirth. This is true of domesticated animals such as cats and dogs as well as wild animals such as antelopes and monkeys, and even of exclusively herbivorous or vegetarian mammals such as guinea pigs, deer, and giraffes. Placenta, they say, is the natural conclusion to the birth process and eating it is nature's way of restoring needed hormones, iron, essential amino acids, vitamins, and nutrients (Janszen, 1981, pp. 366–371).

What do you think? What are your reactions to placenta eating? Elaborate on your feelings about placentophagia and on how your views do or do not fit into notions of ethnocentrism and cultural relativity.

Cultural Relativity and Ethnocentrism

Because of different physical environments, resources, and experiences and contacts with others, societies develop different languages, ways of meeting human needs, artifacts and food and other consumption patterns. The recognition of this fact is expressed in the term **cultural relativity,** the idea that culture is a unique way of adjusting to particular sets of circumstances and that there is therefore no one right or moral way to do things. In order to understand and appreciate the structure and content of any culture, according to this idea, one must first understand its particular circumstances or context. Failure to adhere to this principle results in **ethnocentrism,** the judgment of other cultures using one's own culture as the standard; this is often based on the belief that one's own culture is the only right and good way of life.

All known societies are to some degree ethnocentric. Ethnocentrism fosters feelings of superiority in the members of a group as they judge outsiders or nonmembers to be inferior, bizarre, or stupid. This judgment is often reflected on the labels they use to describe nonmembers. For example, the ancient Greeks viewed all non-Greeks as barbarians, Christians at various times have labeled non-Christians "pagans" and "heathens," and our language is full of negative terms for different kinds of racial and ethnic outsiders. Some people have pointed out that ethnocentrism is even demonstrated in our naming of the baseball playoff games between the American and National Leagues the "World Series," implying that baseball played outside the United States and Canada is inferior or that the United States and Canada are the "world."

Ethnocentrism is not altogether negative. For example, according to a functionalist perspective, ethnocentrism can be a source of unity and stability within a society. By promoting attitudes of superiority toward outsiders, it serves a positive function by promoting group loyalty, solidarity, and stability. Such group solidarity and loyalty are important ingredients of nationalism and patriotism. On the other hand, because ethnocentrism implies attitudes of superiority, it is an obvious source of tension and can lead to divisiveness and conflict between societies as well as within a society. Carried to extremes, ethnocentrism can be very destructive, as Hitler's Nazism and the Jewish Holocaust, South African apartheid, U.S. slavery and the African American Holocaust, ethnic cleansing in Bosnia and Kosovo, and the ethnic war between the Hutu and the Tutsi in Burundi have shown.

The history of human cultures is replete with examples of ideas, practices, or behaviors that seem bizarre or even shocking to outsiders. Some people experience culture shock when reading or learning of some of the cultural practices of other societies. For example, upon the death of a kinsperson, the Ilongots of the Philippines must kill an enemy to obtain a head that they can throw away in order to diminish the grief and rage they feel at the death of their kinsperson. The sixteenth-century Aztecs of Mexico believed that the universe underwent periodic destruction and the only way to prevent disaster was to pluck the hearts from live sacrificial victims to offer to the gods (Robbins, 1993). But the concept of cultural relativity warns us not to judge other cultures as good or bad, right or wrong simply because they differ from our own culture. Rather, we should try to understand "foreign" behaviors in terms of the purpose, function, and meaning they have for the people who perform them. In other words, cultural behaviors and practices can only be understood within the context in which they occur.

However, cultural relativism, like ethnocentrism, also presents problems. As Richard Robbins (1993) and other social scientists have pointed out, cultural relativism can pose a moral predicament that is embodied in the term *relativistic fallacy*—the idea that it is impossible to make moral judgments about the beliefs and behaviors of others. This would mean that no behavior, no matter how terrible or obscene, can be condemned as wrong. For example, we could not condemn the Jewish or African American Holocausts, female genital mutilation, murder and other atrocities in the name of ethnic cleansing, rape, or terrorist acts such as the 1995 bombing of the Murrah Federal Building in Oklahoma City. One way to deal with the dilemmas of ethnocentrism and the relativistic fallacy is to treat cultural similarities and diversity as puzzles through which we can enlarge our understandings of ourselves and others by using them to examine what it is about ourselves that makes others seem so different or bizarre. We must come to understand and appreciate difference and that our ethnocentrism often blinds us to ways of living different from our own (Robbins, 1993).

Diversity within Cultures

Those of us who live in the United States typically think of ourselves as belonging to *American culture.* Likewise, when we travel outside the United States, people view and respond to us based on their notion of Americans and American culture. But what exactly is American culture? The United States is a vastly diverse country and the concept "American culture" does not adequately capture the beliefs, values, and lifestyles of all of its people. The United States is sometimes referred to as a country of immigrants because, from its inception, various groups have migrated here to escape various types of persecutions or simply to seek a "better" way of life. In the 1980s and 1990s alone, some 15 million immigrants have come to this country from Asia, Latin America, and eastern and southern Europe (Divine et al., 1991). In addition, an untold number of "undocumented" immigrants have also come. These people represent diverse religious, racial, and ethnic groups. Further, according to some sources, approximately 32 million people in the United States speak a language other than English (often in addition to English) at home (see Lapham, 1995).

All of these groups have their own unique cultures and lifestyles which, over time, have become incorporated into "American culture." Yet many of these groups are looked upon as outsiders. Many people, from immigrant backgrounds themselves, are intolerant of and often hostile toward immigrants—especially the newly arrived, so-called "undocumented" immigrants—and indigenous peoples such as Native Americans. Barbara Cameron (1993), a Native American feminist scholar, describes this kind of intolerance and ignorance of diversity in this society:

> *Articulate.* I've heard that word used many times to describe third world people. White people seem so surprised to find brown people who can speak fluent English and are even perhaps educated. We then become "articulate." I think I spend a lot of time being articulate with white people. Or as one person said to me a few years ago, "Gee, you don't seem like an Indian from the reservation." (p. 203)

There is not only racial, ethnic, and religious diversity in American society but also diversity in terms of age, geographic region, wealth, sexual preference, education, and occupation, to name a few points. You can see that the United States is not a homogeneous country and, thus, that there is not a single "American culture." Unlike some societies, such as Sweden or Korea, where the vast majority of people share a common culture and are typically from similar social, religious, political, and economic backgrounds, the United States consists of many different subcultures and countercultures.

Subcultures

As our discussion of cultural diversity within societies underscores, not everyone in a society shares the same values and beliefs. Unanimity of beliefs and values among all people within a society is extremely rare, particularly in large complex societies such as the United States. Therefore, when sociologists study a particular society, they often speak of the society's "dominant culture" or "larger culture." A judgment of superiority should not be attached to these labels. Rather, they are intended to refer to the norms, values, and beliefs that are generally shared by the greatest number of people in the society, not, as in conflict theory, to a dominant group that is a powerful elite. Although certain cultural patterns may be dominant, competing cultural patterns exist in the form of subcultural and countercultural lifestyles.

A **subculture** is a smaller culture that exists within the context of a larger, more pronounced culture, sharing most of the larger cultural norms and values while simultaneously holding norms, values, and beliefs that differ from it in some important or even fundamental ways. Racial and ethnic groups such as Native Americans, Latinas(os), Italian Americans, Japanese Americans, and German Americans are subcultures. While they share in the larger cultural system, they also have distinctive sets of cultural values, beliefs, and behaviors that are unique to their groups.

The subcultural values and behaviors of a racial/ethnic group often represent traditional cultural patterns practiced in a homeland and sometimes conflict with those of the dominant culture. The children of immigrants, who usually have more exposure to the dominant culture, sometimes find it difficult to understand and/or accept their parents' cultural traditions.

Religious groups such as the Old Order Amish also demonstrate the concept of subculture. Other examples of subcultures include regional groups, such as Midwesterners or southerners; age groups, such as the "youth subculture" or the elderly; groups based on sexual preference, such as heterosexuals, lesbians, or gays; occupational groups, such as college professors or jazz musicians; and educational groups, such as students.

Countercultures

In contrast to the types of groups mentioned above, some subcultures reject and actively oppose larger cultural norms and values. A **counterculture** is a subculture that exists within the context of a larger, more pronounced culture but whose norms and values are often diametrically opposed to, or at least clash with, those of the larger culture. Countercultures are always subcultures, but the reverse is not always true.

A counterculture is usually at odds with the dominant culture; consciously rejects, at the very least, some or most of the dominant norms and values; and provides what its members consider to be viable alternatives to mainstream culture. Members often develop distinctive styles of dress, speaking, and living that set them apart from the larger culture. Examples of countercultures include the hippies, yippies, and flower children of the 1960s; religious cults, such as the Hare Krishnas; street gangs; organized crime gangs; satanists; survivalists; followers of Scientology; and various hate groups, such as the Aryan Nation, the Ku Klux Klan, and some skinheads. Because countercultures do not agree with major values and behaviors in their society, they either seek to make major changes in the society or they withdraw from the society entirely.

Various kinds of inequality contribute to the development of many countercultures. For example, during the nationalistic and social and political protest years of the 1960s and 1970s, groups such as the Black Panthers, Students for a Democratic Society, the Weathermen, and the Mexican American Youth Organization were very visible and actively engaged in activities counter to those accepted by the larger culture but considered by these groups to be viable alternatives and means for changing society. Although their behavior was countercultural, their activities and social action led to important changes in U.S. society. Other countercultural groups simply withdraw from society, opting for an alternative lifestyle. The hippies, for instance,

withdrew from mainstream society, choosing a communal lifestyle that emphasized personal growth and an expanded consciousness.

The reaction of the larger culture to subcultures and countercultures varies according to their perceived threat to the social system. Subcultures whose norms, values, or behaviors are not seen as threatening to the larger cultures—such as occupational or regional subcultures or those that do not receive much public attention—are usually tolerated by those in the larger society. However, subcultures and countercultures that are perceived as a threat to the very existence of the larger culture are often objects of harassment by police and others having a vested interest in the larger culture and its institutional arrangements.

Multiculturalism versus Cultural Hegemony

The increasing diversity of the U.S. population, the rise and rapid growth of international business and politics, and the increased contact with culturally diverse societies has encouraged Americans to adopt a multicultural perspective. As you learned in Chapter 1, multiculturalism emphasizes respect for and appreciation of cultural diversity and for the cultural contributions, practices, and experiences of diverse groups and promotes equality of all cultural traditions.

The multicultural movement is the direct opposite of how Americans have historically viewed diversity. In the past, the cultural achievements of many groups within the population—such as African Americans, Asian Americans, Latinas/os and Native Americans—were ignored, downplayed, invalidated, or usurped by dominant group members while the achievements of others, particularly Anglo Saxons, were highly visible and prized.

A conflict perspective would explain this cultural history in terms of the social construction of culture and its contents by ruling elites who use their power to impose their views, beliefs, and *ideologies*—ideas and values that rationalize and support particular points of view—on the masses of people. Sociologists refer to this phenomenon as **cultural hegemony**—

the domination of culture by elite groups. Ruling elites are generally able to influence all relevant aspects of a culture because of their control over major societal institutions. Institutions such as education, religion, the government, and the media are used to articulate and transmit the elite's ideologies and to serve their group interests while transforming or making irrelevant ideologies that challenge the status quo. Some sociologists have referred to this hegemony as *framing,* whereby elites assign meaning to and interpret events, behaviors, and conditions in ways that mobilize support for and demobilize challenges to the status quo (see, for example, Snow & Benford, 1988).

In mass societies, the media is the most important instrument of framing used by those in power. The mass media are used to promote the views of the powerful and to dismiss, marginalize, or make invisible those of the less powerful. A classic example of this kind of framing is demonstrated in the contrast between how the U.S. media reported the reactions of some African Americans to the not guilty verdict in the now infamous O. J. Simpson criminal trial and how they reported the reactions of some whites to the guilty verdict in the civil suit brought against Simpson by the Brown and Goldman families. African Americans who cheered the not guilty verdict in the criminal trial were portrayed as racist, clannish, and not intelligent or educated enough to understand the law of evidence or the law generally. Whites who engaged in similar celebratory behavior upon the guilty verdict in the civil trial were portrayed as clearly rational beings who were simply applauding the sanctity and objectivity of the judicial system. Commentators used language that suggested that these were intelligent and educated people who clearly understood the law and were simply showing relief that the system still worked.

While various elite groups exercise considerable control over major mechanisms of communication in democratic societies, they do not have total control. There are therefore always instances of less powerful groups getting their messages and ideologies out to a mass audience. The phenomenon of gangsta rap is a good example of this. Many of the creators of this form of music have used it as a means of communi-cating what they describe as the realities of their experiences in an oppressive, racist, and exploitive social and political system (see the Cultural Snapshot box).

Multiculturalism moves us away from of cultural hegemony and *Eurocentrism,* the dominance of European cultural patterns that has characterized much of U.S. history. Multiculturalists such as Molefi Asante (1993) argue that multiculturalism is not a complicated proposition. In a multicultural society such as the United States, there must be a multicultural curriculum, a multicultural approach to institution building, and so forth. He suggests that a true multiculturalism is one in which there is a mutual respect for difference, dynamism, and decency and in which European Americans work for a national purpose alongside other people, not in a hegemonic position.

Understanding Culture: Theoretical Perspectives of Culture

All sociologists regard culture as a central feature of human life. Thus, a primary task within the discipline has been to analyze and explain culture in all of its variations. Working from the various theoretical perspectives we introduced in Chapter 2, sociologists emphasize different aspects of culture depending on the specific theoretical paradigms they use in their research.

Conflict Perspective

According to a conflict perspective, not only is culture rooted in the material conditions of a society but also it is often created and/or manipulated to serve the material interests of those in power. Who determines the cultural patterns? According to the conflict perspective, cultural practices have been imposed on members of one society by members of another or by groups within society on other groups. An example is a conquering nation using its power to enforce certain types of behavior on those who cannot defend themselves. Another example is

Cultural Snapshot

Sociology and Popular Culture: The Case of Gangsta Rap

Gangsta rap has become a highly visible, controversial, and profitable (it is a multimillion-dollar business) element of American popular culture. At the same time, it is an expression of a counterculture found in many U.S. cities. Although its primary purpose is to entertain, it also provides a medium for individuals and groups to express their feelings and views about themselves, others, and society in general. The term *rap* covers a wide spectrum of music and gangsta rap is simply one form of the larger genre of hip-hop rap music. The raucous language, violent and misogynistic themes, graphic descriptions of sexual behavior, and disdain for the police are typified in the lyrics of N.W.A. (Niggaz With Attitudes), Ice-T, and the late Tupac Shakur. For example, Ice-T sings about "Evil E" who "fucked the bitch with a flashlight/ pulled it out, left the batteries in/so he could get a charge when he begins." Additionally, words such as "bitch" and are normal fare as gangsta rappers sing of "fat bitches," "thug bitches," "shy bitches," and "rough bitches." The violent deaths of gangsta rappers Tupac Shakur in 1996 and Notorious B.I.G. (Biggie Small) in 1997 have been linked by critics to the violence and hatred that encompassed their music. Gangsta rappers, however, say that these lyrics represent the brutality of their experiences in the "hood," or inner city, which they link to economic inequality, police brutality, and white racism.

Sociologists studying gangsta rap might examine the local environments and elements of the larger American culture that spawned it. This might include examining conditions of racism, poverty, crime, violence, and drugs in America; who benefits from this music and who is systematically deprived; and the functions, purposes, and the meanings that such music has for its supporters and detractors. Clearly the phenomena of gangsta rap provides a classic example of the intersections of race, class, and gender in our culture and needs to be studied. According to Michael Dyson (1993), rap is a profound musical and cultural

creation of young African Americans, especially lower- and working-class males, who use it to express their frustrations and desires to reclaim their history, reactivate black radicalism, and challenge the powers of despair and economic depression that are the reality of many African American communities. It is one of the most powerful forms of black music today and speaks, perhaps, to the lives and experiences of millions of voiceless people. For these reasons alone, it should be examined in terms of its healthy and productive aspects as well as its moral content.

However, a double-standard of examination and evaluation are apparent. For example, although some gangsta rappers blur the lines dividing right from wrong, critics treat all of them differently than the generally white creators of gangster films, which also examine the issue of evil and often blur the lines between right and wrong. Further, according to Dyson, although gangsta rap often revolves around pornographic desires, misogynist impulses, and raucous sexual experimentation and although its use of parody expresses a disturbing point of view about women that should not be exempt from cultural and moral criticism, rappers' freedom of expression must be protected. Less obvious sexist attitudes and behaviors are expressed daily in other aspects of popular culture, such as films and advertisement. Indeed, cases for censorship and obscenity could be made against comedian Andrew Dice Clay's white racist and misogynist routines or against the white rock group Guns 'n Roses' homophobic diatribes and racist lyrics, for example. Dyson suggests that gangsta rappers have been singled out in part because of America's repressed attitudes about black sexuality (Dyson, 1991, pp. 7–8).

What do you think? How does gangsta rap compare with other forms of protest music today and in the past? Conduct a brief comparative study of gangsta rap lyrics and those of mainstream protest music of the 1960s and 1970s.

that, although language is a primary carrier of culture, various groups living in the United States, such as Latinas/os, have been increasingly forced by those in power to substitute the dominant language (English) for their indigenous language. Some critics have suggested that recent attempts to make English the official language of the United States is an attempt to totally eliminate a subgroup's culture. The values and norms of a culture as well as the power to enforce them are generally those of the ruling elite and are used to sustain its privileged position.

A strength of the conflict perspective is that it focuses our attention on inequality and the role of cultural norms and values in creating and perpetuating privilege and inequality. It also emphasizes the fact that conflict is not always detrimental and is often, in fact, an engine for social and political change. A limitation is that it ignores the fact that, throughout human history, groups with and without power have created their own cultures.

Feminist Perspectives

Like conflict theorists, feminist theorists focus on the link between culture and inequality, paying particular attention to the ways in which cultural traits benefit male members of society at the expense of females. For example, as we saw in the opening discussion of this chapter, in societies where male culture dominates, all aspects of culture, particularly popular culture, will reflect this dominance. Thus, in the United States, gangsta rap music, dominated primarily by male singers, recordmakers, and distributors, makes millions of dollars for a variety of males at the expense of women's dignity, economic well-being, and in some cases, their safety. A feminist analysis would highlight the role of culture in promoting gender inequality and generating social tensions and conflict between women and men. Some feminist theorists focus on the important role of cultural definitions and belief systems in shaping the social reality of women and men. Thus, for example, in her book *Female Power and Male Dominance,* Peggy Sanday (1981) argues that the cause of women's inequality is a sex-role plan that is deeply rooted

in a cultural orientation that is reflected in "creation myths" that define men as dominant and women as passive.

A strength of feminist analyses of culture is that they raise our awareness of the role that cultural ideologies and definitions of the valuable and important play as central variables explaining women's secondary status in some cultures. Like conflict theory, such analyses are limited by a lack of systematic attention paid to the role of culture in social consensus and order.

Functionalist Perspective

Functionalists view society as an integrated whole based on consensus, harmony, and order, with the various parts serving specific functions for the maintenance of the system. According to anthropologist Bronislaw Malinowski (1929), culture serves both biological and social functions: it helps people meet their biological needs, such as for food and procreation; their instrumental (social) needs, such as for family and education; and their integrative needs, such as for art and religion. As our discussion of values suggested, functionalists believe that values and ideas are commonly shared within a culture, and they examine how these core values and ideas function to maintain the smooth and orderly flow of the cultural system. When people share common norms, values, beliefs, and language (what functionalists refer to as consensus) society is likely to function in an orderly manner. The functional approach therefore explains the presence of particular cultural traits by examining their effectiveness and fit with other cultural traits to maintain the society in an orderly balance. However, not all cultural traits in a society are functional. Some traits are dysfunctional and produce conflicts and problems within society. Our examination of subcultures, countercultures, and cultural diversity suggests that various inequalities and/or cultural diversity often lie at the base of conflict and a lack of consensus about core values and norms.

A strength of the functionalist approach to the study of culture lies in its emphasis on the needs of individuals and society and the significance of consensus and stability for the survival of culture. A limitation is its overemphasis on cooperation, harmony, and consensus and its lack of recognition of cultural traits and practices that lead or contribute to conflict and discord within and across cultures.

Interactionist Perspective

Interactionists examine the ways in which people create, maintain, and modify culture through their day-to-day interactions with one another. As you have learned, language and other symbols are important elements of culture because they represent shared meanings of a people. According to the interactionist perspective, people construct reality and, thus, culture; they use various symbols to communicate and pass on culture from one generation to the next. Cultural elements such as values, beliefs, and norms are the result of ongoing negotiations—interpretations and reinterpretations of social situations and social reality—and are the basis of how people are perceived and treated in a culture.

A strength of this perspective is its focus on how individuals, in interaction with others, maintain and change culture. But a limitation is that, in stressing the shared meanings that people develop in interaction with one another, it

ignores the fact that, likewise, there are many instances of disagreement on the meanings of cultural elements. In addition, it often ignores the macro or larger social structural influences on the creation and maintenance of culture.

Cultural Trends in the Twenty-First Century

As we move into the twenty-first century, cultural diversity and the many issues that it engenders will no doubt continue to be important considerations in U.S. society. Major U.S. institutions such as public education and the job market will continue to face the challenge of widespread cultural diversity as immigration continues.

Culture Wars

The issue of immigration will continue to be the catalyst for major **culture wars**—ideological and/or political conflicts often accompanied by hostility and sometimes violence, rooted in different cultural values. Cultural conflict in

Perhaps nowhere in American culture are ideological and political conflicts more evident than in the debate over abortion. Here pro-life and pro-choice adherents confront one another outside the Supreme Court following a court decision that limited abortion rights.

the United States about issues such as abortion, homosexuality, and family values is also likely to continue well into the next century. According to sociologist James Hunter (1991), these culture wars are essentially a struggle between *traditionalists* and *progressives* to define our way of life. Traditionalists are basically conservatives who view the world in moral terms and who tend to be religious, patriotic, and on the "anti" side of cultural issues such as abortion rights, same-sex marriages, welfare, affirmative action, and multiculturalism. Progressives, although often religious and patriotic as well, tend to view the world in terms of social justice and tend to be on the "pro" side of these same issues. The university campus is not exempt from these conflicts: the curriculum, speech codes, political correctness, multiculturalism, cultural relativism, campus prejudice and racism, the Western canon, Eurocentrism, and Afrocentrism are some of the issues that will continue to provoke solid disagreements between traditionalists and progressives for some time to come.

Hunter, as well as other social analysts, have pointed out the significant role that the media play in culture wars. Richard Eckersley (1996), for example, argues that the media have become the most powerful determinants of U.S. culture, yet we make little attempt to control or direct them in our best long-term interests. The style of public culture dictated by the popular media today is increasingly divisive rather than unifying, fashioning public debate into a battle between extremes.

In the future, sociologists will continue to be challenged to provide meaningful, empirically based insights into the many culture war issues confronting us today. In addition, they will likely be called upon more often to help develop social policies that will mitigate some of these cultural conflicts.

Key Points to Remember

1. Culture is all of the ways of knowing, acting, thinking, and feeling that humans acquire as members of a society. It includes norms, values, beliefs, knowledge, language, and every other custom or capability we acquire as members of a society. Although each of us is a unique individual, culture shapes our sense of who we are by providing us with a framework for viewing and understanding the world.

2. Culture consists of four key components that can be found in all cultures: the symbolic component (symbols and language), the normative component, the cognitive component, and the material component. Language and symbols not only facilitate communication but also shape and structure our reality. Norms can be classified as folkways, mores, and laws. Values (a major part of the cognitive component) are the abstract ideas used to judge what is or is not acceptable to a society. The material component of culture consists of all the physical objects that humans create, use, and share with one another.

3. When sociologists study culture, they usually distinguish between ideal and real culture. *Ideal culture* refers to the norms and values that people claim to hold, while *real culture* refers to the norms and values that people actually adhere to in practice.

4. Culture is not a fixed phenomenon. While there are some general practices that can be found in all known cultures, cultural diversity exists both within and across cultures. Cultural diversity is reflected through race, ethnicity, age, religion, sexual orientation, geographic location, and occupation, to name a few factors. Large, complex societies such as the United States consist of various subcultures and countercultures.

5. Sociologists usually take the position that culture is relative to a particular set of circumstances. In order to understand and appreciate any culture, therefore, we have to understand the particular context in which it occurs. Sociologists refer to this concept as cultural relativism. Failure to follow this principle results in ethnocentrism.

6. Sociologists use a variety of theories to explain culture. A conflict or feminist theorist might focus on cultural hegemony, while a functionalist theorist might focus on consensus and shared values in society and the ways in which they

contribute to order and stability. An interactionist would be much more concerned with understanding aspects such as how people come to share common understandings and reach a consensus about the things that count in a society.

7. In the twenty-first century, U.S. society and societies around the world will continue to face internal cultural conflicts over values, norms, and appropriate forms of behavior. The media play a significant role in shaping these cultural conflicts.

Key Terms

culture
instincts
symbol
language
linguistic relativity hypothesis
norms
folkways
mores

laws
taboos
sanctions
social control
values
cultural universals
incest taboo

cultural diversity
cultural relativity
ethnocentrism
subculture
counterculture
cultural hegemony
culture wars

Key People

C. DeLores Tucker
Peter Berger
Thomas Luckmann

Edward Sapir
Benjamin Whorf

William Graham Sumner
Robin M. Williams, Jr.

Questions for Review and Discussion

1. Some people argue that U.S. culture is in a state of decay, while others argue that it is in a state of renaissance. Take one of these positions and provide evidence for your position. In addition, identify a positive change and a negative change in U.S. culture. What cultural change would you like to see take place in your lifetime? Why?

2. U.S. popular culture is full of ethnocentric statements, artifacts, and other cultural elements. Develop a list of such statements and elements using the various media, T-shirts, bumper stickers, billboards, and conversations, and analyze them in terms of whether they are based on fact, in what ways they distort facts, their meanings and implications, and the val-

ues they imply about the individuals displaying or saying them. What conclusions can you draw from these data about the nature and extent of ethnocentrism in late twentieth-century U.S. culture?

3. Older Americans are an often-overlooked source of information about our past culture. Interview your grandparents or some other older person about a specific cultural topic, such as family values, clothing, marriage ceremonies, raising a family, diversity, the changing role of women and men, food preparation or dishes, and eating patterns, comparing past and present trends.

4. List some of the culture-war issues that are important to you and indicate which side of the is-

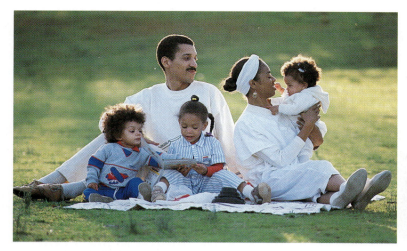

Although many Americans view the two-parent family as the ideal, they are in the minority today. U.S. families are increasingly diverse, covering a range of structures and types including lesbian, gay, multiracial and biracial, and single-parent.

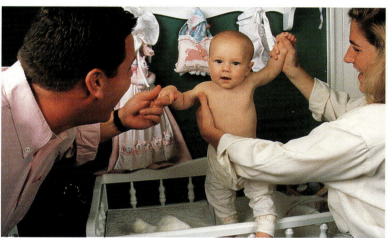

Although the world has grown richer over the last 25 years, not all people have benefited. In some nations, the rate of poverty actually increased. Children are particularly vulnerable to poverty, inadequate nutrition, hunger, and a number of related medical problems.

Although some people believe that Americans are less religious today than in the past, existing data does not support this view. Unlike homogeneous societies that practice a single religion, U.S. culture consists of a wide variety of religious traditions. With this great diversity of religions, Americans have higher rates of church membership and attendance than most other countries.

Although work is central to both individual and societal well-being, in capitalist societies such as the United States, work and its rewards are not equally distributed across populations. Thus some people enjoy greater wealth and higher status than do others. These inequalities, often glaring both within and across societies, are systemic and are passed down from one generation to the next.

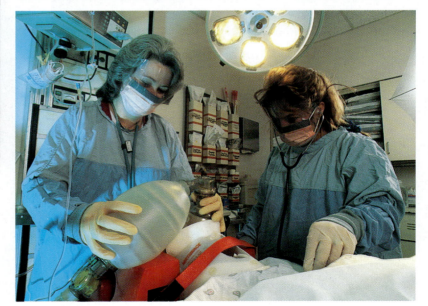

sue you are on. Is there room for compromise on your part? Why do you think people find it hard to compromise on these issues? Can you iden-tify culture wars on your campus? If yes, cite examples and give evidence showing which side of each seems to have the upper hand.

For Further Reading

Barrett, Richard. 1991. *Culture and Conduct.* (2nd ed.). Belmont, CA: Wadsworth. An interesting book that provides a comprehensive examination of the concept of culture. It includes many interesting examples of cultural diversity globally.

Hunter, James. 1994. *Before the Shooting Begins: Searching for Democracy in America's Culture Wars.* New York: Free Press. A provocative discussion and explanation of how various controversial cultural issues are distorted by the media and various activist organizations.

Kephart, William, and William Zellner. 1994. *Extraordinary Groups: An Examination of Unconventional Life Styles.* (5th ed.). New York: St. Martin's Press. A significant sociological exploration of the world of subcultures and countercultures in the United States.

Rooks, Noliwe M. 1996. *Hair Raising: Beauty, Culture, and African American Women.* An interesting examination of the social construction of beauty that focuses on the cultural significance of hair in the lives of African American women.

Sociology through Literature

Baldwin, James. 1965. *Another Country.* New York: Dell. A novel about misery and love in a deviant subculture in New York City.

Kazantzakis, Nikos. 1952. *Zorba the Greek.* New York: Simon & Schuster. A story about a transplanted Englishman in rural Greece who is first repelled, then attracted, and finally influenced by the culture.

West, Dorothy. 1995. *The Wedding.* New York: Doubleday. This novel offers an intimate view of and insights into the subcultural lifestyles, ambitions, norms, values, and beliefs of the African American middle class from slavery to the 1950s.

Internet Resources

http://Jefferson.Village.Virginia.edu/pmc *Postmodern Culture Journal* homepage with insights into the postmodern perspective.

http//www.library.upenn.edu/resources/ssocial/sociology/sociology.html Several indexes of culture and ethnic studies and demographic and statistical sources.

5

Social Structure, Groups, and Organizations

AGENT OF CHANGE: AMNESTY INTERNATIONAL

In 1961, British lawyer Peter Benenson read a newspaper story about two Portuguese students sentenced to seven years in prison for the simple act of raising their glasses in a toast to freedom. Benenson reacted by contacting the *London Observer,* which ran a story, "Appeal for Amnesty, 1961." Benenson asked the paper's readers to write letters asking for the students' release. That letter-writing campaign led to the formation of an international non-governmental organization that campaigns against human rights violations all over the world. Today, Amnesty International has over 1 million members, subscribers, and donors in more than 162 countries and territories.

Amnesty International's main goal is to promote all the human rights enshrined in the *Universal Declaration of Human Rights.* This declaration was passed on December 10, 1948, by the General Assembly of the United Nations in response to the abuses and atrocities of World War II. Article 2 of the declaration states:

> Everyone is entitled to all the rights and freedoms set forth in this declaration, without distinction of any kind, such as race, colour, sex, language, religion, political or other opinion, national or social origin, property, birth or other status. Furthermore, no distinction shall be made on the basis of the political, jurisdictional or international status of the country or territory to which a person belongs, whether it be independent, trust, non-self-governing or under any other limitation of sovereignty.

More than fifty years have gone by since the declaration was passed, but, according to investigations conducted by Amnesty International, in 1997:

- Thousands of actual or possible extrajudicial executions were reported in fifty-five countries, including Myanmar, Mexico and elsewhere in the Americas, and throughout most of the Middle East and North Africa.
- The fate of hundreds of thousands of people in at least thirty-one countries who "disappeared" in recent years remains unknown. Many of them may have been killed.
- Tens of thousands of detainees were subjected to torture or ill-treatment, including rape, in 117 countries, including Afghanistan, Turkey, Myanmar, Israel, and twenty-eight countries in Europe.
- Actual or possible prisoners of conscience were held in at least eighty-seven countries, including Cuba, Indonesia, and twenty-seven countries in Africa.
- Cruel and inhuman punishments, such as amputations, flogging, and stoning, were used in many countries in the Gulf Region, including Iran, Saudi Arabia, and Yemen. (© Amnesty International Publications, 1 Easton Street, London WC1X 8DJ, United Kingdom, from its website http://www.amnesty.org/news/1998/P10000498.html. Reprinted by permission.)

As we can see, many societies, including our own, have not yet guaranteed human rights for all of their citizens. A closer look at these human rights abuses clearly shows that a person's location in her or his society's social structure is often related to how she or he is treated. In many cases, being poor or a member of a social minority can make a person vulnerable to all kinds of harassment by public officials, including arrest, police brutality, or even murder.

The way a society is structured is also related to the kind and extent of human rights abuses that occur within that society. People living under rigid dictatorships, in which freedom of speech and freedom of the press are largely nonexistent, are subject to more harassment than are people living under more democratic forms of government in which these rights are embedded in laws and social institutions. This is true especially for political dissidents and social activists who, all too often, are imprisoned or killed simply because they dared to criticize their government's policies or political leaders (see Data Box). Although democratic societies such as the United States do not, as a rule, have policies deliberately designed to repress particular groups or to violate human rights, abuses can and do occur. In these societies, abuses are more likely to arise from individual misconduct that may be encouraged by an institutionalized failure to hold officials accountable for their actions or by inadequate systems of social control. For example, although not directly ordered to do so, soldiers and police may use excessive force on civilian populations if they perceive that such behavior is tacitly encouraged and approved by their superiors, especially if it has not been punished in the past.

Changes in economic, social, and political climates may also contribute to an increase in abuses. For example, in the United States today, social attitudes support "get tough" measures in the criminal justice system, which may contribute to incidents of police brutality.

Clearly the human rights abuses discussed here represent the more extreme constraints of social structure. Although it is true that social structure constrains our behavior in numerous ways, it is also what makes organized social life possible. In this chapter, we will focus on the meaning and significance of social structure as well as on its component parts.

Understanding Social Structure

As we saw in Chapter 1, the concept of society refers to people who live in a specific geographic territory, interact with one another, and share a common culture and identity. Recall that a key assumption sociologists make about the social world is that human behavior is patterned and

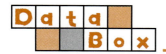

Human Rights Defenders

The following cases represent but a small sample of individuals whose human rights have been violated and on whose behalf Amnesty International continues to work.

- Chechen Republic: Nadezhda Chaykova, a journalist covering the armed conflict in the Chechen Republic, was warned to stop her investigations into misappropriation of funds by leaders of all sides in the conflict if she wanted to stay alive. At age thirty-two, she was killed. Her body was found in March 1996 in a shallow grave near Grozny. She had been blindfolded, severely beaten, and killed by a bullet to the back of her head.
- Mexico: Leticia Moctezuma Vargas campaigned to stop a government-sponsored project that would seriously damage the environment in the Tepoxtlan community in the state of Morelos. She and her young daughters were beaten and received death threats.
- Nigeria: Dr. Beko Ransome-Kuti is a long-time human rights activist in Nigeria and chair of the Campaign for Democracy. He and the vice-chair of the Campaign were sentenced to fifteen-year prison terms for their work on behalf of prisoners convicted in secret treason trials in 1995.
- Pakistan: Zafaryab Ahmed is a journalist and human rights activist who has long opposed bonded labor. After writing about the case of a ten-year-old boy who had been sold in bonded labor to a carpet factory, Ahmed was arrested and charged with sedition.
- Syria: Aktham Nu'aysa and sixteen other members of the Committee for the Defense of Democratic Freedoms and Human Rights in Syria were arrested after issuing a leaflet in 1991 highlighting human rights violations and calling for reforms. He was held in incommunicado detention, tortured, unfairly tried, and sentenced to nine years in jail. Six of those arrested remain in detention.

Source: © Amnesty International Publications, 1 Easton Street, London WC1X 8DJ, United Kingdom, from its website http://rights.amnesty.org/english/stage/news.html. Reprinted by permission.

orderly. Imagine what it would be like to visit another country for the first time not knowing the native language or the local customs. The behavior of the people you would observe would probably seem chaotic, strange, or haphazard at first, but later, when you became more comfortable in your new surroundings, you would see that there was order and organization to their behavior. As you will recall from Chapter 1, sociologists refer to these relatively permanent patterns of interactions and relationships found within a society as social structure. Social structures are created and changed, albeit usually slowly, through people's social interaction, the process by which people act and react in relation to others. This ongoing process gives a dynamic quality to the social order (Sewell, 1992). The efforts of organizations such as Amnesty International are focused on changing social structures that give rise to human rights abuses.

The concept of social structure is one of the most critical concepts you will encounter in your study of sociology. At the same time, it is one of the most difficult concepts to understand fully and to accept, primarily because we are so accustomed to thinking about behavior in terms of individual choices rather than in terms of constraints. Yet it is within the context of ongoing social structures that we learn to become human and participating members of society. Hence, social structure links us to others, influences how we interact with others, and puts constraints on our behavior. As a result, social structure gives order and predictability to social life. The concept of social structure becomes clearer when we examine its key elements: status, role, groups, formal organizations, bureaucracies, and social institutions.

Status

Take a minute to write down your answer to the question, Who are you? Answer the question at least ten times, giving a different response each time. If you are like most people who answer this question, your answers probably went something like this, "I am a student," "I am a female (male)," "I am a daughter (son, parent, wife, husband, sibling)," "I am an employee (employer)," "I am Native American (African American, Asian American, white)," "I am a friend," "I am an athlete." Individuals typically respond to this question in terms of their **statuses** or positions they occupy in the social structure, and, thus, in terms of their relationships to other people. Just these few responses make it clear that each of us occupies multiple statuses at the same time, or what sociologists call a **status set.** The importance of our status set is evidenced in our day-to-day behaviors. For the most part, whenever we interact with others, whether on a conscious level or not, we take our and their statuses into account. For example, although we are happy to share certain jokes and slang language with friends, we are unlikely to use these same expressions with our parents or our bosses.

Some of our statuses fall into the category of **ascribed status,** that is, they are assigned to us at birth and we have little or no control over them. Generally speaking, ascribed statuses cannot be changed, at least not without overwhelming effort and cost to the individual. Although race, ethnicity, age, and sex are determined at birth and, for the vast majority of us, remain constant throughout our lifetimes, some people have felt the need to try to alter these statuses. When some immigrants came to the United States, they Americanized their names to hide their ethnicity in an effort to be more acceptable to this society; some light-skinned African Americans passed as white to avoid the discriminatory consequences of racism; and some individuals, feeling uncomfortable in their bodies, have undergone sex change operations. The social and psychic costs of such "passing" can be enormous: anxiety and worry over acceptance, feelings of guilt for denying one's heritage, and often estrangement from family and friends.

Others statuses, like education and occupation, fall into the category of **achieved status,** that is, they are earned by individual effort. Michael Jordan became a superlative basketball player, Oprah Winfrey a successful talk show host, Itzhak Perlman a famous violinist, and Sandra Day O'Connor an outstanding lawyer and Supreme Court justice only after many years of study, commitment, and hard work. Additionally, there are some statuses, like religion and social class, over which we initially have little choice or control because we acquire them from our parents at birth or adoption. Although it is possible to change the religion and social class position of our childhood, the reality is that for the majority of people, these statuses remain remarkably stable throughout their lives.

Society does not regard all statuses equally. Although people's statuses are, for the most part, fairly consistent with one another, some people experience **status inconsistency,** a situation in which a person occupies two or more statuses of different rank or prestige. For example, in the past, many American artists of color, such as singer Marian Anderson and writer James Baldwin, had to go abroad to exercise their talents and gain recognition. Even across many different occupations and professions today, many women and people of color are not accorded the same respect or treatment as their white male counterparts. As we saw in Chapter 3 and will see again in future chapters, some people react to status inconsistency by challenging society's definition and treatment of them through various forms of individual and collective social action.

Additionally, one status may be seen as more important in our lives than others. A **master status** refers to the position, whether ascribed or achieved, that is perceived as dominant over all others we may hold. As such, it is central not only to our self-perceptions but also to how others view and interact with us. For example, if a person's master status is a U.S. senator or a famous surgeon, she or he is likely to be regarded positively and invited to take other positions in the community, such as member of a country club, member of the Opera Guild, or many others. Conversely, if a person's master status is not highly valued, such as a homeless person or an ex-convict, that person may be stigmatized, isolated, and shut out from many opportunities other people take for granted.

In many societies, including our own, race and gender are each viewed as a master status. Author Barbara Kingsolver movingly describes how a child's master status disrupts the life she and her adopted mother were living when a Native American lawyer, acting on behalf of the

Cherokee Nation, questions both the legality and appropriateness of her adoption (see the Sociology through Literature box). Race and gender are not the only determinants of a master status; other patterns exist as well. For example, for some women and men, being a parent is their major identification and master status; nevertheless, it is more common in our society to measure a person's worth by her or his paid employment. Hence a person's master status is often related to her or his occupation. Thus, William Jefferson Clinton is primarily viewed as "the President" and not as husband, father, church member, or friend.

Societies vary in the degree of importance they attach to these different types of statuses. Some societies, like the traditional Hindus of India, place great emphasis on ascribed status. Marriage, social relationships, and occupation are all determined at birth. As we can see by the story of Govind Dasi in the Cultural Snapshot box, the death of a husband in India, especially when it occurs early, more often than not cuts a woman adrift from her previous social statuses and casts her into a life of poverty. Other societies, like the United States, place a higher value on achieved status. In most industrial societies, the ideology, if not always the practice, is that effort will be rewarded—if people are willing to work hard, the idea goes, they can be anything they want to be. However, the reality is that ascribed status often affects achieved status. For example, the United States has yet to entertain seriously the notion that a woman could be president, although an important barrier to that possibility was overcome when President Clinton appointed Madeleine Albright Secretary of State, the first woman ever to hold that critical position. Indeed, social structures reflect the fact that some people are viewed and treated as more important and receive more power and privileges than others (Ridgeway & Walker, 1995). We will examine the issue of inequality among different segments of our population in more detail in Chapters 9, 10, and 11.

Role

A person's status would be relatively unimportant if it were not for the fact that there is a corresponding role for each status a person occupies. A **role** is a pattern of behavior that is ex-

pected of an individual who occupies a particular status. As Figure 5.1 illustrates, any one status has multiple roles connected to it; these are called a **role set.** Consider the status of a college professor. It involves the role of classroom instructor, the role of student advisor, the role of a peer to other colleagues, the role of department committee member, a research and writing role, and the role of member of the wider college community. Role expectations are defined and structured around the privileges and obligations that the status is believed to contain. For example, professors are expected to be creative, knowledgeable, understanding, and—most important—fair. In return, they expect to be respected, obeyed, and paid. Students are expected to be attentive, hardworking, and prepared. In return, they expect to be rewarded for their efforts with appropriate grades and prospects for a decent job. Thus, roles are reciprocal—the rights of one role are the obligations of another. These shared role expectations fulfill important functions—they link us to other individuals and groups through networks of reciprocal roles and they make behavior fairly routine and predictable, making social order possible.

Role expectations can be dysfunctional as well. If roles are defined so rigidly that behavior and expression are seriously constrained, both the individual and society suffer. Rigid role definitions can lead to the development of stereotypes in which certain characteristics are assigned to an individual solely on the basis of her or his status. Stereotyping is significant because it is frequently used to justify unequal treatment of members of specific groups, often resulting in

FIGURE 5.1 ⟲ **College Student: Status Set and Role Set** In each of these statuses, you enact a variety of role expectations with different role partners.

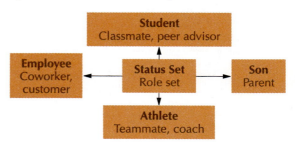

Sociology through Literature

Pigs in Heaven

In her novel *Pigs in Heaven*, Barbara Kingsolver tackles a theme that has occupied the courts since the 1970s. Should race, an ascribed status, be the key factor in adoptions? In the novel, Annawake Fourkiller, a Native American lawyer, is concerned that a Cherokee child called Turtle may have been illegally adopted by a woman named Taylor. The following excerpt details her first encounter with Turtle's adopted mother.

"I work in an office that does a lot of work for the Cherokee Nation. That's what I want to talk with you about. Turtle's adoption might not be valid."

Taylor's cup stops an inch from her lips, and for nearly half a minute she does not appear to breathe. Then she puts down the cup. "I've been through all this already. The social worker said I needed adoption papers, so I went to Oklahoma City and I got papers. If you want to see, I'll go get them."

"I've already looked at the records. That's the problem, it wasn't done right. There's a law that gives tribes the final say over custody of our own children. It's called the Indian Child Welfare Act. Congress passed it in 1978 because so many Indian kids were being separated from their families and put into non-Indian homes."

"I don't understand what that has to do with me."

"It's nothing against you personally, but the law is crucial. What we've been through is a wholesale removal."

"Well, that's the past."

"This is not General Custer. I'm talking about as recently as the seventies, when you and I were in high school. A third of all our kids were still being taken from their families and adopted into white homes. One out of *three.* "

Taylor's eyes are strangely enlarged. "My home doesn't have anything to do with your tragedy," she says. She gets up and stands at the window looking out.

"I don't mean to scare you," Annawake says quietly. "But I want you to have some background on the problem. We need to make sure our laws are respected."

Taylor turns around and faces Annawake, her hair wheeling. "I didn't take Turtle from any family, she was dumped on me. *Dumped.* She'd already lost her family, and she'd been hurt in ways I can't even start to tell you without crying. Sexual ways. Your people let her fall through the crack and she was in bad trouble. She couldn't talk, she didn't walk, she had the personality of—I don't know what. A bruised apple. Nobody wanted her." Taylor's hands are shaking. She crosses her arms in front of her chest and slumps forward a little in the manner of a woman heavily pregnant.

Annawake sits still.

"And now that she's a cute little adorable child and gets famous and goes on television, now you want her back."

"This has nothing to do with Turtle being on television. Except that it brought her to our attention." Annawake looks away and thinks about her tone. Lawyer words will not win any cases in this kitchen. She is not so far from Oklahoma. "Please don't panic. I'm only telling you that your adoption papers may not be valid because you didn't get approval from the tribe. You need that. It might be a good idea to get it."

"And what if they won't give it?"

Annawake can't think of the right answer to that question.

Taylor demands, "How can you possibly think this is in Turtle's best interest?"

"How can you think it's good for a tribe to lose its children!" Annawake is startled by her own anger—she has shot without aiming first. Taylor is shaking her head back and forth, back and forth.

"I'm sorry. I can't understand you. Turtle is my daughter. If you walked in here and asked me to cut off my hand for a good cause, I might think about it. But you don't get Turtle."

"There's the child's best interest and the tribe's best interest, and I'm trying to think of both things."

"Horseshit." Taylor turns away, facing the window.

Annawake speaks gently to her back. "Turtle is Cherokee. She needs to know that."

"She knows it."

"Does she know what it means? Do you? I'll bet she sees Indians on TV and thinks: *How.* Bows and arrows. That isn't what we are. We have a written language as subtle as Chinese. We had the first free public school system in the world, did you know that? We have a constitution and laws."

How do you think Turtle's adoption should be settled? What is the major issue underlying this legal conflict? What does this story tell us about the significance of status and identity?

Source: Excerpt from "A More Perfect Union" from *Pigs in Heaven* by Barbara Kingsolver (pp. 75–77). Copyright © 1993 by Barbara Kingsolver. Reprinted by permission of HarperCollins Publishers, Inc.

Cultural Snapshot

Widowhood In India

The story of Govind Dasi is like that of many Hindu women in India.

Govind . . . was married at 12 in her native village outside Calcutta, widowed at 14 when her teen-age husband died of tuberculosis, then forced to work as an unpaid servant for her mother-in-law for about 30 years. About 15 years ago, penniless and despairing, she boarded a train for the 1,000-mile journey west to Vrindavan, the holy city that has been a point of convergence for Indian widows for at least 500 years.

If Govind does not remember exactly how long she has been here, it is partly because she is illiterate, and partly because of the seamlessness of time. Like the other widows who migrate to this city in central India, she makes her way before dawn each day to one of 4,000 Hindu temples, where she joins in chants to the deity Krishna. Her surname, Dasi, "servant" in Hindi, is adopted by all the widows here to show their religious devotion.

Along with poverty, illiteracy and malnutrition, many Indians regard the plight of the 33 million Hindu widows as one of the darkest blots on the nation's conscience— one that 200 years of social activism and legislation has only partly erased. To be a Hindu widow in the 1900's, at least a poor one, according to Uma Chakravarty, a sociologist at Delhi University, is still to suffer "social death." The core of the problem lies in what Indian sociologists call patri-local residence—the custom of Hindu brides' marrying into their husbands' families, largely severing ties with their own. In many cases, especially when widowhood comes early, this leaves a woman dependent on in-laws whose main interest after her husband's death is to rid the family of the burden of supporting her. . . .

For most, survival is assured by meager handouts of rice and lentils at the temples, coupled with a stipend of two rupees—about five cents—if they chant for four hours in the evening, on top of the four morning hours of holy choruses. Some live beneath stairwells, on verandas or in makeshift shelters, using old jute matting or discarded clothing for bedcovers. . . .

For the younger widows—some barely teen-agers despite laws that forbid child marriages—there is the additional threat of being forced into sex with landlords, rickshaw drivers, policemen, even Hindu holy men. . . .

Govind's life is better than many. Along with her chanting, she works as a seamstress in a garment factory, earning 500 rupees a month to supplement the 125 rupees she gets as a widow's pension. . . .

According to the Skanda Purana, an early Hindu text, widows are to be avoided. [I]n the late 1800's . . . [a] British law remov[ed] the Hindu ban on remarriage. But the taboo on second marriages has remained strong. . . .

Since independence, Indian governments have revised inheritance laws to entrench widow's rights to a share of their husbands' property, and legislated for pensions. But more often than not, laws are circumvented. One study found that inheritance laws often served to entrap women. Their husbands' families, intent on preventing division of land and homes, frequently forced them to remarry back into the family. The old customs mean that many Hindu girls are twice blighted. Parents eager to unburden themselves of a daughter arrange a childhood marriage, and widowhood leaves the woman unwanted again. . . .

Hindu activists are working to improve the lot of the country's widows.

———

How does the status of U.S. widows compare with that of widows in India? What are some of the problems U.S. widows must confront? What steps could be taken to improve the status of widows in India and in the United States?

Source: Excerpted from John F. Burns (1998, March 29) "Once Widowed in India, Twice Scorned." *New York Times,* pp. 1, 12. Copyright © 1998 by The New York Times Company. Reprinted by permission.

———

human rights abuses. For example, women and people of color were viewed as intellectually inferior to white males and were, therefore, denied admission to institutions of higher learning throughout much of United States history; even today, women and people of color are not allowed the full range of opportunities open to most white males. Stereotyping and discriminatory treatment are not confined to the United States. In Japan, the Burakumin, although fully

Japanese and physically indistinguishable from other Japanese, are considered to be mentally and socially inferior to the dominant group. Although the government has outlawed discriminatory practices against the Burakumin, their level of education and income remain considerably lower than that of other Japanese, who still view them as unsuitable marriage partners for their children (Kristoff, 1995c).

Because roles are behavioral expectations associated with a given status, individuals can be viewed as interchangeable in those roles. The role expectations continue regardless of who occupies the position. Regardless of which party is in power, we expect the President of the United States to protect the interests of the United States and to represent those interests to the outside world. Although the country was shocked and saddened when President John F. Kennedy was assassinated, the life and work of the country went on. Vice-President Lyndon Johnson succeeded to the presidency and carried out the responsibilities of that office despite the fact that his personality and leadership style differed from those of President Kennedy. Thus, while the actual behavior of the persons occupying a given status may vary considerably, the accompanying role expectations remain relatively stable.

Role performance is the term used to describe the actual behavior of the person who occupies a given status. If the gap between expected and actual role behavior becomes too great, two things may happen. On the one hand, a person may be forced to exit the role; for example, professors may be fired and students may be dropped for poor performance. On the other hand, the role expectations may be redefined to make them more useful or realistic; for example, some colleges and universities now expect their professors to spend more time and effort on teaching undergraduates than on research and writing than was the case in the past.

Given that we occupy multiple statuses and enact multiple roles, it should not be surprising that at times we experience difficulty in carrying out some of our many obligations. Perhaps you have experienced one or more of the following:

- **Role overload** occurs when the total number of statuses and role sets overwhelm all activity. Many of today's college students are older, married with children, and employed full time. Succeeding in all these endeavors simultaneously requires a difficult balancing act. In reality, what often happens when students struggle to work full time, attend school full time, and raise a family is that all role performances suffer to some degree.

- **Role strain** occurs when a single status calls for incompatible role behaviors. Today, many physicians who have dedicated their lives to healing experience role strain when their patients ask them to relieve their suffering by assisting them to die.

- **Role conflict** occurs when individuals occupy two or more statuses that involve contradictory expectations of what should be done at a given time. A common role conflict for many students today is the conflict they experience as students and workers. It may happen that your final exam is scheduled for a day your employer demands that you show up for work.

These difficulties in carrying out our role obligations can be resolved in a variety of ways. Three common approaches are:

1. *Establish priorities.* This involves making decisions about which activities are more important at a given time. In practice, this may be easier said than done. You may want to make school your highest priority, but you may need to work to pay tuition fees. Thus, although you may want to reduce the number of hours you work, financial obligations may require you to scale back the number of courses you take instead.

2. *Role exit.* This involves disengagement from a role. For example, a student may leave the labor force completely or accept a less demanding job, or conversely a student may drop out of school for a time in order to earn enough money to return to school full time.

3. *Creating public awareness.* This involves making the role strains and conflicts public. For example, Dr. Jack Kevorkian has acknowledged assisting over one hundred people to die. His actions, although contro-

versial, have contributed to the public debate over whether laws should be changed to permit physician assisted suicide, a topic we will return to in Chapter 8.

Social Groups

The second major element of social structure is a **group,** two or more people who interact with each other in patterned ways, share common interests and goals, and experience a sense of identity and belonging. Note the precision of this definition and how it is distinct from other collectivities of people. A *social category* refers to people who have some characteristic in common, for example, voters, Catholics, women, jazz lovers, athletes, parents, teachers, and students. An *aggregate* refers to a gathering of people who have little or no relationship to each other except that they happen to be in the same place at the same time, for example, people waiting for a bus, riding an elevator, or walking through a mall. Although the people in a category share a common characteristic and the people in an aggregate share a common space, they do not meet the other criteria for being a group.

Under certain circumstances, both a social category and an aggregate could evolve into a group. This process of transformation is illustrated in the following two situations. Ted, a college freshman who likes Humphrey Bogart movies, assumes that it is likely that there are other students on campus who share his interest. He puts an ad in the student paper announcing a meeting for anyone interested in seeing and discussing Humphrey Bogart films. Five people show up. They decide to meet on a regular basis, each time renting and discussing a different Bogart film. This social category has transformed itself into a group. Fran, Sarah, and Jean were strangers to one another, although they worked in the same building. One day, they were on the elevator together when it got stuck between floors. It took about thirty minutes for the maintenance workers to free the elevator. The three women were anxious about their situation. To ease their discomfort, they started talking with each other. They found that they had similar interests, and when they left the el-

evator, they agreed to have dinner together later in the week. What started as a chance meeting turned into a long-lasting friendship, a type of group. Conversely, groups can dissolve into categories and aggregates. When the founding members of the Bogart group graduated from college, the other students lost interest and the group eventually disbanded.

Recall that in Chapter 1, we noted that one of the major assumptions of sociology is that human beings are social by nature. From birth until death, human beings depend on others for their physical and psychological survival. Much of our daily life occurs in the context of the many different types of groups to which we belong.

Types of Groups

Sociologists have long recognized the critical importance of groups as well as the diverse forms they can take. Researchers have classified social groups on the basis of their characteristics and functioning. Before examining the different typologies of groups, a word of caution is in order. Most typologies are presented as *ideal types,* abstract descriptions, constructed from a number of cases, that represent the essential characteristics of some phenomenon. These characteristics are presented in exaggerated and idealized forms rather than as empirical descriptions. In reality, any one group may have combinations of characteristics.

Primary versus Secondary Groups   Like the early European sociologists discussed in Chapter 1, Charles Horton Cooley was concerned with how the forces of urbanization and industrialization were transforming social life. He believed that social relationships were moving from more intimate (primary) to more impersonal (secondary) ones, resulting in the weakening of traditional values and social cohesion. According to Cooley, a **primary group** consists of a relatively small number of people who routinely interact on a face-to-face basis, have close emotional ties, and share an enduring sense of belonging. He saw these relationships as primary because within them, individuals have their first social experiences. Through this ongoing and close interaction, individuals begin to develop a sense of who they are and where they fit in the social world. Generally speaking, members of a primary group know one another well, are concerned about each other's welfare, and value their relationships for themselves rather than as a means to other goals. A primary group provides its members with a sense of security and, in turn, its members are expected to provide economic and social support for each other when called upon. As we will see in Chapter 6, primary groups play a critical role in shaping a member's attitudes, values, behavior, and identity. These characteristics are most often found in families and among close friends. It is within these relationships that we can be ourselves, "let our hair down," so to speak, and not worry about being rejected.

In contrast to the primary group, a **secondary group** (a concept implied by Cooley, but formulated by later sociologists) involves larger numbers of people, who interact on a limited, formal, and impersonal basis to accomplish a specific purpose or goal. Work groups, classmates, labor unions, and religious and political organizations are examples of secondary groups. Although members of a secondary group may enjoy and value their relationships, the focus is on the relationships as means to other goals, not as ends in themselves. Interactions in secondary groups tend to follow established rules and individuals participate more as role players than as total personalities. For example, classes meet at specific times and on specific dates and although teachers and students meet regularly to discuss and debate ideas, they generally have only limited knowledge of each other.

Remember, we have been describing ideal types. Think about the many groups to which you belong. No doubt the distinction between primary and secondary groups is not always as clear-cut in some situations as our description makes it. For example, although the majority of families function as primary groups, some families are more characteristic of a secondary group in that the members are emotionally distant from one another and see each other only on a limited basis and then generally in response to a specific need, perhaps a funeral or a financial crisis. Conversely, primary relationships can evolve within the boundaries of secondary groups. For example, coworkers or students, or students and

teachers for that matter, may see each other outside class and their relationships may exhibit both primary and secondary characteristics. Although primary relationships located in secondary groups can offer many benefits, they can also present problems. Friendship between a coach and some of the team members, for example, may cause the coach to spend more time with these players, thus making them feel better about themselves. Even though unintended, the coach's behavior may undermine or compromise the larger group's formal goals and morale. As Figure 5.2 illustrates, the specific groups to which we belong can be located on a continuum ranging from those that most closely resemble the ideal primary group type to those that come closest to approximating the ideal secondary type.

In-Groups and Out-Groups Another way of categorizing groups is in terms of people's sense of belonging. Sociologist William Graham Sumner (1960) distinguished between an **in-group,** a group to which a person belongs and toward which a person directs positive feelings, and an **out-group,** a group to which a person does not belong and about which a person may harbor negative feelings. What makes these groups important is the tendency for in-group members to think of themselves as insiders or "we" and to view the out-groups as outsiders or "they." These groups often develop in the context of larger organizations. For example, students in high school quickly become aware of which stu-

FIGURE 5.2 ⊙ **Continuum of Primary and Secondary Groups**

Primary Groups	←	→	Secondary Groups
Small			Large
Personal			Impersonal
Permanent	Family and peers	Coworkers / Voluntary organizations	Temporary
Informal structure			Formal structure
Broad focus			Narrow focus

dents are in the in-group and which are in the out-group. Feeling excluded by the in-group can be a painful experience, especially for adolescents, who often have strong desires to be accepted. Under some circumstances, out-groups may be perceived as threatening to the in-group. Lewis Coser (1956) called attention to the fact that the existence of a perceived enemy or hostile or competitive group may draw in-group members closer together. At the same time, however, members of in-groups may come to see themselves as superior to out-groups. When the boundaries of an in-group depend on being the "right" race, class, gender, or sexual orientation, there is a high probability that "the other" will be a target of scorn, ridicule, or even violence. In many of our cities today, gangs function as in-groups for some young people, providing them

During the Nazi regime, Jews in Germany were ordered to wear the Star of David on their clothing so they could be identified easily as members of the out-group and thus singled out for discriminatory treatment.

with a sense of "family" and belonging. However, this very cohesion may provoke them to challenge other gang members (outsiders) who happen onto their claimed turf.

Taken to its extreme form, the distinction between in-groups and out-groups can lead to war and genocide. History is replete with such examples. In the United States it was whites against the Native Americans and later African Americans; in Nazi Germany, it was the "Aryan race" against the Jews, Gypsies, and homosexuals; in Rwanda, it was the Hutus against the Tutsis; in Northern Ireland, it was the Protestants against the Catholics, and in the former Yugoslavia, it was the Serbs against the Muslims.

Reference Groups   All of us carry images in our minds of how we would like to be, and we routinely use groups to evaluate how well we are doing. Sociologists refer to such groups as **reference groups,** groups that provide standards for judging our own attitudes, behaviors, and achievements. A classic study of reference groups was conducted by Samuel Stouffer and his colleagues (1949), who examined the military experiences of U.S. soldiers. These researchers discovered that it was not the harshness of their experiences that affected soldiers' morale but rather how they fared in comparison with other groups of soldiers. Thus, regardless of their objective day-to-day situation, the evaluation of their sense of well-being depended on their perception of whether other soldiers were "better off" or "worse off" than they were. This is true in civilian life as well. Evaluations of well-being are affected by our choice of reference groups. If we choose as a reference group a group that is less well-off economically than we are, we are likely to feel relatively prosperous. However, if we compare ourselves to a wealthier group, we may experience feelings of relative deprivation or dissatisfaction. Any group, real or imagined, can serve as a reference group.

Membership is not a prerequisite for a reference group. Although we may attempt to model our dress, goals, values, and attitudes to match the standards of our in-groups of families and friends much of the time, we may try to emulate the standards of a group to which we would like to belong in the future at other times. For example, college students may look to occupational groups, such as business leaders, teachers, doctors, and lawyers for clues to appropriate behavior and values. If the reference groups we select are significantly different from our membership groups, we may experience conflicting images of what is or is not appropriate behavior.

The selection of a reference group is a dynamic process. As we enter new stages in our lives, we are likely to change reference groups. There are sometimes direct attempts to get us to adopt certain reference groups. The advertising industry is a classic example as it targets certain categories of individuals in an attempt to sell its products. In recent years, the tobacco industry has come under intense scrutiny for its advertising campaigns. Its critics allege that ads such as those depicting Joe Camel attempt to attract a new generation of smokers by providing teenagers with a cool, tough, glamorous, streetwise image to emulate (see the Sociological Reflections box).

Social Networks

Our group memberships reach well beyond any individual group boundary and involve us in a much larger web of social relations. Sociologists refer to this web of social relationships that connect us directly or indirectly to other organizations, groups, or individuals as a **social network.** Unlike social groups, members of networks may not have a clear sense of belonging or interact on any regular basis. A quick example will illustrate the complexity of social networks. Take a minute to identify all the friends and acquaintances you have met since starting college, including your professors. Each one of them has the potential to link you to her or his family, friends, acquaintances, and colleagues and through them to other people and their networks. Perhaps one of your professors has already put you in touch with a colleague or other students whose research interests parallel your own. If so, you have already experienced a practice called networking, or making contacts with people who are in positions to provide benefits in some way. The popular expression "Who you know is as important as what you know" exemplifies the important role networks play in social interaction. People often turn to networks when they need help and support, whether it is for

financial advice, choosing a dentist or doctor, finding a date, looking for a job, or any other type of problem solving. Researchers have found that people who are enmeshed in a social network cope better with adversity and consequently suffer less physical and mental illnesses than do people who do not have such a network (Dean et al., 1990; Kraus et al., 1993).

Race, class, and gender affect not only the number and kind of networks people have but also what these networks can deliver by way of tangible benefits. For example, some studies of homeless men have found that either they lack social networks altogether or that their existing networks are so weak and unstable that they can provide only limited amounts of social support (Rossi, 1989; Snow & Anderson, 1993). Conversely, people located at the upper end of the social structure have extensive informal ties with one another that enhance their power and influence (Domhoff, 1974; Knoke, 1990). Historically, women and people of color have been excluded from these relationships, often referred to as the "old boys network." They are increasingly forming their own social networks to further their economic, political, and social interests.

Group Dynamics: The Effects of Group Size

During your college career and in the workplace, you will often find yourself working in small group settings. At times, this activity will be stimulating, productive, and emotionally satisfying, whereas at other times, it will be frustrating and nonproductive. Have you ever noticed how the variable of group size can affect what goes on in a group? German sociologist Georg Simmel (1950) laid the foundation for the study of what has come to be called group dynamics with his analysis of two- and three-person groups.

The *dyad,* or two-person group, is the smallest, most basic, most intimate, but also the most fragile group possible. Think of two best friends or two lovers. There is only one linkage, one relationship involved, so all the energy of these two people can be concentrated on each other. However, if either person leaves the group, it dissolves. Adding a third person to a dyad changes its characteristics in critical ways. The group becomes a *triad;* instead of one linkage,

The Controversy over Joe Camel

Although an increasing number of older adults are quitting smoking, tobacco industry critics contend that the major tobacco companies are seeking "replacement smokers" by aiming advertising campaigns at the young both in the United States and abroad. According to a Health and Human Services Report (INFACT, 1997), 90 percent of smokers begin smoking before the age of twenty-one and 60 percent start before the age of fourteen. Advertising tactics such as cartoon images, free cigarette giveaways, sponsorship of rock concerts and sporting events, and the use of cigarette logos on youth-oriented products have proven effective in recruiting young smokers. The tobacco companies deny targeting young people and point to their own youth nonsmoking programs as evidence. Critics contend, however, that such programs are ineffective and serve only as a public relations ploy. Investigations of the successful RJR Nabisco's Joe Camel campaign appear to support the tobacco industry critics.

According to studies reported in the *Journal of the American Medical Association,* approximately one third of three-year-olds matched Joe Camel with cigarettes, and by age six, children were as familiar with him as with Walt Disney's Mickey Mouse logo. By three years after the introduction of Joe Camel, Camel's share of the youth market had jumped from less than 1 percent to 33 percent. In addition, teen smoking increased by 10 percent. One study reported that U.S. teenagers buy the most heavily promoted cigarettes, and 80 percent of teens consider advertising influential in encouraging them to begin to smoke. What makes Joe Camel so attractive to the young? He is hip, suave, irreverent, fun loving, surrounded by beautiful women, grown-up, independent, and a risk taker—things kids would like to be. He bikes, dances, plays the trumpet, shoots pool, goes to Vegas, and enjoys the high life—things kids want to do.

These patterns are not unique to the United States. Multinational tobacco companies such as RJR Nabisco, Philip Morris, BAT Industries, and American Brands are aggressively pursuing new markets. Numerous studies have documented the success of these efforts: In the last twenty-five years, cigarette smoking has increased by 70 percent in the developing world. Hong Kong children as young as seven years old are addicted to cigarettes. The teen smoking rate in some Latin American cities is 50 percent. Smoking rates among male Korean teenagers rose from 18 percent to 30 percent in one year after the entry of U.S. tobacco companies.

On July 10, 1997, in a statement denying that it was acting due to pressure, Reynolds, a unit of the RJR Nabisco Holdings Corporation, announced that Joe Camel was being retired. He is being replaced with a stylized version of Camel cigarettes' original camel trademark that is more subtle and less cartoonlike. Reynolds's announcement followed closely on the heels of a decision by Phillip Morris to discontinue the cowboy image of the Marlboro Man in its cigarette ads.

Do a content analysis of smoking ads that appear in the mass media. Compare the tobacco ads before and after the demise of Joe Camel and the Marlboro Man. At whom are the ads directed? What messages are being communicated? Do your findings support or contradict the notion that much of cigarette advertising acts as a reference group for young adults?

Source: Information from *INFACT's Tobacco Industry Campaign.* "Tobacco Marketing To Young People." May 20, 1997. http://www.infact.org.

---

one relationship, there are three. The group is now more stable; it can continue to exist even if one member leaves, but the addition of the third member alters the qualitative relationship that existed between the original pair. First-time parents are often surprised at how the arrival of their baby changes their interactions with each other. New fathers sometimes feel neglected because their wives are so involved with the care of the new baby. Even when those feelings aren't present, the couple may find that the baby interrupts their established patterns of intimacy, or they may find themselves disagreeing over the best way to care for the infant. Similarly, when a pair of best friends adds another friend to their ongoing relationship, jealousies may develop if one of the "old" friends seems to spend more time or share more intimacies with the new friend than with the original friend.

As these two examples show, when a dyad becomes a triad, more variety in patterns of interaction become possible. Any one individual member is in a sense less important to the survival of the group. If one member gets angry or unhappy and leaves, there is still a group. Thus, in a triad, there is less need to make concessions to keep every member satisfied. In addition, factions become possible within the group (two against one), and majority rule instead of consensus may become the operating norm. On the other hand, a third person in the group can take the role of a mediator in any disputes between the other two members, thus keeping the relationships in balance.

Figure 5.3 shows how the increase of just a few additional people dramatically increases the possible number of relationships and linkages that can exist within a group. Overall, dyads generally provide for more personal involvement and more emotional satisfaction, whereas larger groups, being more formal and impersonal, are able to absorb new members more easily and are more goal oriented (Carley, 1991).

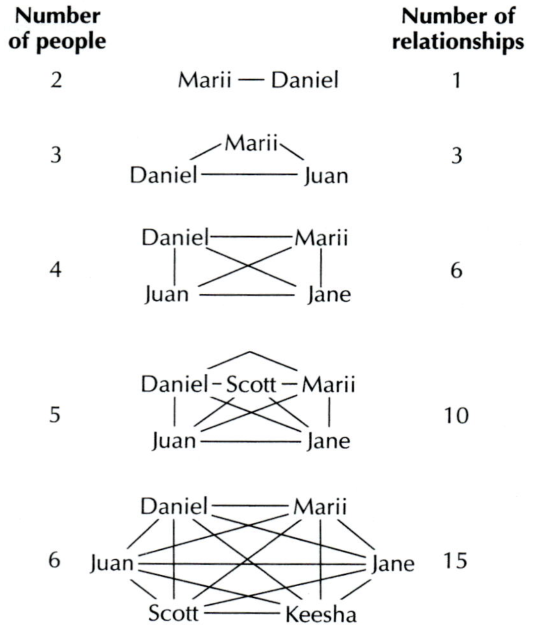

The Power of Groups: Conformity and Groupthink

Social scientists have long been interested in the power of groups. As early as 1935, Muzafer Sherif (1936) called attention to the strong tendency exhibited by individuals to conform to group norms. His experiments on perception focused on how individuals would react in an ambiguous setting. Research subjects were placed in a dark room with only a single point of light where they experienced a phenomenon called the autokinetic effect, in which the point of light appears to be moving even though it is stationary. Because of the darkness, the subjects could not see other objects in the room, thus, they had no reference points. Individuals were first shown the light alone and then later in a group setting. Sherif found that many subjects altered their initial estimates of movement to be more in line with the judgment of the group.

Almost two decades later, Solomon Asch (1952) showed how group pressure could lead individuals to doubt their own judgments and/or to knowingly give incorrect answers. Subjects were placed in groups of seven to nine, all of whom, with the exception of the subject, were confederates of the researcher. The groups were shown two cards: the first card had one vertical line; the second card had three vertical lines of varying lengths. The students were asked to choose which line on the second card matched the line on the first card. When placed in a situation in which choices were made out loud with the confederates answering first and giving the wrong answer, the subjects conformed to the majority view and gave the incorrect choice in about one-third of the cases.

Another classic study of conformity, this time testing people's obedience to authority, was conducted by Stanley Milgram (1974). Subjects were asked to be "teachers" in the study and placed in a separate room with a fake shock

FIGURE 5.3 ♦ **Group Size and Relationships**

generator that indicated a range of shocks from "Slight" to "Danger: Severe Shock" to "XXX." The subjects were unaware that the "learner" in another room was a research confederate paid to act out a prearranged role that included giving incorrect answers and crying out in pain. The researcher, wearing a white coat, instructed the "teachers" to apply an electric shock every time learners gave a wrong answer and to increase the degree of shock in succeeding trials. The reason given for administering the shock was to determine if punishment improves a person's memory. Despite the fact that the vast majority of subjects made prestudy statements that they could not see themselves inflicting severe pain on others, approximately two-thirds of the subject/teachers administered shocks at the highest level. Even though some subjects showed distress while applying the shock treatment, they felt compelled to follow the instructions of the authority figure in the white coat.

The Asch and Milgram studies raise some of the ethical issues we considered in Chapter 2. Subjects in both of these studies were deceived about the real purpose of the study, and a number of them found the experience quite stressful. For these reasons, it is unlikely that such studies would be permitted in university settings today. Nonetheless, these three studies taken together, and now considered classics in the field, clearly demonstrate how groups and authority figures can influence individual behavior even when the groups are artificially constructed. In real group situations, in which strong emotional, economic, and political bonds exist, the pressure to conform is likely to be more intense and the cost of nonconformity much higher. Thus, answers to questions such as How could ordinary German citizens remain silent during the Holocaust? How could U.S. law officials participate in the killing of civil rights activists? How could former Bosnian Serb and Muslim neighbors destroy each other? How could South African police commit such acts of brutality against their black countrymen? require us to look beyond the easy assertion that these are isolated events or aberrations and to focus instead on an examination of group behavior. We should also keep in mind as we do so, however, that in all three of these experiments, as in daily life, many individuals did resist group pressure to conform to existing group norms.

Another major focus of research on groups relates to how group structure influences the way members make decisions. Conventional wisdom holds that in a democracy, group members are free, indeed expected, to express their ideas, share their knowledge, and weigh the pros and cons of alternative strategies in order to arrive at the wisest course of action. In reality, however, group decision making doesn't always follow this pattern. At times, only the voices of the most powerful or loudest members are heard, thus negating alternative points of view. At other times, the pressure to achieve consensus or to maintain positive group feelings may be so strong that individual members may be reluctant to raise a dissenting voice or to seek critical information from outside the group.

Irving Janis (1972, 1982) called such decision making **groupthink,** a process in which group members ignore alternative solutions in order to maintain group consensus and harmony. In analyzing the embarrassing failed attempt by the United States to overthrow Fidel Castro in the Bay of Pigs invasion of Cuba in 1961, Janis found that the initial misgivings among a few of President John F. Kennedy's small group of advisors were dropped in favor of consensus. According to Janis, several conditions are likely to give rise to groupthink: there is a crisis situation; the group is small and tight-knit; the group leader is powerful and actively promotes her or his own plan; and the group members are isolated from the criticism of qualified outsiders. Similar conditions were found to exist in NASA's decision to launch the space shuttle *Challenger* in 1986 despite warnings from Morton Thiokol engineers who were concerned about a possible malfunction in the case of extreme temperatures. Within two minutes of lift-off, the shuttle exploded, killing six astronauts and the first civilian selected to fly, schoolteacher Christa McAuliffe (Moorhead et al., 1991). As these two cases illustrate, groupthink can result in poor, even life-threatening, decisions. The quality of group decision making is generally better when dissent, even if it is a minority opinion, is expressed openly and considered by the majority before a final decision is reached (Nemeth, 1985).

Applying the Sociological Imagination

Consider all the groups you belong to and classify them according to whether they are primary, secondary, in-groups, or out-groups. Does your behavior change when you are in different groups? If so, how do you account for that fact? Have you experienced group pressure to conform when you didn't agree with a group position? Under what conditions is group conformity more likely to exist? Have you ever been part of a groupthink decision? Explain.

Formal Organizations

Earlier, we discussed secondary groups. Some secondary groups, especially those that are large and relatively permanent, develop into **formal organizations,** groups whose activities are rationally designed to achieve specific goals. These organizations accomplish their goals through established personnel and highly defined rules and procedures. Much of our daily life is dominated by a variety of these organizations.

Types of Formal Organizations

Like groups, formal organizations take various forms. They have their own characteristics and culture. They vary in size, goals, and level of efficiency. Additionally, organizations can be distinguished on the basis of their members' motives for participation and the different ways in which control is exerted over members, especially the *lower participants,* those at the bottom of the organizational structure. Using these criteria, sociologist Amitai Etzioni (1975) identified three types of organizations: normative, coercive, and utilitarian.

Normative Organizations   Many organizations are voluntary: members freely choose to belong and membership can be terminated at will. People join these normative organizations, or voluntary associations, for a variety of reasons: for fun, to fill their leisure time, due to shared values and beliefs, due to shared interests, a desire

to meet like-minded people, for self-help, to perform a social service, and/or to promote a special cause. Examples include the Parent-Teachers Association, the Scouts, the National Association for the Advancement of Colored People, the National Organization of Women, the National Rifle Association, Handgun Control, Greenpeace, recovery groups, the League of Women Voters, Young Democrats, Young Republicans, religious organizations, and athletic teams. Many of these normative organizations are part of larger social movements, such as Amnesty International's efforts to promote human rights, which we discussed at the beginning of this chapter.

The tendency of Americans to join and support numerous organizations was identified early in U.S. history. Writing about his visit to the United States in the 1830s, the French social philosopher Count Alexis de Tocqueville (1969:513) observed, "Americans of all ages, all stations in life, and all types of disposition are forever forming associations." Tocqueville saw this participation as strongly related to the development of U.S. democracy and a sense of civic connectedness. Indeed, throughout U.S. history, hospitals, cultural centers, zoos, and social service agencies have depended on legions of unpaid workers whose rewards included satisfaction, a sense of community, and a sense of political effectiveness (Moen et al., 1989). Research shows that the United States has a higher rate of membership in voluntary organizations than other leading industrial countries (Curtis et al., 1992), but some analysts, like Robert Putnam (1996), fear that this sense of civic connectedness is eroding. He argues that this erosion has resulted in less effective social institutions and more negative behavior. Putnam cites findings from the General Social Survey, conducted almost every year over the past two decades, documenting a 25 percent drop in group memberships since 1974 across almost all types of groups. His examination of numerous possible causes for this decline leads him to conclude that the culprit is television. According to Putnam, "A major effect of television's arrival was the reduction in participation in social, recreational, and community activities among people of all ages. In short, television privatizes our lives" (p. 106). His analysis raises many intriguing questions for sociological investigation. For example, will wider access to new communication technologies bring people closer together or fragment them even further?

Coercive Organizations   In contrast to normative organizations, membership in coercive organizations is generally not a matter of choice. People are sent to prisons for punishment and committed to mental hospitals for treatment, most often against their will. To ensure their compliance with rules and regulations, these organizations use a variety of coercive mechanisms—locked doors, barred windows, security personnel, and electronic monitoring. Although some coercive institutions, for example medium security prisons, allow members a degree of freedom of movement, autonomy, and personal responsibility through a variety of mechanisms, many of them take the form of what Erving Goffman (1961, p. xiii) calls a **total institution**—a place "of residence and work where a large number of like-situated individuals, cut off from the wider society for an appreciable period of time, together lead an enclosed, formally administered round of life." During their stay in total institutions, members are told what to do and when to do it, and there is little room for individual autonomy or privacy. Even when membership is not coerced, as in the case of military volunteers, conditions of a total institution may apply for at least a period of time. Louis A. Zurcher, Jr. (1996) analyzed navy boot camp and found that:

> All aspects of the boot's life are conducted in the same place (the center) and under a single central authority (the center commander or more broadly, the U.S. Navy). The recruit does *everything* in the company of others and the expectations for his particular recruit behavior are the same for all his fellow recruits. The day's activities tick off "by the numbers," everything done at the proper time in the proper place, according to an elaborate "plan of the day," published daily and posted by order of the commanding officer. (p. 56)

Although military personnel gain more freedom of movement after completing basic training, they remain under a strict chain of command until their term of service is over.

In Chapter 6, we will examine how such organizations serve as settings for a form of adult learning in which old, established attitudes or behaviors are broken down and replaced with new patterns, a process known as resocialization.

Utilitarian Organizations   Organizations such as corporations, unions, banks, educational institutions, and government agencies are established to accomplish specific tasks. People join them in order to receive some form of direct

Military recruits exist in what Erving Goffman referred to as a "total institution," where members are told what to do and when to do it. There is little room for individual autonomy and privacy.

benefit. For example, a major motivation for attending college is to earn a degree that will provide an advantage in the marketplace. People join labor unions to improve their working conditions. Thus, on one level, membership is voluntary. However, on another level, survival and earning a living is predicated on participation in these utilitarian organizations.

Bureaucracies

By this time, you are probably getting the message that wherever we go, we are all, to varying degrees, caught up in organizations. The food we eat, the products we use, the recreations we enjoy, the work we do, and the education and health care we receive are all provided by organizations. Many of the organizations that we are involved with on a day-to-day basis—workplaces, schools, hospitals, and government agencies—take the form of a **bureaucracy,** a large-scale formal organization in which a complex division of labor based on expertise, hierarchical authority, and written rules is used to achieve maximum efficiency.

The rudimentary beginnings of bureaucratic structures were visible at least 6,000 years ago, when Egypt and Mesopotamia strove to coordinate their complex trade networks (Wallace, 1983). Over the centuries, as societies increased in size and complexity (especially after the advent of industrialization), bureaucratic structures became the dominant organizational form. Industrialists needed an efficient way to mass produce products with a minimum of waste and expense and at the same time to control their growing and more specialized labor force. Max Weber (1968) was one of the first sociologists to identify this new emphasis on efficiency and strategic planning, which he referred to as the *rationalization* of social life. According to Weber, the economy was not the only site for this rationalization. Rather it manifested itself in all aspects of daily interaction in modern society, leading to fundamental changes in the structure and function of educational, political, and even religious organizations as they increasingly took on the characteristics of a bureaucracy.

Characteristics of Bureaucracies

Recognizing the growing significance of bureaucracies in modern life, for both good and ill, Weber (1968) constructed a framework for analyzing them based on a composite of characteristics derived from many existing examples. Weber's resulting ideal type has six essential features:

1. **A hierarchical authority structure.** Each lower office is under the supervision and control of a higher office. Formal lines of authority are represented easily on an organizational chart. The authority is attached to the position, not the person. Thus, organizations are not readily disrupted by anyone's death, retirement, or resignation.

2. **Division of labor and specialization.** Each position in the organization is assigned certain limited duties and responsibilities.

3. **Written rules and regulations.** These standardized rules govern the day-to-day operations of the bureaucracy and are intended to promote efficiency and predictability, and they are typically formalized in a handbook that members receive when they join the organization. Your institution, no doubt, has handbooks for each of its constituencies: faculty, staff, and students.

4. **Expertise or technical competence.** Officials in a bureaucracy are first hired and then later evaluated on the basis of their knowledge and expertise, not on ascribed traits or "connections." For example, most colleges and universities require their faculty to have doctoral degrees before they can be considered for tenure-track positions.

5. **Impersonality.** Bureaucratic rules and regulations are designed to treat members in an impersonal and objective manner, thus eliminating favoritism and ensuring that personal considerations will not impede organizational goals. It is this routinization that makes for bureaucratic efficiency.

6. **Formal, written communications.** Bureaucracies rely on keeping detailed records. These files become the backbone of the organization, guiding all subsequent operations.

Here again we need to remember that Weber was describing ideal types. No one bureaucracy will possess all of these characteristics to the same degree. Thus, your college or university may have fewer rules or a simpler division of labor than ours (see Figure 5.4), but both organizations are bureaucratized to a degree. Further, any given bureaucracy does not conform perfectly to these described characteristics. For example, ascribed traits such as race and gender or whom one knows may be more predictive of getting hired or promoted within a given organization than is individual merit. Also, as we will see shortly, people do violate organizational rules, and bureaucracies are not always as formal and impersonal as they may seem at first glance.

Bureaucratic Dysfunctions

It is likely that when people think about bureaucracy, they are not thinking about these ideal characteristics but rather of their negative experiences within bureaucracies. Although Weber stressed the functional necessity of bureaucracies in modern societies, he also saw that they could take on a life of their own, becoming "iron cages" for those involved with them and having dysfunctions for the larger society as well. Among the most common complaints leveled against bureaucracies are inefficiency and alienation, incompetence, and structured inequality.

Inefficiency and Alienation How is it that an organizational form that was developed to maximize efficiency becomes inefficient? The familiar concept of "red tape" gives us part of the answer. In many bureaucracies, employees are trained to follow the rules and to perform a predetermined set of activities and given few opportunities to exercise personal discretion in the performance of their jobs. George Ritzer (1998) called this rigid control of work activities and the tendency to treat workers as robots the "McDonaldization" effect, referring to the increasing development of work environments modeled after one of the largest fast-food restaurant chains in the world.

One result of such mechanistic job descriptions is what social critic Thorstein Veblen (1922) called a *trained incapacity*—the inability to respond to new situations and a reluctance to exercise personal judgment or independent decision making. This trained incapacity is reflected in the attitudes of some employees who respond to criticisms of their job performance by saying, "It wasn't in my job description," "It's not my responsibility," or, "I was only following orders." All too often, employees become so caught up with following the rules that they lose sight of the organizational goals, a condition Robert Merton (1968) called *bureaucratic ritualism*. This ritualism, coupled with the bureaucratic norm of impersonality, often results in workers treating clients in an uninterested or dehumanizing manner. Forms must be filled out and rules must be followed, despite the client's unique needs. Imagine the feelings and emotions of a family that has fallen on hard times and that, after filling out numerous forms for assistance, is curtly told to come back next week. Thus, bureaucracies often alienate the very people they were created to serve.

C. Northcote Parkinson (1957) saw bureaucratic inefficiency in a different, and some would

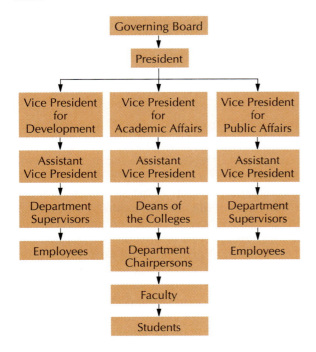

FIGURE 5.4 ❂ **Typical University Organizational Chart**

Governing Board
→ President
→ Vice President for Development
→ Vice President for Academic Affairs
→ Vice President for Public Affairs
→ Assistant Vice President
→ Assistant Vice President
→ Assistant Vice President
→ Department Supervisors
→ Deans of the Colleges
→ Department Supervisors
→ Employees
→ Department Chairpersons
→ Employees
→ Faculty
→ Students

say cynical, light. His view, popularly known as *Parkinson's Law*, asserts that "work expands to fill the time available for its completion." This insight came to him when he realized that after World War I, the number of ships and sailors in the British navy declined while the administrative staff continued to grow. His explanation for this was that employees or bureaucrats, as they are sometimes distainfully called, have a vested interest in promoting and perpetuating the organization in which they work. He reasoned that to protect their positions, employees try to look busy by stretching out work they could complete in a shorter time or else they create new work for themselves. If these efforts are successful, he argues, the bureaucrats are rewarded by getting assistants to help them. Thus, according to Parkinson, bureaucracies grow but do not necessarily become more efficient or productive.

Incompetence   A characteristic reward for working effectively in a bureaucracy is to be promoted to a higher position. According to Laurence Peter and Raymond Hull (1969), these patterns of career mobility can cause problems. Their observations of bureaucratic settings led them to conclude that within bureaucracies, there is a tendency to promote individuals until they reach their level of incompetence. This tendency, popularly known as the *Peter principle*, calls attention to situations in which people find themselves in positions that demand more skills and knowledge than they possess. In short, they are in over their heads and are unable to perform competently, yet because they have performed well in the past, they are not likely to be demoted. Instead, bureaucracies rely on others, usually subordinates, to get the job done.

Structured Inequality   By their very nature, bureaucracies are inherently inequitable. Early in this century, Robert Michels (1966) called attention to the concentration of power in only a few individuals at the top of the bureaucratic pyramid, a characteristic he called the *iron law of oligarchy*. Michels was concerned that this type of concentration of power allowed organizations to operate in undemocratic ways because those at the top have control over information,

organizational resources, and personnel that can be used for personal gain at the expense of others; this control allows those at the top to escape public accountability for their actions. In addition, he noted, those at the top have a tendency to reproduce themselves, that is, to hire people with whom they are comfortable, people with characteristics much like their own.

Historically in the United States, white males have been the dominant group. Hence, women and people of color have traditionally occupied the lowest rungs on bureaucratic ladders. Even when a member of a social minority is allowed to enter a bureaucracy, that doesn't mean that she or he is integrated into the organization's ongoing culture and existing social relationships. Numerous studies show that in a variety of economic organizations, women and people of color are excluded from informal networks and lack mentors who can help promote their careers. Because women and people of color are underrepresented in these organizations, those few who are there become highly visible, a condition referred to as tokenism. Thus, these individuals are likely to feel as if they are on display and, consequently, they become wary of making any mistakes or standing out too much (Feagin, 1991; Kanter, 1977). As we will see in later chapters, there is more diversity in organizations today, but the United States has not yet reached the stage where all its citizens have an equal opportunity to succeed within its existing organizational structures.

Bureaucracy's Other Face: Informal Structures

Although Weber emphasized the formal side of bureaucracy, it has an informal structure as well. As members of a bureaucracy interact with one another, they develop patterns of interaction that are not part of the official hierarchy and which, in fact, may ignore, bypass, or contradict the official rules and procedures of the organization. These informal structures and norms may function in different ways, depending on the situation. On the one hand, these informal structures can promote organizational goals by solving problems when the formal structure is too rigid or unresponsive to do so. For example, your faculty advisor may save you time and effort by helping you cut through some of the formal procedures regulating registration or graduation. On the other hand, informal norms can act to subvert organizational goals. For example, studies at Western Electric's Hawthorne plant in Illinois found that workers in the "bank wiring room" who made parts of switches for telephone equipment deliberately restricted output despite management's offer of financial incentives to improve their productivity. Fearing that if they produced more, management would raise the expected level of output even more or, worse yet, lay off some workers, the men established their own level of productivity for a day's work and created informal rules and sanctions to enforce this norm. Workers who overproduced were criticized as "rate busters," while those who produced too little were ridiculed as "chiselers." Workers who violated these informal norms were "binged" (hit on the shoulder by their fellow workers') (Roethlisberger & Dickson, 1961).

Research such as the Hawthorne studies have focused attention on the importance of informal structures, organizational subcultures, and social networks. Recognizing the validity of these studies, heads of formal organizations have taken a number of steps to build goodwill and loyalty among their members, including organizational sponsorship of recreational activities, recognizing individual and group achievements, and providing increased opportunities for members to be involved in the decision-making process through a variety of means such as focus groups or quality circles. However, when companies attempt to be more competitive through cost cutting and downsizing, these practices often fall by the wayside and employee loyalty declines as a result.

Social Institutions

In ordinary conversation, people often refer to prisons, hospitals, and schools as institutions. However, when sociologists use this term, they are referring to more than a building in which a particular activity is housed. Instead, they define **social institutions** as relatively stable clusters of values, norms, social statuses, roles, groups, and organizations that meet basic social needs.

Sociologists have identified five basic institutions that have endured for generations and existed in virtually all known societies

1. The *family* regulates reproduction and provides care for new generations.
2. *Education* transmits knowledge and skills to the next generation.
3. The *economy* handles the production, exchange, and distribution of goods and services.
4. The *government* maintains order and provides protection for its people.
5. *Religion* imparts a sense of purpose in life.

We will discuss each of the basic institutions in greater detail in subsequent chapters. For now, we simply want to clarify a common source of confusion that students often encounter regarding the appropriate use of the concepts "groups" and "institutions" and to call attention to both the dynamic and the static nature of institutions in general. The concepts of groups and institutions cannot be used interchangeably. In an earlier section, we used families as an example of primary groups. Here we're saying that the family is a basic institution. Both usages are correct, but the contexts are different. When we speak of specific individuals who are connected to one another, we are talking about *a* family (a group) such as the Schwartz family, the Scott family, and your family. When we speak of a cluster of standardized statuses and roles (wives–husbands, parents–children) and patterns of behavior organized to meet societal needs (reproduction, nurturance), we are talking about the institution of *the* family.

The ways in which institutions emerge, are structured, and change vary from one society to another. In some societies, one institution may meet multiple social needs. For example, in simple societies having low levels of technology, the family not only performs reproductive and caregiving roles but also may serve as an economic and political unit. In contrast, social institutions become more differentiated in larger, more technologically advanced societies. Thus, in simpler societies, parents would teach their children the skills and knowledge needed for survival and family elders would settle personal and public disputes. In more complex societies, however, these activities are shared with schools, the mass media, the police, and the military. Nonetheless, even in today's modern, complex societies, this differentiation may be challenged. For example, a growing number of parents today prefer to teach their children at home rather than send them to public schools where they can't control the curriculum or the values being taught.

Although there is widespread agreement that social institutions structure our lives to a marked degree and that, once established, they become deeply embedded in the fabric of society, social theorists approach institutions in different ways. Structural functionalists tend to see institutions as serving the larger social good by providing solutions to problems and giving order and predictability to people's lives. Conflict theorists, using data on poverty, unemployment, and discrimination, argue that the ways institutions are structured benefit some people at the expense of others. Symbolic interactionists remind us that, although much of what goes on in institutional settings is fairly routine and predictable, individuals can and do alter institutions. Their focus of analysis is on how people define and redefine their relationships. In the next section, we will examine just a few of the ongoing structural changes that are likely to continue well into the next decade.

Structural Trends in the Twenty-First Century

Looking back on the twentieth century, we can readily see how technological innovations have altered the social structure of our lives. Let's take one quick example to illustrate this point. Before air conditioning, people had easier access to each other. During warm weather, neighbors kept their windows open and spent considerable time outdoors visiting back and forth on each other's porches and watching the activity unfolding in the streets in front of them. After air conditioning, people stayed indoors with shuttered windows; front porches disappeared from new homes, replaced by family rooms; and communities, now worried about street crime, had to formalize neighborhood watch programs to replace the previous informal supervision of neighbors.

Now, on the verge of a new century, we can see already how the computer is restructuring our lives by briefly considering some of the initial transformations taking place in two of our social institutions—education and the economy. Although the majority of college students today continue to come to a central location or campus on a regular basis to meet with assigned instructors and other students pursuing the same course of studies, this educational delivery system is likely to become obsolete. State governments and educational leaders are designing "virtual" universities without walls, libraries, or classrooms, where students can graduate without ever setting foot on a campus. Such developments will alter the status and role of teacher and student in ways that are not yet clear. Social networks, too, will be affected. For those who have access to computers, social networks will be enlarged and/or changed as people connect and interact with experts and colleagues all around the globe. Some people already spend more time "chatting" on the Internet than they do in face-to-face interaction with family and friends. Similarly, increasing numbers of employees can, by virtue of the Internet, work at home, physically isolated from their colleagues. What these changes will mean in the long run for people's sense of identity, feelings of belonging, or sense of solidarity with coworkers remains an empirical question.

Key Points to Remember

1. *Social structure* refers to the relatively permanent patterns of interaction and relationships found within a society. It links us to others, influences how we interact with others, and puts constraints on our behavior. The key elements of social structure are status, role,

groups, formal organizations, and institutions. A status or social position can be ascribed, acquired at birth, or achieved through an individual's own efforts. *Role* refers to the expectations associated with a particular status. People occupy multiple statuses and enact multiple roles. They therefore sometimes experience role overload, role strain, or role conflict.

2. A group consists of two or more people who interact with each other in patterned ways, share common interests and goals, and experience a sense of identity and belonging. Groups can be classified on the basis of their characteristics and functioning: primary or secondary, in-group and out-group. Our group memberships reach beyond any individual group boundary and involve us in social networks, a larger web of social relationships that connect us directly or indirectly to other organizations, groups, or individuals.

3. The variable of size affects the structure and functioning of groups. As we move from a dyad (two-person group) to a triad (three-person group), the group becomes more stable but the relationships undergo a qualitative change.

4. *Formal organizations* refer to groups whose activities are rationally designed to achieve specific goals. Many of the organizations that we are involved with on a day-to-day basis take the form of a bureaucracy, a large-scale formal organization in which a complex division of labor based on expertise, hierarchical authority, and written rules is used to achieve maximum efficiency. Criticism of bureaucracies include inefficiency and alienation, incompetence, and structured inequality.

5. Social institutions are relatively stable clusters of values, norms, social statuses, roles, groups, and organizations that meet basic social needs. Sociologists have identified five basic institutions that have endured for generations and have existed in virtually all known societies. They are the family, education, the economy, government, and religion.

6. Society and social structures are created and changed, albeit usually slowly, through people's social interaction.

Key Terms

status	role performance	out-group
status set	role overload	reference groups
ascribed status	role strain	social network
achieved status	role conflict	groupthink
status inconsistency	group	formal organizations
master status	primary group	bureaucracy
role	secondary group	social institutions
role set	in-group	

Key People

Peter Benenson	Georg Simmel	Stanley Milgram
Charles Horton Cooley	Muzafer Sherif	Max Weber
William Graham Sumner	Solomon Asch	Robert Michels
Samuel Stouffer		

Questions for Review and Discussion

1. What is meant by social structure? How helpful is the concept of social structure in analyzing social behavior? Explain.

2. Identify and diagram your statuses and role sets. Which are ascribed? Which are achieved? Which are mixed? Do you see potential and/or real problems in any of your role performances? If so, what do you think is responsible for these problems? What can you do to resolve these difficulties?

3. Discuss the Sherif, Asch, and Milgram experiments. What do they tell us about the influence of groups on individuals? Do you have any ethical concerns regarding any of these research studies? If so, what are they? Do you see any relationship to the behaviors revealed in these studies and some of the behavior you read about in newspapers today?

4. Examine your college's or university's organizational structure and functioning. How does it compare to the ideal type bureaucracy described by Max Weber? Compare the formal and informal aspects of your college or university. Which side seems better equipped to meet its goals? Do you see any dysfunctional aspects in the way your college or university tries to meet its goals? If so, what are they? How might your college or university minimize these negative aspects?

For Further Reading

Bellah, Robert N., et al. 1991. *The Good Society.* New York: Alfred A. Knopf. The authors suggest that the U.S. social structure is threatened because citizens are neglecting their institutions. They suggest that this trend can be stopped through participatory democracy.

Giddens, Anthony. 1990. *The Consequences of Modernity.* The author presents a comprehensive examination of the concept of social structure.

Homans, George C. 1950. *The Human Group.* New York: Harcourt, Brace. The author presents a clear discussion of the basic processes and structures of social groups (families, work groups, and gangs).

Lopata, Helen Znaiecka. 1994. *Circles and Settings: Role Changes of American Women.* New York: SUNY Press. The author examines the changing status and roles of American, Chinese, Indian, and Eastern European women and the role strains and role conflicts that accompany these changes.

Sociology through Literature

Golding, William. 1954. *Lord of the Flies.* New York: Coward-McCann. When a ship carrying young English boys sinks and they are forced to take refuge on an uninhabited island, the social structure they had known breaks down. In its absence, they create a new and somewhat fearsome structure.

Kafka, Franz. 1964. *The Trial.* New York: The Modern Library (original publication 1925). Kafka tells the story of Joseph K.—an orderly, industrious chief bank clerk who experiences a bureaucratic nightmare. He is suddenly arrested on his thirtieth birthday and must spend the rest of his life defending himself against an unspecified charge.

Internet Resources

http//lcweb.loc.gov/global/executive/defense.html
Visit the Web site of one of the largest bureaucracies in the world, the U.S. Department of Defense.

Socialization:
The Process of
Becoming Human

AGENT OF CHANGE: ROB CARMONA

On a cold, damp day in March, ninety-one unemployed New Yorkers are gathered in the barren basement of a Harlem housing project. They have come to this basement to participate in an intensive three-week training program, called Strive, hoping to turn their lives around. These clients are poor, out of work, and lack essential job skills. Some of them have been in prison; others are recovering addicts. The cofounder and executive director of the program, Rob Carmona, is a former convict and drug addict who knows first-hand what an uphill struggle this will be. His program is tough, a cross between group therapy and boot camp. To succeed in it, participants must be willing to take a critical look at themselves and to make significant changes in their lives. Getting through the program will not be easy; half the people gathered here will not make it.

At the start of the program, a Strive trainer asks a young man why he didn't raise his hand in response to a question. The young man tells the trainer he didn't feel like it. He is told to leave. Another young man arrives twenty-five minutes late. He is told in no uncertain terms to go back home: "This is not junior high where you roll in when you feel like it. This is the first day of work." Another participant is told to smile. When he does, the trainer tells him, "That's no smile; that's a grin." He protests and is yelled at and made to do it again. This time he succeeds. Next comes Handshake 101. Everyone goes into the hall. Those who don't pass the "smile, shake, greet" test are sent to the back of the line to begin the process all over again.

And so it goes. Participants are told what to wear, how to talk, and even how to style their hair. Staff members try to help these clients see how employers will act towards them if they don't make necessary adjustments in their attitudes and behavior. Toward the end of the three-week program, those remaining must do a mock job interview in front of the group. Strive staffers play the role of employers and they are demanding. The critique at the end of each interview is often brutal. Some participants break down; some cry. Some are made to do it over and over again. Of the original ninety-one people who entered the program that March morning, only half of them graduate. The program is tough, but it does work. Over the last twelve years, Strive has helped more than 15,000 people find jobs.

What is going on here? Are programs like Strive necessary? To answer these questions with any real degree of understanding requires that we step back and analyze how individuals learn to perform social roles such as worker, friend, and citizen. The majority of the population in our society learns these roles without the need for special intervention programs such as Strive. However, many of the Strive participants and millions of other people like them grew up missing out on a lot of experiences that enable individuals to develop their human potential and to learn the knowledge, attitudes, and skills that are deemed socially acceptable and which, in turn, are socially rewarded. In short, not all members of our society begin life with the same kind of socialization experiences. Thus, it should come as no surprise that the life course development of adults varies dramatically. In this chapter, we will explore the dynamic aspects of socialization—how it occurs, its significance for both the individual and society at large, and the forces that give it shape and affect its outcomes. In particular, we will examine how the social constructs of race, class, and gender structure the opportunities and constraints we encounter as we move through our life course and how they shape our self-concepts and the ways other people respond to us (Hess, 1990; Stoller & Gibson, 1997).

Source: Information and quotations from CBS News, *60 Minutes,* May 4, 1997.

The Meaning of Socialization

Socialization is the process of social interaction by which individuals acquire the knowledge, skills, norms, and values of their society and by which they develop their human potential and social identity. This process begins at birth—perhaps even sooner as expectant parents play special music for and talk to their child while it is growing in its mother's womb in the hopes of influencing their child in a positive direction—and it doesn't end until our last breath is taken.

The functions of socialization are twofold. First, it ensures the continuity of the social order by teaching a society's new members the accepted way of doing things. It is through socialization that society and culture are reproduced from one generation to the next. Second, socialization provides the foundation for the development of an individual's **personality**—a relatively stable set of attitudes, values, and behaviors—as well as a sense of **self,** the conscious recognition of being a distinct individual. It is a lifelong process in which individuals learn about themselves through interaction with others.

However, socialization should not be construed as simply a one-way process. From birth on, individuals become active agents in the process (Peterson and Rollins, 1987; Rheingold, 1969). For example, when a child is born, parents immediately alter their behavior to take into account the new member of the household. They adjust their social and sleeping patterns to those of the newborn. However, babies, too, learn early on that crying and smiling will generate specific responses from their parents. And as children mature, they quickly learn to apply their newly acquired interaction skills, often in attempts to get their parents to change their minds on a wide variety of issues ranging from types of discipline to approval of friends, styles of dress, music, and social activities. As people move through their own life courses, their activities and choices influence the reactions of those around them and help to recreate the social world.

Becoming Human: The Nature–Nurture Debate

Consider how you might answer the question, When did you become human? Was it at conception? at birth? when you were a toddler? a child? or are you still in the process of becoming a human being? Although we enter the world with human biological characteristics, we do not become fully human until we are able to function in human groups. Compared to other animals, human beings are the most dependent at birth. Unable to feed or protect ourselves, our initial survival depends on being cared for by others. However, the provision of food and shelter alone is not sufficient to transform biological organisms into functioning human beings. As we will see throughout this chapter, this transformation depends on socialization.

Although there is widespread agreement today that socialization is necessary for the human animal to develop its full potential, there is still some disagreement about how much of an individual's development and behavior is due to an inherited genetic makeup (nature) and how much is due to socialization (nurture). As we saw in Chapter 4, some sociobiologists believe that certain social behaviors (for example, aggression, competition, dominance, shyness, and sexual orientation) seem to be inherited genetically (Kagan et al., 1988; Wilson, 1978). Research on twins who were separated shortly after birth and then raised apart in different social environments provides partial support for their position (Farber, 1981). Despite their different childhood experiences, similar voice patterns, temperaments, and nervous habits were often found in twin pairs. However, these twin pairs also exhibited differences in values and attitudes, thus also providing support for the role of environment in personality development.

Most sociologists today take a middle-ground position, disclaiming that either heredity or environment is all important. Rather, they argue that both biology and environment interact in the socialization process. Genetic inheritance is viewed as raw material that can be developed in numerous ways depending on the kind of environments individuals inhabit. For example, a child may inherit physical characteristics from her or his parents that, if developed, could make her or him a fine athlete. However, if the environment the child inhabits discourages athletics or provides few opportunities to develop athletic skills, it is unlikely that this child will become successful in this area.

The Significance of Socialization

Just as food, water, and shelter are basic human needs, so too is interpersonal interaction. Interaction is necessary for a person to become fully human. If it is missing or inadequate, it can adversely affect an individual's physical, psychological, and social well-being. This deprivation at an early age can lead to lasting and often irreversible damage to the personality.

Isolated Children Sociologist Kingsley Davis (1940, 1947) documented the experiences of two girls who had spent the first six years of their lives in secluded atticlike rooms, isolated from all but minimal contact with others and excluded from family activities. Both girls were rejected apparently because they were born outside of legal marriage. When authorities found the girls, they were in poor physical health and unable to perform any behaviors considered normal for children their age. They were unable to walk or talk and were fearful of strangers. The first child, Anna, was placed in a home for retarded children and initially underwent a period of intensive socialization. Although she never learned to speak, she did learn to walk and to respond to simple commands. Anna never overcame her many health problems and she died at age ten, leaving unresolved the question of whether she could have overcome the damage of her early social deprivation. The second child, Isabelle, fared much better. Within months of undergoing intensive socialization experiences, she learned elementary forms of speech. After two years in a specialized program, Isabelle was behaving in ways characteristic for her age group. One likely explanation for Isabelle's success relative to Anna's was that Isabelle had spent considerable time with her deaf-mute mother, communicating with her through rudimentary sounds and gestures. Thus, however limited it may have been, Isabelle had some experience in forming a meaningful relationship with another human being (Sacks, 1989).

Three decades later, a thirteen-year-old girl was discovered by authorities living in similar conditions (Curtiss, 1977; Rymer, 1993). Like Anna and Isabelle, Genie was deprived of any ongoing contact with others. In addition, her father routinely beat her for making sounds. Not surprisingly, she never learned to speak. Testing showed her developmental level to be similar to that of a one-year-old. Even with an intensive program and the special attention of experts in the field, Genie never progressed much beyond the developmental level of a young child. Unfortunately, Genie's life became entangled in a web of controversy among the professionals involved in her case and she ended up being institutionalized.

Institutionalized and Neglected Children   Social settings do not need to be as extreme as those endured by Anna, Isabelle, and Genie to impair social development. A series of studies dating from the 1940s has demonstrated that even when adequate physical care is provided, individuals will not thrive if there is limited human contact. Dr. Rene Spitz (1945, 1946) studied two groups of infants. The first group of babies had their own caretakers; the second group were raised in an orphanage, where one nurse cared for eight or more infants. The infants in the latter group, while having their physical needs met, received little personal attention. Compared to the first group, they experienced long periods of immobility, engaged in mechanical rocking, and evidenced lower levels of social development. More recently, similar consequences of early deprivation have come to light. When the Romanian President Nicolai Ceaussescu was overthrown in 1989, authorities discovered hundreds of Romanian children living in orphanages where they were fed and diapered on military-style schedules but received little or no love or personal attention. When these children were first observed, many were withdrawn, engaged in rocking be-

havior, and had eating and other behavioral problems. Follow-up studies of many of these children who were later adopted seem to indicate that while early problems fade, they don't disappear completely. The findings from these studies suggest that the severity of the children's problems is proportional to the length of institutionalization, that is, the longer children have been institutionalized, the more behavior problems they have and the longer the duration of these problems (Holden, 1996). The experience of early social deprivation is not confined to institutional settings. Studies of parenting behaviors of depressed and schizophrenic mothers reveal similar social deficits in their offspring (Dodge, 1990; Goodman & Brumley, 1990).

Understanding the Process of Socialization

A great deal of psychological and sociological writing in the twentieth century has been devoted to exploring the actual process by which individuals come to see themselves as distinct entities having specific characteristics and behaviors. Although there is general agreement among social scientists that the self is a social product that emerges through interaction, there is some disagreement as to how the process unfolds. Some, like the psychiatrist Sigmund Freud, saw socialization as an ongoing struggle, much of it at an unconscious level, between the individual and society; others, like Charles Horton Cooley and George Herbert Mead, saw it as a gradual, more complementary blending of the individual and society.

Personality Development: Sigmund Freud

Sigmund Freud (1947) believed that an individual's adult personality was pretty well established during the first five or six years of life. He viewed the personality as composed of three interrelated parts that, taken together, allow the self to function in society. The **id** represents the infant's basic biological urges aimed at obtaining pleasure. If these go uncontrolled, social life would be chaotic, with everyone pursuing her or his own desires with little thought for the welfare of others. Thus, society, through the action of parents and other adults, serves somewhat as a countervailing force on these urges and as a consequence, the individual comes to internalize appropriate norms, values, and feelings. Freud called this internalized part of the personality the **superego,** or conscience. The final element of personality is the **ego,** the rational part of the self whose function is to mediate between the id and the superego, allowing the individual socially approved ways of satisfying the id. According to Freud, if the ego is successful, children grow up to be well-socialized members of their communities. However, he believed that for some people, this process exacted a price in terms of repressed desires that can cause personality problems in later life. Although much of Freud's work focused on the conflicts of childhood, he believed that similar conflicts occur throughout the life course whenever the "childish" desires of the id threaten to overwhelm the rational functioning of the ego.

Although Freud is credited with the discovery and exploration of the unconscious and the recognition of the critical importance of early life experiences, few social scientists accept the view that personality development and socialization are largely achieved by the age of five or six.

Cognitive Development: Jean Piaget

The Swiss child psychologist Jean Piaget (1954) also recognized the self-centeredness of infants as well as the fact that they are at first unable to separate themselves from their surroundings. However, his research focused on cognitive development in children—how they think and understand. Piaget identified four age-related stages of cognitive development, with each new stage involving more sophisticated levels of reasoning. According to Piaget, cognitive development involves both social and biological components. Thus, a given stage cannot be completed until the mind has achieved the appropriate level of physiological development.

1. **Sensorimotor stage** (from birth to about age two). During this period, young children depend on their sensory-based

experiences of touching, looking, sucking, and listening to explore the world around them. Initially, infants do not have a sense of object permanence. For example, they often cry when a parent or caretaker leaves the room because to them, it is as though the person ceases to exist. When this stage is complete, children recognize that objects and people continue to exist even when they are out of sensory range.

2. **Preoperational stage** (approximately from age two to about age seven). In this stage, children learn to use symbols and to communicate with other people through language. However, this process is initially quite limited; they attach words to specific things. Thus, they can describe specific toys, for example, a favorite car, doll, or ball, but they are unable to describe the qualities of toys in a general or abstract way. They do not yet understand abstract concepts. When Piaget showed children two identical glasses, each containing an equal amount of water, they were able to recognize that the amount of water in each glass was the same. However, when Piaget poured one glass of water into a taller, thinner glass, they then said the taller glass held more water. In this stage, children remain egocentric, viewing things from their own perspective only. For example, when asked, a girl may say she has a sister, Mary, but when asked how many sisters Mary has, she may say none, indicating difficulty in seeing herself from her sister's perspective.

3. **Concrete operational stage** (approximately from age seven to about twelve). During this stage, children begin to perceive causal connections in their surroundings. Children this age understand, in Piaget's water glass experiment, that the amount of water remains the same despite a change in the size and shape of the glass. As they mature, children lose some of their earlier egocentrism and they now can imagine themselves from the point of view of another person.

4. **Formal operational stage** (adolescence). This is the stage at which abstract thinking takes place. Objects and events do not

have to be physically present in order to be understood. Children can now analyze hypothetical situations and reach conclusions about them.

Moral Development: Jean Piaget and Lawrence Kohlberg

Piaget was also interested in children's moral development. He believed that it paralleled cognitive development in that children must overcome their egocentrism and be able to take the point of view of others if they are to acquire the ability to act according to abstract ideas about fairness and justice. His observations of game playing among children showed that young children initially have absolute notions of right and wrong. Rules are rules and they should not be broken. As they engage in group play over time, they come to see that rules are created by the group and, therefore, can be altered if the circumstances of the game change. They also become aware that other people may see the same situation differently.

Piaget's work was followed up by the work of Lawrence Kohlberg (1969, 1981) who studied the moral reasoning people used in responding to hypothetical situations involving moral dilemmas. In analyzing subjects' responses to these situations, Kohlberg identified three main stages of moral development. In the *preconventional stage* (seven- to ten-year-olds), children pretty much go by the rules, trying to stay out of trouble. They want to avoid punishment or to gain something. The *conventional stage* (age ten and older) is characterized by a need for social approval. As society's norms and values are internalized, people want to do what is socially acceptable. The *postconventional stage,* achieved by few adults, involves applying general, abstract notions of justice. Kohlberg used the example of "Heinz," who steals a drug to save his wife's life. Reasoning at a postconventional stage would weigh breaking the law against the moral cost of doing nothing. Trying to save a human life may be viewed as worth breaking a law.

Both Piaget and Kohlberg's findings were derived from small samples of mostly middle-class Swiss and Americans. Although most social scientists have found their insights into how socialization contributes to different levels of cognitive and moral reasoning useful, criticisms have been raised about the conclusions they have drawn. Despite the fact that their findings have been supported by studies of other groups, the research done to date remains limited, and therefore, it is as yet unclear how universal these stages of cognitive and moral reasoning may eventually prove to be (Cortese, 1990; Snarey, 1985). A second criticism applies more directly to Kohlberg's findings. He developed his theory using data obtained only from males. The practice of using the behavior of males as the norm for how everyone should behave is being challenged by an increasing number of social scientists.

Gender Differences in Moral Development: Carol Gilligan

Do women and men make moral judgments in different ways? Based on her interviews with girls and women, Carol Gilligan (1982), a former colleague of Kohlberg's, concluded that moral reasoning centers around two distinct themes that reflect gender differences. She argued that women are more likely to make decisions based on norms of caring and responsibility whereas men are more likely to apply abstract principles of justice to their decisions. Gilligan attributes these differences to the different socialization experiences of the sexes. Women are expected to organize their lives around nurturing personal relationships, whereas men are expected to learn the rules of the workplace. Gilligan also challenges Kohlberg's notion that the justice perspective is superior to the caring perspective.

Although subsequent research has confirmed the existence of both care-based and justice-based reasoning, the findings on gender differences have thus far been inconclusive, with some studies reporting gender differences (Stiller & Forrest, 1990; Yacker & Weinberg, 1990) while other studies have found none (Crown & Heatherington, 1989; Pratt et al., 1990; Tavris, 1993). In yet another study, researchers found that sex-role orientation was a better predictor of care-oriented moral reasoning than gender was (Sochting et al., 1994). Thus, it may be that women and men who engage in both breadwinning and child care activities use similar approaches to moral reasoning. Clearly, more research will be necessary before the question of gender differences in moral reasoning can be resolved. Because most of these studies involved white subjects only, we don't know to what extent these patterns exist among different racial and ethnic groups. However, based on some preliminary findings about socialization practices among African Americans, scholars such as Carol Stack (1986) and Patricia Hill Collins (1989) suggest that African American women and men are equally likely to use a "caring" orientation in many situations.

The Development of the Social Self

As we mentioned in Chapter 2, Charles Horten Cooley (1902) and George Herbert Mead (1934) used the framework of symbolic interactionism to show how an individual's self-image is formed. Both men viewed the self as a social product, developed in social interactions with others.

The Looking-Glass Self: Charles Horton Cooley

After observing his own children, Cooley used the analogy of a mirror to illustrate how a person's self-image develops. He used the term **looking-glass self** to refer to the process by which one's self is formulated in response to one's perceptions of the reactions of others toward one's self. According to Cooley, this process unfolds in three closely related phases:

1. We imagine how we look to others— attractive or unattractive, friendly or unfriendly, intelligent or foolish.
2. We imagine how others judge how we look—positive or negative.
3. We develop a self-feeling, such as pride or shame, as a result of our perceptions of these evaluations.

Imagine coming into a classroom in which students are talking and laughing. As you enter the room, the talking and laughter stop. How would you react? You would probably become self-conscious and wonder if you had done something wrong or if something was strange about the way you were dressed. Experiences such as this illustrate what Cooley meant by the looking-glass self and how self-esteem is enhanced or diminished in social interaction. Cooley recognized that the reactions of some people affect us more than those of others. For example, adolescents may be more concerned with peer approval than are members of other age groups. According to Cooley, one's self is always developing

Charles Horton Cooley coined the term "looking-glass self" to describe the process through which we develop a sense of self. Similar to this child's reaction to her reflection in a physical mirror, we develop a self-concept based on our interpretation of the reflections in our "social mirror." Although our self-concept begins in early childhood, its development is a life-long process.

whenever one interacts with others; thus, it can change over time.

Although the looking-glass self contributes to our understanding of how the self develops, it is not without problems. Our perceptions of how others view us can be incorrect. For example, students may misinterpret a professor's response to their questions, concluding that the professor has judged them as silly or dumb. Research examining parent–child interaction suggests that self-esteem itself can be a contributing factor to misinterpretation of the looking-glass self. Richard Felson and Mary Zielinski (1989) found that children having high self-esteem were more likely to pick up on positive responses from parents while children having low self-esteem were more likely to focus on negative responses. Thus, parents need to be sensitive not only to the messages they send to their children but also to the ways in which their children interpret these messages.

Role Taking: George Herbert Mead

Like Cooley, Mead saw the self as developing through social interaction with others. For Mead, the critical factor in this process is **role taking,** mentally putting ourselves in another person's shoes, thus seeing the world as that person does. Taking the role of the other person allows us to anticipate how that person will respond to our actions. According to Mead, this process unfolds over time, becoming more sophisticated with each new stage.

- **Preparatory stage.** During their first two or three years of life, children spend much of their time imitating the role behavior of people around them. Children will put on Dad's hat or pick up the phone like Mom does without fully comprehending the meaning of the behavior they are mimicking. At this age, children do not yet have the ability to take the role of another nor do they yet have a sense of self separate from those around them.
- **Play stage.** During this stage, which begins around age three, children are becoming aware of social relationships and begin to take the role of specific others, especially those Mead called **significant others,** key people who are important in their lives and whose views have the most influence

on their development of self, such as mothers, fathers, and siblings. As children take the roles of "mommy" or "daddy," they learn to imagine the world as their parents do; in the process, they internalize their parents' values and attitudes. Because role taking reflects what children experience, it is likely that children who yell at their dolls or spank them for misbehaving have themselves been yelled at and spanked.

- **Game stage.** As children reach school age, the nature of their play activities changes. As they participate in organized play and team games, they learn to follow rules and they become aware of the interdependency of roles and the need for relating to many different people and groups. Mead used the analogy of a game to illustrate this development. In a baseball game, for example, the pitcher has to be able to take the roles of all the other players simultaneously, knowing when and at whom to throw the ball. Over time, children learn to take on the role of the **generalized other,** Mead's term for the widely accepted cultural norms and values that are used as references in evaluating ourselves.

Mead believed that children, as well as adults, are not just creatures of culture who simply internalize society's values and then mindlessly follow its rules. Rather, he saw people as active participants who negotiate, share, and help create culture (Corsaro & Elder, 1990). He argued that this dynamic process was possible because the self consisted of two distinct but interrelated parts. The *I* is the spontaneous, creative, and subject part of the self. The *I* makes decisions and initiates action. For example, you might tell a friend, "I am going to study tonight," or, "I am going to a movie tonight." The *Me,* on the other hand, is the object part of the self. It allows us to reflect on how others might respond to the actions of the *I.* For example, you might reevaluate your decision about going to the movie by asking yourself, "What will Professor Smith think of *me* if I go to the movie instead of completing my assignment?" According to Mead, the *I* and the *Me* are the basis for thought; they allow us to take others into account even when the others are not physically present and to adjust our actions accordingly.

Although Mead advanced our understanding of the dynamic aspects of the socialization process, he left unanswered the question as to whether members of different groups experience the stages of development in the same way. Later on in this chapter, we'll get some insight into that question when we examine how race, class, and gender affect people's socialization experiences.

Agents of Socialization

Socialization is a process and, as such, its implementation depends on **agents of socialization,** individuals and organizations responsible for transmitting the culture of a society. Among the most significant agents of socialization are the family, peers, the school, and the mass media. As we will see later, children, too, can be an agent of socialization.

Family

Generally speaking, biological parents are the first humans infants encounter. Since infants are dependent on these or substitute caretakers for their survival, parents and other family members become the initial centers of children's lives. It is therefore in the family that children begin to develop their social identities and to internalize the norms and values of their cultures as represented to them by their parents. The vast majority of parents consciously recognize and accept the responsibility for socializing their children and, in general, parents are motivated to do a good job. However, most adults learn to parent based on their own socialization experiences with their own parents. If these were deficient, they, in turn, are at risk for deficient parenting (an issue we will return to at the end of this chapter).

Parenting is a challenging task. At times, parents are baffled when, despite their best efforts, their children fail to meet their expectations or, worse yet, get into serious trouble. People outside the family may add to parental stress by being quick to point an accusing finger

at parents if their children don't measure up to society's standards of what is socially acceptable behavior. Thus, it is important to recognize that socialization is a complex phenomenon and many factors are at work, any one of which can dramatically affect the outcome. First, parents and family members represent only one agent of socialization. Later agents of socialization such as peers, schools, and the media may send out more powerful messages to children. Second, family members themselves may be giving children mixed messages, or a parent may give a verbal message but contradict it with her or his own behavior. For example, a parent may tell a child not to lie or cheat, but then the child observes the parent lying to an insurance company in order to receive unwarranted compensation for an accident. Finally, genetic factors, many of which we do not yet understand, may interact with and influence the socialization process and may help explain the fact that siblings often develop markedly different personalities and behavior patterns (Dunn & Plomin, 1990).

In Chapter 4, we discussed the dominant culture as well as the many subcultures that exist in the United States today. Many parents subscribe to the dominant values of a culture and work to instill those values in their children while at the same time they are members of different racial, ethnic, religious, or class groupings having distinct value orientations of their own. Consequently, there is considerable variation in the content of socialization from one parental group to the next. It is important to recognize these variations because the content of socialization we receive affects the ways in which our personal and group identities develop, how we relate to other individuals, and how the groups to which we belong relate to other groups within society. We will return to these themes when we consider the impact of race, class, and gender on socialization.

Peers

Peer groups are composed of members who are relatively equal in status, of similar age, come together on a voluntary basis, and share common interests. Once children reach the age of three, peers start to become a significant source of information and approval for them. Peer relations remain an important arena for social interaction throughout the life course, but they assume special significance during childhood and adolescence.

Children learn many things from their peers—how to share, how to take turns, how to explore the world beyond the confines of their families, and, as they move toward adolescence, how to deal with authority and how to become independent. One aspect of the development of this independence is the formation of a separate identity and subculture—distinctive dress, language, fads, and fashions, as well as values and behaviors which at times conflict with those of adults, especially with regard to attitudes toward school, music, drinking, and sexual activities. For example, researchers have pointed out how distinct body movements, athletic prowess, sexual competence, and street smarts, including how to fight and defend yourself, are learned in the context of the male African American peer group (Hale-Benson, 1986). Richard Majors (1995, p. 83) describes elements of this process as "Cool Pose," noting that this self-expression develops in response to adverse social, political, and economic conditions and that it functions as a powerful and necessary tool for black men. According to Majors, this coolness can be seen "in black athletes—with their stylish dunking of the basketball, their spontaneous dancing in the end zone, and their different styles of handshakes (e.g., high fives)—and in black entertainers with their various choreographed 'cool' dance steps."

Peer groups often demand a great deal of conformity from members, using ridicule or ostracism to make their point. In his essay "On Becoming Male," sociologist Jim Henslin (1997) writes about how these processes are used to define acceptable boundaries:

> We make fun of anyone who is not the way he "ought" to be. If he hangs around the teacher or girls during recess instead of playing our rough and tumble games, if he will not play sports because he is afraid of getting dirty or being hurt, if he backs off from a fight, if he cries or whines, or even if he gets too many A's, we humiliate and ridicule him. We gather around him in a circle. We call him a sissy. We say, "Shame! Shame!" We call him gay, fag, and queer. We tell him he is a girl and not fit for us. (p. 136)

In adulthood, peers are selected primarily on the basis of similar interests and activities or from the various groups to which we belong; in the younger years, peer groups are generally formed around classmates in the context of school, another critical agent of socialization.

School

By this time, most of you have spent twelve or more years in formal educational settings. Perhaps some of you started attending a day care center even before your first birthday. This would not be surprising in light of the fact that there has been a significant increase in the number of dual-earner families as well as single-parent families. These changes in family structure have occasioned a growth in formal child care settings for very young children. Consequently, the role of the school as an agent of socialization has expanded. Much of what goes on in schools is deliberately designed to provide children with knowledge and skills that will equip them to fill adults' roles in society. The primary mechanism for achieving this goal is a formal curriculum which requires students to study basic subjects such as reading, writing, mathematics, and history, and, increasingly today, to become computer literate.

At the same time, students are exposed to what sociologists call a **hidden curriculum,** values, attitudes, rules, and beliefs that are taught in the schools but that are not part of the formal curriculum. For example, games, math contests, and spelling bees teach lessons about achievement and competitiveness. The allocation of school budgets, space, and the school's various reward systems let students know which activities are valued and which are not. If more money and attention is focused on sports than on the fine arts and academic programs, students quickly get the message of who and what matters in their schools. Additionally, schools introduce students to the impersonal functioning of large organizations. In the family, children are valued for who they are; in schools, children are evaluated on how they perform. At home, children's individual needs are likely to be addressed; in schools, universal rules apply to everyone.

The Mass Media

Consider the fact that over 98 percent of all U.S. households own at least one television set. Table 6.1 shows that access to the mass media is not limited to industrialized countries. Even in some of the more remote and poorest parts of the world today, there are people who have access to newspapers, radios, and even televisions. According to government statistics, the average U.S. household has a television on for seven hours each day (U.S. Bureau of the Census, 1995). In fact, young people spend as many hours watching television, going to movies, listening to music, reading magazines, and, now, using the Internet as they do in school. Thus, it is difficult to argue that the mass media play only an insignificant part in shaping the values, beliefs, and behaviors of modern societies. There are clearly benefits to our exposure to the mass media. Besides being a source of entertainment, much of what we see, hear, and read can enlarge our range of experiences. For example, children can learn to be attentive, to count, to identify colors and objects, as well as a wide range of social skills from watching programs like *Sesame Street* and *Mr. Rogers,* especially when parents are there to guide them and to reinforce these ideas. Watching programs about sports, medicine, criminal justice, space travel, wildlife, and underseas adventures may introduce some young adults to occupations that most likely would otherwise have been outside their realm of experience. Importantly, too, however, our deepest emotions can be triggered by the images conveyed by the media, as evidenced by how people all around the world responded to the death of Princess Diana (see the Cultural Snapshot box).

The media also have the potential to shape our ideas and perceptions in distorted or unrealistic ways. When we ask our students to describe the first images that come to their minds of people living in poverty, their initial responses

TABLE 6.1 ◑ Newspapers, TV, and Radio, by Selected Countries (per 1,000 people)

Country	Daily Newspaper Circulation (1994)	Television (1995)	Radio (1994)
Algeria	46	71	236
Australia	258	482	1,291
Brazil	45	278	393
Canada	189	647	1,051
China	23	250	184
Ecuador	72	148	327
France	237	579	891
Ghana	18	(NA)	229
Iraq	27	(NA)	218
Japan	576	619	912
Russia	267	379	339
Tunisia	46	156	199
United States	228	776	2,122

Source: Adapted from U.S. Bureau of the Census. 1998. *Statistical Abstract of the United States, 1998.* Washington, DC: Government Printing Office, Table 1363, p. 840.

Cultural Snapshot

The Mourning of Princess Diana

In the early morning hours of Sunday, August 31, 1997, Diana, Princess of Wales, died suddenly when the car in which she was riding crashed into a wall in Paris. From the time of her death to her burial the following Saturday, millions of people around the world whom she had never met mourned her death. The outpouring of grief was dramatic. Women, men, and children wept openly. People stood in line for hours to sign condolence books, not only in Britain but in other countries as well. People brought literally tons of flowers and gifts and wrote messages to leave at her home. Thousands camped out in the streets of London for two nights to be in position to watch the funeral procession; millions of others around

the world got up before dawn to watch the televised service. Millions of messages of condolence and shared grief were left on Internet Web pages, discussed in chat rooms, and posted on bulletin boards by Princess Diana's admirers from all corners of the globe. Contributions to a fund set up to assist her favorite charities were projected to reach over a billion dollars.

How do you account for this outpouring of grief for a young woman who wasn't a head of state and whom the vast majority of mourners had never met? Why did they feel a deep emotional closeness to her? What role, if any, do you think the media played in creating this response to her death?

---

are almost always of African Americans, especially of female-headed families. Although this does not reflect the actual composition of the poor in this country, it is consistent with what students see in the media. A recent five-year study of major magazines and national TV newscasts by Yale University professor Martin Gilens found that although most of the nation's poor are white, the media uses pictures of blacks more often than whites to illustrate stories about poverty. Despite the fact that statistics show that only 29 percent of Americans living below the poverty line are black, national news magazines, including *Time, Newsweek,* and *U.S. News and World Report,* pictured blacks 62 percent of the time in stories on poverty; the figure for television was even higher, 65 percent ("Study," 1997).

A stereotypical portrayal, be it on television, in movies, in the classroom, or at home, has the consequence of reinforcing social expectations, resulting in **self-fulfilling prophecies,** the tendency of people to respond to and act on the basis of stereotypes, a predisposition that can lead

to validation of false definitions. Self-fulfilling prophecies can influence the behavior of both dominant and subordinate groups. On the one hand, they provide dominant group members with a justification for prejudicial feelings and discriminatory acts. On the other hand, subordinate group members, seeing themselves depicted as uneducated or in limited roles, may come to believe that school is unimportant and that the future holds little promise or reward for them.

Children and Reverse Socialization

Earlier in this chapter, we discussed the fact that socialization is not a one-way process. In almost any situation, there is a degree of reciprocal socialization, with all actors having some effect on each other. However, there are times when people experience **reverse socialization,** the process in which the supposed targets of socialization influence the supposed socializers. This happens to some extent in all families. As children move into adolescence and young adulthood, they become the mechanism for teaching their parents about the latest trends in music, fashions, and ideas. A more extensive form of resocialization typically occurs in immigrant families in which second- or third-generation offspring help socialize parents and grandparents into the cultural ways of their new country.

Many immigrant parents arrive in the United States as adults and never acquire more than a rudimentary knowledge of English. Once their children reach school age and learn to speak and write English, they become cultural facilitators and mediators for their parents. Children as young as eight or nine accompany their parents to schools, government offices, banks, and stores and act as official translators for their parents. Because the children decide what information to provide, they effectively gain power in the parent–child relationship; at the same time, their parents experience a reduction in power. The more rapidly a culture changes, the more such socialization tasks shift to the younger generation. Today, many parents joke about how their children are responsible for hooking up the family's video recorders and installing computer software.

In sum, socialization is a multifaceted process that requires us to evaluate, ignore, accept, or reject a wide range of ideas and values as we attempt to construct our distinct identity and world view. As we move through the life course, we experience how challenging this process can be as we discover that the ideas and values presented to us by different agencies of socialization often compete or conflict with one another.

Applying the Sociological Imagination

Reflect back on your early socialization experiences. Which agents of socialization had the greatest impact on you? How did these agents influence your attitudes and behavior? Did any of these agents send you conflicting messages? If so, how did you resolve such conflicts?

The Impact of Race, Class, and Gender on Socialization

Race, class, and gender are variants in the overall socialization process. Through what we hear, see, and directly experience, we learn how to think and act as a member of a racial or ethnic group; as a working-, middle-, or upper-class person; or as a female or male. Diana Kendall (1997, pp. 130–131) points to two critical outcomes of this process: "Socialization may legitimize social inequalities by reinforcing patterns of domination and subordination, or it may produce resistance and activism by subordinate group members who seek to bring about social change."

Racial/Ethnic Socialization

Because the United States is populated with people from virtually all the world's cultures, all children receive some racial/ethnic socialization. According to Martin Marger (1994), most children have begun to crystallize racial/ethnic values by the time they are four years old. For example, from early on, Chinese American children learn to have a strong sense of responsibility toward relatives, especially their elders. Although mainstream U.S. culture also stresses respect for parents, filial piety among Chinese Americans requires a much stronger notion of obligation, and Chinese American children are expected to display more overt signs of parental respect (Sue et al., 1983). Many Native American traditions stress teamwork and commitment to the good of the community, in contrast to the dominant culture's emphasis on competition and personal achievement. In some Native American communities, it is considered unnecessary to humiliate an opponent by winning by too great a margin. Such differences in values can cause problems in institutional settings. For example, teachers unfamiliar with these cultural values are likely to interpret a Native American child's hesitancy to volunteer to answer a question or to give a correct answer when another classmate has failed to do so as a sign of low intelligence or uncooperativeness and to treat the child accordingly.

Beyond learning the specific values of their racial or ethnic groups, young children quickly become aware that a racial/ethnic hierarchy exists in society (Marger, 1994). One of the problematic aspects of racial/ethnic socialization is that it often involves socialization into prejudice and discrimination. Symbolic interactionists stress that we come into the world without attitudes, values, or beliefs and, thus, no one comes into the world being prejudiced or having a desire to discriminate. However, if our families and our racial and ethnic groups are prejudiced against other groups, it is highly likely that we will learn to dislike and distrust the members of those groups. Thus, in order to protect their children, besides instilling their own group values, parents who are members of subordinate groups in a society must make them aware of the nature of dominant/subordinate patterns of interaction. Consequently, in the United States, many parents of color prepare their children to live in an environment in which they are likely to encounter prejudice and discrimination by teaching them adaptive strategies. An African American woman, Annette Jones White (1991) describes the adaptive strategies she learned from her mother:

> She taught me how to turn away wrath with a soft answer but without letting anybody make me think I was inferior to them. She also tried to keep me informed of the dangers I might face so that I could avoid situations that would put me in danger. She tried to keep me out of situations that could lead to humiliation and "incidents." For example, on one of the few times she took me downtown, she avoided a confrontation. It was generally known that Blacks were supposed to step off the sidewalk if they were meeting a group of Whites. To not do so invited several things—a tongue lashing, a vicious elbow to the chest or side, or, possibly, arrest. As we walked, we approached a group of Whites. My mother quickly walked to a store window and we window shopped until the Whites passed by. I knew why and she knew I knew why but we never discussed it. That was her way of avoiding an incident. (pp. 190–191)

In other instances, as in the case of parents who attempt to pass as members of another racial or ethnic group, parents do not talk about their racial and ethnic identity until they are forced to do so by external factors. Initially, such a sudden disclosure can be shocking and anxiety provoking for their children, as was the case for Gregory Howard Williams (see the Sociology through Literature box). In contrast to parents of color, white parents, by and large, do not talk about the meaning and experience of whiteness nor do they provide their children with much information about the culture of other racial or ethnic groups, though they often convey attitudes of ambivalence or fear of those different from themselves (Frankenberg, 1993).

People outside the family also contribute to racial/ethnic socialization. This is especially evident when we consider how people use language to convey their ideas, attitudes, and feelings about people based on their race and ethnicity. An examination of the English language shows that there are many derogatory, racist, and stereotypic terms commonly used to refer to various out-groups in our society. The emotional content of words such as *nigger, spook, spic, dago, mick, limey, chink, spade, wet-back, kike, Polack, kraut, honky, slant-eyes,* and *Jap* interfere with learning about and forming relationships with a variety of people. Cultural symbols can also contribute to racial socialization. In our society, we quickly learn that "good guys" wear white hats, ride white horses, and are white knights, while the "bad guys" wear black hats, ride black horses, and answer to names such as Black Bart. A classic example of this use of language to convey symbolically or to perpetuate this good/bad dichotomy is an old children's cartoon program, *Captain Scarlet.* The program is about an organization (Spectrum) whose goal is to save the world from an evil extraterrestrial force (Mysterons). Everyone in Spectrum has a color name, for example, Captain Blue and Captain Scarlet. The one Spectrum agent who falls victim to the Mysterons and works to advance their "evil" goals is Captain Black. On the other hand, the good and noble person who heads Spectrum, the good organization out to save the world, is Captain White (Moore, 1993). This same symbolism is found in many expressions commonly used to describe negative events, for example, "the pot calling the kettle black," "a black mark against an otherwise spotless record," or "s/he is the black sheep of the family."

Sociology through Literature

Life on the Color Line

Life on the Color Line, tells the true story of Gregory Howard Williams who, until the age of ten, lived in 1950s segregated Virginia. After a business failure, his parents divorced. Traveling on a Greyhound bus to Muncie, Indiana, his dark-skinned father, who had been passing as an Italian American, tells Gregory and his younger brother the truth about their heritage.

"Remember Miss Sallie who used to work for us in the tavern?" Dad's lower lip quivered. He looked ill. Had he always looked this unhealthy, I wondered, or was it something that happened on the trip? I felt my face—skin like putty, lips chapped and cracked. Had I changed, too?

"It's hard to tell you boys this." He paused, then slowly added, "But she's really my momma. That means she's your grandmother."

"But that can't be, Dad! She's colored!" I whispered, lest I be overheard by the other white passengers on the bus.

"That's right, Billy," he continued. "She's colored. That makes you part colored, too, and in Muncie you're gonna live with my Aunt Bess. . . ."

I didn't understand Dad. I knew I wasn't colored, and neither was he. My skin was white. All of us are white, I said to myself. But for the first time, I had to admit Dad didn't exactly look white. His deeply tanned skin puzzled me as I sat there trying to classify my own father. Goose bumps covered my arms as I realized that whatever he was, I was. I took a deep breath. I couldn't make any mistakes. I looked closer. His heavy lips and dark brown eyes didn't make him colored, I concluded. His black, wavy hair was different from Negroes' hair, but it was different from most white folks' hair, too. He was darker than most whites, but Mom said he was Italian. That was why my baby brother had such dark skin and curly hair. Mom told us to be proud of our Italian heritage! That's it I decided. He was Italian. I leaned back against the seat, satisfied. Yet the unsettling image of Miss Sallie flashed before me like a neon sign.

Colored! Colored! Colored!

He continued. "Life is going to be different from now on. In Virginia you were white boys. In Indiana you're going to be colored boys. I want you to remember that you're the same today that you were yesterday. But people in Indiana will treat you differently."

I refused to believe Dad. I looked at Mike. His skin, like mine, was a light, almost pallid, white. He had Dad's deep brown eyes, too, but our hair was straight. Leaning toward Dad, I examined his hands for a sign, a black mark. There was nothing. I knew I was right, but I sensed something was wrong. Fear overcame me as I faced the Ohio countryside and pondered the discovery of my life.

"I don't wanta be colored," Mike whined. "I don't wanta be colored. We can't go swimmin' or skatin'," he said louder. Nearby passengers turned toward us.

"Shut up, Mike." I punched him in the chest. He hit me in the nose. I lunged for him. We tumbled into the aisle. My knee banged against a sharp aluminum edge. The fatigues ripped. I squeezed his neck. His eyes bulged. I squeezed harder. *Whap!* Pain surged from the back of my head. Dad grabbed my shirt collar and shoved me roughly into the seat. Mike clambered in beside me, still sniffling.

"Daddy, we ain't really colored, are we?" he asked quietly.

No! I answered, still refusing to believe. I'm not colored, I'm white! I look white! I've always been white! I go to "whites only" schools, "whites only" movie theaters, and "whites only" swimming pools! I never had heard anything crazier in my life! How could Dad tell us such a mean lie? I glanced across the aisle to where he sat grim-faced and erect, staring straight ahead. I saw my father as I never had seen him before. The veil dropped from his face and features. Before my eyes he was transformed from a swarthy Italian to his true self—a high-yellow mulatto. My father was a Negro! We were colored! After ten years in Virginia on the white side of the color line, I knew what that meant.

Imagine yourself in Gregory's position. Why was it so difficult for him to believe what his father told him? What would your reaction be if you were in Gregory's shoes? How would your life change if suddenly you were to discover that instead of being white you were black or instead of being black you were white? Would your self-image be affected? What does Gregory's experience reveal about racial oppression, privilege, and identity?

Source: From *Life on the Color Line: The True Story of a White Boy Who Discovered He Was Black,* pp. 32–34. Copyright © 1995 by Gregory Williams. Used by permission of Dutton, a division of Penguin Putnam Inc.

Political terminology can also convey negative ideas about individuals and groups. For example, *at-risk, culturally deprived, inner-city resident, economically disadvantaged, under-* or *less-developed nations,* and *third world* are all terms that reflect value judgments and often become code words used to refer to a particular racial group. Further, they place the responsibility for their condition on the people being so described (Moore, 1993). How might these terms change if seen from the perspective of the *other*? From the perspective of those so labeled, the idea of being "culturally deprived," for example, might be embodied instead in the concept "culturally exploited."

Social Class Socialization

Melvin Kohn (1959, 1977) was one of the first sociologists to study the effects of social class on parental socialization practices. He found that working-class parents tend to be somewhat authoritarian and strict, stressing respect and obedience in rearing their children, whereas middle-class parents tend to be more lenient, tolerating a wider range of behavior from their children and emphasizing the values of independence and autonomy in their child-rearing practices. Kohn explained these differences in terms of parental education and occupation, two key indicators of social class. Working-class parents by and large have lower levels of education and are concentrated in jobs in which they have little autonomy and are closely supervised. Middle-class parents, by contrast, generally have higher levels of education and are more likely to hold jobs that involve more independence, autonomy, and creativity.

In other studies, Kohn and his colleagues (Kohn & Schooler, 1969; Pearlin & Kohn, 1966) again found evidence of the importance of parental occupation in child rearing. Middle-class parents who held jobs that were closely supervised stressed outward conformity, much as in the working-class model of child rearing, whereas working-class parents whose jobs allowed them more freedom adopted middle-class child-rearing strategies. Although much of Kohn's research was conducted more than two decades ago, his findings remain valid today and extend beyond the borders of the United States. Researchers have discovered similar differences in values based on class and occupation in Poland and Japan (Kohn et al., 1990; Naoi & Schooler, 1985; Slomczynski et al., 1981).

Social class also affects other aspects of socialization. French sociologists Pierre Bourdieu and Jean-Claude Passeron (1990) stress the importance of **cultural capital,** the general cultural background and social assets (including values, beliefs, attitudes, and competencies in language and culture) that are passed from one generation to the next. Wealthier parents can provide their children with a wide variety of growth experiences through books, educational toys, computers, travel, visits to museums and art galleries, attendance at plays and concerts, and elite schools. Lacking this cultural capital themselves, parents in low-income and poverty families may unintentionally socialize their children to believe that education, especially higher education, is unimportant or not for them (Ballantine, 1993); conversely, they may put tremendous pressure on their children to achieve what they could not. Thus, whether consciously or not, the lessons parents teach their children reflect the constraints and privileges they experienced themselves.

Gender Socialization

The process of gender socialization begins before birth. Many expectant parents relate to their fetuses on the basis of whether they believe them to be girls or boys. Perceived female fetuses are thought of as "graceful and gentle," whereas the movements of perceived male fetuses are described as "strong" (Stainton, 1985). The announcement "It's a girl!" or "It's a boy!" sets off a chain reaction that, consciously or subconsciously, separates human beings into two distinct worlds initially indicated by dressing baby girls in pink and baby boys in blue (Henslin, 1997). The clothes children wear send out gender messages as well. Boy's clothing tends to be simple and sturdy, allowing for rough-and-tumble play, whereas girl's clothing tends to be delicate and frilly and, thus, more restrictive. Boys are encouraged to be more active and aggressive in their play than are girls and parents, especially fathers, tend to engage in more rough-and-tumble play with infant and young sons than they do with daughters (MacDonald & Parke, 1986).

Toys also convey messages about gender-appropriate behavior. Boys frequently enjoy a wider range of toys promoting exploration, manipulation, construction, invention, competition, and outdoor play, whereas girls' toys tend to be less varied in type and typically encourage creativity, nurturance, attractiveness, and indoor play (Lott, 1994; Pomerleau et al., 1990). Consequently, play activities are likely to engender different cognitive and social skills in girls and boys.

For this reason, educators have expressed concerns about current differences in the video game playing habits of girls and boys. Computer games are the primary interface between children and computers and one of the main avenues for enhancing their general computer literacy. A 1996 study of the computer gaming habits of approximately 1,000 fourth through eighth graders found that both sexes liked to play computer games. Yet, boys of all ages spend twice as much time playing as girls, with girls' playing time declining in adolescence (Vogt, 1997). This differential has been attributed to a scarcity of girl-oriented software. One estimate is that of the over 3,500 games on the shelf, only about 10 are exclusively for girls. Interviews with girls aged eight to fourteen show that they like to master the same things boys do, but they get bored with kill-or-be-killed action games. These differences can have a deep impact on later occupational opportunities, as evidenced by a recent study by the Educational Testing Service which evaluated the computer-related coursework and career choices of 1 million college-bound seniors. Boys were more likely than girls to report having completed course work in computer programming and literacy; for every ten males who said they were majoring in engineering or math/computer science, there were only two and four females respectively (Vogt, 1997).

Children learn a great deal about adult gender roles from how household chores are distributed. Typically, girls are expected to do domestic work (cooking, washing dishes, and cleaning), and boys are assigned maintenance chores (yard work and emptying the trash). Because girls' chores are done on a daily basis while boys' chores are sporadic, girls spend more time doing chores than boys do (Mauldin & Meeks, 1990). Childhood chores are likely to influence how we, as adults, come to structure the division of labor in our own households. Children also learn gender through observation of adult behavior itself. They are quick to notice whether or not women and men have equal rights to speak, to act independently, and to make decisions.

As in the case with racial/ethnic socialization, language influences how we think about what it means to be female or male. An extensive body of research shows that the English language contains significant numbers of gender and race biases (Lindsey, 1997; Moore, 1993). For example, the word *man* can be used to exclude females—"It's a man's world," "the right man for the job," or "the average man in the street." Other less obvious examples include *college freshman, fireman, policeman, chairman, spokesman, congressman,* and *workman.* Although some people scoff at the notion that these are exclusionary words, researchers have found that most people visualize men when such terms are used (Wilson & Ng, 1988). In a similar vein, other research shows that elementary school children give male-biased responses to story cues that contain the pronoun *he* (Hyde, 1984). When the masculine pronoun is used, as it frequently is, in textbooks to refer to doctors, lawyers, writers, managers, system analysts, bus drivers, or public officials, children tend to associate these occupational roles with males, even though the reality is that many of the people occupying these positions are women. Once learned, language influences our perceptions of what or who is acceptable, appropriate, proper, and representative of humanity. Thus, many children may limit their aspirations to what appear to be gender-appropriate occupations. That this frequently occurs is well documented in Chapter 11. To counter this restrictive influence, many publishers and educators have moved to a more gender-neutral language, using *they, she or he, chairperson, firefighter, police officer,* and *mail carrier* (Schwartz & Scott, 1997).

Socialization through the Life Course

When social scientists speak about the life course, they are referring to an individual's movement through life, analyzed as a sequence of significant life events. Major life events include birth, starting school, puberty, employment, marriage, having children, illness, the death of loved ones, and the onset of old age. A life course perspective allows us to see how our location in the social structure, the historical period in which we live, and our personal attributes influence what happens to us. For example, in "A Time with a Future," Nicholasa Mohr (1997, p. 314) tells the story of Carmela, a recent widow, who recalls how as a young girl she had dreamed of traveling to all the many places she had seen in her geography books and how she would go with her brothers to the docks of San Juan just to watch the freighters and big ships. "When I grow up I'm going to work and travel on those ships." "Carmelita, don't be silly, you can't. Girls can't join the navy or the merchant marines." Carmela's dreams were never realized.

Stages in the Life Course

The life course is divided into a series of stages linked to biological, psychological, and social changes. Each stage presents a person with challenges and requires learning new skills and perhaps unlearning or relinquishing that which is familiar and comfortable. In general, each new stage builds on the foundation of the previous stage and each stage provides members with different rights, rewards, and obligations. The early stages of the life course encompass **primary socialization,** the acquisition of the basic skills, norms, values, and behavioral expectations of a culture as well as the development of the concept of self. As we get older and our social environment expands, we experience **secondary socialization,** the process by which we learn additional skills, values, attitudes, and behaviors and take on new statuses and roles. In so doing, we frequently engage in a related process called **anticipatory socialization,** social learning that prepares us for the statuses and roles we are likely to assume in the future.

Initially, this process is relatively informal; children learn about adult roles by acting them out. Later, the process becomes more formalized. For example, apprenticeships, internships, and probationary periods teach people about the skills, expectations, rewards, and problems that accompany a given work role, allowing them to make meaningful decisions about whether they want to adopt this role. The experience of student teaching leads some education majors to realize that they really don't have the patience, energy, or desire to be teachers, whereas other students readily incorporate being a teacher into their self-identities. Similarly, the participants in the Strive program, whom we met at the beginning of the chapter, were experiencing anticipatory socialization as they prepared for and engaged in mock interviews.

The movement from one stage of the life course to another is generally marked by a rite of passage, a ceremony symbolizing that a transition has been made. Baptisms, Bar and Bat Mitzvahs, graduations, weddings, and funerals are commonly celebrated rites of passage in the United States. In the following section, we will highlight some of the major socialization issues that confront us at different stages of the life course.

Infancy and Childhood (Birth to Age Twelve) As we indicated earlier, an extensive body of literature attests to the importance of providing children with love. The ability to feel love, to express it, and to accept it from others as adults is a learned behavior, acquired through our early experiences in infancy and childhood (Brazelton, 1990; Fromm, 1970). Infants who are held, touched, hugged, and provided with emotional comfort develop a self-love; that is, they come to value themselves because they can see themselves as lovable, important, and worthy of being loved. A person who has failed to develop self-love in infancy and early childhood is likely to have serious difficulties in forming meaningful relationships in adulthood and may become involved in serious antisocial behavior.

In Western cultures, the view of childhood as a responsibility-free stage in life is a relatively modern innovation. Historical records from colonial America reveal that many children were "put out" to other families at an early age to learn a trade, to work as servants, or to be disciplined (Mintz & Kellogg, 1988). Until the twentieth century, child labor was quite common in the United States, and, as we saw in Chapter 1, it remains a fact of life for many children throughout Asia and other parts of the world. Although the dominant culture in the United

States now regards childhood as a time for enjoyment and learning, unencumbered by adult responsibilities, this model still applies primarily to children of the middle and upper classes. Poor and working-class children often have to assume responsibility for themselves and for younger siblings at a fairly young age. Changes in family structures due to divorce or to the necessity of both parents working has shifted more household chores to children and created more *latchkey kids* who must fend for themselves after school until a parent returns from work. Additionally, the view of childhood as a time of innocence is becoming harder to maintain today as many young children routinely observe violence, drugs, or sex in their neighborhoods or see and hear these behaviors discussed or actually portrayed on their home television sets.

Adolescence (Ages Thirteen to Late Teens) Like childhood, adolescence, as a special time in the life course, is a relatively new phenomenon. As European and U.S. industrialization developed in the late 1700s and early 1800s, children as young as eight years old were recruited to work long hours in the new factories. By the late nineteenth century, however, the industrializing countries found that they had more workers than they needed and there was a growing recognition that these societies required a more educated population (Kitt, 1984). In contrast to preliterate societies in which children pass directly from childhood to adulthood, therefore, the teen years in industrial societies came to be defined as a period of time during which children mature sexually, learn specialized skills, and struggle to establish their own identities and to become independent of their parents.

This struggle is more pronounced for some adolescents than for others. Girls, for example, report lower levels of self-esteem than do boys (Goodstein, 1998). One likely explanation for this is that girls receive more negative messages of inferiority, exclusion, and subordination than boys do (Gilligan, 1990). Lesbian and gay youth also have added stress in their lives. Besides the general difficulties associated with puberty and its aftermath, they must deal with an identity that is stigmatized by the larger society— including perhaps their own race, ethnic, or religious groups—and they must struggle with the

Adolescence is a period during which young people mature sexually while they struggle to establish their own identities and become independent from their parents. Being socially accepted by peers is highly valued; rejection can lead to a sense of alienation that on some occasions has manifested itself in violent behavior.

question of whether to reveal their homosexuality to friends or family (Greene, 1994).

Adolescence is often described as a time of turmoil. To be sure, young people may be worldly, moody, rebellious, and reckless. However, data collected from adolescent respondents over the last two decades indicate that the portrayal of adolescence as a period of alienation and ongoing conflict with parents and other authority figures may be overdrawn (see the Data Box). Not only do these studies show that the majority of teenagers have good relationships with their parents, but also they show that teenagers who report feeling close to their families were the least likely to engage in risky behaviors such as smoking marijuana or cigarettes, drinking, or having sex. Emotional closeness was more important than the amount of time that parents actually spent with their adolescents at home, a fact that may give some comfort to working parents (Gilbert, 1997).

Adulthood Scholars have identified three developmental stages covering the adult years: young adulthood, middle adulthood, and late adulthood. Each stage focuses on different problems that must be resolved (Erikson, 1975; Levinson, 1978). In the past, it was assumed that people would enter and exit from social roles at

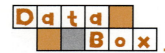

Views and Behaviors of Today's Adolescents (Ages Thirteen to Seventeen)

- "Fifty-one percent said they got along with their parents 'very well,' and 46 percent said 'fairly well.' Nearly two-thirds said their parents were 'in touch with what life is like for today's teen-agers.' . . . But 55 percent agreed that there were times when they had something they wanted to talk to their parents about, but did not. Of these, four out of five said the reason was that their parents 'won't understand,' and most of the rest said their parents were simply too busy. When they go out, 89 percent said, they have to tell their parents where they are going."

- "When asked whom they admired most, 44 percent of girls and 18 percent of boys named their mother. Fathers did not rank as highly; 26 percent of boys and 8 percent of girls said their father was the person they admired most. . . . Nine percent of boys named a sports figure. Five percent of girls named a celebrity."

- "Ninety-four percent say they believe in God."
- "Fifty percent of teen-agers said you could trust the government to do what is right always or most of the time."
- Five percent of girls and 5 percent of boys have a permanent tattoo; another 31 percent of girls and 34 percent of boys would like to get one. An equal percentage of girls and boys (31 percent) don't like tattoos at all. Six percent of girls and 3 percent of boys have body piercing other than ear lobes; 32 percent of girls and 56 percent of boys don't like body piercing at all.
- Twenty-two percent of 13- to 15-year-olds and 58 percent of 16- to 17-year-olds have ridden in a car driven recklessly by another teenager.

Source: Quotations and information from New York Times/CBS News Poll. Laurie Goodstein with Marjorie Connelly (1998, April 30). "Teen-age Poll Finds a Turn to the Traditional." *New York Times,* p. A20. Copyright © 1998 by The New York Times Company. Reprinted by permission.

specific points in time. For example, students would begin college at age eighteen and workers would retire from work at age sixty-five. Fewer people today experience such "orderly" progressions in their lives. Three points are important in this regard. First, there is no one pattern to the life course. Despite similarity in chronological age, birth cohorts (people born during the same time period) exhibit considerable diversity along dimensions of race, class, and gender. Second, although all members of a cohort experience some segments of historical events at similar chronological ages, the impact of these events often varies along these dimensions (Stoller & Gibson, 1997). For example, during the early years of the Vietnam War, many white, middle-class college students were exempt from the draft while their noncollege counterparts were routinely inducted into the military. The end result was that African American men were overrepresented in combat forces.

Third, how people experience events in the life course may differ dramatically from one time period to another. People entering adulthood in the mid-1990s have experienced an unprecedented boom in the stock market and low unemployment rates, a situation quite different from the economic uncertainty and company downsizing that their age counterparts experienced in the late 1980s and early 1990s. Attitudes and values concerning money, spending, and saving are therefore likely to vary among these populations.

Early Adulthood (Ages Twenty to Forty) This period in the life course affords many opportunities for new experiences—going to college, leaving home and living independently, starting a new job, establishing a career, cohabiting or getting married, becoming a parent, or perhaps "breaking up" or getting divorced. Whether these role transitions are smooth or filled with problems will depend on many factors: are they voluntary or involuntary? expected or unexpected? do we have a support network that can provide help in difficult moments? Because this is a period in the life course when we are most likely to enact multiple roles all at the same time (for example, wife, mother, worker, and possibly student) it is also a time that demands skill in balancing conflicting demands.

Middle Adulthood (Ages Forty to Sixty-Five)

Many people use this time period, often characterized as middle age, to evaluate their lives, including coming to terms with unfulfilled expectations. It is also the time during which many people first become aware of the effects of physical aging. For parents, this is often the time when children leave home, thus providing them with the opportunity to redefine their roles. A growing number of women and men see the launching of their children as an opportunity to return to school, to make changes in their work careers, or perhaps to retire. Although many people do gain freedom from major family responsibilities during this period, others find their responsibilities increasing. For example, many people take on the role of grandparent during this stage and must construct meaningful ways for the three generations to interact. This may involve helping their adult children financially as well as helping them out with child care. At the same time, they may also have to care for elderly parents. A federal study found that approximately 40 percent of people in their fifties who had children were helping them and about 30 percent were helping parents financially or in other ways (Kolata, 1993). Gerontologists refer to these people in the middle-aged generation as the *sandwich generation* because of the pressures some of its members experience from both ends of the age spectrum.

Late Adulthood (Ages Sixty-Five and Over)

Although the age of sixty-five has typically been used to mark the onset of old age, there is a growing recognition that chronological age itself tells us relatively little about the content of people's lives. There is a tendency to think of the elderly as a relatively homogeneous population; however, the reality is that the elderly population varies widely by age, sex ratio, marital status, living arrangements, education, income, previous life experiences, race, and ethnicity. In earlier decades, when people could be legally forced to retire at sixty-five, some social scientists argued that there were few norms for older people to follow and that their lives were characterized by disengagement from social roles. They therefore concluded that the elderly occupied a roleless role and that there was nothing to socialize the aged to except perhaps approaching death (Rosow, 1974). Over the past two decades, however, views and expectations about aging and the aged have changed dramatically. Although health issues are prominent in this part of the life course, many of today's elderly remain quite active well into later life. Not only are they involved in family activities, volunteer work, leisure and recreational activities, politics, education, and second or even third careers but also they serve as role models for the younger generations.

In sum, an examination of socialization over the life course reveals two things. Not only do socialization experiences vary tremendously from one group setting to the next but also differential experiences in an earlier phase of the life course frequently result in quantitatively and qualitatively different outcomes in a later stage of the life course. For example, quantitatively, elderly white women and people of color are likely to be poorer than elderly white males; qualitatively, they are likely to live in poorer housing and to experience more constraints in their life style options. This is not an outcome of the last stage in the life course, however. Rather, it represents the cumulative effect of events in earlier stages of the life course. Pensions and life savings are related to earlier occupational experiences, which, in turn, are related to levels of education. White males are more likely to have spent their working years in the primary labor market, which consists of occupations offering higher wages, more benefits, more opportunities for upward mobility, and greater job security. In contrast, white women and people of color are more likely to have spent their work lives in the secondary labor market, where occupations pay low wages and offer few benefits, relatively few opportunities for upward mobility, and little or no job security.

Desocialization, Resocialization, and Total Institutions

Although socialization is a life-long process, it does not always progress in a straight line. Rather, as we move through the life course taking on new statuses and roles, we are faced with a myriad of challenges and conflicting choices which require evaluation and adaptation. This process may involve **desocialization,** the "unlearning" of previous normative expectations and roles. For example, when you graduate from college and enter the work force, you will leave behind certain attitudes and behaviors associated with being a college student in favor of those expected of an employee. People who marry and expect to have the same freedom of movement and independence they had when single are likely to experience considerable marital conflict. Some adults who got off to a rocky start need organizations like Strive to help them acquire the attitudes and skills deemed prerequisites for employment in a technological society. And immigrants may find that some of their culturally approved values and behaviors are incompatible with those of their adopted society.

Role transitions are not all troublesome; some are smooth and require only minor adjustments. At times, however, the process is extensive, aimed at an almost total remaking of the individual. Sociologists refer to this reconstruction process as **resocialization,** learning a new set of norms, attitudes, values, beliefs, and behaviors. This is most likely to occur in the context of what Erving Goffman (1961, p. xiii) called **total institutions,** "places of residence and work where a large number of like-situated individuals, cut off from the wider society for an appreciable period of time, together lead an enclosed, formal, administered round of life." Essentially, this means that people's entire lives are enacted there—all daily activities are carried out within the walls of these institutions. Examples include prisons, mental hospitals, military bases, some religious cults, and, increasingly, boot camps for delinquents and first offenders. In these settings, people are isolated from family and friends; what dominates now is their current status and role. Outside norms are replaced with internal ones. People are closely supervised; the basic daily activities of eating, sleeping, personal hygiene, and recreation are all controlled, as are rewards and punishments.

People are placed in total institutions for the expressed purpose of change. The first step in this process is a *degradation ceremony,* in which "inmates" are stripped of their former identities, publicly stigmatized, and assigned new identities (Garfinkel, 1956). This may involve fingerprinting and photographing as in criminal cases or shaving the head and banning personal dress and fashion in favor of uniforms as in the military and in prisons.

How effective is resocialization in total institutions? The answer to this question depends on many factors. We know, for example, that many attempts to rehabilitate criminal offenders fail. In part, this is due to the fact that while in prison, despite formal programs of rehabilitation, prisoners spend much of their time interacting with other offenders whose values may reinforce the behaviors that got them into trouble in the first place. Although prisoners may outwardly conform to the established rules and procedures, they may inwardly reject and resist any attempts to change their senses of self. Even when they attempt to change, they may slip into old patterns if their families and peers are not supportive of their efforts to lead new lives. On the other hand, for people who seek to acquire new values, ideas, and behavior patterns, as in the case of religious converts, those suffering with a mental illness, and people seeking new careers or lifestyles—such as the cadets at the Virginia Military Institute (see the Sociological Reflection box)—considerable change is possible, especially if they are enmeshed in a supportive network. The more the new behavior is rewarded, the greater the likelihood of change.

Socialization Issues in the Twenty-First Century

No doubt the agencies of socialization we identified earlier in this chapter will continue to shape and nurture societal members well into the new century. However, some aspects of socialization will require well-thought-out policies of inter-

Sociological Reflections

Becoming a "Rat"

On August 20, 1997, 30 young women and 425 young men with close-cropped hair, wearing yellow T-shirts and bright red shorts and carrying white-and-red plastic water bottles, stood at attention in the courtyard. Drill instructors marched ominously into the center of the yard amid a slow beat of drums. As the new class of freshmen stood there, they were verbally taunted by upper classmen who shouted, "You're dead." The freshman class, known as "rats," was starting a six-month initiation ritual known as the "rat line," the purpose of which is to test the cadets' physical, mental, and emotional endurance. They heard Michael Lorence, a senior at the Virginia Military Institute, shout, "Rats, look at the men who stand before you. . . .They will teach and you will learn. Success is a hard choice. For those who fail, you'll be just another name in the matriculation book." When Lorence finished his speech, drill instructors broke ranks and ran randomly at individual freshmen.

They stood nose-to-nose with them, trying to scare and startle the cadets. Drill instructors repeatedly shouted questions at individual cadets, ordering them not to move an inch and insisting on a quick "Yes, sir" in response. If the drill instructor was not satisfied with a cadet's answer, he ordered the cadet to immediately drop to the ground and do pushups.

Would you like to be part of this class? Why or why not? What is going on here? What do you think the drill instructors are trying to accomplish by their actions? Does VMI fit the characteristics of a total institution? Is such socialization necessary?

Source: Adapted from James Warren. 1997. "VMI Women Get the Full Rat-a-tat-tat." *Chicago Tribune* (August 21), p. 1. © copyrighted 1997 Chicago Tribune Company. All rights reserved. Used with permission.

---

vention and ongoing social support to ensure that everyone has sufficient opportunities to reach her or his full potential. We will now consider two issues that are particularly critical for the future: deficit parenting and the rapidly increasing use of the Internet for gaining information.

Deficit Parenting

A recent study reports that children born to teenage mothers are less likely to have received well-baby care in the first year of life, have less cognitively stimulating and nurturing home environments, and obtain lower cognitive achievement scores than peers whose mothers were aged twenty to twenty-one at their births (Moore et al., 1997). These children are also more likely to be victims of abuse and neglect and to be placed in foster care than are the children of nonteens. Further, being the child of a teenage mother substantially reduces one's chances of success as a young adult educationally, economically, and in terms of family formation. Rebecca Maynard

(1997) concludes that by almost any measure, adolescent childbearing has significant adverse consequences for the children involved and that these consequences are costing taxpayers and society dearly, approximately $9 billion annually. Obviously, not all teen parenting results in deficit parenting nor is deficit parenting the exclusive province of the young. Many older parents, for one reason or another, fail to meet the economic, social, and emotional needs of their children. If it has the will to do so, our society can take immediate steps to minimize some of these problems. We can institute parenting classes in the schools and provide quality and affordable child care to assist parents in the important task of socializing the next generation.

Gaining Information through the Internet

In the next century, new information technologies will continue to transform the content and process of socialization in paradoxical ways. First, as Table 6.2 suggests, the new information

TABLE 6.2 ☉ Student Use of Computers at Home by Race and Income, 1984 and 1993

Race/Ethnicity	1984	1993
White, non-Hispanic	13.7%	32.8%
Black, non-Hispanic	4.9	10.9
Hispanic	3.6	10.4
Other	9.0	28.7

Household income	1984	1993
Less than $5,000	2.9%	9.7%
$5,000 to $9,999	3.2	8.0
$10,000 to $14,999	5.0	11.4
$15,000 to $19,999	7.5	15.1
$20,000 to $24,999	9.9	16.8
$25,000 to $29,999	12.8	21.1
$30,000 to $34,999	15.8	24.1
$35,000 to $39,999	19.4	27.1
$40,000 to $49,999	20.4	32.2
$50,000 to $74,999	24.2	43.0
$75,000 or more	22.1	56.1

Source: Adapted from U.S. Bureau of the Census, *Statistical Abstract of the United States, 1996.* Washington, DC: Government Printing Office, Table 263, p. 172.

age may be increasing inequality, dividing society into new categories of haves and have nots—those who have access and those who do not (Ouellette, 1993). People who don't have ready access to the new technologies will see their economic opportunities erode even further as people who do have access to the Internet will be exposed to an ever-widening and diverse range of data which may prove helpful in shaping their personal and working lives.

Second, for those who do have access, children will have greater access to information that may be in conflict with the socialization goals of parents and teachers because there are few controls on what people can post on the Internet. Further, many parents and teachers are not as skilled as their children and students in this new technology. They therefore may not be able to help them develop the critical thinking skills needed to evaluate this information. This is all the more likely given that children and adults frequently use the computer when they are alone.

Society must develop appropriate mechanisms to ensure that these technologies are affordable and easily accessible to all members. Additionally, educational institutions must help students to critically evaluate information that comes over the Internet. Otherwise, we may find ourselves overloaded with information that cannot be applied effectively.

Key Points to Remember

1. Socialization is the process of social interaction by which individuals acquire the knowledge, skills, norms, and values of their society and by which they develop their human potential and identity. To become fully human, people need to interact in a human environment. If human interaction is missing or inadequate in the early formative years, long-lasting and often irreversible damage to personality development is likely to occur.

2. Various theories have been developed to explain how personality develops. According to Sigmund Freud, the self emerges from three interrelated forces: the id, the ego, and the superego. Jean Piaget identified four age-related stages of cognitive development, with each new stage involving more sophisticated levels of reasoning. Lawrence Kohlberg extended Piaget's ideas to moral reasoning and identified three main stages of moral development. Carol Gilligan identified two distinct themes that reflect gender differences in moral reasoning. She argued that women are more likely to make decisions based on norms of caring and

responsibility whereas men are more likely to apply abstract principles of justice to their decisions.

3. Both Charles Horton Cooley and George Herbert Mead used the framework of symbolic interactionism to show how an individual's sense of self is formed. Cooley used the term *looking-glass self* to show that the self is influenced by how we think others respond to us. Mead saw the self as developing through role playing and learning the rules of social interaction.

4. Socialization is a process and, as such, its implementation depends on agents of socialization, individuals and organizations responsible for transmitting the culture of that society. The most significant agents of socialization are parents, peers, teachers, the mass media, religion, and the workplace. Race, class, and gender are important factors in socialization practices. Language plays an important role in the socialization process. The way language is used to describe, include, exclude, or marginalize groups of people is a major factor in the development of an individual's positive or negative sense of self-worth and personal identity.

5. Socialization continues throughout the life course as we exit old roles and acquire new ones. This often involves desocialization, the "unlearning" of previous normative expectations and roles. At times, the process is extensive, aimed at an almost total remaking of the individual. This reconstruction process is called resocialization, learning a new set of norms, attitudes, values, beliefs, and behaviors. Resocialization is most likely to occur in the context of total institutions.

6. Some aspects of socialization will require well-thought-out policies of intervention and ongoing social support to ensure that all members of society have sufficient opportunities to reach their full potentials. Among them are deficit parenting and the gaining of information from the Internet.

Key Terms

socialization	role taking	cultural capital
personality	significant others	primary socialization
self	generalized other	secondary socialization
id	agents of socialization	anticipatory socialization
superego	hidden curriculum	desocialization
ego	self-fulfilling prophecies	resocialization
looking-glass self	reverse socialization	total institutions

Key People

Rob Carmona	Lawrence Kohlberg	George Herbert Mead
Sigmund Freud	Carol Gilligan	Erving Goffman
Jean Piaget	Charles Horton Cooley	

Questions for Review and Discussion

1. Describe the importance of the socialization process from the standpoint of both society and the individual. Are individuals ever completely socialized? What is the relationship, if any, between socialization and free will?

2. What is meant by a life course perspective? Some sociologists argue that the events and changes we experience during adolescence and early adulthood have the greatest impact in creating "generational memories." What events or changes had the most impact on your parents' generation? How did they affect your parents' attitudes, values, behavior, and self-identities? What events or changes do you think will have the greatest impact on your generation? How are they likely to affect your generation's attitudes, values, behaviors, and self-identities? Explain.

3. Assume that you have been asked to serve on a national advisory committee to analyze ways in which socialization practices could be altered to eliminate some of the negative consequences of race, class, and gender stereotyping. How would you go about determining where changes should be made? What changes would you recommend? Provide a rationale for those changes.

4. How does the process of resocialization differ from other types of socialization? Assume that you were asked by public officials to create a program aimed at resocializing juvenile offenders. What kind of program would you recommend? Provide a rationale for your recommendations.

For Further Reading

Berns, Roberta. 1993. *Child, Family, Community: Socialization and Support.* New York: Harcourt Brace. This is a good review of relevant research in the field of socialization.

DeGenova, Mary Kay. (Ed.). 1997. *Families in Cultural Context: Strengths and Challenges in Diversity.* Mountain View, CA: Mayfield. A variety of scholars provide an in-depth look at eleven ethnic family groups. The socialization of children is discussed in most chapters.

Dennis, Everette E. (Ed.). 1996. *Children and the Media.* Rutgers, NJ: Transaction. The contributions in this volume focus on the handling of issues affecting children in the mass media.

Whiting, Beatrice Blyth, and Carolyn Pope Edwards. 1988. *Children of Different Worlds: The Formation of Social Behavior.* Cambridge, MA: Harvard University Press. The authors report on research projects on childhood socialization conducted in other countries.

Sociology through Literature

Miller, Sue. 1990. *Family Pictures.* New York: Harper and Row. This novel tells the story of a family struggling to raise an autistic child and the impact that had on the other siblings.

Owings, Alison. 1995. *Frauen: German Women Recall the Third Reich.* New Brunswick, NJ: Rutgers University Press. This collection of oral histories provides a fascinating account of how ordinary women experienced life in Nazi Germany.

Internet Resources

http://www.missingkids.org/index.html   The National Center for Missing and Exploited Children provides information about child safety and child protection.

http://www.america-tomorrow.com/naeyc/index.html   This is the Web site for The National Association for the Education of Young Children.

7

Societies and Human Sexualities

AGENTS OF CHANGE: DR. NAFIS SADIK, CAROL BELLAMY, AND DR. HIROSHI NAKAJIMA

The practice of female circumcision is increasingly being brought to the attention of the world community. Female circumcision, or more accurately, female genital mutilation (FGM), involves the partial or total amputation of the external female genitalia. Activists, health officials, and development agencies have condemned all forms of FGM, which they regard as one of the most pervasive human rights abuses in human history.

Three leading activists in this regard, Dr. Nafis Sadik, head of the United Nations Fund for Population Activities (UNFPA); Carol Bellamy, Executive Director of the United Nations Children's Fund (UNICEF); and Dr. Hiroshi Nakajima, of the World Health Organization (WHO), have combined their resources and activism in a concentrated effort to eliminate FGM. The trio has developed a joint plan that will considerably improve the health status of millions of women and children in the developing world. It will also be a major contribution to the promotion of human rights and gender equity.

Female circumcision is a cultural practice in at least forty countries—thirty in Africa and the rest in the Islamic Mideast, India, Southeast Asia, Malaysia, Indonesia, and South America. It is practiced by many ethnic groups, from the east coast to the west coast of Africa, in southern parts of the Arabian peninsula, along the Persian Gulf, and among some migrants from these areas in

Europe, Australia, Canada, and the United States ("The State," 1997). FGM is frequently regarded as a religious duty or a necessity to guarantee chastity and, thus, marriage. Mothers arrange for it to be done to their daughters because, in many countries, the male-oriented society demands it: an uncircumcised woman is considered dirty, oversexed, and unmarriageable (Ziv & Claire, 1997). Adult women are under pressure to submit to it in order to ensure the status that marriage and childbearing confer and to demonstrate solidarity with family and community.

It is estimated that between 120 and 130 million living girls and women worldwide have undergone some form of genital mutilation and that at least 2 million girls a year are at risk of mutilation. FGM is often performed by older women who use cutting tools ranging from pieces of broken glass, sharp stones, razor blades, and scissors to special knives which are often reused without sterilization. Anaesthetics and antiseptics are not generally used. The physical and psychological effects of this cultural practice are dramatic: short-term effects include severe pain, urine retention, blood poisoning, hemorrhaging, chronic infection, and shock, all of which can result in death. Long-term effects include chronic severe pain, cysts and absesses, keloid scarring, painful sexual intercourse, infertility and childbirth complications, and permanent psychological trauma (WHO, 1997).

The combined work of Sadik, Nakajima, and Bellamy to eliminate FGM will emphasize a multidisciplinary approach and teamwork, both within the countries where female genital mutilation is practiced and at the regional and global levels. Their plan has the support of women's and professional medical groups in the countries affected, of governments, and of many people in the larger international community. It includes the establishment of national "interagency teams" supported by international organizations, which will assist governments in developing and implementing clear national policies for the abolition of FGM, including, where necessary, the enactment of legislation to prohibit it.

According to these activists, the arguments against FGM are based on universally recognized human rights, including the right to the highest attainable level of physical and mental health. They believe that their joint plan of activism provides the crucial momentum needed to eliminate FGM once and for all. According to Bellamy, efforts such as theirs and others in the practicing countries and in the international community have put pressure on some countries, such as the Cameroon, Egypt, and Burkina Faso, where legislation has been introduced to stop FGM. In a landmark case in 1993, a French court sentenced a Gambian woman to jail for mutilating the genitals of her 1- and 2-year-old daughters. It is believed to be the first time that an African parent has been sentenced to jail for this cultural practice (Simons, 1993).

Although there are activists working around the world to eliminate FGM, the international community overall has not done much to stop the practice. One of the primary reasons that more people have not become involved is a "respect for cultural differences." Those who defend FGM, including some women, say that it is a cultural, not a human rights, issue and that people in Western cultures simply do not understand this cultural practice. FGM is practiced by some African immigrant groups in the United States, and although it is a form of child abuse and a violation of women's and girls' human and sexual rights, no parents have been prosecuted for it in this country to date (Ziv and Claire, 1997). The procedure is illegal in Canada and most of Europe, but it is not yet officially outlawed in the United States. However, Minnesota and North Dakota have made it a felony when performed on minors. In the U.S. Congress, former Representative Patricia Schroeder (D-Colo.) and Senator Harry Reid (D-Nev.) introduced a bill banning female genital mutilation in this country.

The Sociology of Human Sexuality

Being sexual is a vital part of being human. Human sexuality can be, on the one hand, a source of immense pleasure, relaxation, satisfaction, and gratification; on the other hand, it can be a source of guilt, confusion, stress, fear, and ignorance; a pathway to infection; and, as we have seen, a means of exploitation, aggression, control, and even death. Until relatively recent times, the topic of human sexuality received little attention in scientific research and even less attention in institutions of higher education. Human sexuality is perhaps the least understood yet most visible aspect of human social life today. Because it is so broad a topic, there is no one, all-encompassing definition of human sexuality. In a general sense, the term **human sexuality** refers to the feelings, thoughts, and behaviors of humans who have learned a set of cues that evoke a sexual or erotic response. It includes behaviors that are well known to us, such as sexual intercourse and masturbation, as well as behaviors that we do not normally think of as sexual, such as breast feeding, giving birth, and talking affectionately with someone. Human sexuality also includes our emotions, feelings, thoughts, attitudes, and values (Schwartz & Scott, 1997); it expresses our feelings of love, pleasure, tenderness, and intimacy. And, very important, human sexuality involves issues of power, of authority, and of emotional and physical vulnerability.

Human sexuality is an important topic of analysis in sociology because, as you have already seen, it links the personal and the social, the individual and society. Sociologists study human sexuality as a dynamic process that involves psychological and sociocultural dimensions as well as the physiological ones. Although our sexuality is grounded in our bodies, sociologists examine human sexuality in terms of the ways in which it is socially and culturally constructed. Just as we raise issues in this textbook about the social and cultural meanings of female and male, femininity and masculinity, and racial, ethnic, and class categories, we can also examine and analyze the diverse ways in which human sexuality is invested with meaning within particular societies and during particular historical periods. Within every culture, there are patterns, rules, and codes that govern, manage, or control our sexuality and the way it is expressed. In some cultures in which homosexuality, bisexuality, and transsexuality are acceptable, people with these sexual orientations have a positive sexual experience. In cultures such as ours, these forms of sexual orientation have been considered deviant, making the experience of sexuality repressive and stigmatized and subjected to a high degree of public scrutiny, management, and control.

Gender roles and power dynamics between men and women also affect sexual experiences. As we have seen, FGM practices control a woman's sexual behavior and sexual experiences, reinforcing established power relationships in the male-dominated societies in which these practices take place. Not only in these cultures but also in cultures around the world and throughout human history, women have experienced sexuality primarily in terms of reproduction, oppression (powerlessness), and vulnerability (as victims of genital mutilation and/or sexual assault). In contrast, men have experienced sexuality primarily in terms of pleasure: passion and emotions, power and control, and freedom of sexual choice and behavior. For example, the stitching up of the vagina during infibulation (a form of FGM) is meant to reduce a woman's sexual desire at the same time it is meant to enhance male sexual pleasure. This pattern—the social construction of sexuality—is illustrated in the Cultural Snapshot box.

Applying the Sociological Imagination

How do you think the world community would react if 120 to 130 million boys and men had been routinely castrated or had had their penises and scrotums variously mutilated and stitched together and another 2 million boys each year experienced genital mutilation as part of a cultural practice which had as its primary purpose preserving their virginity for marriage and enhancing women's sexual pleasure? Would your reaction be different or the same for both genders? Why or why not? How are your views on this subject related to the cultural values and norms that you hold? What steps should be taken to abolish this practice? What role can grassroots activism play in eradicating FGM?

In addition to the gendered aspect of our sexualities, race and class are important categories of experience that impact and shape our sexualities. For example, the sexualities of various racial groups (particularly Native Americans, African Americans, Latinas/os, and Asian Americans) as well as of poor people of all races have been defined primarily by outsiders. Their sexualities have often been defined in both scientific research and popular culture in negative and stereotypical terms that suggest that they are hedonistic, sexually promiscuous, and deviant from the norms of proper and moral sexual decorum. One of the problems of this lack of power to define one's own sexuality has been that outsiders have used their definitions in conjunction with other racist and class elitist ideologies to rationalize the oppression and unequal treatment of these groups.

Human sexuality is a powerful force in our lives. Throughout our lives, we make sexual decisions and engage in sexual activities based on our experiences, attitudes, cultural norms and values, and societal knowledge. Human sexuality is not static; rather, it changes and evolves as we ourselves change and as societal norms and values shift or change. As we will see in the next section, people of different cultures in different historical periods have engaged in and defined human sexuality in terms of a wide variety of modes of sexual expression and behavior.

Human Sexuality across Time

An examination of some ancient civilizations reveals an early acceptance of homosexuality that changed over time. For example, the celebration of lesbianism in ancient Chinese literature and art reflected the reality of social relationships within households in which several wives, slaves, concubines, and servants lived together and lesbianism was taken for granted. Taoists claimed that men could increase sexual pleasure, improve health and live for thousands of years, if not forever, if they had sexual relations with young, virginal girls and boys or with multiple partners. In other cultures such as ancient Greece or Rome, pure, sexual love between older men and young boys was idealized. In these cultures, for example, homosexuality was accepted much the same as Americans accept heterosexuality today. Male sexual desire and interest in persons of the same sex was assumed to be universal and psychologically normal, although not exclusive. Partnerships with women were for reproductive and domestic purposes, not pleasure. Same-sex relations between Greek men were considered the highest form of love possible. Like the ancient Greeks and Romans, medieval Christian monks experienced passionate desire for members of their same sex.

But not all ancient cultures condoned homosexuality. For example, early Aztecs punished homosexuality by tying men to logs, disemboweling them, covering them with ash, and incinerating them.

Over time, Chinese attitudes toward sexuality changed dramatically. In 1949, Communist officials in the newly established People's Republic of China defined sexual intercourse as a mental disease that wasted both time and energy. Homosexuality was declared lewd, perverse, and immoral, and homosexuals were often sentenced to prison or given electric shock treatments. Today, in a more Westernized China, lesbians and gays are pretty much left alone in places such as Shanghai as long as their activities involve consenting adults. Changing sexual attitudes notwithstanding, there is almost no sex education in China today, and most couples are ignorant of the basics of human sexuality. The dynamics of sexuality in China, however, reflect an attitude among the young favoring sexual freedom. Love and sex are somewhat freely discussed via newspaper advice columns and radio talk shows. Additionally, ideas about love and sexuality are coming into China from other cultures via telephone, fax, and the Internet (Hatfield & Rapson, 1996).

Likewise, sexuality in the West has changed over time, reflecting changing attitudes and

Cultural Snapshot

Human Sexuality across Cultures

Early anthropological studies, although rife with ethnocentrism and racism, nonetheless have been a key source of research data that illustrate how human sexual behaviors are socially constructed. For example, in some cultures such as the Trobriand Islanders of British New Guinea in the South Pacific, sexual expression is open and women and men both enjoy great sexual freedom. Trobrianders do not value virginity and believe that the more sexual partners that a young person has before marriage, the better partner she or he will make after marriage (Weiner, 1988). Further evidence that culture rather than biology shapes sexual impulses and behavior is found in the Mangaian culture in Polynesia. Compared to sexuality in the United States, Mangaian sexuality is much more open and accepted. Girls and boys learn about their sexuality and begin experiencing high levels of sexual desire in early adolescence, and at age thirteen or fourteen, they begin to have sexual intercourse on a regular basis. Following a circumcision ritual, boys are given instruction in the ways of pleasing a girl: erotic kissing, fondling and sucking her breasts, oral sex, sexual intercourse, mutual genital stimulation, and various techniques for bringing a partner to multiple orgasms. After two weeks of training, a sexually experienced older woman has sexual intercourse with the boy to further instruct him on how to sexually satisfy a woman.

Likewise, older women also instruct girls about their sexuality. These women show girls how to thrust their hips and move their vulvas in order to have multiple orgasms. However, ultimately, it is up to a "good man" to teach a young woman how to be orgasmic. If a woman's partner does not satisfy her, she is likely to leave him and she may ruin his reputation with other women by publicly denouncing his lack of sexual skill.

Young women and men are expected to have many sexual experiences before they marry. Up to about age thirty, Mangaian males average about two to three orgasms daily. In Mangaia culture, it is believed that human sexuality is strongest during youth. Therefore, as the Mangaians age, their sexual desire and activities rapidly decline and they cease to be aroused as passionately as they were in their youth. They attribute this phenomenon to the workings of nature and thereafter lead a sexually contented adulthood (Marshall, 1971).

In contrast, among a group of people on a small island off the coast of Ireland (referred to by researchers as Inis Beag), sexual behavior is very restricted. Not only are children forbidden to engage in sexual activities but also sex is never discussed when children are present. Researchers found that the people of this island knew nothing of tongue kissing, oral-genital sex, fondling and/or kissing the female breast, the manual stimulation of the male's penis, or of female orgasm. Unlike in the United States, there was no courtship period and premarital sex was an unknown. Parents arranged the marriages of their offspring, who generally married very late in life. Within marriage, sexual activity was very limited. The Inis Beag residents had great disdain for nudity, so much so that they always changed clothes in private, they never fully undressed to wash (they therefore washed only those parts of the body that were not covered by clothing), and they kept on their underclothes even during sexual intercourse.

As these examples show, although all human beings share the same anatomic structures and physiological capacities for sexual activities and pleasure, societies differ widely in their sexual practices, customs, and attitudes. If human sexuality were completely or predominantly determined by our biology, we would not find this immense diversity across human cultures.

A cross-cultural discussion illuminates the concept of cultural relativity that we learned in Chapter 4. How is our perspective on sexuality related to our location in society, the historical period in which we live, and our race, ethnicity, class, gender, and age? How important is culture in determining how people think and act sexually?

values. In medieval times, for example, religious, medical, and scientific authorities' general condemnation of sexual passion greatly affected individual sexual attitudes and practices. In ancient Jewish traditions, marriage was the only appropriate context for sexual intercourse and gender differences in sexual behavior were prominent. For example, although the norm of premarital chastity applied to both sexes, only women who were not virgins at the time of marriage could be put to death. In seventeenth-century America, Puritan attitudes and values defined sex outside of marriage as sinful and sanctions against premarital and extramarital sex were very rigidly enforced. In the eighteenth century, it was commonly believed that men should conserve their semen in order to maintain their strength and virility. Wasting semen through frequent or frivolous orgasms was linked to a number of physical and mental diseases as well as to moral degeneracy. Women were to be avoided, because sexual attraction to them could lead to semen wastage (Money, 1991).

During the Victorian period (1837–1901), the genders continued to be treated differently as regards sexuality. The attitude that women were the sexual property of men greatly affected sexual behaviors. It was believed that women experienced no sexual desire, only "reproductive desire," which was convenient because they were expected to remain virgins until marriage. For men, on the other hand, sexual desire was acknowledged and premarital intercourse accepted. However, masturbation was considered an unhealthy sexual activity for both women and men; it was believed that it would leave them drained and vulnerable to a wide range of sicknesses and diseases ranging from bad breath, nose pain, and constipation to mental illness, blindness, and genital cancer (Hatfield & Rapson, 1996).

The intersections of race, class, gender, and sexuality are apparent during the eighteenth and nineteenth centuries in the United States. Unlike others in the society, slaves had little or no control over their sexuality, which was governed by a separate set of rules. While sex was considered sacred and ideally restricted to marriage for the white middle classes, slaves were prohibited from legally marrying (with some exceptions) and they were routinely forced to mate with each other to reproduce and increase the slave population. In addition to being forced to mate with male slaves, black women were exploited by white men as mistresses and concubines and were often the victims of rape. Black men, after being used as studs, were often castrated to render them even more powerless and helpless.

Twentieth-Century Sexuality

In the early part of the twentieth century, U.S. sexual codes remained Victorian and the sexual double standard (differing sets of norms based on gender) was largely in force. At the same time, there was a growing emphasis on finding and using successful sexual techniques, particularly among married couples, as a way to express love between partners. By mid-century, sexual attitudes and behavior codes were much less rigid. In the 1960s, a number of cultural, social, political, and economic factors led to dramatic changes in sexual attitudes and behaviors. Economic prosperity, changing cultural ideas about individualism and personal and sexual freedom, advances in birth control methods, the women's movement, and the ground-breaking work of sex researchers such as Alfred Kinsey and his colleagues (1948, 1953) and William Masters and Virginia Johnson (1966, 1970) all contributed to what is commonly referred to as the **sexual revolution**—a radical change throughout society in sexual behaviors and attitudes.

During this period, U.S. society was on the threshold of major social changes, not only in sexual behavior but also in various other aspects of society and culture. The interplay of social, political, scientific, and economic forces—such as the introduction of television, the threat of nuclear war, and the Vietnam War—provided momentum to the sexual revolution. Along with this phenomenon, pop psychology movements cropped up that encouraged sexual expression. In addition, the media began to deal openly with sex, with overt sexual themes and sexual behavior becoming commonplace in films. The civil rights and Vietnam War protests were catalysts for broader protests against conventional morality and perceived government hypocrisy. Among some segments of the population, prohibitions against drugs, casual sex, and even group sex were no longer accepted (Rathus et al., 1997).

These facts notwithstanding, there is some disagreement among academics and other professionals as to whether a sexual revolution really occurred in the United States. Some people cite the broad scope of the changes in Americans' sexual behavior and attitudes as evidence of a "revolution." Sociologist Ira Reiss (1990) proposes that instead of *sexual revolution,* a more appropriate descriptor would be *sexual renaissance.* Others have described the changes in U.S. sexuality as a **sexual evolution,** a gradual process of development and growth toward a new system of sexual ethics. Still others have been very vocal with their viewpoint that what we are going through is a phase of moral degeneracy that is leading to the downfall of the family and other values and institutions that we hold sacred as well as to the eventual downfall of civilization as we know it (Kelly, 1994).

Samuel S. Janus and Cynthia L. Janus (1993) suggest that not only did we have a sexual revolution in the 1960s and 1970s but also a second sexual revolution is now taking place. The first revolution, they say, was about sex and the communication of information and, more important, the acceptance of sexual love as pleasurable and a legitimate end in itself. Janus and Janus believe that their survey of 2,765 Americans points to a second sexual revolution characterized by (1) a willingness to engage in a variety of sexual practices, some of which may once have been defined as deviant or, at the very least, inappropriate and unacceptable to one's social status, and (2) a regeneration of sexual interest and behavior among the older population. Other studies (Libby, 1990; Smith, 1990) suggest that while there has been significant change in attitudes and behavior in some areas of U.S. sexuality, there has not been a significant change in the way Americans view sensitive sexual issues and behaviors such as pornography, teenage sex, extramarital sex, sex education, or homosexuality.

The emergence of the AIDS epidemic in the United States and the AIDS pandemic worldwide in the 1980s is believed to have slowed down the pace of change in human sexual expression. By the end of the 1980s, there was some evidence that the alleged sexual permissiveness of the 1960s and 1970s had decreased and that people were moving back to an emphasis on monogamous relationships, romance, and a limited number of sexual partners. This fact notwithstanding, the sexual behavior of Americans in the 1990s is still considerably less restricted and inhibited than it once was. Despite some people's discomfort with certain sexual acts and the fear of the spread of sexually transmitted diseases, particularly AIDS, most people view sexual pleasure as a worthy goal in intimate relationships. And, among some groups, there does not appear to be a significant decrease in their premarital sexual behavior. In fact, premarital sex among teenagers in this country appears to have increased. The percentage of teens who are sexually active is rising even among teens raised in conservative Christian families (Rubin, 1990). By the time that young people enter high school, over one-third of females and almost half of males have had sexual intercourse (Gibbs, 1993). Although many of the sexual practices glorified in the 1960s and 1970s, such as mate swapping, group sex, and open marriage, are not as openly prominent today, two features of the sexual revolution besides premarital sex have become permanent parts of the social fabric of human sexuality in the United States: the liberation of female sexuality and a greater willingness to discuss sex openly and publicly.

Contemporary Sexual Attitudes and Behavior in the United States

The sexual behavior and attitudes of Americans in the 1990s have become increasingly public, commercial, and politicized, feeding into political skirmishes over issues such as sexual abuse, homosexuality, abortion, and date and acquaintance rape. Sex, it seems, is everywhere. Just read the local newspaper, turn on the television, page through a magazine, or enter cyberspace. What you see and hear is an endless stream of young, hard bodies preparing for, recovering from, or engaging in a constant frenzy of sexual activity (Elmer-Dewitt, 1994). The impression one gets is that life in the United States is one big sexual orgy, full of sexual deviants, flashers, and sex maniacs. Is this really what U.S. sexuality is all about?

Many people believe that U.S. sexuality is a continuum ranging from "inhibited" and "square" at one end to "liberated" and "hip" at

Unlike some cultures, Americans are extremely public with their sexuality. Images of sexuality are everywhere—from the local newspaper, national magazines, television soaps, trashy talk shows, and cyberspace to public displays like that of the couple pictured here.

the other. The inhibited squares are seen as engaging in sex only within the legal confines of marriage and then only infrequently. The liberated hipsters are seen as sexually uninhibited, unattached, and unencumbered; they are worldly, have been there and done that, and are raring to do it more often with more people (Adelson, 1996). But is this an accurate reflection of U.S. sexuality?

Recent research from the most comprehensive sex survey since the Kinsey studies tells us that popular cultural images and definitions of sexuality as well as our preconceived notions about it are all false. The fact is that, by and large, Americans have few sexual partners over their lifetimes, have a modest amount of sex, are faithful to their partners (in marriage and cohabitation), and engage in less exotic sexual practices than those regularly depicted in the media (see Figure 7.1). One of the most interesting findings of the new sex survey is the absence of expected variations in sexuality related to race, ethnicity, class, education, religion, and the like. The typical number of lifetime sex partners for African Americans is four, compared to three for whites and Native Americans, two for Latinas/os, and one for Asian Americans (Laumann et al., 1994). However, there is some variation by marital status or by whether a couple is cohabiting. Once married or living together, people are more likely to be faithful than are single people. In general, Americans are not doing it all day long, every day. Many people report having sex once a week on average, although two-thirds of the population has sex less often. Although men report being more sexually active than women, this result may represent the underreporting of partners by women and/or the overreporting of partners by men. According to Phillip Blumstein and Pepper Schwartz (1983), lesbian couples have sex less frequently than any other type of couple. Among their sample of lesbians in relationships for two or more years, almost half reported having sex once a month or less.

Americans are also pretty conventional in their sexual practices. Contrary to popular belief, vaginal intercourse is far and above all other activities as the most appealing sexual practice, almost universally rated as exciting and pleasurable. And, unlike media representations, it is not the "swinging" singles who are having the most sex. Rather, with the exception of cohabiting singles, married people report having a more lively sex life than their single counterparts. And it is married people and/or people in intimate, exclusive, and committed relationships who report getting the greatest degree of sexual gratification from their sexual relationships (Adelson, 1996). Most women and men, the young and the old, reported that they found sexual practices such as group sex, anal sex, sadomasochism, homosexuality, sex with strangers, and the use of sexual devices and toys unappealing.

Sexual behaviors in the 1990s continue to be shaped by the social networks to which we belong. That is, Americans have sexual relationships with those within their networks and these

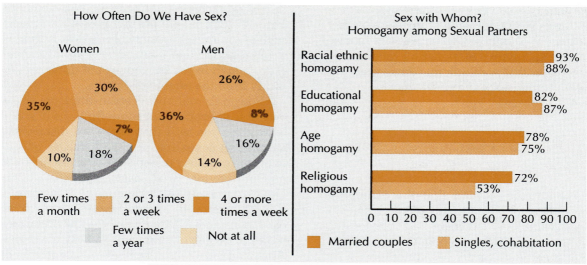

How Often Do We Have Sex?

Women

- 30%
- 35%
- 7%
- 18%
- 10%

Men

- 26%
- 36%
- 8%
- 16%
- 14%

- ■ Few times a month
- ■ 2 or 3 times a week
- ■ 4 or more times a week
- ■ Few times a year
- ■ Not at all

Sex with Whom?
Homogamy among Sexual Partners

- Racial ethnic homogamy — 93% / 88%
- Educational homogamy — 82% / 87%
- Age homogamy — 78% / 75%
- Religious homogamy — 72% / 53%

0 10 20 30 40 50 60 70 80 90 100

- ■ Married couples
- ■ Singles, cohabitation

Reporting Lesbian or Gay

Women		Men
1.4%	Identified themselves as homosexual or bisexual	2.8%
3.5%	Had sex with someone of the same sex at least once since puberty	5.3%
7.5%	Felt desire for sex with a person of the same sex	7.7%
8.6%	Total reporting some same-sex desires or experiences	10.1%

FIGURE 7.1 ◑ **Sex in the United States** *Source:* Adapted from Schwartz, M.A., & Scott, B.M. 1997. *Marriages and Families: Diversity and Change,* p. 148. Adapted by permission of Prentice Hall, Upper Saddle River, New Jersey.

people are usually very much like each other in key experiences such as race, class, religion, and education. People rarely move outside these networks in terms of sexual relationships. When they do, they generally meet with societal disapproval.

If all these statistics reveal the true sexuality of the U.S. population, why are we so misguided about human sexuality? According to psychol-ogy professor Joseph Adelson (1996), what we believe to be true about sexuality is conditioned by a larger set of cultural assumptions and expectations about human nature and the social order. More specifically, when we read about sex or see it portrayed in films, television, or other forms of the media, we do not see its mundane, everyday side. Rather, we see people taking dangerous risks to achieve pleasure or struggling to realize their true selves by means of erotic liberation. For example, if media studies are correct that seven out of eight sexual encounters in television dramas involve extramarital relations, is it any wonder that we think that Americans are sexually promiscuous and unfaithful?

Sociological Theories on Human Sexuality

We have already learned that the Structural Functional Perspective focuses attention on consensus of values, shared goals, and social order. A functional analysis of sexuality would emphasize the functionality of human sexuality when it is channeled into socially agreed upon and productive directions. For example, defining sexual activities between married partners as the only legitimate means of expressing sexuality will encourage people to marry and form families. Various societal institutions act to reinforce this cultural norm by defining sexual orientations other than heterosexuality as well as sex outside of marriage as deviant. The judicial system upholds and reinforces this norm through the enforcement of sodomy laws. For example, a 1986 Supreme Court decision upheld the right of states to define correct positions for coitus, with all other acts defined as sodomy and, thus, as illegal (Hess et al., 1996).

The conflict approach to sexuality focuses on issues of power, authority, inequality, and vulnerability. The institutional regulation of sexuality, for example, through the court system and through religion, is usually controlled by men who have the power to define proper and improper sexuality. In other words, the power to control sexuality is usually in the hands of a dominant group that exercises its power over relatively powerless groups. In most societies, there is a sexual double standard whereby men are presumed naturally to have a greater desire and need for sexual activities than do women. As a dominant group, they often have the power to limit women's sexuality while allowing themselves much greater sexual freedom. As we saw in the chapter opener, this power and sexual freedom often has dire consequences for the health and safety of women, who are relatively power-

less to define and control their own sexuality. The same can be said of other powerless groups, such as various groups of color whose sexuality is often defined as "savage" or "promiscuous" even though in reality, it does not differ significantly from the established norm.

Powerful groups use every institutional means available to propagate their definitions of social reality. As you will find when we discuss the media and sexuality, powerful images of sexuality are routinely transmitted by those in power on a minute-by-minute basis. These images include portrayals of the sexuality of people of color, for example, as significantly more physical and animalistic than that of whites. The sexuality of people of color, particularly of African Americans, is often presented in a way that feeds into other cultural fears and stereotypes that continue to justify racial discrimination and the unequal dispensation of justice for sex crimes. The control of the powerful can and often has been challenged by the less powerful. For example, due to collective action, the U.S. judicial system now recognizes the concept of "marital rape," unmarried people have a legal right to birth control information, and homosexuality is no longer defined as a mental illness.

Similar to the conflict perspective, feminist sociological perspectives on sexuality also focus on power relationships and dominance. According to these perspectives, human sexuality is characterized by male dominance in societies such as ours in which gender inequality exists. In such societies, women's oppression is the direct result of men's control of women's sexuality and the patriarchal institutions that structure sex/gender systems. Catharine MacKinnon (1982, 1983), a noted feminist legal scholar, proposes that men's control of women's sexuality is the central fact of the domination of women and that heterosexuality is the major institution through which men express and exercise their sexual power over women. Men use this power over women in a number of ways, including through rape, incest, violence against lesbians, sexual harassment, and, we would add, the control of commercial sex. These and other acts reinforce male dominance and keep women in their place, submissive and powerless.

Using yet another sociological perspective, the interpretive or social constructionist perspective, our focus is shifted from the macro level to the micro level to explain human sexuality. Using this framework for understanding the development, formation, and maintenance of sexual identities, one focuses on sexuality within the context of social and cultural meanings, values, expectations, and images within a given society. In this context, the emphasis is on social learning through **sexual scripts,** a society's guidelines or blueprints for defining and engaging in sexual behaviors (Schwartz & Scott, 1997). In this sense, one sexual orientation is no more normal than another. In the next section, we examine the link between the macro and micro levels of society through the concept of sexual scripts.

The Social Construction of Human Sexuality

Although many of us have learned that the sexual feelings and desires we experience are natural and beyond our control, the fact is that we are not born knowing how to think, feel, or behave sexually. Within all cultures, there are norms that prescribe and proscribe our sexual behavior. These norms specify what is or is not sexually attractive and stimulating, when and under what circumstances we should be sexually stimulated, why we should or should not engage in sexual behavior, what is and is not appropriate sexual behavior, and how we should or should not feel sexually.

According to social scientists John Gagnon and William Simon (1973, 1987), sexual behavior is not very different from other human behavior. It does not come naturally. Rather, it is socially constructed. Thus, from this point of view, what Sigmund Freud commonly referred to as a *sex drive* is not innate and biologically determined but rather something we have learned in a particular social environment. Our sex drive can be shaped into almost any form. What is "natural" sexual behavior is what our society and culture defines as natural. Little of our behavior is spontaneous or unlearned. Like other behaviors, our sexual behavior is guided by cultural scripts that are similar to the scripts that guide the actions of actors. We begin learning these scripts very early in life through the process of socialization. The scripts we receive and learn greatly affect how we think, feel, and act sexually in adulthood. In learning our culture's sexual guidelines, we in effect create or invent our capacity for sexual behavior.

Sources of Sexual Learning

When we say that human sexuality is neither natural nor innate, it is not to say that we do not experience sexual feelings. Rather, whatever sexual feelings and activities our culture defines as sexual are channeled from the time we are born until death into socially acceptable forms and expressions. As we saw in our discussions of sexuality across time and place, in most cultures, as we are learning other important norms of our culture very early in our childhoods, we are also simultaneously learning about our sexuality. Beside our family and peer groups, we learn about our sexuality through cultural institutions such as the school, religion, and the mass media. Some of the cultural information we receive about our sexuality is consciously presented and learned. However, we learn much of it unconsciously.

Learning Sexuality in the Family As we indicated in Chapter 6, many authorities on early childhood behavior believe that the family is the most significant agent of socialization. Where sexuality is concerned, however, the evidence suggests that children learn very little from their parents. One set of researchers found that almost half of the teens polled in a national survey indicated that if they wanted information about sex, they would not ask their parents. Rather, they would ask their friends, siblings, or sex partners (Coles & Stokes, 1985). In a similar vein, many parents are not comfortable discussing sex with their children. Consequently, sexual information is often presented in the form of prohibitions. For example, exploring their own bodies, including self-manipulation of the genitals and exhibiting their genitals to other children, is normal behavior in all children and is considered by many experts to be positive preparation for adult sexuality (DeLamaster, 1987). However, because parents are often horrified at the discovery of this type of behavior, children often grow up thinking that masturbation is something dirty or bad.

Such parental reactions tend to define children's sexuality generally as something secretive and distasteful. In reality, researchers have found that masturbation is a healthy way of releasing tension, even in children, and that it harms children only if it is reacted to negatively (Packer, 1997).

Parents often perpetuate the myth that children are asexual and that they themselves are asexual as well, going to great lengths to desexualize their children's lives. They stop touching each other or showing any signs of intimacy when the children are around. They do not discuss sexuality around children except in hushed tones, and they often become embarrassed and speechless when their children ask them a frank question about some aspect of sexuality (Schwartz & Scott, 1997). Parents who avoid answering their children's frank questions about their sexuality often convey their own uneasiness about sex and may teach their children that sex is something to be ashamed of.

Another way in which parents send their children negative messages about their sexuality is by using silly words to describe sexual organs. You have probably heard parents talking to their children referring to the genitals with terms such as *wee-wee, pee-pee, kitty-cat,* and *privates.* A study of preschool-age children showed that almost all of the children in the study could give the correct name to the nongenital parts of their bodies but very few of them knew the correct term for their genitals (Wurtele et al., 1992). According to Mary Calderone and Eric Johnson (1989), by using such silly names or no names at all for the genitals, parents are telling their children that their genitals are significantly different, embarrassing, mysterious, or taboo compared to other parts of their bodies, which have correct names that are used openly in conversation.

Sociologists have pointed out that family, social milieu, and degree of optimism regarding success in life are important factors determining the age at which teens will become sexually active (Brewster et al., 1993). Adolescents whose parents are separated or divorced are more likely than those from intact homes to engage in premarital sexual intercourse and teens who feel that they can talk to their parents are less likely to engage in coitus than are those who describe communication with their parents as poor (Rathus et al., 1997). On the other hand, there are many parents who have little problem sharing basic facts of sex with their children and they do so in a tone that is positive rather than negative. In these cases, parents put the sex education of their children into a perspective that encourages children to feel good about themselves, embrace sexual feelings as a joyful part of life, and develop self-control and good judgment in sexual matters.

Applying the Sociological Imagination

What did you learn about sexuality from your parents? Do you remember exploring your body as a child? If yes, how did your parents react to this behavior? Did they use silly names for your genitals? If you have children, have you repeated your own childhood sexual socialization in the family?

Gender Differences in Sexual Scripts Sexual identity is built on the foundation of gender identity. Children learn not only the language that is applied to sexual feelings and events but also cultural and societal expectations for a person of their age and gender. They also learn the reciprocal behaviors, attitudes, and demeanor expected of someone of a different gender. In this way, they become prepared to enact the sexual scripts that are acceptable in their culture (Laws & Schwartz, 1977). Research on female–male sexuality indicates that parents, as well as other early socialization agents, tend to communicate the content of sexual behavior to their children differently depending on the sex of the child. Despite changes in attitudes about gender-specific behavior, certain aspects of the sexual double standard remain, and parents continue to pass these on to their children. For example, girls learn to relate their sexuality to reproduction and morality, whereas boys learn to view sex as a goal-oriented activity and a way to prove their masculinity. Unlike with females, there is little emphasis placed on the tie between boys' sexuality and reproduction and family life. Females are encouraged to play a *gatekeeper role*, taking the responsibility of setting limits on men's sexual behavior and making sure it doesn't get out of control. Males, on the other hand, are encouraged to play the role of the *initiator* in sexual matters, that is, to take control of sexual activities and to be the sexual aggressors and pursuers. This sexual double standard is based on the cultural belief that male sexual needs are stronger and more important than female sexual needs; it is a classic example of the greater power and status given men in U.S. culture.

Parents and others reinforce the sexual double standard in a variety of ways. For example, many parents (1) place more restrictions on their daughters' sexuality than on their sons', (2) watch and warn their daughters more than their sons about sexuality, (3) express greater tolerance for the exposure of the male body than of the female body, and (4) guard and chaperone female movements, social activities, and friendships far more than male activities.

According to Hilary M. Lips (1993), the assumptions underlying this kind of socialization carry enormous implications for the sexual behavior and experiences of women and men and for the power relationship between them. First, it trivializes women's sexuality and sexual feelings; it denies the importance of female sexual desire. Second, it trivializes men, suggesting that they are not capable of self-control and are slaves to their sexual impulses. Some possible fallout from this sexual double standard is that when women become sexually active, they are more often stigmatized than are men. Concurrently, women who have been sexually assaulted, harassed, or raped are often blamed for their own victimization. Fallout may also include men's failure to learn that there are ways of controlling their sexual responses, women's failure to learn about their own capacity for sexual pleasure, and a reluctance of sexual partners to communicate with each other about their feelings.

The liberalization of sexual attitudes over the last several decades and the so-called sexual liberation of women have relaxed the sexual double standard some. However, the sexual script and gender socialization relative to human sexuality has changed very little. Women's bodies continue to be treated differently from men's in advertisements and other areas of popular culture; the same behavior in women and men is interpreted differently (for example, when women have several sex partners they are considered "sluts"; when men do likewise, they are macho and manly); and virginity is still stressed for women while prowess and scoring is stressed for males (Schwartz & Scott, 1997).

Research continues to show that both women and men accept this double standard. For example, a 1991 study found that women and men respondents rated women who engaged in premarital sex as immoral while they accepted male premarital sex (Robinson et al., 1991). But keep in mind that these are generalizations about sexual learning. Not all females and males learn traditional gender-appropriate sexual scripts. The exact content of sexual scripts varies according to a number of factors, including race and ethnicity, social class, and religious orientation. Thus, whatever sexual script we learn, our sexual behavior can and sometimes does change as circumstances change.

Peer Influence   As we indicated in Chapter 6, peers are powerful socialization agents, particularly during adolescence. According to some sources, peer groups are more important than the family in influencing the sexual attitudes and behaviors of adolescents and college students. Unfortunately, much of what they teach each other is actually inaccurate and they therefore frequently mislead and misinform each other. However, peers also provide positive sex socialization. For example, within peer groups, young people can often speak honestly and openly about sex; they can discuss and ask questions about their own developing sexuality or sexuality generally. This is particularly beneficial for those children who cannot or do not get this information and discussion in the family or in formal sex education classes. Moreover, a number of research studies have found that, after physiological readiness, peer pressure is probably the single most important factor that determines when adolescents become sexually active (Smith et al., 1985). Peer pressure to engage in sexual activity is especially strong among young males. Male peers tend to influence each other to explore their sexuality, while female peers encourage secrecy and abstinence.

Sexual Scripts, Popular Culture, and the Mass Media

Popular culture and the media have increasingly played a dominant role in constructing, shaping, and transforming our views and knowledge about sexuality. Unfortunately, this "knowledge" is often inaccurate, distorted, inflated, or outright false. It is often worlds apart from the way that the average person experiences sexuality.

Film One of the most visible popular cultural manifestations of contemporary sexuality is the growth of a multibillion-dollar sex industry. Every major form of the media contributes substantially to this industry. For example, thousands of movie houses across the country still feature X-rated movies, even though X-rated cable television stations have garnered a significant corner of the sex market. Even in mainstream film, sexual behavior is routine. Sex is graphically portrayed as intense, hot, and steamy, and any location remotely conducive to sexual intercourse is fair game: the elevator, the kitchen sink, the bathroom floor. Actresses often achieve film stardom for their sexiness. Sex and violence seem to be the film industry's formula for success. This may explain why the director of the film *Basic Instincts* reportedly walked onto the movie set and asked, "How can we put more tits and cunt into this movie?" (quoted in Strong et al., 1996, p. 9).

Rape is also a regular feature in film and it is often presented as sexy, titillating, provoked, and justified rather than as an act of criminal violence. For example, James Bond films, which are highly popular among the young, routinely depict women being seduced or raped and enjoying it, especially if the rapist is every woman's assumed dream man—James Bond himself (Schwartz & Scott, 1997). Women victims of rape are typically presented as having provoked the rape by dressing, walking, talking, or otherwise acting provocatively or leading a man on. Further, although most women in real life are raped by someone they know who is a person of their same race or ethnicity, the media tends to portray rapists as strangers and dispro-

portionately as African American men preying on white women (South & Felson, 1990; Wilson, 1988).

The sexual double standard is as apparent in film as it is in other cultural institutions. Films of the 1990s are full of female nudity, but men are seldom shown nude in the same way as women. Men are generally semiclad or we see their backsides. Seldom is the penis visible. In contrast, women are often completely nude and we almost always see them from the front.

In comparison to on-screen marital sex, on-screen premarital and extramarital sex is highly passionate, reflecting and reinforcing the idea that nonmarital sexual intercourse is the norm. Images suggesting sexual intercourse and oral sex are commonplace and so realistically portrayed that one can hardly tell that it is just acting. In addition, a whole genre of teenage films presents sex in crude and vulgar detail for teenagers to emulate. Various research studies show that films are a leading source of sex information for white, Latino, and Native American adolescent boys. By the time they are of college age, many males report that pornographic films are important sources of sexual information for them, providing information on subjects ranging from masturbation to oral-genital sex and anal intercourse (Duncan, 1990). Unfortunately, these films typically de-emphasize sexual responsibility. Contraceptives are seldom used and sexually transmitted diseases, including AIDS, are rarely a concern. Given that teenagers are increasingly at high risk for contracting AIDS, such films are, at the very least, irresponsible (Whatley, 1994).

Print Media The print media also contribute to the construction of sexual knowledge. Supermarket tabloids exploit and sensationalize sexuality to make millions of dollars from readers who seldom question the validity or power of those who transmit such information. Sex magazines such as *Playboy* and *Penthouse*—with their centerfolds of playmates or pets of the month and an array of nude pictures, cartoons with sexual content, and articles extolling the virtues of a wide variety of sexual expression—are among the most popular magazines in the world. While the *Sports Illustrated* swimsuit edition exceeds the sales of all other magazines, women's magazines are also increasingly full of sexual content. Magazines such as *Cosmopolitan* and *Redbook* feature sexually staged photographs and contain pages of stories that focus on sexuality. Even in traditional magazines such as *Reader's Digest, Time,* and *Newsweek,* sexual references tripled between 1950 and 1980 (Strong et al., 1996).

Moreover, advertisers routinely use sexuality—particularly female sexuality—to sell their products. Undressed or scantily dressed women implying sexual fulfillment, popularity, and romance are used to sell products ranging from heavy construction equipment and cars to designer jeans, perfume, alcohol, and cigarettes. The personal ads, a feature of most major newspapers, also reflect the increasing openness of today's sexuality. In such columns, women and men publicly advertise for the type of sexual partner or experiences they want. And celebrities have arisen from our new sexual openness. People such as Dr. Ruth Westheimer have developed large followings by talking frankly on radio and television talk shows about almost every conceivable aspect of human sexuality.

Television   Some media scholars describe television as the most pervasive and influential medium affecting our views of sexuality. Sexual behavior is often overt in the content of day- and nighttime television, and is most explicit on cable channels devoted to sexual movies and shows. In most program categories, unmarried heterosexual couples engage in sexual intercourse from four to eight times more frequently than married women and men (Westside Crisis Pregnancy Center, 1997). In action and adventure programs, sexual behavior is often linked with violence or a display of power; it is rarely depicted in the context of a loving or committed marriage relationship or as an expression of mutual affection. As in film, few characters are sexually responsible, despite rampant promiscuity. Women seldom get pregnant and few people contract sexually transmitted diseases.

Perhaps the most vulnerable to television's portrayal of sexuality are adolescents. American adolescents view nearly 14,000 instances of sexual material on television each year. Various researchers have found that watching a high volume of "sexy" television impacts how teenagers view themselves and behave sexually. For example, a study of almost 400 junior high school students reported that those who watched a greater amount of sexy television were more likely than lighter viewers to have become sexually active during the year prior to the survey. Adolescents reported that television is equally or more encouraging about sex than either their best female or best male friend (Westside Crisis Pregnancy Center, 1997).

Soap operas, one of the most popular television genres, are all about the sexual escapades of their stars, who are almost always heterosexual. In the rare episode presenting lesbian and gay sexuality and lifestyles, the treatment is usually stereotypical. Furthermore, characters over the age of forty who are depicted as sexually active are clumsy and unnatural in sexual matters. And, when people of color appear in soaps, they are often involved in interracial affairs that seldom go anywhere and show little if any sexual contact compared to Euro-American couples. According to Linda Lindsey (1994), portrayals of sex on soap operas have a strong impact on adolescent girls, who are heavy viewers of soap operas. These girls have unrealistically high estimates of the extent of extramarital sex and the frequency of intercourse in the general population. Lindsey reports that the most popular soap opera, *General Hospital,* has both the largest teen audience and the highest rate of sexual acts per hour.

On the other hand, some soap operas and other television programming have tried to handle sexuality in a more accurate and responsible way. Several have dealt with social issues such as the consequences of unprotected sex, AIDS, and coming out as a lesbian or as gay to family and friends. Some made-for-TV movies deal with sexuality as a social issue rather than as intimacy. The plots cover a fairly wide range of topics, including teenage pregnancy, rape, sexual harassment, extramarital sex, lesbian and gay love, and sexually transmitted diseases. In many instances, the treatment of these topics is informative, although they sometimes border on sensationalism and exploitation and/or give the impression that these topics are not all that serious.

At the other end of the continuum, television evangelists and religious fundamentalists on religious television networks and programs broadcast their versions of sexuality, sin, and morality to a wide-ranging audience. These views of sexuality stress premarital chastity, opposition to sex education in the schools, and opposition to lesbian and gay love and sexuality, all of which is embodied in what is called a pro-life stance. Ironically, several of the most influential televangelists of the 1980s, such as Jimmy Swaggart and Jim Bakker, lost their ministries because of their own sexual improprieties.

Music   Contemporary music, from popular ballads to rock 'n' roll, heavy metal, rap, and hip hop, is full of lyrics that either are sexually explicit or convey messages about sexuality that are mixed with messages about love, hate, rejection, loneliness, and violence. Much of this music is misogynistic, defining women as sex objects, "whores," and appropriate objects of male fantasy, hatred, and violence. The largest group of consumers of this media fare is made up of adolescents and young adults.

MTV, VH1, and music video programs televise a constant stream of videos filled with sexually explicit lyrics, images, and body movements: gyrating women and men in sexually suggestive clothing, positions, and situations, from a wide variety of men, such as Genuine, holding their crotches and dancing themselves into a frenzy to female artists like Madonna's heavily sexual suggestiveness and innuendo blended with overt female eroticism. For example, in a content analysis of rock lyrics, Michael Medved (1992) counted 87 descriptions of oral sex and 117 explicit terms for female and male genitals in *one* album (*As Nasty as They Wanna Be,* by 2 Live Crew). Sex, violence, and female victimization go hand in hand in this medium. Sodomy or reference to it has become commonplace in these videos, and teenagers and other viewers are fed a constant diet of women asking, sometimes begging, to be raped and sodomized.

Sexual Identities

As we indicated earlier in this chapter, sexual identity is part of our gender identity. In U.S. society, our cultural system recognizes only two sexes: female and male. There is no third, fourth,

or fifth sex; no androgynous orientation; no bisexuality; no mixed cases. As a result, our gender identity is learned in the dichotomous forms of female or male. The female and male sex role scripts include much that is not sexual, such as the expectation that women will be passive rather than aggressive and the expectation that men will be aggressive and in control. This gender identity underlies our **sexual identity,** an individual's awareness of herself or himself as female or male, the knowledge of her or his body and bodily functions, images of femininity and masculinity, and sexual preferences and sexual history. Our sexual identity is not inborn. Rather, it develops through experience (Laws & Schwartz, 1977).

Most individuals in U.S. society find the accepted sexual scripts adequate guidelines for making sense of their own experiences and thus form coherent sexual identities that fall essentially in line with them. For others, the sexual dichotomy of female/male and, therefore, the available gender roles and sexual scripts do not fit their experiences, and attempts to adhere to them can be difficult. In the next section, we discuss sexual identities within the context of **sexual orientation,** the pattern of sexual and emotional attraction toward a person of one's own or another gender. It should be noted that sexual orientation includes not only whom we respond to romantically and erotically but also, more fundamentally, the ways in which we understand and identify ourselves.

Measuring and Documenting Sexual Orientations

Some researchers have suggested that it is almost impossible to get a clear picture of how many people in a given population should be classified as identifying with each sexual orientation because

1. people's answers to questions about their sexual orientations vary according to the questions asked.
2. the people doing the classifying (for example, politicians, moralists, and ministers) often have an interest in classifying as many people as possible as heterosexual. Therefore, their interests and agendas of-

ten shape the way such data are interpreted.

3. it is simply difficult to collect data that would allow an accurate enumeration of people of different sexual orientations (Hatfield & Rapson, 1996).

One problem is the reliance on self-definition in surveys. Elaine Hatfield (Hatfield & Rapson, 1996) reports that while sorting through some old Kinsey files at the Kinsey Institute, she found that self-definitions of sexual orientation do not always match behavior. For example, one man in the Kinsey protocols who identified himself as a "heterosexual all the way" also indicated that he had never had an affair with a woman but also that he had had thousands with men in his occupation of male prostitute (which he said he did only for the money). If, on the other hand, we use sexual desire as a measure of one's sexual orientation, how do we classify the male in the Kinsey study who has plans to marry heterosexually but who also, until he marries, finds sexual release with his male friends? Or, what if we look simply at what people do as the measure of sexual orientation? How, then, would we classify the male in the Kinsey study who is married heterosexually, has two children, and is a devout Mormon who indicates that he is extremely attracted to men but chose to marry heterosexually to fulfill his duty to the church? To have sexual intercourse with his wife is a chore that he endures for the sake of fulfilling his religious duty.

Other pertinent questions arise when we attempt to use people's behavior as an accurate measure of their sexual orientations. For example, do the kinds of sexual activities people engage in in their youth count when measuring their adult sexuality? What about what people do when they are in situations in which the "true" objects of their sexual desire are not available, as in prisons? How many female and male partners does a person have to have before she or he is classified as heterosexual, homosexual, or bisexual? Do we classify a person who has had two partners of the same sex and twenty of the other sex as heterosexual, bisexual, or homosexual? Questions such as these illustrate the difficulty in determining sexual orientation, and they also point up the fact that the boundaries between various sexual orientations are sometimes blurry.

Various researchers have answered these questions in different ways, and some research indicates that the way people identify their sexual orientation is based on the way in which the question(s) is asked. Some social scientists view sexual orientation, like other aspects of our identity, as an ongoing process that can vary over the life course. These social scientists believe that the degree to which we identify ourselves as heterosexual reflects, in part, the extent to which we have internalized our society's messages and definitions of an acceptable sexual orientation or sexual preference. Considering the stigma that is associated with sexual orientations other than heterosexuality, it is not surprising that most people would publicly claim to be heterosexual.

It seems clear that a simple dichotomy of sexual orientation in terms of heterosexuality and homosexuality both is difficult to document with a great deal of precision and accuracy and, equally important, may actually be misleading. For example, in 1948, Kinsey and his associates claimed that few of us are completely or exclusively heterosexual or homosexual. Rather, there are some aspects of both orientations in all of us. That is, sexual orientation forms a continuum from exclusive heterosexuality at one end of the continuum to exclusive homosexuality at the other end, with most people falling somewhere along the continuum and not at either pole. Between these two poles lie people who have various degrees of sexual interest in and sexual experience with people of their own sex (see Figure 7.2). An early study by Phillip Blumstein and Pepper Schwartz (1983) supports this notion of the fluidity of human sexual orientation. They found that homosexual attractions and preferences do not always remain constant throughout people's lives. People sometimes change their sexual preferences because of situational opportunities or because of specific love relationships. Subjects in their study often became homosexual after satisfactory heterosexual lives or heterosexual after years of homosexual identity and behavior. Although rigid categorizations of sexual orientation and behavior have proven to be misleading, many sex researchers continue to hold on to the discreet categories of heterosexual, homosexual and bisexual.

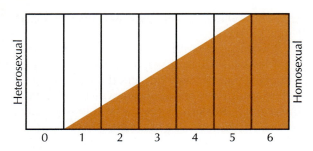

FIGURE 7.2 ⟳ **Heterosexual–Homosexual Rating Scale** *Source:* From Kinsey, A., Pomeroy, W.B., and Martin, C.E. 1948. *Sexual Behavior in the Human Male.* Philadelphia: Saunders, p. 470. Reprinted by permission.

Heterosexualities

In contemporary U.S. culture, a heterosexual orientation and behavior is considered the norm. **Heterosexuality** refers to the preference for having intimate and sexual activities with a person of a sex different from one's own. In a more sociological and political sense, it also includes an individual's community, lifestyle, and core identity. Although it is difficult to know with exact precision what percentage of the U.S. population is heterosexual, the most recent sex surveys suggest a figure of 97 percent (Clements, 1994; Laumann et al., 1994). Our discussion of the difficulty of defining and accurately counting people based on their sexual orientations emphasizes the flexibility and the social construction of sexual orientation. This issue takes on increased importance in that heterosexuality continues to be the barometer by which people in U.S. culture are measured and judged and by which they receive many of the society's social, political, and economic benefits. For example, because heterosexuals (or at least those presumed to be so) have more institutional privileges than do homosexuals, married heterosexual couples may file joint tax returns and, much more often than cohabiting homosexual couples, may get employee benefits such as health and dental care (Andersen, 1997). Adrienne Rich (1980) has argued that "compulsory heterosexuality" in this culture includes the domination and oppression of homosexuality, lesbianism, and other sexualities perceived as "other." It also includes the domination of men's heterosexuality over women's heterosexuality and is perpetuated through dominant social, cultural, and political ideologies and assumptions (Hearn & Parkin, 1995). Religious doctrines and workforce, marriage, and family laws and policies explicitly and implicitly favor heterosexuality, which, according to Rich, restricts the sexuality of females and males alike.

Homosexualities and Bisexualities

Homosexuality, like heterosexuality, refers to both identity and behavior and is the preference for having intimate and sexual activities with a person of the same sex. However, as we discussed earlier, sexual orientation is not always expressed in sexual behavior. For example, some people self-identify as lesbian, gay, or heterosexual long before they engage in sex. Others may choose a celibate lifestyle for religious or ascetic reasons or for a lack of partners. As with heterosexuality, it is difficult to determine with any precision just how many people are homosexual. Despite the fact that Kinsey and his colleagues (1953) reported that 28 percent of his female respondents had experienced homosexual encounters, most studies today report that under 5 percent of women and men actually identify themselves as homosexual. Based upon an examination of data drawn from studies conducted in this country as well as in Asian and Pacific Island countries, Milton Diamond (1993) concluded that only about 5 to 6 percent of men and somewhere between 2 and 3 percent of women across different cultures have engaged in same-sex sexual activities at least once since adolescence and consider themselves exclusively homosexual.

Researchers believe that bisexuality is more prevalent than homosexuality. People who have sexual partners of both sexes either simultaneously or at different times are referred to as **bisexuals.** One of the problems of getting an accurate count of bisexuality in the U.S. population results from the fact that some sex researchers include a large number of people who are actually bisexual in the lesbian and gay category (Kelly, 1994). On the one hand, this practice is supported by a 1990 study that found that among a sample of people twenty-five to forty years old who had engaged in a substantial number of same-sex sexual relationships, few categorized themselves as bisexual. Rather, they viewed themselves as either gay or heterosexual. Even those respondents in the study who had experienced a fairly even number of same-sex and heterosexual relationships considered themselves to be either gay or heterosexual (Pillard, 1990). On the other hand, there are many bisexuals who do not see themselves in an either/or dichotomy; they do not see themselves as gay or straight, and their behavior does not correspond to either. For these reasons alone, it is difficult to know exactly how many people are bisexual. A recent study indicated that around 5 to 6 percent of Americans reported being bisexual since the onset of adulthood. But, in general, sex researchers have put the percentage of bisexuals in the adult population at somewhere between 10 and 25 percent (Maugh, 1990).

Like homosexuality, bisexuality is heavily stigmatized in U.S. culture. However, not all cultures condemn homosexuality and bisexuality. Early in the twentieth century, Aranda men in Central Australia were initiated by having sex with other men until such time as they were eligible to marry (Bullough, 1976). In most tribal societies, homosexual acts of one kind or another are socially acceptable for some members of the society, at least some of the time. For example, among the Siwans of Africa, all men and boys engage in anal intercourse. Men of high status in the society often lend their sons to one another for this purpose, and both married and unmarried men are expected to have both homosexual and heterosexual affairs. If they don't, they are looked upon as peculiar (Ford & Beach, 1951). Likewise, Sambian males of New Guinea illustrate the point that human sexual orientation is malleable and not biologically predetermined. Among the Sambians, young boys of seven or eight years of age begin their sexual lives with older boys. In adolescence, they engage in sexual activities with both sexes, and in adulthood, they move to exclusively heterosexual relationships, losing all sexual desire for men. In some societies, such as the Azande, Dahomey, and !Kung, adolescent girls are expected to have homosexual love affairs (Blackwood, 1986). Other cultures do not care much about homosexuality one way or another. American and European cultures, on the other hand, generally disapprove of homosexual and bisexual lifestyles.

Negative Attitudes   In the United States, there has historically been a generally negative attitude toward homosexual and bisexual lifestyles. Some researchers use the term **homophobia** to refer to strongly held negative attitudes and beliefs, irrational fears, and outright hatred of lesbians and gays and their lifestyles and the term **biphobia** to refer to prejudice, negative attitudes, and misconceptions related to bisexuals and their lifestyle (Kelly, 1994). Public views in this regard have not changed significantly, even after the so-called sexual revolution. People responding in public opinion polls conducted during the 1960s rated homosexuals as the third most dangerous group in the United States; only communists and atheists were considered more dangerous (Aguero et al.,1984). In the 1970s, such polls indicated that although some people were beginning to support some legal rights for homosexuals, the majority viewed homosexuality as vulgar and obscene and homosexuals as people with whom they did not want to associate. An antihomosexual sentiment continued through the next two decades as public opinion research indicated that the majority of the U.S. public (78 percent in the 1980s and 75 percent in the 1990s) believed that sexual relations between two adults of the same sex were always or almost always wrong (Davis & Smith, 1984; Davis & Smith, 1991).

According to much of the survey data, people who are the most rigidly opposed to homosexuality generally hold traditional views, are older, have conservative religious beliefs, hold stereotyped views of the roles of women and men, are relatively uneducated, and live in rural areas (Hatfield & Rapson, 1996). Many young people are also intolerant of homosexuality. For example, studies focusing on the sexual attitudes of college students have found that there is widespread hostility toward lesbians and gays (Kurdek, 1988). College students who have racist and sexist attitudes are more likely also to hold negative attitudes toward homosexuality and bisexuality.

It is because of such attitudes that many lesbians and gays find the college campus less emotionally supportive and less tolerant of change

Although some segments of the U.S. population have adopted a more tolerant attitude toward lesbians and gays, the violent murder of Matthew Shepard in 1998 brought to national attention the ongoing and increasing problem of hate crimes directed toward lesbians and gays. It fanned outrage from citizens across the country and galvanized support for more extensive hate-crime legislation.

and innovation than do heterosexual groups. On some college campuses, lesbians and gays are overtly challenging these attitudes of hatred and intolerance. They have formed lesbian, gay, and bisexual alliances that promote courses on human sexuality and discussions and panels on lesbian, gay, and bisexual issues. In some cases, these measures have had a noticeable effect on promoting more tolerant attitudes and a greater understanding of homosexual and bisexual orientations. However, it is generally those students who are already more liberal and accepting of their own sexuality who are likely to modify their sexual attitudes. In any event, studies show that college men are less accepting of homosexual and bisexual lifestyles than are college women. When change in sexual attitudes does occur, college women seem more likely to change their attitudes than do men (Kelly, 1994).

In the mid- to late 1990s, public figures such as actress Ellen Degeneres, through her television program *Ellen,* have done much to promote lesbian pride and acceptance. In addition, public figures such as Dennis Rodman and Ru Paul have brought the issues of bisexuality and male homosexuality to a new level of visibility and dis-

cussion in this society. Further, Madonna's rebellious sexuality can be interpreted as a conscious masking of her heterosexuality so as to defy patriarchal definition and control of female sexuality. In many of her music videos, she takes a chameleonlike approach to the social construction of her sexuality. That is, she seems to dance around the perimeters of both heterosexuality and homosexuality, creating sexual ambiguity and defying rigid sexual categorization while keeping her audience guessing. Susan McClary (1990, p. 2) defines Madonna's behavior in this regard as a kind of "escape to androgyny," a refusal of rigid gender/sex categories and a deconstruction of women's bodies as objects.

Social Activism   As is heterosexuality, homosexuality is steeped in issues and relations of power and control in this society. Issues related to homosexuality reached an apex in public and political debate in the United States in the 1990s when, for the first time, a candidate for the U.S. presidency made lesbian and gays rights a campaign issue. Lesbian and gay rights advocates have been increasingly active since the 1960s, and they have made some important strides in their efforts to eliminate laws, policies, and practices that discriminate against them purely on the basis of their sexual orientation or lifestyle.

As we stress throughout this textbook, humans are not passive objects acted upon. Rather, they are active agents involved in creating and changing social reality. Lesbians and gays are no exception: as hundreds of thousands have come out and openly affirmed their sexual orientations and lifestyles, they have significantly changed the U.S. sexual landscape. For example, lesbian and gay activism has resulted in the repeal of sodomy laws in half the states that had traditionally maintained them and some cities and states have passed clear policies outlawing discrimination because of sexual orientation. It also contributed to the lifting of the ban against employment of lesbians and gays in the federal government and to the inclusion of gay rights in the platform of the National Democratic Party (D'Emilio, 1997).

However, there has also been a reaction to lesbian and gay activism. For example, in 1992, Colorado became the only state to prohibit legal protection from discrimination for lesbians and gays. Shortly thereafter, several counties in Oregon followed Colorado's lead. And, taking an even more conservative position than Colorado, a county near Atlanta, Georgia, passed a resolution condemning homosexuality. By the mid-1990s antihomosexual legislation was being considered in as many as twenty states (Kelly, 1994).

Thus, although some segments of U.S. society have adopted a more accepting attitude toward lesbians and gays, there is also evidence of increased hostility, continuing discrimination, and repeated acts of violence perpetrated against lesbians and gays. This was made all too evident in 1998 with the violent murder of Matthew Shepard, a twenty-one-year-old gay college student at the University of Wyoming, who was kidnapped, robbed, pistol-whipped, and left tied to a fence in near-freezing temperatures. Shepard's murder fanned outrage and debate over laws on hate crimes, and gay activists have moved to galvanize Congress and state legislatures to pass hate-crime legislation or to broaden existing laws. As of 1998, Wyoming was among ten states having either no hate-crime laws or none based on specific categories (Brooke, 1998a) (see Figure 7.3).

Transsexuality

According to some published reports, there are approximately 15,000 **transsexuals,** people who have undergone plastic surgery in order to change their genitalia to match their gender identities, in the United States. In lay terms, this procedure is often referred to as a sex-change operation. Some researchers estimate that 1 in every 500,000 people over the age of fifteen in the United States is a transsexual. Others suggest that from 50,000 to 75,000 people forgo surgery and live as transsexuals or opposite from the sex

FIGURE 7.3 ↺ **Hate-Crime Legislation in the United States** Although 40 states have some form of hate-crime legislation, only 21 include crimes based on sexual orientation. Ten states, including Wyoming, either have no hate-crime provisions or do not identify hate crimes by specific category. Note: Maryland and Utah require data collection for crimes based on sexual orientation but do not specify such crimes in penalty laws. *Source:* Reprinted by permission of the National Gay and Lesbian Task Force from "Hate Crime Legislation in the U.S.," *New York Times* (October 13, 1998), p. A17.

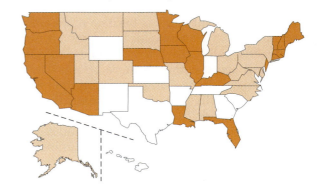

■ Laws include crimes based on sexual orientation

▨ Laws do not include crimes based on sexual orientation

☐ No hate-crime laws or none based on specific categories

they were at birth. Estimates of the number of female-to-male transsexuals are usually much lower than those for male to female, but this may be a function of cultural values more than actual numbers (Brooke, 1998b; Kelly, 1994). Estimates of the number of transsexuals in a population are probably confounded by the fact that not all people living as opposite the sex they were at birth have had sex-change surgery. Social scientists use the term **transgendered** to refer to people who dress and otherwise present themselves as the other sex but have not undergone sex-change surgery.

One of the earliest known sex-change operations was that of Sophia Hedwig in Germany who, in 1882, was surgerically transformed from female to the male Herman Karl (Bullough & Bullough, 1993). Perhaps the most celebrated transsexual in the United States was George (later known as Christine) Jorgensen, who went to Denmark and underwent surgery in 1952 because such surgery was not yet available in the United States. Since then, an estimated 25,000 Americans having *gender dysphoria*—a condition in which a person feels trapped in the body of the wrong sex—have had sex-change surgery. About two-thirds of the sex-change surgeries were performed in the United States from the 1960s through the 1980s and were done in Trinidad, Colorado, which became known as "the sex-change capital of the world."

The experience of transsexuality again points up the flexibility of our gender roles and sexual orientations. Before sex-change surgery, most candidates must go through two psychiatric evaluations, live and dress in their new gender roles for at least a year, and undergo nine months of hormone treatments: testosterone for women and estrogen for men (Brooke, 1998b). As sex-change surgery has become more mainstream and U.S. transsexuals have become more public and politically active, people across the class and age spectra are more openly living transgendered lives. For example, in the fall of 1995, a nationally renowned economic theorist and historian at the University of Iowa announced that he was transgendered and would shortly become a woman. After divorcing his wife of thirty years, Donald McCloskey, at the age of fifty-three, changed his name to Deirdre

and underwent surgery that transformed him from male to female ("Transgendered," 1997).

Like homosexuality and bisexuality, transsexuality is not an issue in all cultures. In some societies, there are alternative gender identities and roles available to people who do not fit into the traditional sex categories of female and male. The Zuni of New Mexico, for example, think of gender as socially, not biologically, acquired. They therefore recognize not only the female and male genders but also a third gender, a *two-spirit* or *berdache,* who is usually a man who assumes the dress, gender role, and status of a woman. Likewise, among some Asian, South Pacific, and other Native American cultures, such as the Plains Indians, there are females, males, and berdaches. Although women can become berdaches, most of the current research indicates that the majority are relatively passive men who enjoy lovers of the same sex and are highly honored in their cultures because they are considered to be members of a third sex that has supernatural powers and combines the best of females and males (Schnarch, 1992; Williams, 1986). Evelyn Blackwood (1984) and others have found that in some Native American cultures, there existed "manly hearted" women who share the activities of men in the society and often live with other women. Among the Mohave, for example, females who wished to pursue a masculine gender underwent an initiation ceremony to become *hwames.* As hwames, they lived much like the men in their culture, although they were not allowed to assume positions of leadership or to participate in war. The male version of this third gender among the Mohave is called an *alyha,* a man who, after an initiation ceremony, adopted a feminine name, performed female tasks, and married a man (Martin & Voorhies, 1975).

A third gender, the *hijra,* can also be found in India. Numbering well over 400,000, with 150,000 in Delhi alone, these men play a prominent social role in Indian society. They combine characteristics and elements of both the female and the male roles, and, as part of their religious devotion to the Goddess Mata, they undergo castration and live a life of sexual abstinence. Many hijras are effeminate because castration results in hormonal changes, but they are not by Indian definition homosexual. They are believed to possess magical powers and to be capable of casting curses on people. Thus, they are a source of blessings for health, prosperity, and fertility, which they typically perform at weddings, religious ceremonies, and the births of children (Nanda, 1990).

The existence of societies in which sexual identity is more a matter of choice than a biological given illustrates the creativity that human beings bring to the production and reproduction of human sexuality. Our biological makeup provides us with broad boundaries of sexual possibilities, but what we do sexually within those boundaries is socially constructed. Thus, the concepts of homosexuality, bisexuality, and transsexuality have meaning only within societies in which only two sexes are recognized, in which female and male sex are assumed to be innate. In societies such as those we have just described, these concepts have little, if any, meaning.

The Exercise of Power through Coercive Sexuality

Hardly a day goes by that we do not hear about allegations of sexual assault and sexual harassment involving a wide array of public figures, celebrities, and politicians as well as the average citizen. Over the closing decade of the twentieth century, public sex scandals have been regular fodder for news organizations, including a sex scandal leading to the impeachment of a sitting president, William Jefferson Clinton.

Sexual Assault: The Case of Rape

Perhaps no other human action better illustrates the unequal power relations between women and men than the act of sexual assault. Millions of women in the United States and around the world have suffered or will suffer some form of sexual assault. **Sexual assault** is a broad term that encompasses any behaviors, either physical or verbal, intended to coerce an individual into sexual activity against her or his will. Sexual as-

sault is extremely widespread in U.S. society, with women and children representing the majority of the victims (Schwartz & Scott, 1997). One of the most extreme forms of sexual assault is rape. **Rape** is legally defined as sexual assault in which a man uses his penis to vaginally penetrate a woman against her will by force or threat of force or when she is mentally or physically unable to give her consent. The legal definition of rape overlooks the fact that men and boys are sometimes victims of rape as well. Consequently, some states have broadened the legal definition of rape by removing sex-specific language. The overwhelming majority of rape victims, however, are female. The Data Box presents some startling statistics on the frequency and nature of rape in the United States.

Historically, estimates of rape have seriously underrepresented its actual incidence. It is believed that estimates of rape would be much higher if they included assaults on young girls by their fathers, stepfathers, and other male relatives (usually categorized separately as incest); cases of statutory rape (that is, sex with girls too young to give consent legally); cases of rape that result in the death of the victim and are therefore classified as homicides; and cases of male rape both inside and outside prisons. Statistics on rape provided by the FBI do not include these categories, nor do they include date and marital rape. Nonetheless, this country has one of the highest rates of rape among modern industrial societies. For example, the rate of *reported* rape in the United States is thirteen times greater than it is in Great Britain and more than twenty times greater than in Japan (Rathus et al., 1997).

Specific sociological data on rape and on who is likely to be raped show that most rapes are committed not by strangers but by people known to the victim. These rapes, involving a rapist who knows or who is familiar with the victim, are called **acquaintance rape.** Date rape is a form of acquaintance rape. Some men who commit date rape believe that a woman's agreement to go on a date is also an agreement to engage in coitus. In the case of *marital rape,* the victim is not only acquainted with the rapist but also intimately involved with him and his life. The typical marital rapist is a man who believes that the marriage license includes his right to

Rape

- Sexual assault is the most rapidly growing violent crime in the Unites States. Ninety-five percent of the victims of sexual assault are female; 1,871 American women are raped every day. It is estimated that a rape against a woman is committed every 1.3 minutes (American Medical Association, 1995–1997; Mental Health Issue of the Month, 1999).
- Eighty percent of rape victims are attacked by husbands, boyfriends, acquaintances, or relatives. Sixty-one percent of female rape victims are under age 18 (American Medical Association, 1995–1997).
- Approximately 81 percent of rape victims are white; 18 percent are black; 1 percent are of other races. About half of all rape victims are in the lowest third of income distribution; half are in the upper two-thirds (TAASA Program Facts, 1997).
- Surveys showing societal attitudes about rape reported that 51 percent of boys and 41 percent of girls in the eleven-to-fourteen-year-old range believe that forced sex is acceptable if the boy spends a lot money on the girl; 76 percent and 56 percent respectively of high school boys and girls believe that forced sex is acceptable under some circumstances; and among male college students, 35 percent admitted that, under certain circumstances, they would commit rape if they could get away with it; 1 in 12 admitted to committing acts that met the legal definition of rape; and 84 percent of men who committed rape did not label it as rape (American Medical Association, 1995–1997).
- In about one-third of rapes, the offender uses a weapon. Approximately one-half of rape victims sustain injuries other than rape injuries and three-fourths of female rape victims require medical care after assault (TAASA Program Facts, 1997).
- The average sentence for criminals convicted of rape is almost 10 years. The average time served for those criminals is just over 5 years. The average sexual assault murderer is a 26-year-old white male (Center Against Sexual Abuse, 1999; SERAPH Security Consulting and Training, 1997).

coitus, whether or not his wife is willing. As indicated in the Sociological Reflections box, this kind of rape is probably more common than other types of acquaintance rape because a sexual relationship has already been established.

Sociological data also reveals a link between a woman's economic status, her race, and rape. For example, African American, teenage, and urban working-class girls are at the greatest risk for being raped (Lott, 1994). Some researchers have suggested that the risk for rape of African American women is so great that elderly African American women are just as likely to be raped as young white women (Gollin, 1980). These statistics take on added significance given that, in general, when violence in the African American community is discussed, its impact for African American women is usually minimized relative to the focus placed on the risk for street violence of African American males. While we do not minimize the devastating impact of African American male street violence on African American women and families, the most devastating form of violence in the life of African American women is sexual assault and domestic violence (Marriott, 1994). Added to the issue of rape in the African American community is the fact that, historically, many people have mistakenly believed that the majority of rapists are African American males who are usually strangers to their victims. Such a myth can have dangerous consequences, not only because it unfairly stigmatizes African American men but also because it diverts the attention of white women away from the most likely sources of their sexual assault: white men. At the same time, it serves as a justification for racist and negative attitudes toward and treatment of African American males, including the act of murder (Schwartz & Scott, 1997). The Sociology through Literature box (p. 192) illuminates this point.

Sociological Reflections

Marital Rape

Although limited, the data on marital rape suggest that a significant number of wives in the United States are raped by their husbands. It is estimated, for example, that one wife in seven is likely to be raped by her husband (Gibbs, 1991). Although the victims of this type of rape seldom report their experiences, the impact of marital rape is no less serious and is sometimes more frightening than that of rape by strangers. Some researchers have found, for example, that the closer the association or prior association of the victim and the rapist, the more violent the rape tends to be (Russell, 1982). Consequently, wives who are raped often suffer greater and longer trauma than other female rape victims do. They often feel betrayed because the rapist was someone they loved or cared for and, generally, someone they continue to live with.

Marital rape can be classified according to the following categories: (1) *force-only rape,* wherein the husband controls the type and frequency of sexual activity within the marriage; (2) *battering rape,* in which the husband humiliates and degrades his wife; and (3) *obsessive rape,* which involves sexual fetishes, sadism, and forcible anal intercourse (Finkelhor & Yllo, 1985). Sociologists have identified a number of important factors associated with marital rape, including the establishment of marital exemption in rape laws, the socially and economically disadvantaged position of women, and the violent nature of U.S. society and its "rape culture" (Pagelow, 1988).

Until the mid-1970s, marital rape was not a crime in this country. In some states today, a husband may be prosecuted for rape only if the wife can show that the assault occurred after legal papers to end the marriage have been filed in court or that the couple were not living together at the time (Russell, 1990). Some states have broadened the scope of rape laws to include sexual acts other than coitus, such as anal intercourse and oral-genital relations, and to apply rape laws to men who rape other men and to women who coerce men into sexual activity or assist men in raping other women (Rathus et al.,1997). Other states, however, have broadened their marital rape exemptions to prevent the prosecution of a man who rapes the woman with whom he is living. Such rape exemptions further limit married or cohabiting women's ability to pursue rape cases in the criminal justice system.

Do you agree with the point of view that married women can be raped by their husbands? How would you characterize your peers' point of view on this issue? Use one or more feminist, conflict, and functionalist perspectives to explain the causes of, effects of, and possible remedies for marital rape.

In addition, age is not a deterrent to rape. Females of all ages are victims of rape. This point is highlighted by the findings of a study of a Washington, D.C., hospital in which victims treated for rape ranged from a fifteen-month-old baby girl to an eighty-two-year-old woman (Benokraitis & Feagin, 1986). Although rape is rape, some people consider child sexual abuse to be more abhorrent than any other type of rape. The term *child sexual abuse* refers to the use of a child for the sexual gratification of an adult; the perpetrator can be a stranger or a family member.

Child sexual abuse within the family is typically referred to as **incest**—the sexual abuse by a blood relative who is assumed to be a part of the child's family. Most definitions of incest include stepfathers and live-in boyfriends as relatives. Most child sexual abuse is perpetrated by family members, but no matter who the adult is, child sexual assault involves an adult using her or his power to force, coerce, or cajole compliance from a child who participates, usually, out of awe, fear, trust, respect, or love for the adult (Tower, 1989). As with every other form of rape,

Sociology through Literature

Your Blues Ain't Like Mine

On Sunday, August 28, 1955, a fourteen-year-old African American boy from Chicago, Emmett Louis Till, was kidnapped at pistol point from his uncle's home in Money, Mississippi, and murdered. Till was kidnapped by two white men, Roy Bryant and his half-brother, J. W. Milam, for allegedly engaging in a sexually explicit act directed toward a white woman: making a "wolf whistle." Emmett Till became the 575th recorded lynching victim in Mississippi since 1882. The novel *Your Blues Ain't Like Mine*, by Bebe Moore Campbell, is loosely based on this real-life murder, and the following passages illuminate the vulnerability of the powerless and how race, class, gender, and sexuality are interlocking systems of experiences that are relative to particular times and places.

The two men sat across from each other at the kitchen table, smoking Marlboros and drinking the strong black coffee Louetta had poured for them. From the window Floyd [Cox] could see Louetta and Lily sitting on the back porch, talking and watching the children play in the yard. He could feel John Earl staring at him as he leaned over and stubbed out the cigarette and then moments later lit another one. Floyd was enjoying the cigarettes and the coffee, the sounds of his wife and child outside. And he was loving being across from his older brother and feeling for the first time in his life that he was the equal of that man, that he had done what his brother would have done. They'd righted a wrong together. Now they shared an intimacy that surpassed what they did with their wives in the dark. Floyd felt calm and ordered and invincible. Peaceful.

"You know they found that boy? You know that, don't you?" John Earl said quietly.

Floyd felt the cup shaking in his hand, and suddenly coffee was spilling all over the front of his pants. He jumped up as the steaming liquid trickled between his legs.

"Take it easy. Take it easy," John Earl said. "Daddy always said you was the nervous type." He grinned at Floyd, who didn't smile back.

"How you know that?"

"I been to town this morning. Everybody's talking about it."

"They know who done it?"

"Yeah. Nigger was still alive when his grandma got to him; he told her. It don't mean nothing; in a couple of days it'll be like it ain't never happened. Ain't a man around here wouldn't have done the same thing. It ain't like the sheriff's gon' come around and take you to Parchman."

"There's just some things a man ain't supposed to stand for."

"That's right. That's right. When a nigger starts talking nasty to a white woman, well . . . And when they start talking about going to school with white children, well, they asking for it. And see, that's another thing. What we done, Floyd, what you done, well, it kind of puts the whole United States of America on notice." John Earl grinned at his brother.

"How you mean?"

"That the Supreme Court ain't gon' ram no integration down our throats, that's what. That we're prepared to take a stand."

"Yeah, I know that," said Floyd.

* * *

[Several days after the murder, the sheriff came to question Floyd, who said he had only talked to the "boy":]
"My wife is carrying my name. What kind of man would I be if I just let any ignorant nigger that wants to talk to her just any old kind of way? A man's got a right to protect his property, his children, and his wife. Ain't that right? Ain't that what America is all about?"

"Well, man's got a right to protect his wife," said Sheriff Barnes, rising from the chair. "And so you're saying that you didn't kill that boy?"

"Never touched him," Floyd said. Lily was silent.

The sheriff smiled and nodded toward Lily. "Sorry to have disturbed you, ma'am."

"Oh, that's all right."

Lily remained in her chair as Floyd walked the sheriff to the door. . . .

Sometimes she didn't understand men, not even her own husband. She thought about what Floyd had said—that a man had a right to protect his property, his wife, and his kids—and the order of the words struck her. She thought that the way he said it made it seem that she and Floydjunior belonged to him same as if he'd bought and paid for them. *I won't think about that,* she told herself. The sheriff had come and gone, and Floyd hadn't been arrested. It was just as he and Louetta had said; there wasn't going to be any trouble.

Explicit in Campbell's novel is an awareness that the justice system is not blind. What is the relationship between race, gender, sexuality, and lynchings in the United States? How do statistics on men incarcerated for rape and other crimes related to the issue of sexuality reflect class and race biases?

Source: Excerpted from *Your Blues Ain't Like Mine* by Bebe Moore Campbell, pp. 52–53, 71–73. Copyright © 1992 by Bebe Moore Campbell. Used by permission of G.P. Putnam's Sons, a division of Penguin Putnam Inc.

the typical victim of child sexual abuse (90 percent) is female (National Coalition Against Domestic Violence, 1996). Some researchers, however, claim that this conclusion is quite misleading because boys are less likely to report a sexual assault. Males who in early childhood are taught to be "strong" and "macho" may be unwilling or unable to admit that they have been victimized in this way. Some researchers, in fact, suggest that boys are almost equally as vulnerable to incest as are girls (Tower, 1989). Given that an alarming amount of child sexual assault occurs within families of all types, we will discuss this issue in more detail in Chapter 12.

It is estimated that fewer than 10 percent of all rape victims are men (Renzetti & Curran, 1992). According to most data, it appears that men are at greatest risk for being raped when they are incarcerated. In addition, men are more often attacked by multiple assailants and are held captive longer than women who are raped (Rathus et al., 1997). Add to this the fact that men are even less likely than women to report that they have been raped. And gay men, like their heterosexual counterparts, seldom report this type of victimization. Contrary to popular wisdom about men, rape, and sexual orientation, the majority of men who are raped are raped by a heterosexual male whose motives tend to be the same as of those who rape women: domination, control, sadism, and degradation.

Although rare, there are reported cases of rape committed by women. Most often, this type of rape involves a woman (or women) helping a man (or men) sexually assault another woman (for example, by holding the woman down while she is raped). There are also reported cases in which men have been raped by women.

Contrary to what some people believe, rape is not about sexual arousal and desire. Rather, it is about anger, sadism, domination, and the violent abuse of power. Regardless of who the victim is, it is an act of violence, an attempted or completed sexual assault instigated by one or more persons against another human being (Doyle & Paludi, 1998). Thus, perhaps more important than knowing exactly how many rapes occur is an understanding that official data on rape can be and often is distorted by a variety of factors that result in underreporting or nonreporting and that rape is about the violent use and abuse of power.

Sexual Responsibility

Women and men living around the world today are perhaps more challenged in their exploration and enjoyment of sexuality than at any other time in human history. **Sexually transmitted diseases (STDs),** diseases acquired primarily through sexual contact, are fairly common in today's society. It is estimated that approximately 333 million people worldwide are stricken with curable STDs each year. In the United States, an estimated 10 million to 12 million new cases are reported each year to the disease control centers; a number roughly 80 times higher than new cases of tuberculosis, HIV infection, and AIDS combined. Some experts say that the United States is experiencing an epidemic of STDs in poor, underserved areas of the country that rivals that of some developing countries. However, the risk is not limited to this population. Recent data show that STDs are becoming increasingly common among teenagers, including those who are white and middle class. The most common STDs are chlamydia, genital herpes, genital warts, gonorrhea, hepatitis B, human papilloma virus, syphilis, and AIDS (Centers for Disease Control, 1998; Stolberg, 1998).

HIV/AIDS is perhaps the most deadly STD to date. It is a threat to female and male, young and old, rich and poor, heterosexual and homosexual of every race and ethnicity around the world. Experts estimate that close to one million people in the United States are infected with the **human immunodeficiency virus (HIV),** the virus believed to be the main cause of AIDS, almost all of whom will eventually develop AIDS. Identified in 1981, **acquired immune deficiency syndrome (AIDS)** is a viral syndrome, or group of diseases, that destroys the body's immune system, thereby rendering the victim susceptible to all kinds of infections and diseases. Because the body is unable to fight off these infections and diseases, they eventually kill the victim. One of the primary ways in which HIV/AIDS is transmitted is through having unprotected sex with someone infected with the virus.

Public figures such as Earvin "Magic" Johnson, the late Arthur Ashe, and the national heavyweight boxer Tommy Morrison who have contracted AIDS have heightened our sensitivities to the problem of STDs generally and AIDS specifically. As a result, city and state govern-ments are increasingly attempting to promote safer and more responsible sexual behaviors. Because of the risks to physical and mental health, because the threat of AIDS and other STDs hangs over every sexual decision we make, we must become more knowledgeable about them and more responsible to ourselves and others in our sexual behaviors (Boston Women's Health Book Collective, 1992). Research shows that certain kinds of behavior place people at greater risk for AIDS and other STDs than do other kinds of behavior. The highest-risk behavior for STDs, including AIDS, is sharing virus-infected semen through oral, genital, or anal sex, followed by behavior related to intravenous drug use and the sharing of needles between drug users. In addition, people who have multiple partners over their lifetimes are at far greater risk than are those who have few sexual partners. Right now, the most basic ways to control the spread of STDs, including AIDS, is believed to be through avoiding high-risk sex (either through abstinence, exclusive relationships, or the use of latex condoms) and through careful monitoring of transfusions of blood and other body fluids.

In the final analysis, each of us has a responsibility to engage in sex in a manner that is protective of both our own and our partners' health and well-being. However, experts in the field argue that there must also be institutional change. For example, prevention programs for AIDS and all other STDs must not only focus on changing individual sexual behavior but also include improvements in the status of women and people of color so that they have more control over when and how sex takes place and better medical care for all people with either HIV/AIDS or other sexually transmitted diseases that can increase the risk of HIV transmission.

The Look of Human Sexuality in the Twenty-First Century

Technological advances, particularly in the fields of communication and entertainment, have broadened the sexual marketplace and played a significant role in the changing meanings of and conventions surrounding sexual intimacy in this country. Without a doubt, our sexual futures will be very different from our pasts, requiring fundamental changes in sexual values and attitudes. The fact that sex is so accessible to children today raises issues far too important for a society to ignore. A fundamental sexual issue in the next century will center on sex in cyberspace, particularly as it impacts children. Some researchers have identified a definite link between cybersex, pornography, pedophilia, and even prostitution involving both children and adults, and they view these types of commercial sex as the most pressing sexual problems we will carry into the next millenium.

As we move into the next century, the struggles between the powerful and the less powerful within the realm of sexuality will continue to focus on issues such as who has the power and right to define pornography and obscenity in art and popular music and who has the power and right to control the reproductive rights of women and people of color. If sexual exploitation of all kinds is to change, the problem of unequal power between women and men will need to be challenged and addressed. We will have to challenge many of our deep-seated beliefs about gender as well as the social institutions that continue to cast women in an inferior role. Until we do, all of the old problems and a host of new ones will continue to haunt us in the twenty-first century.

Key Points to Remember

1. Human sexuality is an important topic of analysis in sociology because it links the personal and the social, the individual and society. Human sexuality is deeply embedded in the structural, cultural, economic, and political fabric of the societies in which we live. Race, class, and gender are important categories of experience that impact and shape human sexuality.

2. Although all humans share the same anatomic structures and physiological capacities for sexual activities and pleasure, societies differ widely in their sexual practices, customs, and attitudes.

3. The sexual behavior and attitudes of Americans in the 1990s has become increasingly public and politicized. There is some debate, however, as to whether a sexual revolution has occurred in U.S. society. Recent sex research suggests that Americans are not the promiscuous sexual beings relentlessly portrayed in the media.

4. Like other behaviors, our sexual behavior is guided by cultural scripts that are similar to the scripts that guide the actions of actors. The major sources of sexual learning are the family, peer groups, popular culture, and the mass media.

5. A major portion of our sexual identities rests upon sex-role categories. In U.S. society, our cultural system recognizes only two sexes: female and male. However, some cultures provide the opportunity for alternative gender identities and roles (including a third sex) for people who do not fit into the traditional sex categories of female and male. It is difficult to measure sexual orientation. Nevertheless, most sex researchers continue to use the rigid and limited categories of heterosexual, homosexual, bisexual, and more recently, transsexual.

6. Millions of women in the United States and around the world have suffered or will suffer some form of sexual assault. Sexual assault takes many forms, the most common of which are rape (date, acquaintance, and marital) and incest.

7. HIV/AIDS and other STDs are fairly common in today's society. Certain behaviors place people at greater risk for these STDs than do others. The challenge is to engage in responsible sex in a manner that is protective of both our own and our partners' health and well-being.

8. The issues and concerns around sexuality in the twenty-first century will include the increasing commercialization of sex, including sex in cyberspace.

Key Terms

human sexuality
sexual revolution
sexual evolution
sexual scripts
sexual identity
sexual orientation
heterosexuality
homosexuality

bisexuals
homophobia
biphobia
transsexuals
transgendered
sexual assault
rape
acquaintance rape

incest
sexually transmitted diseases (STDs)
human immunodeficiency virus (HIV)
acquired immune deficiency syndrome (AIDS)

Key People

Dr. Nafis Sadik
Carol Bellamy

Dr. Hiroshi Nakajima
Alfred Kinsey

Phillip Blumstein
Pepper Schwartz

Questions for Review and Discussion

1. Has there been a sexual revolution in the United States? Would you agree that we are currently witnessing a second sexual revolution? What changes in sexual attitudes and behaviors have you observed among your peers?

2. Consider the environment on your campus. What are the general attitudes and behaviors toward sexual orientations that are not heterosexual? Is there a lesbian and gay student organization on your campus? How do you explain the general political and social climate in regard to issues of sexual orientation?

3. Should condoms be distributed in schools? Can this be considered a way of dealing with sexual responsibility among youth? Is there a high school in your city that distributes condoms? Take a position pro or con, and support it with sociological data.

4. Some sociologists, speaking of sexual assault, have suggested that the United States has a "rape culture." What does this mean? Do you agree or disagree? Why? Provide evidence for your position.

For Further Reading

Bart, Pauline, and Eileen Geil Morgan. (Eds). 1993. *Violence Against Women: The Bloody Footprints.* Newbury Park, CA: Sage. An anthology about various types of crimes perpetrated against women and the cultural, structural, and institutional supports for them.

Ehrenreich, Barbara, Hess, Elizabeth, and Gloria Jacobs. 1986. *Re-making Love: The Feminization of Sex.* Garden City, NY: Doubleday-Anchor. The authors explore the implications of the alleged sexual revolution for women and men and connect changes in sexual behavior to the development of the feminist movement.

Hatfield, Elaine, and Richard L. Rapson. 1996. *Love and Sex: Cross-Cultural Perspectives.* Boston: Allyn & Bacon. A delightful book on the topics of passionate love and sexuality from a multidisciplinary perspective.

Michael, Robert T., Gagnon, John J., Laumann, Edward O., and Gina Kolata. 1994. *Sex in America: A Definitive Survey.* Boston: Little, Brown. A general-interest version of a comprehensive sex survey conducted by the authors. The survey is full of illuminating information on the sexual habits, attitudes, and practices of Americans today.

Sociology through Literature

Lee, Harper. 1960. *To Kill a Mockingbird.* New York: Harper & Row. This classic novel presents a powerful portrayal of childhood innocence and a denunciation of racism and bigotry. It focuses on a southern white lawyer's defense of an African American man accused of raping a white woman.

Lawrence, D.H. 1994. *Lady Chatterly's Lover.* London: Penguin (Original publication 1928). Constance Chatterley, a woman of warm impulses with a physically impotent husband, finds refuge from his demanding individualism and class snobbery by having a sexual relationship with his gameskeeper. A major theme of this novel is that sex without love is a perversion.

Internet Resources

http://www.pilot.infi.net/~susanf/ablinks2.htm
A link to a variety of resources on incest and other forms of sexual assault.

http://www.cdc.gov/nchstp/hiv_aids/statisti.htm
The Centers for Disease Control basic statistics on HIV and AIDS.

8

Deviance

AGENT OF CHANGE: DR. JACK KEVORKIAN

On June 4, 1990, a Michigan pathologist named Dr. Jack Kevorkian sparked a national debate on the controversial subject of physician-assisted suicide by attending the death of a fifty-four-year-old Alzheimer's patient, Janet Adkins, from Portland, Oregon. Adkins pressed a button on a machine that Kevorkian had developed, injecting lethal drugs into her body. Kevorkian was charged with murder, but the charges against him were dropped after a state judge ruled that Michigan had no law against assisted suicide. In October 1991, he attended the deaths of Michigan residents Sherry Miller, age forty-three, who inhaled carbon monoxide, and Marjorie Wantz, age fifty-eight, who used a machine similar to the one Adkins used. Although Michigan suspended Kevorkian's medical license, a state judge dismissed murder charges against him, again ruling that Michigan had no law against assisted suicide. Media accounts of these events referred to the machines used in these deaths as "the suicide machine" and to Kevorkian as "Dr. Death."

In 1992, Kevorkian attended five other deaths. In 1993, a temporary ban on assisted suicide passed by the Michigan Legislature went into effect. During the first year the ban was in effect, Kevorkian attended twelve more deaths and was charged with assisting in several of them. When arrested, he refused to post bond, was jailed, and went on a hunger strike. He was later released from jail after a supporter posted bond for him. The charges were dismissed when Wayne County Circuit Court Judge Cynthia Stephens, acting on a challenge filed by the American Civil Liberties Union, ruled that Michigan's assisted suicide law was unconstitutional. State Attorney General Frank Kelley appealed the decision and the Michigan Court of Appeals ordered the state's ban to remain in effect during the appeal; the Court of Appeals eventually found the ban invalid on technical grounds.

In 1994, Kevorkian attended yet another death. During that year, although two assisted suicide charges against him were also dismissed, Kevorkian was tried in a third case which ended in his acquittal. In December 1994, the Michigan Supreme Court overruled the state's Court of Appeals, stating that the ban, although now expired, was constitutional and that, in any event, assisted suicide was illegal in Michigan under common law. This ruling led to the reinstatement of murder charges against Kevorkian. Following a widely publicized trial, a jury acquitted him of all charges. In November 1998, Kevorkian, who has admitted to assisting 130 people to die, again challenged the Michigan legal system when he gave the CBS News show *60 Minutes* a videotape of himself administering a lethal injection to Thomas Youk, who was suffering from Lou Gehrig's disease. The Michigan authorities subpoenaed the tape and charged him with murder. He was found guilty of second-degree murder.

Kevorkian has supporters and detractors. On the one hand, he is credited with forcing the medical profession and the public at large to confront the ethical issues surrounding the desire of terminally ill people to die with dignity. Kevorkian and others in favor of physician-assisted suicide argue that terminally ill people should not have to suffer and that chronic, debilitating illnesses make life untenable, especially when chronic pain cannot be relieved. Those in favor of physician-assisted suicide believe that people should be allowed to die with dignity and to choose the time and place of their own deaths. On the other hand, critics of Kevorkian maintain that assisted suicide is contrary to natural law and, if permitted, could easily lead society down a slippery slope to the point where the most vulnerable members of society— such as the elderly, the poor, the depressed, and people who have disabilities—would be encouraged to end their lives prematurely. In fact, critics of Kevorkian point out that autopsies have shown that in a few of the deaths he attended, the individuals who died had no detectable physical ailments (Betzold, 1997).

Source: Some of the information is from M. Betzold. 1997. "The Selling of Doctor Death." *New Republic* (May 26): 22–28.

Understanding Deviance

Conflicting views on physician-assisted suicide can help us to understand some of the complexities surrounding deviance. Sociologists define **deviance** as the violation of cultural norms. The violation of norms considered important to a group or society generally results in some kind of social reaction, generally a negative one (Clinard & Meier, 1995). Does physician-assisted suicide violate a social norm, and are physicians who, like Kevorkian, help someone to die deviants? The prosecutors in Michigan believed physical-assisted suicide violated one of their state's social norms and that Kevorkian was indeed a deviant and a criminal. However, until

his recent conviction, in three other separate trials, three different juries disagreed with state officials and acquitted him. Clearly, then, there is more to deviance than just violating a social norm. Several factors must be considered when determining whether any given behavior is deviant. Among these are the norm itself, the actor, the time, the place, and the audience.

Norms

Recall that we discussed in Chapter 4 the normative component of culture, defining norms as the rules or standards and expectations that guide people's behavior. As you will recall, norms differ in the degree to which people in a society feel compelled to conform to them as well as in the strength and intensity of societal reactions to their violation. For example, in Japan, local officials told a father that naming his son Akuma (Devil) didn't conform to social norms and that the child could face discrimination in the future. The father believed that the name would make his son unforgettable, but Judge Hiroshi Tojo said, "Naming a son Akuma is an abuse of the parents' right to give a name. It violates family name registration law" ("Couple Break," 1994, p. 8). Thus, some norms are considered important enough to be codified into laws, whose violation is then considered a crime. We therefore need to distinguish between deviance and crime. Deviance is a broader concept, referring to all norm violations, whereas **crime** is more narrowly defined as the violation of a law. In Kevorkian's case, three juries found him not guilty of violating Michigan law, but many of his medical colleagues felt he had violated medical norms. In October 1995, the general counsel of the American Medical Association (AMA) wrote a letter to Michigan Attorney General Frank Kelley in which he said:

> The AMA established the Code of Ethics for the medical profession. One of the fundamental principles of that code is that physicians must not act with the intent of causing the death of their patients. Physician-assisted suicide is simply incompatible with the physician's role as healer. When faced with patients who are terminally ill and suffering, physicians must relieve their suffering by providing adequate comfort care. Responsible persons may have differing views concerning the propriety of physician-assisted suicide. However, no civilized society should condone assisted suicide as practiced by Jack Kevorkian. Mr. Kevorkian's actions are not those of a primary treating physician. Rather, he serves merely as a reckless instrument of death. (Ohio Right to Life, 1995, p. 1)

Time

What is considered deviance varies from one historical period to another. In the past, it was considered unthinkable for a physician to provide the means to end one's life. However, with the rise of the life-prolonging power of modern medical technology, new concerns have arisen. This technology, which in many cases can delay death but not restore health, can leave patients in a situation that to them and to many observers is far worse than death itself—a seemingly endless period of suffering, pain, and despair (Clark & Liebig, 1996). These changes in medical technology gave rise to a right-to-die movement in the United States (Glick, 1992). In 1991, Washington State voters narrowly defeated legislation aimed at allowing physician-assisted suicide. The following year, voters in California rejected a similar proposal. Although these measures lost, they paved the way for a successful ballot measure three years later in Oregon, making it the first time in U.S. history that voters sanctioned state approval of physician-assisted suicide. However, because of court challenges by opponents of the measure, the law was not put into effect. Voters were given the opportunity to repeal the measure in 1997, but they again reaffirmed their support for the practice by a 60 to 40 percent margin.

Place

Whether a given behavior is deviant or not varies from one place to another. Although physicians can be prosecuted in the United States for helping a patient to die, the Dutch have largely accepted the practice. Beginning in the 1970s and culminating in a 1993 law, court decisions in the Netherlands formed a consensus that physicians would not be prosecuted for aiding a patient's death if they acted in accordance with certain specified conditions: the presence of a confirmed terminal diagnosis; the patient's unwaivering desire, confirmed in writing, of her or his wish to die; the presence of unbearable and incurable physical suffering; and a second medical opinion (DeSpelder & Strickland, 1996).

Actor

Even when behavior is defined as deviance, it does not necessarily follow that the person engaging in that behavior will be considered a deviant. The actor's attributes, such as age, sex, race, ethnicity, social class, and physical and mental states, play a significant role in judgments as to what constitutes deviance. Thus, some people's behavior is considered appropriate or less threatening, whereas the same behavior engaged in by others is considered deviant. For example, Kevorkian was tried and acquitted on three different occasions of helping people to die. His behavior was judged in the context of his medical expertise. However, in another case in which the outcome was the same, the reaction to the actor was quite different. In March 1993, Robert Latimer, a Canadian farmer, put his twelve-year-old daughter, Tracy, who suffered from advanced cerebral palsy that left her body severely twisted and caused her great pain, in his pickup truck, leaving the engine running until the cab was filled with carbon monoxide and she died. Canadian juries twice convicted Latimer of second-degree murder. The first conviction was overturned on a legal technicality (DePalma, 1997); the judge in the second case, believing that the father acted out of love, sentenced Latimer to one year in jail. His decision provoked a national outcry, and an appeals court later overruled him and ordered the father to serve at least 10 years in prison.

Audience

The power to define which behavior is acceptable or not is an important dimension of deviance. People who challenge the status quo, like many of the agents of social change depicted throughout this textbook, are often defined as troublemakers or criminals by those in power who feel threatened by their actions, at the same time, they are hailed as heroes by those whose needs they champion. As the issue of physician-assisted suicide clearly indicates, there are times when there is no clear consensus as to whether a given behavior is deviant or not. Is Kevorkian an unusually clever serial killer, who takes pleasure in assisting people to die, as some have suggested, or is he a compassionate humanitarian performing a much-needed service? What behavior is defined as deviance and which actors are perceived as deviants depend, to a large extent, on who is doing the defining and who has the power to make the definitions stick. In a 1996 Gallup poll, 75 percent of Americans said they favored permitting a doctor to end a patient's life. Another poll taken on June 26, 1997, the day that the United States Supreme Court upheld the rights of states to prohibit physician-assisted suicide, showed that support for physician-assisted suicide had dropped to 57 percent (International Anti-Euthanasia Task Force, 1997). Whether proponents of physician-assisted suicide will ever garner enough support to make it legal throughout the country is unclear.

On the basis of the above discussion, several important conclusions can be drawn. First, no behavior is inherently deviant. Rather, deviance is *socially constructed,* that is, it is a matter of definition. As illustrated in the Cultural Snapshot box about cannibalism, people define behavior as deviant or not based on their views of what is good or bad and right or wrong at a given time. Even a behavior as serious as taking another person's life may evoke quite different reactions. As the current political unrest in the Mideast, Africa, Ireland, and Yugoslavia clearly illustrate, one country's freedom fighters are another country's terrorists. Thus, the label *deviance* is conferred upon a particular behavior by how people react toward it. Second, deviance is relative. What is considered deviant at one time or in one place may not be deviant at another time or in another place. Finally, defining whether something is deviant depends to a large extent on the social context within which the behavior occurs. Baseball fans often see their favorite players spitting as they come to the plate. Little is said about this behavior. Yet, if it occurs on a public street, an individual may be fined for this same behavior in many cities. Similarly, for 364 days of the year, public drunkenness is considered unacceptable, yet it is often tolerated, even expected, on New Year's Eve.

Applying the Sociological Imagination

Survey some of your fellow students about the kinds of behavior they consider deviant. Did any of your respondents include physician-assisted suicide in their lists of deviant behaviors? If not, ask them if they consider physician-assisted suicide deviant. How much agreement and disagreement did you find? Were any behaviors such as financial fraud, insider stock trading, price fixing, or provision of unsafe working conditions noticeably absent from these lists? How might you explain your findings?

Cultural Snapshot

Cannibalism

On October 13, 1972, an airplane carrying fifteen members of an amateur rugby team from Uruguay and twenty-five of their relatives and friends crashed in the Andes mountains. Twenty-seven passengers survived the initial crash, expecting to be rescued quickly. That was not to be; seventy days later, only sixteen remained alive. Their small supply of chocolate and wine, which some had purchased at the airport's duty-free shop, was quickly consumed. The intense cold and starvation began to take its toll. As time passed, several in the group began to realize that their only chance of survival was to eat the flesh of those who had died in the crash. Their bodies lay in the snow near the crash site, perfectly preserved by the bitter cold. Canessa, a medical student, was the first to broach the subject of cannibalism, asserting that the bodies were no longer people; the souls were gone; the bodies were simply meat, like the dead flesh of cattle that they ate at home, he reasoned. The meat was essential to their survival. At first it was merely a discussion, then as days passed and their conditions worsened, serious deliberations began. Some brought God into the picture, arguing that He wanted them to live, that He had provided the bodies so they could. Others agreed that it would not be wrong, but said that they themselves could never do it. Finally, Canessa went outside, cut some strips, and left them to dry on the roof of the plane. Later, summoning every ounce of courage he had, he forced himself to swallow a piece. Another friend did the same, barely managing to wash it down with snow. The next morning, on the repaired radio, they heard that the air force

had ended its search for them. Now their only hope was to send the fittest for help, but none were strong enough to try. Everyone knew there was only one way for them to regain their strength.

Canessa and another survivor went outside and began cutting pieces of the dead flesh. Although some managed to eat the flesh, others could not overcome their feelings of revulsion and refused to eat. The first corpses they ate were those of the crew, strangers to them. Over time, they developed a set of rules. Women's bodies were not eaten; no one could be forced to eat; the meat would be rationed so that only those going for help could eat more than the others. No one had to eat a friend or relative; certain body parts were not eaten. When they had regained sufficient strength, three young men left in search of help. Ten days later, they found a shepherd's hut. Four days before Christmas, the remaining survivors were rescued. When the survivors told their story, there was shock and horror, mixed with fascination.

What is your reaction to the decisions made by this group? Putting yourself in their place, how would you have reacted? How do you think most of the people you know would have reacted? Why? From a sociological perspective, was this behavior deviant? Explain.

Source: Adapted and summarized by permission of the author from Chapter 23 of Henslin, J.M. 1997. "The Survivors of the F-227," in *Down to Earth Sociology: Introductory Readings* (10th ed.). New York: Free Press, pp. 251–259. Copyright © 1991 by James M. Henslin.

The Range and Variability of Deviance

A major difficulty in studying deviance is that there is relatively little agreement on what exactly constitutes it. As our definition of *deviance* implies, people are typically defined as deviant as a result of their behaviors, which can range from the relatively trivial, such as dying their hair green, to the extremely serious, such as violence and murder. However, people can also be considered deviant due to their beliefs or condition (Adler & Adler, 1997).

People who hold extreme, unpopular, or unusual religious or political beliefs are often considered deviant. In 1996, media attention focused on the religious cult Heaven's Gate after thirty-nine of its members participated in a mass suicide. The suicide and the rationale presented for it—the group believed that it was time for the arrival of a spacecraft from the Level Above Human to take them home to Their World—received considerable condemnation. Likewise, people who advocate the use of violence or extremism to obtain a political goal are usually viewed as deviants by the general public. These individuals have an achieved deviant status—they have earned the deviant label as a result of their actions or attitudes. Some people, however, are ascribed a deviant status; that is, they are regarded as deviant simply because of their condition, not because of any action on their part. People who are extremely tall, short, or overweight; who have some physical deformity or disability; or who are mentally ill are frequently regarded as deviant. For example, in the fact-based film *The Elephant Man,* the character John Merrick suffered from a rare disfiguring disease which caused people to turn away from him in revulsion and to consider him as outside normal society. Erving Goffman (1963) argued that this latter category is better characterized as a **stigma,** or an attribute that discredits people, than deviance. According to Goffman, the label *deviant* should be reserved for those people who voluntarily and deliberately violate social norms.

Once again, we can see in all these cases that there is nothing inherently deviant in these beliefs or conditions; rather "they become deviant through the result of a socially defining process that gives unequal weight to powerful and dominant groups in society" (Adler & Adler, 1997, p. 13). Additionally, the amount of deviance existing in society at any given time is a result of the level of social consensus. That consensus can change. Some social scientists, such as U.S. Senator Daniel Moynihan (1993, p. 17), have argued that at various times society "defines deviancy down," normalizing some behaviors that were considered intolerable in the past. Many people were quick to embrace this viewpoint. Critics of popular culture, for example, have attacked daytime talk shows for contributing to this process (see the Sociological Reflections box), arguing that when audiences get a steady diet of behaviors previously considered deviant, they come to assume that such behavior occurs far more frequently than it actually does and then begin to see it as part of the range of normative behavior.

Although there is general agreement about the process Moynihan described, critics such as Andrew Karmen (1994) argue that Moynihan focused only on behaviors that are "politically safe" (in terms of voter appeal), such as the increase in unmarried mothers and crime, and ignored others, such as abortion and the extension of gambling by many states in order to raise tax dollars. In addition, Karmen argued that Moynihan ignored a countervailing trend, "defining deviancy up," the process of discouraging, deterring, forbidding, and outlawing behaviors that used to be overlooked or tolerated. Karmen identified the increased attempts in the last three decades to control child abuse, domestic violence, date rape, hate crimes, sexual harassment, and police brutality as examples of a shift in a more egalitarian direction. By this he meant that the harmful behavior engaged in by people in positions of power and trust is no longer as tolerated as it was in the past.

Forms of Deviance

As we have seen, there is a wide variability in what is defined as deviance. In this section, we will explore three fairly common forms that deviance can take—crime, drug abuse, and deviance in families. Then we will explore some of the consequences of deviance for the social order, after which we will examine the various theories that attempt to explain deviant behavior. The three forms of deviance we will discuss here are not meant to include all deviance nor are they meant to be absolutist. People may disagree about some forms of behavior that we have defined as deviant or, for that matter, that we haven't. In particular, some readers may find it strange to see deviance in families, particularly spouse (partner) abuse, discussed here rather than, as is traditionally done, in the chapter on marriages and families. We have included it here for two reasons. First, we want to emphasize the

Do TV Talk Shows Promote Deviance?

Over the past several years, a controversy has raged over the content of daytime talk shows. On the one side, politicians, religious leaders, and even sponsors have launched attacks on what they call the cultural rot of TV talk shows (Saltzman, 1996). Their criticism focuses on programs that present sleazy and tabloid sensationalism which, they claim, makes the abnormal seem normal and provides audiences with perverse role models. Disenchanted former talk-show host Jane Whitney (1995) described the competitive pressure to produce shows such as "My Wife is Obsessed With Pornography," "I Let My Husband Cheat Because I'm Pregnant," "My Mother Is a Slut," and "Sex for Points." Whitney observed that guests were rarely chided for confessing in public and that they were routinely commended for their "courage" in coming clean—as if they had performed some public service. Criticism of talk TV gained momentum when, three days after the taping of a Jenny Jones show, Jonathan Schmitz, a twenty-six-year-old who had a history of manic depression, shot the gay admirer revealed to him on the show. The jury convicted him of second-degree murder but felt that the show had exacerbated his emotional state.

Journalism professor Joe Saltzman (1996) argues that there is another side to this issue that does not get acknowledged very readily. He argues that, contrary to the critics' opinions, many of these programs do not deal with outrageous topics but instead with parent–child relations, dating, marital relations, sexual activity, reconciliations, physical health, abuse, alienation, physical appearance, and criminal acts—what he calls the stuff of office talk and kitchen chats across the country. Thus, he argues, what people like about TV talk shows is that the guests are like the people viewers know at work, bowling alleys, lunch counters, and retail stores in communities across the country. And viewers can see the kinds of groups they don't see on TV until they are sanitized and homogenized: poor whites, Latinas/os, Asians, and African Americans.

Conduct a content analysis of daytime talk shows. Find out what the show's topics are and who the guests are. What do you observe about the audience reactions to these topics and guests? Do your findings add support to the critics' arguments about the impact of TV talk shows regarding what is normal or acceptable, or do they provide more support to Saltzman's arguments that they more accurately reflect the general population?

---

fact that deviance occurs in all institutional settings, including families. Second, although rates of spouse (partner) abuse are relatively high in the United States, this should not be construed to imply that such abuse is in any way part of normative family behavior. Thus, our purpose here is simply to provide a brief look at some of the various forms that deviance takes and some of the likely settings within which deviance can occur. Although crime represents only one form of deviance, it is perhaps the most widespread form and the form that generates the most concern and fear in the general population. Thus, it is appropriate that we begin this discussion with crime.

Crime

As we noted earlier in this chapter, crime is a violation of the law; yet because crime encompasses such a wide range of behaviors, further distinctions are necessary. The first distinction is made by law enforcement officials, who categorize crimes into *crimes against people,* or *violent crimes,* which involve the threat of injury or the threat (or use) of force against someone, and *property crimes,* which are aimed at gaining or destroying property but do not involve the threat of injury or the threat (or use) of force against intended victims. Violent crimes include murder, forcible rape and attempted rape, robbery, and

Former University of California at Berkeley math professor, Theodore John Kaczynski, is escorted into the federal courthouse in Helena, Montana, after his arrest. Kaczynski, known as the Unabomber, evaded authorities for 18 years, during which time he was responsible for the deaths and injuries of a number of people.

aggravated assault. Property crimes include burglary, larceny-theft, motor vehicle theft or attempted theft, and arson. The media commonly refer to these eight categories as "street crimes," whereas the law enforcement community calls them index offenses. The Federal Bureau of Investigation (FBI) gathers data on these index offenses from official law enforcement agencies across the United States monthly and annually and publishes the results as the *Uniform Crime Reports*. A second perspective on crime is provided by the National Crime Victimization Survey in which details about crime come directly from victims (see the Data Box).

The criminal justice system, charged with prosecuting and punishing offenders, uses another way to differentiate crimes. It recognizes two types of crimes. **Felonies** are crimes considered serious offenses, such as murder, rape, assault, and robbery, which are punishable by heavy fines and/or imprisonment for a year or more. **Misdemeanors** are less serious offenses, such as drunkenness and disturbing the peace, which are punishable by small fines and less than a year in prison. A third distinction is made by sociologists and others who study crime; they look at the characteristics of violators and the settings within which crimes occur. Typically included in these categories are elite deviance, political or governmental crime, organized crime (popularly thought of as "the Mafia" or "the syndicate" as depicted in films such as *The Godfather*), street crime, juvenile delinquency, and victimless crimes. Elite deviance, which encompasses white-collar and corporate crime, and political or governmental crime are not as readily visualized or understood by the general population nor are these acts of deviance as widely studied as are street crimes. Thus, we will focus most of our attention in this section on these two categories.

Elite Deviance   The concept of **elite deviance** encompasses wrongdoing by wealthy and powerful individuals and organizations (Simon, 1996). Traditionally, most research on crime involved studies of street crimes and, thus, unintentionally, contained an inherent class bias that neglected wrongdoing among persons of the upper socioeconomic classes. Edward Sutherland (1949) was one of the first to call attention to this class bias in the study of crime. He coined the term **white-collar crime** to refer to crimes committed by persons of respectability and high status in the course of their occupations. Typical examples of white-collar crime include embezzlement, fraud, bribery, and employee theft. Sutherland was also concerned with what has come to be know as **corporate crime,** illegal acts committed by company officials. His analysis focused on violations of laws involving restraint of trade; false advertising; infringement of patents, trademarks, and copyrights; "unfair labor practices" as defined by the National Labor Relations Board; financial fraud; and other violations of trust. More recent investigations have broadened these lists to include such behaviors as the manufacture and selling of unsafe prod-

ucts, violations of environmental regulations, and providing unsafe working conditions for employees. Although some of these actions are not technically illegal, they are regarded by many people as unethical or immoral and, hence, deviant (Simon, 1996).

White-collar and corporate crime, often referred to as occupational crime, are significant because they counter the misperceptions of many people who believe that crime is a problem more among the lower classes. Although "street crimes" generally generate the most publicity and thus contribute to the public's misperception of who the criminals are, white-collar and corporate crime are far more costly and, in the long term, probably produce more harm and encompass many more victims. Because many occupational deviants occupy positions of trust and leadership in our society—they may be businesspeople, lawyers, doctors, police, or therapists—their acts of deviance may be more profound and damaging than is generally acknowledged. For example, in his book *Elite Deviance*, David Simon (1996,

p. 35) speaks of three types of harms brought about by the acts of elites and/or the organizations they head:

1. **Physical harms.** These include death and/or physical injury or illness. In 1996, there were 6,112 fatal occupational injuries and 3.9 million disabling injuries (U.S. Bureau of the Census, 1998). According to the AFL-CIO, "The median penalty paid by an employer during the years 1972–1990 following an incident resulting in death or serious injury of a worker was just $480" (quoted in Reiman, 1998, p. 77). For example, during the 1970s, the Firestone Tire Company continued to sell its 500-type belted radial tire even after company tests revealed a serious problem with tire separation. A House of Representatives committee reported that Firestone 500 separations "had caused thousands of accidents, hundreds of injuries, and 34 known fatalities" (quoted in Simon, 1996, p. 126).

2. **Financial harms.** Among these are robbery, fraud, and various "scams" not legally defined as fraud but which, nevertheless, result in consumers and investors being deprived of their funds without receiving goods or services for which they contracted. Using a variety of sources, Jeffrey Reiman (1998) estimated the cost of white-collar crime to be $208.5 billion in 1994. He observed that this amount was more than 7,000 times the total amount taken in all bank robberies in the United States in 1994 and more than 13 times the total amount stolen in all thefts reported in the FBI Uniform Crime Reports for that year. For example, it is estimated that at least $100 million of the $1 billion spent annually on health care in this country is lost to fraud. Physician dishonesty includes such practices as "unbundling," which occurs when a doctor charges a patient individually for each part of a procedure that should be charged as one procedure. Unbundling increases the price that a patient and/or the patient's insurance company has to pay the physician (Salinger, 1997).

3. **Moral harm.** Here the deviant behavior of elites forms a negative role model that encourages deviance, distrust, cynicism, and/or alienation among nonelites. In a poll, Lou Harris found that by 1988, 82 percent of the public expressed the belief that business is motivated primarily by greed. Furthermore, seventy percent of Americans now claim that there are no living heroes (Simon, 1996).

Although white-collar and corporate crime are generally more profitable than many street crimes, they are less likely to be detected or punished and, as Table 8.1 shows, when there are convictions, they are likely to result in considerably lighter sentences than is the case for street crimes. There are several reasons for this that relate back to our earlier discussion of the relativity of deviance. First, since elite deviants (the actors) are usually white, middle and upper class, and well educated, they do not fit the widely accepted profile of a "criminal type." Thus, much of their behavior simply is ignored. Second, since white-collar and corporate crimes often involve many parties at different levels, it

TABLE 8.1 ◑ Sentences for Different Classes of Crime (Preliminary) (1994)

	Percentage Sentenced to Prison	Average Sentence (in months)	Average Time Served (in months)
Crimes of the poor			
Robbery	89%	94.6	56.2
Burglary	96%	59.7	23.9
Larceny	31%	25.0	11.3
Motor vehicle theft	77%	86.1	21.3
Crimes of the affluent			
Regulatory offenses	46%	31.7	19.2
Fraud, excluding tax fraud	56%	22.1	15.1
Tax law violation, including tax fraud	37%	15.7	14.0
Embezzlement	40%	14.3	9.0

Source: Adapted from Maguire, K. and Pastore, A.L. (Eds.) 1996. *Sourcebook of Criminal Justice Statistics,* 1995. Washington, DC: U.S. Government Printing Office: Table 5.21, p. 470; Table 5.24, p. 473; Table 5.26, p. 475.

may be difficult to affix individual responsibility in any one case. Third, elite deviants are typically more powerful than their accusers and have the resources to make and argue their case more effectively. Thus, the audience rarely labels or penalizes the "neutralized" actor (Erman and Lundman,1996). Finally, it is only relatively recently that social scientists have begun to critically examine elite deviance in systematic ways. Perhaps over time, as more research on this behavior is conducted and disseminated, public opinion will force officials to make changes in the functioning of the criminal justice system.

Political Crime Sometimes referred to as governmental crime, **political crime** involves misconduct and crime committed within or against a political system. This category of deviance includes a wide range of activities involving the misuse of power. Many political crimes are economic in nature, involving such behavior as granting special favors to companies doing business with the government, ignoring the laws requiring competitive bidding on government contracts, and permitting expensive cost overruns on government contracts. However, other governmental crimes can involve crimes against persons and groups who are perceived as threats to those in power. This latter category can involve crimes of warfare and political assassinations against other nations. Acts against a government's own citizens can include violations of individual civil rights, including illegal surveillance by law enforcement agencies, infiltration of law-abiding political groups by government agencies, and denials of due process of law (Simon, 1996).

Societal reaction to political crime varies, depending on the context of the situation. In cases in which the public has come to see this behavior as common, such as abuses in campaign fundraising, there is relatively little overt reaction. However, if the violation is perceived as flagrant, such as the Watergate scandal or repeated acts of police brutality, there may be a strong reaction in the form of protests and demonstrations, as we have seen in large urban areas like Los Angeles or in the massive demonstrations that helped to end apartheid in South Africa. Political crime on any level can be extremely damaging to the social order. Ironically,

the motives behind many of these activities are to preserve law and order, but the outcome is likely to be the reverse of what is intended. When a government breaks the law, it sows contempt for its own institutions and teaches its citizens to become lawbreakers themselves.

Organized Crime **Organized crime** is crime perpetrated by an illegal business operation. This operation is "defined by a more or less formal structure that endures over time, is directed toward a common purpose by a recognizable leadership operating outside the law, is quite often based on family or ethnic identity, and is prepared to use violence or other means to promote and protect common interests and objectives" (Godson & Olson, 1997, pp. 123–124). Historically, organized criminal activities thrive where there is a demand for illegal goods and services such as prostitution, gambling, loan sharking (making loans at exorbitantly high interest rates to those otherwise without credit), bootlegging alcohol, drugs, and other contraband goods. In addition to conducting these illegal operations, organized crime often infiltrates legitimate businesses such as realty companies, food processing companies, waste disposal enterprises, construction and building services, bars and restaurants, vending machine businesses, casinos, and many others. Although these businesses may simply provide a front to launder money from illegal operations, they also provide major sources of legal revenue (Clinard & Meier, 1995).

Obtaining first-hand data on the characteristics of criminal organizations or their members is extremely difficult and often dangerous work. However, what the data we do have indicate are the existence of many criminal groups operating at all levels of society. These groups, by and large, have been dominated by immigrant and lower-class ethnic groups whose chances for upward mobility through legitimate means have historically been severely restricted. Thus, over time, Italian, Irish, and Jewish Americans were prominent in organized crime. Today, they are being joined or replaced by African Americans, Latinos, and Asians (Albanese, 1989). Organized crime also served what Daniel Bell (1953) called the "queer ladder of upward social mobility" for some immigrants (discussed in Salinger, 1997). Over several generations of a family's involvement, most of the children and grandchildren would become assimilated into the dominant culture and would not become involved in organized crime.

Street Crime   Of all crimes, violent and property crimes are the most feared. This is understandable given that such crimes generally involve direct contact between the criminal and the victim and can take place anywhere—on the street, in public spaces, and, most disturbing of all, in the privacy of our own homes. A common source of information on who commits street crime comes from arrest records. However, because many crimes are not reported and because not all reported crimes end in arrests, such statistics can provide only a broad indication of the characteristics of people who commit these crimes. Arrest rates vary by age, gender, and race. Those arrested are overwhelmingly male (80 percent) and young (44 percent under age twenty-five). In 1995, males were responsible for 85 percent of violent crime arrests and 73 percent of property crime arrests; females were most often arrested for larceny-theft offenses. The under-twenty-five age group accounted for 46 percent of the violent crime arrests and 58 percent of property crime arrests. Sixty-seven percent of arrestees were white, which included Latinos, 31 percent were black, and the remaining 2 percent were Native American or Asian American/Pacific Islander (U.S. Department of Justice, 1996).

Scholars do not agree on the reasons for these differential arrest patterns, but several factors are worthy of note. First, gender roles have traditionally been more restrictive for females than males, thus limiting their opportunities to commit certain crimes. However, in recent years, the increase in arrests of women have been greater than that for men, perhaps indicating both expanded opportunities and less reluctance on the part of law enforcement officials to arrest women. Second, adolescence and young adulthood seem to be crime-prone periods. When there is a decline in this segment of the population, there is often a corresponding decline in crime statistics. Third, the criminal justice system concentrates most of its resources on fighting street crimes in urban areas where African Americans and Latinos are more likely to live. Members of these groups are more likely than whites to be appre-

hended for committing the same offense. For example, according to the National Institute of Drug Abuse, in 1994, more whites (2.3 million) than blacks (789,000) and Latinos (307,000) combined reported using crack cocaine. However, between 1992 and 1994, whites accounted for fewer than 4 percent of all persons prosecuted in the federal courts for crack-related crimes (Weikel, 1995). Further, as we will see in Chapter 9, African Americans and other people of color are more likely than whites to be poor, unemployed, and discriminated against, conditions that foster deviance.

Juvenile Delinquency   Illegal or antisocial behavior on the part of a minor, a person who has not yet reached the age of eighteen, is termed **juvenile delinquency.** Much of this behavior involves *status offenses,* or behavior that only juveniles can commit, for example, being unmanageable at home or school or running away from home or truancy. With the help of family members, increasing maturity, and/or institutional intervention, many of these juveniles straighten out their lives and do not have any future contact with the criminal justice system. However, some juveniles engage in behavior that is comparable to adult criminality—vandalism, shoplifting, car theft, sexual offenses, and even assault and murder. Because of their youth, the courts generally treat them differently from adult offenders. But, in recent years, some young people have so shocked the community by the extreme violence of their behavior that prosecutors have responded by trying them as adults. A recent case in point is that of Michael Carneal, who at the age of fourteen, walked into his Paducah, Kentucky, high school and starting shooting, killing three classmates and seriously injuring five others. He pleaded guilty but mentally ill and will spend at least twenty-five years in prison.

Victimless Crimes   Illegal acts engaged in for the most part by consenting adults are referred to as **victimless crimes.** These are perhaps the most controversial crimes from a criminal justice perspective. Because people choose to participate in these activities—for example, drug use, illegal gambling, selling and buying pornography, and prostitution—the idea of victimization is somewhat ambiguous. In many instances, no one is hurt by these activities; some people are therefore in favor of decriminalizing them to free law enforcement personnel to pursue what are perceived as more serious transgressions. Additionally, the point is often made that the enforcement of these laws is biased in favor of the more powerful, as evidenced by the fact that prostitutes are far more likely to be arrested than those who patronize them. Those who oppose decriminalizing these behaviors argue that there are indeed victims because often naive and underaged individuals are lured into these activities by unscrupulous parties and others may turn to these activities because they have few other economic options. Opponents also argue that decriminalizing these behaviors would be tantamount to saying that they are socially acceptable.

Applying the Sociological Imagination

Check local newspapers over the past week. Were any cases of elite deviance, political crime, or victimless crime reported? If so, were the suspects described and treated the same as or differently from those suspected of street crimes? What were your reactions to these various reports? Should our approaches to these various types of crimes be changed? If so, what do you recommend and why?

Drugs

The issues surrounding drugs are controversial in our society and again reveal the relativity of deviance. Anthropologists report that the use of mood-altering agents appears to be a common characteristic among diverse human cultures. However, what agents are used and under what circumstances vary from society to society. For example, in India, there is a strong religious aversion to using alcohol in the higher castes, but it is common, even expected, that they use Bhang, a liquid form of marijuana mixed with milk or fruit juice at wedding celebrations (Clinard & Meier, 1995). Many Native American tribes routinely used a hallucinatory drug, peyote, in their religious rituals. In the United States

in the nineteenth century, it was legal and common for white middle-class individuals to use drugs such as cocaine, heroin, and opium. People could go to their pharmacies and purchase a mixture of heroin and alcohol to use in treating a wide variety of ailments. Beginning in 1886, Coca Cola drinkers got a boost from an active ingredient used in that drink—cocaine, a stimulant drug derived from the juice of the coca leaf. The cocaine was removed in the early 1900s. Today's Coke drinkers get their boost from caffeine, a milder, but legal, stimulant. As the twentieth century began, societal attitudes toward drugs began to shift. By this time, people were aware of some of the negative properties of these substances. More important, specific drugs came to be associated with groups that were feared or rejected by the larger society. For example, opium came to be associated with the immigrant Chinese who were brought to the United States after the Civil War to build the railroads. Thus, the use of some drugs came to be seen as a problem, and in 1914, the Harrison Act was passed restricting their use.

Today, we are frequently bombarded with mixed messages about these and other drugs. On the one hand, we hear reports about new wonder drugs that promise relief from all kinds of pain and suffering almost weekly. Many drugs are legal and can be purchased over the counter, such as alcohol, tobacco, tranquilizers for relaxation, and barbiturates for sleeping as well as a variety of pain-relieving products. On the other hand, drugs such as cocaine and crack came to be associated with inner city life (Musto, 1997) and have become the focus of the government's war on drugs. According to Marshall Clinard and Robert Meier (1995, p. 219), "Those drugs that are considered the most deviant are likely to be those most used among less powerful groups in this country, including lower-class individuals, those in socially marginal occupations, students, and those not fully assimilated to the United States."

When drugs are illegal, a profitable market for them often develops which, in turn, leads many drug users to commit crimes in order to support their habits. Further, the abuse of these drugs has devastating effects on individuals and whole communities. Estimates of the annual cost of illicit drug use in the United States range from

$76 billion to $150 billion (Angell & Kassifer, 1994). These estimates include the financial impact of premature death, illness, and lost wages because of drug abuse; drug-related crime; and drug-related law enforcement, including incarceration of offenders. In 1995, 14,218 deaths were directly attributed to drug-induced cause. Another 20,231 deaths are due to alcohol-induced causes (U.S. Bureau of Census, 1998). No statistic can hope to reveal the emotional and psychological costs of losing a loved one in this way.

Deviance in Families

One of the dangers of trying to assess deviance in families is the implicit assumption that everyone agrees on what constitutes normative family functioning and structure. That this is not the case is readily apparent in the current debate over family values and the tendency on the part of many people to mourn the loss of what they perceive to be a "golden age of the family." As we will see in Chapter 12, the family, as a social institution, has always taken a variety of forms and, like the rest of society, experiences periods of crisis and transformation. Despite these variations, however, there is general agreement that family members should be cared for and nourished; failure to do so is considered deviant.

Deviance in families is difficult to detect because it is often hidden from public view. However, one form of deviance has become especially visible in recent years, violence in families. Anyone, be it a parent, a child, a sibling, or an elderly member of the family, can be involved in various acts of family violence. In Chapter 7, we discussed one form of deviance this violence can take—coercive sexuality, which includes marital rape, incest, and other forms of sexual assault. We will now examine another type of family violence: spouse (partner) physical abuse.

Although both women and men can experience abuse in any intimate relationship, women have historically been the most likely recipients of physical abuse. In fact, through much of world history, such abuse was socially permissible. Consider that:

- under Roman law, a husband could chastise, divorce, or kill his wife for adultery, public drunkenness, and other behaviors.

- well into the seventeenth century, in many European countries, including England, a man could legally kill his wife for certain behaviors.
- English common law held that men had a legal right to beat their wives as long as the stick they used was no thicker than the husband's thumb.
- sexual assault as well as physical beatings were an integral part of the female slave experience in the United States.
- a nineteenth-century Mississippi court declared that husbands could use corporal punishment on their wives (M.A. Schwartz and B.M. Scott. 1997. *Marriages and Families: Diversity and Change,* p. 304. Adapted by permission of Prentice Hall, Upper Saddle River, New Jersey.)

It was only in 1883 that wife beating was banned in the United States. An examination of cultures around the world led anthropologist David Levinson (1981) to conclude that wife beating is the most common form of family violence. Considerable controversy erupted over some recent findings that suggest that wives and husbands are subject to their partners' violence in about equal numbers (Brush, 1990). Although these studies found that wives reported engaging in violent acts against their spouses, other data show that women make up 95 percent of the victims of spouse abuse (Clinard & Meier, 1995). Two explanations have been offered for these apparently contradictory findings. The first notes that regardless of who strikes the first blow, men are more likely to be bigger and stronger and, therefore, to inflict more damage. The second explanation focuses on the methodology used in most studies of abuse. Michael Johnson (1995) argues that spouse abuse takes two distinct forms. The first he calls *patriarchal terrorism,* which he describes as violence that is almost exclusive to men and that is used to gain and maintain total and absolute control over their female partners. Men's attempts at control over women may involve emotional, sexual, economic, and physical abuse and may extend from verbal assault to murder. This notion of patriarchal terrorism is consistent with the historical tradition of male dominance in the family. Johnson argues that women and men caught up in this behavior are not likely to

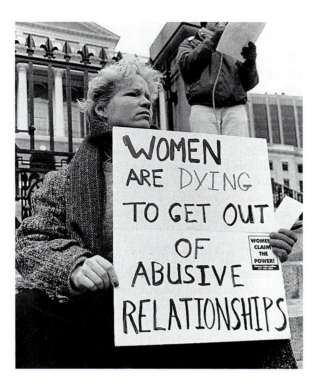

For a large part of U.S. history, physical abuse of women and children was treated as a normal part of family life. It is only in recent years that domestic violence has been legally recognized as deviance, punishable by the criminal justice system.

participate in surveys on domestic violence and that if they do so, they are probably not going to divulge the extent or intensity of their behavior. Thus, he believes that the behavior uncovered in the social surveys fits a form that he calls *common couple violence,* disagreements that get out of hand, which is likely to be mild in form and as easily initiated by women as by men.

Reported cases of spouse (partner) abuse are now treated as cases of assault by the criminal justice system. Persons who are convicted of such assaults are subject to fines and imprisonment. Spouse (partner) abuse can be found in all classes, races, and ethnic groups. Many factors are associated with this behavior. Among them are the use of alcohol or other drugs, economic stress, low self-esteem on the part of both the abuser and the victim, isolation, previous history of family abuse, and lack of social supports. Thus, multiple approaches are needed to combat spouse (partner) abuse.

Becoming Deviant: Theoretical Perspectives

Over the years, two different approaches have been used to explain why some people become deviant and others do not. The first approach, which we will categorize as individualistic, focuses on the individual deviants themselves, seeking to discover what sets deviants apart from nondeviants. The individualistic approach asks: Why did Johnny steal that car? Why did Mary vandalize her classroom? Why did Mr. Smith beat his wife? Why did Mrs. Brown abuse her son? Why did Jack Kevorkian assist in someone else's death? In contrast, the second approach uses a sociological perspective and concentrates its attention on factors outside the individual, examining the social environment in which deviance occurs. Thus, the sociological approach asks: Is physician-assisted suicide considered deviant, and, if so, by whom? Was it always considered deviant? If not, when and how did it come to be considered deviant?

Individualistic Explanations for Deviance

Included in the individualistic approach are several variants of biological and psychological theories. In general, biological theories assume that the explanation for deviance can be found in the genetic makeup or genetic predisposition of individuals, whereas psychological explanations tend to focus on the personality traits of people identified as deviant.

Biological Theories   In the latter part of the nineteenth century, an Italian physician, Caesare Lombroso, put forth one of the first modern biological explanations for deviance and crime. He argued that people who had certain physical characteristics—abnormal skull formations, low foreheads, large jaws, and long arms—were more inclined to engage in criminal behavior. This theory was discredited when Charles Goring (1913), a British physician, undertook a study of both criminals and noncriminals and found no physical differences between the groups. Lombroso, who studied only prison inmates, had failed to include a control group in his research.

However, several decades later, psychologist and physician William Sheldon and his colleagues (1949) hypothesized a link between body type and crime. They checked the records of hundreds of young men and classified them according to body types, concluding that deviant behavior was more common among mesomorphs, boys who had strong, muscular builds. Later, Sheldon and Eleanor Glueck (1950) confirmed this finding in their research but observed that the nondelinquent population also contained young men with that body type; they concluded that body type in itself did not cause delinquency. Rather, they reasoned biological factors exist and interact in a social environment. For example, if you were going to get in a fight, steal a car, or burglarize a home, you would be more likely to choose a fast and agile mesomorph as your accomplice than a slow, puffing endomorph (boys with fat and round body types).

More recently, the attempt to discover whether there is a genetic basis to some crime has led some investigators to examine whether crime is more frequent in twins than in other siblings. Adrian Raine (1993) analyzed ten such studies and concluded that there was some basis for the heritability of crime in that identical twins had a much higher probability of both being criminal than did fraternal twins or siblings. Raine also analyzed studies of crime in biological and adopted families across fifteen states and found that the majority of the studies reported some genetic tie to crime in that they reported that adopted children whose biological parents were criminal had higher crime rates than did adopted children whose biological parents were not criminal.

Critique What are we to make of these biological theories? Critics point to the fact that many research findings are inconsistent and deal with only a small percentage of the population that engages in deviant behavior. Even in the twin studies discussed above, in the majority of cases in which one twin had committed a crime, the other had not. Additionally, many people who have been convicted of crimes have biological parents who have not. Further, a remaining problem in this approach is the question of how and why some behaviors come to be defined as deviant while others do not. Edwin

Sutherland and Donald Cressey (1978, p. 123) point this out when they say that it is "obviously impossible for criminality to be inherited as such, for crime is defined by acts of legislatures and these vary independently of the biological inheritance of the violators of law." Thus, the most we can say with any certainty is that a person's overall genetic makeup, in combination with social influences, may account for some of the variations in deviant behavior.

Psychological Theories Psychological explanations of deviance, like biological theories, focus on the individual norm violators. For the most part, psychological approaches attempt to identify personality traits that distinguish deviants from nondeviants. Among the traits frequently investigated in such regard are aggression, weak emotional attachments, hyperactivity, immaturity, and feelings of inadequacy. David Tennenbaum (1977) reviewed a wide range of such studies and found that 82 percent of these studies found some differences between criminals and noncriminals. However, the differences were small and there was no way of telling whether the personality characteristics contributed to the deviance or whether the characteristics were an outcome of the deviance. Other psychological approaches have attributed some forms of deviant behavior, especially those that take extremely violent forms, to mental illness, especially to what has been called an antisocial personality disorder. People diagnosed with this disorder are thought to be impulsive, out of touch with reality, and without guilt or remorse for their behavior.

Critique Even though it may be comforting to think that people who violate cultural norms are "sick" or somehow psychologically different from conforming members of society, the empirical evidence does not justify this position. According to Clinard and Meier (1995), comparisons with control groups have revealed no series of traits distinguishing deviants from nondeviants in general nor do studies show that all deviants have a specific trait that is absent in nondeviants. Rather, some deviants are "emotionally insecure," but so, too, are some nondeviants. Similarly, not all people identified as antisocial are criminals nor are the vast majority of criminals antisocial (Cleckley, 1976). Finally, psychological explanations, like biological explanations, may provide insight about specific individuals, but they do not help us to understand how definitions of deviance arise and why some people are defined as deviants whereas others are not, even though they engage in the same behavior. To understand these processes, we must look to factors outside the individual.

Sociological Theories of Deviance

Although there are several different sociological theories that can be applied to the study of deviance, they all share a common concern with the process by which something or someone comes to be defined as deviant. Generally speaking, these theories tend to focus on deviance that is disapproved of and that generally elicits negative reactions.

Structural Functional Theories   Structural functional theorists see deviance not as a characteristic that inheres in an individual but rather as a property of the social structure. Functional theorists, beginning with Emile Durkheim (1964), have argued that deviance, even a severe form such as crime, is a natural and inevitable part of all societies. Along with Durkheim, other sociologists, such as Lewis A. Coser (1956) and Edward Sagarin (1975), have called attention to the fact that deviance fulfills important integrative functions for society as a whole (Bynum & Thompson, 1996):

- **Deviance promotes conformity**. When a person is punished for violating norms, others may take notice and adapt their behavior to avoid similar consequences. For years, many motorists living in congested Chicago neighborhoods routinely ignored city parking restrictions and tickets, leaving their cars in alleys, cross walks, at bus stops, or near fire hydrants. However, after the introduction of the Denver Boot, a mechanical device that immobilizes a car and can be removed only by a trained crew of city workers at a high cost to the owner, these parking violations decreased dramatically.

- **Deviance reaffirms and clarifies norms**. When deviance occurs and the deviants are punished, other members of society may engage in a widespread discussion of the seriousness of the violation and the appropriateness of the punishment. In this way, the normative aspects of social life are brought into clearer focus. For example, the 1997 trial of Louise Woodward, a nineteen-year-old au pair from England convicted of the murder (later reduced to manslaughter) of an eight-month-old boy left in her care by two working parents, ignited an intense debate on both sides of the Atlantic about the problematic aspects surrounding the policies and practices of child care here in the United States. Similarly, the controversy surrounding the actions of Dr. Jack Kevorkian have forced a public debate over physician-assisted suicide.

- **Deviance promotes social cohesion**. When a group feels threatened, as is frequently the case when a criminal is on the loose in a community, members are drawn together to "fight the common enemy." Local businesses respond to such threats by posting warning notices for their customers, often posting a suspect's picture to aid the police in apprehending the suspect. Neighbors volunteer to watch out for each other and to report any suspicious activity to their local officials. Additionally, community members often contribute their time, labor, and funds to help victims cope with their loss or injury, as was clearly evident in the aftermath of the bombing of the federal building in Oklahoma City in 1995.

- **Deviance contributes to social change**. In many cases, people violate norms that they perceive to be unjust, inappropriate, or outdated. Such challenges call attention to the fact that, at least for some people, the social system is not working well and requires reexamination and probably change. In 1957, when Rosa Parks refused to move to the back of the bus so that whites could have her seat, her deviation from the Jim Crow segregationist norm not only focused national attention on the inherent injustice of racial segregation but also became the impetus for the Montgomery bus boycott and the civil rights movement, which eventually resulted in the outlawing of segregationist legislation.

Robert Merton and Structural Strain Theory
To explain deviance, Robert Merton (1957) adapted Durkheim's notion of anomie, a social condition in which people who feel weak ties to a social group or the larger community find it difficult to know what to do because social norms are unclear or have broken down. Merton attributed deviance to the strain people experience as a result of the disjuncture between cultural goals and the socially approved means for achieving these goals. In the United States, most children quickly learn that economic success is a highly valued and sought-after goal that is measured by material possessions such as a nice home, a car, and the latest fashions. They are also taught socially acceptable ways to become successful—follow the rules, work hard, get a good education, and save your money. In an ideal world, everyone would have equal access to the approved means for getting ahead. However, in the real world, many Americans, especially the poor and lower classes of any race, are at a disadvantage—they have little formal education and few economic resources with which to create opportunities for themselves. Thus, Merton reasoned, they are the most likely to experience strain which results in a feeling of anomie, or normlessness, which, in turn, can easily lead to nonconformity and deviance. He identified five modes of adapting to this goal/means dilemma, each mode depending on whether people accepted or rejected societal goals and/or the legitimate means to achieve them (see Table 8.2). Only the first adaption in Merton's typology, conformity, involves following the norms; the four remaining are deviant adaptations to the conditions of anomie.

1. **Conformity.** Merton listed this as the first and the most common response to the goal/means dilemma, with people accepting both the cultural goal of success and the legitimate means to accomplish it. For example, you are here in college to obtain knowledge, skills, and a degree which you hope to parlay into a well-paying job or career.

TABLE 8.2 ⊘ Merton's Strain Theory of Deviance

Mode of Adaptation	Accepts and Seeks Cultural Goals	Accepts and Uses Approved Means
Conformity	Yes	Yes
Innovation	Yes	No
Ritualism	No	Yes
Retreatism	No	No
Rebellion	No—substitutes new goals	No—substitutes new means

2. **Innovation.** This response differs from conformity in that only the goal is accepted. The means are rejected, often because they appear out of reach, and replaced with unconventional, inappropriate, or outright illegal means. But the goal of success is still very much intact. Instead of studying, some students cheat to get good grades. Other people may steal, extort, or sell drugs or their bodies to obtain the material symbols of success.
3. **Ritualism.** In this mode of adaptation, the individual adheres to the means for success in a ritualistic, mechanical way but doesn't feel she/he will ever really achieve success. People working in large-scale bureaucracies often lose sight of organization goals and insist on rigidly adhering to the rules regardless of the outcome.
4. **Retreatism.** Retreatists reject both cultural goals and the accompanying institutionalized means to these goals. Many drug addicts, chronic alcoholics, and homeless derelicts have, in effect, dropped out of society. Although there is a tendency to associate this mode of adaptation with low-income and destitute people, it can cut across all income groups.
5. **Rebellion.** Like retreatists, rebels also reject both the goals and the means, but rebels go a step further and substitute new goals and means and actively seek to change society

through a variety of means, ranging from demonstrations, civil disobedience, and even armed insurrection.

Although Merton identified some of the consequences of structural strain, a gender and class bias is inherent in his structural strain perspective. Given women's more limited opportunity structure (see Chapter 11), structural strain theory should predict that they would commit crime in numbers similar to men. That is not the case. Although the female crime rate is increasing, it is considerably lower than men's (Beirne & Messerschmidt, 1995). One possible reason for this is that women do not internalize the success goals to the same degree that men do and perhaps, as we will see in the next section, that illegitimate means may be closed to women in somewhat the same way that legitimate means are.

Opportunity Theory   Richard Cloward and Lloyd Ohlin (1960) argued that illegitimate opportunities must be available before deviance can occur. They identified three different forms of delinquent subcultures that can develop as a response to the various types of illegitimate opportunities available in a given community. In some neighborhoods, young people may become part of a *criminal subculture* whereby they learn the knowledge and skills necessary to succeed through criminal behavior, for example, stealing and selling drugs. Studies of gangs have shown that young people often join gangs because they provide a means to be "successful" in terms of either money, belonging, or status (Esbensen & Huizinga, 1993). Other neighborhoods may lack even these opportunities and give rise to *conflict subcultures,* in which individuals may try to obtain some measure of respect by demonstrating their toughness through violent behavior. Still other areas may promote a *retreatist subculture* via the abuse of alcohol and/or other drugs.

Control Theory   While Merton, Cloward, and Ohlin were attempting to explain why some people engaged in deviant behavior, others focused their attention on the factors that seemed to prevent deviance. Echoing a theme identified by Durkheim, Walter Reckless (1967) suggested a theory of social control that put forth the idea that people can be "insulated" from deviance if

they have a strong, supportive network of family and friends who provide adequate supervision and reasonable social expectations, thereby enabling them to learn responsibility and to develop self-control. Researchers have found that delinquency rates are lower among young people who exhibit strong interpersonal ties to parents, teachers, peers, and others who disapprove of deviance (Gottfredson & Hirschi, 1990). Conversely, when such ties or social bonds are weakened, there is a greater likelihood for deviance to occur.

Overall, structural functionalist theories tend to focus our attention on disadvantaged people, but they do not explain why they are far more likely to be reflected in the crime statistics than are people in higher classes. Conflict theory helps to explain these patterns.

Conflict Theory   Conflict theorists who study deviance in capitalist societies generally use Karl Marx's notion of the importance of "ruling class ideas." In so doing, they argue that the more powerful groups are able to create laws that serve their own interests, regardless of how such laws may impact those having less power. Thus, laws tend to favor the interests of management over workers, landlords over tenants, men over women, and adults over children. According to Richard Quinney (1980), the powerful define certain behaviors that they perceive to threaten their own interests as deviant and often pass laws against these behaviors. This may explain why well-dressed individuals rarely encounter resistance when they sit in a public space or browse in a department store while poorly groomed or attired individuals doing the same thing in the same place may find themselves under suspicion, denied entrance, or even arrested for violating "antiloitering" ordinances. Similarly, Steven Spitzer (1980) argues that the powerful are quick to apply deviant labels to people who challenge the capitalist system—either directly, by their action, or indirectly, by their inaction—as a means of discrediting the legitimacy of their challenges. For example, the antiwar activists during the Vietnam era, union organizers, and today's environmentalists are depicted as "troublemakers," "rabble rousers," "rioters," or, in the period of the Cold War, "commies" and "pinkos," and welfare recipients are often portrayed as "lazy" and "non-contributing" members of society.

Most of the support for the conflict theory comes from data, like that in Table 8.1, that shows that elite deviants are less likely to be prosecuted for their offenses and that, when they are prosecuted, they receive lighter sentences than "street criminals." Conflict theory also gives us insight into the types of crime people commit. Women, for example, are more likely to commit property crimes such as shoplifting, passing bad checks, and welfare fraud than to engage in elite crime such as embezzlement and business fraud, all in keeping with women's more subordinate position in society.

Nevertheless, not all efforts at lawmaking or enforcement are focused on protecting only one segment of society. Clearly, all classes of the population share an interest in living in a safe environment, and there is widespread consensus that certain behaviors are a threat to everyone. In fact, households having incomes of less than $7,500 have crime victimization rates over twice that of households having incomes of $75,000 or more (U.S. Bureau of the Census, 1998). Additionally, not all members of powerful groups limit their activities to their own interests; many members of the middle and upper classes are strong advocates for improving the lives of those less fortunate than they are. Finally, conflict theory, like structural functionalism, tends to view deviance as a product of society and does not address the specific manner by which a person comes to be a deviant. For this, we turn to symbolic interactionism.

Symbolic Interactionism As we have already seen, symbolic interactionism is concerned with the subjective interpretations that shape our understanding of the world and the processes by which we learn these meanings. Two of the best known interactionist theories of deviance are differential association theory and labeling theory.

Differential Association Theory Edwin Sutherland (1939) coined the term **differential association** to describe the process of social interaction through which people learn deviance. Sutherland advanced the notion that we learn to be deviant in the same way we learn to conform—from the people around us. So if par-

ents or friends show by word or deed that it is okay to speed, to cheat, or to violate societal norm in other ways—or conversely if they stress conformity—chances are pretty good that that's what we will learn. However, this is not simply a one-to-one process. Given the many different agents of socialization we experience, we may receive a wide variety of mixed messages. Sutherland argues that it is the "excess of definitions" that leads to conforming or deviant behavior. If more of these definitions are favorable to deviance, we are likely to be deviant. Thus, for Sutherland, the frequency, duration, and degree of intimacy of people's interactions were key to their learning conforming or nonconforming attitudes and behavior. Although this theory helps us to understand how individuals learn deviance, it does not tell us why some people are perceived to be deviant and others aren't even though they engage in similar behavior. Labeling theory helps us to understand this aspect of deviance.

Labeling Theory In contrast to the other theories we have discussed, **labeling theory** does not focus on the causes of deviance; rather it sees deviance as the product of others who react to the norm violator. It also examines how the norm violator is affected by that reaction. Sociologist Howard Becker (1963, p. 90) succinctly described the first part of this process when he wrote, "Deviant behavior is behavior that people so label." Thus, the crucial factor here is not the behavior itself but the social reaction to the behavior. Becker himself labels those who have the power to label others *moral entrepreneurs;* they use their own view of right and wrong, good and bad, to establish rules that they then apply to persons who have less power.

Everyone violates norms at some time in their lives. Maybe, as an adolescent, it was drinking under age, skipping school one afternoon, cheating on a test, soaping someone's window on Halloween, or stealing candy from the corner store on a dare. Most people who engaged in those behaviors probably gave them little thought, believing them to be a way to have fun or a part of growing up. Edwin Lemert (1951) coined the term **primary deviance** to refer to violations like these that a person commits for the first time and without consciously thinking about them as deviant.

However, someone else may see these same behaviors as early signs of delinquency, label them as such, and punish the violator for her or his actions, thus initiating a second step in the labeling process. The label may stick, and people may start to treat that person in a different way. A teacher may react by showing that she or he doesn't trust that student, a friend's parent may refuse to let her or him associate with the "troubled" youth, or an employer may refuse to hire the "truant." As a result of being labeled deviant and treated accordingly, a person's self-image may change to include the deviant label. The person may then try to live up to this label by repeating these or similar norm violations and thus become a career deviant. Lemert referred to deviation that results from social reaction as **secondary deviance.**

Labeling theory reinforces the view that deviance is relative, that what is deviant depends on the reactions of others toward the behavior in question and that this, in turn, depends on factors such as time, place, actor, and audience. Further, this perspective allows us to see how deviance is created through interaction on a daily basis. Parents and teachers who label children as "lazy" or "stupid" or as "troublemakers" may find that they have unwittingly created such children; they come to believe this label about themselves and, consequently, to incorporate the associated behavior into their self-concepts. Individuals who have been convicted of a crime and imprisoned may believe the label "ex-con" will prohibit them from getting a fair shake and so continue to commit crimes.

Like all of the theories we have discussed, labeling theory also has its weaknesses. First, the theory does not explain why primary deviance occurs in the first place nor does it deal with "deviance" that nobody sees. If no one is around to label an act deviant, does that mean deviance has not occurred? Second, not all labels carry the same weight or stigma for all groups. For example, being labeled sexually promiscuous may have more profound consequences for women and people of color than for white males. Third, not everyone who is labeled a deviant accepts that label or continues in a deviant direction. People see themselves in many ways, and some of these identities have greater salience than others. For example, someone who has been labeled a thief may see that behavior as a one-time occurrence, a mistake, or poor judgment and may concentrate on her or his other identities as a hard worker, a parent, or a friend.

Feminist Theories   Feminist theorists have pointed out that most theories of deviance were constructed on samples that were primarily or exclusively male, thereby raising questions about their applicability to female deviants. Such theorists acknowledge the relativity of deviance and the importance of class in determining who and what gets labeled as deviant, but they also call attention to the important role that gender plays in the defining process.

For example, in the past, it was assumed that, with the exception of prostitution, crime was pretty much the province of males. Women who committed crimes or engaged in prostitution were thought to be abnormal or promiscuous. However, as feminist analyses point out, women historically had few opportunities to commit crime, and prostitution was often a response to their low economic status. Feminists argue that now that increasing numbers of women are moving into the labor force, many in occupations once the exclusive domain of men, they have more opportunities to commit white-collar or corporate crimes.

At the same time, however, many women remain in low-paying jobs, and many others are seeing their economic well-being decline as a result of divorce. Thus, some of these women may feel pressured to engage in property crimes for economic survival. Poor, young women of color may be especially vulnerable in this regard. In addition, feminist theories point to the role of victimization and subsequent contact with the criminal justice system. For example, researchers have found that a high percentage of women offenders had been victims of physical and/or sexual abuse at the hands of parents or relatives (Chesney-Lind & Rodriquez, 1993).

Feminist researchers and theorists are increasingly focusing attention on finding answers to questions such as these: Will the levels of deviance among women continue to increase as family and economic structures change? Are these changes and the subsequent reactions to them the same or different for white women and women of color? How different are the patterns and motivations of female and male deviants?

Deviance and Social Control

Now that we have some understanding of the "causes" of deviance, let's examine the practical implications of social control and the attempts to encourage conforming or at least socially tolerated behavior. Although deviance can serve important social functions, too much deviance in society can jeopardize the social order. To minimize the possibility of such disruptions, groups and societies develop systems of social control that rely on two basic processes. The first is the *internalization of group norms* which comes about through the process of socialization we discussed in Chapter 6. If socialization is effective, people not only learn their group's norms but also acquire a desire to conform to their group's expectations. The majority of people obey traffic signals, pay their income taxes, respect other people's property, and support their families not because they are being physically coerced or because they fear being caught but rather because they have internalized cultural norms and believe that these are the right and customary ways of behaving. Thus, they are likely to judge themselves in terms of how well they meet group expectations, feeling good about themselves when they do "what is right" and feeling ashamed or guilty when they violate the norms. These self-feelings enable individuals to exercise self-control over their own behavior and lessen the need for external social controls.

Despite this rather efficient way of controlling deviance, however, everyone at some time or another is likely to violate a social norm. For the most part, these are minor violations, but in some cases, these may be serious violations. Societies use a second process of social control, the *application of sanctions,* in an attempt to keep such violations down. As we saw in Chapter 4, these sanctions may take a variety of forms; they can be positive (rewards) or negative (punishments), informal (enforced in day-to-day social interactions) or formal (enforced through legal authorities).

In general, informal sanctions are most effective in small groups, in which people know one another and under circumstances in which people are concerned with what others think about them. Negative informal sanctions such as gossip, ridicule, reprimands, and frowns are meant to show that others disapprove of our behavior, whereas smiles, praise, and applause signify approval of our behavior.

In contrast, formal sanctions are administered by specialized agencies and organizations and involve laws, rules, and policies that specify the conditions under which people should be rewarded or punished for their actions. Although the police and the courts come quickly to mind in this regard, other agencies—including employers, churches, professional associations, labor unions, educational institutions, clubs and other organizations—also administer formal sanctions. The police and the courts exercise their control through negative sanctions such as fines, imprisonment, and even, on occasion, execution (see Sociology through Literature box, p. 222). Other agencies and organizations are more likely to use formal positive sanctions such as certificates of merit or diplomas, cash bonuses, promotions, and other rewards to encourage conformity to their norms. However, when a violation of norms is perceived as serious, these same agencies and organizations will use whatever formal negative sanctions they deem necessary to control the behavior of their members.

Consider, for example, the behavior of Latrell Sprewell, a guard on the Golden State Warriors basketball team, who physically assaulted his coach, P. J. Carlesimo, during a Warrior practice on December 1, 1997. As a result of that behavior, Sprewell's employer, the Golden State Warriors, terminated his four-year, $32 million contract and the National Basketball Association Commissioner David Stern suspended him for one year, the longest penalty for a nondrug offense in the league's history.

Deviance and Social Control in the Twenty-First Century

As we look forward to the next century, it is well to keep in mind Durkheim's admonishment that deviance is an inevitable part of society and that it serves some critical functions. The task for any society is to maintain the appropriate balance between conforming and deviant behavior and an ongoing awareness of the new trends and developments that can easily result in decreased amounts of certain types of deviance or lead to new and/or expanded forms of deviance. Three issues seem particularly relevant here: creative sentencing, deviance and crime in cyberspace, and the increased opportunities for international organized crime.

Creative Sentencing

As Figure 8.1 shows, the U.S. prison population has increased by more than five times since 1970, giving the United States the highest incarceration rate of any industrialized country. Given the economic costs of keeping a person in prison ($20,000 to $30,000 a year) as well as the fact that many offenders sentenced to long, mandatory terms have no record of violent crime (Goldberg, 1997), some criminal justice experts are questioning the efficacy of current sentencing policies and are recommending that judges be permitted to use more discretion in sentencing when an offender does not have a serious criminal record. A few judges are experimenting with "creative" sentencing in an attempt to relieve prison overcrowding as well as trying to educate the offender and others away from committing similar behavior. For example, rather than sending a nineteen-year-old man to prison for ten years, for drunk driving that killed two people, Texas Judge Ted Poe ordered him to serve six months

in jail. In addition, during the next ten years he must carry the pictures of the two people he killed in his wallet, visit their gravesites, do community service at a hospital emergency room, and periodically stand outside a bar wearing a sign saying, "I drove while drunk and killed two people." The judge also ordered that violation of any part of the sentence will result in his immediate imprisonment. In the future, we can anticipate more of these innovative approaches as officials attempt to decrease the prison population.

Cyberspace: The New Frontier of Crime

In December 1997, law enforcement officials from the major industrial nations met to discuss strategies to combat a growing global computer crime wave that U.S. Attorney General Janet Reno called the "new frontier of crime" (James, 1997). Criminals and deviants are no longer restricted by state or national boundaries. The potential for individuals or organized groups to do great harm using information networks is already a reality. For example, Russian computer hackers in St. Petersburg broke into a Citibank electronic money transfer system and transferred $10 million from Citibank branches around the world to accomplices' accounts in places as far flung as Israel and Finland. Although it is difficult to quantify the scope of the computer crime problem, public reports estimate that computer crime costs between $500 million and $10 billion per year (Litt, 1997). Further, because computers control sizeable parts of a nation's critical services, such as telephone or electrical services, the possibility of electronic sabotage or cyberterrorism also exists.

Several other developments have sounded the alarm about deviance and crime in cyberspace: the ease of sending and receiving pornography over the Internet; the opportunity "chat rooms" have given pedophiles to make contact with unsuspecting children right in their own homes; the tendency of some personalities to become "addicted" to the Internet, causing disruptions in interpersonal relationships; and, on our university campuses, cheating is as easy as "point and click"—thousands of term papers can be downloaded any time of the day or night. These problems, in turn, have generated calls for "policing" the Internet.

FIGURE 8.1 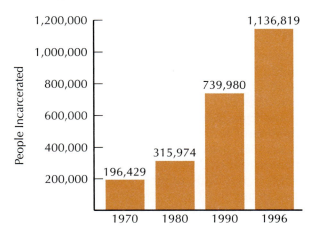 **The Growth of U.S. State and Federal Prison Populations** *Source:* Adapted from U.S. Bureau of the Census. 1998. *Statistical Abstract of the United States, 1998.* Washington, DC: U.S. Government Printing Office, Table 377, p. 229.

Sociology through Literature

Compulsion

In 1924, eighteen-year-old Richard Loeb and nineteen-year-old Nathan Leopold, Jr., two brilliant students at the University of Chicago, deliberately planned and carried out the brutal murder of fourteen-year-old Robert Franks. These young men believed that they were superior in intelligence to all others and that they could pull off a "perfect crime" and get away with it. The media quickly dubbed the murder "the crime of the century." After their arrest, the young men confessed to the murder. Feelings ran high against Loeb and Leopold, sons of millionaires; many called for the death penalty. Their families hired the controversial lawyer Clarence Darrow, a staunch opponent of capital punishment, hoping he would be able to get them a life sentence instead of the death penalty. The excerpt below is from Meyer Levin's novelized account of this crime and the sensational trial that followed. Here Darrow, called Jonathan Wilk in the book, presents part of his closing argument; the defendants are referred to as Judd Steiner and Artie Straus.

> "As a rule, lawyers are not scientists. They think that there is only one way to make men good, and that is to put them in such terror that they do not dare to do bad."

And then he spoke of an aspect of the crime that few had considered. Going back over the record of hangings, he showed that a recent change had taken place. For years,

no minor had been hanged in Chicago, not even on a jury conviction. Not from 1912 until 1920. "In 1920, a boy named Viani was convicted by a jury and hanged, a boy of eighteen. Why did we go back to hanging the young? It was 1920; we were used to young men, mere boys, going to their death. It was 1920 just after the war. And that time is still with us, Your Honour.

"We are anew accustomed to blood, Your Honour. It used to make us feel squeamish. But we have not only seen it shed in bucketsful, we have seen it shed in rivers, lakes, and oceans, and we have delighted in it; we have preached it, we have worked for it, we have advised it, we have taught it to the young, until the world has been drenched in blood and it has left stains upon every human heart and upon every human mind, and has almost stifled the feelings of pity and charity that have their natural home in the human breast. . . .

"We read of killing one hundred thousand men in a day. We read about it and rejoiced in it—if it was the other fellows who were killed. We were fed on flesh and drank blood. I need not tell Your Honour how many bright, honourable young men have come into this court charged with murder, some saved and some sent to their death, boys who fought in this war and learned to place a cheap value on human life."

Wilk turned toward Judd and Artie. "These boys were brought up in it. The tales of death were in their homes, their playgrounds, their schools; they were in the newspapers that they read; it was part of the common frenzy.

International Organized Crime

Like the global economy today, organized crime has developed a global character. Members of organized crime syndicates have increasingly become interconnected in areas such as drug smuggling, money laundering, and numerous financial schemes aimed at defrauding people around the world. With the collapse of communism, many of the countries that were former states of or allied with the Soviet Union began to experiment with capitalism. Organized crime, like legitimate businesses, has rushed in to establish a niche in these countries. Today's international criminal organizations (ICOs) have become powerful enough to challenge and sometimes to destabilize small, weak states. For example, in countries such as Myanmar, Colombia, and Peru, the international drug cartels have challenged governmental authority, eroded public order, and drained economic resources (Godson & Olson, 1997). Large, industrialized countries such as the United States are not immune from these problems either: witness the number of resources that have been mobilized to combat illegal smuggling of drugs across our borders. Since these ICOs operate across many borders, it is difficult for law enforcement agencies in any one country to stop their activities. During the 1990s, a number of tentative steps

What was a life? It was nothing. One of them tells us how he was haunted by a war poster, how he dreamed of rape and of killing.

"It will take fifty years to wipe it out of the human heart, if ever. No one needs to inform me that crime has a cause. It has as definite a cause as any other disease. I know that growing out of the Napoleonic Wars there was an era of crime such as Europe had never seen before. I know that Europe is going through the same experience today; I know it has followed every war and I know it has influenced these boys so that life was not the same to them as it would have been if the world had not been made red with blood. I protest against the crimes and mistakes of society being visited upon them. All of us have our share in it. I have mine. I cannot tell and I shall never know how many words of mine during the war might have given birth to cruelty in the place of love and kindness and charity. . . .

"I do not know how much salvage there is in these two boys. I hate to say it in their presence, but what is there to look forward to? I do not know but what Your Honour would be merciful if you tied a rope around their necks and let them die: merciful to them, but not merciful to civilization, and not merciful to those who would be left behind. To spend the balance of their days in prison is mighty little to look forward to, if anything. Is it anything?

"They may have the hope that as the years roll around they may be released. I do not know. I do not know." He gazed at the defendants. "I will be honest with this court as I have

tried to be from the beginning. I know that these boys are not fit to be at large. I believe they will not be until they pass through the next stage of life, at forty-five or fifty."

The words fell heavily, as if he had prophetically sentenced them.

"I would not tell this court that I do not hope that sometime, when life and age has changed their bodies, as it does, and has changed their emotions, as it does, they may once again return to life. I would be the last person on earth to close the door of hope to any human being that lives, and least of all to my clients. But what have they to look forward to? Nothing."

What theory of deviance is implicit in Wilk's arguments? Although not explicitly stated in Wilk's argument, there is an underlying assumption that capital punishment does not deter crime. What evidence can you find either to support or to dispute this notion? If the death punishment does not deter crime, why do thirty-eight states in the United States use it? Survey your classmates. What opinions do they hold regarding the efficacy of capital punishment?

Source: Excerpted from Meyer Levin. 1956. *Compulsion* (pp. 372–374). New York: Carroll & Graf Publishers. Reprinted by permission of the author and the author's agents, JABberwocky Literary Agency, P.O. Box 4558, Sunnyside, NY 11104-0558.

were taken to foster more international cooperation among law enforcement agencies worldwide in an effort to stem the threats posed by ICOs. The challenge in the decades ahead will be to ensure that law enforcement agencies around the world will have the determination, the skill, and the tools to more than match those of the ICOs.

Key Points to Remember

1. Deviance refers to the violation of cultural norms. Several factors must be taken into account when determining whether any given behavior is deviant or not. Among these are the norm itself, the actor, the time, the place, and the audience. No behavior is inherently deviant; rather, deviance is relative, socially constructed, and depends on the social context within which behavior occurs.

2. One form deviance takes is crime. Crime is a violation of the law. The FBI distinguishes

between crimes against people (violent crimes) and crimes against property. Elite deviance encompasses wrongdoing by wealthy and powerful individuals and organizations and includes white-collar and corporate crime. Although elite deviance is far more costly to society, it is generally punished less severely. Other forms of crime include political crime, organized crime, juvenile delinquency, and so-called victimless crime.

3. Drugs and spouse (partner) abuse reflect other forms of deviance and illustrate the fact that deviance can take place in any type of institutional setting.

4. Deviance is both functional and dysfunctional for society, and all societies must struggle to maintain a balance between conforming and deviant behavior.

5. There are two major approaches to explaining deviance, individualistic and sociological theories. Individualistic theories focus on the norm violators, whereas sociological theories focus on the process by which someone or something comes to be defined as deviant. Among the sociological theories are: structural strain theory, opportunity theory, control theory, conflict theory, differential association theory, and labeling theory. Feminists have been critical of the male bias in much of the research on crime and deviance.

6. All social groups and societies develop ways to limit deviance and maintain social order. There are two basic processes of social control—internalization of group norms and the application of sanctions. Sanctions can be positive or negative, formal or informal.

7. Three trends will be particularly important in the twenty-first century: creative sentencing, deviance and crime in cyberspace, and international organized crime. Dealing with these three trends requires the United States to review the functioning of its criminal justice system and to work cooperatively with other law enforcement agencies around the world.

Key Terms

deviance

crime

stigma

felonies

misdemeanors

elite deviance

white-collar crime

corporate crime

political crime

organized crime

juvenile delinquency

victimless crimes

differential association

labeling theory

primary deviance

secondary deviance

Key People

Dr. Jack Kevorkian

Edward Sutherland

Daniel Moynihan

Emile Durkheim

Robert Merton

Howard Becker

Edwin Lemert

Questions for Review and Discussion

1. Reflect on your past experiences and those of people you know. Can you identify any situations in which people were treated differently although they engaged in the same behavior? If so, how and why were they treated differently?

With what consequences? Should efforts be made to change such patterns? Explain your position.

2. Compare and contrast the various theories that have been offered to explain deviance. Which

do you think provide the greatest insights? the least? Feminists have argued that there is a male bias in these theories, that they do not really reflect women's experiences. Do you agree or disagree? What suggestions would you make for strengthening any one of these theories and making them inclusive of women's experiences?

3. There has been controversy over whether we are "defining deviancy up" or "defining deviance down." What position do you take on this issue? What evidence can you provide for your position? What does this discussion tell you about the nature of deviance?

4. Based on what you have read and your own personal experiences, critically evaluate the functioning of the criminal justice system in the United States. What are some of the problems confronting the system? What recommendations would you make to improve the system? Which social control strategies do you favor for promoting conformity to society's norms?

For Further Reading

Campbell, Anne. 1984. *The Girls in the Gang: A Report from New York City.* London: Blackwell. The author provides a rich ethnography of female gang members, giving insights into the causes of their involvement.

Mann, C.R. 1993. *Unequal Justice: A Question of Color.* Bloomington: Indiana University Press.

The author provides a thought-provoking analysis of the racial inequities in the functioning of the criminal justice system.

Wright, Richard A. 1994. *In Defense of Prisons.* Westport, CT: Greenwood Press. The author presents a balanced view of the strengths and weaknesses of U.S. prisons.

Sociology through Literature

Berendt, John. 1994. *Midnight in the Garden of Good and Evil.* New York: Random House. The book explores the mysterious death of a young man in Savannah and describes people in that city whom many would consider deviants.

Hughes, Langston. 1950. *Simple Speaks His Mind.* New York: Simon and Schuster. A story about a

humorous sage who has not had much education, but is a wise person who is able to drive home his point with good-humored wit. This story raises questions as to what is deviant and what is normal.

Internet Resources

http://www.odci.gov/cia/pulications/95fact The CIA World Factbook contains statistics on crime in other countries.

http://www.fbi.gov/ The FBI homepage with links to current investigations and crime statistics.

http://www.useoj.gov/ U.S. Bureau of Justice contains links to a variety of other resources on crime.

Social Stratification: The Structure of Inequalities

AGENT OF CHANGE: MITCH SNYDER

Community and social activist Mitch Snyder spent a significant portion of his life as an activist and advocate for the homeless. A one-time federal prison inmate, Snyder turned his life around and left prison with a cause—to eliminate homelessness in the United States. As director of the Washington, D.C., based Community for Creative Non-Violence (CCNV), he focused legal and public attention on the fact that U.S. society allows people to live on the street and to eat out of garbage cans. He drew public attention to the unequal distribution of resources in our society and to the devastating consequences for many people of that distribution. He consistently challenged the privileged, comfortable, and high-status members of society to think about how their own lives and consumption played a part in the creation of homelessness and other forms of persistent poverty in the United States. And he suggested that others get involved in the lives and misery of the poor, not just on a theoretical or theological level, but by making an actual, personal commitment to making a difference.

During his involvement at CCNV, the group helped thousands of homeless women, men, and children in the nation's capital. Under his leadership, the group also relentlessly called upon the federal and municipal governments to respond to the needs of the homeless with prompt, appropriate action. Snyder made tremendous inroads into cutting through the apathy that allows poverty to flourish amid prosperity. He saw the first step toward reintegrating society's homeless as providing them with an unstructured base from which they would have the opportunity to build for themselves. His activism on behalf of the nation's poor and homeless helped to raise enough donations to improve the quality of life for some homeless people, won enough lawsuits to raise roofs over the heads of some people who would not otherwise have had them, and raised enough social awareness to get politicians promising to do something for the homeless.

Although he never hit upon the combination needed to solve the problem of homelessness, Snyder unquestionably succeeded in bringing national attention to the problem. For example, during the 1984 national election, CCNV backed an initiative that would mandate shelter for the homeless with a five-week series of demonstrations. In addition, Snyder and CCNV gained access to an abandoned federal building near the Capitol, which became the home of CCNV and a shelter for Mitch and up to 800 homeless people. Their refusal to leave the building led to a confrontation with the federal government that lasted well over a year. It culminated with a highly publicized fifty-one-day hunger strike led by Snyder and eleven community members, which he declared would be until death or until the federal government agreed to provide sufficient funding to operate a shelter in that would be a model for the rest of the country. Public awareness and sympathy resulting from his actions convinced President Ronald Reagan to promise to build a $5 million "model shelter." The publicity surrounding the confrontation led to a made-for-television movie, *Samaritans: The Mitch Snyder Story.* Snyder and CCNV used the national attention garnered by the movie as leverage to help create a social movement that carried out a nationally coordinated day of action against the scandal of homelessness in the United States.

In 1988, attention and support for the National Affordable Housing Act was generated through actions in over seventy cities across the country. Most involved building take-overs and other acts of civil disobedience. In October 1989, the movement that Snyder helped create brought over 140,000 people to the nation's capital to demand increased federal support for affordable housing.

In July 1991, Mitch Snyder committed suicide. Most people who knew him believed that he took his life because of a string of defeats—locally in D.C. and nationally—which left him depressed and disillusioned about the prospects for success for the movement he helped create. His suicide however, does not diminish the prophetic and inspirational nature of his life, his advocacy, and his activism. His singular commitment to the nation's poor and homeless led to many changes in homelessness, and he has been not only remembered for his work but also emulated by hundreds of others.

An annual award is given in Snyder's name to women and men across the country whose lives and efforts exemplify the selfless commitment and courage that Snyder demonstrated during his life. It is meant to encourage people to be edified by and to emulate Snyder's example, and it is rooted in Snyder's belief that until those who enjoy lives of relative comfort and privilege recognize that their good fortune comes at the expense of others, there will be no significant diminishment in the suffering and degradation endured by the homeless (Congregational United Church of Christ, 1998).

Source: First Church Shelter. 1998. "About the Mitch Snyder Awards." http://www.gis.net/~1stshelt/MITCH2.html.

The Study of Social Stratification: Defining Concepts

Mitch Snyder's social activism on behalf of America's homeless offers insight into many of the key concepts in this chapter. The fact that some people live in high levels of comfort while others live on the streets and eat out of garbage cans clearly indicates a pattern of **social stratification,** an institutionalized form of inequality in which categories of people are ranked in a graded hierarchy on the basis of arbitrary criteria, which then serves to create and perpetuate unequal access to rewards, resources, privileges, and life chances in a society. The resources and opportunities available in society are distributed according to a person's placement in the social hierarchy. For example, those at the top of the social hierarchy have access to a larger share of the material wealth, social honor and prestige, and political power in society than do those at or near the bottom of the social hierarchy.

The dynamics of a stratified society result in, at minimum, two culturally distinct groups: a culturally dominant group and a culturally subordinate group. The dominant group is able to remain dominant by controlling the production and distribution of valued goods and services and resources; they are able to do so because of their greater access to the *opportunity structure*—circumstances that provide chances for people to acquire valued goods, services, and resources. By means of their ownership or control of major valued resources such as education, health care, housing, and the criminal justice system, the wealthy members of society can decide who will have access and what that access will be. In contrast, the poor and homeless are often unable to improve their status/rank within the social stratification hierarchy because they lack access to the necessary resources.

To be sure, the United States does not stand alone as a stratified society. All known societies have some system of stratification. Although the nature and content of the stratification system may vary from one culture to another, the result is similar: some individuals and groups are considered more worthy, are ranked higher, and receive more of the society's scarce and valued resources than do others. In this chapter, we will examine the nature, causes, and consequences of social stratification.

Social Stratification and Inequality: A Persistent Link

Social stratification is one of the most important areas of sociological study. Social stratification refers to **structured inequality,** a recurrent pattern of differential access to goods and services and the things that count in a society. This kind of inequality is built into the social structure and is determined by socio-historical and polit-

ical forces, not by biological differences such as race and sex. As you will see in Chapter 10, there are many who argue that racial differences have *no* biological basis, that race is purely a social construct. However, these biological attributes are given social meaning and importance and used as a rationale for the unequal distribution of valued resources. For example, the race of people in the United States, in and of itself, was not relevant in patterns of social inequality in this country until it was used to differentiate one group from another and given importance by being incorporated into the attitudes, values, and beliefs of the people of this country.

The patterning of social stratification can be seen in almost all aspects of a society. Social inequality becomes built into the social patterns of societal institutions. The control of society's resources by institutions further entrenches the inequality system. The patterning of inequality can be seen, for example, in the socialization process. Through the institutions of the family and education, each generation of people learns and internalizes the society's norms, values, and beliefs. Poor children and rich children as well as all others learn early on the attitudes and values of their culture; they learn who is valued and who is not and what their status is in the social hierarchy.

Social Differentiation and Social Inequality

As this discussion points up, *difference* is a key feature of social stratification. In all cultures, people differ from each other along some dimension. Differences contain no inherent basis for inequality. However, every society evaluates and ranks certain characteristics and attributes depending on the values of the society. In addition, the culture of a society supports inequality by promoting values that support the stratification system.

All systems of stratification are accompanied by a prevailing *ideology*, a system of beliefs and ideas that represent the interest of some category of the population and serves to legitimize, rationalize, and justify the subordination of some groups of people and the elevation of others. Although the exact content of these belief systems varies across societies, the fact is that all such ideologies serve to promote, legitimate, and reinforce the stratification system and its attendant inequality. It is not surprising, therefore, that poor and homeless people receive far fewer of the benefits and rewards in U.S. society than do wealthy people, given the society's ideological belief that individuals are fully responsible for their own economic fates such that character flaws and motivational deficiencies are the causes of failure, poverty, and economic insecurity. In this context, then, we assume that financially successful people deserve their good fortune because of their individual hard work and desire. Conversely, we assume that the poor, homeless, or otherwise economically insecure deserve their plight because they lack initiative, hard work, and desire to succeed, or because they have innate character flaws such as laziness.

Variations in Systems of Stratification and Inequality

Not all stratification systems operate in the same manner. However, despite the variation in inequality systems, each one falls somewhere along a continuum between the two extremes of **closed systems,** in which people are ranked on the basis of ascribed characteristics and in which mobility within the system is not possible, and **open systems,** in which people are ranked on the basis of merit, talent, ability, or past performance and movement upward or downward in the system is possible. Beside the degree of openness or closure of a stratification system, sociologists also examine

1. how positions are filled in the system (by ascription, achievement, or both) and the resulting impact this process has on people's life chances.
2. the rigidity of the system, that is, how hard it is for people to change their status categories.
3. the extent to which there are restrictions on social interaction between people of different categories or strata.

Although there are five general systems of stratification—slave, caste, estate, class, and apartheid—we will examine only class, caste,

and estate systems here. We will examine slavery and apartheid in the next chapter. These systems of inequality should be understood as ideal types for purposes of analysis. There is no scientific evidence that any stratification system exists in the ideal or pure form. Therefore, keep in mind as you read this section that any given society may include elements of more than one of these types of stratification systems.

Caste Systems of Inequality

Castes are very rigid and static hereditary systems of rank, usually religiously dictated, that tend to be fixed and permanent. Movement from one group to another is highly restricted by both law and custom. The classic example of a caste system of inequality is the Hindu caste system of India that existed prior to World War II. It is distinguished not so much by physical distinctions between groups as by people's social descent (Marger, 1985). In its classic form, there were four major castes based on occupation, called *varnas,* and a fifth category, referred to as *untouchables,* considered to be so lowly and unclean as to have no place within this system of stratification. The Brahmins (priests and scholars) represented the highest caste and were viewed as spiritually pure. The Brahmins were followed by the warriors, merchants, artisans, and then, at the very bottom, by the untouchables.

Although no longer sanctioned by the Indian government, the caste system still operates in many of India's 650,000 villages, and it continues to dominate the lives of rural Indians, who make up close to three-fourths of the Indian population. Caste membership is hereditary; it is established at birth. It is a closed system in which individuals cannot move from one caste to another, although whole castes can and do move and change their positions within the caste system. Each caste is clearly defined, and caste membership usually determines one's occupation and social roles. Caste rules are strictly enforced, and interaction between the castes in intimate social settings is minimal to nonexistent. Members are expected to live with, eat with, interact with, and marry other members of their caste. The restriction of social interchange across castes greatly reduces the likelihood that caste barriers will be breached. This system of inequality is strongly buttressed by the Hindu belief in reincarnation (rebirth of the soul), which holds that individuals who fail to abide by the rules of caste stratification will be reborn in inferior positions in their next lives. Given the continuation of some forms of the caste system in India and the historical view of untouchables as outcasts, it is noteworthy that an untouchable, K. R. Narayanan, a seventy-six-year-old former scholar, diplomat, and Cabinet minister, was recently installed as president (see the Cultural Snapshot box).

Estate Systems of Inequality

The term **estate system of stratification** refers to a system of inequality based on noble birth and ownership and/or control of land. The estate system of inequality characterized feudal European society, but it has also existed in various Asian nations as well. Similar to the caste system, the feudal estate system consisted of different levels of social position, called estates, each with its own set of legal rights and obligations and each ranked according to its functions. However, unlike castes, estates were of equal importance, at least theoretically. The three major estates in the feudal system were the nobility, whose wealth, power, and prestige were based on their noble birth and their large land holdings; the church, possessing somewhat lower status than the nobility but nonetheless possessing distinct privileges and often exercising enormous power (for example, the church owned a tremendous amount of land and exercised a good deal of influence over the power of the nobility); and the peasants, consisting of serfs, merchants, artisans, and free peasants. Within each estate, people were stratified by a hierarchy of positions.

Buttressed by religion and tradition, the estate system was a somewhat open system in that some limited intermarriage and individual mobility between estates were possible. For example, serfs who had distinguished themselves in some way were occasionally freed and given land, some peasants were allowed to enter the priesthood, and peasants were sometimes knighted for having performed special services for the monarch or for having excelled in the military. Some vestiges of the estate system remain in some modern societies that maintain a landed gentry and inherited titles of nobility, such as the United Kingdom, where the Queen and her family are still recognized and enjoy high status, some political power, and wealth, although they no longer have the power to rule.

Class Systems of Inequality

The term **class stratification** refers to the institutionalized system by which some groups have more economic resources and power than do others. The concept of social classes is most associated with modern industrial societies such as the United States. Contemporary sociologists define and analyze **class** in many different ways. However, the concept generally refers to any group of people who occupy a similar economic position in society. Members of a class tend to share a common lifestyle and to have relatively similar resources and life chances. Class is an important social construct not only because it creates different opportunities and privileges or disadvantages for individuals and groups but also because society is structured in terms of class relationships. Class is not just a matter of individual resources; it also involves the relationship between class groups and whole social systems. It is thus a structured or institutionalized system of privilege and inequality (Andersen, 1997).

Class, along with race and gender, is an essential dimension of life in the United States because it influences the access different groups have to economic, social, and political resources. Where people are located in the class hierarchy determines how well societal institutions serve them. For example, poor people have far less access to quality health care; primary, secondary, and higher education; political power and clout; and other cultural resources than do the middle, upper, and elite classes. Although social class is based primarily on economic position, as you will learn in our later discussion of Max Weber and social stratification, economic position is strongly related to prestige and power as well.

Class systems are most characteristically found in industrial societies having market economies because such societies create more opportunities for achieving wealth and status than do societies having centralized economies.

Cultural Snapshot

An Untouchable Takes Office as India's President

During the second half of the twentieth century, India's adherence to the caste system has been slowly eroding. A noteworthy change took place in 1997.

> Half a century after Mohandas K. Gandhi led India to independence with a vision of a society that would rid itself of its ancient system of caste discrimination, a member of Hinduism's lowest caste took the oath . . . as the country's President and declared his elevation as proof that "the concerns of the common man" have finally taken precedence in the nation's affairs.
>
> K.R. Narayanan, a 76-year-old former scholar, diplomat and Cabinet minister who once served as India's Ambassador to the United States, was chosen for the ceremonial post last week by an electoral college comprising all the country's federal and state lawmakers. While others have risen to be senior Cabinet ministers, top judges and high-ranking military officers, Mr. Narayanan is the first to realize Gandhi's standard of proof that India was finally resolved to stamp out the humiliations of the caste system—the election of an untouchable as President.
>
> Real power in India rests with the Prime Minister and the Cabinet. But at a time when India seems destined to elect politically unstable coalition governments, some Indians believe that the President's role in choosing the Prime Minister and the Cabinet, judging who is most likely to be able to command a majority in Parliament, could see Mr. Narayanan emerge as crucially important political figure.
>
> For the 150 million Indians who call themselves Dalits, a Hindi word meaning "the oppressed" that is now commonly used when referring to untouchables, Mr. Narayanan's story has the elements of a fable. He grew up in the southern state of Kerala in the 1930's at a time when untouchables were routinely denied the right to enter Hindu temples, draw water from wells reserved for Brahmins and other members of the higher castes, or walk along some village pathways; these restrictions still apply, even if they are unlawful, in many of India's 650,000 villages. . . .
>
> In his address in the ornate Central Hall of India's Parliament, Mr. Narayanan, who previously served as Vice President, began with a salute to the lawmakers who chose him in a ballot last week in which he won 95 percent of the votes, defeating the only other candidate, a former election commissioner, T. S. Seshan. Mr. Seshan, a well-known maverick, greeted his defeat with an angry outburst, telling reporters that it was "an insult" to Mr. Narayanan that the mainly upper-caste lawmakers chose him, in Mr. Seshan's words, "only because he was a Dalit."

The more surplus produced in a society, the more stratified it will be and the more complex its class system will be. As some scholars have observed, although the United States is often touted as the epitome of an open system of stratification, the fact is that it not only consists of social classes but also contains castelike characteristics as well. For example, as we will show in Chapters 10 and 11, the intersections of race, ethnicity, and gender often present castelike barriers to the mobility of many people in the U.S. class system.

Many people think of the U.S. class system as a **meritocracy,** a system of social stratification based on ability and achievement rather than social background. This is certainly not accurate. In fact, ascription sometimes outweighs achievement in determining one's upward or downward mobility. People born into wealthy families are generally more likely to enjoy high status than are people born into poor or working-class families. For example, any offspring of the wealthiest private individual in the world, Bill Gates, will find the class system far more open and will have greater access to the things that are valued in this society, including high social status and education, than will, say, the more than one million homeless individuals in U.S. society. This fact notwithstanding, what people *do* is also important in determining their status in a class sys-

Mr. Narayanan made it clear that he thought Mr. Seshan had gotten matters upside down.

"That the nation has found a consensus for its highest office in someone who has sprung from the grassroots of our society and grown up in the dust and heat of this sacred land is symbolic of the fact that the concerns of the common man have now moved to the center stage of our social and political life," he said. "It is this larger significance of my election rather than any personal sense of honor that makes me rejoice on this occasion."

Mr. Narayanan went on to offer a stinging rebuke to the country's politicians, who applauded him repeatedly even as he politely condemned them.

With barely three weeks to go to the 50th anniversary of India's independence from Britain, he recalled Gandhi's ambition that a free India would "wipe every tear from every eye" by eliminating the country's ancient scourges, including poverty, disease, illiteracy and caste discrimination—ills that are still pervasive, leaving India close to the bottom of virtually every international index of social progress. Among other things, India's official statistics say nearly 350 million of the country's 960 million people still live in deep poverty. . . .

"Excessive obsession with the pursuit of pure politics has often overshadowed the social, economic, and developmental needs of our people," he said. "Can we not sink our differences, as we have done on critical occasions in our history, and devote our undivided attention, for a time, to the development of the economy and the welfare of the people?"

But many Indian commentators shared Mr. Seshan's view that there was tokenism in Mr. Narayanan's appointment, and others said Mr. Narayanan had been co-opted by the Brahmins and other upper-caste Indians who still dominate in the country's politics, civil service, and top corporations. . . .

But another view was that Mr. Narayanan could play a key role in encouraging lower-caste Indians to believe that there is a place for them in a caste-free society. . . .

The Indian Express, one of the county's most powerful newspapers, expressed the hope that Mr. Narayanan's arrival as President would quell the turn toward caste-based politics. It said in an editorial that the appointment "advertises the fact that social mobility is no mere directive principle—it can be an actual fact."

Source: Excerpted from John F. Burns. (1997, July 26). "Lowest-Caste Hindu takes Office as India's President." *New York Times*, p. 3. Copyright © 1997 by The New York Times Company. Reprinted by permission.

---

tem. For example, completing medical school and making sound economic decisions will greatly impact and enhance a person's status.

Both ascribed and achieved statuses have important consequences for a person's chance to enjoy wealth and high social status in the United States. Its persistent pattern of economic inequality results in masses of people being systematically limited in their access to the opportunities and resources in U.S. society—for example, to full and equal participation in major U.S. institutions such as employment, education, politics, health care, and housing. Yet participation in these institutions is essential to an individual's or group's **life chances**—the likelihood that individuals and groups will have access to important societal resources, positive experiences, and opportunities for long, healthy, and successful lives.

The Impact of Social Class on Life Chances As our discussion thus far reveals, a major consequence of the hierarchal placement of people in society is that the rewards and things that count in a society, such as wealth, power, prestige, income, and adequate housing, are unequally distributed. This differential access to scarce goods and resources produces differences in life experiences.

Differences in life chances across social class are quite apparent in the United States.

According to sociologists, poverty lowers and closes life chances while wealth enhances life chances in that it allows for greater access to quality education, safer neighborhoods, and high-quality housing, health care, nutrition, and police protection (Ruane & Cerulo, 1997). That is, social class affects what neighborhood and the type of housing we will live in, what schools we will attend, what lifestyles we will follow, what our leisure activities will be, and whom we will have major interactions with, whom we will marry, and at what age we will marry. Unlike in the caste system, whose groups are clearly delineated, the lines are blurred and sometimes overlap and people often do not fit neatly into one class or another in a class system. Where, for example, would a person who has a doctorate degree in sociology from Harvard University but who drives a taxi because of the scarcity of jobs in higher education fit in the class system? Because the boundaries of class are so flexible, most people (except those in the higher classes) do not display a class consciousness.

A close examination of the connections between class and life chances makes it clear that the difference between upper-class and lower-class status, between wealth and poverty can literally have life-and-death consequences. For example, as we will discuss in some detail in Chapter 15, research on the **mortality rate,** the number of deaths per 1,000 members of the population, suggests that one's longevity is greatly influenced by one's socioeconomic status.

The term **socioeconomic status** refers to a particular social location, defined with reference to education, occupation, and financial resources. In the United States, those who have the highest socioeconomic status live significantly longer than do those of the lowest status. In fact, according to some sources, a privileged person's life span can exceed that of a disadvantaged person by as much as 6.5 years (Ruane & Cerulo, 1997). Likewise, **infant mortality,** the number of deaths of children under one year of age per 1,000 live births, is twice as high among the poor as it is among the wealthy. The link between social class and mortality stems, in part, from the fact that the lower classes have significantly less access to high-quality health care than do members of higher socioeconomic classes. Given the debilitating consequences of class

stratification for those at or near the bottom of the class hierarchy, why have societies been unable to eliminate class stratification? In the next section, we take a brief look at some of the sociological explanations of continuing socioeconomic stratification.

Theoretical Perspectives on Socioeconomic Stratification

Sociological theories of social stratification and inequality present a variety of ways of explaining why inequality exists, why it varies from one society and historical period to another, how it is maintained, and why it persists. Most of the classic theorists did not consider race and gender in their analyses of social stratification. Because they were developing explanations of the stratification that resulted from the industrial revolution, economic inequality was clearly a major variable of concern. Although race and gender are clearly important dimensions that account for inequality, they do not account for the entire range of socioeconomic levels in the United States and most other industrial countries.

Even a cursory look at U.S. society confirms the existence of pervasive inequalities. Masses of people live in poverty; a few are very rich. A majority of people enjoy some degree of affluence, although most must scrape to make ends meet. If the masses of people who live in poverty acquired wealth today or tomorrow, would they remain politically powerless? Or if they somehow jostled power away from the ruling elites, would they still have low social status?

Questions such as these have challenged sociologists to try to explain the reasons for the unequal distribution of wealth, power, and prestige in human societies. While contemporary answers to such questions have their basis in the works of Karl Marx and Max Weber, most sociologists today tend to take either a functional or a conflict perspective. Functionalists argue that stratification is a necessary and inevitable piece of machinery that keeps society functioning efficiently. The conflict view regards stratification as the result of the selfish struggle between individuals for scarce rewards and as persisting not because it is functional but because those who have power are determined to preserve their power and advantage by dominating and exploiting those who do not. Thus, sociologists are deeply divided over the root causes of inequality, and despite decades of scientific research, they are still far from agreeing on how and why humans become unequal.

A Conflict Perspective of Inequality: The Tradition of Karl Marx

Karl Marx believed that in order to understand social order, we must recognize and understand who controls the means of economic production in a society. He viewed the material basis of society as the key to social structure. Thus, for Marx, social stratification and social structure were one and the same. Marx's key insight into social stratification was in his discussion of social class and social conflict. He believed that every aspect of a society is an outgrowth of—and at the same time perpetuates—the society's class structure. For Marx, the structure of a society is based on its level of production, and it is one's relationship to the means of production (that is, where they work in the economy), rather than innate abilities, talents, drives, or needs, that determines one's class level, personality, and social consciousness. So the critical factor in creating stratification systems (for example, social classes) is the ownership of the means of production.

Marxian stratification theory suggests that social classes are formed as a result of a struggle to acquire scarce and desirable social resources. He argued that this struggle results in two clearly conflicting economic interest groups in any society:

1. **The ruling class.** This class is made up of those who own and/or control the means of production and whose interests lie in maintaining their privilege and power and in preventing the lower classes from wresting social resources for themselves. Thus, the ruling classes use the labor of the lower classes to preserve their privileged position by purchasing their labor at the lowest possible cost in order to maximize profits for themselves.
2. **The subordinate class.** This class is made up of those who own little or nothing, who work for wages with which they buy the basic necessities of life, and who have an interest in changing the system so that they can receive a greater share of society's resources.

Thus, social stratification is created and maintained by one group in order to protect and enhance its economic interests. It exists only because those in the ruling class are determined to preserve their advantages; they do so by exploiting those in the subordinate class. That is, some people are wealthy because some people are poor. According to Marx, social inequality is maintained by the use of power by those who control the means of production. They control the distribution of resources and shape people's outlooks and experiences in life.

Marx predicted that the gap between the ruling and subordinate classes would increase as capitalism became more deeply entrenched and also that the ruling class would shrink in numbers as a result of their endless competition, the middle class would disappear into the working class, and the increasing poverty of workers would spark a successful revolution. Although Marx failed at predicting the future of industrial capitalism, it does not invalidate his basic insight that conflict over scarce resources leads to the creation of class systems and that in every case, the interests of the dominant class are served by the ideology and the power of their class position. This Marxian insight continues to form the basis of some contemporary scholars' work on stratification and inequality.

Post-Marxist Theory: Erik Olin Wright   Since the early 1970s, there has been an explosion of theory and research within the Marxian tradition. This theory has done much to transform the problems of a classic Marxian analysis of inequality such that it is more applicable, for example, to an analysis of the contemporary class structure in the United States. A major proponent of this post-Marxian theory is Erik Olin Wright. His theory both builds on Marx and addresses a problem with traditional Marxian theory.

One of the major problems posed by a classic Marxian analysis of stratification in contemporary industrial societies is Marx's polarization of class into two antagonistic classes: owners and nonowners of the means of production. Such a polar view of workers and class leaves us with the question of what to do with those in the middle. In this context, Wright (1985, 1989a, 1989b, 1996) defined classes in terms of their members' control over money, physical capital, and others' labor. He offered the following four criteria for placement in the modern class structure: (1) ownership of the means of production, (2) purchase of the labor of others (employing others), (3) control of the labor of others (supervising others on the job), and (4) sale of one's own labor (being employed by someone else). Class locations are determined, then, by ownership and authority.

Wright uses the concept of *contradictory locations* to broaden the definition of class to include a total of four classes: (1) the capitalist class, (2) the managerial class, (3) the small business class, and (4) the working class. Figure 9.1 illustrates Wright's conceptualization of social class and is based on his research of the average annual income, from all sources, of people in each class stratum. According to Wright, the two classes that were central to Marxian theory represent the largest differences in people's ability to exploit property, authority, and expertise in modern society and can be found at each end of Figure 9.1 (in the top left corner and the bottom right corner). The remaining cells represent the middle classes, which hold contradictory positions. Wright suggests that in advanced capitalist societies, a given position does not necessarily have to be located within a given class and that, in some cases, a position may be simultaneously proletarian and bourgeois (thus, contradictory). For example, many managers and CEOs could be viewed as simultaneously capitalists (insofar as they dominate the labor of workers and maximize profits) and workers (insofar as they do not own the means of production and sell their labor power to capitalists).

The Tradition of Max Weber

Take a moment to think about your social position in society. What position do you occupy in the social stratification system? Take a look at others around you. Where do you think categories of people such as students, doctors, college

FIGURE 9.1 ☉ **Erik Olin Wright's Neo-Marxist Typology of Social Class in Capitalist Society** *Source:* Adapted from E.O. Wright. 1984. "A General Framework for the Analysis of Class Structure." *Politics and Society*, vol. 13, no. 4, Table 4 (p. 410). Copyright © 1984 by Sage Publications. Reprinted by permission of Sage Publications.

	Assets in the Means of Production				
	Owners of Means of Production	Non-Owners (Wage Laborers)			
Owns sufficient capital to hire workers and not work	1. Bourgeoisie	4. Expert managers	7. Semicredentialed managers	10. Uncredentialed managers	+
Owns sufficient capital to hire workers but must work	2. Small employers	5. Expert supervisors	8. Semicredentialed supervisors	11. Uncredentialed supervisors	> 0
Owns sufficient capital to work for self but not to hire workers	3. Petty bourgeoisie	6. Expert nonmanagers	9. Semicredentialed workers	12. Proletarians	−
		+	> 0	−	Organization Assets

Skill Credential Assets

Note: The typology is divided into two sections, one for the owners of the means of production and the other for nonowners. For wage earners, social class location is distinguished by two subordinate relations of exploitation characteristic of capitalist society: organization assets and skill credential assets.

professors, college presidents, sports figures, movie stars, laborers, the unemployed, or individuals such as the president of the United States, Bill Gates, Oprah Winfrey, Barbara Walters, or John Doe the cab driver are located in this system? What criteria do you use to locate yourself and others in the stratification system? Is it public recognition, wealth, political power, or some other factor? In contrast to the unidimensional view of inequality put forth by Karl Marx, sociologist Max Weber offered a multidimensional view of social stratification and placement in the social hierarchy that included three major dimensions: wealth, prestige, and power (Weber, 1968).

While acknowledging the importance of economic causes in the formation of social strata, Weber insisted that noneconomic sociocultural factors are also influential. In fact, they are often more influential than economic factors in controlling the distribution of material and symbolic benefits. Whereas Marx believed that social stratification was a result of economic conflict, Weber believed that it was a reflection of the unequal distribution of power—the chance of a person or a number of people to realize their will in a social action even against the resistance of others. Therefore, although Weber agreed that economic forces were important, he did not see them as operating independently. Rather, he saw multiple sources of rankings. Although there is a good deal of interplay among these dimensions, Weber believed that each could be analyzed separately.

Wealth is based on the ownership of capital goods and property. According to Weber, wealth and property stemming from economic activities represent one source of ranking in society, which leads to the *formation of classes.* For Weber, *economic class* refers to the distribution of people into various strata based upon their economic assets. Essentially, Weber expanded Marx's view of economic or class divisions to take into account not only ownership versus nonownership of the means of production but also people's more general relationship to the marketplace. In other words, equally important as ownership/nonownership are the opportunities for income that people have, for example, the skill level a worker possesses. The higher the skill level, other things being equal, the more return

(income or wealth) a worker is able to obtain for her/his labor. According to Weber, class is a complex, multidimensional social phenomenon that involves status and power as well as economic factors.

Prestige, or status, refers to the social esteem or social honor accorded to people by others. Every position in a society is awarded a different degree of status. For example, the positions of lawyer and doctor are highly valued in the United States; as a result, lawyers and doctors enjoy high status by virtue of their positions. Social status involves lifestyle, is tied to the consumption of goods, and is a source of ranking, creating *status groups.* For example, we tend to give high social ranking to the rich and famous—to people who live in luxurious homes, have servants to attend their needs, purchase expensive art, and vacation in glamorous places around the globe—and low social ranking to people who have no home or who live in small, inconspicuous homes. In Marx's view, a person's relationship to the means of production—*how* she or he earns a living—determines her or his social status in the inequality system. Weber, on the other hand, believed that the way people *spend* their earnings is equally important in determining social status. It also depends on how highly a society values certain characteristics such as education, race/ethnicity, occupation, sex, age, and family background. In U.S. society, for example, the type of work people do is an important source of social prestige. In other countries high prestige or social honor is accorded to the elderly.

Power, the ability to realize one's will, even against the resistance of others, is another valuable resource in society that is unequally distributed. It can be valued for its own sake, or it can be the means by which individuals or groups raise themselves either economically or socially. The status, and often the profits, of a law firm, for example, can be significantly enhanced if one of its members holds a political office. In the Weberian sense, power is based partly on class and partly on status.

According to Weber, these multiplicity of resources generate unequal rankings in a society. He recognized that while these three dimensions of stratification are frequently interrelated, they often appear independently of one another.

While a person's power, status, and income levels are usually the same, there are sometimes discrepancies. For example, gaining power in a crime syndicate or a street gang does not necessarily enhance one's social status in society at large. Wealth does not automatically confer a place in "high society"; nor is the richest person in a community necessarily the most respected. A well-known artist may be accorded high status or social honor based on her work but have little power to affect the actions of others.

Although Marx saw power as always rooted in the economic conditions of life, Weber argued that it is possible to have wealth but possess little power or prestige. High-priced prostitutes can earn considerably more money than the typical worker, but their lifestyle is viewed in this society with disdain and they are unlikely to possess any real political power. Most often, however, one can use economic wealth to obtain prestige and political power, and, conversely, one can use prestige (for example, in the form of noble birth or skin color) to secure economic benefits or prestige (Rossides, 1997).

Davis's and Moore's Functionalist View

It is obvious that valued resources such as money or income and wealth are distributed unequally in U.S. society. Why does this disparity exist? Is inequality natural and inevitable? Is it necessary for society's proper functioning? Marx saw this inequality as an inevitable result of capitalism and a situation that would lead to conflict. Functionalists also see the inevitability of inequality, but they believe that it is functional for society. In this view, just as various elements or parts of society exist and persist over time because they serve a necessary function in the overall maintenance of society, so does inequality.

Over half a century ago, in one of the most widely cited and debated theses on stratification, sociologists Kingsley Davis and Wilbert Moore presented what is now a classic functional theory of stratification. In their article *Some Principles of Stratification,* Davis and Moore (1945) asked why some occupations such as lawyer are more highly rewarded than others such as farm worker. They argued that economic inequality exists because it meets society's needs for productivity by motivating people.

According to Davis and Moore, there are certain critical jobs that require prolonged and difficult training and a high level of responsibility and accountability in every society. Mistakes may affect a large number of people or lead to injury or death. In addition, these jobs are often very stressful and require more hours of work than the average job. Because these jobs are difficult but essential, society must provide ample rewards to entice people to take them on. These rewards are high salaries and high social prestige. For example, anyone can learn to dig a ditch in a few days, but it takes years of costly schooling and special skills to become a doctor. In addition, doctors often work long hours, are almost always on call, and are responsible for the longevity and good health of their clients. If people capable of filling such jobs are to get the extra training and endure the stress related to making life-and-death decisions, they must be motivated to do so. If people could earn the same money working at a low-stress, eight-hour-a-day job that required little training, wouldn't it be harder to get people to become doctors? According to Davis and Moore, the differential reward system leads to individual motivation, which is the key to ensuring society's survival. Without this system, they believe, many essential tasks would not get done. As a consequence, rewards and their distribution are built into the social structure, giving rise to social ranking and social inequality. In this sense, social inequality is only incidental to or a by-product of a functional society.

Not all important jobs are hard to fill. Important jobs that are easy to fill do not get high rewards. For example, teachers may be as important as doctors, but because teaching jobs are easier to fill, require less accountability, and do not necessarily involve life-and-death decisions, teachers receive less compensation and fewer rewards than do doctors. Essentially, then, the Davis and Moore thesis suggests that inequality is both necessary and functional. The reward system ensures that the functionally most important roles are filled by competent people through their status striving. The magnitude of the reward is a consequence of the functional importance of the job. Although stratification is found in all known societies, its specific form will vary depending on the major functions of a society. However, at the basis of all such systems is functional importance and relative scarcity. Most people in society accept the reward system and cooperate in preserving the existing distribution of rewards and opportunities. Therefore, according to Davis and Moore, the entire society benefits in the long run.

Applying the Sociological Imagination

Do you agree with the Davis and Moore thesis? Make a list of occupations in U.S. society and evaluate how important they are to society. Then collect some data about the typical income and other social rewards attached to these occupations. Would you agree that the salaries, social recognition, and rewards for each occupation are commensurate with the value of the occupation to society? If not, how else might you explain the differences in rewards?

Some Principles of Social Stratification: A Critique

As with any theory of human behavior, the Davis and Moore theory of social stratification has been subject to great scrutiny and critique. As with functional theory generally, a major critique centers around the notion of *functional importance.* In this case, for example, how do we determine that one occupation is more critical or functionally more important than another? How do we determine, for instance, that the occupation of doctor is more important than that of garbage collector? As has been amply pointed out in the scientific literature, regular and effective garbage collection and disposal are far more important in lowering death rates in a society than are highly trained doctors. Furthermore, some studies of the degree to which rewards are actually related to the importance of a job or the scarcity of qualified people to fill it show that the importance of positions is unrelated to rewards; they show little support for the functionalist contention that incomes will be higher when the supply of workers for a given position is small (Cullen & Novick, 1979; Wanner & Lewis, 1978). Interestingly, in 1998, occu-

pational data indicated that there was a substantial oversupply of physicians in the United States, both generalists and specialists. Consequently, if the Davis and Moore thesis is correct, shouldn't we expect that physicians' salaries will come down?

Conflict theorist Melvin Tumin (1953) presented a classic critique of the Davis and Moore thesis of social stratification specifically and of functional explanations generally. In an article titled "Some Principles of Stratification: A Critical Analysis," Tumin pointed out several major flaws or shortcomings in the logic of the Davis and Moore thesis. He argued that contrary to the Davis and Moore thesis, inequality does not facilitate competition for socially important jobs. Rather, it limits the competition to those who can afford the training, thereby eliminating people who may be equally or better qualified for the job. Basically, there is a vast waste of potentially brilliant doctors, lawyers, teachers, and others who may be too poor to attend college. Although a few poor people might get the training needed to secure high-status jobs, the vast majority will not. Over 20 percent of all doctors and over 40 percent of all professionals follow in the footsteps of their parents. Thus, in a stratified society, the vast majority of talent, energy, and potential among the lower classes is often lost.

Furthermore, according to Tumin, the Davis and Moore thesis does not consider the motivation of the masses other than to say that people accept the stratification system and believe that they get what they deserve. However, the riots in U.S. cities in the 1960s and 1990s demonstrate clearly that marked inequalities create distrust, hostility, and suspicion between different segments of the population, a condition that can hardly be called functional. People who are struggling to survive in a society that favors the rich and powerful have little incentive or motivation to abide by norms and respect the culture.

Tumin also questioned whether some of the jobs that receive high rewards are really more critical to society than other jobs. This is certainly not always the case. How many millionaires perform work that is actually essential to society's survival? Tumin points out that if factories had all managers and engineers and no line workers, they could produce nothing. Similarly, if hospitals had only doctors and no nurses,

nurses' aides, clerical workers, janitors, and other cleaning personnel, they could not save many lives. Therefore, low-status, poorly paid workers can be as important to the functioning of society as those who earn high salaries and receive valued rewards such as power and prestige. In fact, given the increasingly specialized character of the modern division of labor, one could argue that every individual makes an essential contribution. And, even if we agree that those at the top have the more functionally important positions, how necessary is the vast inequality in salaries to ensuring that people choose these positions over unskilled ones? For example, there is a tremendous gap between the salaries of CEOs of major corporations in the United States and the salaries of unskilled and other workers in the same corporations. According to Graef Crystal (1995), the average salary of the CEOs of 424 of the largest U.S. corporations in 1993 was 170 times the average salary of factory workers. Even if some economic incentive is necessary to motivate people to fill certain essential roles or jobs in society, it is difficult to see how inequality as extreme as this is either functional or inevitable.

Is the United States a Meritocracy?   Implicit in the Davis and Moore thesis is that everyone is where they are in the stratification system because of merit. As Tumin points out, however, the Davis and Moore notion of a meritocracy overlooks the importance of inheritance in people getting important positions and owning or controlling major valued resources in society. In all too many cases, it is not what you know but who you know that matters. Membership and high status is frequently passed on from one family or generation to another. For example, two thirds of those on the 1997 Forbes Fortune 400 listing of the 400 richest Americans started with at least some substantial start-up capital, and 42 percent inherited enough wealth to rank in the 400 at birth (Werbe, 1998). Various organizations and institutions contribute to this process; it is not just the extremely wealthy who inherit and gain control of valued goods and resources. Trade unions, for example, have historically passed on membership to sons, and women and people of color have been denied access until recent times.

The Davis and Moore thesis implies that everyone has equal life chances when in reality they do not. As we discussed earlier, life chances are unequally distributed in U.S. society, and they are highly dependent on key factors such as race, social class, and gender. The fact is that the majority of those at the top of the stratification hierarchy are white males. Of the 400 richest Americans reported in the 1997 Forbes Fortune 400 listing, for example, only one (Oprah Winfrey) was an African American, and most of the 15 percent who were women acquired their wealth through inheritance, marriage, or both. Based on the Davis and Moore thesis, the fact that so few women and even fewer people of color are represented on the Forbes list would suggest that this is because women and people of color have not contributed anything beneficial to society, that they do not have the talent, skills, or motivation to perform highly rewarded positions in society. In many respects, the Davis and Moore thesis blames the victim for her or his inequality: it implies that people are poor because they choose to be poor by being lazy and unmotivated. In implying this, it leads us to overlook the structural and institutionalized features of inequality such as race and gender discrimination, lack of education and job opportunities, and inadequate funding of public education.

Social Stratification: A Synthesis   Criticisms of them notwithstanding, both the structural functional and conflict perspectives offer key insights into social inequality. Harold R. Kerbo (1993), for example, points out that, on the one hand, the notion of supply and demand explains some aspects of the unequal distribution of rewards in the occupational structure, while on the other hand, economic conflicts are some of the most important sources of division in modern capitalist societies.

Several sociologists have developed a tradition of synthesizing these two important theoretical paradigms. For example, Gerhard Lenski (1966) concurs with the functionalist view that the major resources in society are distributed as rewards to people who occupy important positions and that stratification fosters a rough match between scarce talent and social rewards. However, he also points out that as societies advance technologically, they become capable of producing surplus goods and services. As surplus increases, conflicts emerge over its distribution.

In the United States, there is a strong ideological belief that everyone has an equal opportunity to be successful. However, the stark contrast between how the wealthy and powerful live and how people like this homeless woman live raise serious questions about our image of America as a meritocracy.

Those individuals and groups who have greatest access to power and authority are able to control social wealth, and they build inequality into the society, which results in a system of stratification. In essence, Lenski argues that inequality is necessary and desirable under conditions of low surplus. It arises out of society's need to fill social statuses and from group competition and conflict. Although stratification is prevalent, some of it is neither necessary nor inevitable. In many societies, some of the social rewards are fairly allocated, but most are not. Thus, while stratification facilitates some aspects of societal functioning, it impedes other aspects. Lenski suggests that inequalities remain and are unlikely to be eliminated because of the division of labor and greed.

Socioeconomic Stratification and Inequality in the United States

In the United States, people are separated into class-based, homogeneous residential, educational, and other groupings. As we learned in Chapter 6, we acquire our personalities through the socialization process; our personalities therefore result, in large part, from our social class background. In the next two sections of this chapter, we examine the distribution of income and wealth and take a closer look at social classes in the United States. In general, this discussion is framed around questions such as Is inequality increasing or decreasing? Is the United States really a land of golden opportunities? If so, for whom? Are hard work and initiative the primary roads to economic success?

The Distribution of Income and Wealth in the United States

Although many people tend to think of the United States as a meritocracy where people just have to work hard and pull themselves up by the bootstraps to be financially successful, this is clearly not the reality for millions of working Americans whose bootstraps are frayed just from the attempt to make ends meet. This romantic vision of U.S. society clouds people's view of the existence of vast inequalities. Two major indices of inequality are **income,** the amount of money an individual or family earns from occupational wages or salaries and from investments, and **wealth,** the total value of money and other assets that individuals or families own, less all outstanding debts. Let's briefly examine each of these indices to get a picture of who is rich and who is poor in the United States.

Income   Although they work, over 10 million Americans and their families live in poverty. Most of them are minimum-wage earners who in 1997 earned an average of $5.15 per hour or $10,712 per year working full time, year round. Although the minimum wage has increased a little more than 20 percent since 1995, real wages decreased between 1973 and 1997 and the distribution of income continues to be extremely unequal. According to Jill Lawrence (1997), the economic boom of the 1990s was largely a bust for those at the bottom of the socioeconomic ladder. The new prosperity of the nation is definitely not reaching the working poor or welfare recipients or wage earners generally. Consider the following point about income: in Gutherie Center, Iowa, farm women have flocked to jobs that typically pay $5.50 per hour to help make

family ends meet. In contrast, in his heyday, Michael Milken, the "junk-bond king," received in excess of $1.5 million *a day* in salary and commissions (Braun, 1997).

According to recent U.S. Census data, the income gap between the rich and poor is increasing. As Figure 9.2 shows, the top 20 percent of the population receives slightly less than one-half of all income in this country (47.2 percent). In stark contrast, the bottom 20 percent of U.S. citizens receive only 4.2 percent of all income. The higher one goes up the income scale, the greater the rate of capital accumulation. Not only have the top 20 percent of the population grown more affluent compared with everyone below but also the top 5 percent have grown richer

FIGURE 9.2 ◑ How the Economic Pie Is Sliced

Source: U.S. Bureau of the Census. 1998. "Historical Income Tables-Families." In *Statistical Abstract of the United States.* Washington, DC: Government Printing Office, Table F-2.

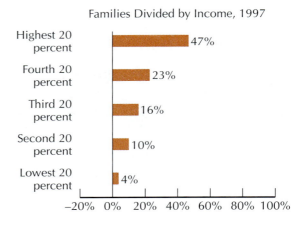

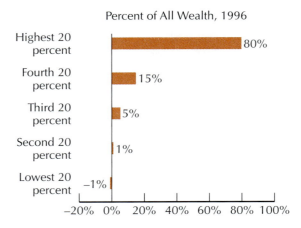

compared with the next 15 percent. Likewise, the top 1 percent have become richer compared with the next 4 percent. It has been estimated that if children's play blocks represented $1,000 each, over 98 percent of us would have incomes represented by a pile of blocks no more than a few yards off the ground, while the top 1 percent would stack blocks many times higher than the Eiffel Tower (Parenti, 1998) (see Figure 9.3).

In summary, with peaks and valleys, large disparities in income between American workers exist. As we move into the twenty-first century, real income has declined and relative income inequality is greater than at any time in the past forty years. The numbers of poor people are increasing, homelessness is increasing, and the middle classes are becoming increasingly poorer as their incomes have dropped. Children of baby boomers who are now working have suffered the greatest deterioration in income. As a

consequence, they are increasingly locked out of the American Dream. Only a very small percentage of the American population has reaped benefits from recent U.S. economic policies and the rise of the world economy. Although women, poor rural farmers, African Americans, undocumented immigrants, and other workers have made some economic gains over the past twenty years, these groups continue to be easily exploited in the labor market (Braun, 1997). In fact, a 1998 study of hunger in the global economy found that the United States has the greatest level of wage inequality of any industrialized nation (Bread for the World Institute, 1998).

Wealth   The income gap in the United States is large, but the gap in wealth is even larger. There is unbelievable wealth in the United States, but it is concentrated in the hands of a few individuals and families, and the gap between this small

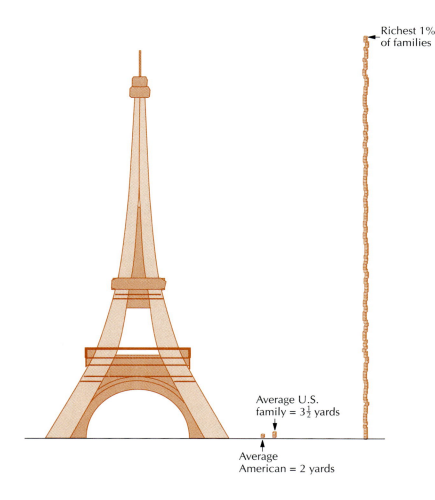

Richest 1% of families

Average U.S. family = 3½ yards

Average American = 2 yards

FIGURE 9.3 ♻ An Income Pyramid: Inequality of U.S. Income
Source: Data from M. Parenti. 1998. "The Super Rich." *Z Magazine,* http://www.lol.shareworld.com/zmag/articles/parentimar98.htm.

minority and the poverty of millions is almost inconceivable. It should be noted that wealth and income inequality are not one and the same, although they are obviously closely related. Wealth is derived almost totally from ownership in stocks, bonds, and capital goods, whereas income derives mostly from job-related earnings. For example, *Fortune* magazine estimated in 1996 that Steve Forbes of Forbes, Inc., had a personal net worth of $439 million, mostly from his inherited stake in the family publishing and land empire. In addition to his income, the magazine estimated that Forbes's personal wealth included: (1) a 35 percent stake in Forbes, Inc., worth $407.4 million, (2) a New Jersey house and farm worth $26.5 million, and (3) stocks and other investments worth $5 million.

Many Americans have some wealth equity, such as a house or pension investments, and an increasing number own stocks (about one half of all stocks are now owned by U.S. workers). However, the top 1 percent of families owns 60 percent of all corporate stock in the United States. These families also control one-third of all wealth in the country. Figure 9.2 on p. 242 shows that the top 20 percent of U.S. families own nearly all of the financial net wealth (80 percent). Although there is a correlation between income and wealth, at the lower end of the income scale, increases in income bring only modest increases in wealth.

How rich are the truly wealthy in the United States? The answer is staggering. In 1998, the combined income of the three richest Americans alone was $132 billion (see Table 9.1). It is not a cliché to say that the rich keep getting richer. According to a recent study published by United for a Fair Economy, a Boston think tank, not only are the rich getting richer at the expense of the classes below them but also the pace of this trend is accelerating (cited in Werbe, 1998). For example, the average net worth of the wealthiest 200 individuals increased by almost one fourth from 1997 to 1998. Bill Gates's net worth grew by an astounding $400 million a week from 1996 to 1997 and by another 40 percent from 1997 to 1998. At the same time that wealth was increasing for a very small percentage of the population, the net worth of the bottom 40 percent of the population decreased, with a large percentage of this group going deeper into debt. Moreover, an increasing number of Americans had stagnating incomes, declining savings, and limited retirement options.

Huge gaps in wealth between racial and ethnic groups can also be seen. Although many individuals among various groups of color have made some net gains in wealth over recent

TABLE 9.1 ◑ Forbes Ten Richest Americans, 1998

Individual	Wealth (in billions)	Source of Wealth
1. William H. Gates, III	51,000	Microsoft Corp.
2. Walton family	48,000	Wal-mart Stores
3. Warren Edward Buffett	33,000	Berkshire Hathaway
4. Paul Gardner Allen	21,000	Cofounder, Microsoft Corp.
5. Edward Forrest, Sr., family	13,500	Mars Candy
6. Jay A. and Robert A. Pritzker	13,500	Financiers
7. Michael Dell	10,000	Dell Computer Corp.
8. Haas family	8,200	Levi Strauss & Co.
9. Fisher family	8,000	The Gap
10. Gordon Earl Moore	7,500	Intel Corp.

Source: Gorham, J. 1998. "The Forbes 400: The Richest People in America." *Forbes.* (October 12) Vol. 162, No. 8, pp. 165–169.

decades, the fact remains that currently, for every one dollar of median net worth held by a white household, Latina/o households have about eleven cents and African American households have a little over eight cents. This lack of wealth hinders families of color from upward mobility and, as research has shown, it also offers little protection from downward mobility. The existing pattern of the unequal distribution of wealth in the United States functions to intensify racial and ethnic inequalities and tensions while passing them on from generation to generation (Braun, 1997).

The Distribution of Power and Prestige in the United States

Political power and prestige in industrial societies tends to be organized around class relationships. According to Marx, dominant class members tend to hold a disproportionate share of political power and prestige and the other classes are subordinate to the dominant class to differing degrees. A study of the power elite by sociologist C. Wright Mills (1956) supports Marx's view. According to Mills, this power elite was composed of top business leaders, the executive branch of the government, and the military. Mills argued that of these elites, the heads of huge corporations were the most powerful because of their unique ability to parlay their vast wealth into political power. The masses of the population are relatively powerless and vulnerable to the exercise of political power by the wealthy few.

The wealthy typically acquire political power through campaign contributions, through special interest lobbies, and by becoming politicians themselves. Think about some of the people who exercise great political power in the United States. Do names such as Kennedy, Reagan, Bush, and Gore come to mind? These are not average eight-hours-a-day, five-days-a-week wage earners. They have enough wealth not to work for wages and to devote considerable time to running for public office if they so choose. It is clear that in the United States, being wealthy is closely connected to being nominated for political office and, often, to winning the office. It is no accident that almost half the current U.S. senators are white male millionaires. It was only in 1992 that the first African American woman,

Carol Mosley-Braun, and the first Native American, Ben Nighthorse Campbell, were elected to the U.S. Senate.

Sometimes, simply running for office can make one politically powerful and able to affect policy. For example, millionaire Ross Perot, using much of his personal wealth, was able to shape many of the issues of the 1992 presidential debates. This is not to say that others in society have no political power. Although power is unequally distributed, the masses of people have some degree of political power, primarily through their exercise of their constitutional right to vote. The ability of the vote, of course, does not measure up to the ability of the wealthy to affect public policy, and its relative influence depends on whether people actually vote and the degree to which they base their votes on issues rather than on personalities.

Like power and socioeconomic status, prestige is unequally distributed in the United States. As in most places in the world, prestige is associated primarily with one's occupational position. Sociologists have used prestige rankings of occupations for over fifty years to measure prestige as a social reward by asking large samples of the public to rate various occupations in terms of desirability and admirability. From these answers, sociologists have constructed what are now classically referred to as Occupational Prestige Scales; these are commonly used by researchers as part of their measure of social class in the United States.

Over the years, these surveys have usually yielded remarkably similar responses, indicating some stability in how the public views various occupations. Table 9.2 is an occupational prestige table developed from national survey data collected between the years 1972 and 1996. The highest ranking is 100 and the lowest is 0. As the table shows, physicians, attorneys, dentists, and college professors rank high in terms of occupational prestige while equally important occupations such as janitor, farm worker, and garbage collector rank at the lowest end.

These rankings are fairly consistent with the amount of financial remuneration these occupations command. Occupations at the bottom of the ranking are typically low-paying, dead-end jobs, held overwhelmingly by women and people of color, while those at the top are typically

TABLE 9.2 ⊙ Occupational Prestige Rankings of Selected Occupations in the United States

Occupation	Prestige Score	Occupation	Prestige Score
Physician	86	Funeral director	49
Attorney	75	Insurance agent	47
College professor	74	Mail carrier	47
Dentist	72	Legal secretary	46
Clergy	69	Plumber	41
Registered nurse	66	Typist	41
Secondary school teacher	66	Farmer	40
Athlete	65	Child care worker	36
Accountant	65	Barber/beautician	36
Elementary school teacher	64	Teacher's aid	36
Sociologist	61	File clerk	36
Police officer	60	Retail sales clerk	30
Actor	58	Garbage collector	28
Librarian	54	Taxicab driver	28
Firefighter	53	Waiter/waitress	28
Social worker	52	Household laborer	23
Electrician	51	Janitor	22
Computer operator	50	Shoe shiner	09

Source: Adapted by permission from National Opinion Research Center. 1996. *General Social Surveys 1972–1976: Cumulative Codebook.* Chicago: NORC, pp. 1077–1085.

white-collar or professional jobs requiring high levels of education and commanding higher salaries and held disproportionately by whites and males. Researchers have found that the prestige ranking of various occupations in the United States is similar to those in other societies (Lin & Xie, 1988; Nakao & Treas, 1990). According to some researchers, the impact of race and gender is reflected in these rankings in that when people are told that the hypothetical person holding a given job is a woman or a person of color or if they perceive the job to be held primarily by women or people of color, they are more likely to rank it low (Bose, 1985).

The Class Structure and Accompanying Lifestyles

Sociologists use a variety of measures to identify social classes. For example, one of the earliest methods of measuring class was the *reputational approach,* in which the researcher asked a select group of respondents to rank people in their community socially. A second method used by sociologists is the *subjective method,* which asks subjects to identify their location in the class system. However, most often, sociologists use an *objective method,* wherein they assign people to a particular class based on an objective measure of socioeconomic status using the Weberian concepts of wealth, status, and power, paying particular attention to differences in consumption patterns and lifestyles. Using this method, they have identified anywhere from three basic classes to nine classes, including four subclasses. Here we will examine four basic classes—upper, middle, working, and under—paying some attention to distinctions within classes. Figure 9.4 illustrates these classes using the symbol of stair steps.

Upper Class The upper class consists of a small, elite group of individuals, comprising about 1 percent of the total population (Gilbert & Kahl, 1998). It includes major corporate heads; people who have inherited great wealth from their parents; people who have accumulated large sums of money through real estate, stocks and bonds, or other investments; some of the top-earning entertainers, such as movie and television stars; the most successful and highest-paid athletes; and a few others. Upper-class privilege rests on two major characteristics that we have already discussed: the possession of enormous resources of wealth and power.

Members of the upper class typically use their political influence to protect their economic empires. They also segregate themselves socially to maintain their privileged status and protect their assets. For example, it is difficult to penetrate the upper class because its members are highly selective in social networks, social ties, and social memberships. They are socialized to practice *endogamy*—cultural norms prescribing that people marry within their own social group or category: they live, eat, sleep, and recreate with others like themselves. This class exclusiveness solidifies and enhances their status privilege.

Some social scientists distinguish the very top of the upper class from the lower portion. The *upper-upper,* as it is called, includes the super rich who have amassed huge fortunes and live lifestyles that most people cannot even imagine. They generally own several homes in different locations; have servants, huge art collections, and other expensive artifacts; send their children to the best schools; and vacation regularly in exotic places. Their class consciousness is reflected by such things as their choice of schools and being listed in the *Social Register,* a book of "blue bloods" that lists the highest-status and wealthiest 0.1 percent of the U.S. population. In the past, this upper-upper crust consisted primarily of "old money" families such as the Rockefellers, Vanderbilts, Du Ponts, Fords, Chryslers, and Mellons, whose wealth had been in the family for several generations.

FIGURE 9.4 ☉ **Social Class in America: Up and Down the Class Stairwell** *Source:* Adapted from *American Class Structure in an Age of Growing Inequality,* 5th ed., by Dennis Gilbert. © 1998. Reprinted with permission of Wadsworth Publishing, a division of International Thomson Publishing. Fax 800/730-2215.

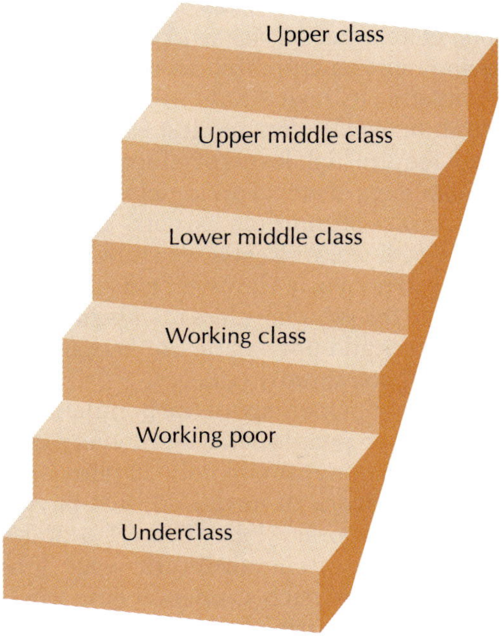

	Education	Occupation	Percent of Population
Upper class	Prestigious university	Investors, heirs	1%
Upper middle class	College, university, professional degree	Professionals, upper-level managers	14%
Lower middle class	High school, some college	Semiprofessionals, lower-level managers, supervisors	30%
Working class	High school	Factory workers, clerical workers, craftspeople, salespeople	30%
Working poor	Some high school	Laborers, service workers, low-paid salespeople	20%
Underclass	Some high school	Unemployed, part-time workers, odd jobs, welfare or some other assistance	5%

The *lower-upper class* consisted of the "newly wealthy," who had amassed their fortunes within the last generation or so. The emergence of a global economy has contributed greatly to an increase in the numbers of millionaires and billionaires in the United States since World War II. In many cases, although their wealth is new, lower-upper class members often have more wealth than do members of the old monied class. Although the lines denoting upper-upper and lower-upper are invisible to most of us and probably of little interest (rich is rich, after all), those among the upper class are often very cognizant of it. For example, although Oprah Winfrey has made the Forbes 400 list for several years and is more wealthy than some of the upper-upper stratum, her name does not appear in the *Social Register*.

Middle Class   As with the upper class, sociologists typically describe or analyze the middle class in terms of upper and lower divisions. Some have suggested that the middle class is the least well-defined class. When asked, most Americans identify themselves as middle class, most likely because of their general belief that this is a classless society. Few people identify themselves as poor or working class because of the stigma attached to these labels. At the same time, they know they cannot pass themselves off as rich. They tend to think of themselves as "average" or middle Americans and see others that way as well. The middle class consists of approximately 44 percent of the population (Gilbert & Kahl, 1998). Once largely white, the U.S. middle class today has expanded to include a considerable number of people of color.

The *upper-middle class* consists of business executives, high-level politicians and administrators, skilled technicians, and professionals such as doctors, lawyers, engineers, college professors, and small entrepreneurs. About 14 percent of the population is upper-middle class (Gilbert & Kahl, 1998). Their lifestyle includes ownership of luxury items, elegant homes, and other pricy items of conspicuous consumption. A distinguishing feature of this stratum is its high level of education and occupational prestige. The greatest majority have four-year degrees and many have graduate and postgraduate degrees. They perpetuate themselves by providing the best possible education for their children and preparing them for stable and high-paying upper-middle class jobs.

The *lower-middle class* consists of lower management and technical workers, elementary and high school teachers, nurses, and an array of white-collar workers. Estimates are that around 30 percent of the population are members of this stratum (Gilbert & Kahl, 1998). Their incomes are typically lower than the upper-middle class's incomes, although two-career lower-middle class families can make more money. Members of this stratum are almost always high school graduates, and many have some college education or a college degree. Like other Americans, they want the best educational experiences for their children, although they are not as able to pay for it as those in the strata above them. According to some sources, there is quite a bit of movement between the lower- and upper-middle classes as members of the lower-middle class return to college and earn graduate and professional degrees and change to occupations commensurate with their educational attainment.

Working Class   The working class represents about one half of the population if we combine the traditional working-class category with the working-poor category. The *traditional working class* includes semiskilled and skilled factory workers, trade union workers such as mechanics and plumbers, secretaries, service workers, and salespersons and represents approximately 30 percent of the population (Gilbert & Kahl, 1998). Members of this stratum usually earn modest wages in jobs that do not require high levels of education. In order to make ends meet, working-class families typically consist of multiple earners. Traditionally, members of working class were not likely to have college experience. However, today, a growing number of the working-class members are attending colleges and universities, although most of them attend community colleges.

A significant percentage of the population is made up of poor people who work every day. The *working poor,* approximately 20 percent of the population, work in unskilled, low-paying dead-end or temporary jobs (Gilbert & Kahl, 1998). These are often minimum wage jobs and/or seasonal jobs, such as migrant farm work, sharecropping, domestic service, and day labor.

This group has traditionally been defined as the lower class. However, we believe that the descriptor *working poor* is a more accurate reflection of this group of people.

Although they may have graduated from high school, the schools the working poor attend usually lack the resources, human and physical, needed to provide a quality education. With little job stability, low income, low levels of education, few marketable skills, and low-prestige jobs, the working poor live very tenuous lifestyles; they are constantly in debt, and many depend on supplemental incomes to make ends meet. African Americans, Latinas/os, and other groups of color are disproportionately represented among the working poor. This stratum, more than any other, is extremely vulnerable to unscrupulous businesspeople who sell them inferior goods at exorbitant prices and high interest rates and to "absentee landlords" who charge high rents for inferior housing. The toll this takes on people's self-esteem and the energy they must expend on routine daily tasks is revealed in Sandra Cisneros's novel *The House on Mango Street* (see the Sociology through Literature box).

Underclass   Popularized in the work of sociologist William Julius Wilson (1978), sociologists have increasingly used the category of *underclass* to define the group of people found at the very bottom of the class hierarchy. Representing about 5 percent of the population, this group used to be called the *ghetto poor,* signifying the disproportionate number of inner-city residents, many African American and Latina/o, who are trapped in this castelike stratum (Gilbert & Kahl, 1998). The majority of those in the underclass can be found in the nation's largest inner cities, and most are members of generations of families trapped in a cycle of poverty. Those in this stratum are viewed by some researchers as occupying a position *beneath* the class system because they have little or no connection to the job market. Those who do work typically work in menial, low-paying temporary or seasonal work. Most are welfare dependent, and an increasing number are homeless. Their lack of access to adequate education, jobs, and other opportunities forces them to live in poor neighborhoods plagued by many of the problems of disadvantaged communities. In his so-titled book, Wilson (1987) referred to this underclass as the *truly disadvantaged.* While the globalization of the job market has greatly benefitted those at the top of the class hierarchy, it has reduced further the underclass's access to the job market.

A Closer Look at Social Class in the United States

According to some observers, despite the severe inequities in U.S. society, many people are either not aware of social class or tend to reject the existence of social classes. In general, Americans have very little awareness of class as a comprehensive system that determines the distribution of opportunities and other social benefits. Americans show less **class-consciousness**—an awareness and identification with the interests of a particular social class and an understanding of the ways in which society operates to produce class inequality—than do people in many other societies (Braun, 1997).

The myth that there are plenty of opportunities for everyone to advance through hard work is reinforced in the media and throughout popular culture. If people think that it is the individual's fault that she or he is not rich or better off, they are not apt to try to change the system. However, if they perceive the system to be unfair and unequal, they are more likely to seek actively to change it. From time to time, we are made aware of the class stratification system: labor unions highlight the inequities experienced by workers; various civil rights and women's movements and groups point out institutionalized race and gender inequality. Is social mobility real in U.S. society? Or is it simply a figment of the ruling class's "pull yourself up by the bootstraps" ideology?

Social Mobility: Ideology and Actuality

Social mobility, the movement (or lack of movement) by individuals and households from one social position to another in the stratification system, is an important part of the American dream. An important ideology in U.S. society is that, despite a person's social and family origins, hard work and a future orientation (the

Sociology through Literature

The House on Mango Street

The following narrative is the opening vignette of Sandra Cisneros's novel *The House on Mango Street*. It poignantly illustrates the impact of social class on self-esteem and mobility aspirations.

We didn't always live on Mango Street. Before that we lived on Loomis on the third floor, and before that we lived on Keeler. Before Keeler it was Paulina, and before that I can't remember. But what I remember most is moving a lot. Each time it seemed there'd be one more of us. By the time we got to Mango Street we were six—Mama, Papa, Carlos, Kiki, my sister Nenny and me.

The house on Mango Street is ours, and we don't have to pay rent to anybody, or share the yard with the people downstairs, or be careful not to make too much noise, and there isn't a landlord banging on the ceiling with a broom. But even so, it's not the house we'd thought we'd get.

We had to leave the flat on Loomis quick. The water pipes broke and the landlord wouldn't fix them because the house was too old. We had to leave fast. We were using the washroom next door and carrying water over in empty milk gallons. That's why Mama and Papa looked for a house, and that's why we moved into the house on Mango Street, far away, on the other side of town.

They always told us that one day we would move into a house, a real house that would be ours for always so we wouldn't have to move each year. And our house would have running water and pipes that worked. And inside it would have real stairs, not hallway stairs, but stairs inside like the houses on T.V. And we'd have a basement and at least three washrooms so when we took a bath we wouldn't have to tell everybody. Our house would be white with trees around it, a great big yard and grass growing without a fence. This was the house Papa talked about when he held a lottery ticket and this was the house Mama dreamed up in the stories she told us before we went to bed.

But the house on Mango Street is not the way they told it at all. It's small and red with tight steps in front and windows so small you'd think they were holding their breath. Bricks are crumbling in places, and the front door is so swollen you have to push hard to get in. There is no front yard, only four little elms the city planted by the curb. Out back is a small garage for the car we don't own yet and a small yard that looks smaller between the two buildings on either side. There are stairs in our house, but they're ordinary hallway stairs, and the house has only one washroom. Everybody has to share a bedroom—Mama and Papa, Carlos and Kiki, me and Nenny.

Once when we were living on Loomis, a nun from my school passed by and saw me playing out front. The laundromat downstairs had been boarded up because it had been robbed two days before and the owner had painted on the wood YES WE'RE OPEN so as not to lose business.

"Where do you live?" she asked.

"There," I said pointing up to the third floor.

"You live *there?*"

"There." I had to look to where she pointed—the third floor, the paint peeling, wooden bars Papa had nailed on the windows so we wouldn't fall out. "You live *there?*" The way she said it made me feel like nothing. *There.* I lived *there.* I nodded.

I knew then I had to have a house. A real house. One I could point to. But this isn't it. The house on Mango Street isn't it. For the time being, Mama says. Temporary, says Papa. But I know how those things go.

Source: From *The House on Mango Street,* pp. 3–5. Copyright © 1984 by Sandra Cisneros. Published by Vintage Books, a division of Random House, Inc., and in hardcover by Alfred A. Knopf in 1994. Reprinted by permission of Susan Bergholz Literary Services, New York. All rights reserved.

---

ability to defer gratification) will lead to upward mobility. We are often reminded of this possibility by those few (for example, President Bill Clinton and Oprah Winfrey) who come from humble beginnings but make it up near to or actually to the top of the socioeconomic and status hierarchies. These successes notwithstanding, however, the American dream of upward mobility is tempered by lived experiences such as race, ethnicity, and gender.

When movement in the stratification system is upward or downward, we call it **vertical mobility.** Vertical mobility occurs in two major ways: intergenerationally or intragenerationally. For example, if the child of a postal worker goes to college and becomes a college professor, she has experienced **intergenerational mobility,** movement upward or downward in the stratification system compared to her or his parents. On the other hand, if a computer programmer becomes wealthy after developing and selling a computer chip to Microsoft for millions of dollars, this person has experienced **intragenerational mobility,** movement upward or downward in the stratification system over the life course.

According to most sociologists, another type of mobility, **structural mobility**—movement upward or downward in the social class hierarchy as a result of changes in the structure of society as opposed to individual effort—is key to understanding the degree to which mobility is a reality in the United States. Changes in society such as the creation of new technologies can cause both upward and downward mobility. For example, advancing computer technology has opened up many new jobs, and many people have taken advantage of this surge in jobs by getting the training needed to move upward or horizontally. However, many people who cannot afford such training have been left behind to languish in low-paying jobs or have actually been replaced by those having the new computer skills. Thus, while some have benefitted from changes in technology, others have suffered disadvantage. However, most important, in both cases, changes in social status was primarily a result of structural changes and not individual effort. Without such changes, social mobility would be almost nonexistent.

The Limitations of Social Mobility Studies

In 1967, sociologists Peter Blau and Otis Dudley Duncan (1967) published a landmark study on occupational mobility in the United States. Their analysis was male-specific, measuring mobility strictly by comparing men occupationally with their fathers. It led them to conclude that social mobility was simply a function of education and social origins and that no other conditions affect chances for mobility in the United States. Some observers have suggested that the Blau and Duncan research ignored women because in previous generations, mothers usually did not work outside the home and derived their social and economic status from their husbands. Clearly, this is problematic because many women, including a large percentage of African American women, did work outside the home, and this percentage has risen dramatically over the last twenty years. Although much of the subsequent mobility research was flawed in that it followed the Blau and Duncan pattern, recent research has begun to include women and people of color in examinations of social stratification and social mobility (Beeghley, 1996; Higginbotham and Weber, 1992; Scott, 1988).

Applying the Sociological Imagination

How will thinking about social stratification and social mobility change when we include women and people of color in our analyses? Some researchers have suggested that the calculation of women's mobility should be based on women's own work and thus carried out separately from the status and work history of their fathers and/or husbands. Do you agree or disagree? How might this change our overall view of mobility in this country? Think about your own family. What contribution have women members made to the overall mobility of your family?

The Distribution of Poverty in the United States

Powerful stereotypes dominate people's views of the poor. Close your eyes for a moment. Think about the poor. What visions do you have? If you are like many Americans, you probably pictured the poor as unkempt persons, wearing tattered or worn clothing and having poor hygiene. Many people also tend to think of the poor as welfare dependent. However, as we have already indicated, the vast majority of poor people in this society work every day and/or live in households in which individuals work full time but make very low wages.

How Do We Measure Poverty? The United States Census Bureau collects income statistics that are used to classify people as poor. The poverty threshold, which is revised each year to account for inflation, is calculated based on an estimation of the cost of a minimally nutritious diet for a typical family. Because it is estimated that one-third of the budget of a poor family goes for food, the costs are multiplied by three to allow for nonfood costs. The poverty threshold varies depending on a family's characteristics. A larger family has more members to feed; it therefore needs more money. The elderly need less money because their food consumption is typically lower. Critics of the government's measure of poverty point out that the measure is outdated. It also has many methodological flaws, such as the use of twenty-year-old nutritional standards in assessing people's level of poverty.

Sociologists studying poverty often distinguish between absolute and relative poverty. The term **absolute poverty** refers to the condition in which people do not have the means to secure the most basic necessities of life. People living in absolute poverty are often homeless people who have little if any means of obtaining basic necessities such as food, shelter, and clothing. Absolute poverty can therefore have life-threatening consequences. Those falling below the poverty threshold are most likely to live in absolute poverty.

The term **relative poverty,** on the other hand, refers to a fluid standard of deprivation by which people compare their lifestyles to others in the society or elsewhere. Thus, people are judged to be relatively disadvantaged or advantaged depending on the comparison group.

Although the economic recovery of the early 1990s lifted over 1 million people out of poverty by the mid-1990s, the U.S. poverty rate continues to rank among the highest in major industrial societies. Observers note a number of reasons for the persistent rate of poverty in this country. Although debate about the cause of poverty often centers on individual characteristics, it is nonetheless possible to identify some important structural causes. Without doubt, one cause of the rising rate of poverty is the decreasing number of middle-income jobs. A second important reason for the rising poverty rate is tied to low wages. A significant number of people who work do not earn enough wages to rise or stay above the poverty threshold. For example, a full-time minimum-wage job in 1997 still left a family of four $4960 below the poverty level.

Who Are the Poor? Poverty rates are not randomly distributed across the population. Although there is no single defining feature of

poverty, a number of social characteristics increase the risk that individuals and families will live in poverty. Race, class, and gender are, of course, significant factors in the risk for poverty.

Race and Ethnicity If we use the poverty threshold of $12,802 for a nonfarm family of three and $16,400 for a family of four, 35.6 million people lived in poverty in 1997. The poverty rate was 13.3 percent. As Figure 9.5 shows, 46.4 percent of all poor people in the United States are non-Latina/o whites. However, the poverty rate for non-Latina/o whites was unchanged at 8.6 percent, whereas the rate for African Americans was 26.5 percent and the rate for Latinas/os was 27.1 percent (Weinberg, 1998). People in both these groups are about three times as likely as white people to be poor (see Figure 9.5). Among the traditional groups of color, Asians and Pacific Islanders have the lowest rate of poverty at 14 percent. Poverty among Native Americans is said to parallel that of African Americans, although on some individual Native Reservations, the poverty level is as high as 64 percent (Kanamine, 1992; Snipp, 1992) and some Native Americans live in conditions of poverty that most people, even the poor, cannot fathom. For example, one study of Native American poverty found that 70 percent of Navajo households in three different states were without running water, sewer facilities, or electricity (Benokraitis, 1993).

Age, Family Patterns, and Gender Although the elderly used to be at the highest risk for being poor, the poverty rate for those aged sixty-five and older has dropped dramatically. However, the poverty rates of different racial/ethnic groups hold fairly consistent for the elderly in each group. This translates into the fact that African American, Native American, and Latina/o elderly, like their youthful counterparts, are two to three times more likely to be poor than are elderly whites (Braun, 1997). Despite the fact that most U.S. families were able to stay afloat in terms of real income over the last two decades, 7.3 million families continue to live in poverty. Nonetheless, this number represents a decline of 384,000 from 1996 to 1997. African American families accounted for more than half of the decrease. Although there have

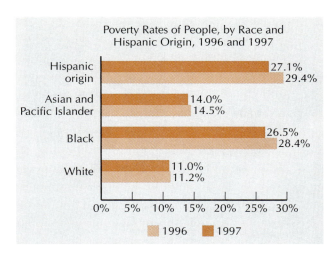

Poverty Rates of People, by Race and
Hispanic Origin, 1996 and 1997

Hispanic origin: 27.1% (1996), 29.4% (1997)
Asian and Pacific Islander: 14.0% (1996), 14.5% (1997)
Black: 26.5% (1996), 28.4% (1997)
White: 11.0% (1996), 11.2% (1997)

■ 1996 ■ 1997

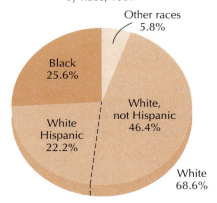

Proportion of People below Poverty Level,
by Race, 1997

Other races 5.8%
Black 25.6%
White Hispanic 22.2%
White, not Hispanic 46.4%
White 68.6%

Note: People of Hispanic origin are
23.4% of the population.

FIGURE 9.5 ● **Poverty American Style** *Source:* Weinberg, D.H. 1998. "Income and Poverty 1997." Press Briefing on 1997 Income and Poverty Estimates. Washington, DC: U.S. Census Bureau, Housing and Household Economic Statistics Division, Chart 8.

been decreases in the number and rate of poverty for some groups, the overall number of poor people remains statistically unchanged, and there has been no change in income inequality (Weinberg, 1998).

Gender is also a significant factor in who is at risk for being poor. Almost two-thirds of poor people over the age of eighteen are women. Of the 7.3 million poor families, 54 percent are headed by single women whereas only 7 percent are headed by single men.

The high risk for poverty of women heads of families means that the poverty rate for their children is also high. Sixty-four percent of children under the age of six living in a family headed by a woman are poor, compared to 12 percent of children under the age of six living in married-couple families. Children of all ages are 40 percent of the poor although they are but 26 percent of the population. Their poverty rate is higher than for any other age group, at 19.9 percent in 1997 (Weinberg, 1998). Moreover, poverty is much greater among Latina/o (42 percent) and African American children (44 percent) than among other children such as whites (17 percent), although as is true with adults, in absolute numbers the majority of poor children (9 million) are white (Children's Defense Fund, 1996).

Sociologists link three important factors to the significant increase in the numbers of women and children who are poor. They refer to the trend whereby women are disproportionately represented among the poor as the **feminization of poverty** and suggest that it is caused by (1) increasing divorce rates, (2) increasing births to girls and women who are not legally married, and (3) the significant inequality gap in the wages of women and men.

Explaining Poverty: Personal Trouble or Public Issue?

How do we explain poverty, particularly in affluent nations such as the United States? Historically, scholars have offered explanations of poverty that focus on either the individual, the cultural, or the structural level.

Individual Explanations: Blaming the Victim   Social Darwinists such as Herbert Spencer used the concept of the survival of the fittest to explain that people were poor because they were not biologically fit to compete. Given the U.S. ideology of individualism and the importance we place on individuals' strivings and success in competitive settings, it is not surprising that many people blame the victim in a number of situations. Explanations that blame the poor for being poor direct our attention to various

Poverty is often viewed as an urban problem, however, many of the 7.3 million poor American families live in rural areas. Despite extreme poverty, this rural Oklahoma family struggles to provide loving support for each other.

personal characteristics and deficiencies to explain what is viewed as poor people's failure (not the system's failure) to achieve success. Contemporary politicians, policy makers, and yes, even some sociologists, continue to endorse this blaming-the-victim ideological approach emphasizing, for example, poor people of color's alleged cultural inferiority. The most recent revival of this blaming-the-victim approach is in *The Bell Curve: Intelligence and Class Structure in American Life,* by Richard Herrnstein and Charles Murray (1994). The authors present a biological determinist argument of racial inferiority based on questionable data on racial and class differences in IQ scores. Essentially, they claim now that equality of opportunity for advanced education is a reality in our culture, poor people as well as people of color lack the innate cognitive ability needed to achieve high income via demanding, intellectual jobs. Their argument has been severely critiqued on several grounds: its flawed methodology and data; its faulty conceptualization of intelligence; the failure to address seriously the impact of educational, social, or environmental effects upon achievement; and

an overstatement of the genetic heritability of intelligence (Braun, 1997).

Cultural Explanations: The Culture of Poverty Consistent with the blaming-the-victim explanatory approach is the cultural inferiority argument, a viewpoint that is incorporated in the concept of the culture of poverty. As put forth by anthropologist Oscar Lewis (1966), this argument maintains that by the time poor children are six years old, they have fully internalized the basic values, attitudes, and behaviors of a subculture of poverty and that, as a result, they are unable to compete in the larger culture. Some of the major characteristics of the alleged culture of poverty are a fatalistic view of the world and one's place in it, a present-time orientation, a tendency toward female-headed families, a high rate of abandonment of women and children, male superiority and frequent violence, a high rate of alcoholism, and a martyr complex among women. Although Lewis recognized that these characteristics could be viewed as a response to the conditions of poverty, he maintained that, over time, these values and behaviors become well-entrenched cultural traits that are then passed on from one generation to the next. Edward Banfield (1974), picking up on the "present orientation" trait pointed out by Lewis, claimed that people's time orientation was an important factor in explaining their poverty. For example, he argued that a distinguishing feature between the poor and the middle class is that poor people are unable to defer immediate gratification, to give up something in the present for the sake of realizing greater gain or profit in the future, whereas middle-class people are able to defer their gratification. This future orientation is allegedly a key factor in keeping middle-class people in the middle class and out of poverty.

As with the blaming-the-victim explanation, this explanation of poverty has not gone unchallenged. Some critics point out that Lewis's basic argument blames the victim for failing to adopt middle class norms and values rather than blaming the exploitative and racist socioeconomic system that makes escape from poverty difficult to almost impossible for most. It is quite possible, some critics argue, that these so-called cultural traits are simply adaptive patterns that would be discarded once the material conditions of poverty were removed (Marger, 1985; Ryan, 1976).

Despite the strenuous critique of this view, many people still adhere to it. For instance, poor people who are welfare dependent are accused of developing, maintaining, and perpetuating a welfare culture. The recent debates about welfare and the restructuring of the welfare system under the Clinton administration is rooted, in part, in this kind of culture-of-poverty explanation. Implicit in the recent restructuring of the welfare system and the accompanying workfare program for welfare recipients are the assumptions that individuals are responsible for their poverty and that their condition can be changed by a change in their behavior (hard work) and attitudes (a desire for upward mobility).

More recent cultural explanations of poverty use the concept of *cultural capital,* which as you will recall, refers to the cultural values, beliefs, attitudes, and competencies necessary for one to succeed in society. This kind of explanation suggests that poor people lack adequate cultural capital to function in a competitive global economy.

In general, critics of cultural explanations of poverty argue that they divert attention from what the critics believe to be the real sources of poverty and shift the blame from the rich and powerful to the poor and powerless (Sidel, 1996). In contrast to the cultural explanation, William Julius Wilson (1996) argues that when work disappears—when jobs move out of inner cities—there are not enough opportunities for people to support themselves and their families, causing high levels of poverty. His argument places the blame on society, and he suggests that any lack of ambition that poor people may exhibit is a consequence of insufficient opportunities rather than a cause of poverty.

Structural Explanations: Functionalist and Feminist Views   Those who take a structural approach to the study of poverty direct our attention to the social structure of society, and how it contributes to, maintains, and perpetuates poverty. The major question they try to answer is, What are the societal and historical conditions that promote the institutionalization of poverty? In a classic statement on the functions of poverty, sociologist Herbert Gans (1995) pointed out that an individualistic approach to explaining poverty misses the structural functions that poverty serves in society. Gans argued that society actually benefits from the existence of the poor, and he identified a number of social, economic, and political functions of poverty, including the following:

- Poverty makes it possible for the "dirty work" in a society to be done. Most people stay away from boring, underpaid, menial, undignified, and unpleasant jobs. However, someone has to do them. Because they cannot do better, poor people are compelled to take such jobs.
- Within a hierarchical society, the existence of poor people guarantees the higher status of the more affluent.
- Poverty creates a whole set of middle-class jobs—the jobs that service the poor, such as legal jobs, public health jobs, welfare workers' jobs, social workers' jobs, and police. Poverty also creates illegal jobs, such as gambling runners, loan sharks, and drug dealers.

Feminist approaches to the study of poverty would also direct our attention to the social structure. It is not by accident that women are disproportionately found among the poor. The United States has the largest gender gap in poverty of any industrial country. For example, U.S. women are 41 percent more likely to be poor than U.S. men. This compares to 34 percent for Australian women, 29 percent for German women, and 19 percent for British women; in Sweden, women are *less likely* than men to be poor (Casper et al., 1994). We have already pointed out some of the structural factors a feminist analysis would emphasize, such as the patriarchal structure and sexist ideology that uphold gender inequality. The structure of the gender-segregated job market ensures that women are more likely than men to be poor because women are paid, on average, lower wages than men, even when they do comparable work (see Chapters 11 and 14).

Stratification and Inequality beyond the United States

For the last three decades or so, global competition for new markets has intensified. Individuals and families in wealthy and poor countries alike are hearing that they must adapt to this increased competition, yet the benefits and the burdens of this adaptation are not shared evenly. Although we have focused much of our discussion on social stratification in the United States, we know that inequality exists throughout the world. Today, the wealthiest fifth of the world's population controls about 85 percent of total economic activity as measured by gross national products, domestic savings and investments, and world trade. The poorest fifth controls about 1 percent (United Nations Development Program, 1991). In fact, the gap between rich and poor is so great that the world's 358 wealthiest people have assets equal to the combined income of 2.3 billion people, just less than half of the global population (Schaffer, 1996).

Although the world has grown richer over the past twenty-five years, the world's nations have vastly unequal wealth. And although this increase in world wealth has improved the standard of living for many of the world's people, not all nations, and not all people in the richer nations, have benefitted. Some countries, primarily in Africa and Latin America, have experienced a net decline in gross domestic product (GDP), while many countries that have achieved a higher GDP have also experienced an increase in the number of people living in extreme poverty. Moreover, the gap in national income between the richest and the poorest nations continues to increase, as does the gap between the rich and poor people within nations.

Widening gaps between the rich and poor are also emerging in China and the postcommunist states of Eastern Europe and the former Soviet Union. Until recently, the economic gap between the rich and poor had been kept relatively narrow in these countries by state policy. However, with the onset of capitalism, the economic well-being of the lowest strata of these societies has become considerably worse, while the newly formed entrepreneurial class has been able to accumulate considerable wealth and to display it in highly conspicuous ways (Klare, 1997).

Perhaps most notable in the growing hierarchy of inequality around the world is the plight of women and children. Despite improvements in education and health, the rate of poverty for the world's women has increased almost twice as fast as it has for men. In the West, the liberalization and the dominance of the world market has meant that those having the least earning power—women with children—have suffered most (van der Gaag, 1997).

Global Inequality: Theoretical Perspectives

A number of theories have been developed to explain the vast differences in wealth, prestige, and power among various nations of the world. We conclude this chapter with a brief look at some of these explanations and a look ahead to social inequality in the twenty-first century.

Modernization Theory One of the classic statements on global inequality can be found in modernization theory, which holds that the industrial revolution and industrial technology in conjunction with creative entrepreneurial enterprises created new wealth in the world at an unprecedented rate. Although this new wealth benefitted only a few in the beginning, the standard of living for everyone, even poor people and nations, gradually began to rise. Wherever nations industrialize, such as in middle-income nations in Asia and Latin America, they too become wealthier. Without industrial technology, low-income nations change very little.

There are a number of criticisms of modernization theory, among them:

1. that it is simply a rationalization for capitalism.
2. that it fails to recognize how rich nations often use their positions of global strength to block the opportunities for development for poor and powerless nations.
3. that it has an ethnocentric bias in that it suggests that industrialized or the most-developed countries of the world are superior and the gauge by which all others should be measured.
4. that it contains a blaming-the-victim implication that the causes of global poverty lie in the poor nations themselves.

Dependency Theory   As the critique of modernization suggests, another way of looking at global inequality is to focus on the historical exploitation of poor nations by wealthier ones. Dependency theory maintains that rich nations have systematically exploited poor nations, leaving them impoverished and dependent on them. In other words, the wealth and power of rich nations can exist only because other nations are poor and powerless. European expansion and colonization of Africa, Asia, and Latin America, from the fifteenth century through the early twentieth century, for example, left the colonized nations impoverished and dependent while the European nations themselves prospered. Even today, although much of the old colonialism has disappeared, the economic relationship between rich and poor nations reflects a continuing pattern of colonial domination and dependency. According to dependency

theory, this neocolonialism is at the heart of today's capitalist world economy.

World Systems Theory   Using a systems approach to explaining global inequality, sociologist Immanuel Wallerstein (1974, 1984, 1990) maintains that economic relations are no longer confined within national boundaries. Rather, they form an international capitalist *world system* held together by economic ties. From this viewpoint, global stratification is a function of the operation of a very complex world system in which the nations of the world are divided into a hierarchy based on the mode of incorporation into the capitalist work economy. At the top are *core nations,* such as the United States, Germany, and Japan, which are highly industrialized and urbanized. At the bottom are *peripheral nations,* such as most countries in Africa, South America, and the Caribbean, which have little or no industrialization and urbanization and are dependent on core nations for capital. In the middle are *semiperipheral nations,* such as South Korea, Mexico, Brazil, and India, which are more developed than peripheral nations but less developed than core nations. Essentially, the wealthy, economically diversified, and powerful industrial nations of the northern hemisphere act as an international upper class. These rich core nations own or control the means of production on a global level, and the less-developed nations of the southern hemisphere serve as an international lower class whose raw materials and human resources (labor) are exploited by the core nations. In addition, the wealthy within the peripheral nations benefit from the exploitation of the labor of the poor and from their relationship with core nation capitalists, whom they support in order to maintain their own personal wealth.

Not everyone agrees with this theory of global stratification. However, most academics do agree that a small, elite group of nations and transnational corporations operate as a kind of upper-class elite controlling the global economy. How they define the future of global inequality depends largely on their theoretical viewpoint. In any event, persistent and increasing poverty around the globe as well as the increasing global domination of transnational corporations will likely continue to present human development and human rights issues well into the next century. On the other hand, the increasing sophistication of modern technology could result in a reduction in global poverty in the next millennium.

Inequality in the Twenty-First Century

As we close this century and open the next, great inequalities in this country and around the world will continue to exist. Many different inequalities exist that we have not detailed in this chapter, but they will continue to nag at us well into the next century. For example, as we indicate in Chapter 10, slavery continues to exists in many parts of the world. You will recall that in Chapter 1, we discussed the exploitation of child labor around the world. A significant number of these children are forced into slave labor. In addition, the sexual exploitation of women and girls for economic profit will continue to have profound consequences for individuals and families. The exploitation of cheap labor will also continue to be a characteristic of the world system of stratification. The global assembly line connects low-wage workers in the second and third worlds with elite manufacturers and clothing and shoe designers in the first world. For example, over one-fourth of the clothes we wear result from exploited labor of peoples in this stratification system. And the exploited laborers in poor and nonindustrialized countries are increasingly mobile, moving from their home countries to wherever they can sell their labor. Finally, the exploitation of migrant farm workers in the United States will also continue to be a stratification and human rights issue that we will take into the next century.

This outlook may seem bleak to you. Focusing on the extent to which inequality exists and on the huge gaps in life chances for people around the world may suggest to you that inequality is so pervasive and entrenched that positive change is not only improbable but next to impossible. After reading this chapter, you might feel depressed. However, history teaches us that problems can be solved and that concerned people can find solutions to these problems. History as well as the chapter openers in this textbook also tell us that needed changes can and have been won through various individual and collective actions. For example unionism, civil rights, and feminist movements have all been successful in reducing inequalities.

Key Points to Remember

1. Social stratification is an institutionalized form of inequality that can be found, in some form, in all known societies. It is elaborate and institutionalized and upheld by an ideology that justifies the exploitation of some by others.
2. Stratification systems vary along a continuum between two extremes: open and closed systems of inequality. Caste, estate, and class systems of inequality can be distinguished, in part, by their degree of openness to mobility, how positions are filled in the stratification system, how unequal access to benefits is institutionalized, and the extent to which there are restrictions on social interaction between strata.

3. Sociological explanations of inequality are rooted in the works of classical writers such as Karl Marx and Max Weber as well as in the contemporary works of scholars such as Erik Olin Wright, Kingsley Davis and Wilbert Moore, Melvin Tumin, and a variety of feminist theorists.
4. Most sociologists agree that there is no one single dimension of inequality. Rather, there are many, the most prominent of which are wealth, status, and power. There are glaring gaps in the distribution of income and wealth in the United States. The richest 1 percent of Americans owns and/or controls the majority of the

country's wealth and income. Likewise, the distribution of political power and prestige is concentrated in the hands of a small elite. The U.S. class system can be broken down into the following classes: upper, middle, working, and the underclass. The probability of living a long and healthy life depends on which of these classes one belongs to.

5. According to data on socioeconomic class and poverty, social mobility might be more a figment of ideology than an actuality. Although past social mobility studies had serious limitations, such studies today are much more likely to take into account the intersections of race, class, and gender.

6. Like wealth and income, poverty is unevenly distributed in society. Over 35 million Americans live in poverty. This includes over 10 million working-poor people. Statistics show that women, children, and people of color are disproportionately poor. Explanations of poverty typically focus on one of three factors: individual characteristics of the poor, cultural features of society, or the socio-structural nature of poverty.

7. Stratification in the United States is part of a larger global system of inequality. Social scientists have described and explained this global system using modernization, dependency, and world systems theories. Whichever explanation is used, statistics show a clear and increasing gap between the wealth, income, and life chances between people in developed and in less-developed countries.

8. Issues involving inequality in the twenty-first century will include child labor exploitation, the sexual exploitation of women and girls, and the economic exploitation of millions of workers on the global assembly line.

Key Terms

social stratification	life chances	social mobility
structured inequality	mortality rate	vertical mobility
closed systems	socioeconomic status	intergenerational mobility
open systems	infant mortality	intragenerational mobility
castes	prestige	structural mobility
estate system of stratification	power	absolute poverty
class stratification	income	relative poverty
class	wealth	feminization of poverty
meritocracy	class consciousness	

Key People

Mitch Snyder	Max Weber	Melvin Tumin
Karl Marx	Kingsley Davis	Gerhard Lenski
Erik Olin Wright	Wilbert Moore	

Questions for Review and Discussion

1. Discuss the differences in life chances that exist for yourself and for homeless individuals. In addition, compare the life chances of people in core nations with those of people in peripheral nations. In both cases, should we be concerned about the differences that exist?

2. Hypothetically, you have been invited to a White House conference on the "Differential Distribution of Life Chances in the United States and Globally." Prepare a position paper on this issue to present to a conference audience. Share it with your class.

3. How does the U.S. ideology of individualism and self-reliance explain the public's criticism and negative views of welfare and other programs of assistance to the poor? Are public views about welfare consistent for all class levels and individuals who receive such assistance? For example, explain why the public does not criticize or view negatively those who are beneficiaries of college financial aid, home mortgage deductions, farm subsidies, and so forth. Can you think of other ways in which the middle and upper classes are beneficiaries of programs of assistance but are not criticized for them?

4. Looking ahead to the twenty-first century, where do you think you will fit in the stratification system? What about family and friends? Will they be located in the same stratum as you? Why? Why not? Which of the models of stratification presented in this chapter seems the most accurate method for determining your class location and that of your family and friends?

For Further Reading

Allen, Michael P. 1987. *The Founding Fortunes: A New Anatomy of the Super-Rich Families in America.* New York: Dutton. An interesting examination of the lifestyles, values, and beliefs of the traditional wealthy elite in the United States.

Berrick, J.D. 1995. *Faces of Poverty: Portraits of Women and Children on Welfare.* New York: Oxford University Press. A well-written book of biographies of five women on welfare who dispel many of the myths and stereotypes about the poor and welfare families.

Frazier, E. Franklin. 1957. *The Black Bourgeoisie: The Rise of a New Middle Class.* New York: The Free Press. A classic and still relevant analysis of the rise of the African American middle class focusing on the intersections of class and race in the mobility experiences of this group.

Lamphere, Louise. (Ed.). 1992. *Structuring Diversity: Ethnographic Perspective on the New Immigration.* Chicago: University of Chicago Press. An excellent book based on research studies of immigrants in six U.S. cities examining how they experience U.S. society's stratification system as newcomers.

Sociology through Literature

Naylor, Gloria. 1983. *The Women of Brewster Place: A Novel in Seven Stories.* New York: Penguin Books. A refreshing novel in the voice of African American women that highlights the intersections of race, class, and gender in the lives of African American women.

Orwell, George. 1993 (originally published in 1945). *Animal Farm.* New York: Signet. A classic fiction which is excellent for discussions of stratification and inequality.

Internet Resources

http://www2.ari.net/home/nch/   This is the home-page of the National Coalition for the Homeless. It includes facts, policies, and issues pertaining to homelessness and the voices of the homeless themselves.

http://risya3.hus.osaka.u.ac.jp/shigeto/ssm/ ssmE.html   Survey data on social inequality and social status in Japan.

http://www.pscw.uva.n1/sociosite/TOPICS/   A rather large listing of resources on stratification, poverty, and classes.

http://www.census.gov/org/hhes/income/index.html   The Annual Report of the U.S. Bureau of the Census on Income and Poverty can be found here.

10

Race, Ethnicity, and Structured Inequalities

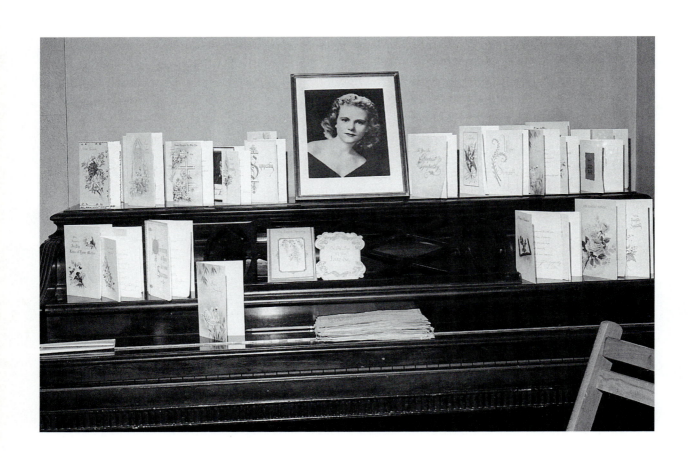

AGENT OF CHANGE: VIOLA FAUVER GREGG LIUZZO

Viola Fauver Gregg Liuzzo, a civil rights activist, stands tall among the many people who gave their lives for racial justice in the United States during the heyday of the civil rights movement. In March 1965, when she was thirty-nine, Liuzzo was murdered as she drove to Montgomery, Alabama, to transport marchers to housing in Selma. By most accounts, Liuzzo was an incredible woman, and her activism had begun long before her fatal trip to Montgomery. At age thirty-six, the mother of five went back to school to become a medical lab technician. After graduating with top honors, she worked for a few months and then quit her job to protest how female secretaries were being treated. She joined the National Association for the Advancement of Colored People (NAACP), becoming one of its few white members, and soon immersed herself in the civil rights struggle. After hearing reports of Alabama troopers attacking marchers in Selma and of the murder of Reverend James Reeb and watching on television the "bloody Sunday" clash in Selma, Liuzzo decided to go to there to assist the freedom marchers. Leaving her children and husband in Michigan, she drove alone to Alabama, where she worked with the marchers for six days and became known as a cheerful and tireless worker and activist.

On March 25, 1965, Liuzzo and a young African American activist, LeRoy Moton, made several trips to Montgomery to pick up marchers and drive them to Selma. On a return trip to Montgomery, four Ku Klux Klansmen drove beside Liuzzo's car on Highway 80 and shot her twice in the head, shattering her skull; Moton escaped uninjured by pretending to be dead.

Within two days of the murder, an outraged President Lyndon B. Johnson announced the arrest of four members of the Ku Klux Klan in connection with the death of Liuzzo as well as a congressional investigation of Klan activities. Three of the Klansmen were indicted for her murder but were acquitted by an all-white jury in the Alabama State Court; the fourth was identified as an FBI informant. After their acquittal, the three Klansmen marched in a Klan parade and were given a rousing ovation. However, in 1966, based on the testimony of the FBI informant, they were convicted of violating Liuzzo's civil rights and sentenced to ten years in prison.

After Liuzzo's murder, her family was besieged with hate mail and phone calls, and the Klan circulated a number of untrue attacks against Liuzzo's character, which were repeated in FBI reports. In 1978, the three Klansmen named the FBI informant as the person who had fired the fatal shots killing Liuzzo, and he was indicted for murder. However, the federal courts ruled that he could not be tried and a Justice Department inquiry found "no credible evidence" that the informant had fired the fatal shot. In 1983, a federal court rejected the Liuzzo family's $2 million negligence suit against the FBI.

Perhaps beyond the horror and notoriety of the death of this civil rights activist, Liuzzo's work and death had a great impact on women. Viola Liuzzo represented what women had been doing for years both inside and outside the civil rights movement. During her life, as during the lives of many women, her contributions were significant. In some ways, her death signified that women's role in the movement had taken on a new facet. Women who actively participated in the movement for civil rights were now as much a target as active men, and the Klan, if no one else, recognized their activism as a threat to racism, segregation, and racial oppression and as a push for a more racially equal society. Congress mentioned Liuzzo's name when it passed the Voting Rights Act in 1965. Viola Liuzzo, like so many others before and after her, took an active role in something she believed in, and paid with her life (Lowery & Marszalek, 1992).

Sources: Information and some paraphrasing and quoting from the following sources: http://www.sage.edu/html/RSC/programs/globcomm/division/students/liuzzo.html; John Hayman. 1996. *Bitter Harvest: Richmond FLowers and the Civil Rights Revolution.* Montgomery, AL: Black Belt Press; Jared Taylor. 1995. "The Many Deaths of Viola Liuzzo," *National Review,* vol. 47 (July 10): 38–39; http://thesource.net; Charles D. Lowery and John F. Marszalek (eds.). 1992. *Encyclopedia of African American Civil Rights: From Emancipation to the Present.* New York: Greenwood Press, pp. 319–320.

Race, Ethnicity, and the Sociological Imagination

I had flown from San Francisco to Norfolk and was riding in a taxi to my hotel to attend a conference on multiculturalism. . . . My driver and I chatted about the weather and the tourists. . . . The rearview mirror reflected a white man in his forties. "How long have you been in this country?" he asked. "All my life," I replied, wincing. "I was born in the United States." With a strong southern drawl, he remarked: "I was wondering because your English is excellent!" Then, as I had many times before, I explained: "My grandfather came here from Japan in the 1880s. My family has been here, in America, for over a hundred years." He glanced at me in the mirror. Somehow I did not look "American" to him; my eyes and complexion looked foreign.

Suddenly, we both became uncomfortably conscious of a racial divide separating us. . . . I said goodbye to my driver and went into the hotel, carrying a vivid reminder of why I was attending this conference.

Questions like the one my taxi driver asked me are always jarring, but I can understand why he could not see me as American. He had a narrow but widely shared sense of the past—a history that has viewed American as European in ancestry. "Race," Toni Morrison explained, has functioned as a "metaphor" necessary to the "construction of Americanness": in the creation of our national identity, "American" has been defined as "white." (Takaki, 1998:52–53).

Sociologist Ronald Takaki's experience is a profound yet simple statement about race in U.S. society. That the racial divide continues to exist and separate groups defined as races is one thing. The consequences of that division are quite another. Racial inequality is one of the most vital issues confronting contemporary U.S. society. Issues of racial and ethnic identity and equality were drastically reconceptualized during the civil rights struggles of the 1950s and 1960s. The deaths of civil rights activists such as Viola Liuzzo as well as the overt violence and brutality of institutionalized racism and discrimination and of individual acts such as those perpetrated by members of the Ku Klux Klan fostered public indignation that led to many improvements. According to various scholars and analysts, however, the task today is to identify and challenge the new, less overt forms of racism and racial injustice left in the wake of the civil rights movement, the implicit and tacit forms of contemporary racial inequality that are difficult to see and thus difficult to combat.

According to Paul Sniderman and Thomas Piazza (1996, p. 44), "The deepest obstacle to understanding the new politics of race—to recognizing what the conflicts over race are now about—is the universal, if unspoken, assumption that we already understand the place of race in contemporary America." Unfortunately, many people do not understand the history of race and race relations in the United States, and many say that whatever problems the country once may have had with race have been resolved such that race is no longer an issue. However, as Takaki suggests, the racial divide is still very much a part of the fabric of U.S. society and the issues that surround it are complex, systemic, and ongoing. The sociological imagination allows us to view and analyze issues such as racial and ethnic diversity within the context of social and historical factors rather than in terms of innate characteristics and tendencies of individuals. In applying the scientific method to their studies of race and ethnic relations, sociologists show us

that much of what we take for granted as common-sense knowledge about race and ethnicity is not nearly as simple as we think.

Racism as Ideology: Creating Racial, Ethnic, and Minority Groups

Whenever social stratification or inequality occurs as a result of race or ethnicity, we have a phenomenon known as racism. The concept of racism has been so widely and differentially used that some scholars question its usefulness as an explanatory concept. Moreover, among the lay public, the concept evokes very strong reactions from people regardless of race, ethnicity, age, and social class, and different groups define racism differently. Whites, for example, tend to define racism in very narrow terms to refer only to those people who overtly espouse white superiority and claim that all other groups are inferior. By locating racism only in terms of extreme attitudes, reactions, or behaviors, the majority of whites can absolve themselves of the sin. On the other hand, many people of color think of racism more broadly, including both attitudes and behaviors, intentional or not, that disadvantage some while advantaging others (Renzetti & Curran, 1998).

Likewise, many sociologists also take a broad view of the term *racism,* defining it in terms of both an ideological and a behavioral component. In this context, **racism** is an ideology of domination and a set of attitudes, ideas, and social, economic, and political practices by which one or more groups define themselves as superior and other groups as inferior and then systematically deny these groups the dignity, freedoms, opportunities, and rewards that the society has to offer. As an ideology or a belief system that holds that one race or ethnic group is naturally superior (or inferior) to another, this form of racism is often referred to by sociologists as *ideological racism* or *racist ideology.*

Classic examples of racist ideology include the belief undergirding slavery that Africans and their descendants were uncivilized and less than human; the belief under Adolf Hitler and

Nazism that Aryans were a master race; the belief supporting eighteenth- and nineteenth-century European imperialism and expansion that European peoples and cultures were superior to all others; and the belief of British colonizers in North America that Native Americans were savages. This kind of ideology implies that differences among various groups defined as racial groups are innate and permanent, and it ignores the impact of the social environment on such things as intelligence, personality, and even lifestyle. Moreover, ideologies are not synonymous with reality. In fact, they often reflect myths and untruths about people and behavior. However, through constant articulation, they become accepted as unquestioned truths.

Racist ideologies are much more prevalent in societies in which there are clear physical differences between groups, such as between African Americans and whites in the United States and Africans and Europeans in South Africa. As we will discuss later in this chapter, racism is not limited to situations involving people whose physical appearances are clearly visible. Neither is it limited to groups defined as races nor only to people defined as blacks and whites; rather, it applies also to ethnic groups, whether distinguishable by race or culture. Jews, for example, were not physically distinct from Germans; nonetheless, Nazi Germans developed a racist ideology labeling Jews as innately inferior and Aryans as superior that rationalized the murder of over 6 million Jews.

Race as a Biological Concept

Race is one of the most used, misused, and misunderstood concepts of our time. Much of the confusion surrounding this concept can be attributed to the fact that race has, in the past, had both biological and social meanings. Today, however, the biological concept of race has been shown to have absolutely no validity. The notion of racial classifications has been discredited because, according to such schemas, race is supposed to be defined on the basis of shared genetic material; a combination of physical traits such as skin color, body type, facial features, and so forth that have stayed the same for long time periods are used to represent underlying genetic similarities. However, shared physical traits don't necessarily have a genetic basis. Such similarities could be attributed to environmental influences. Also, there is no classification scheme that can encompass the entire human race. There is far too much variability (Kottak, 1994). Although many school textbooks and encyclopedias still define races in terms of a classification based on skin color (for example, white, black, and yellow), contemporary scientists have not been able to distinguish physical characteristics that would allow them to unequivocally classify individuals into distinct racial categories, nor have they been able scientifically to document racial differences in such things as intelligence, aptitude, or behavior.

According to most scientists today, in both biological and genetic terms, we (human beings) are more similar than different, regardless of how we look physically or how we are racially classified (Jaret, 1995). African Americans and whites, for example, have more genes in common than the ones that distinguish them. The variability between the average African American and the average white, in genetic makeup and physical appearance, is less than the variability within each group (Delgado & Stefancic, 1997). Based on DNA samples from peoples around the world, geneticists have concluded that traits that determine cultural ideas about race—skin color, eye shape, and color—are irrelevant. In addition, as shown in Figure 10.1, through genetic footprinting scientists have corroborated archeological evidence that the first modern humans came from Africa about 100,000 years ago and we are all their descendants (Salopek, 1997).

Race and Ethnicity as Social Constructions

From a sociological perspective, physical differences alone mean nothing. They are only important when we evaluate them, give them meaning—by creating definitions of and a set of beliefs about various groups as races—and then respond to them as if our definitions and beliefs about them are real and immutable. Most sociologists view race as a *social construction,* a set of beliefs and cultural meanings attached to different types of physical attributes. The nature, importance, and consequence of the differences

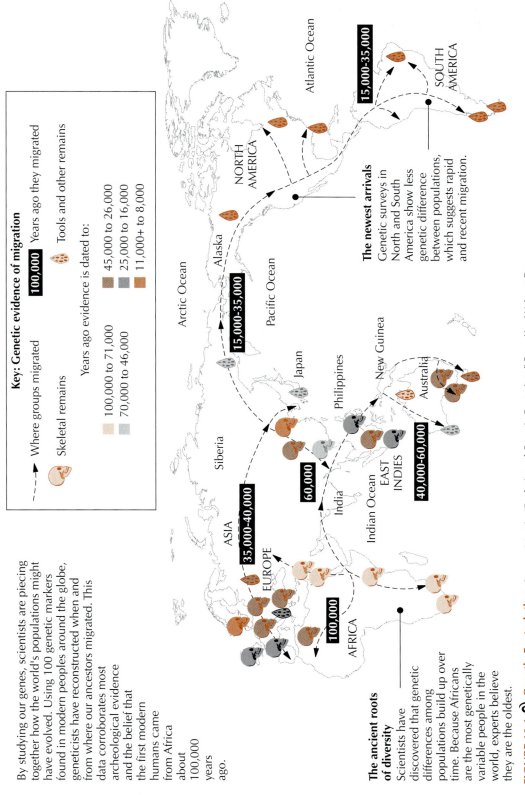

By studying our genes, scientists are piecing together how the world's populations might have evolved. Using 100 genetic markers found in modern peoples around the globe, geneticists have reconstructed when and from where our ancestors migrated. This data corroborates most archeological evidence and the belief that the first modern humans came from Africa about 100,000 years ago.

The ancient roots of diversity
Scientists have discovered that genetic differences among populations build up over time. Because Africans are the most genetically variable people in the world, experts believe they are the oldest.

Key: Genetic evidence of migration

→ Where groups migrated   100,000 Years ago they migrated

Skeletal remains   Tools and other remains

Years ago evidence is dated to:

- 100,000 to 71,000
- 70,000 to 46,000
- 45,000 to 26,000
- 25,000 to 16,000
- 11,000+ to 8,000

The newest arrivals
Genetic surveys in North and South America show less genetic difference between populations, which suggests rapid and recent migration.

100,000

35,000-40,000

60,000

40,000-60,000

15,000-35,000

15,000-35,000

15,000-35,000

Atlantic Ocean

Arctic Ocean

Pacific Ocean

Indian Ocean

NORTH AMERICA

SOUTH AMERICA

ASIA

EUROPE

AFRICA

Alaska

Siberia

India

Japan

Philippines

New Guinea

Australia

EAST INDIES

FIGURE 10.1 ◑ Genetic Footprinting *Source:* Map in "Evolution of Genetic Footprints." From Ken Weiss at Pennsylvania State University, National Institutes of Health, Mike O'Neill at Perkin-Elmer Applied Biosystems, "The History and Geography of Human Genes," "The Human Dawn," "Genetics and Evolution." Chicago Tribune/Celeste Bernard, Rick Tuma. In Paul Salopek. 1997. "Basically, We Are All the Same," *Chicago Tribune* (April 27), sec. 1, pp. 10–11. © copyrighted 1997 Chicago Tribune Company. All rights reserved. Used with permission.

267

are created, maintained, contested, and changed by social activities over time (Hall, 1997). People are assigned to a racial category not because of actual difference but by social definition by the powerful agencies of the elite. Racial classifications in the United States have historically functioned to restrict the distribution of goods, services, entitlements, and social status as narrowly as possible to those whose power is already entrenched. Thus, from a social constructionist perspective, racial categories are neither objective nor natural but rather ideological and constructed. In this sense, race is not so much a category but a practice—*people are raced* (Jones, 1997).

Historically, race has been an artifact of social and political processes, as well as of social scientists, statisticians, and a variety of physical and biological scientists who have variously created racial categories. Therefore, definitions of race vary not only from one society to another but also within societies from one historical period to another. Michael Omi and Howard Winant (1986) call this sociohistorical process *racial formation,* whereby racial categories are created, inhabited, transformed, and destroyed. Federal agencies, legislation, and the legal system have been instrumental in the process of racial formation. Although most people have come to believe that racial/ethnic classifications are "scientific" and immutable, the fact is that they are entirely subjective, whimsical, changeable, and unscientific (see the Sociological Reflections box).

In 1997, golf great Tiger Woods appeared on a nationally televised talk show and expressed his annoyance with the fact that most Americans persist in defining him only as an African American. As a youngster, Woods developed the term *Cablinasian* (starting with the first two letters of each of the three major parts of his ancestry and ending with his Asian ancestry) to describe his mixed ancestry: one-eighth Caucasian, one-fourth African American, one-eighth Native American, one-fourth Thai, and one-fourth Chinese. However, regardless of how Woods views himself, most Americans view him racially as African American. Certainly, white golfer Fuzzy Zoeller saw only Woods's African American heritage when he made his infamous reference to Woods eating fried chicken and collard greens, dishes recognized in popular culture as African American. The situation of Woods and many other biracial people whose ancestry includes African points out the conscious and unconscious acceptance by many Americans across race of a historical American standard called the *one-drop rule.*

The **one-drop rule** defines as a black person anyone who has any trace of black heritage (at least a drop of black African blood) in her or his ancestral history. For example, as late as in 1982, a Louisiana woman, Susan Phipps who was descended from an eighteenth-century slave and a white planter challenged a 1970 Louisiana law that legally defined her as black because she had more than one thirty-second of "Negro blood (stemming from a Great, Great, Great, Great Grandparent)." Although experts testified at the trial that the ancestry of most whites is one-twentieth or more African, Phipps and six family members nevertheless lost the court case. Phipps argued in court that the assigning of racial categories on birth certificates is unconstitutional and that regardless of the one-drop law, she was white. The assistant attorney general of Louisiana defended the law, saying that it was necessary in order for the state to comply with federal record-keeping requirements and to keep track of people at risk for certain diseases. In 1986, the U.S. Supreme Court upheld the Louisiana court ruling ("Descendant of Slave," 1982).

Uniquely, the one-drop rule applies only to African Americans. Whereas a mere drop of African blood is sufficient to define one as black, a person must have at least one-eighth Native American ancestry to be legally defined as Native American. Even an abundance of "white blood" does not qualify one to be defined as "white" if there is any trace of African heredity. This contradiction can be understood within the context of politics and power. According to Adrian Piper (1997), the reason for this contradiction is economic. A legally defined Native American is entitled to financial benefits from the government, so those in power make this classification difficult to attain. On the other hand, a legally defined black person is not entitled to financial, social, or inheritance benefits from her or his white family of origin, so those in power make assignment to this category not only easy but also automatic.

Sociological Reflections

Racial Formation and the U.S. Census Bureau

It is significant that as we close the twentieth century, one of the most hotly debated racial issues is that of how race will be defined in the year 2000 U.S. Census. Popular discussions and debates about how to address multi- and biracial people are linked to hearings held by the U.S. Congress for the purpose of helping to decide how the federal government will measure race and ethnicity in the year 2000 census. This debate is not new. Historically, the federal government has created, defined, changed, and/or modified the meanings of racial and ethnic categories from one time period to another. For example, up to 1962, U.S. Census Bureau statistics stated that there were only three races in the United States: White, Black/Negro, and Indian. In 1962, the U.S. Bureau of the Census revised its definition of racial categories, adding new distinctions from the old three-category classification to produce an expanded model of five racial categories: Negro, Spanish-American, Oriental, American Indian, and White. Over time, Negroes became black and Spanish-Americans became "Spanish-surnamed" and, later, Hispanic. Interestingly, the classification of Hispanic entered the Census lexicon in 1970 only after the Census Bureau found that, when the Census form mentioned "South Americans" as a category, over a million residents of Alabama, Mississippi, and other southern states said that they were South American.

The contradictions of U.S. Census Bureau classifications of race are many. For example, language, a common factor among ethnic group members, is not a common factor in the Census classification: more than 10 percent of California residents who have Spanish surnames do not speak Spanish but are classified as Hispanic. In addition, Argentineans, who are primarily of European ancestry, are considered white in Argentina but Hispanic in the United States. Further, because of the pervasiveness of mestizo influences, most Mexicans could be counted as Native Americans if they were born in the United States but are instead counted as Hispanic. This conceptual quagmire led to the rearticulation of the Hispanic population from a racial group to an ethnic group. Thus, by 1977, the federal government's classification of race in the United States had evolved into an odd fivefold, simplistic classification of the world's peoples as represented by their emigrants and descendants in this nation: non-Hispanic whites, non-Hispanic blacks, Hispanics (black or white), Asians or Pacific Islanders, and American Indians or Alaskan natives. The Hispanic or non-Hispanic classifications represent ethnic group classifications, whereas everything else refers to race.

Finally, in the 1990 Census count, officials indicated that Americans used a write-in blank on the census form to identify nearly 300 "races," 600 Native American groups, 70 Latino groups, and 75 combinations of multiracial ancestry, including one person who self-identified as "black/Hmong." In addition, more than 2 million people said that they were Native American, an impossible increase over the 1980 Census Count. Further, some 5 million people said that they had Native American "heritage" even though they did not classify themselves as Native American. It is estimated that at least half of these people will claim themselves to be Native Americans in the 2000 census, doubling the number of Native Americans with no increase in the Native American birthrate. Harold Hodgkinson estimates that if the 2000 Census provides a box labeled "multiracial," meaning any racial/ethnic mixing backed by four or more generations, approximately 80 percent of African Americans and a majority of Americans in general would check the box. In such a scenario, the current population labeled African American of 34 million could dwindle to less than 7 million. Obviously, the diversity of national origins among the various groups in the United States raises important questions about the meaning and utility of U.S. racial classifications. As these examples make clear, race and ethnicity are social constructions. If we can create race and ethnicity, we can uncreate them.

Sources: Orlans, H. 1989. "The Politics of Minority Statistics." *Society* (March/April): 24–25. Hodgkinson, H.L. 1997. "What Should We Call People?" In P.B. Morrill (ed.), *Societies: A Multi-Cultural Reader* (3rd ed.) New York: Longman, pp. 48–49. Morganthau, T. 1995. "What Color is Black?" *Newsweek* (February 13):63–65.

Race is not reducible simply to black and white, although that is the way most people in the United States think of race. The increasing presence of a wide variety of people of color, the existence of multiracial people, and the changing meaning of "whiteness" highlights the fact that many people do not fit into one neat, mutually exclusive racial category. For example, according to some sources, ten thousand people each year cross the visible and invisible color line and become "white." As you may remember from Chapter 6, this process of crossing the color line and its attendant behaviors are referred to as "passing for white"—presenting oneself as and living a lifestyle defined as white. People who "pass" typically believe that becoming white will afford greater economic, political, and social security; grant access to a panoply of public and private privileges; and ensure that one will not be the object of others' domination (Martinez, 1997). The reality of "passing" not only provides support for the notion that race is a social construction but also calls into question the use of skin color as a means of identifying people racially. This point is illustrated, for example, in the following passage from Shirlee Taylor Haizlip's (1994) book describing her search for family:

> I am a black woman, but many of you would never know it. . . . My skin is as light as that of an average white person. The skin of my sisters and brother is as light as, if not lighter than, mine. But we have lived as, worked as and mostly married black people. Our psyches, souls and sensibilities are black. Sociologists would say we have been "socialized" as black people. (p. 13)

> . . .

> I began the search for my mother's family believing that I was looking for black people "passing for white." And they did indeed pass. But what I ultimately found, I realized, were black people who had become white. After all, if you look white, act white, live white, vacation white, go to school white, marry white and die white, are you not "white"? (p. 266)

The phenomenon of passing also suggests that the United States is not what it presents itself to be racially. Some geneticists have said that 95 percent of "white" Americans have widely varying degrees of black heritage. The longer a

person's family has lived in this country, the higher the probable percentage of African ancestry. Furthermore, according to *The Source: A Guidebook to American Genealogy,* 75 percent of all African Americans have at least one white ancestor and 15 percent have predominantly white blood lines. It is interesting that we do not refer to people as "passing" for Mexican, Asian American, African American, and so on. If we applied the one-drop rule to whites, a significant number might become black, and if we applied the rule in reverse to blacks, a significant number of black people might become white.

Historically, there has been a striking absence of attention, debate, and scholarship focused on questions of whiteness as race, privilege, and social construction. Those researchers who have studied race in terms of white identity (for example, Carter, 1997) have found that most whites have not thought much about their race. Few, when asked to identify themselves by attributes, name whiteness among their primary characteristics. When asked to reflect on their race, whites often respond that they never thought about themselves (or their whiteness) in terms of race. Rather, they always thought of race as something that belonged to others: persons of color. Researchers suggest that unlike people of color, who typically know they have been classified according to some societal notion of race and that this racial categorization has meaning and significance for their personal identity, whites are typically unaware of race as a group and personal characteristic. However, according to sociologist Charles Gallagher (1997), whiteness is in a period of fundamental transformation for at least two reasons: (1) as a reaction to the entrance of historically marginalized racial and ethnic groups into the political arena and the ensuing struggle over social resources, and (2) a perception by whites of current and future material deprivation and the need to delineate white culture in a nondemonized fashion. Gallagher suggests that whites have gone through a process of racialization which is shaped by a decline of ethnicity, a rise of identity politics, the perception that whiteness is a social and economic liability, and the ideology of neoconservative racial politics.

It is ironic that whites most often say that they are not aware of themselves as white given that through various social, political, and institutional means, whites maintain racial divisions in this society. Although most researchers have concluded that much of this effort is unintentional and indirect, the ramifications are nonetheless powerful in terms of the racial exclusion of whole groups of people and the maintenance of a system of white dominance and privilege. Some social scientists have described this conviction of white superiority as **cultural racism**—the conscious or unconscious conviction that white or Euro-American cultural practices and patterns, as reflected in values, language, belief systems, styles of interpersonal interaction, behavioral patterns, social roles, politics, economics, music, art, religious tenets, and so forth, are superior to those of other visible racial/ethnic groups (Carter, 1997).

Ethnicity, like race, can be best understood as a dynamic, constantly evolving category applied both to individual identity and group organization. The term *ethnicity* emerged in the 1960s. Prior to that, groups we now know and define as ethnic groups were defined as races or nationalities (Glazer & Moynihan, 1975). In simple terms, an **ethnic group** is a group within a larger society that shares (or is believed to share) a common cultural heritage that sets it off from the society's mainstream or modal culture. According to most definitions of ethnicity, people do not have to share a common ancestry in a real sense. Like race, ethnicity is an important basis for ranking people in the U.S. stratification system and a key determinant of who gets what in society.

Applying the Sociological Imagination

How do you classify yourself racially? Are you white? Do you have friends or relatives who are white? If yes, how do you know you are white? That your friends and relatives are white? If no, how do you know you are not white? Is there congruency between the racial label ascribed to you by U.S. society and how you self-define racially? Does the one-drop rule have any conscious or unconscious effect on how you define yourself racially? Can you look at a person and determine her or his race? What criteria do you use to determine race?

The Social Construction of a "Minority" and a "Majority" Group

Race, ethnicity, and minority/majority group are such interrelated concepts that it is near impossible to discuss them as separate constructs. Like race and ethnicity, minority and majority groups are social and political constructs created as a means of categorizing and differentiating groups of people who share certain physical and/or social traits defined as inferior from those who share certain physical and/or social traits defined as superior. The significance of such labeling is apparent when such groups are categorically singled out for different treatment resulting in either disadvantage or privilege. Christopher Doob defines these two concepts in the following manner: a **minority group** (often referred to as a subordinate group) is any category of people having recognizable racial or ethnic traits that place it in a position of restricted power and inferior status so that its members suffer limited opportunities and rewards. In contrast, a **majority group** (often referred to as a dominant group) is a category of people within a society who possess distinct physical or cultural characteristics and maintain superior power, authority, and resources (Doob, 1996).

Minority and majority status are both ascribed and socially constructed. They are ascribed in the sense that people sharing certain hereditary physical traits are defined as inferior or superior. They are socially constructed in that they are categories or labels "given" to people who share certain cultural traits and who are defined as inferior or superior. In both types of groups, members come to share a common awareness of their status in society and this awareness helps to create and maintain a sense of belonging to the group. Minority status has traditionally been assigned to those groups in U.S. society whose histories include patterned subordination and oppression vis-à-vis groups defined as majority and superior. These groups are Native Americans, African Americans, Asian Americans, and Latinas/os.

It should be made clear that minority and majority status are social constructs used by sociologists and have little relationship to numerical presence. For example, the indigenous population of Africans in South Africa under apartheid constituted a minority group even though it made up about 80 percent of the total population. Africans were a minority group in the sociological sense because (1) being European was made the norm, (2) Europeans were in power, and (3) the indigenous population of nonwhites was excluded from full participation in South African culture and mainstream life. They had little or no access to political and economic power, they were assigned the lowest occupational positions, and their access to the opportunity structure was grossly unequal to that of Europeans.

Most often, social scientists have focused their attention on "minority groups," giving little attention to how those who are part of the "majority group" secure, maintain, and perpetuate their power, dominance, and privileged position. However, this pattern is changing. Sociologist Peggy McIntosh (1998), for example, provides a provocative analysis of skin color privilege and its relationship to minority/majority, dominant/subordinate relations. McIntosh suggests that white privilege is an "invisible backpack" of unearned assets, and she lists twenty-six privileges that whites enjoy, often without realizing it. Three examples typify the elusive but ever-present white-skin-color privilege. According to McIntosh, as a person defined as white:

1. "If I should need to move, I can be pretty sure of renting or purchasing housing in an area which I can afford and in which I would want to live."
2. "I am never asked to speak for all the people of my racial group."
3. "I can be pretty sure that if I ask to talk to 'the person in charge,' I will be facing a person of my race." (p. 97)

McIntosh's analysis provides evidence against the notion that the United States is a meritocracy. It is not that people who possess these privileges are bad people, nor is it that these privileges aren't things that everyone would want to enjoy in a democratic society. But not to recognize that various statuses and conditions such as skin color are either assets or disadvantages depending on how society defines them is to overlook the importance of the social, economic, and political nature of these various designations based almost exclusively on socially constructed definitions of race.

Attitudes and Action: Prejudice, Racism, and Discrimination

The first American settlers' written records indicated that they considered Native Americans as "depraved, savage brutes, as impious rascals who lived in filth and ate nasty food (Jacobs, 1985, p. 110). A "white" Harvard professor, writing circa 1890, recorded his feeling about Jews this way:

> Many Jews have personal and social qualities and habits that are unpleasant. . . .These come in large measure from the social isolation to which they have been subjected for centuries, by the prejudice and ignorance of Christian communities. Most Jews are socially untrained, and their bodily habits are not good." (Steinberg, 1981, p. 235)

Similar examples of prejudice exist for almost every racial/ethnic group in this country. For example, a colleague of ours recently related to us a story about a white female student in one of her classes who blurted out in a classroom of about thirty-five students, "I hate black people. I have had black student aids who worked for me and they are lazy and unskilled." One of the interesting things about this student's outburst was that, when called on her hate speech, she denied being prejudiced. Exactly what is prejudice? How pervasive is it? Do only a few people today, like the student mentioned above, hold negative feelings and attitudes toward other groups?

Prejudice   Although it often guides actions and behavior, **prejudice** is an attitude, generally negative, based on any categorical and unfounded overgeneralization about selected groups. It can take the form of beliefs about a group, negative feelings toward a group, or the desire to discriminate against a group. In each of these cases, prejudice involves an automatic reaction to a group or to a person's group membership. Both the American settlers writing about Native Americans and the Harvard professor writing about Jews probably would have insisted that their remarks were not indicative of prejudice. Rather, they might have argued that their opinions of these groups were based on social reality. However, prejudice is less often based on reality and more often based on stereotypes.

A common type of prejudice, a **stereotype** is an exaggerated belief about the appearance, behavior, or other characteristics of a group of people, an assumption that all people in a group share certain characteristics. Racial stereotypes are particularly abundant in our culture and are expressed in often-heard phrases such as "lazy blacks," "drunken Irish," "Italian mobster," "dumb Polack," "racist southern redneck," and "breeding Latinas/os." Each one, like all stereotypes, is a gross overgeneralization or exaggeration. Certainly, some people within these categories fit the stereotype, but so do others who are not part of the particular group. Further, not all people in any group are exactly the same. Although some stereotypes are positive, they can still have a negative impact when applied to individuals and groups. A good example is the stereotype that all Asian Americans are high academic achievers, especially in math and science. Fueling the myth of Asian Americans as a *model minority,* this stereotype diverts our attention from the persistence of poverty, racism, and discrimination faced by many Asian Americans. The use of stereotypes of any kind indicates a lack of understanding of the culture and heritage of a people and is generally offensive to the people who are the object of the stereotype. Although some people view stereotypes as "innocent humor,"others see them as a form of racism.

Racism   One of the most powerful and often destructive forms of prejudice is racism. As we indicated earlier, many people think of racism as hatred, hostility, contempt, and the harmful intentions and behaviors of individuals who have ill will toward other races. In this sense, racism is viewed as conscious and deliberate. However, as pernicious as this type of racism is, it is only a small part—and perhaps not the most important part—of what scholars and social critics today mean by the term racism (Zack, 1998). Let's turn our attention to some of the many ways in which racism is manifested.

Individual and Institutional Racism   As our discussion thus far suggests, racism can be overt or covert. On the one hand, it can be manifested when individuals or groups self-defined as superior act against individuals whom they define as inferior. According to Stokely Carmichael and Charles Hamilton (1967) in their now classic work *Black Power: The Politics of Liberation in America,* this behavior can be defined as **individual racism.** It is expressed through personal attitudes and behavior directed toward certain racial or ethnic groups by individual people. It can range from individual acts such as derogatory name calling, biased treatment during face-to-face contact, and avoidance to overt acts by individuals that cause death, injury, or the violent destruction of property. This type of racism can often be observed in the process of commission, such as the brutal beating of Mexican immigrants in Los Angeles or the brutality committed against an African American female motorist by a highway patrolman, videotaped by his own police camera. This kind of individual racism receives the most media attention. Although the impact of these acts extends beyond the individuals involved, they are nonetheless individual actions from which "respectable" members of society can divorce themselves. Although individual racism is most often intentional, it need not be. For example, one could argue that individual racism occurs when a white student seeking the chairperson of an academic department within a university setting approaches two people (one white and one African American) and addresses the white person, assuming that this individual is the person in charge. By most accounts, individual racism remains a common feature of U.S. life. Sociologists such as Joe Feagin (1991) and Lois Benjamin (1991), for example, have documented widespread individual racism in the everyday lives of middle-class and elite African Americans.

On the other hand, racism can be manifested when one entire community acts against another entire community. This behavior can be defined as **institutional racism**—established customs, laws, and practices that systematically reflect and produce racial inequalities in a society, whether or not the individuals maintaining these practices have racist intentions (Newman, 1995). Institutional racism involves discriminatory racial practices that are built into various societal institutions such as the political, economic, and educational systems.

Institutional racism is far more subtle and far less easy to identify in terms of specific individuals committing these acts than is individual racism. However, it is no less destructive to human life. For example, when a group of people are made wards of the government and forced to live on reservations and to assimilate, this is an example of institutional racism. It has its origins in the operation of established and respected forces in the society and thus receives far less public attention, scrutiny, and condemnation than do individual acts of racism. The concept of institutional racism is distinctly sociological in that it emphasizes that social structures establish norms that guide people's behavior. By accepting the norms developed and maintained in racist structures, individuals inevitably perpetuate discriminatory conditions and practices. Thus, institutional racism is the primary means by which racism is maintained (Doob, 1996). Although both types of racism are damaging to individuals and groups, the consequences of institutional racism dramatically limit whole groups of people's chances for success.

Symbolic and Aversive Racism Although people of color and members of other groups continually make serious efforts to advance their social position in the face of persistent racism, prejudice, and discrimination from the wider society, many whites deny that there is any racial inequality present in U.S. society. They generally believe that the U.S. system is a fair one and that everyone has opportunities for success equal to or greater than those of whites. They therefore believe that if groups are disadvantaged, these groups themselves are responsible for that disadvantage (Kluegel, 1990). This type of racial attitude on the part of some whites is consistent with what some scholars have described as **symbolic racism,** the denial of the presence of racial inequality in society and the opposition to any social policy that would enable disadvantaged groups to escape their position of disadvantage in U.S. society (Kinder and Sears, 1981; McClelland and Auster, 1990; Pettigrew, 1985).

Symbolic racism is sometimes explained in terms of the distorted images of people of color held by whites. Recent national survey data, for example, suggest that what whites think they see

relative to people of color may affect their beliefs. For example, as Table 10.1 shows, many white Americans indicate that they believe that the average African American is fairing as well as or better than the average white in such areas as jobs, education, and health care. Researchers studying the relationship between knowledge and attitudes suggest that it is not a big leap to imagine that the images that people hold about certain groups will affect their beliefs about those groups. Symbolic racism is a contemporary form of racism that is most often attributed to people who identify as political conservatives. However, the data presented in Table 10.1 suggest that such attitudes may be more widespread—that is, they cannot be categorized and attributed to a single group. Conversely, people who identify as political liberals are said to exhibit *aversive racism* more often. The data presented in Table 10.1 also calls this assumption into question.

Psychologist John Dovidio (1997) uses the term *aversive racism* to describe contemporary forms of racism. Whereas traditional forms of racism and prejudice are direct and overt, contemporary forms are indirect and subtle, or aversive. Dovidio defines **aversive racism** as a modern form of prejudice that characterizes the racial attitudes of many whites holding egalitarian values who regard themselves as nonprejudiced but who nevertheless discriminate in subtle, rationalizable ways (Gaertner et al., 1997). Although aversive racism is far more subtle and unintentional than the type of racism prevalent at the time of Viola Liuzzo's death, it can, and often does, contribute to distrust, tension, conflict, and fear among racial and ethnic groups. Because it is often subtle and covert, it often goes unnoticed and unchallenged.

Discrimination In general, **discrimination** is the unfair actions or practices of an individual, group, or subpopulation of individuals that deny another individual, group, or subpopulation of individuals access to valued resources. Within the context of race and ethnic stratification, *racial and ethnic discrimination* are the actions or practices of members of more powerful and dominant racial and/or ethnic groups who deny the members of other, less powerful and subordinate racial and/or ethnic groups full access to any of the things the society values (Aguirre &

TABLE 10.1 ⟳ Is There a Link between Perceptions and Attitudes?

Do people's perceptions about various racial groups influence how they think about issues related to those groups? Respondents were asked whether the average black was faring better than, worse than, or the same as the average white in six categories: income, jobs, housing, education, job security, and access to health care. Government statistics show that the average white is faring better in all of these categories.

	Number of whites	
Attitudes that are affected by awareness	Most Informed*	Least Informed[†]
Favor cuts in food stamp spending	34%	62%
Favor cutting aid to cities	48	58
Favor cuts in Medicaid spending	53	38
Are willing to pay more in taxes to help low-income minorities	34	68
Believe that minorities can overcome prejudice and work their way up without special help from the government	41	82
Believe that affirmative action should be limited	43	63
Attitudes on which awareness has little effect		
Believe low-income minorities need to become less dependent on federal government	90	94
Oppose cuts to public housing spending	62	59
Oppose cuts to Medicare spending	57	60

*Most informed gave correct answers to five or more questions
[†]Least informed gave incorrect answers to five or more questions
Source: Adapted from "How Perceptions Affect Attitudes." 1995. Washington Post/Kaiser Family Foundation/Harvard University Study. In Richard Morin, "A Distorted Image of Minorities: Poll Suggests That What Whites Think They See May Affect Beliefs," *Washington Post,* October 8, 1995, sec. A. © 1995 The Washington Post. Reprinted with permission.

Turner, 1998). Although prejudice refers to an attitude and discrimination to behavior, it is not always easy to distinguish between the two. One reason is that attitudes and actions toward members of various racial and ethnic groups may fluctuate within different social contexts. For example, depending on the social context, not everyone who is prejudiced will discriminate and not everyone who discriminates is prejudiced. On the other hand, some people are both prejudiced and discriminators while others are neither prejudiced nor discriminators.

Sociologist Robert Merton (1968) developed a typology of prejudice and discrimination that illustrates this point (see Table 10.2). According

to Merton, *all-weather liberals* accept the societal ideal of equality and do not discriminate against minorities. An example would be a person who has friends across racial groups and will date people from various racial groups. Her/his attitudes and actions are consistent. At the opposite end of this continuum are *active bigots*, whose attitudes and behavior are likewise consistent: they are overtly prejudiced and do not hesitate to let this attitude lead them to discriminate if an opportunity arises. Members of any number of hate groups around the world would fit this category. The next two categories illustrate Merton's belief in the situational context of prejudice and discrimination. For

TABLE 10.2 ⚙ **Robert Merton's Typology of Prejudice and Discrimination**

	Does Not Discriminate	Discriminates
Unprejudiced	All-weather liberal (unprejudiced nondiscriminator)	Fair-weather liberal (unprejudiced discriminator)
Prejudiced	Timid bigot (prejudiced nondiscriminator)	All-weather bigot (prejudiced discriminator)

Source: Merton, R. 1976. *Sociological Ambivalence and Other Essays.* New York: Free Press, pp. 189–216.

example, *timid bigots* are persons who are prejudiced and hold stereotypic views about minorities but will not discriminate because of situational norms. If a situation requires fair treatment of a racial or ethnic group, although prejudiced against the group, the timid bigot will treat the group fairly. An example would be a department head who does not like Latinas/os and believes that they are less intelligent than whites but who hires affirmatively in order to avoid penalties against discrimination. Finally, Merton described *fair-weather liberals* as persons who do not hold prejudiced feelings but who will discriminate if the situation calls for it. Many whites, for example, do not hold prejudicial feelings toward various racial and ethnic groups, but some might discriminate against them for the sake of expediency. An example would be a person who believes that people of various racial and ethnic backgrounds should get along and be friendly with one another but who will not invite friends of color home or to parties for fear that her/his white friends and family would not understand or accept this practice.

Although Merton presents us with ideal types, he makes the point that social pressures and the costs of discriminating or not discriminating will often determine whether or not prejudice and racism will be translated into action. If the costs are perceived as great, prejudiced people will often not discriminate. Likewise, relatively unprejudiced people may discriminate if pressured to do so. Merton's typology suggests that prejudiced attitudes and discriminatory behavior are not static. They can and do change. Researchers, for example, have documented the decline in prejudice in the U.S. South (at least as measured by people's responses

to questionnaires) after federal laws ordered desegregation of public facilities.

Today, the term *reverse discrimination* is sometimes used to suggest that programs designed to overcome the effects of past discrimination against members of various subordinate groups deny some members of the dominant group equal access to society's valued resources. Reverse discrimination is a highly charged concept that provokes many emotions. On the one hand, those among the dominant group who believe that they have been denied resources feel cheated and angry, and they argue that they do not discriminate and should not be held responsible for the behavior of their foremothers and forefathers. On the other hand, those who have to live with the legacy of past as well as present discrimination believe that some remedy is necessary to overcome the effects of discrimination and further, that reverse discrimination is not possible in a society in which all institutional, cultural, social, political, and economic structures favor the dominant group. No matter which side we come down on, the fact is that the process of discrimination is the most important force sustaining racism and inequality in a society (Aguirre & Turner, 1998).

The Declining or Inclining Significance of Race?

One of the most controversial articulations of the very complex issues surrounding analyses of race and racism in contemporary U.S. society is that of sociologist William Julius Wilson. His suggestion that race has declined in its significance as a major force of inequality in the lives of African Americans is at the basis of much scholarly work and discourse.

According to Wilson, race relations in the United States are shaped by the system of production characteristic of the society. After 1945, U.S. race relations have been shaped by a period of progressive transition from race inequalities to class inequalities. Since the civil rights movement of the 1960s, Wilson argues, improving economic conditions, declining discrimination, and government policies such as equal employment programs and greater access to higher education have enabled a growing number of African Americans to attain middle-class status, distancing themselves from a growing, poverty-stricken African American underclass. In turn, this has created a dual labor market in which middle-class African Americans do better in every way than poor African Americans. Unprecedented job opportunities in the public and private sector have put them on a par with whites having equivalent qualifications. At the same time, there is a huge African American underclass that is subject to class subordination and unable to enter the U.S. mainstream. Many whites and other groups of color are subject as well to this class subordination. Thus, according to Wilson, it is no longer the color of one's skin but the economic status of the family into which one is born that affects one's life chances. What is needed are widespread public policies and programs that focus on class inequality (Wilson, 1978).

Charles V. Willie, one of the earliest detractors of the Wilson thesis, argues that discrimination on the basis of race persists, despite the gains made by a small segment of the African American population. While recognizing the gains made by African Americans in various areas of social, economic, and political life, Willie argues that African Americans have not progressed as far as Wilson would have us believe and that the reason continues to be race and gender. Willie counters with the argument that the significance of race is increasing, especially for middle-class African Americans who, because of school desegregation and affirmative action and other integration programs, are coming into direct contact and competition with whites for jobs, education, and other social and political opportunities. Although African Americans continue to make gains, no matter how high they rise in socioeconomic terms, their presence is still firmly resisted in various institutions and social arrangements, for example, residential areas, high-level jobs, board rooms, and social arrangements (Willie, 1989). Considerable sociological research supports Willie's contention that race has not diminished in significance as a major determinant of the quality of life for individuals living in the United States today (see, for example, Feagin, 1991; Feagin & Vera, 1995; Thomas, 1993; Thomas et al., 1994).

Some scholars have argued that neither Wilson's nor Willie's argument is sufficient by itself. Wilson's focus on class is in the right direction, but it is incomplete. A missing piece is his inattention to the fact that racism has been a function of class interest throughout U.S. history, beginning with slavery, continuing with racist segregation and discrimination in favor of both the white property and the white working classes, and up to today where racism is supported by a theory of equal opportunity and competition through civil rights, busing, and affirmative action. African Americans continue to be subordinated by the system of production. The African American middle class is small and has made its gains through employment, not business ownership, and much of these gains have been made through employment in the public sector, where African Americans may have some degree of status but little or no power. Moreover, the current antiurban policies of many businesses have hurt the African American middle class as well as the poor. However, although race continues to be an important factor in the life chances of various U.S. groups, it is also the case that by the mid-1990s, the U.S. corporate economy was thoroughly entwined in the world market, where cheaper global labor operates directly counter not only to the interests of groups of color but also to the interests of white workers and even some white professionals (Rossides, 1997).

Theories of Race and Ethnic Inequality

Why are some people prejudiced? Is prejudice inevitable? Various social scientists, including sociologists, have attempted to answer questions such as these by focusing either on the individual psyche or on macro-level intergroup processes that occur between racial majority and minority groups.

Social Psychological Theories

Social psychological theories of racial and ethnic inequality focus on the attitudes of people. In general, these theories argue that people's social situations and experiences influence their attitudes and beliefs. These situations and experiences lead some people to develop prejudiced attitudes and beliefs, usually as a result of misplaced frustration and aggression, personality needs, or social learning.

Frustration–Aggression An early psychological theory of prejudice, associated with the work of John Dollard and associates (1939), explains this attitude in terms of people's hostility and rising frustration. The basic idea of this thesis is that prejudice originates in a buildup of frustration; people who are frustrated in their efforts to realize some highly desired goal tend to respond with a pattern of aggression. Because either they do not know the source of their frustration or the source is too powerful to confront directly, they single out a convenient substitute, or scapegoat to blame unfairly. Sociologists typically define a **scapegoat** as a racial, ethnic, or religious group in close proximity that is not capable of offering protracted resistance to the hostility or aggression of others. Although scapegoats are not the true source of prejudiced people's anger, they serve as effective targets for their displaced aggression. For example, recent immigrants and undocumented workers rather than the policies of capitalists are blamed by some members of U.S. society for social problems such as unemployment and low wages. Although the frustration-aggression thesis is logical, social scientists have pointed out a number of questions unanswered by this theory (Marger, 1994): (1) Under what conditions will frustration *not* lead to aggression? (2) Under what conditions will aggression be directed inward, and when will it be directed at the true source of frustration? (3) Why are some groups chosen as scapegoats rather than others?

The Authoritarian Personality Theodor Adorno and his colleagues (1950) developed the theory of the *authoritarian personality,* which links a particular personality type with prejudiced attitudes. Based on their analysis of the hate speeches and writings of groups such as the Ku Klux Klan and the Nazis, Adorno and his associates found a consistent relationship between antiblack and anti-Semitic attitudes and a set of characteristics that they defined as an authoritarian personality. This type of personality is characterized by excessive respect for and submissiveness to authority, conformity, superstition, aggression, worry about sexual "goings-on," insecurity, rigid stereotypic thinking, and cynicism. They argued that people possessing this personality type are authority oriented, intolerant, and preoccupied with power. Adorno found that adults having authoritarian personalities had usually experienced harsh discipline as children. As a consequence, they held intense anger, feared self-analysis, and had a strong tendency to blame their troubles and shortcomings on people whom they perceived as inferior to themselves.

Historically, the aggression and hostility of the authoritarian personality has been directed toward African Americans, Jews, and various other groups defined as subordinate and inferior. Adorno found that people who displayed strong prejudice toward one minority group were usually prejudiced toward all minorities. Several researchers have confirmed Adorno's finding of scapegoating and projection among many prejudiced people. Moreover, subsequent studies have found that people who are less educated, older, and from a lower socioeconomic status in society and who have harsh and demanding parents are more likely to possess an authoritarian personality.

Social Learning Theories Social learning theories of prejudice suggest that people are prejudiced because of the environments in which they are socialized. This would explain, for example, the pervasive antiblack prejudice of some people in the U.S. South. They learn prejudice from observing and emulating significant others, such as parents, other relatives, neighbors, and peers. The process of learning prejudice is much the same as that for learning other attitudes and behaviors. Prejudice is sometimes taught directly and intentionally; for instance, parents who are self-professed white supremacists often report that they consciously teach their children to mistrust and hate Jews, African Americans, and various other groups that they view as inferior. However, prejudice is most often learned in an unconscious manner when parents, peers, and other significant influences informally transmit their attitudes and beliefs about certain groups to their children or peers. Children as well as adults pick up racial cues from these individuals and groups as well as from the mass media. For example, some researchers have found that by the age of four, U.S. children have been exposed to the ethnic hierarchy, especially the black–white dichotomy, and they have begun to develop a fairly crystallized set of racial/ethnic values and attitudes (Porter, 1971).

Researchers suggest that this type of learned prejudice is different from that based on personality needs in that it is easier to change. For example, when people who have learned prejudice in a prejudiced environment move to environments where their significant others are relatively unprejudiced, their prejudice levels often fall. In short, people can learn to be prejudiced or nonprejudiced depending on their learning environments, whereas for people who have a personality need to be prejudiced, the need remains regardless of the environment they are in (Marger, 1994).

Social Structural Theories

Whereas social psychological theories of race relations focus on individuals and their personality development and needs, sociological theories focus on social structural determinants of prejudice and discrimination. While the former type of theories gives clues as to how prejudice and racism are transmitted and sustained, the latter gives clues as to the origins of racial and ethnic tensions, prejudice, and discrimination.

Functional Theory   According to functionalists, if a pattern such as racism and discrimination persists, it is assumed that it does so because it serves some positive function either for individuals, for society, or for both. Although those who take a functionalist approach do not necessarily advocate racism, racial aggression, and hostility,

they point out that it serves positive functions, at least for those who are prejudiced and who discriminate. For example, prejudice provides a moral justification for discrimination and the denial of equal rights. If we can define Africans and later African Americans as inferior and less than human, we can justify their enslavement and the various other atrocities committed against them, such as mass lynchings (Nash, 1962).

On the other hand, a functionalist analysis might find racial/ethnic prejudice and discrimination dysfunctional as well. For example, when individuals and groups are denied full access to the opportunity structure of society, the society suffers from a loss of a large pool of talented and creative leaders. Prejudice and discrimination are also dysfunctional in the sense that they are highly correlated with various costly social problems, such as poverty, crime, and unemployment (Rose, 1997).

Conflict Theory   Most contemporary sociological analyses of race and ethnic relations approach the topic from a conflict perspective. Unlike functionalism, a conflict perspective does not view racial and ethnic inequality as resulting simply from cultural differences and ethnocentrism. Rather, a conflict perspective focuses on the competition between groups and the resulting subjugation and oppression of some racial and ethnic groups and the privilege and power of others. A classical Marxist analysis of racism would argue that racism and racial oppression exist because they benefit the ruling economic class. Marxists believe that racial competition and antagonism are primarily mechanisms that are used by the owners to divide the working class. For example, they would suggest that employers encourage white workers to believe that they are threatened by workers of color. In this way, whites come to see these groups rather than the employer as their enemy. By dividing the working class along racial lines, it is unlikely that its members will work together to advance their common interests. Those in power, then, are able to use prejudice as a strategy to divide workers and protect their own privileged position. Labor history in this country offers considerable support for this viewpoint.

Oliver Cox (1948) and others, using this Marxian *exploitation theory,* have shown that racism keeps minorities (for example, Latinas/os and undocumented workers), in low-paying jobs, thereby supplying the capitalist economy with an ever-ready and ever-present pool of cheap labor to exploit. At the same time, it allows the capitalists to regulate the wages and working conditions of all workers. When workers from the majority group demand higher pay, they are threatened with the loss of their jobs and replacement by minority group members, who have few options but to accept the low-paying jobs. Although this theory explains a significant aspect of prejudice and racism, it does not account for the fact that not all minority groups have been exploited or are exploited today to the same extent. And some groups (for example, religious groups such as the Quakers) have been victimized by prejudice for reasons other than economic ones (Schaefer & Lamm, 1998).

Feminist Sociological Theory

A feminist perspective on race and ethnic inequality suggests that race as a social construction overlaps with other socially constructed categories, such as class, gender, and sexual orientation. As a result of these intersections, racism combines with other types of prejudice and discrimination, such as sexism, heterosexism, and class elitism, to form patterns of social relations that develop into hierarchical orders. Feminist sociologist Patricia Hill Collins (1991) refers to these hierarchical orders as a *matrix of domination* in which each type of inequality reinforces the others so that the impact of one cannot be fully understood without also understanding the others. These relations are institutionalized into stratified structures, resulting in different forms of social, racial, and ethnic inequality in different historical and societal contexts. Similarly, Ester Ngan-Ling Chow, Doris Wilkerson, and Maxine Baca Zinn (1996) suggest that these relations form structural and symbolic bases for both the objective conditions and the subjective meanings of women's and men's lives. A feminist analysis, then, requires us to focus our analysis on the interactive, reciprocal, and cumulative effects of racism and racial and ethnic inequality.

Historical Patterns of Race and Ethnic Relations

Groups defined in racial and ethnic terms have historically encountered each other, and varying patterns of contact and of long-term relationships have developed as a result of these encounters. Based on our discussion thus far, we know that one outcome of this contact has been the development of racial and ethnic stratification systems fostered by prejudice and discrimination. But there are also other aspects of racial and ethnic relationships that interest social scientists. Sociologists typically describe these relationships and patterns of interaction in terms of assimilation, pluralism, segregation, colonization, slavery, population transfer, expulsion, and genocide.

Assimilation

Assimilation is a broad term used to describe the process whereby racial and ethnic minority groups gradually adopt patterns of the majority group and become absorbed into the larger societal mainstream. Ideally, complete assimilation creates a new homogeneous society in which there are no longer distinct racial and ethnic groups and race and ethnicity are not a basis of social differentiation. One of the most fundamental and persistent viewpoints about U.S. society is that it represents the ultimate model of racial and ethnic assimilation. Historically, and even today, many people think of the United States as a great *melting pot* in which immigrant groups of varied nationalities and racial and ethnic backgrounds have blended together to form a new and distinct national identity and way of life. The problem with this "melting pot" view is that it reflects an ideal. In actuality, assimilation occurs in varying degrees. Without a doubt, for some groups, assimilation occurred and they *melted* into the mainstream (for example, Germans and the Irish). Sociologists refer to this pattern as **cultural assimilation,** a process whereby various cultural groups in a society become more similar to one another so that the differences that form the basis for prejudice and discrimination are minimized or eliminated (Gordon, 1964). However, for other groups, whether desired or not, less melting has taken place (for example, Italians and Koreans). For still others, assimilation, to the extent that it has occurred, has been forced upon them (for example, Native Americans and African Americans). **Forced assimilation** is the process whereby the majority group either prohibits or makes it difficult for a minority group to practice its language, religion, and other customs.

Pluralism

A pattern of racial/ethnic relations in which a variety of subcultures live side by side but maintain their respective cultures and lifestyles is called **pluralism** or *multiculturalism*. This phenomenon has led conflict theorists and others to describe societies in which this occurs as *plural societies.* Under **cultural pluralism,** various racial and ethnic groups maintain most or all of their cultural patterns but share some elements of the culture with the larger society.

The United States is often described as a pluralistic society. On the surface of it, this would appear to be true. Ideally, all societal institutions operate on the principle of equal access to all people. And, at the same time, U.S. society is full of visual indicators of its diversity: specific and identifiable ethnic neighborhoods with their distinctive restaurants, shops, churches, and other cultural symbols. However, although many white ethnic groups, such as Jews, Poles, and Italians, may have the option to maintain their subcultural patterns and still be accepted in the larger culture, some racial/ethnic groups have had their cultures attacked and used to justify prejudice and discrimination against them. Interestingly, at the same time that these cultures are under attack, various elements of them (for example, music, food, and dress) have been co-opted by the larger culture.

Some groups have developed and maintained groups, organizations, and institutions that are separate from the dominant culture. For example, various groups of color have developed and maintained separate churches, alternative schools, and their own theaters and other recreational organizations, not because they are separatists but because they have been excluded from mainstream institutions. Sociologists refer to this pattern of race relations as *structural pluralism.*

Segregation

One of the most common patterns of relations between racial and ethnic minorities and majorities

U.S. society is full of visual indicators of its diversity, such as San Francisco's Chinatown, with its distinctive restaurants, shops, churches, and other cultural symbols.

is **segregation,** the physical and social separation of racial/ethnic groups in a society. This pattern of race relations generally results not only in the separation and isolation of some groups from the dominant group, but also it generally happens that because the groups are considered inferior, the conditions under which they are forced to live are inferior to those of the dominant group. Some groups, for instance religious minorities such as the Amish, segregate themselves. Others, however, are involuntarily excluded from the cultural mainstream. For example, under the past system of *apartheid* in South Africa, hundreds of laws and acts were passed mandating racial separation in almost every conceivable area of human life, thus severely restricting the rights and opportunities of the indigenous population.

The most pervasive pattern of racial/ethnic segregation in the United States occurs in housing. Early studies of *residential segregation* predicted that as racial/ethnic groups rose in socioeconomic status, residential segregation or restrictions on where certain racial and ethnic groups could live would disappear. For most European American groups, this prediction has held true and, to some extent, it also has for Native Americans, Asian Americans, and Mexicans. However, by and large, it has not held true for African Americans. In general, African Americans have been forced, first by law—*de jure segregation*—and now by custom and norms—*de facto segregation*—to live separately from whites. When African Americans have attempted to live outside of "black belts" and "bronzevilles," they have faced not only "white flight" but also, often, physical violence to their persons and property. Although some research suggests that there have been modest decreases in residential segregation in the United States over recent decades (Farley, 1995), other research documents the continued widespread segregation of African Americans in many U.S. inner cities. This *hypersegregation* is said to affect almost 20 percent of African Americans, whereas it affects only a few comparably poor whites (Jagarowsky & Bane, 1990).

Today, many U.S. suburbs are experiencing what happened in major inner cities following World War II, when whites fled to the suburbs to escape residential integration. Today, the pattern has reversed. As an increasing number of African Americans and Latinas/os (many of high socioeconomic status) have sought better housing and safer neighborhoods in the suburbs, whites are fleeing to new, predominantly or all-white suburbs or returning to central cities by buying or renting high-price, prime real estate. Thus, residential segregation persists, whether in cities or suburbs, because most whites choose not to live in the same communities with members of some racial groups and they are able to keep these and other unwanted groups out of certain residential areas through a variety of real estate practices.

In segregated areas where members of minority groups predominate, unemployment, underemployment, poverty, and dependency on government support are generally greater than in areas where dominant groups live. These conditions severely limit the chances to live a long and healthy life. Involuntary segregation often creates situations of hostility and conflict but, as we saw with the case of Viola Liuzzo and others, the actions of individuals and groups can often make a difference. As a result of the gains of the civil rights movement, for example, public facilities and accommodations were desegregated.

Subjugation and Extermination

In many societies in which groups have been defined as subordinate and/or inferior, patterns of subjugation often take on an increasingly inhumane character. Subjugation often progresses from colonization of a group to expulsion of the group from its homeland to the actual destruction of the group through genocide.

Colonization: External and Internal   In its traditional meaning, **colonization** refers to a powerful country's establishment of control over a foreign country and its people. European countries, for instance, came to control much of Africa. Typically, the indigenous people of the colony are assigned a status lower than that of the colonizers. The colonizers take and use the natural resources of the colony, often along with the coerced labor of the indigenous group, to enrich the colonizing country. Sociologists have used the concept of *internal colonization* to describe a similar process that occurs when the colonizer and colonized live within the same society. Internal colonization involves societal policies of exploitation and oppression of minority groups. Slavery and apartheid are extreme examples of internal colonization.

Slavery and Apartheid *Slavery* is the most extreme form of legalized and sanctioned inequality for individuals and groups. It is distinguished by the ownership of some human beings by others. The enslaved population is defined and treated as chattel property, the equivalent of other property such as livestock, pets, and household furnishings, although it is not always treated as well. A clear example of this can be seen in the passage from the book *Amistad* in the Sociology through Literature box. The role of ideology in supporting any system of stratification is evidenced in the conversation between the slave broker and the slave ship's captain. As their conversation reveals, definitions of slaves as property were not only rationalized and justified on the basis of a profit motive but also rationalized and justified on the basis of an ideology of **manifest destiny**—a set of beliefs about white supremacy that rationalizes the exploitation of people defined as inferior on the basis that it is the God-ordained destiny of whites to direct inferior people's movement toward participation in modern political and technological life.

Slave systems have varied over time. In the ancient Greek and Roman societies, the mass of slaves consisted primarily of captives of war and piracy. Although slave status could be inherited, it was not necessarily a permanent condition. In stark contrast, the more contemporary slave systems in the United States and Latin America were based solely on race and were permanent conditions. In the United States, for instance, anyone of African descent was a slave. Even free blacks could be enslaved at any time. The best-known estimates of the number of slaves brought to the so-called New World range between 9 and 15 million, with perhaps half dying during the infamous *middle passage* from Africa to the Americas (Doob, 1996). Skin color became the visible symbol of slave status in the United States, and a rigid racist ideology developed to buttress the system. In addition, racial and, in most instances, legal barriers prevented the freeing of slaves. Every aspect of slave life was controlled by the slave owner and was explicitly legitimized by slave codes: slaves could not own property, testify in court, inherit property, hire themselves out, or make contracts; laws forbade teaching them to read and write. This rigid system of slave stratification and inequality was enforced not only through the legal system of slave codes but also through an informal etiquette, in which physical contact was not uncommon but the social spaces of whites and slaves were clearly marked.

Whenever and wherever slavery has existed, it has been based upon extreme coercion and oppression in order to maintain the privileges and profits of the slave owners. However, throughout history, slaves have fought back against their oppression and enslavement. For example, there were many documented slave revolts during the history of U.S. slavery. Most were unsuccessful, however, because of the significant resources that the ruling elite controlled and utilized in crushing such collective actions and maintaining a system of involuntary servitude. In the United States, the slave-labor system of inequality eventually broke down, not so much because of moral indignation but because it was no longer an economically efficient system for the ruling elites. However, the racist ideology that was developed to support the slave system continues to influence not only the perception of African Americans by whites but also the life chances of African Americans as we move into the twenty-first century. Although slavery as a formal and legitimized system of inequality ended in North and South America over one hundred years ago, slavery has not disappeared from the world. Notwithstanding the fact that as late as 1948, the United Nations made a Universal Declaration of Human Rights which declared that no one shall be held in slavery or servitude and that slavery and the slave trade shall be prohibited in all of their forms, it is estimated than more than 100 million people around the world are still enslaved.

Apartheid, a system by which white supremacy is assured and separation between groups is legally maintained, developed in South Africa. It has been variously described by scholars of stratification as a racial caste system, in which the castes are defined based upon race, or as twentieth-century slavery, in which the

Sociology through Literature

La Amistad

Amistad, by David Pesci, combines historical scholarship with the art of literature to chronicle what was until lately only a footnote in the history books on the subject of slavery in America: the real revolt by African slaves aboard the ship *La Amistad* in 1839. The excerpt below illuminates the issue of slaves as property and the rationalization of and justification for the enslavement of human beings. Here, the American slave broker Shaw and the ship's captain, Alonzo Frederico Miguel Figeroa, with whom Shaw has contracted to transport 600 slaves from Lomboko Africa to Cuba, share their views on the humanity or inhumanity of slaves. This conversation takes place after Shaw has stopped a sailor from killing the slave Singbe and has subsequently beaten Singbe to make his points that he owns him and all the other African captives and that they will obey his rules and the rules of the slave ship.

Figeroa took a long drink out of his mug, then went back to his pipe. "Some men, whip the niggers until the life is almost gone from their bodies," he said. "Others, let them get too soft, worried about damaging the cargo. They let them get away with anything, which ends up making more work and risk for the ship's captain and crew. But you Señor Shaw, you know exactly how to walk the line with these animals. You keep them in fear, but you keep them intact."

"Perhaps that is because I don't see them as animals, Captain Figeroa. Rather, I see them as they are. As men."

. . . "Men? As you and I are men in the eyes of God? Of course, you are not serious."

"Yes, I am. They are men . . . perhaps they are not as learned and cultured and scientific as we. Perhaps they are a little closer to Eden in their way of life. But they are men, just the same."

"I do not believe that. I do not believe that you believe it, either. They are ignorant, godless creatures. A lower breed, closer to the monkeys in the trees of their homeland than to any white man."

"When you transport female slaves, do you take one to your bed to keep you warm at night?"

"Of course. In fact, I was very disappointed to see that you were not bringing any negresses onboard this trip."

"The demand is stronger for the men, though I never mind giving a wench over to a ship's captain to add comfort during his voyage. After all, it is customary, and, as I see it, a courtesy. However, I detest having my property roughed over by the crew. It can depreciate their value, especially if the females are going to be purchased for breeding."

"A good point, Señor Shaw."

"Actually, my point rests on a question, captain. You bed-down female slaves on your voyages, yes?"

"Si."

"So, do you mean to tell me that you have been fornicating with animals sir?"

Figeroa's lips parted into a smokey grin. "Let us say, animals with a human form."

"Nonsense, captain. They can reason, they can speak, they have families and farms and laws. They have governments and wars and take slaves of their own. Show me monkeys that do that. As for ignorance, well, I have seen black servants in America and the Indies who have been taught to read and cipher and speak English, Spanish, and French as well as any white man. No, they are men. They are people, as are you and I."

"If you believe such a thing, then how can you do what you do, buying and selling them as cattle, as slaves to other men?"

"There have always been slaves, my friend, in almost every human society since time began. In the Bible, the Israelites were slaves in Egypt, and before that the Jews had slaves themselves. Slaves are the spoils of the conqueror. And, at this point in history, Christian white men are masters of the earth. The Africans are men, but their simple ways and societies are no match for our science and weapons or our politics or resolve."

Write a short reflection paper reacting to the logic/rationale used by each of these men to justify slavery. In what ways do vestiges of this type of ideological thinking remain a part of the racial stratification system in the United States today? Give examples.

Source: From the book *Amistad: A Novel,* by David Pesci, pp. 21–23. Copyright © 1997 by Marlowe & Company. Appears by permission of the publisher, Marlowe & Company.

ruling white numerical minority (14 percent of the population) owned and/or controlled the majority of the land and the indigenous population of Africans (86 percent of the population) were forced to sell their labor for whatever price the ruling elite were willing to pay. Africans under apartheid, as under U.S. slavery, had few, if any, legal rights. Their lives were completely governed by a complex system of laws that mandated racial separation in almost every conceivable area of human life, severely restricting the rights and opportunities of Africans and reinforcing the racial ideology of white supremacy. Their every movement was governed by passbooks, which was similar to the U.S. slavery rule that slaves had to have a written note to validate being off the plantation.

Under the apartheid system of racial stratification, people were identified first and foremost by their race, which then profoundly impacted every aspect of their lives, determining where, and with whom, they could live, work, eat, travel, play, learn, sleep, and be buried. The problems we have discussed concerning the definition of race based on skin color and ancestry are all too evident under apartheid. For example, under apartheid, racial classifications were in some sense arbitrary because people could appeal and even change their classification. Sociologist Joan Ferrante (1998) reports that when South Africans applied for a change in racial classification, the board hearing such appeals paid careful attention to the tint of a person's skin color, facial features, and hair texture. In a typical twelve-month period under apartheid, the many changes in racial classification included: 150 coloreds (people of mixed racial ancestry) reclassified as white, 10 whites reclassified as colored, 2 coloreds reclassified as Chinese, 10 Indians reclassified as coloreds, 1 Indian reclassified as white, 1 white reclassified as Malay, 4 blacks reclassified as Indian; and 3 whites reclassified as Chinese. Adding to the arbitrariness of the concept of race in South Africa was the fact that the Chinese were officially classified as a White subgroup and the Japanese, most of whom were not residents but visiting businessmen, were given the status of "honorary whites." Absurd? Ferrante says yes, if this had been fiction rather than a chilling historical reality that was part of the most complex system of human oppression and control in the world.

Although apartheid has been dismantled and South Africa has its first African president, the long-term effects of the economic damage, human misery, and daily indignities of racial and economic oppression inflicted on the non-white population cannot be estimated. Huge and significant economic, educational, and health gaps between whites and Africans will not disappear over night. In this sense, racial inequality still exists in South Africa. Progress toward a more egalitarian system in South Africa lies in dismantling the effects of years of oppressive conditions on the relationships between the majority and minority populations.

Population Transfer and Expulsion   In some instances, a dominant group has exercised its power and control through *population transfer,* the voluntary or involuntary movement of racial/ethnic groups to designated geographical areas. In 1838, the U.S. government forced the Cherokee people from their homes in Georgia and the Carolinas to reservations in Oklahoma. It is estimated that over one-third of the Cherokee people died under the harsh and brutal conditions involved in this process of population transfer that came to be called the Trail of Tears. More recently, Serbs in the former Yugoslavia forced Muslims and ethnic Albanians out of Serb-controlled communities. In other instances, the dominant group has expelled racial/ethnic groups from the country entirely. For example, in the nineteenth century, millions of Jews were driven out of Russia, and during the late twentieth century, over 1 million ethnic Chinese, who came to be known as Chinese boat people, were expelled from Vietnam.

Genocide   The most extreme form that racial and ethnic relations have taken is **genocide,** the extermination or wholesale killing of a racial or ethnic group. However horrendous this action, it has been attempted all too frequently in human history. Often, the practice of genocide has been based on an attempt by more powerful groups seeking to *racially purify* or *ethnically cleanse* their race and the territories within which they live. For example, the murder of Jews, Gypsies, and others in Nazi Germany during World War II was tied to the ideology of racial purity; the wholesale murder of Muslims, Croats, and ethnic Albanians by Serbs was tied to the concept of ethnic cleansing; and in Rwanda, over a million people were slaughtered within a ninety-day period in the name of ethnic cleansing.

Moreover, the early genocidal policies and practices of European settlers in North America resulted in the annihilation of millions of Native Americans, although not expressly for the purpose of achieving racial or ethnic purity. Native Americans numbered somewhere around 5 million when Europeans first settled in North America. By both the direct and indirect actions of Europeans, there were only half a million Native Americans at the beginning of the twentieth century. Likewise, although there is no official count of the millions of Africans who were murdered or otherwise died during the middle passage or of the millions who were murdered or otherwise died under U.S. slavery, the policies and actions of Europeans and European-Americans toward African Americans and their ancestors represent a form of genocidal annihilation.

The Social Construction of Race and Ethnicity in the United States

A discussion of each of the individual racial/ethnic groups in the United States is not possible (and perhaps not even desirable) in an introductory sociology textbook. Therefore, to illustrate the patterns of racial and ethnic relations in the United States, we will limit our focus to six groups or categories: the four major groups that continue to be defined and treated in racial/ethnic terms—Native Americans, African Americans, Latinas/os, and Asian Americans—new immigrants, and European-Americans (see Figure 10.2).

Native Americans

Native Americans are the first Americans. Their ancestors migrated from Asia over 20,000 years ago, and for many centuries, they were the sole

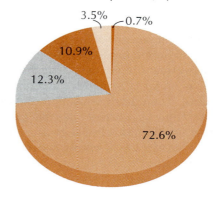
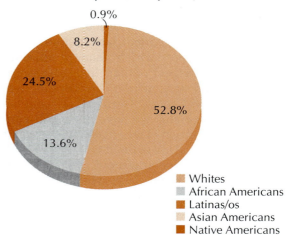

FIGURE 10.2 ↻ **Distribution of U.S. Population, 1997**
Source: U.S. Bureau of the Census. 1998. *Statistical Abstract of the United States, 1998.* Washington, D.C.: U.S. Department of Commerce, Table 19.

inhabitants of this land. As shown in Figure 10.3, the label "Native Americans" represents a wide variety of groups having a diverse array of cultures, most distinguishable in terms of language, family organization, and religion. Approximately half live in rural areas, and the large majority live on reservations. Two-thirds of those living on reservations are concentrated in Oklahoma, Arizona, New Mexico, California, and the Dakotas.

After the Civil War, the U.S. government established reservations, ostensibly to assimilate Native Americans into the U.S. mainstream. In

1871, Native Americans became wards of the federal government, whose assimilationist policies demanded the abandonment of traditional Native American culture and the adoption of European culture. But Native Americans were not granted U.S. citizenship until 1924 (Rose, 1997).

Today, Native Americans are often referred to as an *invisible minority* because most Americans are hardly aware of them. United States policies toward Native Americans have vacillated between domination and oppression and total neglect. As a result, Native Americans have the highest rates of poverty, unemployment, poor health, suicide, and alcoholism of any of the groups defined as minorities in the United States. The average life expectancy of Native American women is forty-six and of Native American men is forty-five. In addition, the suicide rate of Native people is twenty times higher than the national average (Munson, 1997). In spite of improvements in health care and education since World War II, discrimination and racism continue to limit Native Americans' opportunities for advancement and achievement (see Table 10.3).

Of those who have given up their status as wards of the government, some have been successful in assimilating into the mainstream, but the majority have faced the same or similar conditions of racism and oppression as have other minority groups. On the positive side, since winning a series of legal battles in the 1960s that restored their control over the land and their right to determine economic policy, many Native American groups have opened businesses on their land, ranging from industrial parks to gambling casinos. Some gains over the past decade include:

- The recognition of 150-year-old treaties about fishing rights.
- The Suquamish tribe and some fifteen others in the state of Washington were finally assured the legal right to harvest shellfish from private beaches and state parks.
- Some tribes have been granted special status and been exempted from certain taxes and zoning regulations, allowing them to expand giant enterprises on their own lands.
- Members of the Choctaw tribe in Mississippi have become a primary employer, owning five car-part factories and other businesses that give the tribe an employment rate of 80 percent.

In Connecticut, the once-poor Mashantucket Pequot Native Americans have become fairly wealthy by establishing a huge gambling casino. Native American groups have established over 300 casinos in twenty-six states. Not all Native Americans agree with the practices of gambling and of the establishment of casinos on their land, but Native Americans have earned over $4 billion in new revenue from these business

FIGURE 10.3 Native American Population in North America by Selected Ancestry Group and Region, 1990
Source: U.S. Bureau of the Census. 1998. *Statistical Abstract of the United States, 1998.* Washington, DC: U.S. Department of Congress, Tables 30, 54.

Distribution of Largest Native American Groups

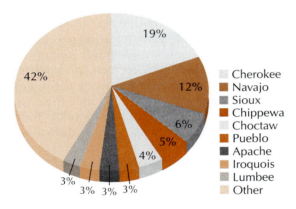

Native Americans by Region*

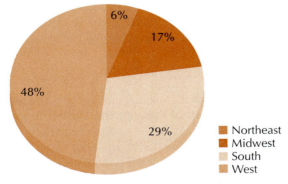

*American Indian, Eskimo, and Aleut population

TABLE 10.3 ⊙ Comparative Well-Being in the United States by Race, 1997

	Median Family Income	Percentage of White Income	Percentage Unemployed	Percentage of Individuals below Poverty Level	Percentage Who Own Home	Education*	Life Expectancy
Whites	44,756	—	2.8	11.2	69	25	76.1
Native Americans	21,619	48	NA†	31.2	NA	9	NA
African Americans	26,522	59	6.5	28.3	46	13	69.1
Asian Americans	49,105	110	3.2	14.4	52	42	NA
Latinas/os	26,179	58	5.3	29.4	43	10	NA

*4 or more years of college

†Data not available

Source: U.S. Bureau of the Census. *Statistical Abstract of the United States, 1998.* Washington, DC: U.S. Department of Commerce, Tables 19, 51, 54, 55, 126, 127.

enterprises, and, for the most part, they have invested these monies in areas that have improved the lives of their entire reservations (Deloria, 1995; Rose, 1997). At the same time, their ability to increase their casino profits is being challenged by white gambling executives in Nevada and Atlantic City, New Jersey, who are pressuring the U.S. Congress to restrict Native American casinos (McAuliffe, 1996).

Although Native Americans have clearly made important economic gains, they have not yet been able to overcome two hundred years of European American oppression. The majority still remain members of an oppressed minority situated in the bottom tenth of the economic hierarchy and at the bottom of the class hierarchy (Rose, 1997). And the Bureau of Indian Affairs (a branch of the U.S. Department of the Interior) still maintains administrative control over most Native Americans today.

As have other individuals and groups, Native Americans have challenged the forces of oppression and racism. Various Native American groups have actively engaged in recovering and honoring their cultural traditions and in challenging a system that they view as having done little of a positive nature and much that was destructive to Native American people. Perhaps the most dramatic and widely reported examples of Native American social and political activism have been their occupation of the abandoned Alcatraz Island in 1970 and their two-month siege of Wounded Knee in 1973. Today, some Native American activism is directed toward eliminating a form of cultural abuse and institutional racism that is widespread in education and sport: the use of Native Americans and their culture as school, athletic, and sports mascots, logos, and team names (for example, Indians, Braves, Warriors, and Chiefs). The use of Native Americans as logos, mascots, and nicknames creates, supports, and maintains stereotypes of Native Americans, and many Native people view them as a mockery of their culture.

African Americans

People of African descent currently represent the largest group of color in the United States. Andrew Billingsley (1968) points out three important elements that distinguish the experience of African Americans from that of other groups in the United States: (1) unlike most of their colonial contemporaries, African Americans came to America from Africa and not from Europe; (2) African Americans were uprooted from their cultural and family bases and brought to the United States as slaves; and (3) from the beginning and continuing even today, African Americans were systematically excluded from participation in the major institutions of U.S. society. Numerous research and scholarly writings on African Americans in the United States have traced contemporary conditions of African American life to the historical experience of slavery. Clearly, slavery has had a devastating impact on African Americans. Under slavery, African Americans were stripped of their cultural traditions and forced to assimilate Euro-American culture and traditions while at the same time being denied treatment as *full* human beings. However, as we stress throughout this textbook, most people are not passive players in the theater of life. Thus, very often, through both overt and covert actions, African slaves managed to maintain some elements of their culture.

The end of slavery did not bring full freedom and equality to African Americans. White supremacy continued under Reconstruction and Jim Crow laws, which were designed specifically to deny African Americans the same constitutional rights other Americans had and to segregate them from whites in all areas of public and private life. In addition to legal discrimination, segregation, and oppression, African Americans faced the threat of and actual violence committed by groups such as the Ku Klux Klan that murdered and maimed an untold number of African American women, men, and children.

As you read in the chapter opener, however, at the height of the civil rights movement, for example, African Americans and others who believed in racial justice and equality were actively engaged in the struggle to demolish then-existing patterns of racial segregation and inequality throughout the South and the North. In 1954, the Supreme Court outlawed segregated schools, defining them as inherently unequal. This decision sparked increased social and political activism for equal rights for African Americans. The landmark 1964 Civil Rights Act banned discrimination in public facilities, the 1965 Voting Rights Act banned literacy tests as the hoop African Americans had to jump through to exercise their constitutional right to vote, and the 1968 Civil Rights Act expanded African American rights under the Constitution. In addition, as a result of increased enrollments in college and gains in employment over the last few decades, the African American middle class has expanded.

Native Americans and their supporters protest the Cleveland Indians' "Chief Wahoo" logo as racist and demeaning. Many also object to the team names and other Native American cultural symbols routinely used by sports teams across the country.

However, although African Americans have made important political and economic progress, they by and large continue to lag far behind whites in major institutional areas such as health, economics, employment, and education (see Table 10.3). Its gains notwithstanding, the civil rights movement did little to transform U.S. institutions and left institutionalized racism and discrimination basically intact. Visible examples of the economic gains by some African Americans are embodied in the persons of celebrities such as Oprah Winfrey, Michael Jordan, and Bill Cosby. However, the small handful of successful African American entertainers and other celebrities does not constitute the majority of the African American population, and a focus on their status and income camouflages the persistent pattern of racism and discrimination faced by African Americans at all income levels. Although the African American middle class has become somewhat more prosperous, members still do not enjoy full citizenship rights and the rewards of their success. African Americans, across class, continue to have experiences that include police brutality, poor service in public facilities, difficulty getting a cab, and being watched and/or followed in shopping centers and stores. Moreover, overt acts of racism and violence directed against African Americans, regardless of their social class standing, continue in the tradition of earlier attacks by hate groups such as the Ku Klux Klan. The 1991 beating of motorist Rodney King, the 1997 brutal beating of a thirteen-year-old boy in a white working-class community in Chicago, the 1998 grisly murder of James Byrd, Jr., in Jasper, Texas, and numerous other hate crimes continue to be facts of life for many African Americans. Perhaps the most heinous of such crimes since the 1955 lynching of fifteen-year-old Emmet Louis Till, James Byrd, Jr.'s, decapitated body was found after he had been abducted, chained to the bumper of a pickup truck, and dragged three miles along a backwoods road by three white men. According to police reports, two of the three men charged with his murder sported white supremacist tattoos and were believed to have ties to the Ku Klux Klan. One of the three told police that Byrd was killed at random, for no better reason than the color of his skin. Hate crimes such as these are sinister reminders of how deeply ingrained racial hatred is in the American psyche.

Asian Americans

Asian Americans are a diverse group that has long been the target of prejudice and discrimination in the United States. Over the last two decades, Asian Americans have become the fastest growing group of color in the United States, although they remain only a small percentage of the total U.S. population: They make up less than 2 percent of the population in most states (see Figure 10.4). The largest number of Asian Americans includes people of Chinese, Filipino, Japanese, Asian Indian, Korean, and Vietnamese descent. Asian Americans are highly urban (94 percent live in urban areas) but tend to live in less segregated neighborhoods than do other groups of color.

Asian Americans are often lumped together and touted as the model minority, allegedly because they have succeeded despite the limitations of racism and discrimination: they work in a wide range of occupations, many are active in politics, and some hold high elected offices. Sociologists have traced this success to at least four major features: (1) close family ties, (2) a supportive community, (3) high educational aspirations an achievement, and (4) assimilation into the U.S. mainstream. Their high average educational attainment, occupational status, and household income seem to negate the idea that they are a disadvantaged group in the United States (Lee, 1998). The "model minority" ideology has been used to blame other groups for their alleged failure to pull themselves up by the bootstraps. It also ignores the ethnic and class diversity among Asian Americans, which contradicts the model minority stereotype. For example, although some Asian Americans have made it and earn six-digit incomes, others live below the federal government's poverty index and still others are welfare dependent. Southeast Asians living in the United States, for example, have the highest rate of welfare dependency of any racial or ethnic group. And Asian Americans generally continue to experience racial prejudice in various forms and of various levels of intensity.

Ethnic Origins of Asian Americans

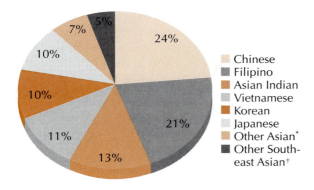

- Chinese — 24%
- Filipino — 21%
- Asian Indian — 13%
- Vietnamese — 11%
- Korean — 10%
- Japanese — 10%
- Other Asian* — 7%
- Other Southeast Asian† — 5%

Asian Americans by Region

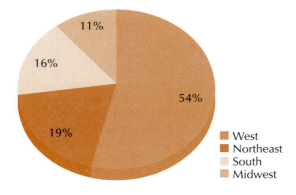

- West — 54%
- Northeast — 19%
- South — 16%
- Midwest — 11%

*all other Asian American ethnic groups
†Cambodian, Hmong, and Laotian

FIGURE 10.4 ⟳ **Asian Americans in the United States, by Selected Ancestry Group and Region, 1997** *Source:* U.S. Bureau of the Census. 1998. *Statistical Abstract of the United States, 1998.* Washington, DC: U.S. Department of Commerce, Table 30. Lee, S.M. 1998. "Asian Americans: Diverse and Growing." *Population Bulletin* 53, no. 2: Figure 1, p. 6.

Chinese Americans Chinese Americans were the first Asian group to establish themselves in the United States in large numbers; almost one quarter of a million Chinese immigrated to this country between 1850 and 1880. A sociologist using a conflict perspective might point out that the Chinese were encouraged to come to the United States as a new source of cheap labor. As unskilled laborers they were used, like other racial/ethnic groups before them, to perform the dirtiest, lowliest work for very little pay vis-à-vis the profits their labor generated. As the number of jobs diminished, many white workers came to resent the presence of the Chinese, viewing them as undercutting them in the labor market. Their use as a cheap source of labor essentially ended when white Americans, particularly the middle class, organized and put an end to Chinese immigration, both legally and by discouraging new immigrants with physical and racist attacks such as lynchings. For example, in Los Angeles in 1871, twenty-two Chinese were lynched, and in 1885 in Wyoming, twenty-nine Chinese were massacred. Furthermore, the Chinese Exclusion Act of 1882 legally halted further Chinese immigration and prevented Chinese American residents from becoming U.S. citizens. Because of prejudice and discrimination, Chinese Americans were relegated to ethnic enclaves where they kept pretty much to themselves. Due to their high visibility as well as their refusal to give up their cultural ties to their ancestors and homeland, they have never become completely assimilated into the U.S. mainstream.

Since World War II, there has been a noticeable rise in Chinese American communities and in their general standard of living. Today, the Chinese American community is witnessing an influx of immigrants from Hong Kong and Taiwan and, as Figure 10.4 shows, Chinese Americans represent the largest Asian American group in the United States, totaling a little over 1.5 million people. Some Chinese Americans have entered the U.S. mainstream through high-paying, prestigious jobs, and notably, in 1996, Chinese American Gary Locke became the first Asian American to be elected governor of a state on the mainland (Washington) and Fred Lau became the first Chinese American to head a police force in a major U.S. city (San Francisco). These milestones notwithstanding, many Chinese immigrants live and work under abhorrent conditions, including their exploitation in illegal sweatshops at less than minimum wages.

Japanese Americans After the Immigration Act of 1882 limited Chinese immigration into the United States, the Japanese were brought in as the next significant source of cheap labor. As they entered the United States, they first settled in Hawaii. However, when Hawaii was annexed by the United States, the Japanese began to spread out on farms in California and all along the West Coast. When they arrived, they found anti-Asian attitudes already established and easily transferred to them. Thus, they quickly became the main targets of racism and discrimination. While Japanese immigration was similar to Chinese immigration in many ways, the Japanese typically came from a more middle-class background than had the Chinese. The Japanese were primarily rural peasants but pretty middle class and entrepreneurial in attitude. Even as they were used as cheap labor, many Japanese Americans became successful enough in U.S. agriculture and in small businesses to draw attention to themselves. Their industriousness and success, even though it mirrored the American dream, incited racist attacks upon them and a series of laws were enacted on the West Coast designed to prevent them from becoming too successful. For example, in 1913, the Alien Land Law was enacted which prohibited aliens (effectively, the Japanese) from owning land.

Perhaps the most organized, institutionalized, and vicious act of racism perpetrated against Japanese Americans came in 1942. After Japan's attack on Pearl Harbor, over 100,000 Japanese, the greatest majority U.S. citizens, were forced from their homes and businesses and imprisoned in so-called "relocation centers," which some described as nothing short of "concentration camps." This act was carried out even though federal agents had not found any instances of sabotage or espionage on the part of Japanese Americans. Moreover, although we were also at war with Germany, in glaring contrast to the way in which the federal government treated Japanese Americans, few, if any, German Americans were sent to "relocation" or "evacuation camps," even though there were some instances of subversion by German Americans (Hosokawa, 1969). In 1983, a federal commission on Wartime Relocation and Internment of Civilians found that the detention of Japanese Americans had been motivated by racial prejudice, war hysteria, and a failure on the part of the political leadership of the time. It therefore recommended reparations to all surviving Japanese Americans who had been held in relocation camps during the war. This recommendation was followed in 1988 by legislation entitled the Civil Liberties Act, in which the federal government apologized for the forced internment of Japanese Americans and agreed to establish a $1.25 billion fund to pay $20,000 in compensation to each survivor (Lee, 1998; Molotsky, 1988; Takezawa, 1995).

Today, Japanese Americans as a group lead successful lives, exceeding many whites in terms of major stratification indicators such as family income and occupational and educational attainment. However, the rate of poverty among Japanese Americans also exceeds that of whites. Although many have been successful, Japanese Americans as a group still face prejudice and discrimination, albeit in much more covert and subtle forms than in the past.

Korean Americans   Although roughly equal to the Japanese American population, Korean Americans have been largely ignored in sociological discussions of Asian Americans. There have been three major waves of Korean immigration into the United States, with the most recent (since 1964) bringing the largest number of Koreans to this country. Most of these immigrants came with high levels of education and professional skills and the money or backing to open businesses soon after their arrival. However, because of racism and discrimination, many Koreans are underemployed.

Many Korean Americans have opened small retail businesses, preferring inner-city, poor, and working-class African American communities as places of opportunity. An increasing hostility has developed between African Americans and Korean Americans as a result of a number of social and economic factors. African Americans have accused Korean shop owners of being arrogant and racist toward their African American clientele, of selling inferior products at high prices, of refusing to hire people from the communities in which they make their money, and of seldom interacting with African Americans outside the owner/customer relationship. On the other hand, many Korean Americans view African Americans in stereotypic terms, assuming that all are thieves and not to be trusted in their shops. These clashing viewpoints were apparent in the 1992

South-Central Los Angeles uprisings, in which Korean American–owned shops in the city's poorest areas were targeted for destruction, reflecting the anger and hostility on both sides. As the relationship between these two groups illustrates, the cost not only of the larger issue of racism but also of internalized racism between and among various oppressed groups is often deadly. On the other hand, although far less publicized in the media, many African Americans and Korean Americans are working collaboratively to improve relations between the two groups. These attempts have included actions such as joint church services, joint musical performances and poetry readings, donations by Korean merchants to African American community and youth programs, African American teachers volunteering in classes for Korean immigrants studying for citizenship examinations, and Korean translations of African American history materials (Kim, 1993).

Latinas/os

According to current U.S. definitions of race, Latinas/os are neither a "race" nor an "ethnic group." Rather, they are a disparate collection of nationalities variously descended from Europeans, Africans, and Native Americans. Nonetheless, they have suffered racism and discrimination characteristic of many other groups defined and treated in race terms. As with other groups that we have discussed, Latinas/os represent an extremely diverse collection of people, including Americans whose ancestors come from Mexico, Puerto Rico, Cuba, and Central and South America. Concentrated in four states, California, Florida, New York, and Texas, Mexican Americans represent the largest Latina/o group (see Figure 10.5). The fastest growing segment of the Latina/o community is new immigrants from Central and South America and the Caribbean. The increasing number of Latinas/os in the U.S. population has not only changed the U.S. cultural milieu but also given rise to contentious debates on issues such as bilingualism and immigration. A number of Latinas/os have entered the United States by means other than those sanctioned by the Department of Immigration and Naturalization and are referred to pejoratively as "illegal aliens." Many in the United States perceive these immigrants as taking jobs away from citizens and as an economic burden to taxpayers. The role they play in society is the issue at the center of one of the most heated political debates in the United States today, especially in states where there is a large number of Latina/o immigrants. The Latina/o population is expected to be the largest group of color in the United States as early as the year 2010. Compared to non-Hispanic whites and Asian Americans, Latinas/os as a group are worse off on all indicators of well-being and fall far behind whites in terms of median family income and educational and occupational attainment. However, Latinas/os are a diverse group, and country

FIGURE 10.5 ○ **Latina/o Population in the United States, by Selected Ethnic Group and Region, 1997**
Source: U.S. Bureau of the Census. 1998. *Statistical Abstract of the United States, 1998.* Washington, DC: U.S. Department of Commerce, Table 30.

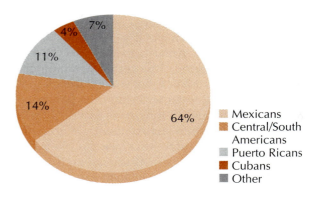

Distribution of Latina/o Population

- Mexicans
- Central/South Americans
- Puerto Ricans
- Cubans
- Other

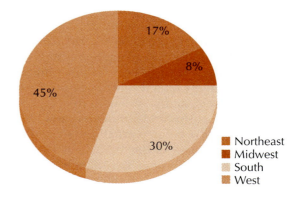

Latinas/os by Region

- Northeast
- Midwest
- South
- West

of origin is significant here. For example, Cuban Americans score much higher than other Latinas/os on indicators of well-being, and Puerto Ricans score the lowest.

Mexican Americans Living primarily in the Southwest and along the West Coast, not all Mexican Americans are descended from immigrants nor are they immigrants themselves. Many are descendants of Mexicans living in the territories annexed by the U.S. government after the Mexican-American war of 1848. Indicative of the U.S. obsession with skin color as a marker of race, race privilege, and disadvantage, lighter-skinned Mexican Americans who were of pure Spanish ancestry and who adopted a Euro-American world view were assimilated into the U.S. mainstream, while those of a darker skin color who maintained their heritage, particularly the Indian part of that heritage, were defined as inferior and have experienced extreme levels of racism and discrimination. Historically, Mexican Americans have been used as cheap labor in the U.S. labor market. This has been particularly evident in their exploitation by farm owners, who often hire their workers from the large group of undocumented Mexicans living in the United States. As a group, Mexican Americans are very family oriented and religious (the majority are Catholics), two characteristics that some scholars suggest have helped them withstand the patterned racism and inequality they have faced in their predominantly white environments. A growing Mexican American activism since the 1960s has focused on challenging institutional racism and pursuing the interests of Mexican Americans as a collective.

Puerto Rican Americans Puerto Ricans living in Puerto Rico have been U.S. citizens since 1917. The largest populations of Puerto Ricans in the United States can be found in New York City and in Chicago. Puerto Ricans, like other groups of color, particularly African and Native Americans, face extremely high levels of poverty, low educational levels, and poor health in comparison to their Euro-American counterparts. As with other groups of color, particularly since the civil rights movement of the 1950s and 1960s, Puerto Ricans have become increasingly active on behalf of Puerto Rican rights in the United

States and the political destiny of the island of Puerto Rico itself. Today, Puerto Rico is a commonwealth, but the debate over whether it should remain independent or become the fifty-first state in the United States continues, even though as recently as 1998, the people of Puerto Rico rejected statehood.

Cuban Americans While Cuban Americans had a presence in the United States as early as 1831, the largest wave of Cuban immigration began after the 1959 Cuban revolution, when Fidel Castro assumed power. Almost a quarter of a million Cubans migrated to the United States during this wave of migration, many of whom were professionals having fairly high levels of education. However, immigrants coming in the most recent wave from Cuba are not nearly as educated or skilled. Miami is the home of the largest number of Cubans outside of Cuba. In fact, 53 percent of all Cuban Americans live in Miami, and they represent the majority of residents in that city. The experiences of Cubans in the United States have been mixed. The earlier wave of educated professionals was able to become more upwardly mobile than later Cuban immigrants. In addition, the historic anticommunist sentiment in this country was often manifested in racist and discriminatory practices perpetrated against Cuban immigrants. Like other Latinas/os, Cuban Americans are underrepresented in positions of power and authority in U.S. society.

European Americans

The overwhelming majority of the U.S. population consists of descendants from Europe. As Figure 10.6 shows, dominant among this group are the descendants of Northern and Western Europeans. The majority of those in the U.S. elite are WASPs (White Anglo Saxon Protestants). WASPs are primarily English, although a few are Scottish and Welsh. Although WASPs are now outnumbered by Germans and the Irish, U.S. society is still dominated by the English language, English law, and the Protestant religion. Moreover, WASPs hold and/or control the most important positions in the major social, economic and political institutions in U.S. society, although an increasing number of Irish and Germans are gaining ground. American cul-

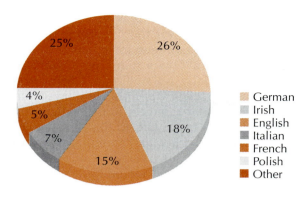

FIGURE 10.6 ○ Americans of European Descent, by Selected Ancestry Group, 1990 *Source:* U.S. Bureau of the Census. 1998. *Statistical Abstract of the United States, 1998.* Washington, DC: U.S. Department of Commerce, Table 58.

Pie chart legend:
German 26%
Irish 18%
English 15%
Italian 7%
French 5%
Polish 4%
Other 25%

ture is essentially WASP culture, and assimilation has been primarily aimed at getting other groups to adopt WASP culture. However, in recent years, the multicultural movement has challenged this sort of assimilation and emphasized the importance of the cultures of all people. This movement has generated some new hostilities and antagonisms in that some WASPs perceive multiculturalism to be a threat to their culture and feel that various groups of color are receiving special treatment at their expense (Baltzell, 1994; Brookhiser, 1991).

Groups that are generally referred to as white ethnics in the sociological literature are descendants of Eastern and Southern Europeans. These groups include Italians, Poles, Russians, Hungarians, Bohemians, Slovaks, Jews, and Czechs. Some members of each of these groups live in ethnic enclaves in most major U.S. cities and continue to identify primarily in terms of their ethnicity. Their communities have been named by outsiders and reflect their countries of origin: Little Italy or Russian Town, for example. Others have assimilated into the U.S. mainstream and their ethnicity is no longer a major part of their identity. In addition, as we indicated earlier, few whites (including white ethnics) view themselves as a racial category. And, although sociologists and other social scientists make the distinction between white ethnics and WASPS,

most groups, particularly groups of color, do not see these distinctions in a society in which skin color, and not ethnicity, is the major factor that privileges or disadvantages people. Although white ethnics are underrepresented in the ruling elite of this country, they are not nearly as underrepresented as the four major groups of color we discussed earlier.

White ethnics and various groups of color have a history of antagonism and hostility between them. One way that sociologists have looked at these antagonisms is through the lens of economic conflict and competition. For example, much of the hostility between these various groups is a consequence of the competition for jobs, housing, education, and other social and political opportunities that the society has to offer. On the one hand, the subordinate status of some white ethnics vis-à-vis WASPs raises some of the same basic issues of stratification and inequality as raised by groups of color in the stratification hierarchy. On the other hand, because of skin color privilege, their plight is fundamentally different from that of various groups of color. For example, historically, as with every major group that migrated into the United States, various white ethnic groups were defined and treated in race terms and exploited as cheap labor. Each group experienced antiforeign prejudice and restrictive practices. Like groups of color, they were denied access to various jobs, schools, fraternities, restaurants, and private clubs. It was not unusual to see signs that read, "Irish Need Not Apply" and "No Jews Allowed." Restrictive legislation in the early twentieth century, such as the law requiring that immigrants had to demonstrate an ability to read, was designed primarily to limit the migration of white ethnics (southern and eastern Europeans) (Rose, 1997). However, those who were most like the dominant group, both in terms of physical appearance (including skin color) and culture, and who were willing could and did more easily assimilate into the WASP mainstream and became less and less defined and treated as a minority group. Today, it is difficult, if not impossible, to tell them from mainstream whites.

As has been pointed out by other scholars, white ethnics are often stereotyped as conservative, racist, uneducated, and lower or working class. However, this is not an accurate picture of white ethnics. Rather, there is a higher number of white ethnics in the middle class than of any other group. In addition, white ethnics have a high rate of college attendance, and, according to survey data, they are more liberal on social issues such as welfare and less racially prejudiced than other Euro-American groups (Farley, 1995; Feagin & Feagin, 1996).

Jewish Americans   Representing about 2 percent of the U.S. population, Jews have been scapegoats for the hatreds and prejudices of dominant groups around the world for thousands of years. In the United States, Jews have been variously regarded as a religious group, a racial group, and an ethnic group. They have been socially defined on the basis of alleged physical or cultural characteristics and treated as an oppressed group. As late as the 1940s, they were considered by many whites as a biologically inferior race. Today, they are most often treated as an ethnic group distinguishable primarily on the basis of cultural characteristics, particularly the Jewish religion.

Despite a history of intense prejudice and discrimination, a substantial number of Jews have been able to prosper, and many have surpassed other racial/ethnic groups as well as WASPs in upward mobility. This is not to say that they have achieved parity with the ruling elites. Jews are still few in number in top management positions, and anti-Semitism continues to exist, although it is abating, in the corporate world. And, contrary to the stereotype of the rich Jew, a significant number of Jews are poor. To some extent, the success of some Jews has increased the level of animosity and hostility toward them.

On the one hand, like African Americans, Jews continue to be the targets of the hate speech and actions of groups such as the Ku Klux Klan, Neo-Nazis, and Skinheads. It is notable that the rise of German Nazism evoked some sympathy among Euro Americans and several new hate groups sprang up to defame Jews. On the other hand, reactions to the horrors of the Nazi regime served to reduce anti-Jewish sentiments greatly, and there continues to be some decline in anti-Semitism in this country today.

As with other groups we have discussed, Jews were faced with the choice of assimilating or maintaining their rich cultural heritage. Some

Jews have assimilated, as is evident in the rising concern of rabbis over the increasing number of Jews marrying non-Jews (over half of all Jewish marriages involve a non-Jew). Others are somewhat socially isolated, partly because of discrimination but also because they have steadfastly maintained their cultural practices and traditions. Jews in the United States are prominent in the global Jewish community because they represent the largest concentration of Jews anywhere in the world, including Israel (Rose, 1997).

The New Immigrants

As you have learned, historically, the majority of immigrants to the United States came from Europe. Only a small trickle came from Asia, Africa, and Central and South America. Today, however, this trend has been turned on its head. Since 1965 and a revised immigration act that removed all racial/ethnic quotas for immigrants to this country, the majority of immigrants have been people of color. As Figure 10.7 shows, in 1996, the majority of immigrants were from Asian, Latin American, and Caribbean countries. Less than twenty percent of the new immigrants were from Europe, whereas 51 percent came

FIGURE 10.7 ◑ **The New Immigrants by Birth, 1996**
Source: U.S. Bureau of the Census. 1998. *Statistical Abstract of the United States, 1998*. Washington, DC: U.S. Department of Commerce, Table 8.

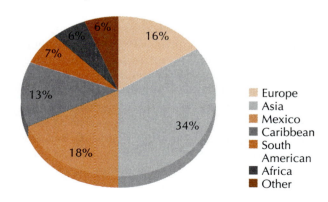

from Mexico, China, the Philippines, Vietnam, and the Caribbean. By comparison, 97 percent of the immigrants that came one hundred years earlier were from Europe or Canada (U.S. Bureau of the Census, 1998).

Although the U.S. government has welcomed many new immigrants, that welcome has been highly selective. For example, in the 1980s, immigrants from communist nations were welcomed but those who were simply attempting to escape harsh political regimes and grinding poverty, such as Haitians, got less of a welcome. In fact, the Immigration and Naturalization Service held thousands of Haitians in detention while their petitions for asylum were reviewed suspiciously.

There is always a danger in lumping members of a group together to make general statements about them. Such lumping together, for example, hides the diversity within groups. For example, there are considerable differences between Colombian dentists and Mexican cotton pickers that the label "Latino" does not capture, nor does the label "Asian" capture the differences between Korean chemical engineers and Pakistani nurses' aides. New immigrants have come to the United States for the same reasons past immigrants have come. Although some have come as political refugees, most are responding to the population and economic pressures of their countries of origin, and most seek economic betterment and improved social conditions. The racial and ethnic background of the new immigrants, the continued immigration at the current level and from the current countries, as well as natural increases means that in the future, U.S. society will be populated by people very different from those who populated it fifty to one hundred years ago. It is estimated, for example, that Latinas/os alone will account for 28 percent of the total population growth by the year 2010. Moreover, in major cities across the country, large numbers of new immigrants already represent significant percentages of the total population. For example, in New York, approximately one-third of the total population is foreign born; in Los Angeles, 44 percent of adults are foreign born; and in Miami, 70 percent are foreign born.

Today's immigrants are changing U.S. society, bringing with them new colors and languages, a new vibrancy and vigor. They have begun to have a significant impact on the ethnic flavor of U.S. society, and, at the same time, they have introduced new problems and questions of ethnic relations (Marger, 1994). Currently, for example, there is a growing debate over whether the United States should restrict immigration and admit only those who will contribute to the economy and society. For many people of color, this is code language used to mean "limit immigration to those who are educated, job skilled, English speaking, and white. Some of the new immigrants agree that new immigration should be selective, as do others in the general population, while still others see this talk of restrictionism as, at base, racism. Whatever the future holds for U.S. society, it seems that, unlike their earlier counterparts, today's immigrants will neither melt into the U.S. mainstream nor remain aloof and distinct from one another.

Race and Ethnicity in the Twenty-First Century

Although considerable progress has been made in U.S. race relations since the 1960s civil rights movement, a number of issues and events have emerged and occurred over the last decades of the twentieth century that inform us that issues of race and racism are neither things of the past nor simply a matter of a few isolated cases of individual racists' actions. For example:

1. The restructuring of the economy has dislocated workers across race and class.
2. As the United States has become more multicultural and multiracial, issues of race, racial identity, and racial politics have become increasingly important.
3. White pride and a white racial consciousness has emerged, in part in response to a perception of affirmative action policies in education and the workplace as unfair or reverse discrimination.
4. Political campaigns and politicians increasingly use race-baiting strategies to get elected to office.

5. Racial tensions have escalated around the country and hate crimes, particularly those directed at people of color and Jews, have increased.

6. Despite evidence of continued racial inequality and institutional racism, major retreats have been made in policies related to affirmative action, school desegregation, voting rights, and, in general, social and legal supports for racial equality have been eroded.

7. Most Americans, both within and outside the political arena, feel that race is no longer a significant factor in determining life chances. The fact that this mistaken view exists is a primary issue confronting American society as we move into the twenty-first century.

And finally, in the next century, we are also likely to be confronted with increased activism around the issue of *reparations*—compensation and recognition of past injustices—for African Americans for more than 250 years of slavery and another 100 years of segregation. We close this chapter with a brief look at a critical issue surrounding the compensation of disadvantaged groups: affirmative action.

Affirmative Action or Reverse Discrimination?

Affirmative action refers to any special effort by an employer or a college admissions office to hire or admit more females or people historically defined as members of minority groups and/or to upgrade their positions. Affirmative action was conceived as a remedy to institutional racism and discrimination: it was designed to enhance justice and opportunity for African Americans, members of other ethnic and racial groups, and women. Because the U.S. constitutional right of various racial and ethnic groups to equal opportunities in work and education had been so violated for so long, legislation was enacted beginning in the early 1960s that was meant to reverse the cumulative disadvantage caused by prolonged discrimination. Heretofore, white men have been the primary beneficiaries of racial ethnic and gender biases.

Affirmative action remains a prominent issue that divides people along racial lines. Opponents of affirmative action or those who severely criticize current methods of affirmative action argue that it has become a kind of reverse discrimination, giving those previously discriminated against an unfair advantage. The concept of reverse discrimination suggests that affirmative action has created a new set of victims, namely white males. Proponents of affirmative action argue that given that racism and discrimination are systemic problems, their solutions require institutional remedies such as those offered by affirmative action legislation. Even if direct forms of discrimination no longer exist, indirect and institutional forms continue to perpetuate disadvantages for people of color and women in the labor market and in higher education. Moreover, there is little evidence, if any, that white men have suffered displacement by unqualified people of color and women (Leonard, 1991). Further, researchers on affirmative action have found that both white and African American workers, women and men, gain both materially and politically from affirmative action. They make more money, and whites who work with African American workers have more antiracist attitudes. Whites who work in the most segregated occupations and workplaces have the most racist outlook and voice the greatest opposition to affirmative action (Herring & Collins, 1995).

Controversies concerning the persistence of discrimination and the proper remedies to its cumulative effects and who should and should not benefit from policies of affirmative action and other types of remedies have grown in significance over the years. At present, affirmative action remains in place in many of U.S. institutions and organizations. However, on some local levels, such as the California higher education system, affirmative action based on race has been eliminated by popular referendum (Zack, 1998). It is too soon to tell what the long-term effects of such changes will be for the overall goals of racially egalitarian public policy. In addition, although President Clinton launched his 1997 "Initiative on Race" amid much hoopla, with the intent of closing the racial divide in the twenty-first century, its outcomes and its impact on U.S. race relations are not yet known.

Key Points to Remember

1. Race and ethnicity are among the most divisive issues facing Americans today. The sociological imagination allows us to view and analyze issues of racial/ethnic diversity within the context of social and historical factors rather than in terms of innate characteristics of individuals.

2. Whenever social inequality occurs because of race or ethnicity, we have a phenomenon known as racism. Race as a biological concept has been shown to have no validity. Most sociologists view race as a social construction—people are assigned to a racial category not because of actual difference but by social definition by the powerful and agents acting on their behalf. Although we recognize people of color as raced, seldom do U.S. whites think of themselves and their experiences as racialized.

3. Ethnicity, like race, is a social construction, and, like race, ethnicity is an important basis for ranking people in a culture's stratification system. Race, ethnicity, and minority/majority group are interrelated concepts, and each represents social and political constructs created as a means of categorizing and differentiating groups of people as inferior and superior.

4. Prejudice refers to an attitude, whereas discrimination refers to behavior. Racism is one of the most powerful forms of prejudice. It is manifested both in individual attitudes and actions and in institutional practices. Sociologists have identified modern, more subtle forms of racism, which they refer to as symbolic and aversive racism. Sociologist Robert Merton developed a classification of prejudice and discrimination that shows that attitudes and behavior toward members of various racial and ethnic groups may vary within different social contexts.

5. Sociologists do not agree about the relative significance of race and social class in determining the social and economic experiences of African Americans. In general, explanations of race and ethnic inequality include social psychological theories that focus on attitudes and personality types, social learning theories, and social structural theories such as functionalism, conflict theory, and feminist theories.

6. Historical patterns of race and ethnic relations include: assimilation, pluralism, segregation, colonization, population transfer, expulsion, and genocide.

7. Although there are many well-established racial and ethnic minorities in the United States, there are four that have been historically defined and treated in racial/ethnic terms: Native Americans, African Americans, Latinas/os, and Asian Americans. However, the overwhelming majority of the U.S. population consists of descendants of Europe. WASPs, who predominated among the earliest immigrants to the United States, continue to hold high social positions today. Groups that are generally referred to as white ethnics in the sociological literature are descendants of Eastern and Southern Europeans, whose early history in the United States includes racism and discrimination similar to that faced by groups of color today. White ethnics include Jews, a group whose members have been scapegoats for the hatreds and prejudice of dominant groups around the world for thousands of years.

8. Fewer than 20 percent of today's immigrants are from Europe. The majority of new immigrants are people of color from Mexico, Asia, Africa, and the Caribbean.

9. Some of the most vital issues that Americans will confront in the next century are bilingualism, immigration policies, multiculturalism versus U.S. pluralism, reparations, and affirmative action.

Key Terms

racism	ethnic group	prejudice
one-drop rule	minority group	stereotype
cultural racism	majority group	individual racism

institutional racism
symbolic racism
aversive racism
discrimination
scapegoat
assimilation

cultural assimilation
forced assimilation
pluralism
cultural pluralism
segregation

colonization
manifest destiny
apartheid
genocide
affirmative action

Key People

Viola Fauver Gregg Liuzzo
Ronald Takaki

Robert Merton
Theodor Adorno

William Julius Wilson
Charles V. Willie

Questions for Review and Discussion

1. Why is there no one-drop rule for whites in U.S. society, and what does this say about race as a meaningful biological concept? What does it say about power in U.S. society? Can we get beyond race in U.S. society? If we did, what would that mean for social, political, and economic relations in society?
2. How has recent immigration changed U.S. culture? Write a concept paper debating the validity of U.S. racial categories. Discuss the reasons for and against using such labels.
3. Is the belief in "white power" different from the belief in "black" "red" or "Latina/o power"?

Can people living in the United States believe in white power and take pride in their whiteness without being racists? without defining themselves as superior and members of other races as inferior?

4. Research one of the social change movements centering around issues of racial and ethnic social justice and civil rights, such as the American Indian Movement (AIM), the Black Power movement, and La Raza Unida, and answer the following questions: What has the movement accomplished for members of the group? Has it been effective in promoting social change?

For Further Reading

Delgado, Richard, and Jean Stefancic. (Eds.). 1997. *Critical White Studies: Looking behind the Mirror.* Philadelphia: Temple University Press. An excellent anthology of work by a wide variety of writers of vastly different persuasions whose analyses of race in the United States focus on an examination of whiteness.

Fanon, Franz. 1967. *Black Skin White Masks.* New York: Grove Press. A classic, this book examines the black psyche in a white world; it centers on racism and colonialism and its impact on the identity of African Americans.

Fine, Michelle, Weis, Lois, Powell, Linda C., and L. Mun Wong. (Eds.). 1997. *Off White: Readings on Race, Power, and Society.* New York: Routledge. An excellent reader that attempts to address the absence of attention, debate, and scholarship on questions of whiteness in scholarly discussions of race; it examines whiteness as race, and as privilege, as social construction.

Parillo, Vincent. 1990. *Strangers to These Shores.* (3rd ed.). New York: Macmillan. A comprehensive text that provides a sociological framework for the study of a wide variety of racial/ethnic groups that are part of the racial/ethnic landscape of U.S. society.

Sociology through Literature

Momaday, N. Scott. 1969. *House Made of Dawn.* New York: Signet. An excellent novel that deals with the life of quiet desperation led by many Native Americans.

Kingston, Maxine Hong. 1976. *The Women Warrior: Memoirs of a Girlhood among Ghosts.* New York: Knopf. A good feminist analysis of the Chinese American experience.

Walker, Alice. 1982. *The Color Purple.* New York: Pocket. Walker examines the life of poor southern African Americans prior to World War II. An excellent portrayal of the intersections of race, class, gender, and sexual orientation as systems of oppression, disadvantage, and advantage.

Internet Resources

http//www.efn.org/~dennis_w/race.html An Antiracism Resources Homepage that links to a variety of Web sites that provide antiracism resources as well as resources directed to specific groups.

ftp//heather.cs.ucdavis.edu/pub/README.html This site contains information and issues of concern to people of color, including issues such as the affirmative action debate.

http://www.georgetown.edu/crossroads/asw/race.html A comprehensive listing site that deals with general issues pertaining to race and ethnic relations as well as to a variety of racial and ethnic groups.

Inequalities of Gender and Age

AGENT OF CHANGE: KAREN NUSSBAUM

Many of the agents of social change featured throughout this textbook experienced a defining moment that ignited their social activism. Karen Nussbaum's defining moment came in 1973 while she was working as a secretary at Harvard University. One day, she was alone in the office when a male student entered, looked her right in the eye, and asked, "Isn't anybody here?" (Witt, 1994). Nussbaum quickly realized that besides low pay (she was making two dollars and fifty cents an hour), a major problem facing women clerical workers like herself was a general lack of respect. Armed with this insight, she organized meetings where women workers could compare notes. The women soon realized that they shared common problems as workers and as women that were not likely to be solved on an individual level.

These meetings evolved into an organization known as 9 to 5, the National Association of Working Women. Nussbaum quit her job to put out a newsletter and to run the fledgling organization full time. In 1976, the organization received a charter from the Service Employees International Union, becoming a union, District 9 to 5. Nussbaum was elected its first president and later served as its executive director. Today, the union bargains collectively for over 9,000 workers nationwide. Its sister organization, the 15,000 member national association, has twenty-five chapters involved in public policy research, training, and education.

For years, Nussbaum worked to organize "pink-collar" workers to improve their wages and working conditions. Some of the experiences of the women she helped to organize were depicted in the 1980 film *9 to 5,* starring Jane Fonda, Dolly Parton, and Lily Tomlin. In 1993, President Bill Clinton appointed her to the position of Director of the Women's Bureau in the Department of Labor, where she led efforts to make working women aware of their rights regarding sexual harassment, pregnancy discrimination, and the Family and Medical Leave Act. During her tenure at the Women's Bureau, her major focus was on helping women to balance work and family responsibilities. However, in that position, Nussbaum could not do the organizing that she believed essential to making substantial gains in the workplace. So after two years, she left her government post to become head of the AFL-CIO's Working Women's Department. (AFL-CIO stands for American Federation of Labor-Congress of Industrial Organizations. It is the umbrella organization representing union members across the country.) Her belief that unions can help working women is borne out by a report by the U.S. Bureau of Labor Statistics that shows that in 1996, women who were union members earned $549 per week; nonunion women earned only $398.

However, union men still made more than union women, $653. Nonunion male workers made $520 per week (Wickham, 1997). A recent AFL-CIO survey of 50,000 women nationwide showed that despite economic growth during the late 1990s, women still earn less than men and they continue to worry about job security and finding affordable child care. These concerns are not unique to women in the United States, but rather, as we will see, they are experienced by women around the world.

In the previous two chapters, we examined social inequalities based on economic as well as racial–ethnic stratification. In this chapter, our focus will be on the social constructions of both gender and age and their consequences for daily life. We will see that both gender and age are socially significant because they define what is appropriate for or expected of individuals because they are female or male, young or old.

Source: Information from various sources, including the following: (1) D.E. Lewis. 1996. "Founder of '9 to 5' Group to Launch Working Women's Unit at AFL-CIO," *Boston Globe* (June 4). (2) L. Witt. 1994. "Woman Warrior," *Mother Jones* (September–October).

Understanding Gender Stratification

Early in her working life, Karen Nussbaum learned about **gender stratification,** the unequal distribution of a society's wealth, power, and privilege between females and males. Not only was she paid less than similarly educated males but also society valued her work less than that of her male counterparts. Yet gender stratification differs from the other forms of stratification discussed in Chapters 9 and 10 in a significant way. In cases of class, race, and ethnic stratification, the dominant and subordinate groups rarely have intimate contact with each other. In contrast, from infancy on, both females and males are involved in many intimate and loving relationships with both dominant and subordinate group members—our mothers and fathers, grandmothers and grandfathers, sisters and brothers, aunts and uncles, and female and male cousins and friends. The majority of the population grows up and marries members of the other sex and shares the advantages and disadvantages of a class status with them. But, as you can see in the Sociological Reflections box, gender inequities exist even in marriage. Why do such gender inequities exist?

Beginning with Karl Marx, a number of theorists have sought answers to this question in the concrete, historically specific aspects of gender stratification systems. Their analyses focused on the family, where women's childbearing and lactating functions initially affected the division of labor between the sexes, leaving women respon-

Sociological Reflections

How Much Is a Corporate Wife Worth?

The recent divorce case of Lorna and Gary Wendt clearly illustrates that, even in marriage, some partners are more equal than others. Gary Wendt, the chief executive of GE Capital, offered his wife of thirty-one years a $10 million divorce settlement; instead, she took him to court, claiming that his offer was a small percentage of her contribution to their relationship and a small percentage of the value of their estate. The Wendts were high school sweethearts who married after college but before either had visions of being wealthy. He got his MBA while she worked as a public school teacher. Thereafter, she ran the house, raised their two daughters, and supported his career, mostly by entertaining his business associates. During that time, he worked in real estate in Texas, Georgia, and Florida before moving to Connecticut and GE Capital, where, after eleven years, he became chief executive.

Most divorce cases are settled out of court and out of the public eye, but this case drew considerable media attention because it involved the rich and raised new questions at a time when family values are being widely discussed. In the past, U.S. courts have shied away from awarding the wife half when the value of an estate is more than $10 or $15 million, preferring instead to award her what she needs to live in the style to which the couple had become accustomed.

Reactions to this case have varied with some people siding with Gary Wendt who claimed that his wife was not responsible for his success and that he had created and preserved their assets. Others sided with Lorna Wendt, who said the case was not about money but about the fact that she entered into the marriage as a partner and contributed as a partner. In the end, Lorna Wendt was awarded $20 million.

Survey your family and friends to see whether they agree with the judge's decision. Ask them to explain their reasoning. Which side did your respondents support? What do their answers suggest about how these two marital roles are valued in our society? How do the specifics of this divorce case relate to the larger issue of gender stratification?

Source: Information from Judith H. Dobrzynski. 1997. "Divorce Executive Style, Revisited." *New York Times,* January 24, C1.

---

sible for domestic and child-rearing tasks, regardless of what other work they did. According to these theorists, the roots of gender inequality can be found in a sexual division of labor in the family by which males initially provided much or all of the family subsistence. In essence, they argued that the system of gender inequality is marked by an almost total separation of domestic and child-rearing tasks from paid work outside the home (productive labor). With the former assigned to women, they are left vulnerable to total dependence on their wage-earning husbands. This historical division of labor, fueled by an ideology that supports and sustains a system of patriarchy or male dominance, gave rise to economic and social policies that proved immensely profitable for capitalists (employers). Consequently, when women moved into the paid labor force, they found themselves working in jobs that were segregated by sex and earning less than male workers. Therefore, as Karen Nussbaum discovered, even when women work in the paid labor force, they remain exploited and oppressed, both by low wages and limited opportunities and by continued responsibility for domestic and child-rearing labor.

According to Marxist-feminist theories, capitalists control the society's political and cultural as well as economic institutions; thus, they possess the power to realize their goals very effectively. Moreover, as the argument goes, capitalists are generally supported by working class men, who also profit from a system of gender inequality even though they also suffer exploitation under capitalism. Two powerful incentives lead many male workers to support existing gender inequities. The first is that women provide the domestic labor that maintains male workers, and the second is male's competitive advantages over women in the wage labor market. In addition, as the influence of capitalism spreads worldwide, the oppression of women deepens and takes on new dimensions in heretofore noncapitalist societies. Borrowing from other feminist theories, Marxist-feminists argue that patriarchy (male domination) constitutes an analytically and historically distinct system that has been affected by and has affected economically based class systems. Women and men of the proletariat and the bourgeoisie lack a commonality of interest because of the interpenetration of capitalism and patriarchy. The oppression of women is both different from, and greater than, that of male proletariats (Chafetz, 1988).

The Data box on gender stratification highlights several of the inequalities we'll focus on and try to explain in this chapter.

Distinguishing between Sex and Gender

Before proceeding any farther, it is important to clarify some concepts that are key to understanding the process of gender stratification. Al-

though the terms *sex* and *gender* are often used interchangeably, they refer to quite different attributes. **Sex** refers only to the biological characteristics that differentiate females from males. These include external genitalia (vagina and penis), gonads (ovaries and testes), sex chromosomes (XX for females, XY for males), and hormones (estrogen, progesterone, and androgens). At puberty, as the production of hormones increases, secondary sex characteristics emerge— larger breasts, wider hips, narrower shoulders, more fatty tissue, and menstruation for females and a deeper voice, greater height, more muscle mass, and more facial and bodily hair for males.

Although an extensive body of research has tried to determine other differences between females and males that are rooted in biology, the weight of the evidence seems to show that the similarities are far greater than any differences that exist and, furthermore, that the differences that do exist are not of great significance, especially in modern, technological societies. Thus, the biological category of sex, in and of itself, cannot answer the question of why one sex is more highly valued than another. To answer this question, we must focus our attention on **gender,** the socially constructed cluster of behavioral

Gender Stratification

- The majority of women earn, on average, about three-fourths of the male wage for the same work outside the agricultural sector, in both developed and developing countries.
- Women's unemployment rates run from 50 to 100 percent greater than those of men in many industrialized countries.
- Women hold fewer than 6 percent of senior management jobs in the world. The International Labor Organization estimates that, at the present rate of progress worldwide, it would take 475 years for parity to be achieved between women and men in top managerial and administrative positions.

- In developed countries, women work at least two hours per week more than men, and often five to ten hours more per week.
- In developing countries, women spend 31 to 42 hours per week in unpaid work (in the home). Men spend between 5 and 15 hours in unpaid work.
- Women make up nearly 70 percent of the world's poor and 65 percent of the world's illiterate.
- Of the approximately 100 million children in the world who have no access to primary education, 60 percent are girls.

Source: Adapted from Lin Lean Lim. 1996. *More and Better Jobs for Women: An Action Guide.* Geneva: The International Labour Organization, pp. 11, 14.

patterns and personality traits that are associated with being female or male, or what we commonly call *femininity* and *masculinity*. Over the past three decades, a number of studies have found a broad consensus among different groups of people regarding the existence of different personality traits associated with each sex. For example, in a 1990 Gallup poll, adults were read a list of thirty-one personality traits and asked which were more characteristic of women or of men. Women were most often described as emotional, talkative, sensitive, affectionate, patient, romantic, moody, cautious, and creative, whereas men were most often described as aggressive, strong, proud, disorganized, confident, courageous, independent, and ambitious (De-Stefano & Colasanto, 1990). It is important to remember that this type of research indicates only people's awareness of gender stereotypes; it does not tell us whether they believe they are true nor does it tell us whether people would have created a similar list if simply asked to list traits they associated with females and males.

These notions of gender would not be terribly significant if it were not for the fact that society also has behavioral expectations for its female and male members, what sociologists call **gender roles.** Anthropologist Margaret Mead (1963) was one of the first researchers to call attention to the fact that the content of gender roles is not universal but rather varies from one culture to another. Mead studied three tribes living in New Guinea. One tribe, the Arapesh, were a gentle and passive people; both females and males had characteristics that would be labeled "feminine" by our standards. In contrast, the Mundugumors were combative, fierce, and aggressive, and both sexes exhibited what appear to us as "masculine" traits. The last tribe, the Tchambuli, had distinct gender traits based on sex, but it was the women who were dominant and provided most of the food. Males, in contrast, were more passive. Mead's research and a growing body of cross-cultural research that followed show a great deal of flexibility in gender roles and point quite convincingly to the fact that gender roles can and do change in societies over time. The existence of flexibility and change in gender roles can be illustrated by examining the history of work and gender in the United States.

Work and Gender in the United States

For most of U.S. history, people did not see work as separate from the rest of their lives. In agricultural America, both women and men worked, and they consumed most of what they produced; few people were paid for their labor. It was only in the nineteenth century that production moved off the farms and into factories. With this industrialization, work come to be defined as a paid activity which, until quite recently, was characterized as predominantly male. Although a significant number of women and children accompanied husbands and fathers into the factories, a specialized role, known as the "good provider," emerged around 1830; this held that a man's major contribution to his family was economic. Masculinity came to be equated with being a successful and, for the most part, sole provider (Bernard, 1984). At the same time, an ideology developed that the so-called true woman was the woman who did not work but rather stayed home and provided domestic service for her family (Welter, 1978). However, the option of staying home never applied to all groups of women—women in poor and working-class families, women raising children on their own, most women of color, and most white immigrant women could not afford to stay at home. Nevertheless, these ideologies became embedded in a system of gender stratification that attaches different values and rewards to the work that women and men do even today. The effects of these ideologies can be seen in three major areas: labor force participation, occupational segregation and concentration, and a gender earnings gap.

Labor Force Participation

Although women have always worked, they were not always (and still aren't in many countries) counted in the labor force because much of their work was done in the home and, therefore, was unrecognized and unpaid. The **labor-force participation rate** is the percentage of workers in a particular group who are employed or who are actively seeking employment. Not counted in these statistics are many people who are working at home. For example, many women, especially in other countries, produce goods and services at home, some of which later may be sold in a marketplace. Yet these individuals are generally not counted as part of the labor force. In 1900, only 20 percent of women aged fourteen and older were in the labor force, compared with approximately 86 percent of men in that age category, and the majority of these women workers were young, single, poor, and women of color (U.S. Bureau of the Census, 1975). The comparable rates ninety-six years later were 59.3 percent for women and 74.9 percent for men sixteen years of age and over; the gap between white women and women of color had equalized to a marked degree—60.4 percent for African American women, 59.1 percent for white women, and 53.4 percent for Latinas (U.S. Bureau of the Census, 1997). The labor-force participation rates for women and men are moving in opposite directions, with the result that women now constitute 46 percent of all workers, up from 18 percent in 1900.

Looking at working women around the globe, we find that the composition of the labor force varies enormously from one country to the next. As Figure 11.1 shows, women make up only a small percentage of the labor force in countries such as Qatar and Saudi Arabia, but their participation rates approach nearly 50 percent in countries such as Tanzania, Vietnam, Finland, and the Czech Republic. The ability of women to participate in the paid labor force is influenced by many factors, including their skills, their levels of education, and, probably most important, cultural norms. In many countries, including Bolivia, Guatemala, Lesotho, Swaziland, Syria, Togo, the United Arab Emirates, and Zaire, husbands have the legal right to restrict or even prohibit their wives' working in the paid labor force (Seager, 1997:118). Even when women are free to choose to enter the labor force, however, they often find themselves segregated and concentrated in certain jobs.

Occupational Segregation and Concentration

Where people are located in the occupational structure has a major impact on their working conditions and on their earning power. Two processes are relevant here. The first is **occupational segregation,** the tendency for women and

FIGURE 11.1 ☺ **Labor Force Participation Rates by Gender, Select Countries, 1994** *Source: Data from Seager, J. 1997. The State of Women in the World Atlas (2nd ed.). London: Penguin Reference, pp. 96–103.*

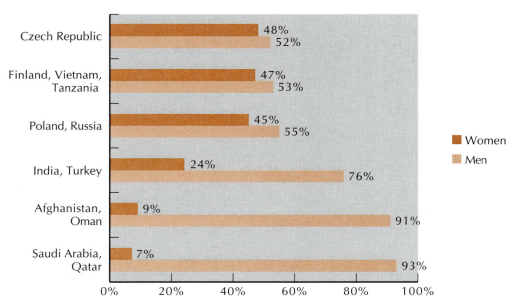

men to be employed in different occupations. This process creates the second, **occupational concentration**—the overrepresentation of women in a limited number of occupations. Although we are likely to see interesting news features on people who enter nontraditional occupations—for example, women coal miners and construction workers and male nurses and child care workers—as Table 11.1 shows, although some changes have taken place in the past decade, most occupations remain either female or male dominated. Furthermore, women are heavily concentrated in low-paying clerical or service jobs, and, although slightly more women than men are working in professional specialties, they tend to be working in the lower-paid professions such as nursing, whereas men are more concentrated in the higher-paid professions of law and medicine. In 1997, only 26.7 percent of all lawyers and judges and 26.2 percent of physicians were women. Race is also a factor. African Americans and Latinas/os were underrepresented as lawyers and judges, accounting for only 3.4 percent and 2.9.1 percent respectively. Similarly, African Americans and Latinas/os accounted for only 4.5 percent and 5.1 percent of all physicians (U.S. Bureau of Census, 1998). Men have been more reluctant than women to enter nontraditional occupations. Thus, some job categories remain overwhelmingly female, for example, nursing (93.5 percent female), and secretarial work (98.6 percent female). To achieve occupational integration, approximately 53 percent of the female labor force would have to shift to mostly male occupations (Reskin & Padavic, 1994). This pattern of occupational segregation by gender is common in other industrialized countries as well—even in Sweden, which has one of the highest rates of women's labor force participation in the world.

Occupational segregation has several consequences for the well-being of all workers. Foremost, it restricts what people can do, regardless of their talents and abilities. It also creates a gendered environment which can prove troublesome for workers when they enter nontraditional occupations. Nontraditional workers, usually women and people of color, often encounter prejudice and hostility, which lead to high levels of stress. This hostility often leads to exclusion from informal work groups that are so necessary

TABLE 11.1 ◐ **Occupational Segregation and Concentration, 1983 and 1997**

	1983	1997
Female Dominated Occupations	Percent Female	
Secretaries	99.0	98.6
Receptionists	96.8	96.5
Private household workers	96.1	95.4
Registered nurses	95.8	93.5
Bank tellers	91.0	90.1
Librarians	87.3	80.5
Male Dominated Occupations	Percent Male	
Firefighting and fire prevention	99.0	96.6
Airplane pilots and navigators	97.9	98.8
Engineers	94.2	90.4
Police and detectives	90.6	83.6
Physicians	84.2	73.8
Lawyers and judges	84.2	73.3

Source: Adapted from U.S. Bureau of Labor Statistics. 1984. *Employment and Earnings, January.* Washington, DC: U.S. Government Printing Office; U.S. Bureau of the Census. 1998. *Statistical Abstract of the United States, 1998.* Washington, DC: U.S. Government Printing Office, Table 672, p. 419.

to successful job performance and advancement. In contrast, men who enter nontraditional occupations are less likely to experience discriminatory treatment from their coworkers and, in fact, are likely to experience a rapid rate of advancement. Researchers have found, for example, that women in nontraditional occupations often encounter a "glass ceiling" that limits their advancement but that men in nontraditional occupations experience a "glass escalator" that propels them to higher positions in that field (Williams, 1992). Occupational segregation also results in an earnings gap between women and men and between whites and people of color which limits the resources available to them and to their families.

The Earnings Gap

In the United States, as in most nations, women earn substantially less than men. As Table 11.2 shows, this pattern exists across all race and ethnic groups. In 1997, on average, women earned seventy-four cents for every dollar men made, up from sixty cents in 1979. This improvement can be attributed to a number of factors: women's higher levels of education and professional training, fewer and shorter interruptions in women's work lives as more women continue to work after marriage and the birth of children (a pattern increasingly resembling men's), the willingness of employers to support more equitable pay scales, and a stagnation or actual decline in men's wages. According to a recent study, the typical female worker's pay rose 6.1 percent (16.4 percent for women in upper-level jobs) whereas the pay for male workers decreased by 11.7 percent between 1973 and 1993 (Harris, 1996). Despite some improvement, the gender gap in earnings continues even when women and men share the same occupation, although the size of the gap varies from one occupation to the next. For example, female nurses make 95 percent of what male nurses do, but female accountants and auditors earn only 73 percent of what their male colleagues earn.

Such disparities in earnings exist in other countries as well. As Figure 11.2 shows, the average gender gap in earnings is between 30 and 40 percent. The wage gap is narrowest in countries such as Vietnam (92 percent), Australia (91 percent), and Iceland (90 percent) and widest in countries such as Japan (41 percent) and Russia (40 percent).

Explaining Gender Inequities in the Workplace

How can we account for the continued existence of occupational segregation, occupational concentration, and the earnings gap? Human capital theory and gender discrimination theory are most commonly used to explain these patterns.

Human Capital Theory   The economic theory that assumes that labor markets operate in a nondiscriminatory fashion, rewarding workers for their productivity, is called **human capital theory** (Reskin & Padavic, 1994). It assumes that if women are worse off than men, it is because they are less productive workers. However, productivity is not easily measured in many jobs. Thus, researchers examine the characteristics assumed to increase productivity—the skills, experiences, effort, and commitment that workers bring to their jobs, that is, their human capital. This model assumes that workers make an investment in themselves through education, training, and experience which increases their productivity and, in turn, their earnings. Hu-

---

TABLE 11.2 ♻ **Median Annual Earnings of Full-Time, Year-Round Workers, by Sex, Race, and Ethnicity, 1995**

			Earnings		
	Total	White	Black	Latino	Asian/Pacific Islander
Women	$22,500	$22,900	$20,700	$17,200	$24,900
Men	31,500	32,200	24,400	20,400	31,600
Ratio (W/M)	0.71	0.71	0.85	0.84	0.79

Source: Adapted by permission of the Population Reference Bureau from Bianchi, S.M., and Spain, D. 1996. "Women, Work, and Family in America." *Population Bulletin* (December): Table 8, p. 25.

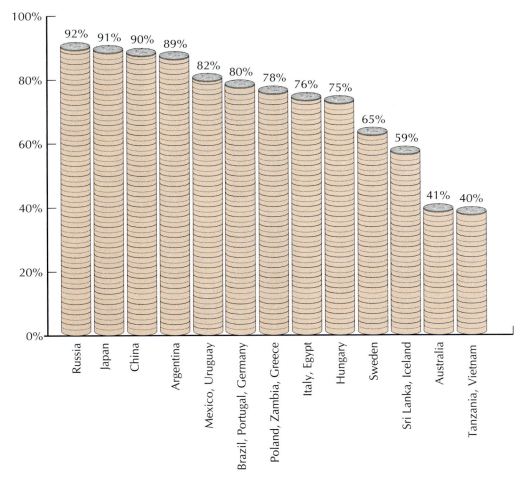

FIGURE 11.2 ⟳ **The Earnings Gap in Selected Countries, 1995** *Source:* Data from Seager, J. 1997. *The State of Women in the World Atlas* (2nd ed.). London: Penguin Reference, pp. 68–69.

man capital theorists assume that men make a greater investment in their human capital than do women. Women, by contrast, are believed to invest less in education and training and to choose occupations that are less demanding because of their anticipated family responsibilities. Similarly, because employers believe that women will not stay with an employer for as long as male workers will, they invest less in training them. The human capital theory predicts that as women's commitment to employment increases, they will invest more in education and training and employers will provide

them with more on-the-job training, believing that such an investment will now pay off.

How valid is this theory? Paula England (1997) reviewed a number of studies testing it and concluded that neither education nor effort is particularly relevant to the gender gap in pay because, on average, women have as much, and in some cases more, education as men and exert as much or more effort as men do on their jobs. However, women's fewer years of seniority and overall employment experience, and the intermittency of such experience, explains some proportion (between one quarter and one half) of the gender gap in pay. Thus, we must look farther to find an explanation for the remaining portion of the earnings gap.

Gender Discrimination Theory   As we discussed in the previous chapter, discrimination is an act of unfair treatment directed against an individual or a group. Throughout recorded history, evidence exists to show that employers have discriminated on the basis of sex, as well as on the basis of race, ethnicity, national origin, age, appearance, and sexual orientation (Reskin & Padavic, 1994). The reasons for this are varied. Employers, like other members of society, learn gender stereotypes. Thus, employers may discriminate against women because they believe that they are not capable of doing the work or that they will be less productive or more costly to employ because of the priority they give to their family roles. Sociologists refer to the practice of treating individuals on the basis of beliefs about groups as **statistical discrimination.** The fact that this practice is illegal in the United States has not prevented employers from utilizing it.

Some employers are concerned about the impact that hiring or promoting women will have on their male workers or clients. For example, until a U.S. Supreme Court decision required them to change their practices, airlines would hire only women as stewardesses because of their assumption that the flying public would not accept male flight attendants. Clearly, this proved not to be the case as male flight attendants are a common fixture on airlines today. Because many employers fear a hostile reaction from their male workers, they are reluctant to promote women to positions in which their responsibilities would include supervising men. A recent Gallup poll seems to confirm their fears. The poll found that 46 percent of those surveyed would prefer to work for a male boss; only 20 percent said they would prefer working for a woman. Surprisingly, more women reported a preference for a male boss, 54 percent compared to 37 percent of the men. Although the poll did not ask why, Anne Ladky, executive director of Women Employed, offers a plausible reason for this response, suggesting that women may prefer to work for men because they tend to be more powerful than women (Brotman,

Today it is no longer rare to see women and men in nontraditional occupations. However, the more common pattern is for women to move into jobs that were once the sole province of males, such as this woman working in the fishing industry.

1996). Additionally, many employers assume erroneously that women who choose traditional female jobs are not interested in promotions and, therefore, are willing to accept lower pay because, unlike their male counterparts, they are not oriented to paid work and are just working for extra money (Reskin & Padavic, 1994). According to Alice Kemp (1990), data show that approximately 50 percent of the pay gap is due to discriminatory factors.

Clearly, society pays a price when it fails to utilize the abilities of all of its citizens. The challenges of a global economy, environmental deterioration, war and violence, poverty, and crime cannot be resolved without the talents and efforts of both women and men. Solutions to the problems of inequality in the workplace require an integrated, proactive policy at the national and international levels.

Several policies have already shown signs of effectiveness. For example, the aggressive wage equality laws in Italy and Scandinavia have narrowed the wage gap between those countries' female and male workers (Seager, 1997). Although not widely implemented as yet, *comparable worth* policies in the United States also engender more equitable pay scales. Essentially, these policies adhere to the principle of equal pay for different jobs of similar worth and require evaluating jobs in terms of education, experience, and skill as well as the job's value to the community. When implemented, these policies go a long way toward equalizing the return on women's investment in education, even if women remain in jobs traditionally viewed as "woman's work." These policies have been more readily adopted in the public sector. In the private sector, employers have resisted them, claiming they would be too expensive to implement.

Additionally, the movement on the part of some employers to make their training programs and policies more equitable has allowed some women to move into higher-paying positions. Finally, when there is an equitable sharing of family responsibilities, including housework and child care, women are better positioned to balance the demands of home and work and to take advantage of work situations that can lead to upward mobility for them and their families.

Applying the Sociological Imagination

Think about your career goals. Do they reflect what you thought you wanted to be when you were a child? If not, how did they change? Did anyone encourage or discourage your goals? What factors influenced your choice of career goals? Have you or anyone you know experienced any inequities in the workplace because of gender? Do you think that you might experience any kind of inequity in the workplace as a result of choosing this career? If so, what do you think you could do to change that?

Educational Inequities

The fact that you are sitting in a college classroom suggests that you believe in the value of education. As we saw in Chapters 9 and 10, formal education is one of the most important sources of opportunity in any culture because it is associated with many of life's chances—the kind of job we have, the amount of money we make, our level of political influence, and even our health. Yet, an estimated 965 million people—a quarter of the world's adult population—cannot read or write. About two-thirds of them are women. Jamaica is the only country where there are significantly more illiterate men (21 percent) than women (12 percent). A more typical pattern is that found in countries such as Afghanistan, where the illiteracy rates are 56 percent for men and 87 percent for women (Seager, 1997). Generally speaking, high rates of illiteracy for both women and men are indicators of a country's extreme poverty. Higher illiteracy rates for women reflect a pattern of gender discrimination in countries where women are restricted primarily to reproductive roles and social roles associated with caring for families. This pattern is particularly evident in developing countries, where girls are much less likely than boys to start school. When they do start school, their presence in school decreases as they move up the educational ladder, dropping off dramatically at the university level.

The consequences of illiteracy are enormous for both women and men in that it constrains their economic opportunities. The higher rates of illiteracy for women increase their dependency on men by limiting their ability to control or even to understand their own property, wealth, health, and legal rights. And, as the principal care givers for children, they pass this legacy to the next generation. According to Economist Lin Lim

(1996), investment in the education of girls will return large dividends. Each additional year of schooling has been shown to raise a woman's earnings by about 15 percent (compared with 11 percent for a man), to reduce fertility rates by 5 to 10 percent, and to avert 43 infant deaths per 1,000 educated girls.

Unlike most developing countries, industrialized countries, like the United States, require mandatory education for both sexes to a certain age, usually about sixteen, and, by and large, encourage both women and men to attend college. In fact, in 1997, 54 percent of all U.S. first-year college students were women, and women earned 54.6 percent of all bachelor's and 55.1 percent of all master's degrees awarded in 1995 (U.S. Bureau of the Census, 1998). African American women were the first group to earn more bachelor degrees than their male counterparts, achieving this distinction in the late 1970s. By 1993, white, Native American, and Asian American women did the same (Bianchi & Spain, 1996).

Nevertheless, gender discrimination in education does exist in the United States, but it takes more subtle forms than in developing countries. Although U.S. society has become more conscious of gender inequities in the educational system and has taken some steps to alleviate them, serious problems remain in many schools and classrooms around the country. Some teachers continue to structure classroom activities along gender lines that emphasize competition rather than cooperation between the sexes—math or spelling contests with girls versus boys, for example. In addition, the allocation of space is still gender specific on many playgrounds. Because boys are expected, indeed encouraged, to play team sports during their free time, they usually end up occupying large open spaces while girls contend with more limited space for their activities—frequently closer to the school building and with adult supervision. Such use of space conveys subtle messages that girls need more protection than boys and that boys are entitled to more space. Similarly, classroom chores may be allocated on the basis of gender, with girls watering the plants and doing the dusting while the boys are handling equipment and running errands.

Other gender messages are communicated to students by how teachers interact with them. Educational researchers have found that, regardless of educational level, many teachers provide more assistance and challenges for boys than for girls (Sadker & Sadker, 1994a). In a similar vein, other investigators found that teachers are more likely to praise girls for conforming behavior whereas they are more likely to praise boys for creative behavior (Grossman & Grossman, 1994). These issues are even more complicated when the race of the student is taken into account. Teachers, like many others in our culture, often perceive Asian American students as model students and treat them accordingly (Basow, 1992). Conversely, teachers provide less feedback and academic encouragement to African American girls than they do to white girls. Boys have their problems, too. Regardless of race or ethnicity, boys are more likely than girls to be referred to special education programs and to be identified as having learning problems (U.S. Department of Education, 1997).

These gendered messages from teachers are frequently reinforced by the curricular materials used in the classroom. Although, in general, both sexes are depicted in less stereotypical ways today than in the past, many children's readers still present boys engaging in a wider range of activities than girls (Purcell & Stewart, 1990). Textbooks still exhibit language bias in the form of the exclusive use of masculine pronouns and nouns and in content bias as seen in the omission of the contributions of and scholarship by women (Sadker & Sadker, 1994a). Other countries are dealing with this issue as well. A study of primary and secondary school textbooks in use in Zurich, Switzerland, revealed similar biases. Men and boys are depicted in Swiss texts as much as ten times more frequently than women and girls ("Textbook Sexism," 1992).

The use of sex-typed materials in the classroom and the nature of many teacher-student interactions often result in girls being directed toward fields of study that will later limit their career choices. A considerable body of research points to the constraining outcome of these gender inequities—an increase in sex-typed attitudes, especially among young children. Conversely, the use of sex-equitable materials in schools helps students develop more flexible gender-role attitudes, which allow them to make educational and career choices based on their own interests rather than on preconceived notions of what is "right" for a female or male (Scott & Schau, 1985). However, Table 11.3 shows that gender tracking in fields of study is still the dominant pattern in higher education. Although more women are entering fields dominated by men, men for the most part continue to avoid fields long thought to be women's domain.

TABLE 11.3 ☉ **Percentage of Bachelor's Degrees Earned by Sex, Selected Fields of Study, 1971 and 1995**

Major Field of Study	Percent Female	
	1971	1995
Agriculture and natural resources	4.2	36.0
Architecture and environmental design	11.9	34.4
Area, ethnic, and cultural studies	52.4	63.3
Biological sciences/life sciences	29.1	52.3
Business and management	9.1	48.0
Computer and information science	13.6	28.4
Education	74.5	75.8
Engineering	0.8	15.6
English language and literature	65.6	65.7
Foreign languages	74.0	69.2
Health sciences	77.1	81.9
Home economics	97.3	88.2
Library and archival sciences	92.0	96.0
Mathematics	37.9	46.8
Philosophy, religion, and theology	25.5	31.0
Physical sciences	13.8	34.8
Psychology	44.4	72.9
Public affairs	68.4	78.8
Social sciences	36.8	46.8
Visual and performing arts	59.7	59.4

Source: U.S. Bureau of the Census. 1998. *Statistical Abstract of the United States, 1998.* Washington, DC: U.S. Government Printing Office, Table 325, p. 200.

Gender and Political Structures

Given our discussion of gender inequities in the workplace and in education, it probably will not surprise you to find that across the globe, women occupy only a small percentage of positions having real decision-making power. In Kuwait, women are not allowed to run for office. In another five countries (Bhutan, Djibouti, Mauritania, the United Arab Emirates, and Papua, New Guinea), there are no women in their national legislatures. Of the other countries for which data are available, forty-five have 5 percent or fewer women in their main political bodies. These countries tend to be primarily in Africa, the Middle East, and Eastern Europe. The main political bodies in the majority of the world's countries, including the United States, contain only 5.1 percent to 15 percent women. Twenty-one countries' political bodies contain from 15.1 percent to 25 percent women. Among these countries are Argentina, South Africa, Chad, Canada, China, Spain, Italy, Switzerland, Austria, and Italy. Only nine countries' political bodies contain 25 percent or more women. Sweden leads this group (which includes other Scandinavian countries and Germany), its national legislature containing 40.4 percent women (Seager, 1997).

This lack of political representation is related to women's lack of voting rights in most countries until relatively late in the twentieth century (see Figure 11.3). Women in New Zealand were the first of their sex to win the vote, in 1893. Their sisters in Australia won it nine years later, and in 1906 Finland followed suit. The United States did not extend suffrage to women until 1920. The biggest surge in voting rights for both women and men followed in the wake of World War II and again in the late 1950s, when decolonization was taking place. However, all women do not yet have the right to vote. Kuwait specifically denies women the vote and in Bhutan, women are effectively disenfranchised by a "family vote" system (Seager, 1997).

A number of other factors contribute to women's low representation rates in the political structures of their countries. The first factor

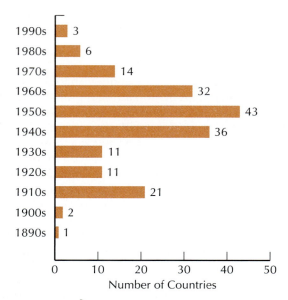

FIGURE 11.3 ⟳ **Number of Countries in Which Women Won the Vote, by Decades** *Source:* Data from Seager, J. 1997. *The State of Women in the World Atlas* (2nd ed.). London: Penguin Reference, p. 89.

is their low level of education. However, even when these levels match or exceed men's, women are underrepresented in fields that traditionally lead to political careers, such as law and business. Second, because women still have major responsibility for household tasks and child care, they have less time to devote to political activity. Finally, and perhaps most important of all, women do not have the same access to resources such as money, organization, and political mentors as men do.

Fortunately, this pattern seems to be changing. In the United States, political action committees such as Emily's List (Early Money Is Like Yeast), dedicated to providing financial support to women across the country, have helped increasing numbers of women win political office at the state and national level. Women have been particularly active at the local and state levels. For example, in 1999 slightly over 22 percent of state legislators were women, up from just under 5 percent in 1969 (Verhovek, 1999). It is likely that some of them will be able to use that

experience to move to higher offices. This is a critical issue for, if women continue to be excluded from political decision making, their needs and issues are less likely to be addressed and the lower status they currently have will be passed on to their daughters. We can gain some insight into the significance of this fact by examining how two male-dominated governmental and military bodies devalued women by systematically raping and sexually abusing them and then refusing to take responsibility for their actions (see the Cultural Snapshot box).

Although the U.S. government has been a strong advocate for improving human rights around the world, it is only recently that some of the systematic violations of women's rights have moved to the front of the political agenda. For the past two decades, the U.S. State Department has issued an annual report of human-rights violations that routinely included horrors such as the Siberia gulags, torture in Iran, and the imprisonment of political dissidents in China and the former Soviet Union and Eastern Bloc countries. At the same time, it has largely ignored the mistreatment of women around the world. However, that changed in 1993 when the report highlighted some of the problems women face globally. For example, Moroccan law permits a husband to injure or kill his wife if she commits adultery but prohibits a wife from physically harming her adulterous husband. In India, if a groom and his family think a bride's dowry is too small, she may face persecution or even death resulting from an "accidental" kitchen fire. In Thailand, young, mostly rural, women are recruited as prostitutes, usually by procurers who give parents new homes in exchange for their daughters' services. Estimates are that up to 1 million women may be working in Thai brothels (Seter, 1994).

Despite this recent concern, the United States Senate has not yet ratified the United Nations Convention on the Elimination of All Forms of Discrimination Against Women (CEDAW), signed by President Jimmy Carter nearly two decades ago. Its aim is to ensure equality in education, inheritance, property rights, citizenship, marriage, and child custody. According to the treaty, participating nations are obliged to incorporate the principle of gender equality in their laws or constitutions and to take all appropriate measures to eliminate discrimination against women by any person, organization, or enterprise. The United States is one of only thirty-five nations, the only major industrialized nation, and the only nation in the Western Hemisphere that has not ratified this international treaty. Critics of the treaty in the United States claim that it is vaguely worded, unpredictable in its legal effect, and unnecessary. Proponents of the treaty argue that current U.S. legal protections for women, based on the concept of equal protection under the fourteenth Amendment, are far weaker than the guarantee of equality in CEDAW (Choo, 1998).

Sexual Harassment

In a 1993 ruling on sexual harassment, the U.S. Supreme Court defined **sexual harassment** as any sexual conduct that makes the workplace environment so hostile or abusive to the victims that they find it difficult to perform their jobs. While this definition is specific to workplace sexual harassment, this kind of sexual behavior can and does occur in a wide variety of cultural spaces; it ranges from unwanted sexual remarks, sexual jokes or comments, sexual innuendos, and sexual leers or overtures and physical contact to actual rape.

Sexual harassment falls within the category of sexual coercion which we discussed in Chapter 7 in that it generally occurs within the context of power, dominance, and control. Most often this power, dominance, and control is exercised by men. Contrary to the role reversal characterized in the recent film *Disclosure,* men seldom experience (or are more reluctant to report) sexual harassment. The rate of sexual harassment of males, reported to be about 15 percent (Townsend & Luthar, 1995) is still quite low compared to that of sexual harassment of females. Women can and do sexually harass subordinates. However, because men hold a majority of the positions of authority, the more common pattern is for men to harass women (Shoop & Edwards, 1994). Regardless of the sex of the victim, however, sexual harassment is about power, and it involves a more powerful person victimizing a less powerful person. And, like rape and other coercive sexual acts, it has much more to do with the abuse of power than with sexual desire.

Sexual Harassment at Work and School Sexual harassment is not a new phenomenon. As early as 1908, *Harper's Bazaar* published stories about women who carried knives to work to protect themselves from being sexually harassed in the factories where they worked (Betz & Fitzgerald, 1987). Today, women constitute approximately 46 percent of the U.S. labor force, yet despite this trend toward numerical equalization, relationships between female and male workers are often full of problems. Because women generally occupy lower-status positions, have less power in decision making, and are paid less than their male counterparts, they are vulnerable to sexual harassment. Like other forms of sexual victimization, it is difficult to gauge the actual extent of sexual harassment. Nevertheless, a number of surveys suggest that sexual harassment is quite widespread in a wide variety of work and educational settings both in the United States and in other countries (see the Data box on page 320). Despite the wide extent of sexual harassment, only thirty-six countries have legislation targeted specifically against such behavior.

Race, socioeconomic status, sexual orientation, age, and marital status affect experiences of sexual harassment. Women of color are more likely to experience sexual harassment than white women, and the harassment is likely to include racial stereotypes (Fain & Anderson, 1987). Sexual harassment also appears to be more prevalent in male-dominated occupations in which some male workers seek to maintain control over women rather than to recognize them as equals. Single and younger women report being sexually harassed more often than do their married and older counterparts. In addition, lesbians and gays experience physical and verbal harassment because of their sexual orientation (Shoop & Edwards, 1994).

Consequences of Sexual Harassment Workers and students who are sexually harassed report a number of problems both physical (headaches, chronic neck and back pain, gastrointestinal disorders, insomnia, and loss of appetite) and psychological (decreased motivation and feelings

Cultural Snapshot

Mass Rape: A Weapon of War

In a historic move, the International Criminal Tribunal on the Former Yugoslavia that is investigating war atrocities in Bosnia has declared that rape used as a weapon of war is a war crime, "a crime against humanity." Although wartime rape has a long history, it is only now being recognized as an instrument of government policy.

In one modern instance of government-sanctioned wartime rape, the Japanese military during World War II operated what were in effect rape camps that it euphemistically called "comfort stations." Although no one knows the exact numbers, it is estimated that as many as 200,000 Korean, Chinese, and other Asian women were abducted into these camps and forced to sexually service Japanese soldiers during their occupation of Korea. Some "comfort women" were school-age children. Many were tortured and some died during their captivity. Those who made it home suffered for the rest of their lives. Some had contracted syphilis; others carried the scars of beatings. All had a misplaced sense of shame; all kept their tragic experiences locked deep within themselves. Some never married; some suffered extreme psychological distress. No relief organizations or rape-victim support groups were organized for them. The postwar International Military Tribunal largely ignored them and the Japanese government denied that their victimization had ever happened. These women were hidden behind a wall of silence. In 1990, fifty years after the fact, a survivor broke the silence and told her story. Her courage enabled other women, now mostly in their

seventies, to come forward. They demonstrated in front of the Japanese Embassy in Seoul, demanding an official response to their suffering. After eight years of trying to avoid taking any responsibility for the military's actions, the Japanese prime minister made a personal apology. A private fund was established in Japan to provide some compensation to these women.

About the time that the "comfort women" started to tell their story, warring factions in Bosnia began their campaign of terror. The organized character of the mass rapes in Bosnia was revealed early in the war through an interview with a seventeen-year-old victim. She and her mother and about two dozen other women between the ages of twelve and forty-five were rounded up and imprisoned in the basement of a building. For four months, she and her mother had to watch as the other was gang-raped about three times a day. She and two other victims were released only when they became visibly pregnant. This is a typical tactic. Women are raped repeatedly until pregnancies are confirmed; then they are detained until it is too late for them to obtain safe abortions.

Mass rape is an act of conquest and subjugation of whole societies, involving deliberate national humiliation as a means of suppression and social control. Its effect is to destroy the enemy as an organic community. A policy of mass rapes and other forms of sexual violence can be used domestically against ethnic minorities and opposition groups as well as against foreign populations. In Bosnia-Herzegovina, it became a major technique for "ethnic cleansing." Rape and the threat of rape

---

of humiliation, helplessness, embarrassment, anger, and fear). As a result, their work and school performance suffer. Many victims of harassment leave their jobs, change careers, or drop out of school. Data collected by the International Labor Organization (1995) reveal that one out of twelve women were forced out of a job after being sexually harassed. The majority of those reporting harassment on various surveys do not

file formal complaints because they believe nothing will be done or that, like many other victims of abuse who go to court, they will experience a second victimization. They fear that they will be retaliated against, blamed for the harassment, viewed as liars, or simply dismissed as being overly sensitive or poor sports.

These fears were crystallized for many women by the negative treatment University of

are terror tactics that drive people out of their homes and villages, making it easier for enemy forces to extend their control over territory. Also, potential male combatants are removed from the enemy ranks when they flee with their families in an effort to protect them.

The rape of a family member devastates family life. Frequently, family members are forced to witness the atrocity as a way to maximize its effectiveness in achieving social, emotional, and cognitive disorientation, terrorizing the community and making it easier to control. Those forced to watch feel powerless because they can't stop it. The consequences for the victims are long-lasting—they may grow to fear sexual intimacy and to develop an impaired capacity to trust. Some go insane; others commit suicide.

Despite the positive move by the Tribunal in declaring mass rapes a war crime, it is unlikely that anyone will be prosecuted for these crimes. The reasons for this are both personal and political. On a personal level, even though they are blameless, rape victims are ashamed of what happened to them and many desperately want to conceal their terrible experience from public view. Being raped creates a social stigma in cultures in which shame is connected to the loss of female chastity. In these cultures, women who are raped are regarded as tainted even though they had no control over their situations. Single women become unmarriageable. Married women become outcasts in their own families. Thus, a raped woman is humiliated twice, first by her attacker and second by her fear of rejection by her family. In a culture in which women do not speak easily with strangers of either sex, it is difficult for women to speak about something so intensely personal as rape.

The social and legal repercussions of coming forward are such that they act to shield the rapists who commit their crimes during war, and the political bodies overseeing the Tribunal have not taken adequate action to prevent this. Although the Tribunal established a Victims and Witnesses Unit to cover their travel expenses to the Hague where the trials are held, no procedures have been developed nor are funds available to protect victims from reprisals when they return home or resettle after testifying. Because few of the rapists are in custody, there is a strong possibility that women will encounter their rapists on the streets, and many of these rapists are now wearing the police uniforms of the new Serb Republic in Bosnia.

How is this behavior consistent with what you have learned about gender inequality? What does it tell you about gender roles in these societies? Why did the Korean women wait so long to tell their story? What steps do you think societies can take to keep this kind of behavior from recurring?

Source: Information from Shanker, T., and Hundley, T. 1997. "Uncovering Campaign of Horror." *Chicago Tribune* (May 18):1; Lord, M. 1996. "The Comfort Woman's Cry." *U.S. News & World Report* (December 16):62–65.

Oklahoma law professor Anita Hill received when she testified before a 1991 Senate Judiciary Committee during the confirmation hearings for Supreme Court nominee Clarence Thomas. Thomas was confirmed, but Hill's televised testimony that she was sexually harassed when she worked under his supervision at the Equal Employment Opportunity Commission (EEOC) brought national attention to this problem. New sexual harassment complaints filed with the federal EEOC jumped from 6,127 in 1990 to 15,342 in 1996, a jump of 150 percent; over 90 percent of the complaints were filed by women (Reynolds, 1997).

In 1993, the Supreme Court, in a unanimous ruling, broadened the legal definition of sexual harassment, making it easier for victims of harassment to win their cases as they no longer

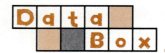

Reports of Sexual Harassment

- A 1987 survey of the U.S. Department of Labor showed that 37 percent of its women employees believed that they had been sexually harassed (Kleiman, 1991, cited in Stanko & Miller, 1996).

- A 1988 survey by the U.S. Merit Systems Protection Board of 10,648 female federal employees showed that 42 percent believed that they were harassed on the job (Kleiman, 1991, cited in Stanko & Miller, 1996).

- A 1989 study of female doctors and medical students indicated that 27 percent believed that they had experienced sexual harassment; that same year, a survey of 3,000 female lawyers showed that 85 percent had experienced or observed sexual harassment during the previous two years (Kleiman, 1991, cited in Stanko & Miller, 1996).

- A 1990 survey of the 1,300 members of the National Association of Female Executives indicated that 53 percent believed they had been harassed by male supervisors (Kleiman, 1991, cited in Stanko and Miller, 1996).

- According to a recent Pentagon study, more than half of the women in the U.S. military have been objects of harassment ("Pentagon Survey," 1996).

- A 1993 study of 1,632 students in grades eight through eleven from seventy-nine schools across the United States suggested that 85 percent of the girls and 76 percent of the boys experienced unwelcome sexual behavior that interfered with their ability to concentrate at school (cited in Doyle and Paludi, 1998).

- A recent study reported that 30 percent of undergraduate women experienced sexual harassment from at least one of their instructors during their college years. The rate in undergraduate populations increases to almost 70 percent when sexist remarks are included (Paludi, 1996).

- A study of working women in twenty-three industrialized countries found that up to 30 percent reported frequent harassment on the job (International Labor Organization, 1993). This study also found that some men experience sexual harassment, especially men of color and gay men.

have to prove that they have suffered severe psychological damage. Employers can now be held responsible for any actions that create or allow a workplace environment that a reasonable person would perceive as hostile. Specific actions that could create a hostile workplace include a pattern of threatening, intimidating, or hostile acts and remarks; negative sexual stereotyping; and the display of degrading materials.

Ignoring the problem of sexual harassment can be an expensive proposition for employers. The total damages paid for the 15,342 EEOC cases filed in 1996 totaled $27.8 million. This figure does not include jury awards such as the recent $80.7 million award given to a United Parcel Service manager who said the company retaliated against her after she accused a driver of poking her in the breast ("UPS," 1998). Nor does it include costs linked to absenteeism, low productivity, and employee turnover. Although stricter enforcement of equal employment laws will help to reduce cases of harassment, sexual harassment will not be eradicated until societies move to an acceptance of a more egalitarian conceptualization of gender-role ideology which then becomes an essential part of the functioning of their economic, political, and social institutions.

Gender Inequality in the Twenty-First Century

As the twentieth century draws to a close, it is clear that the status of women has improved in many ways both in the United States and around the world. Nevertheless, nowhere on earth can it be said that women and men are truly equal in terms of their access to power, prestige, and property. Besides the continuing problems of job seg-regation, pay inequity, and sexual harassment, millions of women around the world contend daily with many restrictions on their movement, public presence, dress, and public and private behavior. For example, the seclusion of women is an accepted practice among some ethnic and religious groups in countries such as Morocco, Tunisia, Saudi Arabia, Iran, Afghanistan, Pakistan, and India. In Saudi Arabia, women are not allowed to drive cars; in Qatar, to do so they need permission from a male relative. Women who want to obtain a passport or to travel abroad must first have permission from their father, husband, or male guardian in a number of African and Middle Eastern countries. In the Sudan, Saudi Arabia, Iran, and Afghanistan, there are compulsory government-mandated dress codes for women. Attacks on women for "immodest" dress have been reported in some of these countries as well as in Algeria, Nigeria, and Pakistan (cited in Seager, 1997).

Many of these practices originated in fundamentalist interpretations of religious doctrines. As we will see in Chapter 13, the influence of fundamentalism in most of the world's major religions is on the increase, and many people fear that this will lead to more legal and social restrictions for women. At the same time, however, a growing number of social critics, religious authorities, and feminists are challenging these interpretations as misrepresentations of religious teachings and offering alternative interpretations that suggest a more egalitarian treatment for women. This struggle will continue well into the next century and will, by its nature, raise questions about human rights abuses and political repression of men as well.

Gender inequality is only one of the many conditions that will challenge societies in the decades ahead. Many societies are aging and must find creative ways to meet the needs of their elderly members.

AGENT OF CHANGE: MAGGIE KUHN

In 1970, at the age of sixty-five, Maggie Kuhn was told by her superiors that it was time for her to retire. Kuhn was an executive in the national office of the Presbyterian Church, and the church, like most employers in the United States at that time, had a policy of mandatory retirement at age sixty-five. Kuhn had no desire to retire. She met with four friends who shared similar concerns: They objected to the practice of mandatory retirement as well as to the condescending way older people were viewed and treated in society. They were critical of the media's portrayals of the elderly as unproductive, sexless, and senile, portrayals which they argued encouraged younger people to fear growing old and the elderly to withdraw from meaningful social lives. They advocated acknowledgment of the capabilities and contributions the elderly make to society as well as the

creation of more opportunities for meaningfully productive roles for the elderly, both in and out of retirement. They also believed that the young and old shared common goals, among them opposing the Vietnam War. So they called a public meeting in New York City to discuss these issues; over one hundred people showed up. This meeting represented the birth of a seniors' rights organization known as the Gray Panthers. Today, the organization has over 40,000 members in thirty-two states and six countries and continues to have an intergenerational focus.

Kuhn believed that **ageism**—a term coined by Robert Butler (1975), the former director of the National Institute of Aging, to describe age stereotypes and the discriminatory treatment applied to the elderly—was as fundamental and poisonous a force as racism and sexism and needed to be fought just as vigorously. The Gray

Panthers used grassroots tactics that included marches on Washington, picketing, writing letters, lobbying legislators, and public town meetings to attract attention to their cause and to fight against mandatory retirement and age discrimination. Their efforts paid off with the passage of the 1978 and 1986 amendments to the

Age Discrimination in Employment Act, which prohibited the use of age as a criterion for hiring, firing, and discriminatory treatment on the job.

Source: Information from various sources, among them "Maggie Kuhn, One of the Founders of the Gray Panthers." 1995. *Chicago Tribune,* April 23: 6; Bruce Shapiro. 1995. "Corliss and Maggie," *The Nation,* 260, 21 (May 29): 744.

Aging and Society

Although today's Maggie Kuhns cannot be forced out of their jobs by a policy of mandatory retirement, the reality is that many employers still find ways to get rid of older workers who would like to continue working, especially higher-paid workers or those who are close to earning handsome retirement benefits. Despite laws against age discrimination in employment, employers have devised a number of tactics—such as unnecessary shift changes, requiring additional work without additional pay, or demotion to a lower position—that essentially force older employees to quit. Aided by a recent Supreme Court decision, employers can now argue that layoffs of older workers are economically necessary to keep a company competitive. And employers may offer incentives for some workers to take early retirement. The economic value of these early retirement packages vary tremendously, providing a secure future for some but offering little more than a subsistence level of income for others. It is often difficult for displaced older workers who need or want to work to find reemployment, in large part due to the erroneous belief that older workers are less productive than younger workers.

Conversely, however, many older workers look forward to retirement, seeing it as a just reward entitlement for their years of productive activity. The current trend in the United States is for workers to retire before age sixty-five: the average age of retirement in the United States is 63.5 years. Workers in many other industrialized countries are also retiring at earlier ages: the av-erage retirement age in Austria is 59.9, in Japan it is 61.5, in Germany 61.4, and in France 62.4 (Kristof, 1996).

Social gerontology, the study of the impact of sociocultural conditions on the process and consequences of aging, shows us that aging is not one process but many, with a diverse range of positive and negative outcomes. Throughout the remainder of this chapter, we will examine the differing realities of the elderly in the United States. This approach requires that we balance the strengths and satisfactions of the elderly with the real problems many of them confront on a daily basis and that we recognize the impact that the interaction of race, class, and gender has on the experience of aging.

The Graying of America and the World

As Figure 11.4 indicates, the composition of the population of the United States is changing dramatically. In 1900, only 3.1 million people in the United States were aged sixty-five or over. By 1996, this age group accounted for approximately 34 million people. By 2040, the number of elderly is expected to climb to more than 67 million people. Between 1900 and 1996, the percentage of Americans aged sixty-five and over has more than tripled (from 4.1 percent to 12.8 percent). Additionally, the elderly population itself is getting older. In 1996, the sixty-five to seventy-four age group (18.7 million people) was eight times larger than in 1900, but the seventy-

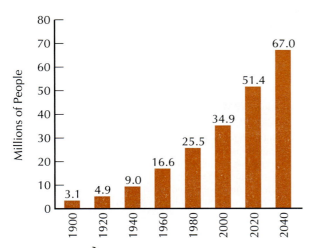

FIGURE 11.4 ☉ **Number of Persons in the United States Aged 65 and Over, 1900 to 2040** *Source:* U.S. Bureau of the Census. 1993. *Population Projections of the United States.* Washington, DC: U.S. Government Printing Office.

ters provides some insight into what it is like to reach this milestone (see the Sociology through Literature box).

It is not just that individuals are getting older; societies are aging as well. Due to low birth rates and increased longevity, the median age of U.S. society has changed dramatically in the past 150 years (Figure 11.5). In 1850, the median age was 18.9 years ("the median age" means that half the population was younger than that age and half the population older). In 1997, the median age was 34.9. By 2050, it is projected that it will be 38.1.

One of the consequences of this changing age structure is an increase in the **old-age dependency ratio,** the ratio of elderly people to working-age adults. In 1990, there were 22.3 retirement-age people for every 100 working adults. This number is expected to rise to 35.1 by the year 2025 (Kristof, 1996). The United States, like many other industrialized countries, established old-age insurance for its elderly citizens, paid for out of the taxes of current workers. This intergenerational transfer system which funds the Social Security system worked relatively well for the last sixty years or so. However, many analysts fear that as the ratio of retirees to workers increases, the system may collapse. Polls of young adults show that many believe that Social Security will not be there for them when they retire. The debate over Social

five to eighty-four age group (11.4 million people) was sixteen times larger and the eighty-five or older group (3.8 million people) was thirty-one times larger. Already, 57,000 Americans are one hundred years of age or older (U.S. Bureau of the Census, 1997). The story of the Delany sis-

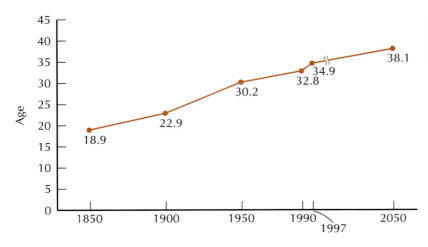

FIGURE 11.5 ☉ **Median Age of the U.S. Population, 1850 to 1996, and Projections to 2050** *Source:* Adapted from U.S. Bureau of the Census. 1998. *Statistical Abstract of the United States, 1996.* Washington, DC: U.S. Government Printing Office, Table 13, p. 14.

Sociology through Literature

Having Our Say

In *Having Our Say,* the Delany sisters, Bessie (age 101) and Sadie (age 103), recall their experiences growing up with eight other siblings. Their father was born in slavery yet became the nation's first elected black Episcopal bishop. They experienced their first days of Jim Crow and legal segregation in North Carolina, but they later migrated to Harlem during World War I. Both sisters favored careers over marriage—Bessie became a dentist and Sadie a high school teacher. In the following excerpt, Bessie reflects on growing old.

Tell you the truth, I wouldn't be here without sister Sadie. We are companions. But I'll tell you something else: Sadie has taken on this business of getting old like it's a big *project.* She has it all figured out, about diet and exercise. Sometimes, I just don't want to do it, but she is my big sister and I really don't want to disappoint her. Funny thing about Sadie is she rarely gets—what's the word?—depressed. She is an easygoing type of gal.

Now, honey, I get the blues sometimes. It's a shock to me, to be this old. Sometimes, when I realize I am 101 years old, it hits me right between the eyes. I say, "Oh Lord, how did this happen?" Turning one hundred was the worst birthday of my life. I wouldn't wish it on my worst enemy. Turning 101 was not so bad. Once you're past that century mark, it's just not as shocking.

There's a few things I have had to give up. I gave up driving a while back. I guess I was in my late eighties. That was terrible. Another thing I gave up on was cutting back my trees so we have a view of the New York City skyline to the south. Until I was ninety-eight years old, I would climb up on the ladder and saw those tree branches off so we had a view. I could do it perfectly well; why pay somebody to do it? Then Sadie talked some sense into me, and I gave up doing it.

Some days I feel as old as Moses and other days I feel like a young girl. I tell you what: I have only a little bit of arthritis in my pinky finger, and my eyes aren't bad, so I know I could still be practicing dentistry. Yes, I am sure I could still do it.

But it's hard being old, because you can't always do everything you want, exactly as *you* want it done. When you get as old as we are, you have to struggle to hang onto your freedom, your independence. We have a lot of family and friends keeping an eye on us, but we try not to be dependent on any one person. We try to pay people, even relatives, for whatever they buy for us, and for gasoline for their car, things like that, so that we do not feel beholden to them. . . .

Truth is, I never thought I'd see the day when people would be interested in hearing what two old Negro women have to say. Life still surprises me. So maybe the last laugh's on *me.*

I'll tell you a little secret: I'm starting to get optimistic. I'm thinking: *Maybe I'll get into Heaven after all.* Why, I've helped a lot of folks—even some white folks! I surely do have some redeeming qualities that must count for something. So I just might do it: I just might get into Heaven. I may have to hang on to Sadie's heels, but I'll get there.

Sadie died on January 25, 1999, at age 109; her sister Bessie died in 1995. She was 105.

Do you want to live to be one hundred? Why or why not? What lessons can we learn from Bessie about growing old? What are some of the challenges and adjustments we face as we grow older? Reflecting on Bessie's life, what actions can people take in their younger years to prepare themselves for successful aging?

Source: Reprinted with permission from *Having Our Say* by Sarah L. and A. Elizabeth Delany and Amy Hill Hearth, published by Kodansha America, Inc., pp. 207–210. Copyright © 1993 by Amy Hill Hearth, Sarah Louise Delany, and Annie Elizabeth Delany.

Security raises the specter of future intergenerational conflict. To avert this potential conflict, public officials are proposing ways to strengthen Social Security as well as to ease the burden on the working population. Some of the suggestions currently being considered are raising the age of eligibility, which would probably have the effect of requiring people to work longer; cutting benefits; and, the most controversial, privatizing all or part of the pension system.

The United States is not the only country that has a growing elderly population. As we can see in Figure 11.6, some industrialized countries have even higher percentages of elderly than the United States, and they are struggling with similar old-age dependency ratio problems. Of perhaps even greater impact is the finding that the greatest growth in the elderly population is taking place in developing countries, particularly those in Asia and Africa where societal resources are more limited (Hobbs, 1996).

Changing Age Norms

All societies develop specific **age norms,** expectations and guidelines about what people in a given life stage are allowed to do and to be as well as what they are required to do and to be. Like other norms, these are socially defined and vary from one culture to the next. Some norms apply very generally to items of dress, personal appearance, or demeanor across a variety of social roles. For example, older people are sometimes ridiculed or admonished "to dress their age" if they are perceived to be adopting styles that are perceived as too youthful for them. Other age norms regulate the entry into, incumbency in, and exit from social roles, such as the "appropriate" ages at which to marry, start a job, and retire.

Some age norms make good sense. For example, driving an automobile requires a degree of skill and maturity that is generally not found in ten- and twelve-year-olds, and we know that divorce rates are higher among those still in their teen years than among older adults. However, the assumptions underlying many age norms are often based on stereotyped images of what people at various ages are capable of doing rather than on empirically established facts. Consequently, these norms and their underlying assumptions often limit opportunities for people at both ends of the age structure. For example, children are often told that they are too young to make decisions for themselves without regard for their individual level of maturity and older workers are often bypassed when it comes to promotions or training opportunities on the assumption that "you can't teach an old dog new tricks."

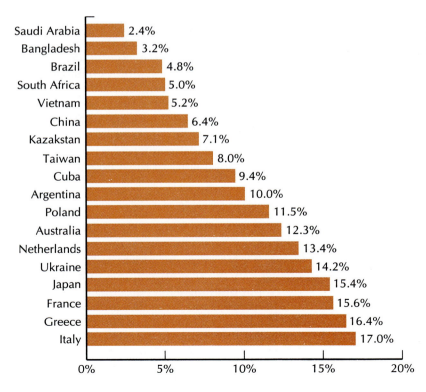

FIGURE 11.6 ○ **Percentage of the Population 65 and Over in Select Countries, 1997** *Source:* Adapted from U.S. Bureau of the Census, 1997. *Statistical Abstract of the United States, 1997.* Washington, DC: U.S. Government Printing Office, Table 1335, p. 832.

Reaching one's 100th birthday is no longer a rare event. Jeanne Calment looks at her birthday cake as she celebrates her 121st birthday at her retirement home in Arles, France. In 1996 Calment was identified as the world's oldest person according to verifiable birth records.

Over the last several decades, the growing numbers and diversity of the elderly population have become more visible and, as a consequence, age norms are showing signs of being less restrictive than in the past. For example, three decades ago, the typical college class was composed of students between the ages of eighteen and twenty-two, and these students were expected to graduate in four years. Today's college classrooms are populated with people of all ages and they may take four, five, or even eight years or more to earn their degrees. In the past, many universities, especially at the graduate level, made a practice of not accepting applicants if they were over thirty years of age based on the assumption that they would have too few productive years left to warrant the investment made in

them. As we discussed earlier, in the 1960s and 1970s, people typically retired at sixty-five whether they wanted to or not. In contrast, a number of today's elderly are starting new careers at the age of seventy, while younger adults are opting or being induced to retire at age fifty-five.

Applying the Sociological Imagination

What is your attitude toward aging and growing old? Do you see it as primarily a positive or a negative experience? Explain. How is your life likely to be affected by having aging relatives? Interview several persons who are sixty-five or older and ask them about their experiences of aging. Have they experienced constraints on their behavior because of age norms? What advantages and disadvantages have they encountered (or do they expect to encounter) because of their age? Are their experiences similar to or different from each other?

America's Elderly

Earlier, we pointed out that not everyone experiences aging in the same way. Part of what contributes to the multifaceted experiences of aging is that the aged do not constitute a homogeneous population. In this section, we will examine the diversity of this segment of the U.S. population; after that, we will explore some of the ways in which the social constructs of race, class, gender, and marital status interact with age to produce different quality of life outcomes.

Race and Ethnicity

Table 11.4 presents some of the projections made by the U.S. Census Bureau for the years 1995 and 2050. They reveal an interesting pattern of changes in the overall composition of the elderly population. The percentage of elderly whites is projected to decline from 85.0 percent in 1995 to only 67 percent in 2050; correspondingly, the percentage of elderly people of color is expected to increase from 15 percent in 1995

TABLE 11.4 ⓞ **Projections for Population Aged 65 and Over by Race/Ethnicity, 1995 and 2050**

	1995	2050
Native Americans/Eskimo/Aleut	0.4%	0.6%
Asian/Pacific Islander	2.0%	7.0%
Black	8.0%	10.0%
Latina/o origin	5.0%	16.0%
Non-Latina/o white	85.0%	67.0%

Source: U.S. Bureau of the Census. 1993. *Current Population Reports* (Series P-25-1104). Washington, DC: U.S. Government Printing Office, Table 2.

to approximately 34 percent in 2050. Although all groups will experience change, the highest growth rate is expected to be among Latinas/os. By 2050, one in six elderly likely will be Latina/o. The higher fertility and immigrant rates among Latinas/os in recent years account for these projected changes, which have social policy implications. Because elderly people of color tend to be disadvantaged in the labor market earlier in their lives, they are less likely to save enough money to carry them through their retirement years. This means that we can anticipate a fairly large increase in the number of elderly who will require economic support in the next century.

Gender and Marital Status

Gerontologists often refer to aging as a primarily female experience because elderly women, especially those in the oldest category, significantly outnumber elderly men. In 1997, the **sex ratio** (the number of males for every one hundred females) was 69.8 for those sixty-five years and over (U.S. Bureau of the Census, 1998). Among those eighty-five and older, the sex ratio is even more lopsided. It is projected that in the year 2000, there will be only 38 males per 100 females in that age category (Atchley, 1997). This pattern developed relatively recently with the decline in female deaths connected with pregnancy, childbirth, and infections beginning in

the 1930s. Although scientific research has yet to unravel all of the reasons for the gender difference in mortality rates today, it is likely that it is a combination of genetic and socioenvironmental factors.

Longevity for women has a double edge. On the one hand, it provides more time to accomplish life's goals. On the other hand, it often means living alone on dwindling resources. In 1996, 42.6 percent of women aged sixty-five and over were married, as compared to 75.6 percent of their male counterparts. Gender differences in survivorship rates are significant because older women across all racial and ethnic groups have fewer financial resources and are more likely to experience poverty in old age than are elderly men. In the first section of this chapter, we examined some of the gender inequities that exist in the labor market. Women, regardless of race or ethnicity, when compared to men, earn less money, are segregated into less prestigious jobs, and are more likely to work part time and to have their work life interrupted by child rearing. Consequently, women have less access than men to pension plans and receive fewer benefits when they do have access.

Aging and Poverty: Intersections of Race, Ethnicity, and Gender

In the 1960s, Americans were shocked to learn that 35 percent of the elderly lived in poverty and that 80 percent of the elderly survived solely on Social Security (Atchley, 1997). Clearly, the post–World War II prosperity was not shared by all. In subsequent years, however, activist social movements raised the nation's consciousness about numerous social injustices, including the plight of the elderly. Under the leadership of President Lyndon Johnson, the nation declared a War on Poverty. In 1965, Congress passed the **Older Americans Act,** which established an Administration on Aging as part of the Department of Health, Education, and Welfare (the name was later changed to the Department of Health and Human Services). That same year, the Social Security Act was amended to establish Medicare to provide financing for health services for the elderly. Two years later, Congress passed the Age Discrimination Employment Act, which, as

TABLE 11.5 ☉ Median Incomes for Persons Aged 65 and Over

	Median Income
White males	$15,276
White females	8,579
Black males	8,031
Black females	6,220
Latinos	9,253
Latinas	5,968

Source: Hobbs, F.V.B. 1996. *65+ in the United States.* Washington, DC: U.S. Government Printing Office.

you will remember, prohibited the use of age as a criterion for hiring, firing, and discriminatory treatment on the job. Other legislation aimed at improving conditions for the elderly followed in the 1970s.

By 1980, however, there was a more conservative mood in the country, and many social-welfare programs were reduced or eliminated during the Reagan and Bush administrations. Nevertheless, the programs that benefitted the elderly remained largely in place, and there were even some new additions. For example, Social Security benefits were improved by providing for increases in the cost of living. Many companies instituted private pension plans, which have provided workers with additional retirement income. Businesses instituted discount programs for senior citizens regardless of economic need. Attempts to reduce or eliminate these programs have been resisted by effective political lobbying by groups such as the American Association of Retired Persons (AARP), which has 32 million members.

The net effect of all these programs can be seen in current statistics. By 1997, poverty rates for the elderly had fallen to 10.5 percent. However, all groups did not benefit from these programs in the same way. The poverty rate for elderly whites is only 9.4 percent, but it is 25.3 percent for elderly blacks and 24.4 percent for el-

derly Latinos/as (U.S. Bureau of the Census, 1998). Poverty rates are even higher among people who are seventy-five years of age or older across all race and ethnic groups and among women. About 2.7 million, or 15.7 percent, of noninstitutionalized women aged sixty-five or older live below the poverty threshold, compared with only 7.6 percent of elderly men (Task Force on Aging Research, 1995). Thus, although a smaller proportion of the elderly are poor today than in the past, poverty remains a problem for millions of elderly, especially for the oldest-old.

How can we account for these economic differences? As we saw in Chapter 9, one's life chances are in large measure, dependent on social class position. As we can see in Table 11.5, women and people of color have fewer economic resources in old age than do white males. This is not surprising given the disadvantages they faced in the labor market in earlier years: low-paying jobs, longer and more frequent unemployment, and racial discrimination. As we indicated earlier, this, in turn, generally means fewer health insurance or Social Security benefits or supplementary retirement incomes from private pensions. Meeting the needs of the growing numbers of the elderly without engendering intergenerational conflict will be a major challenge for decades to come.

Sociological Explanations of the Aging Process

Sociologists have developed a number of theories to explain the aging process, ranging from a microlevel analysis of the ways in which individuals adapt to changing roles to a macrolevel analysis of the inequalities resulting from age-based stratification.

Structural Functionalism

One of the earliest theories on aging emerged from structural functionalism and came to be known as **disengagement theory,** the view that as people age, they gradually withdraw from specific roles and activities and simultaneously are relieved of social responsibilities (Cumming & Henry, 1961). Such a withdrawal is seen as functional for both the individual and society. For example, retirement allows the elderly to concentrate their energies on themselves while providing employment opportunities for the next generation. The major criticism of this theory is its failure to recognize the diversity of the aging population and its implied assumption that older people should be encouraged to withdraw from meaningful social roles. Although some elderly people are happy to relinquish social roles, others are not. Elderly people who get satisfaction from their work and community roles often want to continue them, at least in some capacity. Losing these roles may have negative effects—loss of self-esteem, loneliness, and poor health. Similarly, society may suffer if its most experienced workers and community leaders are forced to leave these roles prematurely.

Symbolic Interactionism

In contrast to the structural focus of disengagement theory, symbolic interactionists examine the meanings and values that the elderly attach to their social roles, and they see a relationship between meaningful social activity and a high quality of life. **Activity theory** takes the view that the more active and involved older people are, the more likely they are to experience life satisfaction. Proponents of activity theory argue that it is healthy for people to continue their middle-adulthood roles through late adulthood or to take up new ones to replace those that are lost. This view seems to be supported by research that shows that elderly people who are involved in desired roles and activities report higher levels of life satisfaction than do disengaged individuals (Idler & Kasl, 1992). However, although activity theory recognizes the diversity of the elderly population, it ignores the fact that some elderly are blocked from actively participating in society because of structural constraints such as ageism and poverty.

Conflict Theory

Like symbolic interactionists, conflict theorists recognize the diversity in the elderly population, noting that race, class, and gender differences affect the elderly in much the same way that they affect younger generations. Thus, for example, the wealthy elderly enjoy better medical care and greater security, status, and opportunities for personal satisfaction than do their poorer counterparts. At the same time, however, conflict theorists call attention to the prejudice and discrimination that many elderly people experience in capitalist societies. For example, older workers generally earn more than younger workers and cost more in benefits such as health and life insurance, thus, employers may be motivated to push them out before they are ready to retire. Conflict theorists also call attention to the fact that the elderly are often targets for abuse and perceived as easy prey by scam artists. Conflict theory has been criticized for emphasizing only the ways in which capitalist societies devalue older people and ignoring the ways in which capitalist societies have enhanced the quality of life for their elderly members.

Aging in the Twenty-First Century

Beginning in 2011, the first of the baby boomers will turn sixty-five. This development portends great opportunities as well as difficult challenges for the nation as a whole. First, its sheer numbers alone will focus attention on the problems faced by this age cohort. Many of the baby boomers are better educated and wealthier than was the case in previous generations, and they have already demonstrated their considerable political clout. Their active involvement in the civil rights and women's movements of the 1960s and 1970s helped to change the U.S. landscape. Their anti–Vietnam War protests effectively removed Lyndon Johnson from the 1968 presidential race and ultimately forced the government to end the war. Given its past history, it is unlikely that this generation will take a passive role if it feels that its welfare is being threatened by cuts in Social Security benefits, Medicare, or other programs to which it feels some degree of entitlement. Many in this generation will remain active economically and politically, thus altering the attitudes and normative expectations about aging in a more positive direction.

All this notwithstanding, however, there will be another side to aging in the twenty-first century which will not be as positive. For example, the increased numbers of elderly will put greater pressure on the already beleaguered Social Security and health care systems. According to the U.S. Bureau of Census (1998), over nearly 16 percent of the population (41.7 million Americans) are without health insurance coverage. Although there is relatively little difference between females (14.2 percent) and males (17.1 percent), there is a wide gap between whites (14.1 percent) and people of color (21.7 percent for African Americans and 33.6 percent for Latinas/os). If unchanged, these patterns will contribute to the creation of two very distinct groups of future elderly: those who are vital and healthy as a result of their access to high-quality health care and those who are ill or disabled because of their history of inadequate care (Conner, 1992). Policy analysts argue that keeping future health care costs in check requires investing more dollars in wellness programs today, a strategy that is sorely lacking in many parts of the country. In addition, many of tomorrow's elderly—especially today's women, children, and people of color—are already living in poverty. Without intervention programs in education and job-training today that will lead to better pay and pension plans tomorrow, the number of people entering old age who will require financial assistance just to survive will greatly increase, putting a severe strain on the nation's budget.

Last, but not least, the kinship structure for many families now and in the foreseeable future will contain more elderly than younger members. Thus, it is unlikely that the nation will be able to continue to count on the informal support and care giving of family and friends to take care of many of the needs of the elderly. Rather, it will have to move to a more formal care giving system (for example, adult day care, visiting nurses, housekeeping services) or some combination of the two. This process may be mediated, however, if our society comes to recognize the tremendous reservoir of skills and abilities that exist among the elderly. For example, some public schools and universities, already recognizing this fact, have initiated intergenerational partners projects in which the elderly serve as tutors and teachers' aides (Aday, Rice, & Evans, 1991). Other programs already underway involve the elderly as "foster" grandparents and as business, craft, and hobby mentors. In the future, increasing numbers of the elderly could be encouraged to use their talents for the social good through either paid employment or various forms of volunteer work.

Key Points to Remember

1. Gender stratification refers to the unequal distribution of a society's wealth, power, and privilege between females and males.

2. Although *sex* and *gender* are often used interchangeably, they refer to quite different attributes. *Sex* refers only to the biological characteristics that differentiate females from males. *Gender* refers to the socially constructed cluster of behavioral patterns and personality traits that are associated with being female or male, what we commonly call femininity and masculinity. Gender roles are the behavioral expectations that society has for its female and male members.

3. Women have always worked, but they were not always counted in the labor force because much of their work was done in the home and was unrecognized and unpaid. Women now constitute 46 percent of all workers in the United States, up from 18 percent in 1900.

4. The workplace is characterized by occupational segregation and occupational concentration. In effect, this means that women are heavily concentrated in low-paying clerical or service jobs. Despite some recent improvements and regardless of how earnings are measured, women's wages are below those received by men, regardless of race, ethnicity, or country. Two theories

have been used to explain gender inequities: human capital theory and gender discrimination theory.

5. Although women earn more bachelor's and master's degrees than men do, the U.S. educational system contains many forms of gender discrimination in terms of teacher–student interactions, the allocation of tasks, and the use of physical space as well as biases in curricular materials. Research has shown that the use of sex-equitable materials helps student to develop more flexible gender role attitudes and to make more informed career choices.

6. Around the globe, women are underrepresented in the political structures of their country. The vast majority of women did not win the right to vote until the mid- and latter part of the twentieth century. The fact that women generally occupy lower status positions, have less power in decision making, and are paid less than their male counterparts leaves them particularly vulnerable to sexual harassment.

7. The United States is an aging society; the number of elderly is projected to reach 70 million by the year 2040, putting pressure on Social Security and health care programs. With the increased longevity and visibility of the elderly, many age norms show signs of being less restrictive than in the past.

8. The elderly are a heterogeneous group that experiences the aging process in a variety of ways. Elderly women and elderly people of color are overrepresented in the ranks of the poor because of earlier experiences of discrimination and gender inequities. Disengagement theory, activity theory, and conflict theory have contributed to our understanding of the experience of aging.

Key Terms

gender stratification
sex
gender
gender roles
labor force participation rate
occupational segregation
occupational concentration

human capital theory
statistical discrimination
sexual harassment
ageism
Age Discrimination in Employment Act
social gerontology

old-age dependency ratio
age norms
sex ratio
Older Americans Act
disengagement theory
activity theory

Key People

Karen Nussbaum
Margaret Mead

Maggie Kuhn

Robert Butler

Questions for Review and Discussion

1. Assume that you are asked to give a presentation on the social construction of gender to a high school class. How would you go about defining that concept? What are the

implications of seeing gender this way? What evidence would you offer to support your position? How can this concept be used to end some of the gender inequities that exist in the United States and around the world?

2. How do you explain the increased female labor-force participation rates in the United States and around the globe? Why hasn't women's entrance into the labor force put them on a more equal footing with men in their societies? Which theoretical perspective do you find the most useful in explaining gender inequities in the workplace?

3. What is sexual harassment? How would you respond to someone who says that alleged vic-tims of sexual harassment are being too sensi-tive? Why don't more victims report being sexually harassed? What can employers and workers do to minimize the possibility of sexual harassment?

4. What is ageism? Why does it occur? Have you observed any indicators of ageism in your family, neighborhood, or community? Should there be age norms in a society? If so, what should they be? If not, which of the current age norms that operate in our society would you eliminate? Do you think there is a possibility of intergenerational conflict in the future? Explain.

For Further Reading

Bank, Barbara J., and Peter M. Hall. (Eds.). 1997. *Gender, Equity, and Schooling: Policy and Practice.* New York: Garland. This volume takes on the tough questions of how to define and obtain gender equity in the next century.

Dunn, Dana. 1997. *Workplace/Women's Place.* Los Angeles: Roxbury. The articles in this anthology offer an interdisciplinary and insightful look at the important trends in women's lives and provides both quantitative and qualitative evidence to explain these trends.

Friedan, Betty. 1993. *The Fountain of Age.* New York: Simon & Schuster. Friedan contrasts the stereotypical images of aging and the elderly and the reality of vital elderly people whose lives contradict the expectations of decline and loss so often associated with the aging process.

Stoller, Eleanor Palo, and Rose Campbell Gibson. 1997. *Worlds of Difference: Inequality in the Aging Experience.* Thousand Oaks, CA: Pine Forge Press. The introductory essays, short stories, and poetry bring the aging experience of women and people of color into sharp focus.

Sociology through Literature

Kidder, Tracy. 1993. *Old Friends.* Boston: Houghton Mifflin. Two male residents of a nursing home become friends as they struggle to reconcile their personal histories and confront the last stage of their lives.

Piercy, Marge. 1976. *Woman on the Edge of Time.* New York: Fawcett Crest. Piercy takes you on a wondrous journey with Connie as she tries to fight her way out of a mental hospital, where she is being held against her will, and into a future that holds promise.

Internet Resources

http://www.now.org/issues/wfw/ The National Organization for Women (NOW) is a grassroots political action organization; its Web site provides information on sexual harassment.

http://www.dol.gov/dol/wh/ The Women's Bureau is an agency within the Department of Labor. This Web site provides access to press releases and special reports related to women's issues in the workplace.

http://www.aarp.org/ This is the homepage for the American Association of Retired Persons and offers information about issues affecting older people as well as on the benefits of membership in the AARP.

http://www.aoa.dhhs.gov The Administration on Aging's Web page includes information about AoA, the aging network, and the Older Americans Act programs and statistical information on aging.

12

Marriages and Families: Intimacy in Social Life

AGENT OF CHANGE: ANDREW VACHSS

Andrew Vachss is a lawyer whose only clients are children and youth. His practice encompasses everything from defending children accused of crimes to representing children who are crime victims as well as everything in between—civil litigation, adoptions, and representing children who are the battlegrounds in divorces. Vachss is one of the few—if not the only—lawyers in private practice whose clients are exclusively children and youth. He also writes novels as an extension of his work, hoping to reach a larger jury than any courthouse could offer.

While Vachss was a director of a prison for violent youth, he decided to go to law school and represent children exclusively. Since that time, he has become a leading authority on child abuse and an outspoken advocate for its victims. Child abuse cases constitute the majority of his work, which he often does free of charge or at one-eighth of what the average lawyer gets for a case.

When asked why he has dedicated himself to fighting child abuse, Vachss says that there are two things that people can do with their lives: spend their time in introspection or spend their time *doing something*. For Vachss, the question is not why is he but instead why aren't others doing something.

On the topic of the family and family rights, Vachss says that he is totally opposed to family being defined by biology. For him, families should be defined operationally. For example, in the case of abused children, efforts at family preservation should be made, but, if they fail, children should have the opportunity to be raised by a "real" family that provides care and support rather than by a biological one that doesn't.

Andrew Vachss's advocacy and activism on behalf of children force us to take a hard look at how we think of and treat children in U.S. society. On the one hand, we claim that children are our most valuable resource. However, we often don't treat them that way. Clearly, issues surrounding the welfare of children within families has become highly politicized as different groups compete with each other over who is most pro-children. For example, during the 1996 presidential elections, the Democratic platform included the following stance on "Stronger Families": "The first and most sacred responsibility of every parent is to cherish our children and strengthen our families. The family is the foundation of American life." On the other hand, cases of child abuse (at least reports of it) have increased dramatically over the past twenty years. Common reports of child abuse claim that one out of every four children in the United States today will have been sexually abused by the age of eighteen. The issue of child abuse raises a series of important questions about families and their roles in socializing and protecting the young. In addition, it also raises important public policy issues. These issues are related to issues of power and control and the ability of individuals and institutions to exert their will over others. Power gives one the leverage not only over the behavior of others but also to set public policy based on a particular set of beliefs, which in turn impacts the ways in which various individuals are treated. If the family is the foundation of American life, what is happening to that foundation?

Source: Information from the following four sources, all available at Andrew Vachss's Web site, http://www.vachss.com. Vachss, A. 1998. "A Hard Look at How We Treat Children." *Parade* (March 29); "Voices for Children: Andrew Vachss." 1997. *Children's Voice,* 6, no. 2; Layman, Richard. 1990. "Perspective: Attacking the Problem." *Current Issues, 1: Child Abuse;* Luker, K. 1992. "Avenger of the Abused Child." *Sober Times* (September).

Contrasting Views of Families

It seems that almost everyone today has an opinion of what is happening to marriages and families in modern society. People—ranging from politicians, Sunday morning evangelists, radio call-in show hosts and audiences, and an array of social scientists—suggest either that the family is crumbling under the weight of a loss of family values or that it is simply changing to reflect the increasing diversity of contemporary life. Some proclaim that the restoration of family values and the two-parent family will restore the foundation of U.S. society. Others argue that "family values" means "valuing families," appreciating their contributions regardless of their structure and form (see for example, Skolnick & Rosencrantz, 1994).

Many people who believe that marriages and families are in grave danger today feel that the tradition of human family life is being replaced by an alien and destructive set of relationships that is tearing at the very heart of U.S. society. These critics of the modern family deplore the increasingly violent nature of families. They contend that individuals are more sexually promiscuous than in the past, as evidenced by the increase in sexual activity among nonmarried people and the high rate of teenage pregnancy. They argue that family values and morals are collapsing, as evidenced in the visibility of lesbian and gay lifestyles, the high rate of welfare dependency, the high divorce rate, and the growing number of public disclosures of sexual, emotional, and physical abuse of children in families. Certain trends, such as the tendency to delay marriage, the growth in the number of people not marrying at all, and the alleged popularity of extramarital relationships, are viewed as signs of a general disregard for marriage. Consequently, people who hold this point of view typically embrace themes that call for a "return to family values," by which they mean a return to a "traditional family structure" and a set of values that supposedly characterized the lives of earlier generations. They believe that this structure was more virtuous and harmonious than the family structures that exist today.

A contrasting point of view is that current events and trends in marriage and family life are indicative of the redefinition of marriages and families in the context of changing social, economic, and political circumstances in U.S. society. Those who take this perspective on modern marriages and families are equally concerned about the problems of modern families. Although they concede that marriages and families are experiencing some problems, they argue that marriage and family life are still extremely important to most people in the United States. They cite census data that indicate that the United States has perhaps the highest marriage rate in the world. Although young people may delay marriage, almost everyone gets married—at least once. In 1997, 93 percent of women and 91 percent of men ages forty-five to fifty-four either were currently or had been married (U.S. Bureau of Census, 1998). And although the United States has one of the highest divorce rates in the world, the overwhelming majority of divorced people remarry. Furthermore, various survey results report that most people in the United States hold the family in high regard and report high levels of satisfaction with their own family lives. Those who hold this point of view refute the idealized version of families of the past and give us instead a picture of a traditional family that was often rigid and oppressive. They remind us that traditional families were often based on a clear division of labor along age and gender lines that often resulted in a very restrictive life, especially for women and children. They also question the premise that family values and traditional family structure are one and the same and that both are synonymous with stability (Schwartz & Scott, 1997).

According to family historian Stephanie Coontz (1995, 1998), families face serious problems today, but proposals to solve them by romanticizing "traditional" family forms, values, and gender roles and calling for their revival will not enable families to develop moral and ethical systems relevant to 1990s realities. Calls for the revival of the traditional family miss two points. First, no single traditional family existed to which we could return, and none of the many varieties of families in our past has had any magic formula for protecting its members from the negative impact of socioeconomic change; the inequities related to race, class, and gender; or the consequences of interpersonal conflict. Violence, child abuse, poverty, and the unequal distribution of resources to women and children have occurred in every historical period and every type of family. Second, the strengths found among many families of the past were rooted in socioeconomic and cultural circumstances different from those that exist today.

Marriages and Families: Basic Concepts

Marriage and family are among the oldest human social institutions. The family, and marriage as a process that generates it, exists in some form in all societies and is created by human beings in an attempt to meet certain basic individual and social needs such as survival and growth. Implicit in Andrew Vachss's suggestion that we define families operationally is the notion that family is a social as well as a biological unit. Many sociologists today argue that the family is socially constructed—that is, it is defined distinctively in different cultures and historical time periods. Thus, the meaning of family and its social functions vary across cultures and time periods (Gittins, 1998). Accordingly, we define **family** as any relatively stable group of people who are related to one another through blood, marriage, or adoption or who simply live together and who provide one another with economic and emotional support. In addition, a family can be a group of people who define themselves as family based on feelings of love, respect, commitment, and responsibility to and identification with one another. This concept of family has a subjective element in that it takes into account people's feelings of belonging to a particular group. Thus, communes as well as cohabiting individuals (of either the same sex or different sexes) who identify themselves as a family meet these criteria and can be considered families (Schwartz & Scott, 1997).

Marriage has been defined in the United States as a legal contract between a woman and a man who are at or above a specified age and who are not already legally married to someone else. Although some people still regard this definition as adequate, as with the historical definition of family, an increasing number of scholars and laypersons alike consider this definition of marriage to be too narrow. For example, by focusing on the legal aspect of marriage alone, it excludes a variety of relationships—such as some heterosexual and homosexual cohabitive relationships—that function in much the same way as legally sanctioned marriages: partners are economically interdependent and have a sexual relationship with the expectation of permanence. In fact, we can think of these relationships as *social marriages*. Such a broader view of marriage is becoming more widely accepted and cohabiting couples, heterosexual and homosexual, are increasingly accorded some of the legal rights and responsibilities of legal marriage (Kramer, 1991). Thus, we utilize a more encompassing and reality-based definition of **marriage** as a union between people (whether widely or legally recognized or not) that unites partners sexually, socially, and economically; that is relatively consistent over time; and that accords each member certain agreed-upon rights.

Contemporary Family Forms

According to many observers of contemporary marriages and families, *the* American family does not exist. Rather, this chapter will examine the many American families of diverse styles and forms and the impact of race, class, gender, and sexual orientation on the family experience.

Types of Families   Sociologists use a wide variety of terms to identify these diverse family forms. For example, *nuclear families* consist of a mother and father and their natural or adopted offspring, whereas *voluntarily child-free families* consist of couples who make a conscious decision not to have children. *Single-parent families* (resulting either from divorce, unmarried parenthood, or the death of a parent) consist of one parent and her or his children. These families are sometimes specifically described as *female-* or *male-headed families.* In either case, legal marriage is not a criterion for family status, as the parent may or may not have been legally

married. Second marriages often bring together people from unrelated backgrounds. For example, *reconstituted, blended,* or *stepfamilies* are formed when a widowed or divorced person remarries, creating a new family that includes the children of one or both spouses. *Lesbian* and *gay families* are composed of individuals of the same sex who live together and identify themselves as a family; these relationships may or may not include natural-born or adopted children. A growing number of U.S. families are *biracial* or *multiracial.* As you learned from the example of golfer Tiger Woods in Chapter 10, such families have partners whose immediate ancestry includes two or more different racial/ethnic groups and, if there are offspring, the children are products of more than one racial/ethnic classification. An increasing number of people living in the United States, especially children, live in foster families. A *foster family* consists of one or two parents and one or more children who have been taken away from their biological families and become wards of the state. While they are under their care, foster parents typically raise these children as their own.

Other contemporary forms of the family include: fathers working away from home and stay-at-home mothers; mothers and fathers both working away from home; mothers working away from home and stay-at-home fathers; families of color; white ethnic families; immigrant families; heterosexual couples; working-class, poor, middle-class, and wealthy families; married and unmarried couples with and without children; multiple-generation families; two families living in the same household; homeless families; and what some social scientists call the *surrogate* or *chosen family*—a set of roommates; a group of people, of either different or the same sex, who choose to share the same household and who define themselves as family; and people simply living together sharing a *feeling* of family. The Data box illustrates the diversity of today's families.

Historically, marriages and families have undergone transformations as changes have occurred in the macrostructure of society, including shifts in the economic structure, as changes have occurred in the demographics of the population, and as individual and collective activism have provided an impetus for family

reform. Nonetheless, it is difficult to make simple generalizations about how marriages and families have changed because there has been a polarization of experiences. On the one hand, marriage is far more likely to end in divorce today. On the other hand, those marriages that last are described by their participants as happier than those in the past and they are far more likely to confer such happiness over many years. Likewise, while some fathers (and some mothers, too) desert their children, others have developed a new commitment to childrearing and child care (Coontz, 1995). Many fathers spend more time with their children than ever before, and they feel more free to be affectionate with them. Others, however, feel more free simply to walk out and abandon their families (Furstenberg, 1988). In addition, an increasing number of people have experienced one or more of the following: cohabitation, getting married at a later age, serial marriages, single parenthood, nonresident parenting, stepparenthood, stepgrandparenthood, and openly romantic, committed relationships with a person of the same gender (Marsiglio & Scanzoni, 1995). Beside these macro-level changes in families, micro-level changes are also part of individual family experiences, as illustrated in the Sociology through Literature box.

Changing Fertility Patterns in the United States

Another change in marriages and families today is the decrease in the fertility rate, resulting in a decline in the typical family size in the United States. Demographers use the term **fertility rate** to refer to the number of births per 1,000 women in their childbearing years (fifteen to forty-four). Evidence suggests that the fertility rate in the early history of the United States was quite high. For example, the **total fertility rate** (the total number of births the average woman will have given current birth rates) in 1790, when the first census was taken, is estimated to have been 7.7 (Gill, Glazer, & Thernstrom, 1992), in contrast to approximately 2.0 today. As the United States moved from an agricultural to a postindustrial society, the economic value of children declined and it became more costly to raise and educate them. At the same time, birth control became more effective, which contributed to the decline in the birth rate. Similarly, among the more developed countries, the total fertility rate is 1.6,

Sociology through Literature

Changing Family Roles

In the following excerpt, Ann Tracy describes two significant changes taking place in her family. One involves the expansion of the family through an interethnic marriage, and the other comes in the form of role changes between mother and daughter.

Murphy's getting married. Surprise, surprise! We had him pegged for a lifelong bachelor (no rarity in this under-mated family) but he was, it seems, just being frugal with his dating money. Now he's fetched a fiancé back from Winnipeg, where he's been doing graduate study, and my mother and I are giddy with the novelty. We haven't added a family member since Murphy himself was born, and now there'll be a whole new relative, bringing along her own story like a character in a hypertext novel. We're delighted with Zirka from the start: she's bright and agreeable and funny, and comes with a bonus of cultural exoticism—she laughs at our struggle to say her name right, while we find her lapses into Ukrainian consonant sounds no end endearing, and she knows how to cook ethnic things we never heard of. She's at first a bit stunned by the skylarking of the family women, having come from a house where nobody whistles or fools around in front of the icons, but she rallies—she's clearly made of the right stuff. Only a few years from now she'll be wearing black leather skirts and driving a vicious bargain in Tibetan bazaars, and nobody will be surprised.

Her family are somewhat stunned too, at having acquired a hairy American. American popularity in Canada is even lower than usual. Murphy not only isn't Ukrainian, he isn't even Catholic, though at least (as a kind aunt points out) the Baptists have a radio program. But the match is made, and in Winnipeg they welcome us to the most exciting wedding we've ever seen, with gold crowns and book-kissing and exhortations in a tongue as mysteriously religious as glossolalia.

In the half day before our plane leaves, my mother and I go shopping at The Bay. By the time we're through at the regional gifts section we've lost our bearings completely, have no idea which way we came in. I stand around vaguely, waiting for my mother to lead, as she has, after all, done for my whole life. In a bit it occurs to me that nothing is happening. I look at her, and she's looking at me, clearly waiting for *me* to lead *her* out, this short, white-haired person that I'm suddenly supposed to be responsible for. I'm appalled. I can't believe that a major transition would happen this way, with no discussion. It's not as though one of us had just turned a milestone age. My mother has never announced, "I'm sixty-five now and retiring from management," or, "You have now officially entered middle age and become the leader." What is going on in her head and how did she arrive at this point? She just gives me a trustful, dependent look. There's a moment when I can't catch my breath and I want to scream and protest that I'm not ready for this changing of the guard. But what's the use?

"I think it's over this way," I say, and she follows me.

What were the contrasting emotions of the narrator of this story in relationship to the changes taking place in her family? How do you account for these different reactions? What major changes have taken place in your family in recent years? Was there any advanced discussion or preparation for these changes? How did family members react to these changes?

Source: Excerpted by permission of the author from Ann Tracy, "Between the Funerals" (1992). In Eleanor Palo Stoller and Rose Campbell Gibson (1997). *Worlds of Difference,* (2d ed., p. 242). Thousand Oaks, CA: Pine Forge Press.

---

but among the less developed countries (excluding China), the rate is 4.0 (Population Reference Bureau, 1997).

Although the national total fertility rate is slightly under the population replacement level of 2.1, the rate is not uniform across all racial and ethnic groups. As Figure 12.1 shows, Latinas/os have the highest total fertility rates, Asian and Pacific Islanders and whites have the lowest, and African Americans and Native Americans, Eskimos, and Aleuts have intermediate rates. However, there is great diversity even within these general categories. For example, in 1990, Mexican Americans averaged 3.2 children, whereas Cuban Americans averaged only 1.5 children. Similarly, within the Asian/Pacific Islander group,

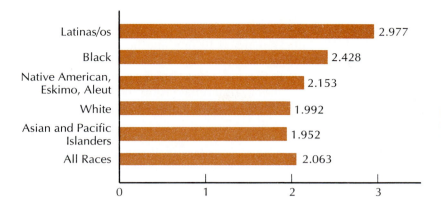

FIGURE 12.1 ⊙ Projected Total Fertility Rate, by Racial/Ethnic Group, 1996 *Source:* Adapted from U.S. Bureau of the Census. 1998. *Statistical Abstract of the United States, 1998.* Washington, DC: U.S. Government Printing Office, Table 98, p. 79.

Hawaiians averaged 3.2 children, whereas Japanese Americans averaged 1.1 children (National Center for Health Statistics, 1993). Age, cultural norms, and class combine to explain these rate variations. Asian Americans tend to marry later than other groups and are more likely than other groups to delay childbearing until their late twenties and thirties. In contrast, Native Americans, Eskimos, and Latinas/os begin childbearing at early ages.

Marriages and Families Cross-Culturally

Despite the changing nature of families, there is still the persistent notion that there is some universal family form that is constant across cultures and time. However, two useful methods of analyzing families enable us to *deconstruct* the idealized, white, middle-class and traditional family models and enable us to understand how present ideas of marriages and families have been socially constructed over time and across cultures. One method of analysis is to shift the focus away from the dominant culture within a society to the marriage and family experiences of all groups. When we do this, we integrate the voices and experiences of diverse marriage and family forms. The second method seeks to understand marriages and families as social constructions through the use of historical and comparative analyses.

In general, marriages across cultures is restricted to heterosexuals and is typically either monogamous or polygamous. **Monogamy** involves one person married to one other person of the other sex. Although *monogamy* legally refers to heterosexual relationships, any couple can be monogamous if the partners are committed exclusively to each other sexually and otherwise during the course of the relationship. Although monogamy is the dominant pattern in the United States, it is more accurately classified as **serial monogamy,** by which individuals may marry more than once, with each prior marriage ended by death, divorce, or annulment. **Polygamy** is a broad category that refers generally to one person of one sex married to several people of the other sex. It can take one of two forms: **polygyny,** in which one male has two or more wives, and **polyandry,** in which one female has two or more husbands.

Polygyny is the most common form of polygamy and is often found in societies in parts of Africa, the Middle East, and Asia in which there is a shortage of males. For example, among the Siwai of the South Pacific, more wives mean higher status for males (Oliver, 1955). Polyandry, on the other hand, is rare but can be found in societies in which widespread female infanticide results in a shortage of women. Polyandry is practiced among the Toda of India whereby a woman who marries a particular man is then considered to be married to all of that man's brothers, including any brothers unborn at the time of the marriage (Goldstein, 1971). Many Americans tend to view polygamy as an exotic relationship that occurs in some societies far remote from the United States. However, although both forms of polygamy are illegal in the United States, some religious groups here routinely practice polygyny. For example, among a dissident Mormon sect in Colorado City, Arizona, the typical household consists of a husband and three or more wives. In fact, as discussed in the Sociological Reflection box, in some states such as Utah and Arizona, *plural families* have become increasingly visible and part of the middle-class mainstream. A third form of marriage is **cenogamy,** or group marriage, in which all of the women and men in a group are simultaneously married to one another. Like polygamy, this form of marriage is also illegal in this country. In the mid-1800s, however, the Oneida Community, a communal group living in New York, practiced cenogamy until they were forced to disband.

Now take a moment to think about the composition of your family. If you are like most unmarried people, you probably described your **family of orientation,** the family into which a

Sociological Reflections

Polygamy in Suburbia, U.S.A.

Jim Harmston and Rocky Baker are among a growing number of polygamists living in Utah. Polygamy is a felony in that state, notes an article in the *New York Times,* "but it is no longer prosecuted, said Eric A. Ludlow, the Washington County Attorney, in southern Utah where a number of plural families live. Polygamists, he said, get around bigamy statutes [laws that prohibit the marrying of one person while still legally married to another] by legally marrying only one wife; the others are recognized by religious leaders, or simply by the individuals themselves. . . . 'It's a consensual relationship between adults.' "

With some degree of tolerance, prosperity and creativity, increasingly these plural families are entering the American mainstream. Some observers are now referring to them as a "polygamous bourgeoisie" because they are often upper-middle class with the economic resources that enable them to live in spacious expansive homes, such as the bed and breakfast converted by Jim Harmston, the 12,000-square-foot house where Ray Timpson, a fundamentalist Mormon, and his 65 siblings and half-siblings grew up, and the 35,000-square-foot home that serves another polygamist, his 10 wives and their 28 children.

Many of these polygamists consider themselves to be orthodox Mormons. For example, according to the *Times,* Mr. Baker "belongs to one of several growing sects of fundamentalist Mormons, who cling to the original divine revelations—including plural, or celestial marriage—of the church's founder, Joseph Smith. Although the official Church of Jesus Christ of Latter-Day Saints renounced polygamy in 1890 as it was embarking on a bid for statehood for Utah and now excommunicates polygamists, the practice of plural marriage is more visible than ever. Based on interviews with sect leaders, Ogden Kraut, a fundamentalist publisher and historian in Salt Lake City, estimates there are 30,000 to 35,000 practicing polygamists, counting all family members, in the United States." The polygamy practiced by these fundamentalists is polygyny; polyandry is far rarer.

The *Times* continues: "After the Mormons banned plural marriages in 1890, many outlaw polygamists colonized remote areas throughout the West, Canada and Mexico, housing their families as best they could. Today, polygamists are more openly carving out their domestic niches. . . ."

"In much the same way the single-family suburban home evolved to accommodate postwar notions of privacy and female domesticity," says the *Times,* "the modern, middle-class polygamous household reflects its own social values, including a strong division of labor, the imperative to be fertile and a belief in efficiency and strict child-rearing. Thomas Carter, an associate professor of architectural history at the University of Utah, pointed out that the houses reveal a major power imbalance, somewhat like a traditional harem, reinforcing the relative mobility of the man and the relative immobility of the women and their availability to him."

person is born or adopted and in which s/he is raised. This includes, for example, you, your parents, and your siblings, if any. In contrast, when we marry or have an intimate relationship with someone or bear or adopt children, we create what sociologists call the **family of procreation.** Some of us were born into a **nuclear family** consisting of a mother, father, and siblings. Although this was once the typical pattern in U.S. families, this is no longer the case. The recognition of many other family structures, such as lesbian and gay families, reflects our awareness that the traditional nuclear family now describes fewer than one-third of families with children (Brettell & Sargent, 1997). Furthermore, some of us were born into an **extended** or **multigenerational family** consisting of one or both of our parents, our siblings, if any, and other relatives, including grandparents, aunts, and uncles living in the same household. In both urban and rural areas of the United States, a form of the traditional extended family is often evident. That is, in many neighborhoods, especially those with ethnic or poor and

An often pressing issue among plural families is the allocation of space and the responsibilities of wives and the husband. The philosophy of Rocky Baker, according to the *Times,* is this: "It is important . . . for each of his wives to be responsible for preparing food for her children. Mr. Baker, a modern polygamist, is quick to point out that he cooks one night a week (usually pizza). . . . He typically rotates where he eats (and sleeps) every night. With . . . separate but equal kitchens facing a central living room, he's always just a shout away from any of his [13] children."

For the sake of unity and separation between "sister wives," some polygamists have constructed separate quarters for each wife and set of children. For example, Brady Williams divided the family home into three equal apartments. The *Times* says: "Each wife has her own entrance, her own floor plan and her own furnishings. . . . The only space that the women share is a utility room for laundry and a family room. Mr. Williams keeps a few shirts in each apartment, and he rotates his meals and nights between wives, but the entire family eats together on Sunday. In a considerate gesture he designed the house so that no master bedroom is directly above, below or next to any other master bedroom."

In the 35,000-square-foot house mentioned earlier, the *Times* notes: "All the wives share a central kitchen. By schedule, they rotate child-care duties, cooking, cleaning, yard work and gardening." How do the wives feel about each other and their plural arrangement? The first wife says, according to the *Times,* " 'Naturally

some wives get along better than others. . . . Every day it takes an effort. We have to want to get along.' . . . The wives have worked out a pro-rata system for child-care based upon how many infants they have contributed to the pool."

Some analysts view polygyny as beneficial to men but divisive for women, especially when wives must compete for the husband's attention and resources. Others, however, including many plural wives, view plural marriage as beneficial to wives in that it provides an environment within which cooperative relationships develop between women who share domestic work and become part of a social network of mutual emotional support.

The idea of polygamy goes against traditional U.S. values and is hard for some people to accept. Would you consider living in this type of marriage? Explain. What are some of the advantages and disadvantages of polygamy? What is the relevancy of monogamy in U.S. society today?

Source: Information and excerpts from Florence Williams. 1997. "A House, 10 Wives: Polygamy in Suburbia," *New York Times* (December 11): B1, B11. Reprinted with permission from Florence Williams.

working-class groups, a variety of relatives live not necessarily in the same household but in very close proximity to one another (upstairs, next door, down the block, around the corner), interact on a frequent basis, and provide emotional and economic support to one another. Some sociologists have labeled this family form the **modified extended family.**

In research that focuses on marriages and families across cultures, families are defined in terms of kinship systems and lineage or descent patterns rather than of specific family forms. **Kinship** refers to relationships resulting from blood, marriage, or adoption or among people who consider one another family (Schwartz & Scott, 1997). Such studies typically examine the relationship between domestic and political domains, highlighting the contrasting power and authority of women and men in kinship groups. Some of those conducting this research view marriage as a political transaction involving the exchange of women between men who wish to form alliances. From such a perspective, women are viewed primarily in terms of the rights their kin have to their domestic labor, to the property they might acquire, to their children, and to their sexuality (Brettell & Sargent, 1997). According to Caroline Brettell and Carolyn Sargent (1997), this viewpoint is androcentric and ignores the dynamic, affective, and even interest-oriented aspects of women's kinship. A gendered approach to cross-cultural studies of kinship focuses specifically on how kinship patterns and dynamics affect the status and power of women. These studies have found that among horticulturalists, women have higher status in societies characterized by *matrilineal descent,* descent through the female line from a common female ancestor, and *matrilocal residence,* living with the wife and her kin after marriage (see the Cultural Snapshot box), than in societies characterized by *patrilineal descent,* descent through the male line from a common male ancestor, and *patrilocal residence,* living with the husband and his kin after marriage.

In matrilineal family systems, descent group membership, social identity, rights to land, and succession to political office are all inherited through one's mother; however, inheritance of property and position is usually traced from the maternal uncle (mother's brother) to his nephew

(mother's son). When matrilineality is combined with matrilocal residence, a man marries into a household in which a domestic coalition exists between his wife and her mother, sisters, and broader kin relations. These women work cooperatively with one another and provide mutual support. Although in a matrilineal system, a man retains authority over his sisters and her children, the cooperative systems between kin-related women often provide them with power and influence both within and without the household. The important point here is that women's higher status is not attributable to the descent system per se but to the organization of the domestic group.

In contrast, in patrilineal and patrilocal family systems, women do not have their kin nearby. Women enter the husband's household as a stranger. However, as researchers have pointed out, opportunities do arise for women in these marriage and family systems to enhance their power and status usually by having sons. The Taiwanese marriage and family system, for example, is patrilocal and patrilineal. Taiwanese women marry into the households of their husbands, pay homage to their husband's ancestors, obey their husband and mother-in-law, and bear children for their husband's patrilineage. Although Taiwanese women will never appear in anyone's genealogy as a name connecting the past to the future, they play a key role in providing the links in the male chain of descent by giving birth to a son (or sons). In fact, the only way to ensure their economic security is to give birth to male offspring (Brettell & Sargent, 1997).

In most industrialized countries, the majority of married couples live in a *neolocal residence,* a pattern in which a married couple moves into its own residence apart from both the wife's and the husband's parents. Although the neolocal residential pattern is typical of families in the United States, during periods of economic hardships and downturns, some U.S. families have lived in either traditional extended families or modified extended families. The typical structure of descent and inheritance in the United States is *bilateral,* meaning kinship and inheritance is traced through both partners' families.

The residential pattern of families and where they live are related in obvious ways to the distribution of power and authority in marriages

Cultural Snapshot

The Khasis of Meghalaya

For centuries, the Khasis of Meghalaya in northeastern India have had a matrilineal society in which property and the family name pass from mother to daughter. In the past, when the Khasi people were under attack from other tribes and Khasi warriors spent months away from home in order to defend their borders, Khasi women ran the family, looked after their villages, and carried out the religious and traditional rites of the tribe. Today, the matrilineality of this group continues. Women run many businesses in Shillong, the state capital, and in the home, they play an important role in domestic decision making. Traditionally, the only male who holds any importance in family matters is the maternal uncle, the brother of the mother of the house.

Upon marrying, the Khasi husband must go to live in the house of his wife's family and must defer to the authority of his mother-in-law. In Khasi homes, female babies are greeted with much joy, whereas a boy is less welcome. Recent surveys show that many Khasi families will invest more in the education of their daughters, who will inherit the family name and care for their parents, than in the male offspring. In some rural areas, some Khasi boys may never get to school, while their sisters may be educated to the university level. Under this system, the youngest daughter inherits the family property because it is believed that she will probably marry last and live the longest; thus, she is the best one to look after her parents in their old age. She is something like a custodian of the family wealth.

In recent times, a growing number of radical Khasi women and young men are challenging this ancient tribal tradition. They, along with many urban Khasi women, believe that the matrilineal system has destroyed the confidence of their men and that it is time to replace it with the patrilineal system that is found in the rest of the world. A female Khasi journalist and teacher said that the Khasi men are little more than "breeding bulls" whose children cannot even bear their names. However, there is powerful opposition to any attempt to dismantle the traditional matrilineal system. Some of the most ardent supporters of the matrilineal system are Khasi men who are content in their role and find that the system has many good points. For the time being, there is a kind of uneasy peace between the two camps. But given that the total population of India is nearly 1 billion people, it seems that the long-term chances of the Khasi matrilineal system surviving in one small pocket of the vast subcontinent are fragile.

Some radical Khasi women have called for changing the village's matrilineal system to a patrilineal system in order to value men and get them more involved in the family. If this occurs, what do you think will happen to women? Using your sociological imagination, why do you think some Khasi women are willing to give up the "advantages" of a matrilineal system for a patrilineal system? What are the advantages and disadvantages of both systems?

Source: Adapted by permission of the author from Haslam, N. 1996. "Reluctant Rulers: Matrilineal Tribe Tries to Shape Up Its Men." *Chicago Tribune* (April 7), sec. 13, pp. 1, 6.

---

and families. Traditionally, families in the United States, as in many other cultures, have had a patriarchal family structure. A **patriarchal family** is a family in which the male (husband or father) is the head of the family and exercises authority and decision-making power over his wife and children. In contrast, a **matriarchal family** is one in which the female (wife or mother) is the head of the family and exercises authority and decision-making power over her husband and children. This form of family authority is far less common than patriarchy, and even in societies in which women have major power, authority and decision making are shared with men. Many families in the United States, particularly during the height of the contemporary women's movement, moved toward an **egalitarian family** structure whereby both partners share power, authority, and decision making equally. As women become less and less economically dependent on men, it is likely that the occurrence of this family pattern will increase. However, U.S. families today generally remain tilted toward a patriarchal structure.

Some researchers studying female-headed families, particularly among African Americans, have referred to them as matriarchal. However, others have pointed out that defining female-headed families as matriarchal (1) overestimates women's power and decision making, and (2) diverts attention away from the essential patriarchal nature of families generally and the network of family relations throughout various societal institutions that negatively impact single female heads of families. Still others have used the term *matrifocality* to refer to a complex of characteristics, including female-headed families, women's control of household earnings and decision making, kinship networks forged and linked by women, and the absence of resident men. The intent is to focus on the central position and power of the mother within the household. Rather than viewing such families as pathological and disorganized, researchers using this concept focus on the adaptive strategies of and advantages for women who head their families (Prior, 1997).

Although much of this research has focused on African American and Afro-Caribbean families, such a family structure can be found in other cultures as well. For example, in fishing towns along the coast of northern Portugal, there is a longstanding pattern of male emigration which has led to women-centered families. The absence of husbands leads to **consanguine ties** (the primacy of blood ties over marital ties) over **conjugal ties** (the primacy of marriage over blood relations), inheritance by women, and the tendency for matrilocal or neolocal residence near the wife's family (Cole, 1997). An extensive body of literature points out the social and ritual importance of kinship for women. Through kin work, women typically set up a network of valuable and long-term obligations within a circle of social relations as well as a mechanism for economic survival (Cole, 1997; di Leonardo, 1997; Prior, 1997; Stack, 1997; Yanagisako, 1977). For example, in a report on her study of African American families in a Midwestern town, Carol Stack (1997) emphasizes the fluidity and flexibility of female-headed families and how they are tied together by complex networks of female kinship and friendship. Through these women-centered networks, women exchange a variety of goods and services, including child care. They depend on one another, and, through collective actions, they keep one another afloat.

Theoretical Views on Marriages and Families

The sociology of marriages and families is an important subdiscipline of sociology. In general, it focuses on the patterns of marriage and family life and structure across groups and cultures. Family sociologists typically work within the theoretical frameworks of functionalist, conflict, interaction, and feminist theory.

Functionalist Theory

A functionalist perspective of families views the family as a universal system of biological and social relations that serve important functions that are essential to the well-being of both individual family members and the society. According to this perspective, the division of labor contributes to greater efficiency in all areas of social life, including marriages and families, while at the same time imposing certain limitations on some people. The division of labor makes it possible for families to fulfill a number of functions that no other institution can perform as effectively. These functions include regulation of sexual behavior, reproduction, socialization of the young, provision of economic and psychological support, and social placement.

Regulation of Sexual Behavior In most societies, sexual behavior is regulated and enforced within the context of families. Although the norms governing sexual behavior may vary among societies, as we learned in Chapter 7, all societies define and regulate who may have sex with whom through the enforcement of exogamous norms, the practice of having sexual relations with and marrying outside one's own family grouping, and endogamous norms, the practice of having sexual relations with and marrying within certain groups. For example, all societies prohibit incest or sexual relations between certain blood or close relatives. Exogamy promotes alliances between families, reinforces their social independence, and prevents or minimizes sexual jealousies and conflicts within families. However, within some royal families, such as in ancient Egyptian and Hawaiian societies, incest was practiced to enable the family to maintain its power and property and prevent the splintering of its estate through inheritance.

Violations of these rules can have serious consequences, as was recently shown in Karachi, Pakistan, where endogamy is the norm; the marriage between a couple from rival ethnic groups sparked widespread ethnic violence. The husband was arrested and charged with having sex outside of marriage even though the woman was his lawful wife. He was later shot as news of the marriage set off ethnic rioting. The wife went into hiding after her father and members of her tribe's council of tribal elders sentenced her to death for marrying someone outside her tribe (Associated Press, 1998a).

Moreover, in most contemporary societies, sexual relations are linked with marriage. Even in those societies in which they are not, their members' sexual behavior is nonetheless regulated so that it reinforces the social order. For example, among the Masai (a polygynous pastoral group in Africa), whose men dominate in the family, young wives of older men are allowed discreetly to take lovers from the unmarried warrior class. If the wife becomes pregnant from such a relationship, family stability is not disrupted. The children from these unions simply belong to the husband and further increase his wealth and prestige. In the United States, endogamous norms have been reinforced by formal laws. As late as the 1950s, for example, over thirty U.S. states legally prohibited marriage between whites and African Americans. Despite the repeal of these laws in 1967, informal endogamous norms continue to discourage marriage across racial lines.

Reproduction   To perpetuate itself, a society must produce new members to replace those who die or move away. In most societies, families are given the primary responsibility for reproducing the species. The reproductive function of families is considered to be so important that many societies employ a variety of practices to motivate married couples to have children. For example, in the United States, couples typically receive tax exemptions and other tax breaks for each child they produce. Couples who cannot or consciously choose not to have children are penalized by tax laws and are sometimes stigmatized by society's members. In addition, sexual intercourse that occurs outside marriage or that will not produce children, such as lesbian or gay sexual relations, is highly stigmatized and discouraged. In contrast, in certain societies, the concern with reproduction translates primarily into a concern with population control. Families are motivated not only to reproduce but also to keep society manageable through population control. For example, in China, material incentives such as work bonuses, free medical care, and other privileges are given to married couples who agree to limit their reproduction to one child.

Socialization   Human infants are not born with the knowledge of the norms, values, and role expectations of their society. However, they soon learn what their society considers to be appropriate ways of acting, thinking, and feeling. Children's social development as well as the continuation of society depends on the socialization process. Today, as in the past, families are the primary transmitters of culture to each new generation of the young. Compulsory education, however, has placed a significant amount of the socialization function in the hands of the state and schools. In addition, the increasing need for mothers to work outside the home has placed part of this function in the hands of child care workers and the mass media, especially television, each of which have become important agents of socialization.

Provision of Economic and Psychological Support
Families have physical and economic needs as well as social needs. Family members must be fed, clothed, and sheltered. Providing for these needs is the basis of the economic function of families. In the past, families consumed

Today, as in the past, families are the primary transmitters of culture to each new generation. As the center of emotional life, families can provide love, care, and emotional support that cannot be obtained easily outside the family context.

primarily goods that they produced. Although the economic security of marriages and families today is tied to the workplace and to macrolevel economic systems, as we will see later in this chapter, marriages and families nonetheless continue to produce goods and services within their respective units.

A great deal of sociological and psychological research indicates that in addition to the necessities of life, human infants also need warmth and affection. Furthermore, even as adults, humans need intimacy and psychological and emotional support and often need other human beings for care and protection during periods of illness, disability, or other dependencies. Ideally, families function to provide an intimate atmosphere and an economic unit in which these needs can be met. As the center of emotional life, families can provide love, care, and emotional support that cannot easily be obtained outside the family context. For many of us, throughout our lives, our families will be our most important source of comfort and emotional support.

Social Placement When new members are born into society, they must be placed within the social structure with a minimum of confusion and in a way that preserves order and stability. The status placement function of families occurs at a number of levels. On one level, families confer statuses that orient members to a variety of interpersonal relationships, including those involving parents, siblings, and a variety of relatives. In addition, simply by being born into or raised in a particular family we automatically inherit membership and status in certain basic groups, including racial, ethnic, religious, class, and nationality.

Taken together, these functions contribute to the continuity, stability, and longevity of families by ensuring that new members are born and properly socialized. However, any given family may or may not perform any or all of these functions. The family as an institution is so diverse that not all families fulfill all of these functions, and some families who do, do not always fulfill them well. That we live in a time of transition and change is unquestionable. Thus, as we reported earlier, many of the activities previously identified by social scientists as family functions have been taken over by or are shared with other societal institutions such as schools, mass media, religious organizations, and government agencies. The socialization of children and stabilization for adult family members, however, remain two of the primary functions of families.

Conflict Theory

Conflict perspectives of marriages and families take a view of these institutions that opposes the functionalist view. Conflict theorists agree that families serve important functions in society, but they reject the notion that marriages and families operate harmoniously for the benefit of individuals and society. Rather, they argue that marriages and families are sources of social inequalities and conflict over values, goals, and access to power and other resources (Benokraitis, 1993). Along with other societal institutions, marriage and family serve the interests of the dominant groups in society. And the accepted form that they take is generally that which is consistent with the values and benefits of the dominant groups. For example, the traditional family with its patriarchal structure serves the interests of men by enabling them to dominate women and children. The dominant groups protect themselves against threats to their privilege and domination by controlling various institutions such as the media and the schools, through which they transmit the notion that monogamy, nuclear or traditional families, and private ownership of the means of production are best for everyone.

Looking at the production and reproduction of gender inequality within the family, conflict theorists consider the relationship between wives and husbands to be similar to those between capitalists and workers. Just as workers exchange their labor power for wages, wives also exchange their domestic labor and sexual availability for economic support. As such, husbands, like capitalists, enjoy the greater privileges and advantages in such relationships, and this privilege and advantage is reinforced by other social institutions. For example, the economy pays men more than women for similar labor. This gives men a decided advantage over women both inside and outside of marriages and families. This fact notwithstanding, some conflict theorists examine the impact of married women working outside the home on the balance of power within the family. When a man is the sole breadwinner, he tends to hold the balance of power and decision making within the family. However, when women work for pay outside the family, there is a reshuffling of power within the family with women gaining increased power and authority.

Feminist perspectives on marriages and families, like conflict analyses, view marriages and families as institutions that reproduce inequality between women and men. Feminist analyses have been in the forefront of defining family violence within the context of the patriarchal structure of marriages and families and showing that violence against women within marriages and families is part of broader societal patterns of violence against women and that it is reinforced by other social institutions. As we discussed in Chapter 8, 95 percent of all spousal or partner assaults are committed by men. Although domestic violence is against the law, male offenders are seldom arrested; if arrested, they are usually not convicted of a criminal offense. When they are convicted for their violence, judges tend to be lenient and seldom sentence them to prison terms. Moreover, men who kill their wives or partners are less severely punished than are women who kill their husbands or partners (Bannister, 1991).

Symbolic Interaction Theory

Symbolic interactionists focus on the meanings that people give to their marital and family relationships. Understanding what people think as well as what they say and do is very important in understanding the dynamics of marriages and families. For example, in her classic study of *The Future of Marriage*, sociologist Jessie Bernard (1972, 1982) highlighted the fact that women and men perceive and experience marriage and family life differently. When asked identical questions about their marriages, wives and husbands answered so differently that Bernard called their marriages "her marriage" and "his marriage." Wives and husbands disagreed on basic things such as how much housework they do. Even when asked basic questions like how often they had sexual relations or who made family decisions, wives' and husbands' responses were so different it was as though they were talking about two different marriages. How is it that wives and husbands view the same relationship so differently? The key lies in the social construction of meaning by wives and husbands as they interact with one another. The experiences of wives and husbands in traditional marriages contrast so sharply that each one, like social actors in any form of social interaction, give different meanings or interpretations to situations and events that occur within the marriage, resulting in *hers* and *his* marriage.

Developing Intimate Relationships

Love and marriage are important sources of intimacy for most people. Nonetheless, these experiences do not always bring intimacy; if it is achieved, they do not guarantee that it will continue. Although the methods by which people develop intimacy vary from one culture to another, the expression of some form of intimacy is universal.

Courtship and Marriage

Most people who are interested in meeting prospective mates, developing a dating relationship, falling in love, and marrying think that when the time is right, "it will happen." Yet, as sociologists point out, in most societies, courtship and marriage are not random activities. Rather, with relatively few exceptions, they are predictable and structured by a number of social and demographic factors such as race and ethnicity, age, level of education, social class, religion, geographic residence, historical time period, and cultural norms and values. Because of the principles of endogamy, exogamy, and homogamy (the tendency to meet, date, and marry someone having characteristics very similar to our own), the freedom to choose a mate is restricted, even where mate selection is said to be open. For example, in the United States, a white, Catholic male with a graduate degree whose parents are both attorneys is likely to marry a white, Catholic female slightly younger than himself who is also a college graduate and whose parents are probably professionals as well. Likewise, we can predict with fair certainty that a male high school dropout whose parents are blue-collar workers who themselves did not finish high school probably will not marry a highly educated female who comes from the upper class.

Although according to an old proverb, "there is someone out there for everyone," some people who are interested in dating and marriage cannot find a partner. For example, if you are a female born after World War II, you are in a pool that has more women than men who are eligible for marriage and looking for a partner. Sociologists have defined this imbalance in the ratio of marriage-aged men to marriage-aged women as a **marriage squeeze,** whereby one sex has a more limited pool of eligibles than does the other. Recently, demographers have predicted a worldwide shortage of men by the year 2050, particularly in the over-sixty age group, in which women will outnumber men almost two to one (*Good Morning America,* 1998). Thus, women over sixty looking to date and/or marry will find a severe shortage of potential partners to choose from.

Although the marriage squeeze has reversed itself for some groups (Latinas/os, African Americans, and whites), many women continue to find their options for dating and marriage extremely limited even though there are theoretically more eligible men than women. Another factor that affects the availability of potential dating and/or marital partners is the *marriage gradient.* In the United States, because women tend to marry into a higher socioeconomic status and men to marry downward, men at the top of the class hierarchy have a much larger pool of eligible mates than do men at the bottom. The reverse is true for women: those at the top have an extremely small pool of eligibles, whereas those women at the bottom have a wider range of men to choose from. In essence, this pattern works to keep some of the highest-status women and lowest-status men from marrying. Although this pattern describes marital patterns, the same general trend operates prior to marriage as well and has been called by some a *dating gradient.*

Applying the Sociological Imagination

The relative scarcity of men by the year 2050, especially in the older age groups, has moved some observers to suggest that because many heterosexual women will not be able to share intimacy with a male partner, they will have to develop other options for intimacy. Among the options suggested are polyandry and/or lesbian relationships. Should women, particularly older women, consider these as viable options for intimacy? Explain. Can you suggest other options?

Not everyone is interested in marriage. For example, in Japan, many young women would like to have a boyfriend but say that they do not want to get married. As more and more young Japanese women establish themselves in careers and achieve financial independence and personal freedom in a traditional, male-oriented culture, they are postponing marriage, having fewer children or not getting married at all because they believe that becoming a traditional Japanese wife will cost them their new-found freedom. Having experienced independence, Japanese women are less interested in the responsibilities of being a wife and mother, which include not only running the household but also caring for the husband's parents. Because women are delaying marriage, Japan's birthrate has dropped dramatically and is now one of the lowest in the world (see Figure 12.2). Although Japanese women do not consider their rejection of marriage a political statement, it may, in a sense, be looked at as a scathing critique of Japan as a male-dominated society (Lev, 1998).

Although most marriages are between heterosexuals of the same race and class, gay, interracial, and interethnic marriages are gaining some degree of acceptance in the larger society. For example, a growing number of universities, municipal governments, cities, and corporations, including Disney and Lotus Development Corporation, openly recognize lesbian and gay domestic partnerships, and many states now have provisions for lesbians and gays to register their relationships officially. Yet in the U.S., legal marriage per se is still a civil right that applies only to heterosexual couples. Interracial and interethnic marriages no longer have to overcome legal restrictions, but sociocultural constraints keep these marriages to a minimum. Three decades ago, less than 1 percent of all marriages

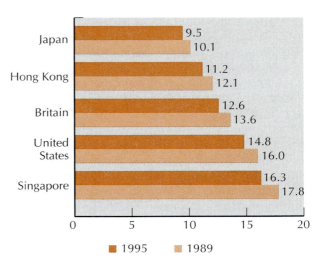

FIGURE 12.2 ⟳ **Birth Rates for Selected Countries, 1989 and 1995** *Source:* Data from United Nations Population and Vital Statistics Report. In Lev, M.A. 1998. "Japan Worries as Women Turn from Marriage." *Chicago Tribune* (March 30), p. 1; corrections published April 1.

in the United States were between interracial couples, whereas today the percentage has increased to 2.3 percent (U.S. Bureau of the Census, 1998). Although many people interpret *interracial marriage* as referring to black–white couples, interracial marriages actually involve a wide range of combinations, including not only blacks and whites but also Native Americans, Asian Americans, and Latinas/os. In fact, Asian Americans are most likely to marry outside their race, usually to someone white. Almost one-fourth of all Asian Americans marry a non-Asian American. Japanese Americans, who have the highest socioeconomic status among Asian Americans, also have the highest rate of interracial marriage (Lee & Yamanaka, 1990). Native Americans also have a high rate of interracial marriage, while whites are the least likely to marry someone of a different race. Sociological data show that interracial marriage is most common among college-educated, middle-income people of all races.

The United States is not alone when it comes to racial endogamy in dating and marriage. Interracial relationships and marriage are sensitive issues in many countries, and racial endogamy is the norm. A case in point is the attitudes and behavior toward interracial couples in South Korea. There, people are particularly concerned about romances between South Korean women and foreign men, and parents go to great extremes to stop interracial dating (for example, locking their daughters in the house for extended periods, making them call in sick at work, and lecturing against "mixing blood"). Because of the patriarchal structure of South Korean society, the same restrictions on dating and marriage are not imposed on men. Thus, Korean men dating Western women is far less taboo, and the marriage of South Korea's founding president to an American never became a major political issue. Sometimes, the Korean reaction to interracial dating and marriage turns violent. For example, recently, a U.S. soldier who touched the buttock of his South Korean wife in public set off a brawl that led to his arrest. A few years before this incident, a U.S. soldier was beaten to death by a South Korean man who objected to the American escorting his South Korean girlfriend. These antagonisms are particularly deep when the American is black, as many U.S. soldiers stationed in Korea are (Kristof, 1998).

The Parenting Decision

Among the most critical decisions we can ever make is whether to become a parent. For many couples, parenting is a deliberate choice; for others, it is an unplanned event or a response to pressure from relatives and friends. Frequently, would-be parents have a romanticized view of childrearing—instant intimacy with gurgling, laughing, adorable infants and toddlers. The reality of chronic crying and temper tantrums may come as an unexpected and unnerving shock to the unprepared. Parenthood, like any other social activity, involves both costs and benefits that vary over the family life cycle; people seldom evaluate them before taking on this lifetime role.

Costs and Benefits of Parenthood   According to a 1996 survey by the Department of Agriculture, new parents will spend, on average, $149,820 to raise a newborn to the age of seventeen. The survey found that it costs about $8,300 a year, or $694 per month, to raise one child in a two-child, two-parent, middle-income family (Asso-

ciated Press, 1997a). Besides money, parents must be prepared to invest time, energy, and emotions in childrearing. Infants and toddlers are totally dependent on parents for all their physical and psychological needs. As children reach school age, parents confront new concerns for their safety. The easy access to drugs, the lure of gangs, and random violence put many children in harm's way. Childrearing tasks can also disrupt previously satisfying lifestyles in a number of ways: children often interrupt lovemaking and sleep, alter household routines, and interfere with their parents' social lives and recreational pursuits.

Despite these costs, parenthood conveys many benefits. Heading the list of benefits is the opportunity for mutual expressions of intimacy. For many parents, their children are a tangible symbol of the love they share and the means for establishing "a real family life" (Neal, Groad, & Wicks, 1989). This is especially true for people who experienced happy childhoods. Children also enlarge their parents' social network by providing connecting links to other family members (grandparents, aunts, uncles, cousins) and to the larger community via schools, churches, neighbors, and places of recreation. Parenthood also provides a recognition of adult status, personal fulfillment, and an ongoing legacy. Both women and men, but especially women, are socialized to see themselves in the adult parental role. Childrearing can impart a sense of pride and a feeling of immortality—even after death, something of their parents can live on through children and grandchildren.

In addition, children may provide tangible benefits as well. Children of parents who farm, run small businesses, or have trouble making ends meet are likely to contribute their labor or wages to the family. And, as parents age and perhaps become frail, they can generally count on their adult children for care and support. Last, but not least, children are fun; they allow adults to recapture the wonders of their own childhood as they join in their children's new discoveries and delights. For example, childrearing allows parents to enjoy all kinds of toys, games, and leisure pursuits.

Remaining Child Free   Although it is widely assumed that having children is the normal course of development for married couples, some couples consciously reject parenthood, and others find that they are infertile and unable to have children without medical intervention. Our focus here is only on women who remain child free by choice. Because only women give birth, research on parenting choices tends to focus on women. The U.S. Census Bureau began tracking the child-free option in 1976. Forty-two percent of women between the ages of fifteen and forty-four are child free today, compared to 33 percent in 1976, even as the rate of infertility remained stable. The increase is most pronounced among thirty-five- to thirty-nine-year-old women, increasing from 10.5 percent in the mid-1970s to 19.7 percent in the mid-1990s (Childless by Choice, 1998). Women having higher levels of education are more likely to remain child free than are women having less education. For example, among women thirty-five to forty-four years of age, 34 percent who had graduate or professional degrees were child free in 1994, compared to 9 percent of women who had less than a high school education (Spain & Bianchi, 1996). Race is also a factor; child-free women are most likely to be white. Remaining child free can be a conscious choice or the result of delaying childbearing to the point where the biological clock has run out. Among the conscious reasons both women and men give for remaining child free are a desire to avoid work/family conflicts that typically accompany dual-earner parenting; career, relationship, or recreational priorities; other responsibilities; and doubts about their own parenting aptitudes and skills. Improved birth control techniques and legal abortion make these choices possible today.

Some social scientists express concern over the increasing number of child-free adults, calling attention to the possibility that, if alternative social networks aren't created, these people will enter the final phase of the life cycle deprived of a support system that adult children usually provide for elderly parents. However, having children is no guarantee of being cared for in old age. Even in Japan, many of the elderly, who themselves cared for elderly parents and in-laws in accord with their culture's deeply embedded norm of filial responsibility, fear that they will be left to fend for themselves. They cite the geographical mobility of their children and the erosion of cultural traditions as the leading causes for their concerns (Kristof, 1997a).

The Intersection of Work and Family

In 1940, only 14 percent of married women were in the labor force (Thornton & Freedman, 1983); twenty years later, the corresponding figure was 31.9 percent. This upward trend continued at a dramatic pace, almost doubling to 61.6 percent by 1997 (U.S. Bureau of the Census, 1998). As you will recall from our discussion in Chapter 11, women today constitute almost half of all workers (46 percent). This movement toward gender equalization in the labor force reveals only part of the story, however. Prior to World War II, the majority of women workers were young, single, poor, or women of color. As late as 1975, as Figure 12.3 shows, only 36.7 percent of all married mothers with children under six years of age were in the labor force. However, almost 54.9 percent of black mothers were in the

FIGURE 12.3 ☉ **Labor Participation Rates of Married Women with Children under Age 6, by Race, 1975–1997**
Source: Adapted from U.S. Bureau of the Census, 1998. *Statistical Abstract of the United States, 1998.* Washington, DC: U.S. Government Printing Office, Table 655, p. 409.

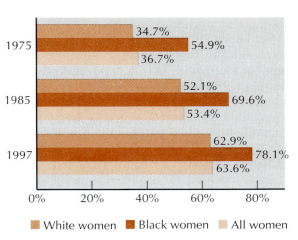

labor force, compared to 34.7 percent of white mothers. Twenty-two years later, 63.6 percent of all married mothers with preschool children were in the labor force and the gap between the participation rates of black and white mothers had narrowed somewhat, 78.1 percent versus 62.9 percent.

Work and Family Structures

The rapid movement of married women with children into the labor force has altered family life in many ways. A variety of work and family structures have emerged as a response to these economic and social transformations, creating both opportunities and challenges for families.

Variation on the Traditional Nuclear Family As we saw earlier, the number of traditional nuclear families has declined in recent decades, and within that family form, there are a number of variations. Included within this family type are one-earner families, in which either women or men stay home to care for home and family while their spouses work. In 1993, 325,000 men aged twenty-five to fifty-four were not in the labor force because they were keeping house, up 26 percent since 1990 (Russel, 1995). These individuals engage in activities that some authors are now calling *home production:* the nonmarket production of goods and services, usually for the family but occasionally on a volunteer basis for schools, churches, or other groups. If these non-paid home production workers were paid for their labor, such compensation would amount to billions of dollars per year. Another variation of one-earner families is the form described by Hanna Papanek (1973) as the *two-person career.* This model is found primarily in middle- and upper-class families in which a husband has a business, professional, or political career. His wife is incorporated into his career through the expectation that she will entertain his business and professional associates, engage in volunteer activities that will enhance his organization's image, be an attractive and supportive companion for him, provide childcare, and keep the household running smoothly. The classic example of this role is our nation's First Lady.

The social role of homemaker, like all social roles, has advantages and disadvantages. On the one hand, it allows some freedom in scheduling activities and the opportunity to be the primary guide in children's daily lives. On the other hand, many household tasks are boring and repetitive and their successful completion often generates little intrinsic satisfaction or public recognition. Finally, with only a sole provider, family members may be economically vulnerable if illness, death, or divorce disrupts the breadwinner's role.

Dual-Earner Couples Approximately 80 percent of all married couples are dual earners (Rivers & Barnett, 1997). Although there have always been families in which both parents worked, they were found primarily among the lower classes, especially among people of color, in the past. Today's dual-earner families cut across all classes, races, and ethnic groups. They enjoy a financial advantage over one-income families. Government statistics show that in 1996, the median income for dual-earner couples was $64,278, compared to $40,999 for couples in which only the husband worked (U.S. Bureau of the Census, 1998). Some dual-earner families take the form of *commuter marriages,* marriages in which each partner works in a different geographic location and, therefore, maintains a separate residence. In the early 1990s, there were about 1 million commuter marriages (Maines, 1993). Most people involved in commuter marriages do not readily choose this option but are more or less thrust into it because they are unable to find suitable jobs in the same locations as their spouses' or for one reason or another one spouse is unable to or won't relocate when the requirements of her/his partner's job necessitates a geographical move. Although each spouse enjoys a considerable amount of freedom in such situations, there may be considerable stress, especially if children are involved. The biggest challenge of such relationships is to maintain social intimacy and support from a distance. Research comparing commuting and non-commuting dual-earner couples found that commuters are more satisfied with their work life and the time they have for themselves but are more dissatisfied with family life, their partner relationships, and with life as a whole (Bunker, Zubek, Vanderslice, and Rice, 1992).

The Impact of Changing Work/Family Patterns

When both spouses work, adjustments are generally made in family roles and responsibilities. Three of the most significant issues dual-earner couples confront involve marital decision making, the division of household labor, and child care. The manner in which they resolve these issues bears significantly on their perceived level of marital happiness.

Marital Power and Decision Making   When we discussed stratification in Chapter 9, we pointed out the strong correlation between income and the exercise of power. This correlation is found within families as well. For example, compared to homemakers, working wives exercise considerably more power and have greater authority in family decision making (Godwin & Scanzoni, 1989). Recent research suggests that a new form of marriage is emerging: the collaborative couple—a wife and husband who share the breadwinning and parenting roles. This pattern is characterized by flexibility and cooperation between the couple with relatively little or no conflict over who has more power in the marriage. The collaborative couple marriage appears to be taking hold across most racial and ethnic groups (see, for example, Mindel, Habenstein, and Wright, 1988), although some researchers have found that black marriages tend to be more egalitarian than white marriages (John, Shelton, and Luschen, 1995). This finding is not surprising given the long history of high rates of labor-force participation among African American women (McAdoo & McAdoo, 1995). The meaning couples attach to women's paid employment or unpaid household labor also influences how power and decision making are distributed in the relationship. For example, if unpaid household labor is valued by the working spouse, that spouse is more likely to share decision making (Pyke, 1994). Conversely, if couples believe that men should be the primary breadwinner and, correspondingly, have the final say in most decisions, men will have more power in the rela-

tionship, regardless of the earnings of either spouse (Thompson & Walker, 1989).

Division of Household Labor   Although working women have more to say in family decision making, this exercise of power has not resulted in a major restructuring of household labor yet. Beginning with research in the 1960s, study after study has found that, regardless of how housework is defined or measured, working wives still do more of it than do husbands. Arlie Hochschild (1989) called this pattern a *second shift*. In her study of fifty dual-earner couples, she found that employed women perform about an extra month of full-time work each year because of this second shift. An analysis of data from the National Survey of Families and Households found that, across family types and regardless of women's employment status, women performed two to three times more housework than their husbands or cohabiting partners (Demo & Acock, 1993). Women averaged between forty and forty-four hours a week of household labor across family types, whereas men averaged 13 hours a week.

However, a recent study by the Families and Work Institute suggests that men are beginning to assume a greater share of responsibility for household chores. The study involved 3,551 telephone interviews with a nationally representative sample of employed adults. Results were compared with those from a similar study done in 1977 by the Department of Labor. Men reported spending more time, and women less, on household chores, than was the case twenty years ago. In 1997, men reported spending 2.1 workday hours and 4.9 nonworkday hours on household chores, compared to the 1.2 and 4.0 hours reported in 1977. In contrast, a comparison of women's reports show a decrease in time spent on chores from 3.3 workday hours to 2.8 and from 6.7 nonworkday hours to 5.8 (Lewin, 1998c). A word of caution is in order. This research relied on self-reports, which may be biased in the direction of providing socially approved responses. Ongoing research in this area is needed to verify the accuracy of such reports.

The extent of men's involvement in household labor is associated with several factors. Among them are age, the percentage and value of the wife's contribution to the family income, and spousal gender role attitudes. Younger males seem to be more receptive to changing gender role expectations than are older males, especially those younger males who were exposed to egalitarian ideologies and saw their mothers as competent individuals who shared equal status with their fathers (Barnett & Rivers, 1996). The greater the percentage of and value a wife's earnings have to the welfare of the family, the more time the husband spends on household tasks (Coltrane, 1995; Ross, 1987). In the early 1990s, working wives contributed about 30 percent of their family's income; this increased to 40 percent when they worked full time, year round (Hayghe & Bianchi, 1994). Men who see themselves as coproviders with their wives do more household labor tasks than do men who still believe in the good provider role (Perry-Jenkins & Crouter, 1990). For example, Lilian Rubin (1994) found that Latinos and Asian American men, especially those who live in ethnic neighborhoods where traditional gender roles remain strong despite women's employment, do relatively few household tasks.

Child Care   Earlier in this chapter, we saw that one of the primary functions of the family is the care and socialization of children. With the advent of the good provider role in the early nineteenth century, the care of children was increasingly viewed as women's prime responsibility. Even today, women, who now make up 46 percent of the labor force, still do the majority of child care. However, recent studies, such as the survey conducted by the Families and Work Institute discussed earlier, indicate that in dual-earner families, fathers are spending more time in activities with their children than fathers did twenty years ago. Compared to fathers in 1977, who reported spending 1.8 workday hours and 5.2 nonworkday hours with their children, today's fathers reported spending 2.3 workday hours and 6.4 nonworkday hours with their children. In comparison, today's working mothers reported spending slightly fewer workday hours—3.0—with their children than the 3.3 hours reported by mothers in 1977 but more time on nonworkdays—8.3 hours, up from the 1977 reports of 7.3 hours (Lewin, 1998c).

Dual-earner couples with overlapping work schedules and single parents who must combine breadwinning and homemaker roles whose children are not old enough to enter the school system on a full-time basis face the daunting task of finding alternative child care arrangements. Figure 12.4 shows the distribution of primary-care arrangements for children whose mothers worked thirty-five or more hours per week in 1995. Eighty-eight percent of these children were in some form of nonparental child care arrangement, the most common being a center-based program. Thirty-nine percent of the children were in a daycare center, head start program, or some other early childhood program. The remaining children were almost equally divided into those cared for by a relative (33 percent) and those cared for by a nonrelative (32 percent).

Although all parents seeking child care confront three major problems—quality, cost, and limited availability—the problems are especially acute for poor parents. For example, the Human Resources Administration which runs New York

FIGURE 12.4 ↻ **Type of Nonparental Child Care Arrangements for Children Under 6 Years Old, 1995**
Source: Adapted from U.S. Bureau of the Census. 1998. *Statistical Abstract of the United States, 1998.* Washington, DC: U.S. Government Printing Office, Table 634, p. 394.

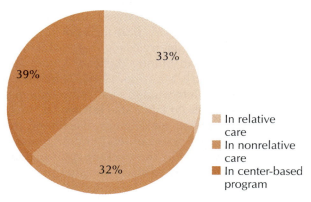

Note: Percentages may add up to more than 100 because some women reported more than one type of child care arrangement.

City's welfare programs reports that New York lacked child care facilities for 61 percent of the children whose mothers were supposed to participate in workfare in 1998. This translated into 21,000 slots that were needed in order to move women from welfare to work. Many of the facilities that do exist are overcrowded, staffed by inadequately trained care givers, and lack proper equipment (Swarns, 1998). Similar problems can be found throughout the country and highlight some of the contradictions that exist in America's attitude toward child care. The United States lags behind other industrialized nations in providing a national program of child care, in large part due to the deeply embedded cultural ideology that still holds that mothers (but only if they are not on welfare) should stay at home with their children and that child care is the responsibility of individual families. The impact of a mother's employment (but rarely a father's) on the well-being of children has been the subject of debate and study ever since World War II, when mothers were encouraged to join the labor force to support the war effort. Contrary to popular belief, the weight of research evidence shows that children who receive quality child care suffer little, if any, negative consequences from maternal employment (Hamburg, 1992).

There are indications that employers are becoming more responsive to their employees' child care needs. In 1980, fewer than 200 companies provided employer-supported child care; in 1997, approximately 10,000 did so (Neikirk, 1998). Work-site child care programs allow parents to visit their children during work or lunch breaks, thus relieving parents of worry over how their children are managing and the quality of care that they are getting. However, these benefit plans cover only a fraction of workers and they are generally not available to minimum wage workers, who are most in need of child care assistance.

Marital Happiness   The gender gap in the provision of household labor and child care holds more than scholarly interest; it can affect marital happiness and satisfaction. The expansion of a highly competitive global economy, attended by company downsizing, often results in the loss of the male breadwinners' jobs or in the dimin-

ishment of their wages and their wives' entrance into the labor market. According to Caryl Rivers and Rosalind Barnett (1997), such economic realities are at odds with a patriarchal marriage ideology that proclaims that men should be "heads of households" and sole breadwinners. The experience of paid employment often leads women to become less traditional. As women become competent employees and managers, it becomes difficult for them to step into a subservient role at home. Recent national surveys show that increasing numbers of men report deriving satisfaction from their families and want more flexibility in their employment so that they can be more involved with their families (Cose, 1995). But if a husband is or remains more traditional than his wife, the quality of marriage goes down for both. Numerous studies show that an equitable division of family work between spouses is associated with higher levels of marital satisfaction and psychological well-being for women; wives who feel overburdened are less satisfied with their marital relationships (Ahlander & Bahr, 1995; Lennon & Rosenfield, 1994; Thompson & Walker, 1991). If the level of dissatisfaction becomes too great, spouses may seek a divorce as a way to improve their personal well-being.

Divorce

No doubt most people mean it when they promise, "Till death us do part." Nevertheless, for every two new marriages in recent years, there has been one divorce. Statisticians estimate that if this trend continues, over one-half of new first marriages will end in divorce (National Center for Health Statistics, 1996). The rate is slightly higher for remarriages. Why is that promise, sincerely made, so difficult to keep, and why is it, as Table 12.1 shows, that the United States has one of the highest divorce rates of all the industrialized countries?

Socioeconomic Changes and Divorce

In her controversial book, *The Divorce Culture,* social historian Barbara Dafoe Whitehead (1997)

TABLE 12.1 ◑ Divorce Rate per 1,000 Married Women, by Country, 1970 to 1995

Country	1970	1995
United States	15	20
Canada	6	11
Denmark	8	12
Italy	1	2
Japan	4	6
Netherlands	3	10
Sweden	7	14
United Kingdom— England and Wales only	5	13

Source: Adapted from U.S. Bureau of the Census. 1998. *Statistical Abstract of the United States, 1998.* Washington, DC: U.S. Government Printing Office, Table 1346, p. 832.

Whitehead's argument overlooks two important factors. First, with few exceptions, most notably during the Depression and the decade following World War II, this nation has experienced an ongoing upward trend in divorce rates for well over a century. Second, although the divorce rate was considerably lower in the earlier part of this nation's history, in large measure due to more restrictive religious, legal, social, and economic factors, it did not mean that families necessarily remained intact. When divorce was not an option, many people simply walked away. Rates of desertion, the abandonment of a spouse or family, were quite high throughout much of U.S. history. Further, shorter life expectancies brought an early end to many marriages. Today, life expectancy for women is approaching eighty years, while for men it is almost seventy-three, with increasing numbers of people living well into their eighties and nineties. We can only speculate whether marriages in the past would have endured for fifty or sixty years under similar life expectancies.

The above factors notwithstanding, Whitehead is on target in two respects. First, compared to many other societies, there is relatively little stigma attached to divorce in the modern United States. This attitudinal change has been reflected in more liberal divorce laws, making divorce more accessible to a broader share of the population. Prior to the introduction of **no-fault divorce** (the dissolution of a marriage on the basis of irreconcilable differences), most courts granted divorces only on the basis of proven misconduct, such as adultery or cruelty and mistreatment, on the part of one or both partners. In state after state after 1970, couples could apply for a divorce without attributing blame for misconduct to either spouse. Since the introduction of no-fault divorce laws all across the country, the divorce rate has increased in all but six states (Nakonezny, Shull, & Rodgers, 1995). Even in Japan, where the divorce rate is considerably lower than in the United States, attitudes are changing. A recent poll commissioned by the prime minister's office found that 54 percent of the respondents approved of divorce, up from only 20 percent in 1979 (Associated Press, 1998b).

Second, in many other cultures, especially in those characterized by marriage arrangements,

attempts to answer these two questions. Although Whitehead acknowledges that divorce has existed in America for over 300 years (the first recorded divorce occurred in Massachusetts in 1639), she argues that it was only in the latter part of the twentieth century that divorce became a socially accepted institution in the United States. Prior to that time, she maintains, divorce was seen as a failure having serious negative consequences for children and unhappiness alone was not considered a sufficient reason to divorce. Even today, despite the higher divorce rate, some people remain in marriages that are unhappy. They do so for a variety of reasons: inadequate resources to live on their own, fear of being alone, adherence to religious prohibition against divorce, a desire to keep daily contact with their children, lack of a better alternative, and simple inertia. Nevertheless, Whitehead believes that there has been a significant change in people's attitudes regarding divorce that was brought on by the affluence of the 1960s. With increased economic security, couples could afford to put more emphasis on their sense of emotional well-being; the resulting rise in emotional expectations led to a growing sense of marital dissatisfaction.

the goal is to find a suitable partner, not necessarily an exciting, romantic one. Hence, expectations for the quality of the marital arrangement are not as high as in the United States, which places a heavy emphasis on romantic love. In the United States, when romance fades, as it often does when economic and other stresses intrude on the relationship, the potential for divorce increases (Cherlin, 1992). Also, with the rise of dual-earner families, increasing numbers of spouses can be economically independent of each other to a marked degree. Thus, in contrast to an earlier time, if marriages are unsatisfactory, economic ties are less likely to sustain them. These macrolevel changes are not unique to the United States. As we saw earlier, other industrialized countries have also experienced a rapid increase in their divorce rates since 1970. The trend is also apparent in industrializing countries: Economic reforms in China, for instance, have put pressure on marriages by providing both women and men greater personal freedom and lifestyle choices than they had in the past. China's divorce rate has reached 10.4 percent, low by comparison with the United States, but historically high for China (Faison, 1995).

Marital Risk Factors, Marital Problems, and Divorce

An extensive range of research has documented a number of factors in addition to these overall societal changes that put couples at greater risk for becoming divorced. Among the most significant factors are early age at marriage, especially age younger than twenty (Sweet & Bumpass, 1987); low levels of education and income (Martin & Bumpass, 1989); interfaith marriages and lack of attendance at religious services (Glenn and Supancic,1984; Lehrer & Chiswick, 1993); parental divorce (Keith & Finlay, 1988; Saluter, 1994); overall differences in social backgrounds (Wineberg, 1994); premarital pregnancy (Norton & Miller, 1992); and being child free (Heaton, 1990).

When members of the American Association of Marriage and Family Therapists were asked to rate the frequency, severity, and treatment difficulty of twenty-nine problems commonly found among couples experiencing marital dissatisfaction, they identified poor communication, unrealistic expectations of marriage or spouse, power struggles, serious individual problems, role conflicts, lack of loving feelings, lack of demonstration of affection, alcoholism, extramarital affairs, and sex problems as the most damaging. The therapists identified alcoholism, lack of loving feelings, serious individual problems, power struggles, other addictive behaviors, value conflicts, physical abuse, unrealistic expectations of marriage or spouse, extramarital affairs, and incest as the most difficult problems to treat (Geiss & O'Leary, 1981). These lists can be useful in that they suggest that constructive measures can be taken to resolve problems, such as improving communication skills and developing more realistic marital expectations. Knowing that some problems, like alcoholism, are difficult to treat effectively can serve as a warning sign that marriage to a person experiencing such a problem is best postponed until she or he has resolved it.

Consequences of Divorce

As we have seen, marriage is an important institution that fulfills critical social functions. Thus, marital disruptions, even when they are not acrimonious, have wide-reaching consequences that extend beyond the divorcing couple. Some of these can be positive—divorce can free people from unhappy and/or conflict-ridden relationships (Lund, 1990); divorce can also function as a mechanism for personal growth (Riessman, 1990). Nevertheless, divorce can also cause pain, uncertainty, guilt, and a sense of failure for the entire family, including children, who often believe that somehow they are responsible for their parents' divorce. In the wake of divorce, which often entails residential moves, the entire family may experience health problems (both physical and psychological), loneliness, and the loss of other previously supportive relationships, such as neighbors, friends, and former in-laws. Further, divorce does not end intimacy or sexual needs. Divorcing couples must decide whether and then how to resume the dating process and whether or not to be sexually active. After a divorce, some individuals may desire a sexual involvement to validate a sense of self-worth that may have been seriously eroded during the divorce process. These decisions do not come

Although the decision to divorce is the result of a number of marital problems, a lack of communication is often at the heart of marital discord. This problem often carries over into efforts to dissolve a marriage amicably. Recognizing problems such as this, some divorcing couples take a constructive approach to resolving their relationship by using the services of a divorce mediator.

easily at any age, but they are particularly problematic for older divorced people, especially for those who retain custody of their children (Morgan, 1990).

The economic impact of divorce can be enormous, even to the point of impoverishing a significant number of women and children. Two opposing trends generally follow a divorce—a woman's standard of living declines by about 27 percent on average, whereas her former spouse's increases by about 10 percent (Peterson, 1996). These trends result from a combination of three key factors: (1) women are far more likely than men to have custody of their children (86 percent to 14 percent), (2) on average, working women are paid less than working men, and (3) the courts are often reluctant to award alimony and child support, and when they are awarded, spouses often fail to make payments. Courts award alimony in fewer than 17 percent of divorces, and payment is received only 75 percent of the time. Similarly, in 1991, the courts awarded child support to approximately 55 percent of all custodial parents, but only 51.5 percent of these received the full amount awarded; 23.8 percent received partial payment, and 24.8 percent received no payment at all. The average

amount of child support received was $2,961 (U.S. Bureau of the Census, 1998).

Divorce affects children, too. Some studies have found higher absentee rates, lower levels of academic performance, higher drop-out rates, and more incidents of misbehavior on the part of children of divorced parents than among children from intact families (Children's Defense Fund, 1992; McLanahan, 1994). However, several factors must be taken into account in interpreting findings such as these. First, many of the problems of children of divorced parents predated the divorce and arose because of the conflicts between their parents. Second, many of these problems are associated with the economic impact of divorce—the lower the income of the custodial parent, the more likely children are to experience problems (Cherlin & Furstenberg, 1991; Hetherington & Clingempeel, 1992).

Strengthening Marriages

This country's high divorce rate, along with its attendant economic and social costs, especially for children, has generated much debate. However, there is little consensus on what should be done to lessen the prospects of divorce. On the one hand, there is pressure to change divorce laws, making it more difficult to divorce. Advocates of this approach point to countries like Chile, Malta, and the Philippines, where divorce remains illegal. Many states are in the process of considering legislation to make marriage or divorce or both harder to get. In 1997, Louisiana passed a "covenant marriage" act that allows couples to choose between the standard marriage contract with which a couple can later get a no-fault divorce and a tougher optional marriage contract that requires premarital counseling and all but eliminates the possibility of an easy, no-fault divorce. Instead, a spouse would have to prove abuse, adultery, abandonment, or "habitual intemperance, excesses, cruel treatment or outrages" (Associated Press, 1997b).

Opponents of this approach point out that simply making divorce more difficult to get doesn't solve the problems generated by unhappy marriages as indicated by high rates of separation, desertion, and cohabitation in countries where divorce is illegal. Instead, they argue for more education and parenting classes in the schools, premarital counseling before any couple can receive a marriage license, and parenting classes for any couple with children seeking a divorce. A recent Time/CNN survey conducted by Yankelovich Partners Inc. found popular support for this position. Sixty-four percent of the respondents felt "people should be required to take a marriage-education course before they get a marriage license." There was more ambivalence about the government's role in divorce matters. Only 37 percent wanted the government to make it more difficult for people to get a divorce, even though 50 percent believed "it should be harder" to get a divorce than it is now and 61 percent believed it should be harder for couples with young children to get a divorce (cited in Page, 1997). Finally, others argue that there needs to be more support for families in terms of affordable child care and help in balancing the demands of work and family. It is too early to predict what the outcome of such proposals will be. However, there are some indications that couples may be dealing with this issue themselves. Voluntary premarital counseling appears to be increasing, couples are marrying at later ages, and the divorce rate has leveled off in recent years.

Applying the Sociological Imagination

Conduct interviews, involving respondents from several generations. Among the questions to ask: Is a lifetime marriage commitment a realistic goal in today's society? Should people in unhappy marriages stay together for the sake of the children? Should states make it more difficult to get married? divorced? Explore the reasons for their answers. Did you find any differences in response by race, sex, gender, or age?

Single-Parent Families

One obvious consequence of the high divorce rate is the growth of single-parent families. In 1997, 32 percent of all family groups in the United States were single-parent families, up from 13 percent in 1970. Twenty-six percent of white families with children, 36 percent of Latina/o families with children, and 64 percent of African American families with children have only one live-in parent. Approximately 84 percent of these families are headed by women (U.S. Bureau of the Census, 1998). Single-parent families are not new. Parental death rates in late-seventeenth-century Virginia were so high that most children spent part of their growing up years in a single-parent family (Darrett & Rutman, 1979). It is estimated that one-half to two-thirds of all children born in the 1990s will live in single-parent families sometime before their eighteenth birthdays. However, today divorce, not parental death, is the major factor in their creation, followed by births to unmarried women. Unmarried women accounted for nearly one in three births in 1995, compared with one in five in 1980 and one in ten in 1970. A common misperception is that teenagers produce the most out-of-wedlock births. The reality is that the rate is highest for women in their early twenties (72 births per 1,000 unmarried women), followed by women in their late twenties (59 per 1,000), and then teenagers (46 per

1,000). The percentage of births that occur to unmarried women varies by race and ethnicity. In 1994, Asian and Pacific Islander ethnic groups (with the exception of native Hawaiians) had the lowest rates, ranging from 7 to 19; the rate for white non-Latinas was 21; African Americans (71), Native Americans (57), and Latinas (43) had the highest rates (cited in Bianchi & Spain, 1996, pp. 6, 8). Although a significant number of well-educated and professional women are opting for parenthood without marriage, unmarried childbearing is more commonly found among women having lower levels of education and income.

Although the structure of a single-parent household is different, single parents must accomplish the same parenting goals as two-parent families, and they face many of the same problems and rewards of parenting as other types of families. Thus, just as two-parent families are not always secure and happy, neither are single-parent families inherently deprived or dysfunctional. This is not to say they are without problems. To examine this issue, Sara McLanahan and Gary Sandefur (1994) undertook an intensive secondary analysis of four major sets of survey data. The findings from these four studies were consistent. Compared to children living in families with both biological parents, children living in single-parent and stepfamily households were at a distinct disadvantage. They were more likely to perform poorly in school, drop out of school, and not expect to and generally not to attend or graduate from college. However, further analysis showed that about half of the differences found for children living in single parent families were explained by a low family income. McLanahan and Sandefur argued that the remaining differences can be explained by several factors: single mothers have lower aspirations for their children and less time to supervise or interact with them, and they move more often. Although the authors found that income levels and supervision are fairly equivalent between stepparent families and those with two biological parents, children living in stepparent families are more likely to have changed schools and experienced other disruptions in their support networks. Thus, differences in life chances between children living with both biological parents and children living with a single parent or in a stepparent family disappear when there is adequate income, supervision, and stability of place and fewer disruptions in social networks.

Death of a Spouse

Our discussion of divorce should not obscure the fact that millions of couples have been able to fulfill the promise "till death us do part." In fact, approximately 3 percent of the population celebrate golden wedding anniversaries. Eventually, however, all married couples must confront one of life's most stressful events, the death of a spouse. Widow- and widowerhood often bring significant role changes. Social networks are disrupted; not only have the widowed lost their main source of intimacy and support, but also social interaction with in-laws and friends brought into the relationship by the deceased partner may gradually decrease. The death of a spouse also causes radical changes in life's routines—day-to-day conversations, shared meals, and activities in and around the household as well as leisure pursuits shared by both partners. Although over time, most people adjust to these major shifts in lifestyles, the result is often less human interaction and sense of belonging (Atchley, 1997). Cultural norms also play a major role in both the treatment of remaining spouses and their adjustment to widow- or widowerhood. Throughout the world, widows have few rights and face many restrictions. For example, in Gabon, Africa, the husband's family must issue written authorization for the widow to inherit property. Widows themselves can be considered "property" and may be inherited along with other goods, as is true in some regions of Nigeria (Seager, 1997).

Remarriage

Despite the high divorce rate, marriage remains a popular institution in the United States. About two-thirds of divorced women and three-fourths of divorced men eventually remarry. These gender differences are explained by two factors: women are more likely to retain custody of children, thus reducing their "marriage marketability," and cultural norms allow men to choose new spouses from a larger age pool than they do women.

When divorced or widowed parents remarry, they create a new family form. On the surface, remarried families may look just like nuclear families. The reality is far different, however. Family structure and functioning are more complicated in remarried families, often involving stepsiblings, half siblings, or both. The need to manage relationships with former spouses and in-laws as well as to establish emotional ties with newly acquired stepchildren, stepparents, and stepgrandparents can seem overwhelming, especially in the absence of clear-cut guidelines for how to behave in stepfamilies. Although the biological parent–child relationship is legally well defined, the legal rights and responsibilities of stepparents remain ambiguous. Cultural stereotypes of the "wicked stepparent" contribute to conflicts over money, discipline, and parental authority, all of which can strain the marital relationship to the breaking point. Because of these added stresses, the risk of divorce is higher in second marriages. Nevertheless, second marriages can be as happy and satisfying as good first marriages (Coleman & Ganong, 1990). Factors associated with marital happiness and stability in remarriage include a strong social support system, realistic expectations about the challenges of living in a stepfamily, flexibility, and good communication (Ihinger-Tallman & Pasley, 1994; Kelley, 1995).

Marriages and Families in the Twenty-First Century

As we have seen throughout this chapter, marriages and families have changed significantly in the last several decades in response to a number of economic and social trends. So, too, the shape of families in the twenty-first century will be affected by trends unfolding today. The consequences of some trends seem relatively easy to predict. For example, although overall fertility rates remain relatively low, immigration and higher fertility rates among different groups are contributing to a shift in the racial and ethnic composition of the population which will have implications for future marriage prospects. As life expectancy increases, more families will confront the issues of how best to care for elderly relatives. The impact of other trends and changes are more difficult to predict, but two troubling and complex issues will remain with us well into the next century: child abuse and neglect and welfare reform.

Child Abuse and Neglect

Societal attitudes regarding what constitutes child abuse and neglect vary over time and from one culture to another. For example, in modern Sweden, a parent can be imprisoned for striking a child, whereas in ancient Rome, a father had the power to sell, abandon, and even kill his own child (Radbill, 1980). For much of recorded history, children have been defined as the property of families, and infanticide, the killing of infants and young children, was common. Even today, in countries like China and India where male babies are preferred, female infants are often put to death, abandoned, or placed in orphanages. Further, it is not always easy to know where to draw the line between parental concern and abuse because parents often use physical measures to discipline children, including spanking, physical work details, denial of privileges, and scolding.

In an attempt to set guidelines for both parents and policy makers, Congress passed the Federal Child Abuse Prevention and Treatment Act of 1974, which defines child abuse and neglect as the physical or mental injury, sexual abuse, or negligent treatment of a child under the age of eighteen by a person who is responsible for the child's welfare under circumstances that indicate that the child's health or welfare is harmed or threatened. Child abuse is extensive in the United States. In 1996, over 3 million children were reported to the authorities as probable victims of abuse or neglect. Investigations substantiated that about 1 million of these children were abused or neglected (U.S. Bureau of the Census, 1998). Approximately 52 percent of the cases involved neglect and approximately 24 percent involved physical abuse. The majority of the victims were female, and almost 40 percent were five years of age or younger. Many factors correlate with child abuse and neglect: parental youth, marital discord, stress, unemployment, low income, inadequate parenting skills, physical and emotional problems on the part of either parent or child, social isolation, and, in general, lack of support in the parenting role. Thus, to combat child abuse in the future will require more than punishing parents for their behavior; it will require therapeutic intervention to teach parents to deal with their feelings of anger and frustration and to become more knowledgeable about children; but it also will require fixing many of the underlying structural problems in society.

Welfare Reform: Its Impact on Families

In 1996, the U.S. Congress passed, and President Clinton signed, the Personal Responsibility and Work Opportunity Reconciliation Act, ending the federal government's Aid to Families with Dependent Children (AFDC) as of July 1997. AFDC was established in 1935 to help poor widows raise their children at a time when societal norms strongly disapproved of the employment of married women, especially those with children. Over time, the program was expanded to include impoverished divorced and unmarried mothers and their children as well. In 1996, over 11 million people, down from 14 million in 1993, received benefits from the program, averaging $383 a month per family (U.S. Bureau of the Census, 1998).

By this time, the call for welfare reform was already well underway. Numerous factors fueled the welfare debate. First, as the United States economy shifted to a service economy, the demand for women employees increased and the sentiment against working women gradually moderated. During the 1980s, the labor force participation rate of married mothers caught up with the participation rate of single mothers, thus raising a question of fairness—why should some mothers be "rewarded" for not working while others have to work (Bianchi & Spain, 1996)? Second, during the 1980s and early 1990s, federal deficits skyrocketed, leading to demands for cutbacks in government spending. Third, conservative critics of welfare, such as Charles Murray (1984), author of *Losing Ground: American Social Policy, 1950–1980,* argued that welfare itself contributed to the decline of two-parent families by discouraging fathers from supporting their children and encouraging out-of-wedlock childbearing. In contrast, liberal critics argued that the decline in two-parent families stemmed primarily from a lack of economic opportunity—that a lack of jobs and poverty, not the availability of welfare, encouraged marital dissolution and nonmarriage and undermined the ability of low-income fathers to support their children.

Although there is as yet no national assessment of the full impact of the provisions of the new law (greater state involvement, tighter restrictions on welfare eligibility, and workfare—the need to become employed after two years of receiving welfare benefits), initial reports coming from the various states are mixed. State officials are quick to announce cuts in welfare rolls, but follow-up investigations indicate that relatively few recipients are landing jobs that lift them out of poverty. For example, in New York City, fewer than a third of the people cut from the welfare rolls got jobs. Those who did often became cheap labor for the city, cleaning and maintaining streets, parks, and buildings for minimum wages while city workers who were paid higher wages for doing the same work lost their jobs. Mothers are being pushed to take jobs even though there are only enough licensed child care slots in the city's neediest sections for one out of every three or four children (Jackson, 1998). The goal of having people achieve economic self-sufficiency is deserving of widespread support. However, the stark reality is that unless resources are found to provide education and training for jobs that pay a living wage and to increase child care options, the current mode of welfare reform, rather than strengthening families as intended, is likely to undermine them even further.

Key Points to Remember

1. Almost everyone today has an opinion about the "problems" of modern families. Some view the family as crumbling under the loss of family values, while others argue that family values mean valuing all families regardless of their structures or forms.

2. Marriage and family are among the oldest human social institutions. Definitions of marriages and families should be broad enough to account for the wide diversity in structure, form, and interactions within these institutions. Race, class, gender, and sexual orientation are part of the total fabric of experience for all families. Although these categories are different aspects of social structure, individual families experience them simultaneously.

3. Cross-cultural studies of marriages and families reveal a variety of marriage forms, family types, residential patterns, and ways in which power and authority are distributed as well as ways in which descent and inheritance are traced.

4. Sociological views on marriages and families include: functionalist theory, conflict theory, and symbolic interactionist theory. Functionalism examines the major social functions of families. Conflict theory focuses on the sources of inequalities and conflict over values, goals, and access to power and resources within marriages and families. Likewise, feminist theories examine inequality in marriages and families, often with a focus on the patriarchal structure of these institutions. Finally, interactionists are concerned with the meanings that people give to their marital and family relationships.

5. Intimacy is a universal feature of human societies, yet the manner in which people seek to achieve and maintain intimacy varies across cultures. In some cultures, people engage in dating and courtship rituals with the goal of marriage; in others, marriages are arranged and love and intimacy follow rather than precede marriage. In either case, the selection of intimate partners is not random; rather, it is structured by a number of factors: race, ethnicity, age, education, social class, religion, geographic residence, historical time period, and norms and values.

6. Among the most critical decisions people make is whether or not to parent. The costs of parenthood include monetary, time, energy, and emotional investments as well as lifestyle disruptions. Benefits include the exchange of love and affection, provision of adult status, personal fulfillment, fun, enjoyment, and a sense of immortality. Some people choose not to parent; others are not able to because of infertility.

7. Social and economic changes have led to major transformation in work and family roles. Today, women constitute 46 percent of all workers. Approximately 80 percent of all married couples are dual earners. Working wives exercise considerable more power and have greater authority in family decision making than do wives who don't work outside the home. Although men are taking on greater responsibility for both household tasks and child care, women still do the majority of these tasks. Women's marital happiness and satisfaction is higher when family work is equitably divided.

8. The United States has high divorce and remarriage rates. Divorce is more socially acceptable today than in the past. Following divorce, the standard of living of women and children declines, whereas men's standard of living generally increases. A number of states are considering ways to make divorce, marriage, or both more difficult to enter. Men are more likely to remarry than women. The structure of remarried families is more complicated than that of first marriages.

9. Divorce, births to unmarried mothers, and the death of a parent have combined to increase the number of single-parent families in the United States today. The differences in life chances between children living with both biological parents and children living with a single parent or in a stepparent family disappear when there is adequate income, supervision, and stability of place and fewer disruptions in social networks.

10. Widow- and widowerhood bring significant role changes, and although most people adjust to these major shifts in lifestyles, the result is often less human interaction and sense of belonging. The marriage gradient and women's longer life expectancy contribute to the excess number of widows compared to widowers.

11. Families in the twenty-first century will be affected by many of the economic, social, and demographic trends unfolding today, including the controversial 1996 welfare reform act.

Key Terms

family
marriage
fertility rate
total fertility rate
monogamy
serial monogamy
polygamy
polyandry

polygyny
cenogamy
family of orientation
family of procreation
nuclear family
extended family
modified extended family
kinship

patriarchal family
matriarchal family
egalitarian family
consanguine ties
conjugal ties
marriage squeeze
no-fault divorce

Key People

Andrew Vachss
Stephanie Coontz

Barbara Dafoe Whitehead
Sara McLanahan

Gary Sandefur

Questions for Review and Discussion

1. The issue of family values is the centerpiece of most contemporary discussions of U.S. families. What does the concept of "family values" mean to you? In what ways does government policy reflect a particular view of family values? Give examples. What policies would you recommend in support of your view of family values?

2. In a democratic society, should all members be allowed to participate in and benefit from the institutions of marriage and family? Should definitions of marriage and family be extended to include a much wider range of household forms, relationships, and lifestyles? In your opinion, which is more important, the structure of a family or the interactions between its members?

3. Describe the ways in which families have been affected by the economic transformations of the last two centuries. How does the division of household labor and child care affect marital functioning and satisfaction? Should the government and employers take any responsibility for helping families to balance the demands of work and family? Explain your position.

4. What special problems are associated with divorce, widow- and widowerhood, single parenthood, and remarriage? What can individuals and the larger society do to help minimize these problems?

For Further Reading

Hochschild, Arlie. 1997. *The Time Bind: When Work Becomes Home and Home Becomes Work*. New York: Metropolitan. The author interviewed working parents and found that many took refuge from the pressures of family life by working longer hours.

No culture is completely static. Social change occurs everywhere and at all levels. However, the rate of change can vary dramatically from one society to another. In the United States, the rate of change is rapid. In other societies, indigenous people continue to follow traditions and practices similar to those of their ancestors. To the outside observer, as well as to individuals within those societies, change may go almost unnoticed.

Social change occurs in many ways. Sometimes people act individually to resist or promote certain patterns of behavior. For example, a simple act of mentoring could lead to meaningful change. At other times, collective action is used to either resist some societal practice, such as institutional racism or sexism, or to promote new patterns of racial and gender equality.

The increasing globalization of the world has facilitated the spread of diverse products and practices from one society to another, thus bringing about social and cultural change. For example, it is no longer unusual to see some Western fast-food restaurants in less-developed countries.

Hood, Jane C. (Ed.). 1993. *Men, Work, and Family: Research on Men and Masculinity.* Newbury Park, CA: Sage. A collection of contemporary research on how men balance their work and family commitments and the impact of public policy on men's experience of family and work.

Sherman, Suzanne. 1992. *Lesbian and Gay Marriage: Private Commitments, Public Ceremonies.* Philadelphia: Temple University Press. A thought-provoking book that documents the debate regarding lesbian and gay marriages.

Stacey, Judith. 1996. *In the Name of the Family: Rethinking Family Values in the Postmodern Age.* Boston: Beacon. Based on interviews with single mothers and working class families, this book documents the strengths of these families compared to families of the past.

Toth, Jennifer. 1997. *Orphans of the Living.* Needham Heights, MA: Simon and Schuster. In this well-written but alarming book, the author examines the plight of the half a million children in foster or substitute care and provides compelling reasons for reforming the system.

Sociology through Literature

Guest, Judith. 1976. *Ordinary People.* New York: Penguin. This compelling story of the Jarrets, who from all outward appearances are the ideal American family, reveals how the tragic and untimely death of one son uncovers a deep emotional schism in the mother's relationship with the surviving son which ultimately leads to the disintegration of the Jarrets' marriage.

Murayama, Milton. 1975. *All I Asking for Is My Body.* Honolulu: University of Hawaii Press

(originally published 1959). An excellent Japanese American novel about Asian values of family and community. Murayama explores the issue of justice in terms of an individual's rights versus one's obligation to one's family.

Smiley, Jane. 1992. *A Thousand Acres.* New York: Fawcett Books. A compelling story of a father and his daughters, examining the relationships of sisters, wives, and husbands, and depicting the harsh realities of life on a family farm.

Internet Resources

http://www.ag.ohio-state.edu/~ohioline/lines/ fami.html   Information and Web links to social scientific sources on family studies.

http://www.tmn.com/cdf/index.html   The Web site for the Children's Defense Fund, a private, nonprofit children's advocacy organization.

http://www.umanitoba.ca/faculties/arts/ anthropology/kintitle.html   Provides links to information on diverse family systems.

http://www.cdc.gov/nchswww/nchshome.htm   The National Center for Health Statistics provides data on births, marriages, divorces, and deaths in the United States.

13

Religion and Education

AGENT OF CHANGE: RENNY GOLDEN

At the age of nineteen, Renny Golden entered the Dominican order of nuns. Her desire to serve others led her to break off an engagement and to change her life radically. Her first assignment as a novice nun was teaching first grade in a poor area of Detroit. It was at this same time that the civil rights movement was gaining momentum. Her firsthand look at poverty and the struggle for civil rights caused her to question her role in the convent as well as the role of the authority structure in organized religion and its effectiveness in dealing with these critical social issues. After deciding she could be more effective outside the convent, Golden came to Chicago to teach in a poor community on the West side. With another teacher she started an adult-education program for parents who did not have high-school diplomas. She used the methodology of Brazilian educator Paulo Friere, author of *Pedagogy of the Oppressed,* who had taught illiterate peasants to read and write in twelve weeks. He also taught them to question their place in the world and to engage in the practice of radical democracy to overcome their political and economic oppression.

In 1975, Golden began teaching at Northeastern Illinois University in Chicago, where her educational philosophy and religious and political beliefs became even more closely integrated when she was introduced to *liberation theology,* a blending of Christian principles with political activism. Often Marxist in character, liberation theology was introduced in South America in the late 1960s by Roman Catholic priests and nuns working to help people improve their lives. After learning about the widespread killings of thousands of peasants and activists by the military in El Salvador, Golden began her work in Central America. She was instrumental in organizing a task force on Central America that helped fleeing Salvadoran and Guatemalan refugees find sanctuary churches and synagogues throughout the United States. Later, she traveled to El Salvador and spoke to women living and working in the war zone. Just the act of talking to a North American put these women at great risk, so their stories had to be gathered clandestinely and the interview tapes had to be smuggled out past checkpoint security guards.

Golden told of the suffering and the sacrifices of these women in her 1991 book, *The Hour of the Poor, the Hour of Women*. She continues her work for social justice through writing, teaching, and personal activism. She has written a book about the U.S. child welfare system and is currently working on a book on San Salvador's Archbishop Oscar Romero, whose assassination is rumored to have been the work of a military death squad. Her commitment to social justice serves as a role model for her students at Northeastern Illinois University, the majority of whom volunteer at social service agencies, working in soup kitchens, homeless shelters, and in the juvenile court system. She routinely leads student groups to El Salvador and Guatemala so that they, too, can experience Friere's method of education—applying what you have learned to change the world. Golden's commitment to social justice is simple: "My freedom is tied up with everybody else's struggle. I don't think I can be free if other people aren't free" (Hamburg, 1998).

Source: Adapted by permission of the author from Hamburg, Gail Vida. 1998. "A Quest for Justice." *Chicago Tribune* (May 24), sec. 13, p. 3.

The Interactive Influence of Religion and Education

In this chapter, we will examine two independent but closely related social institutions: religion and education. Both religion and education are cultural universals, and both are important agencies of socialization in that, as illustrated in Renny Golden's life, they help to shape people's attitudes, values, and behaviors. The separate impact of these two institutions is somewhat difficult to assess because they overlap in many situations. For example, in the United States, religious activists have attempted to influence the curriculum in the public schools in a variety of ways, resulting in the politicization of education and religion as well as in law suits regarding who should decide what is to be taught in U.S. public schools. Such behavior is part of a long history of public discourse and debate on the appropriate relationship between religion and public education. For example, it was not until 1967 that teachers in the Tennessee school system could legally teach evolution, the theory that humans evolved from lower primates. The ban on teaching evolution was based on the premise that it denied creationism, the divine creation of humans as taught in the Bible (see the Sociology through Literature box).

The evolution versus creationism debate is but one of the many issues that underscore the intersection of education and religion. Other issues include the teaching of moral education, sex education, school prayer, and the subject and content of textbooks and library books. In 1998, two Maryland high school districts removed the books of two of the nation's best-selling female authors, Toni Morrison (*Song of Solomon*) and Maya Angelou (*I Know Why the Caged Bird Sings*), from the English curriculum because parents had complained about sexually

Sociology through Literature

Inherit the Wind

During the scorching days of July 1925, John Scopes went on trial in Dayton, Tennessee, for teaching evolution in violation of state law. He was defended by noted lawyer Clarence Darrow. The prosecuting attorney was the brilliant orator William Jennings Bryan. The trial was background for the play *Inherit the Wind;* a brief excerpt is presented below. The characters in the play are the teacher, Bertram Cates, his defense attorney, Henry Drummond, and the prosecuting attorney, Matthew Harrison Brady.

Drummond: Your Honor, I wish to call Dr. Amos D. Keller, head of the Department of Zoology at the University of Chicago.

Brady: Objection.

Drummond: On what grounds?

Brady: I wish to inquire what possible relevance the testimony of a Zoo-ology professor can have in this trial.

Drummond: It has every relevance! My client is on trial for teaching Evolution. Any testimony relating to his alleged infringement of the law must be admitted.

Brady: Irrelevant, immaterial, inadmissable.

Drummond: Why? If Bertram Cates were accused of murder, would it be irrelevant to call expert witnesses to examine the weapon? Would you rule out testimony that the so-called murder weapon was incapable of firing a bullet?

Judge: I fail to grasp the learned counsel's meaning.

Drummond: Oh. (*With exaggerated gestures, as if explaining things to a small child.*) Your Honor, the defense wishes to place Dr. Keller on the stand to explain to the gentlemen of the jury exactly what the evolutionary theory is. How can they pass judgment on it if they don't know what it's all about?

Brady: I hold that the very law we are here to enforce excludes such testimony! The people of this state have made it very clear that they do not want this zoo-ological hogwash slobbered around the schoolrooms! And I refuse to allow these agnostic scientists to employ this courtroom as a sounding board, as a platform from which they can shout their heresies into the headlines!

Judge: Colonel Drummond, the court rules that zoology is irrelevant to the case.

Drummond: Agnostic scientists! Then I call Dr. Allen Page—Deacon of the Congregational Church—and professor of geology and archeology at Oberlin College.

Brady: Objection!

Judge: Objection sustained.

Drummond: In one breath, does the court deny the existence of zoology, geology, and archeology?

Judge: We do not deny the existence of these sciences: but they do not relate to this point of law.

Drummond: I call Walter Aaronson, philosopher, anthropologist, author! One of the most brilliant minds in the world today! Objection, Colonel Brady?

Brady: Objection!

Drummond: Your Honor! The Defense has brought to Hillsboro—at great expense and inconvenience—fifteen noted scientists! The great thinkers of our time! Their testimony is basic to the defense of my client. For it is my intent to show this court that what Bertram Cates spoke quietly one spring afternoon in the Hillsboro High School is no crime! It is incontrovertible as geometry in every enlightened community of minds!

Judge: In this community, Colonel Drummond—and in this sovereign state—exactly the opposite is the case. The language of the law is clear; we do not need experts to question the validity of a law that is already on the books.

Drummond: In other words, the court rules out any expert testimony on Charles Darwin's *Origin of the Species* or *Descent of Man*?

Judge: The court so rules.

What does this play suggest about the relationship between religion and science? How does what people believe about the relationship between science and religion affect their views of what is an appropriate educational curriculum? Who should control what is taught in public schools?

Source: From *Inherit the Wind* (pp. 72–74) by Jerome Lawrence and Robert Edwin Lee. Copyright, as an unpublished work, 1951 by Jerome Lawrence and Robert Edwin Lee. Copyright © 1955 and renewed 1983 by Jerome Lawrence and Robert E. Lee. Reprinted by permission of Random House, Inc.

explicit descriptions and language in the texts (Weldon, 1998). Concern over these and similar issues has led to hotly contested school-board elections. Groups such as the Citizens for Excellence in Education, dedicated, among other things, to restoring school prayer and teaching the story of creation, have helped to elect over 10,000 school board members nationwide who share their views (Impoco, 1995). Other parents deal with these issues by choosing to educate their children at home or send them to schools affiliated with a specific religion as a way to ensure that their children will be taught in accordance with their own personal beliefs and values. We will begin our discussion with religion and conclude the chapter with an examination of education.

The Meaning of Religion

There are probably few, if any, places in the world where one could visit and not encounter some historical and/or modern religious symbols, beliefs, and behaviors. Thus, sociologists include religion as one of the universal institutions and study its impact on individuals, groups, and society at large. One need only pick up a daily newspaper to see that the role and importance of religion in modern society is a topic of considerable debate and emotional intensity. For example, some critics of modern life attribute many contemporary behaviors—such as an increasing number of births outside marriage, high divorce rates, and escalating levels of violence—to an erosion in religious values, while others, rather than seeing an erosion in religious values, point to a growth in membership in religious organizations and a resurgence of religious activism in societies around the globe. In order to assess whether either of these arguments have merit, we need first to have a clear understanding of what religion really is.

In his classic work *The Elementary Forms of Religious Life,* published in 1912, Émile Durkheim (1947) attempted to identify the elements common to all religions. Although in his survey of world religions, Durkheim found no common belief or practice, he did find that all religions he studied made a distinction between

the **profane,** or ordinary, aspects of everyday life and the **sacred,** those things that transcend the ordinary, are associated with the supernatural, and inspire awe, respect, worship, and even fear. For Durkheim, the latter category defined the essence of **religion,** a "unified system of beliefs and practices relative to sacred things" (p. 37). This system of beliefs and practices includes **rituals,** specialized rites and ceremonies that, along with a set of rules, believers use to guide their daily behavior. He referred to the people who were united by their religious practices as a *moral community* or church.

Durkheim argued that the identification of an object as profane or sacred resides not in the object itself but in the meaning believers attach to it and the context in which the object is used. Thus, at any given moment, an object can be either profane or sacred. For example, Catholics may drink wine with dinner or to relax in a social setting. If wine is spilled in these circumstances, it is of little consequence. During the religious ritual of Mass, however, Catholics believe that this ordinary object, wine, is transformed into the blood of Christ. If it is spilled, great care and reverence accompany its removal. All religions have sacred things. They may take the form of writings (for Christians the Bible, for Jews the Torah, for Muslims, the Qur'an or Koran); revered persons (Christ, Moses, and Mohammed); important symbols (the cross, the Star of David, and the crescent moon and star); places of worship (a church, a synagogue, or a mosque); religious holidays (Christmas, Yom Kippur, and Ramadan); and even "holy" cities (Bethlehem, Jerusalem, and Mecca).

Sociological Perspectives on Religion

Since Durkheim's pioneering work, the relationship between religion and society has become a common focus of sociological investigation. In general, sociologists employ the same methodologies and theoretical approaches to the study of religion that they do to other kinds of social behavior. In so doing, they examine religion as a social institution created by human actors. Thus, sociologists do not investigate whether God or any other supernatural force or being exists, nor do they try to ascertain the validity of one system of beliefs over another. As individuals, sociologists may profess particular belief systems in their own personal lives, but as professional sociologists studying religion, they investigate the social aspects of religion, identifying, as did Durkheim, elements that are common to all religions: the various organizational forms religion may take, the functions and dysfunctions of religion, the conflicts within and among religious groups, the impact religion has on people's attitudes and behaviors, and the relationship between religion and other social institutions. Four major theoretical perspectives have been utilized to study religion: the functionalist, conflict, feminist, and symbolic interactionist perspectives.

The Functionalist Perspective

Although the social functions of religion include maintaining order and social solidarity, religion can also serve as an agent of change. Durkheim's study of Australian aborigines convinced him that the essential function of religion was the preservation of the social order itself. According to Durkheim, when people believe the same things and engage in the same rituals, they create social bonds with one another. These bonds give them a sense of social solidarity and community, a feeling of belonging to a group. The more that people come together to worship and to express their beliefs, the more likely they are to strengthen those bonds.

Religion contributes to the maintenance of social order by establishing rules for people to live by. The fact that these prescriptions are anchored in a supernatural authority and define what members must do in order to attain salvation make them highly effective in controlling people's behavior. The values evoked in these normative guidelines often reinforce those found in secular laws and other social institutions, for example, prohibitions against murder, theft, and doing harm to others as well as prescriptions for supporting the common good through fulfilling civic duties such as paying taxes, serving your country, and maintaining your family and personal property.

Although religion often supports the status quo, it can serve as an agent for change as well.

An examination of the civil rights movement in the United States shows that a significant number of leaders and volunteers in the fight for racial justice came to participate in marches, lobbying, sit-ins, and freedom rides through their involvement with a religious organization such as the Southern Christian Leadership Conference. Anglican Archbishop Desmond Tutu was an important voice for social change in South Africa. Throughout many of the poorer countries in the world today, religious personnel are challenging unjust situations and are actively working for social change.

On a personal level, all religions attempt to provide answers to troubling questions about life and life after death as well as events in people's lives and environments that appear to be beyond human understanding. Suffering, untimely deaths, evil, and natural disasters can make life seem random and aimless. Religion gives life meaning and purpose. Religion also provides psychological and social support for individuals. Faith and prayer actually seem to relieve anxieties and to contribute to a sense of well-being. For example, David Myers (1993) found that people who are religiously active tend to be healthier and happier than those who are not. Harvard Medical School researchers found that praying can lower brain wave activity and heart and breathing rates and thus relieve pain (Wronski, 1995). Additionally, in times of trouble, religious institutions often provide people with sanctuary, food, clothing, and other goods. When social services traditionally provided by the government are cut, religious bodies often feel called upon to pick up the slack.

Functionalists recognize that religion also has latent or unintended and hidden functions which are more difficult to discern and which may turn out to be dysfunctional. Thomas O'Dea and Janet O'Dea Aviad (1983) point out that each of the above functions, if taken too far, can have negative consequences. For example, if people identify too strongly with their own religions, believing that they alone have the "truth," they can become intolerant of the beliefs of others, engaging in persecution and even genocide of the "unbelievers." Throughout history, wars and conquests have been conducted in the name of religion. In the Middle Ages, for example, Christian Crusades were launched to drive the Moors out of Spain; Catholics and Protestants clashed in seventeenth-century Europe and again in twentieth-century Northern Ireland; Jews and Arab Muslims continue to battle in the Middle East; Hindus and Muslims have yet to resolve their differences in India and Pakistan, whose very countries were created because these two religious groups could not coexist within the same geographical boundaries. Such divisiveness diminishes social solidarity and makes social control more problematic on the societal level. At the same time, however, having an "external" enemy can increase the internal cohesion of a group. Resolving religious differences is especially difficult when they, as they so often do, coexist with political, social, or economic inequalities.

Given these apparent paradoxes, what are we to make of the functionalist view of religion? Clearly, one of functionalism's main contributions to the sociology of religion is its recognition of the important role religion plays in people's lives. What remains questionable, however, is the extent to which religion can fulfill functions for "the larger society," especially in modern societies that are multiracial, multiethnic, multireligious, and multiclassed. For example, in places where there is consensus around a major religious tradition, religion can help to maintain order and to promote solidarity on the societal level. However, in countries where the population is divided among different and conflicting religious traditions, finding common ground among all parties may be elusive and religion may prove to be divisive rather than cohesive. For example, in the United States today, religious fundamentalists and those following a more liberal tradition often engage in heated debate over issues such as abortion, capital punishment, homosexuality, and a myriad of other issues. This interreligous strife, called **sectarian conflict,** can turn violent, as we have seen in recent years with the shootings and bombings at abortion clinics.

The Conflict Perspective

Nothing represents the conflict view of religion as much as the words of Karl Marx (1964, p. 27): "Religion is the sigh of the oppressed creature, the sentiment of a heartless world, and the soul of soulless conditions. It is the opium of the people." As you will recall from our discussion of Marx in Chapter 2, he saw capitalist societies as composed of two opposing and hostile classes, the capitalists, or ruling class, and the proletariat, or laboring class. According to Marx, religion reflects the power relationships in a society and serves the economic interests of the ruling class by "drugging" the oppressed with the belief that worldly suffering is only temporary and a route to a better afterlife. This belief, coupled with another that views what happens in life as part of a divine plan, can become an obstacle to social change. Marx argued that, like opium, religion offers relief and escape from pain and keeps people from seeing the true source of their troubles—their exploitation and domination by the ruling class. Marx believed that people who accept these religious teachings are unlikely to challenge the existing order or take action to end their suffering.

History provides many examples of how religion has been used to legitimize the social order and to justify social inequality. In ancient Egypt, religion taught that the Pharaoh was God. In the Middle Ages, monarchs proclaimed their "divine right" to rule. Consequently, in both cases, it was assumed that subjects had a moral obligation to obey their rulers. When European countries explored and colonized Africa, Asia, and the Americas, they took along Christian missionaries for the purpose of converting the "heathens," thus justifying their economic actions in the name of religion. As we saw in Chapter 9, for centuries, Hinduism perpetuated inequalities in India through its caste system by teaching its members that each caste had to follow certain rules. A failure to follow the rules or any attempt to move out of one's caste would be punished by rebirth into a lower caste. This belief system effectively minimized organized efforts to change the status quo. In a similar fashion, religion was used to justify slavery in the United States. According to historian Kenneth Stampp (1956), slave holders used the Bible to teach slaves that God expected them to be obedient and, if they were, they would be rewarded in the next life.

The major contribution of the conflict analysis of religion is its observation that religion does not benefit everyone in an equal manner and that powerful groups, consciously or unconsciously, often utilize religion to support and maintain their positions. Marx and other conflict theorists have called attention to how religion can retard social change. Nevertheless, other sociologists, such as Max Weber, have called attention to conditions under which religion can also be a catalyst for producing social change. As we saw in Chapter 1, Weber argued that the Protestant ethic, originating in the religious teachings of John Calvin, was instrumental in the rise of capitalism. And, at the outset of this chapter, we saw that in Latin America, for example, Roman Catholic clergy and social activists like Renee Golden have employed liberation theology to help people free themselves from poverty and oppression. Similar efforts have taken place across a wide range of societies and in many different historical periods. Religious leaders like America's Reverend Martin Luther King, Jr., South Africa's Archbishop Desmond Tutu, India's Mother Teresa, San Salvador's Archbishop Romero, and numerous other rabbis, priests, and religious personnel of all denominations have risked their lives to work alongside the poor and oppressed to end injustices and secure a more equitable share of society's resources for everyone. Although religious beliefs played a significant role in the maintenance of slavery and apartheid, they also were instrumental in their abolition. And, as we have seen with the functionalist perspective, religion meets the needs of many people along a number of dimensions that are unrelated to economic factors.

The Feminist Perspective

The feminist perspective, like the conflict perspective, focuses its attention on the relationship between religion and social inequality. However, besides issues of race, class, and ethnicity, the feminist analysis pays close attention to issues of gender and sexual orientation. For example, feminists argue that over the centuries, symbols of female power as represented in female deities such as the Greek Demeter and the Egyptian Isis were displaced from the major religions and replaced with a pattern of male dominance. According to feminists, a literal reading of the sacred writings of many of the major religions project, wittingly or unwittingly, a subordinate status for women compared to men. For example, the Qur'an states that "Men are in charge of women because God has made one to excel over the other . . ." (quoted in Haddad, 1985, p. 294). The Bible contains numerous references to male dominance such as "Wives, be subject to your husbands, as to the Lord. For the husband is the head of the wife as Christ is the head of the church. . . ." (Eph. 5:22–23). A daily prayer for male Orthodox Jews includes the words "Blessed art thou, O Lord our God, King of the Universe, that I was not born a woman."

Feminist scholars also point out that although in the United States more women than men define themselves as religious (see the Data box), a "stained glass ceiling" exists that denies women important leadership roles in religious institutions. However, there is some indication that the ceiling is cracking, albeit slowly. Although the Roman Catholic Church, Orthodox Judaism, and the Islamic faith continue to prohibit female ordination, the Association of Theological Schools recently reported that women now make up 22 percent of the enrollments at five of the nation's largest divinity schools, and the Episcopal Church reports that 20 percent of its priests, deacons, and bishops are women (Norman, 1998). Feminist scholars are not concerned only with issues of gender; they also examine patterns of discrimination against lesbians and gays as clergy and as members of the laity. Although more religions are welcoming homosexuals, with some even blessing same-sex unions, such actions continue to generate controversy (Niebuhr, 1998).

The Symbolic Interaction Perspective

According to symbolic interactionists, religion provides a reference group that helps people to define themselves (Chalfant, Beckley, & Palmer, 1994). People internalize their religious teachings and use them as a yardstick by which they measure their social conduct. In this way, religious beliefs help people to define a situation, to determine how to interpret that situation, and, thus, how to act in it. For example, as we saw earlier, many people in Dayton, Tennessee, in 1925—as many people do today—believed in the literal interpretation of the Bible and, thus,

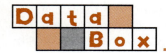

Gender and Religion in the United States

- Sixty-seven percent of adults imagine God in masculine terms.
- Sixty-nine percent of women say that religion is important to them, compared to 51 percent of men.
- Fifty-five percent of women say they get a great deal of consolation from religion, whereas only 38 percent of men say that.
- Women are more likely than men to believe that God works miracles and is with them at all times and that religion is relevant to most of life's challenges and difficulties.
- Women of all generations are more likely than men to be actively connected to religious institutions.

Approximately 75 percent of women belong to a church or another religious group. The corresponding figure for men is approximately 67 percent.

- Almost half of all women say that they attended a religious service in any given week; less than 40 percent of men do so. Women are considerably more likely than men to watch religious television.
- African American women tend to be more religious than both white women and African American men.

Source: Data from Robert B. Fowler and Allen D. Hertzke. 1995. *Religion and Politics in America.* Boulder, CO: Westview Press, pp. 167–168. See also National Opinion Research Center. 1994. *General Social Survey,* p. 127.

---

found it difficult, if not impossible, to accept the validity of evolutionary theory. Similarly, the strength of religious attitudes and the role they play in people's behavior can be observed in current controversies over abortion, homosexual rights, and physician-assisted suicide.

Symbolic interactionism provides insight into the process by which people create religious meaning and shows how those meanings then shape people's attitudes and behaviors. However, this micro-level approach is limited in that it generally pays little attention to the larger historical and social structural context in which people interact and in which religious meanings and behaviors are constructed; it thus overlooks the critical issues of power and inequality.

Forms of Religious Organization

Slightly over 15 percent of the world's nearly 6 billion people view themselves as nonreligious. Another almost 4 percent are atheists, people who deny the existence of God. The majority of the world's population belongs to just six of the world's religions (see Table 13.1). Most of the major world religions contain subdivisions which may differ significantly in organization and structure. Ernst Troeltsch (1931), a student of Max Weber's, attempted to differentiate between types of religious organizations by dividing them into two polar types: churches and sects. Other sociologists, recognizing that this classification did not encompass all forms of religions, added denominations and cults to the typology. Here again, it is important to realize that this classification is intended as an ideal type which allows us to examine the similarities and differences among religious organizations in terms of a variety of characteristics such as size, professionalization of clergy, authority structure, membership requirements, and degree of integration within the larger society. As Figure 13.1 illustrates, religious organizations can be placed along a continuum according to these differences, with a church at one end and a sect at the other end. Cults represent an organizational variant that is qualitatively different and thus cannot be as easily placed on the church–sect continuum.

TABLE 13.1 ⊘ Religious Population of the World, 1996

Religion	Adherents; Percent of World's Population	Founder; Date	Belief System
Christianity	1.9 billion; 33.7%	Jesus Christ; first century	Monotheistic (one God); Jesus Christ is the son of God; salvation comes through moral behavior and God's grace
Islam (Muslims)	1.1 billion; 19.4%	Muhammad; about 622 C.E.	Monotheistic; those who follow the teachings of the Koran will go to an eternal Garden of Eden
Hinduism	800 million; 13.7%	Aryan invaders of India mixed their Vedic religion with that of the natives; about 500 C.E.	Polytheistic; life in all its forms is an aspect of the divine; there is a cycle of birth and rebirth determined by one's past deeds
Buddhism	325 million; 5.6%	Siddhartha Gautama; about 525 B.C.E.	Nontheistic; through right meditation and deeds, people can free themselves from desire and suffering, escape the cycle of eternal rebirth, and reach nirvana (enlightenment)
Judaism	14 million; 0.2%	Abraham; about 1300 B.C.E.	Monotheistic; God established a particular relationship with the Hebrew people; by obeying God's law, they would be witness to His justice and mercy
Confucianism	5.1 million; 0.1%	Confucius; around 500 B.C.E.	Nontheistic; sacred philosophy that emphasizes ethical principles

Source: Adapted and summarized from U.S. Bureau of the Census. 1997. *Statistical Abstract of the United States, 1997.* Washington, DC: Government Printing Office, Table 1333, p. 828; *The World Almanac and Book of Facts.* 1998. New York: World Almanac Books, pp. 654, 659.

Churches

A **church** is a large religious organization that is well established and well integrated into society; it is characterized by a formal, bureaucratic structure, including a professional clergy arranged in a hierarchy of authority. A church has a fairly elaborate and highly prescribed ritual and belief system and tends to be relatively stable over time, having as members many generations of the same family. A church may take the form of either an ecclesia or a denomination. An **ecclesia** is a church that is formally allied with the state and is the "official" religion for the society. Aided by the government, an ecclesia typically maintains a religious monopoly by ignoring, coopting, or sometimes repressing other religious groups (Mc-Quire, 1992). Generally, an ecclesia works in harmony with the government, each reinforcing the other's power and control over its respective sphere of influence. Contemporary examples of churches that approximate the ideal type ecclesia include Lutheranism in Sweden, Judaism in Israel, Islam in Pakistan and Iran, Buddhism in Myanmar (formerly Burma), Anglicanism in England, and Roman Catholicism in Spain.

The range of citizen involvement in an ecclesia varies considerably. For example, some Catholics in Spain are members in name only, an accident of birth, and they limit their participation to rituals associated with major life changes such as baptism, marriage, and funerals. Al-

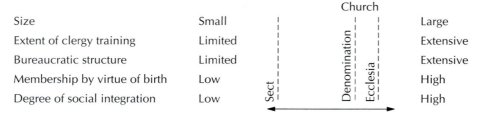

Size	Small	Church	Large
Extent of clergy training	Limited		Extensive
Bureaucratic structure	Limited		Extensive
Membership by virtue of birth	Low		High
Degree of social integration	Low	Sect ← Denomination Ecclesia →	High

FIGURE 13.1 ○ Church-Sect Continuum

though Roman Catholicism remains the state religion in Spain, people are free to choose the extent of their religious involvement. In contrast, people living in Iran find that the majority of their life experiences, including political beliefs, are circumscribed by the teachings of the ecclesia and enforced by the state. For example, in Iran, women must wear the chador (long cloak) and hejab (veil) in public; female athletes are restricted to playing five sports in international competitions so that they may wear the hejab during the games. Social contacts between women and men are strictly controlled. For example, women are not allowed to be spectators at men's sporting events (Hersh, 1998), and mixed parties among the sexes are prohibited.

The majority of modern societies do not recognize an ecclesia. However, even when there is a conscious effort to separate church and state, religion may still play a prominent role in political life. Robert Bellah (1970) refers to the set of beliefs, rituals, and symbols that makes sacred the values of a society as **civil religion.** Although civil religion is not tied to any one denomination or religious group, many of the religious symbols used in community logos and other public places are reflective of Christian traditions. Given the increasing religious diversity in the United States, public expressions of civil religion have engendered controversy. Some people object to symbols that are perceived as representing only one religious tradition (see the Sociological Reflections box); others who identify themselves as atheists, like Illinois's Rob Sherman, have sued to have religious symbols removed from all public venues.

A **denomination** is a religious organization, independent of the state, that is generally toler-

ant of religious diversity and that competes with other denominations for members. Although people can and do join a denomination voluntarily, most members are there as a result of ascription. They are born into the religion of their parents, and unless they become disillusioned or simply stop attending, they remain members for life. Denominations flourish in societies that have a separation between church and state. The United States, with approximately 300 identified denominations, has more religious diversity than any other country in the world. This is due in large measure to its history as a nation of immigrants who brought with them a wide range of religious experiences.

Sects

Sects are on the opposite end of the religious continuum from churches. A **sect** is a relatively dogmatic and homogeneous religious group that is considerably smaller in size and less well integrated into society than a church. Most sects are formed when a group of church members disagree over some aspect of doctrine or ritual and split off to begin a new organization. For example, the Methodist denomination originated out of a protest against the formality of the established Church of England. Typically, a sect is neither bureaucratic nor hierarchal; its clergy is often part-time and not professionally trained. Max Weber (1922) observed that sect leaders often exhibit charisma, an aura or mystique that compels people to listen to their message. Such leaders are perceived as being divinely inspired and are able to elicit strong support from their followers. Most sects stress *evangelism,* the active recruitment of new members who then be-

Sociological Reflections

A Struggle over Symbols

In the United States, the First Amendment mandates the separation of church and state. Because of this, controversies have arisen in some communities.

> [In 1990,] on a whim, Marilyn Shexsnayder entered a contest to design a logo for her hometown. She was a stockbroker, not an artist. But using her colored pencils and her computer she drew an outstretched hand, and, to portray the centrality of religion in this old railroad town with more than 25 churches and about 8,000 people, she sketched the simple fish that she regarded from childhood as a universal symbol of faith. . . .
>
> Mrs. Shexsnayder won the logo contest and $100 prize, and for eight years the logo with the fish . . . adorned Republic's trucks, flags, street signs, stationery, business cards, and Chamber of Commerce brochures.
>
> [Then] suddenly, the little fish [was] causing a big splash in this town just southwest of Springfield. Someone complained about the fish to the American Civil Liberties Union, and . . . the organization sent a letter asking the Mayor to delete the logo because it was "unmistakably identified with Christianity."
>
> "The fish symbol, also known as an ichthus, first appeared in the second century and was used as a secret sign of Christianity," said the letter. . . . "Thus we believe the City's seal violates the First Amendment's prohibition against the establishment of religion" . . .
>
> Instead of changing its logo, like a nearby town . . . faced with a similar warning from the A.C.L.U., Republic . . .

> vowed to fight. Many residents . . . [said] they must stand for their local autonomy against meddling outsiders like the A.C.L.U., and for the Christian faith of the town's majority.
>
> "The logo represents the town over all," said Paula Howell, an office manager at an accounting firm and a third generation Republic native, "and I don't see anything wrong with that because the majority of our community are very religious. This is the Bible Belt, and a number of churches we have per person is pretty high. It ranks right up there with fast-food restaurants." . . .

[Others, including the logo's designer, are not in favor of keeping the fish and are unhappy at the divisiveness that has ensued.]

> If Mrs. Shexsnayder had to do it all over again, she said she would try to find a symbol that was truly universal. "Maybe," she offered, "a halo."

What issues are involved here? As a student of sociology, what advice would you give to Republic's town leaders on how to handle this conflict? What can be done when a community that has been religiously and ethically homogeneous for generations begins to feel a threat to its communal identity when diversity begins to emerge?

Source: Excerpted from Laurie Goodstein (1998, June 23). "Town's Logo Becomes a Religious Battleground." *New York Times*, pp. A1, A17. Copyright © 1998 by The New York Times Company. Reprinted by permission.

---

come "converts" or who feel "born again" when they accept the teachings of the sect. Some sects, like the Jehovah's Witnesses, actively recruit members by going door to door. While many people who join sects are poor and estranged from much of society, increasing numbers of middle-class people are joining sects because they feel spiritually empty or the sect offers them a more emotionally satisfying sense of community than they found in their larger denomination (Iannaccone, 1994).

Sects perceive themselves not as "new" but rather as "true" faiths in contrast to the church

they left, which they see as having become too accommodating to a secular society (Stark & Bainbridge, 1985). Consequently, sects tend to be more doctrinaire, less tolerant of differences, and more demanding on their members than churches. Many sects are short-lived, failing to attract enough new members to maintain themselves. Others become institutionalized, often withdrawing from society by forming their own community characterized by a distinctive dress, speech, and lifestyle. For example, members of the Old Order Amish sect preserve their culture by living in rural enclaves in Iowa, Ohio, New

York, and Pennsylvania; wearing the simple clothing of their ancestors; and rejecting modern conveniences such as electricity, motorized vehicles, and formal education beyond the eighth grade. They limit their contact with the larger community, restricting it primarily to shopping in town, conducting necessary business transactions, and relying on natural reproduction for new members (Hostetler, 1981). Still other sects successfully increase their membership by recruitment. In the process, they become more diverse and broaden their belief systems, gaining social respectability and acceptance, eventually evolving into a denomination as the Methodists did.

Cults (New Religious Movements)

Thus far, the religious forms we have been describing are all related in some way to existing religious faiths that are perceived as more or less coventional within the dominant culture. In contrast, a **cult** is a dissident religion, organized into a tight community in great tension with the larger environment (Fowler & Hertzke, 1995). Typically, cults are relatively small in size and headed by a charismatic leader. Cults tend to flourish in times of social stress and rapid social change and to recruit most of their members from people who feel alienated from the larger society. While membership in a cult is short-lived for many, cults can mean moral survival for certain individuals, giving them a sense of meaning and purpose (Tipton,1982).

Cults may be home grown—such as Scientology, which was founded in California in 1959 by science fiction writer L. Ron Hubbard—or imported from other cultures. Two examples of the latter are "The Moonies," named after the followers of the Reverend Sun Myung Moon, founder of the Unification church in Korea in 1956, and the Hare Krishna, whose members wear saffron-colored robes, shave their heads, and hand out their literature in public places. This cult traces its origins to a meditative religion in Asia. Like sects, cults may be of short duration or they may evolve into other types of religious organizations. Some of the largest religions in the world today, such as Christianity, Judaism, and Islam, began as cults. However, in recent years, highly publicized cases of mass suicides of cult members (Heaven's Gate, 1997) and standoffs with federal authorities ending in many deaths (the Branch Davidians in Waco, Texas, 1993), have imbued the term *cult* with a negative meaning that conjures up images of brainwashing, communal lifestyles, and bizarre behavior, thus weakening its usefulness as a social category. For this reason some sociologists suggest that the term *cult* be replaced with terms such as *new religious movement, alternative religion,* or *unconventional religion* (Fowler & Hertzke, 1995; Chalfant, Beckley, & Palmer, 1994).

Applying the Sociological Imagination:

Using the traits in Figure 13.1 (p. 378), analyze the structure and organization of a religious organization with which you are familiar. Where would you place that religious organization on the church–sect continuum? What problems, if any, did you encounter in your analysis? For example, do some traits overlap? What other characteristics could you employ in a comparative analysis of various religious groups?

Religion in the United States

As noted earlier in this chapter, some people perceive that Americans are less religiously inclined today than in the past. Existing data do not seem to substantiate this, however. A Gallup Poll conducted in 1944 found that 96 percent of Americans professed a belief in God or some higher power. That figure remained stable in a 1994 survey. Further, in 1995, 58 percent of Americans surveyed said that religion was very important in their lives, compared to 52 percent in 1978. A comparative study of other countries, but excluding India and Muslim countries, found that only South Africans had higher ratings (cited in Koenig, 1997, pp. 33, 36). In 1997, 67 percent of adults said they belonged to a church or synagogue, ranging from a low of 63 percent for those eighteen to twenty-nine years of age to a high of 75 percent among those sixty-five years and older. Forty percent of adults surveyed reported attending a church or synagogue in the last seven days (U.S. Bureau of the Census, 1998, p. 72). Whether these latter figures reflect actual behavior or socially accepted answers, Americans have higher rates of church membership and attendance than in most Latin American and European countries. Religious preferences in the United States are depicted in Figure 13.2.

Although why Americans have higher rates of religious involvement than people in other countries is not entirely clear, two factors are probably relevant. First, historically, religious and ethnic identity were important to many of the groups that migrated to the United States (Parillo, 1994). Second, compared to other countries, the United States is home to many denominations, sects, and cults that actively compete for members, giving people the opportunity to choose a structure which best meets their needs. Indications are that religious diversity will continue to increase in the United States as patterns of migration shift. As you learned in Chapter 10, today's immigrants come as did most earlier imigrants, not from Europe, but from Asia and Latin America, and they bring with them a wide range of religious traditions, including Islam, Hinduism, Buddhism, and Sikhism, as well as Protestantism and Catholicism. Indications are that the fastest growing religion in the United States, and in the world at large, is Islam. There are about 6 million Muslims in the United States, nearly half of whom are African Americans who are attracted to the Islamic message of hope, discipline, and self-improvement. The remaining adherents are foreign-born immigrants from Muslim countries (Peart, 1993).

Religion in the Information Age

Throughout history, religious leaders have explored new ways to bring religion to the population. In earlier times and even today, church missionaries traveled to far-away places in an effort to win converts. With the invention of the radio and later television, electronic preachers called "televangelists" became popular, bringing their message to thousands and even millions of listeners at one time. There are now some 1,400 radio stations and 220 television stations devoted exclusively to religious broadcasting, representing about a $2 billion enterprise. In recent years, the development of the Internet has created additional opportunities for the distribution of religious materials and the recruitment of new members. It is now possible to attend a virtual church any time of the day or night by clicking on a mouse. Menus allow you to select scripture readings, hymns, prayers, and sermons, and to join chat rooms with like-minded individuals. How this new technology will affect church membership and attendance in the coming years awaits empirical study.

Religion in the Twenty-First Century

Two trends currently underway are having a profound impact not only on U.S. culture but also on the way in which nations relate to one another, and it is likely that these patterns will continue into the next century. Mainstream churches have lost membership, while the fundamentalist churches, perceived by many to offer more emotional involvement and clear answers to today's problems, have increased their numbers. In some countries, fundamentalism is fueling the rise of religious nationalism.

The Fundamentalist Revival

The fundamentalist revival is not limited to the United States; it is occurring in many parts of

FIGURE 13.2 ☉ Religious Preferences in the United States *Source:* Adapted from U.S. Bureau of the Census. 1998. *Statistical Abstract of the United States, 1998.* Washington, DC: U.S. Government Printing Office, Table 90, p. 72.

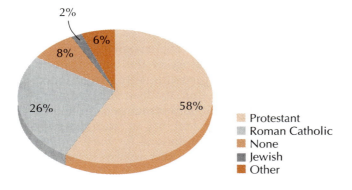

- Protestant
- Roman Catholic
- None
- Jewish
- Other

the world. **Fundamentalism** refers to a religious orientation characterized by the belief in strict and unambiguous rules and by a literal and dogmatic acceptance of scripture exactly as written. Among fundamentalists, whether the Taliban in Afghanistan (see Chapter 3) or the coalition of conservatives and fundamentalists known as the Religious Right in the United States, there is a sense that modern culture is increasingly corrupt. Alcoholism, permissive sex, abortion, pornography, drugs, gambling, changing gender expectations, and lesbian and gay rights are all targets of fundamentalist criticism. To counter these trends, fundamentalists have mobilized their resources, becoming politically active in an effort to set a political agenda in keeping with their religious beliefs. Such activities have engendered a negative response among the nonreligious and those who believe religion should be a matter of personal conscience and not a subject for legislative action. They voice fears about a loss of freedom and privacy as well as the potential for discriminatory treatment on the basis of religious beliefs. Fundamentalist revivals are most likely in times of rapid change, when many people long for what they perceived as a "better and more moral" existence. Closely related to this trend is the rise of religious nationalism.

The Rise of Religious Nationalism

The political face of the globe changed dramatically in the last half of the twentieth century. The reach of the global economy pushed the forces of modernization into more traditional societies, altering centuries-old norms and roles. The collapse of the Soviet Union, the end of the Cold War, the ethnic conflicts in Yugoslavia and Africa, and the continuing power struggles in the Middle East have altered political boundaries, contributing to mass migrations of populations. As a result, millions of people with deeply embedded religious and cultural ties to one area are now forced to live in another. These tensions and changes have provided fertile ground for the rise of religious nationalist movements in a number of countries.

Adherents of these movements want to rid their nations of outside control, nonbelievers, and what they see as the corrupting influences of modern secular states like the United States and its Western allies and to return to a more religiously based culture. Many are willing to use violence to achieve their goals. Israeli Prime Minister Yitzhak Rabin was killed in 1995 by a Jewish religious nationalist who believed that Rabin's policies violated God's will for Israel. Islamic nationalists have gained control in Iran and of large areas of Afghanistan, Egypt, Algeria, Sudan, Pakistan, and parts of the Middle East, replacing secular law with a system of Islamic law and justice, purging Western practices and fashions and establishing religious control over political decisions. Hindu nationalists have gained more influence in India's political institutions, and, as we saw earlier, fundamentalist Christians have gained political influence in the United States. The challenge in the years ahead will be for religiously based governments and secular nations to find ways to accommodate to each other's diverse political orientations. Failing that, a "new cold war" is likely to emerge (Juergensmeyer, 1993).

Education as a Social Institution

Like the family and religion, education is an important social institution in human societies. In the United States, education has become one of the nation's most dominant institutions, one that is strongly linked today not only to religious ideology but also to achievement and opportunity. **Education,** the transmission of the knowledge, skills, and cultural norms and values of members of a society, creates options for individuals in economic, social, and political life. As this definition implies, the process of education imparts far more than the three Rs (reading, writing, and arithmetic); it also helps shape people's values and ways of living in society.

In the early history of the United States, when it was still a predominantly agricultural or early industrial nation, the lack of a **formal education,** systematic and structured training in school, or even an inability to read and write were not serious limitations for most people. Until the nineteenth century, relatively few people had formal education. Formal education was largely restricted to the wealthy and well-connected, generally white, men of the upper class. It was considered irrelevant for most free people and dangerous and even illegal for the enslaved (Sapiro, 1994). However, U.S. society today requires literacy—not only the ability to read, write, and count but also, increasingly, the acquisition of specialized skills.

Today, education is a primary mechanism by which individuals attain high status and earn respect. It is also one of the most important institutional components of the U.S. race, class, and gender system. For example, despite programs designed to create equal opportunity through the U.S. education system, substantial sociological and other research demonstrates that race, class, and gender continue to affect students' experiences and educational outcomes (Disch, 1997). Researchers such as Jonathan Kozol (1991), for example, have provided substantial description of how race and poverty intersect in impoverished communities and schools producing savage inequalities in educational experiences and outcomes in many U.S. cities. Similarly, a 1995 report based on research commissioned by the American Association of University Women Educational Foundation documented the effects of gender, race, and class on educational achievement.

Sociological Perspectives on Education

Public debate about the purposes and future directions of U.S. education is as lively and spirited as ever. The wide variety of interest groups in this arena reflects a broad spectrum of academic viewpoints ranging from various sociological, behaviorist, and feminist perspectives to cognitive developmental perspectives as well as nonacademic humanistic perspectives. Of particular concern to contemporary sociologists is the purpose and consequences of education in society. Although sociologists have divergent perspectives on this issue, each perspective helps us understand various aspects of education, including its purposes, functions, benefits, costs, and limitations as well as the process of education itself.

The Consequences of Education: A Functionalist Perspective

According to a functionalist perspective, one of the major functions of education is to teach the common morality. Indeed, one of the most compelling responsibilities of U.S. schools is, and has always been, the preparation of young people for their moral duties as free citizens of a free nation. When the public school movement began in the United States in the 1830s and 1840s, the notion of universal public schooling as a mechanism for instilling a sense of national identity and civic morality was supported (Schultz, 1993). Beside the teaching of a common morality, functionalists have identified a number of other manifest as well as latent functions and dysfunctions of education:

1. **Socialization.** The socialization function of education consists of the teaching of knowledge and skills. This includes not only technical skills and knowledge such as reading, writing, and arithmetic but also social skills such as obedience to authority, cooperation, and punctuality. Schools also promote national unity and patriotism by teaching young people to pledge their allegiance to their country and by teaching them a history of the culture, which is not always the complete history. For example, in the United States, until recently, the history that students were taught in schools was primarily Eurocentric, focusing on the positive contributions of Euro-Americans, past and present, with little integration of the history of the diverse groups that have historically made up the U.S. motif. Moreover, students were often taught an idealized and distorted version of U.S. history. Few, if any, history lessons, for example, spoke to the massive murder of Native Americans by European settlers, the taking of their land, and the systematic destruction of their cultures. Today, multicultural curricula have changed, to some degree, how history is taught in some schools. However, there is still a definite ethnocentric, Western bias in the teaching of U.S. history. Likewise, other countries play up their national achievements in history and civic lessons while watering

Besides teaching basic academic skills, schools promote national unity and patriotism by teaching young people to pledge their allegiance to their country and by teaching them a history of the culture. The history taught, however, is often idealized and often ignores the contributions of many of its citizens.

down or omitting negative acts. For example, in Japan, students are not taught about the Japanese massacre of thousands of Chinese civilians in the city of Nanjing, including how some civilians were used for target practice and others were buried alive (Kristof, 1995a; Sayle, 1982).

2. **Cultural transmission.** Schools play an important role in the transmission of culture by teaching students society's core values. In U.S. society, values such as individualism, patriotism, and competition are interwoven into virtually all educational activities. Activities such as spelling bees, placement on the honor roll, and course grading (such as grading on a curve) are based on individuals competing or being measured against one another. Although ostensibly they imply cooperation and unity, oftentimes even team activities promote individual competition.

3. **Assimilation and social control.** Schools function to assimilate or mainstream culturally distinct individuals into the larger culture. Schools expose students from diverse backgrounds and in all regions of the country to a common curriculum, thereby helping to create and maintain a common cultural base. Students of color are often educated out of their racial or ethnic subcultures into society's mainstream. Schools also teach young people to conform to societal norms and values.

4. **Social placement.** Schools play an important role in determining who will eventually occupy high and low status positions in society. **Gatekeeping,** determining who will enter what occupations, is another term for the social placement function of education. Credentialing is an example of how gatekeeping works. Credentials such as diplomas and degrees are increasingly used to determine who is eligible for what job. For example, although a Ph.D. in the social sciences such as sociology does not prepare students to teach in a college classroom, nonetheless university hiring committees routinely require the doctorate as a credential for who gets teaching jobs. In this sense, credentials function as sorting devices, weeding out those who presumably do not have the knowledge or skills to perform a given job. In reality, however, credentials do not guarantee ability, skills, or knowledge. It is quite often the case that one does not have the credentials but does have the ability, skills, or knowledge to perform a given job. Like-

wise, it is sometimes the case that one has the credentials but not adequate knowledge, skills, or ability to perform a job.

5. **Change and innovation.** An important function of schools is that they act as agents of change. To meet the changing needs of students, schools often offer new courses and curricula such as women's studies, AIDS education, computer science, black and chicana studies, and gay and lesbian studies. This function is particularly evident at the college and university level where, through the conduct of scientific research, knowledge is produced and reproduced.

Today, structural functionalists stress the positive functions of education while focusing on the needs of an increasingly complex industrial society. In this context, functionalists hold that mass education fills the need of complex industrial societies for skilled workers, moral and social consensus, and equal opportunities. Accordingly, the creation of new occupations in the early part of the twentieth century, the massive in-migration of foreign workers to U.S. cities and factories, the information explosion of the mid-twentieth century, and widespread acceptance of egalitarian ideas have all contributed to the dramatic expansion of formal education today (Thompson, 1994). However, although high-level skills in reading, writing, math, and computer technology are needed in today's workplace and the global economy, U.S. education has not functioned positively to prepare the majority of students to compete with citizens of other industrialized countries. For example, U.S. high school students score lower on math and other tests of academic achievement, literacy, and knowledge than do their counterparts in most other countries (Bennett, 1988; Stevenson, Lee, & Stigler, 1986). Mastery of these skills and knowledge as well as of computer technology is a must for survival in the global economy.

Education and Social Inequality: A Conflict Perspective

By focusing primarily on the positive functions of education, a functionalist perspective does not readily focus our attention on who is most likely to fail in the educational system and why.

The implication of a meritocracy diverts our attention from the consequences of social class location, that is, what it means to be rich, poor, or middle-class and a student in the U.S. educational system. The fact is, students do not succeed in the educational system solely because of ability. Rather, as a conflict perspective suggests, well-to-do parents are able to parlay their wealth and other resources into a quality education for their offspring and, at the same time, influence education policy and practices. Conflict theorists contend that formal education has been designed by and maintained by the ruling elite (capitalists) in order to further their dominance and their own goals. For example, during the early twentieth century, schools were designed to turn immigrant and rural children into obedient workers; later the emphasis shifted to developing white-collar skills and loyalty to the capitalist system. Contrary to the functionalist perspective, conflict theorists argue that schools do not promote egalitarian ideals; rather they protect the status quo by using tests and other allegedly objective measures that favor students of upper- and middle-class backgrounds and by maintaining the illusion of equal opportunity (Thompson, 1994).

Conflict theorists point out that schools teach not only reading, writing, and arithmetic but also a **hidden curriculum,** the unwritten rules of accepted behavior and attitudes, such as competition and other cultural values. They argue that the hidden curriculum teaches young people to be obedient and to conform in preparation for life in the industrial working class (Dale, 1977). Conflict theorists also point out that there is a race, class, and gender bias deeply embedded in both the formal and the hidden curriculum. For example, through curriculum materials and classroom treatment by teachers, female and poor and working class students as well as students of color are often made to feel inadequate and less important than white and/or male students. Over time, the hidden curriculum undermines these students' self-esteem and negatively impacts their educational outcomes (Raffalli, 1994). Perhaps the most consistent argument put forth by conflict theorists about the education system is that it reproduces inequality. It does so in a number of ways, including tracking, providing unequal access to quality education, and providing unequal funding to schools.

Tracking and Sorting Out as Tools for Maintaining the Status Quo

Almost as soon as students enter school, they are stratified (overtly or covertly) by the **tracking system**—sorting students into different educational programs (such as college preparatory, vocational education or remedial programs) on the basis of real or perceived abilities. Objective and, often, subjective criteria are used to channel students into different programs.

Although proponents of tracking argue that it ideally benefits both gifted students and slow learners by providing programs structured to address their unique needs, the reality is that such tracking produces positive effects for those in the high-ability groups and negative effects for those in low-ability groups. Various sociological research has documented the fact that teachers often have lower expectations for students assigned to low-ability groups and give them fewer opportunities and incentives to learn than those in high-ability groups (see for example, Oakes, 1985). This lowers their self-esteem and expectations for educational success and fosters a poor attitude toward school which, in turn, impacts their achievement level. Sociological research has also shown that tracking is closely related to ascribed characteristics such as race, class, gender, and religion, key factors in determining who succeeds and who fails in the educational system. The lower track is generally characterized by a curriculum that is often distinctly inferior to that in upper tracks and disproportionately filled with people of color and those from the lower classes. African American and Latina/o students in particular are found disproportionately in the lower tracks. This serves to increase the gap between high- and low-track students, reproduce the hierarchial social class structure, and perpetuate society's social class divisions.

Thinking sociologically, we are reminded that societal institutions such as education are rooted in cultural norms, customs, values, and attitudes. Thus, educational practices, like other cultural practices, vary across cultures. For example, although both German and U.S. schools practice tracking, it is a much more systematic process in Germany. After fourth grade, German students are seriously tracked into one of three high school tracks and the kind of secondary school one attends has lasting life consequences (see the Cultural Snapshot box). In contrast, Japanese schools do not practice tracking or ability grouping at all. Typically, children from both poor and rich families attend the same school. In the Japanese educational system, the emphasis is neither on separating students by abilities nor on stressing competition. Rather, the emphasis is on keeping the whole class moving through its academic work at the same pace, with the higher achievers assisting their slower classmates. The similarity of all students; the importance of the group, group participation, and loyalty; and the responsibility of the individual student to the class as a group is emphasized. Teachers seldom address students individually or overtly recognize differences in their individual aptitudes, and they minimize situations in which children compete individually with each other. Working and playing together so closely over a long period of time, Japanese students come to know each other intimately and to think of themselves as a group. Habits of group loyalty, a preference for uniformity, and the learned skill of building a group consensus through patient negotiation prepare Japanese children for the all-important work groups in their adult life (Duke, 1986; Kristof, 1995b; Schneider & Silverman, 1997).

Differential Access to Education: Race, Class, and Gender

According to some reports, differences in access to education between white and some children of color begin before they reach the formal school setting (kindergarten). For example, in the early part of the 1990s, 30 percent of African American three- and four-year-olds were in nursery school programs, compared to 40 percent of whites. This may be due to the combined effects of race and class because most preschools are private and, on average, African American and Latina/o families have less income than whites (U.S. Department of Education, 1992).

This pattern of unequal access is apparent for students of color at every education level. Although public institutions such as community colleges and state universities are not free and tuition costs in these institutions have increased dramatically in recent years, the cost of attending them is relatively low compared to private institutions. Thus, students of color and poor and working-class students are disproportionately found in these institutions. While the prestigious colleges and universities do supply scholarships to a certain number of qualified lower-income students, most are barred from entry because they can not afford it. An annual tuition sometimes as high as $30,000 is way beyond the means of poor and working class students. Thus, race and class factors such as the increasing cost of education reproduce and reinforce the class system. This can be seen in the differential educational attainment of people by race and class shown in Table 13.2.

After centuries of inequalities, women and men now have almost equal access to most areas of education. Inequities, such as in sports programs and scholarships for female athletes, are gradually being addressed as the impact of Title IX is felt. **Title IX** is a federal law that prohibits discrimination on the basis of sex or gender in all federally assisted education programs in all institutions, public and private, that receive monies from the federal government. In fact, according to recent statistics, college campuses that for decades were dominated by males are fast becoming a place where the "boys are not." Colleges in the United States are beginning to ask, "Where have all the men gone?" as women increasingly

outnumber men at colleges and universities. This gender imbalance began in the 1980s and has grown every year since (see Figure 13.3). The U.S. Department of Education projects that by 2007, almost two-thirds of college students will

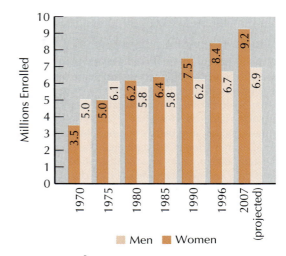

FIGURE 13.3 ☉ The New Gender Gap in Higher Education *Source:* Data from Lewin, T. 1998. "American Colleges Begin to Ask, Where Have All the Good Men Gone?" *New York Times* (December 6): 1, 28; U.S. Department of Education, National Center for Education Statistics. 1997. *Digest of Education Statistics,* Table 172.

TABLE 13.2 ☉ Educational Attainment, by Race

	African American	Asian/Pacific Islander	Latina/o	White	Other	Native American
Not high school graduate	25.7%	6.5%	46.9%	17.2%	18.9%	—
High school graduate	35.1	21.7	26.0	33.9	23.7	65.6%*
Some college/no degree	18.8	19.8	13.2	17.3	13.7	—
Associate degree (2 yr.)	6.7	—	3.6	7.3	7.3	—
Bachelor's degree	10.0	41.7[†]	6.6	16.1	23.7	9.4[‡]
Advanced degree	3.6	—	2.6	8.1	12.7	—

*This figure represents precentage of Native Americans completed high school or higher
[†]This figure represents percentage of Asians/Pacific Islanders completed four or more years of college
[‡]This figure represents percentage of Native Americans completed B.A. or higher
Source: U.S. Bureau of the Census. 1997. *Statistical Abstract of the United States: 1997.* Washington, DC: U.S. Government Printing Office, pp. 50, 51, and 160.

Cultural Snapshot

Education in Germany

Although all societies have some system of training their members to live and function in their environments, the context within which education takes place and its goals and objectives can differ significantly from one society to another. This is because societal institutions such as education are firmly rooted in the norms, traditions, values, and beliefs of a people. A cross-cultural examination of education can help us better understand education as a social institution as well as help us gain an understanding of how education is directly and indirectly related to other societal institutions such as the economy, politics, and religion. Moreover, an examination of education cross-culturally can also help us understand where contemporary U.S. students fit in terms of global competition. For example, global standardized test score data show that students in various industrialized countries such as Switzerland, Germany, and Japan outscore U.S. students on math and science tests. Because many of these countries are making significant economic gains that place them ahead of the United States, some observers have attributed this advancement to the superiority of their educational systems. Even students in newly industrialized societies such as Singapore and South Korea outscore U.S. stu-

dents on these tests. A brief look at the German education system provides a comparison and contrast to the U.S. education system and some insight into its effectiveness for German citizens.

Germany has a highly effective educational system. The average adult has completed almost twelve years of school. Ninety-five percent of children attend public school. Primary schools are neighborhood schools; unlike the race- and class-segregated schools in the United States, rich and poor children in Germany often attend school together because neighborhoods often have diverse populations. Teachers are paid by the state and salaries are standard. There is no tracking (ability grouping) at the primary level; all the children are taught the same lessons in heterogeneous classes. However, at the end of the fourth grade (in some states sixth), based on grades, teachers' assessments, and their parents' wishes, students will transfer to one of three types of secondary school. From then on, German schools are seriously tracked into one of three high school tracks and the kind of secondary school one attends has lasting life consequences.

Students considered to have the highest academic ability go to Academic High School (or Gymnasium), which they attend to around age nineteen. Academic high school is roughly equivalent to U.S. high school

be females. Women outnumber men in every category of higher education: public, private, religiously affiliated, four-year, two-year. And among part-time students, older students and African Americans, the skew is much larger. Although there is no clear consensus on why men are not pursuing higher education at the same rate as women today, some education experts suggest that it is probably a combination of factors, from girls' greater success in high school to a strong economy that may give boys a sense that they can make it without higher education, whether in computer work or the military. Some schools are responding to the gender imbalance by having

easier admissions standards for boys than for girls. Others are repackaging themselves to attract more male students. These data notwithstanding, in terms of issues of gender equity in educational access, we should be cautious in how we interpret these statistics. For example, although women are the majority at most liberal arts schools, men are still the majority at most engineering and technical schools. Although the gender imbalance is not extreme, it does raise questions about the consequences of fewer men getting advanced education and of the fact that the liberal arts education may become a women's domain (Lewin, 1998a).

plus one or two years of college. In the 1990s, roughly 31 percent of German students attended Academic High Schools, most of whom were from middle-class families. Whereas many universities in the United States have an open-door policy, only those students who have attended academic high schools, get good grades, and pass rigorous entrance exams are permitted to attend the university in Germany. Again, unlike higher education in the United States, which is increasingly more and more expensive, German universities do not charge tuition and German students are given allowances for living expenses so that they do not have to work while they are in school.

Approximately 28 percent of German students move from primary school to technical institutes, or *Realschule* where they get some academic education but they specialize in commercial or technical fields. Students attend these vocational schools through tenth grade and when they graduate (usually around age sixteen) they go on either to an apprenticeship or to a technical college, where they train for a career such as in accountancy or nursing.

The third and largest track is the *Hauptschule*. Over one-third of German students attend these vocational high schools until age fifteen; they are prepared for apprenticeship, or they work in manual, clerical, and un-skilled service jobs. These schools have low prestige, and the majority of the students are from working-class backgrounds. The majority of Germans who do not attend the university enroll in apprenticeships, a German tradition and well-respected alternative to a university education. Even here, however, there is an expectation of high achievement, and those in technical and vocational education, like those with a university education, must show their grades to employers when they seek jobs. Thus, in every track, education is taken very seriously by both teachers and students, and at every level, education culminates in marketable skills that enable students to find good, full-time jobs immediately after graduation.

In recent years, the German tracking system has been modified to allow for students who start out poorly academically but later decide that they want to go to a university. Also, technical school students can now switch over to an academic high school after graduation, although they may lose a year or two in the transition. In addition, the German educational system now provides some adult education courses which prepare people for college entrance later in life.

Source: Adapted by permission from Schneider L., and Silverman, A. 1997. *Global Sociology: Introducing Five Contemporary Societies.* New York: McGraw-Hill, pp. 245–248.

Although the gender gap in terms of access to most classrooms seems to have narrowed considerably or, in some cases, to have disappeared for women, they still lag far behind in terms of access to jobs in the field of education, particularly higher-status, better-paying jobs having some assurance of longevity in higher education. For example, although women represent approximately one-third of all higher-education faculty, they are clustered in the lowest-status and lowest-paid positions in most universities and colleges. Women of color are particularly invisible representing only 4 percent of all college faculty members compared to 28 percent for white women. As Figure 13.4 shows, taken together, African American, Latina/o, Asian, and Native American women and men constitute only 12 percent of all higher-education faculty members. To date, Title IX has done little to eliminate these gender disparities in education. Like the educational reform and policies directed at educational differences in school processes and outcomes by race discussed later in this chapter, reform directed at gender discrimination has narrowed the differences but has not eliminated the problem. As we move into the twenty-first century, educational opportunity in the United States continues to be

Percentage of Faculty Members, by Color

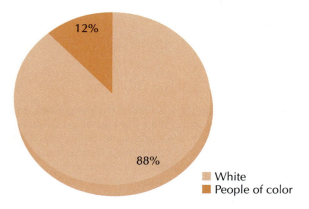

12%

88%

- ■ White
- ■ People of color

Percentage of Faculty Members, by Sex

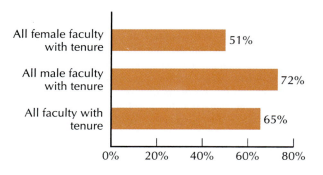

15%

52%

33%

- ■ White males
- ■ White females
- □ Other

Percentage of Faculty Members, by Race

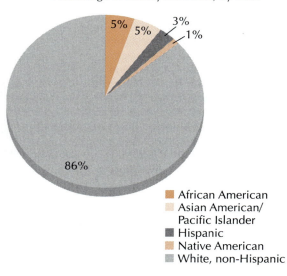

5% 5% 3% 1%

86%

- ■ African American
- □ Asian American/ Pacific Islander
- ■ Hispanic
- ■ Native American
- ■ White, non-Hispanic

Percentage of Faculty Members with Tenure, by Sex

All female faculty with tenure	51%
All male faculty with tenure	72%
All faculty with tenure	65%

0% 20% 40% 60% 80%

FIGURE 13.4 ↻ **Percentage Distribution of University Faculty by Race and Sex** *Source:* U.S. Department of Education, National Center for Education Statistics. 1997. *Digest of Education Statistics,* Table 226.

highly unequal across race, ethnicity, class, and gender (Mickelson & Smith, 1997).

Per Pupil Expenditures: Unequal Funding Like access, funding to schools is a source of inequality in education. Most public schools are funded from local property taxes and from appropriations from the state legislature. Children living in central cities often attend public schools in districts whose property tax bases have been seriously eroded by the exodus of significant industries and middle-class families. Many middle- and upper-income families live in the suburbs which generally have stronger tax

bases. Because many families living in central cities live at or below the poverty level, public education is usually their only option.

Historically, state appropriations to public schools have created "rich" and "poor" school districts characterized by differential access to the latest in instructional materials and state-of-the-art equipment, including computers, and new school buildings. According to Jonathan Kozol (1991), poor schools are often housed in dilapidated buildings having outdated facilities. In addition, poor schools are often overcrowded and have fewer and less-experienced teachers and other resource personnel than private and suburban public schools. In stark contrast, rich schools typically have the best teachers, state-of-the-art buildings and equipment, well-maintained campuses, and up-to-date and innovative teaching materials.

The distribution of funding and resources for schools has become a political football. On one side are those who argue that the equalizing of school funding would eliminate poor and rich schools and would serve to close the gap in school achievement between low- and high-status students. Others argue that spending more money on a school will not necessarily improve the education that children receive. Some empirical research support this latter position, suggesting that school expenditures do not make a significant difference in school achievement. Nonetheless, a number of state legislatures have revamped their equalization formulas in an attempt to close the gap between poor and rich school districts. As we will discuss later, there have been many attempts in recent years to reform school funding, including legal actions and a school voucher plan as methods for equalizing school funding.

Education as Process:
An Interaction Perspective

A major limitation of a conflict analysis of the educational system is that it is almost wholly macroscopic; as a result, it offers us very little understanding of the micro aspects of the educational process, such as how individuals' thoughts and actions within the environment in which teaching and learning occur impact student achievement or lack thereof. When symbolic interactionists look at education, they focus on the face-to-face interactions that take place within the institution of education, such as within the classroom. For example, scholars using this perspective have found that teachers' attitudes and expectations profoundly impact the achievement of their students. If teachers have high expectations for their students, those students are likely to perform well. If, on the other hand, teachers view students as low achievers and have low expectations for them, these students are likely to perform at a low level. Educational researchers have referred to this phenomenon as the *pygmalion effect.*

The pygmalion effect takes its name from a Greek myth about a sculptor named Pygmalion who fell in love with a statue of a woman he had created. Pygmalion prayed to the goddess of love who brought the statue to life. In a sense, because his expectations brought the statue to life, they were self-fulfilling. Similarly, educational researchers have found that teachers' expectations for their students can be self-fulfilling. A wide range of studies have shown that children readily perceive their teachers' attitudes and expectations toward them, and they can be greatly affected by what their teachers think of them and what they can accomplish. Some researchers have suggested that stimulation and teaching based on positive expectations seem to play a more important role in a child's academic achievement than does the community environment from which s/he comes (Clark, 1965). Research also indicates that teacher expectations strongly influence student self-images and thus students' ability to adjust and learn in the classroom. It is an unfortunate reality that some teacher expectations and preferences are influenced by race, ethnic, class, and gender stereotypes. For example, some teachers come to the classroom with preconceived notions about the abilities and behaviors of certain students. They expect poor achievement and discipline problems from these students and they therefore receive it.

A number of researchers have tested the pygmalion effect in the classroom and have found this hypothesis to be true. Robert Rosenthal and Lenore Jacobson (1973), for example, tested the pygmalion effect hypothesis by giving all the children in a particular elementary school an IQ test. Then they randomly assigned the label high achiever to a small number of the low scorers and told their teachers (falsely) that these children scored very high on the test. Near the end of the school year, the researchers went back to the school and retested all of the students. They found that those students whom they had falsely labeled high achievers did in fact perform better than those who were not so labeled, confirming their hypothesis that teacher expectations influence student performance. Similarly, in Scotland, a computer was incorrectly programmed and, as a result "low-ability" students were sent into the high-ability track and the "high-ability" students were sent into the low-ability track. When the mistake was uncovered nearly one year later, authorities found that the "low-ability" students were behaving as though they had high ability and the high-ability students were behaving as though they had low ability.

Feminist Perspectives

A feminist analysis of education would typically begin with the situation or experiences of women and girls in the educational institution, it would examine the world from their distinctive viewpoint in the schools, and it would be critical and activist on behalf of women. Some feminist perspectives have focused specifically on the diversity of women's experiences, paying particular attention to factors of subordination and oppression, such as race, class, gender, and sexual orientation. Thus, such an analysis might probe the interrelationships of these interactive categories of oppression and how they interact structurally and dynamically in the educational setting to create oppression, inequality, and/or privilege. Sociologist Ruth Sidel (1997), for example, analyzes the climate for women students, students of color, Jewish students, and lesbian and gay students on college campuses. Citing incidents from many campuses of racism, sexism, homophobia, sexual harassment, rape of women, and anti-Semitism, Sidel presents findings that reflect tensions and conflict in the wider society. According to Sidel, members of these groups have been perceived and treated as "the other." That is, they have been viewed as an object to be manipulated and controlled on college campuses. Over the past several years, racism, sexism, homophobia, classism, and anti-semitism have been catalysts for hostile acts against women, gays and lesbians, Jews, and some groups of color on college campuses. According to Sidel, both academic and popular discourse have focused far more on affirmative action and political correctness than on the hate incidents and violence that continue to occur on college campuses. Feminist perspectives on education are quite useful in helping us understand the unique experiences of women in the educational setting. Such perspectives help us understand not only why or how it is, for ex-

ample, that girls are the only group in this society who begin school scoring ahead and leave school scoring behind but also how various factors of oppression impact the school experiences for various groups of women differentially.

Challenges and Issues in Contemporary Education

The growing mass number of functionally illiterate people graduating from U.S. educational institutions, the mediocrity of U.S. education, inequality of educational opportunities, generally low academic performance, high dropout rates, the high cost of a college education, the slowing productivity growth of workers, drug use, and the increasing violence in schools are some of the major challenges facing schools today. Added to these challenges is that of teaching and providing adequate resources for children who have special needs, such as children with physical and emotional handicaps and, increasingly, children whose mothers were addicted to crack cocaine when they were born. These challenges are national in scope and have serious consequences not only for our schools and colleges but also for the future of individual citizens and the collective life of U.S. society and culture.

Violence in Schools

In contemporary U.S. society, it is not surprising that many students across the country fear for their safety in their schools. In a typical one-month period, over 157,000 crimes occur in U.S. schools. Furthermore, it is estimated that 135,000 guns are brought into the schools each day, and approximately fifty students are killed on school grounds during the school day during each academic year (Applebome, 1995). A Department of Education study released in 1998 found that more than 6,000 children were expelled in 1997 for bringing guns to school. In a country in which one-third of all households have at least one gun, it is not surprising that U.S. students know where to get guns and many of them pack them to school. As Figure 13.5 shows this trend has become more and more deadly. In

a little more than three years, from February 1996 to April 1999, there were fifteen violent incidents in U.S. schools, many resulting in multiple deaths (see the Data box).

Although kids bringing guns to school and school-based violence are most often viewed as an urban problem, the fact is that kids in rural areas are two times more likely to bring guns to school than are their urban counterparts. As the urban youth (fourteen to twenty-four years of age) homicide rate was dropping dramatically in the 1990s, there was a corresponding rise in small-town school shootings. When the guns, violence, and killing occurred in urban inner city schools, there was much talk of inner city children as "diseased by pathology." Curiously, however, there is little talk of pathology to describe the new wave of school violence, in which the shooters are all young white males. Rather, intellectuals and various professionals are searching for a new vocabulary to describe this growing phenomenon of white kids gunning down other white kids and whoever else gets in their gun-sights.

The American Psychiatric Association attributes much of the growing problem of school violence to past suicide attempts, social isolation, poor peer relationships, alcohol or drug abuse, bullying behavior, and easy access to weapons. According to recent surveys, one in four students in grades seven to twelve consider suicide each year (Deardorff, 1998). Few researchers today dispute the impact of media violence on behavior. In addition, there is the whole genre of video games built around the model of hunt and kill, such as Nintendo's Mortal Kombat 3 and Golden Eye, a game in which the player spends nearly all of her/his time drawing a bead on her/his victims down the barrel of a gun (Lacayo, 1998).

Responses to violence in U.S. schools have included violence prevention programs that focus on conflict resolution, limiting the number of school entrances, installing metal detectors and mounting surveillance cameras, hiring more security staff, conducting personal searches, and proposed legislation such as that suggested by Georgia state legislator Mitchell Kaye, who proposed allowing at least a few teachers to carry concealed weapons at school. He says that he was inspired to propose this law after the assistant principal in Pearl, Mississippi, used his own handgun, which he kept in his truck, to hold the sixteen-year-old boy who was arrested in the Pearl school killings (Page, 1998). A growing number of schools has responded to school violence by instituting mandatory or voluntary dress code policies that require students to wear

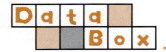

U.S. School Children: Armed and Dangerous

April 20, 1999—Littleton, CO. In the worst school massacre in American history, two male high school seniors, seventeen and eighteen years of age, killed thirteen people and wounded twenty-three others before killing themselves at Columbine High School near Denver.

June 15, 1998—Richmond, VA. A male teacher and a female guidance counselor were shot at a Richmond High School.

May 21, 1998—Springfield, OR. A fifteen-year-old male, expelled the day before for bringing a gun to school, allegedly walked into his high school cafeteria and opened fire on his classmates, killing two and injuring twenty-two others, four critically. Later the same day, police found his parents shot to death in their home.

May 21, 1998—St. Charles, MO. Police uncovered a plot by three sixth-grade boys to kill classmates on the last day of school.

May 21, 1998—Onalaska, WA. A fifteen-year-old boy took his girlfriend off a school bus at gunpoint and took her to his home, where he shot himself to death.

May 21, 1998—Houston, TX. A gun in the backpack of a seventeen-year-old suburban high school student went off and wounded a fifteen-year-old female fellow student.

May 19, 1998— Johnston, RI. Two boys were suspended from school after being accused of writing and giving threatening notes to their classmates. The notes included things such as, "All your friends are dead."

May 19, 1998—Fayetteville, TN. An eighteen-year-old honor student at Lincoln County High School

shot to death a classmate who was dating his ex-girlfriend.

April 28, 1998—Pomona, CA. A fourteen-year-old boy was charged with killing two teenage boys and wounding a third as the boys played basketball at their elementary school in Pomona.

April 24, 1998—Edinboro, PA. A fourteen-year-old middle school student shot a science teacher to death in front of students at a graduation dance.

March 24, 1998—Jonesboro, AR. Two boys, eleven and thirteen years of age, armed with three rifles and seven guns, fired off twenty-two shots wounding nine classmates and one teacher and killing four girls and one teacher.

December 1, 1997—West Paducah, KY. A fourteen-year-old student was charged with killing three of his classmates and wounding five others as they sat in a prayer circle in a hallway at his West Paducah high school.

October, 1, 1997—Pearl, MS. A sixteen-year-old boy was accused of killing his mother and then going to his high school and shooting nine of his classmates, two of whom died.

February 19, 1997—Bethel, AK. A sixteen-year-old student killed his high school principal and a student and wounded two other students.

February 2, 1996—Moses Lake, WA. A fourteen-year-old boy dressed in a trenchcoat and carrying a hunting rifle, shot and killed a junior high school algebra teacher and two students and wounded a third student.

Source: Data from the following: ABC News and Starwave Corporation. 1998, online; Richard Lacayo. 1998. "Toward the Root of Evil," *Time* (April 6): 38–39; Sebreana Domingue. 1998. "Public Domain: To Answer the Unanswerable," online; CFRA, Canada, a division of CHUM Radio Ltd. 1998 (March 25), online.

---

uniforms. Advocates of a school dress code believe that school uniforms will help curb gang violence, crime, and truancy; ease peer pressures; and even instill self-esteem. President Bill Clinton is counted among those who advocate such a policy. Recently, the president suggested mandatory uniforms as a tool to focus on discipline and

learning in public schools. Although there is not much systematic data on the impact of uniforms in schools, some administrators have reported that since the institution of uniform dress codes in their schools, there have been fewer incidents of vandalism, assault, and robbery; improved behavior; better test scores; and higher attendance.

Applying the Sociological Imagination

How might using the sociological imagination help us understand this phenomenon? Is it enough to dismiss kids killing kids as "emotionally disturbed" youngsters in an otherwise healthy youth culture? Or is there something going on in U.S. society and its youth culture that is driving young people to commit murder and other violence against their peers? Is the incessant violence of the mass media and video games desensitizing young people to violence generally and the consequences of their violent actions specifically? What can be done to change this growing trend in U.S. schools?

Educational Reform

As conflict and feminist theorists have pointed out, the U.S. educational system is far less than equal. Since the inception of mandatory formal education in the United States, there have been numerous efforts to improve the educational system. Given the significance of race and racism in U.S. social, political, and economic history, many of the educational policies and reforms historically have been attempts to redress the most egregious forms of inequality based on race (Mickelson & Smith, 1997).

School Desegregation and Resegregation   The school desegregation movement which culminated in the 1954 *Brown vs. the Board of Education of Topeka* decision, which outlawed de jure segregation in schools, was one of the first systematic attempts in the United States to deal with the issue of educational inequality based on race. **Desegregation** refers to the abolishment of legally sanctioned racial and ethnic separation in public and private facilities. The movement to desegregate schools has not been without resistance and even violence. Where it has been successfully implemented, it has reduced inequality. Research has shown that all students, regardless of race, benefit academically and socially from well-developed and well-run desegregation programs and policies (Mickelson & Smith, 1997). Unfortunately, although desegregation has been fairly successful

in the South (the South of today is the least segregated region of the country), outside of this region, public schools are *more* segregated today than they were four decades ago. Although desegregation efforts have enjoyed some limited success in small towns, rural areas, and some suburban areas, this trend is reversing in large cities due to white flight and several rarely discussed Supreme Court decisions in the 1990s have opened the door for the abandonment of desegregation (Orfield, 1996). *White flight* refers to a trend in cities whereby whites move to the suburbs or enroll their children in private schools that are racially homogeneous (Armor, 1989; James, 1989; Kantrowitz and Wingert, 1993).

Despite the efforts and early victories of the desegregation movement, most children living in the United States today attend schools segregated by race, ethnicity, and class. In fact, according to some writers, the nation's schools today are becoming increasingly resegregated for both African American and Latina/o students (Brooks & South, 1995; Mickelson & Smith, 1997). For example, a year after the Supreme Court's 1971 decision mandating school busing as a tool to achieve school desegregation, 64 percent of African American students attended schools where less than one-half of the student body was white. Almost fifteen years later, the percentage had not changed. However, by the mid-1990s, the percent had actually risen to 67 percent. Similarly, whereas 55 percent of Latina/o students attended predominantly nonwhite schools in 1968, today 74 percent do so. The patterns of school segregation vary across the country. In 1994, the states with the most segregated schools for African Americans were Illinois, Michigan, New York, and New Jersey, and for Latinas/os they were New York, California, Texas, New Jersey, and Illinois (Taubman Center, 1998).

Gary Orfield and colleagues (1996), of Harvard's Graduate School of Education, argue that the current trend toward school *resegregation* by race is particularly troubling because it is linked to segregation by class. Eighty-eight percent of schools having 90 to 100 percent African American or Latina/o children have student bodies that are also more than 50 percent poor. Conversely, only 5 percent of the schools that are 90 to 100 percent white or Asian have such concentrations of poverty. There is an abundance of research that has documented the fact that students in schools having large numbers of poor students tend to underperform compared to their socioeconomic counterparts in schools having economically diverse student populations. Accordingly, Orfield has suggested that the bridge from the twentieth century may not be leading to the twenty-first century; rather, it may be leading us back to the nineteenth century.

Compensatory Education   *Compensatory education* refers to a wide variety of programs that were initiated in public education following the passage of the 1965 *Elementary and Secondary Education Act.* These programs are aimed at children who are both poor and underachieving and provide them with developmental preschool or a variety of individualized programs in math, reading, and language arts once they are in elementary school. The underlying premise upon which such programs are based is consistent with Oscar Lewis's "culture of poverty" thesis; that is, they are rooted in the notion that poor children and children of color are "culturally deprived" and need to be somehow compensated for their alleged cultural and social deficiencies so that when they come to school, they will be able to compete without the handicap of their "disadvantaged" background.

Among the better-known educational programs that fall under the rubric of compensatory education are: (1) Head Start and other early childhood education programs; (2) Follow Through programs, which continue where Head Start programs leave off, and Even Start programs specifically designed for some Native Americans; (3) bilingual education, (4) Chapter 1 programs, which provide language arts and math programs as well as food, medicine, and clothing to students in elementary schools who are identified as needy; and (5) higher education programs designed to identify potential college students in high schools and special admissions, transition, and retention programs for qualified students going to college (Mickelson & Smith, 1997).

Compensatory education has both supporters and detractors. Some critics argue that the underlying premise of compensatory education is both racist and elitist. Other critics, such as Arthur Jensen, argue that compensatory education is a total waste of time and money because the achievement scores of some students, such as African Americans, indicate that they are less intelligent than whites. However, Jensen's redi-

There is an enormous increase in the number of children in American schools whose first language is not English. They are often poor and labeled "underachievers." Under the Compensatory Education Act, many schools offer programs such as bilingual classrooms to help bring these students to parity with others. Here students are creating posters in both English and Spanish about people such as Dr. Martin Luther King.

rection of the debate over the link between poverty and education to one based on race is not supported by credible data, and it totally ignores the fact that many compensatory education students are white and the majority of African American students neither need nor participate in such programs. Although the achievement gap across race and class remains, recent research nevertheless indicates that compensatory programs produce cognitive and social benefits to their recipients. This fact notwithstanding, compensatory education has not brought about educational parity in terms of school outcomes.

School Choice   School choice, or the *voucher system,* as it is also called, first surfaced in the late 1960s and early 1970s and was based on the simple notion that competition among schools would create better schools. Such a system would allow parents and others to choose where they would go to school, the assumption being that freedom to choose will create competition for students among various schools. That is, in competing with each other and with private and parochial schools, good public schools would attract many students and poor public schools would be forced to either improve or shut down. Currently, most students attend schools in the neighborhoods in which they live, regardless of the quality of the school. The school voucher system would allow parents and students a wider range of choices as to where to go to school. Essentially, parents, not the schools, would receive public monies in the form of a voucher which they could then use to pay for their children's education in the school of their choice.

Not everyone embraces the school voucher system. Some parents, teachers and their unions, as well as some civil rights groups are critical of the system, suggesting that, among other things, it would reinforce race- and class-segregated schools by encouraging white parents so inclined to choose schools on the basis of race and ethnic prejudice. This could do nothing less than perpetuate the existing racial and class divisiveness inside and outside schools. In addition, some critics have argued that the voucher system would include giving government money to religious schools, which would violate the separation of church and state mandated by

the U.S. Constitution. The idea of the voucher system lay dormant for most of two decades but was revitalized in the early 1990s, partially in response to school problems of overcrowdedness, violence, and low academic achievement. Today, a number of states have instituted school choice programs, but their success in the venue of school reform remains to be demonstrated.

School Restructuring

As our previous discussion has shown, there have been numerous efforts to improve and reform education in the United States. Some of the reforms include restructuring the curriculum from preschool through the university level of education in an attempt to address a myriad of issues facing educators today. Prominent educational restructuring has occurred in terms of both specific curriculum content and the overall structure and delivery of educational content.

Multiculturalism   Like the society generally, U.S. public schools are becoming increasingly racially and culturally diverse. As you learned in Chapter 9, immigration into the United States over the last several decades has brought millions of people, representing a wide variety of cultures and speaking many different languages, into this country. Consequently, U.S. public schools consist of an increasing number of children having limited proficiency in English. In some states, such as Texas, New York, and Colorado, over a quarter of the students do not speak English as a first language. In fact, some demographers predict that within five years, a majority of the total U.S. elementary and secondary school student body will be composed of children of color (primarily, Native, African and Asian American and Latina/o). The multicultural character of public education presents special challenges for teachers, parents, students, and educational administrators.

In response to the growing diversity of U.S. society and its schools, a movement to restructure the academic curriculum to more adequately and sensitively address the diverse cultures and backgrounds not only of the U.S. student body but of peoples around the world has gained increasing momentum. Like the civil rights movement of the 1950s and 1960s, the multicultural education movement is based on a powerful movement for equality. Equal human worth is at the core of the concept of multiculturalism. **Multicultural education** is teaching and learning about the equal human worth of distinctive groups of people acting in customary spheres of social life. Although the multicultural education movement is diverse, a common theme is that education should empower students with a constructive sense of social consciousness and a willingness to transcend racial, ethnic, and other social barriers that confront them in their schools and their communities (Schultz, 1995).

Alternative Schools and Home Schooling   Alternative schools emerged in response to what some critics of public education viewed as the repressive nature of U.S. education. Rote learning, strict discipline, obsession with rules and regulations, and conformity and obedience were typical characteristics of public education, and some sociologists, such as Harry Gracey (1999), have likened it to military boot camps. In contrast, alternative schools are structured such as to encourage students to be creative in their thinking and to allow them the freedom to choose learning materials within the classroom. In alternative schools, teachers facilitate learning rather than lead or direct it. Ideally, the classroom is a resource center where teachers become mentors rather than rulers. Since the late 1960s and early 1970s, the alternative school movement has become an influential force in public and private education. Whereas there were only a few hundred such schools in 1972, today, there are approximately 10,000 alternative schools in the United States. Because their small class size allows for individualized instruction, these schools have been remarkably successful in educating students across race, class, and gender backgrounds.

Like the alternative school movement, the home school movement has grown considerably over the last several decades. Today, there are over half a million children who receive their formal education at home rather than in a traditional classroom. The home school movement was initially made up primarily of religious fundamentalists who took their children out of public schools for religious reasons: they typically believed that public education either completely ignored or grossly mistreated religion in the curriculum. However, as the movement has grown, those opting for home schooling for their children are increasingly parents who are fed up with public education for secular, not religious, reasons. For example, they believe that public schools are unsafe, overcrowded, and overrun with drugs and violence and that the instruction is of poor quality. A profile of these parents shows that they typically are white, are college educated, and have a median income between $35,000 and $50,000 (Lewin, 1995; McArdle, 1994). Much of what we know about the success of home schools is based on anecdotal data. However, there is some systematic data that indicates that students educated at home score higher on standardized tests than do their counterparts in conventional schools (McArdle, 1994).

Single-Gender Education   Single-gender schools represent yet another way to restructure schools to meet the needs of a specific student population. Single-gender schools for women are not new. In the early history of formal education in the United States, because women were denied access to institutions of higher learning, women's colleges were built to educate women in what those in power deemed appropriate subject matters. Today, across the United States, parents and teachers, concerned about gender bias in the educational system, have begun to take action.

One such action for change is a renewed movement for girls-/women-only education. Although not everyone agrees, most research to date shows that girls in single-gender schools achieve more, have higher self-esteem, and are more interested in subjects such as math and science. In the last several years, scattered public schools in cities such as Illinois, Maine, New Hampshire, New York, and California have created single-gender classes or all-girls' schools, like the recently established Young Women's Leadership Academy in Harlem (Lewin, 1998b). Even some coed schools are experimenting with single-gender classes. For example, a public school in Ventura, California, offers an all-female algebra class, and in 1994, an Illinois public coed residential math and science academy for gifted students offered for the first time an all-girl calculus-based physics class. Girls in these experimental classes report feeling more enthusiastic and motivated to learn than when they were in their coed classes (Sadker and Sadker, 1994b).

Likewise, when women's academic experiences in single-gender higher education institutions are measured by scholarship, degree aspirations, leadership, and self-confidence, the research results are again favorable for single-gender education. Women from single-gender colleges outperform their counterparts in non-single-gender schools, and they are much more likely to attend graduate or professional school. Research also indicates that women's colleges also offer people of color and returning, non-traditional-age students a much more hospitable learning environment (Lindsey, 1997).

The pros of single-gender classes include the fact that female students feel safer about voicing their opinions and their uncertainties in all-girls classes and they feel that the environment is more comfortable. Critics of single-gender schools point out the negative effects of an already pervasively gender-segregated society. Some research findings suggest that while within-gender solidarity is enhanced through gender segregation in school, between gender understandings are diminished. Rather than developing gender-segregated classes and schools, classrooms and schools generally should be restructured to reflect not only a more gender-sensitive environment and culture but also one that is beneficial to both females and males (Lindsey, 1997). Other critics consider single-gender education to be a defeatist approach that gives up on girls and boys learning equally, side by side.

In addition, in 1998, the American Association of University Women (whose 1992 study of girls and education suggested that public schools shortchanged girls), in a controversial new report entitled *Separated by Sex: A Critical Look at Single-Sex Education for Girls,* backpedaled from their original stand on girls in coed schools. According to this new study, single-gender education is not a good solution, after all, to the problems of sex inequities in the schools. Although girls appear to prefer single-gender classes and they report greater confidence and better attitudes about traditionally male subjects, they do not leave these classes with measurably better skills. This research did, however, find evidence of positive effects from single-gender schools, but cautioned that some of this effect was related to class. For example, greater income and educational level of the parents of students at these schools correlated highly with greater student achievement. A precautionary note: this study is not based on original research but on a review of dozens of studies on single-sex education. It is far from the last word on the subject of all-girls schools and classes.

In the recent past, there was a movement for all-African American male schools. This movement was led by educators and others who believed that, because of racism and stereotypical treatment of African American males in the larger society generally and in public education specifically, these males could benefit from separate schools. Although the movement for all-African American male schools has lost considerable steam and has run into legal problems, the movement is not dead. For example, in Detroit, the Malcolm X Academy, an elementary and middle school, teaches young African American males about their history and culture so that they will develop a strong sense of pride in their racial and ethnic heritage. Opened in 1990 as an all-boys school, Malcolm X Academy was forced to admit girls after a judge ruled in the same year that single-sex schools violated Title IX. Today, the school is coed but the overwhelming majority (92 percent) of the students are African American males. After evaluating the poor academic performance of many African American males in its public school system, the Milwaukee School Board contemplated the creation of three all-boys schools in 1990. However, after the Detroit decision, the Milwaukee School Board instituted changes in the general curriculum instead (Pitts, 1994).

Education in the Twenty-First Century

Clearly, issues of access and equal educational opportunity have not been resolved. These issues will continue to challenge educators, students, parents, and the public generally well into the next century. As competition in the domestic and global economies continues to heat up, another challenge educators will face will be to develop programs and curricula that match education and skills to jobs in the twenty-first century. As has been pointed out elsewhere, in recent times, the nature of work has changed considerably. We are now living in a postindustrial society, in which the majority of the members provide services, including producing, managing, and distributing information, increasingly with the aid of electronic technologies, especially computers. Therefore, jobs in the next century will increasingly require a literate workforce. Unfortunately, recent statistics on literacy indicate that 40 to 44 million U.S. adults are **functionally illiterate,** or unable to use reading, speaking, writing, and computational skills in everyday life situations, and another 50 million are defined by the U.S. Department of Education as low-literate adults, those whose skills are a bit more varied but still quite limited (U.S. Department of Education, 1993).

Looming high on the educational horizon of the twenty-first century is the issue of how education will be delivered in the future in light of recent rapid advances in technology. While the literacy problem must be addressed, there is ample reason to believe that students will enter the workforce with a fairly sophisticated understanding of technology because schools are utilizing the technology to teach. On the elementary and secondary levels, the computer is beginning to assume a position of master teacher, replacing the traditional classroom teacher. Instruction is presented in an entertaining and informative manner, and the classroom teacher often becomes an assistant to the electronic teacher, helping students to understand the presented materials and occasionally expanding on them. At the college level, increasingly, instead of gathering at a central place (such as the lecture hall), students go to several satellite rooms to see the professor on a video monitor as s/he delivers course materials. The presentation becomes interactive through a video camera and microphones in each satellite room that are linked to the professor, who is able to answer student questions (Wilber, 1997).

The advancing use of technology in education means that students, especially those at higher levels, may never need to step foot on a traditional campus in order to earn a degree. The virtual university, which uses technology to deliver courses, is a growing reality as we move into the next millennium. For example, in 1998, the Western Governors University spanned sixteen states and was made up of twenty-one colleges and corporations, representing most of the sixteen participating states and Guam. Eventually, students anywhere in the world will be able to enroll in this virtual university. The virtual university can help rein in the costs of educating ever larger numbers of students and it can provide access to students who might not otherwise be able to access higher education. However, there are some anticipated problems, including fears about quality control of content; pressure on nonvirtual university professors to teach more students with technology, reducing the quality of their teaching; and the concern that universities will hire low-paid, part-time adjuncts to handle the distance students rather than expand their permanent faculties (Blumenstyk, 1998).

Whatever the pros and cons of technology in education, it is clear that as we prepare to move into the next century, educators will face new and increasing challenges brought on by the revolution in computer-generated learning resources. Providing equal access to educational technology is but one of the challenges in this regard. Although an educational goal is to use computer and television technology to broaden educational opportunities, according to some observers, the reality is that technology is simply reinforcing the disparity that already exists in public education—the rich are getting richer and the poor are getting poorer (Virshup, 1997). Although 97 percent of schools nationwide have computers, only 20 percent of students have access to their own computer (Martin, 1997). There is already a significant disparity in the quality as well as in the inventory of technologies in rich and poor schools. And poor children and many children of color have limited access, both at school and at home. Nonetheless, computer-based learning is sure to become widespread in the near future. How we meet the challenges that it creates depends on what we do today.

Key Points to Remember

1. Religion is a unified system of beliefs and practices relative to sacred things, which include rituals or specialized rites and ceremonies along with a set of rules that believers use to guide their daily behavior. Religions make distinctions between the profane, or ordinary, aspects of everyday life and the sacred, those things which transcend the ordinary, are associated with the supernatural, and inspire awe, respect, worship, and even fear.

2. The sociological study of religion focuses on the social aspects of religion, identifying elements that are common to all religions: the various organizational forms religion may take (ecclesia, denomination, sect, and cult), the functions and dysfunctions of religion, the conflicts within and among religious groups, the impact religion has on people's attitudes and behaviors, and the relationship between religion and other social institutions.

3. Studies have found that Americans have higher rates of church membership and attendance than do people in most Latin American and European countries. The United States also has the highest number of denominations of any country.

4. Mainstream churches have lost membership while fundamentalist churches, perceived by many to offer more emotional involvement and answers to today's problems, have increased their numbers. In some countries, fundamentalism is fueling the rise of religious nationalism.

5. In the early history of U.S. society, few people had a formal education. Today, education is a primary mechanism by which individuals attain high social status and earn respect. Sociological perspectives on education vary in their focus. Functionalists focus on the functions and dysfunctions of education; conflict and feminist theorists focus on issues such as unequal access to education; and interactionists examine micro interactions between teacher and students.

6. Although all societies have some system of training their members to live and function in their environments, the context within which education takes place and its goals and objectives differ significantly from one society to another.

7. Educators, parents, students, and society at large face a variety of challenges and issues in contemporary society. One of the most pressing issues is violence in the schools. In response to this issue, schools have implemented a number of procedures to ensure the safety of students.

8. Since the inception of mandatory formal education in the United States there have been numerous efforts to improve the educational system. These efforts have taken the form of reform movements and movements to restructure the system and include desegregation, compensatory education, school choice, multicultural education, alternative schools and home schooling, and single-gender education.

9. Issues of access and equal educational opportunity will continue to challenge educators, students, parents, and the general U.S. public well into the next millennium. Other challenges will include raising the level of adult literacy and determining how education will be delivered in the future in light of recent rapid advances in technology.

Key Terms

profane	civil religion	gatekeeking
sacred	denomination	hidden curriculum
religion	sect	tracking system
rituals	cult	Title IX
sectarian conflict	fundamentalism	desegregation
church	education	multicultural education
ecclesia	formal education	functually illiterate

Key People

Renny Golden
Émile Durkheim

Max Weber

Gary Orfield

Questions for Review and Discussion

1. In the beginning of this chapter, we pointed out two contrasting views of religion in today's society: some people attribute current social problems to an erosion of religious values, while others see a resurgence of religious activism. Which position seems the most accurate to you? What evidence is there to support your position?

2. Compare and contrast the functionalist, conflict, feminist, and symbolic interactionist perspectives on religion. Which perspective or perspectives do you think provides the best insight into religious behavior in the United States today? Explain your answer.

3. Observe one of your classes to see what patterns of behavior exist vis-à-vis student–student and student–teacher interactions relative to race, class, gender, and sexual orientation. Describe and analyze these patterns. What, if any, changes would you recommend to improve the classroom environment in this regard?

4. Assume that the federal government has offered a handsome reward to social scientists who can offer viable ways to improve the quality of education in the United States and promote a curriculum that meets the needs of those who will be working and raising families in the twenty-first century. Thinking as a sociologist, what methods of improvement would you suggest? What information in this chapter would you draw upon to come up with viable ways to improve education? What kind of resources would be needed to implement your plan?

For Further Reading

Berliner, David, and Bruce Biddle. 1995. *The Manufactured Crisis.* Reading, MA: Addison-Wesley. An interesting rebuttal of the argument that U.S. public education is getting worse.

Marty, Martin E., and R. Scott Appleby. 1992. *The Glory and the Power: The Fundamentalist Challenge to the Modern World.* Boston: Beacon Press. The authors examine fundamentalist movements in a variety of places, including the United States, Israel, and Egypt, and explain their popularity.

McKenna, Francis. 1993. *Schooling in America.* Dubuque, IA: Kendall/Hunt. A collection of articles that deal with a number of key educational issues, such as reform and equality, in the U.S. educational system.

Sadker, Myra, and David Sadker. 1994. *How America's Schools Cheat Girls.* New York: Scribner and Sons. A well-written book that documents how teachers and schools unwittingly shortchange girls up and down the educational ladder.

Stanton, Elizabeth Cady. 1999/1895. *The Women's Bible.* Amherst, NY: Prometheus Books. Stanton challenged the religious status quo by attacking the scriptural suggestion that sin and death were introduced into the world by women.

Stark, Rodney. 1997. *The Rise of Christianity.* New York: HarperCollins. The author presents a highly readable account of the early development and growth of Christianity.

Sociology through Literature

Braithwaite, E.R. 1977. *To Sir With Love*. New York: Jove Books. In this story, a dedicated teacher overcomes his students' hostility and rebelliousness and helps them to find respect and hope.

Brink, Andre. 1979. *A Dry White Season*. New York: Penguin Books. A moving story of a white schoolteacher in suburban Johannesburg who confronts the destructive aspects of the apartheid system.

Kingsolver, Barbara. 1998. *The Poisonwood Bible.* New York: HarperFlamingo. A fictional account of the experiences of an American missionary and his family in a remote village in the Belgian Congo in 1959. The novel explores the themes of religion, conscience, imperialism, and many paths to redemption.

Potok, Chaim. 1976. *The Chosen.* New York: Fawcett Book Group. A now-classic story of two Jewish boys in Brooklyn—one modern Orthodox and the other Hasidic—who form a friendship in the wake of Israel's war for independence. The novel focuses on the two boys and their fathers, as well as the pressures on all of them to pursue the religion they share in a way that is best suited to each.

Internet Resources

http://www.freenet.edmonton.ab.cal~cstier/religion/ toc.htm This Web site contains resources and information on a wide variety of world religions.

http://www.academicinfo.net/religionindex.html This Web site provides a directory of internet resources for the study of religion.

http://eric-web.tc.columbia.edu/ This Web site provides information about various aspects of education, including school reform, urban teachers, and compensatory education.

14

The Economy, Work, and Politics

AGENTS OF CHANGE: CESAR CHAVEZ, DOLORES HUERTA, AND THE UNITED FARM WORKERS

Throughout this century, agricultural workers have been among the most exploited groups of workers in the U.S. economy. Millions of temporary workers were imported from Mexico to work in the agricultural fields of the United States under the Bracero program, which lasted from World War II to 1964. This program allowed growers to hire workers for less pay than that given to domestic workers. Language barriers put workers at a disadvantage vis-à-vis the growers and their agents. Anyone complaining about conditions could be easily intimidated by threats of being fired. State laws regarding working standards were largely ignored. There were few, if any, facilities for sanitation in most fields. Workers were forced to drink water from the same cup, and in some fields, growers charged for the water. Worker housing consisted of unheated metal shacks, often infested with bugs, often having no indoor plumbing or cooking facilities. Workers were segregated on the basis of race, and groups were played off against each other. Despite laws against it, child labor was common. Little attention was devoted to safety measures aimed at preventing accidents. The average life expectancy of a farm worker was forty-nine years.

Although there were ongoing efforts to change these conditions by organizing farm workers in the 1940s and 1950s, the growers were able to prevent any major changes again and again. These efforts took on increased significance with the founding of the United

Farm Workers (UFW) under the leadership of Cesar Chavez (1927–1993) and Dolores Huerta. Both learned about injustice early in life. Chavez's father was swindled out of his home by dishonest Anglos. Forced off their land in Arizona, the Chavez family moved to California to become migrant workers. Cesar left school to help support his family by working in the fields. At seventeen, he joined the Navy. Later, he became an organizer for the Community Service Organization (CSO), a grass-roots Mexican American rights group, where he met Dolores Huerta, a founding member of the Stockton, California, chapter of the CSO. Huerta's mother, a community activist, operated a restaurant-hotel in a diverse neighborhood in Stockton and often let indigent farmworkers stay for free. Huerta became an elementary school teacher, but after seeing her students come to school hungry and in need of shoes, she decided she could do more by organizing farm workers than by trying to teach their hungry children.

After the CSO turned down his request to organize farm workers in 1962, Chavez and Huerta resigned and formed the National Farm Workers Association, the predecessor of the UFW. Using a variety of nonviolent tactics (demonstrations, grape and lettuce boycotts, picketing, strikes, and lobbying), the two worked tirelessly together to build an organization that would give dignity to farm workers. In 1966, Huerta negotiated the first contract between the United Farm Workers Organizing Committee and the Schenly Wine Company, the first time in the United States that a committee composed of Mexican American farm workers negotiated a collective bargaining agreement with a U.S. corporation. Other contracts followed, but the struggle wasn't easy. Chavez put his life on the line many times, fasting for weeks on end to draw attention to the farm workers' struggles and spending time in jail for his union activities. Huerta was arrested more than twenty-two times for disobeying illegally imposed injunctions. In San Francisco in 1988, while protesting President George Bush's opposition to the UFW's Grape Boycott, she was beaten by a police officer, suffering three fractured ribs and a ruptured spleen.

During the late 1960s and early 1970s, the union enjoyed widespread liberal support throughout the country and its membership grew to approximately 80,000. However, by the end of the decade, the political climate had shifted. Conservative Republicans were elected both to the White House (President Ronald Reagan) and to the California State House (Governor George Deukmejian). Many growers refused to renew contracts, and the union's membership dropped to fewer than 20,000. After Chavez's death in 1993, his son-in-law Arturo Rodriguez, who holds a bachelor's degree in sociology and a master's degree in social work, took steps to revitalize the union. An activist since college, UFW President Rodriguez continued Chavez's policy of taking a salary comparable to a farm worker's ($8,610 in 1993) and living in a union-provided house.

Today, shouts of "*Usí se puede!*"—"It can be done!" the rallying cry of the UFW, can be heard echoing across California's strawberry fields, where a major union campaign is under way to organize the 20,000 migrant farm workers who, each spring, pick $650 million worth of strawberries. Many of these farm workers are undocumented workers, often preferred by the growers because they can be controlled more easily. Imagine what it must be like being hunched over for ten or eleven hours a day in the hot California sun, picking strawberries off foot-tall plants; after the seven-month season ends, like the average strawberry picker, you have made just $8,500. Like many farm workers, you, too, might call the strawberry *la fruta del diablo*—the fruit of the devil. (Puente, 1998; UFW; http://www.ufw.org/98.htm).

Source: Information from the following: Teresa Puente. 1998. "On the Record." *Chicago Tribune* (February 22): sec. 2, p. 3; United Farm Workers website, http://www.ufw.org, especially: (a) Julie Felner. 1998. "Woman of the Year: Dolores Huerta" (January–February), http://www.ufw.org/ms.htm. (b) "The Story of Cesar Chavez," http://www.ufw.org/cecstory.htm. (c) Steven Greenhouse. 1997. "Chavez's Son-In-Law Tries to Rebuild Legacy." *New York Times* (June 30): 8 (at http://www.ufw.org/nyt630.htm).

Types of Economic Systems

Throughout history, societies have created a variety of different ways to produce and distribute the goods and services needed for their survival. As the story of the United Farm Workers illustrates, these processes can involve competing interests and overt conflict among the different participants. Over the centuries, two major economic systems have emerged and become dominant in the modern age: capitalism and socialism. As you read and think about these systems, it is important to keep in mind again that we are describing ideal types. As Figure 14.1 reveals, what exists in the real world is a continuum, with some societies more closely approximating capitalism and other societies more closely approximating socialism. In between, there are a number of mixed economies, sharing characteristics of both capitalism and socialism. Each economic ideal type can be examined by asking three questions:

1. Who owns the means of production (land, machines, capital, and factories)?
2. Who is responsible for economic planning and decision making?
3. What is its ultimate goal? (Ford, 1988)

Underlying each system is a distinct ideology which governs how it operates. Each system also has both strengths and weaknesses for each of the system's different players.

Capitalism

Capitalism, as you learned in Chapter 1, is an economic system based on private ownership of property, competition in the production and distribution of goods and services, and the maximization of profits. Although economic planning is concentrated primarily in the hands of the owners and/or managers of individual businesses, consumers also play an important role in this process in that they decide where and on what to spend their money. Thus, to a degree, the supply and demand of the marketplace allocates resources and sets prices. However, like other economic systems, capitalism has undergone numerous changes since its inception. In the early 1800s, the dominant mode was *laissez-faire* (unregulated) capitalism. The British economist Adam Smith (1723–1790) espoused the principle of laissez-faire in his book *The Wealth of Nations* (1776). Smith believed in a natural economic order that functions best when individuals are free to pursue their own interests and profits through unrestrained trade and unregulated production. He argued that since people are motivated by the same goal, to own property and to accumulate wealth, the ensuing competition among them will ensure that no one controls the entire market; governmental interference or regulation is not needed because a freely competitive economy regulates itself by the "invisible hand" of the laws of supply and demand. According to Smith, the market will, by itself, produce the goods people want at appropriate prices, thus benefitting society as a whole.

However, as history shows, laissez-faire capitalism did not develop in the way Smith had predicted nor were its effects as benign as Smith had hoped. In the United States, some early capitalists, like oil's John D. Rockefeller, were able to drive out their competitors and create a **monopoly,** a market controlled by a single business firm which can then dictate prices and set quality standards. Such control leaves consumers little choice. If they want or need the product, they must accept the firm's conditions. And, unfettered by regulation, some firms produced unsafe products and millions of people were forced to work in unhealthy and dangerous conditions. The U.S. Congress came to view these conditions as a threat to public health and even to capitalism itself and responded by passing the Sherman Antitrust Act

FIGURE 14.1 ☉ **The Economic Continuum**

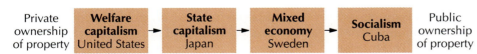

| Private ownership of property | Welfare capitalism United States | State capitalism Japan | Mixed economy Sweden | Socialism Cuba | Public ownership of property |

in 1890 to restrict monopolies and the Pure Food and Drug Act in 1906 to safeguard products.

Today's form of capitalism is referred to as *welfare capitalism.* Although individuals continue to own the means of production, make economic decisions, and pursue profits, the government plays a significant role in seeing that competition is fair and the public welfare is protected. To this end, government regulations cover such issues as child labor, minimum wages, the safety of products, environmental protection, working conditions (including collective bargaining between workers and management), and the constraint of competition and trade. Recently, the U.S. Justice Department began questioning whether some of the business practices of the giant Microsoft Corporation, maker of the popular Windows computer software, are anticompetitive and in violation of antitrust laws. Microsoft has approximately an 85 percent share of the market for operating software. Senator Orrin Hatch, Chairperson of the Senate Judiciary Committee which held hearings on this issue, characterized Microsoft's practice of giving away its World Wide Web browser free to consumers who buy their Windows product as predatory behavior (Bendavid, 1998). Testifying at this hearing, Bill Gates, president of Microsoft, disputed the charges, claiming that software makers had created more than 2 million jobs, had contributed $100 billion to the economy in 1997, and had generated significant technological advances. Sounding somewhat like a modern-day Adam Smith, Gates argued that innovation in technology will continue as long as it is not restricted by government (Lohr, 1998).

Although the United States has tried to prevent companies from dominating the marketplace, fewer than 1 percent of all corporations produce over 80 percent of the private sector output (Parenti, 1995). Much of this concentration has been made possible by mergers and acquisitions, and the pace of such transactions is increasing. According to Securities Data, in the first two months of 1998 alone, 1,506 domestic transactions valued at $142.2 billion dollars were announced, surpassing the previous high value of $128 billion involved in the mergers announced in the first two months of 1997, continuing record increases for the fourth year in a row. This merger phenomenon is not limited to the United States.

In 1997, 45 percent of all mergers were outside North America (Holson, 1998). Although such mergers and acquisitions can lead to a greater market share and higher profits for the firms involved, the increased concentration of capital often reduces competition and increases prices. Many positions in the merged companies are often eliminated outright, and duplicate positions in the merged companies are combined into one position with a resulting loss of jobs. Additionally, the acquiring company must spend much of its earnings on paying off its debt rather than investing in new plants or creating new jobs.

Beside its rather limited role in regulating the marketplace, the U.S. federal government itself is deeply involved in several key industries: the postal service, the railroad system, public education, and some utilities. The government also makes use of fiscal and monetary policies to accelerate or slow down economic growth, to prevent inflation, and to maintain economic stability. In this regard, the government has proven itself not adverse to acting to prevent the collapse of a business when it believes the common good is involved. For example, in the 1980s, at a high cost to taxpayers, the government bailed out the savings and loan industry, which was on the verge of collapse as a result of speculative practices and bad loans.

Yet another version of capitalism has emerged in some Asian countries such as Japan, South Korea, and Singapore. They practice what economists call *state capitalism.* Under this system, companies are privately owned, but they maintain a close working relationship with their governments, often receiving help from the government in the form of financial assistance and controls on the importation of foreign products. These practices are intended to help domestic companies remain highly competitive in world markets (Gerlach, 1992), but they have led other nations, such as the United States, to charge them with engaging in unfair trade practices.

Socialism

In contrast to capitalism, **socialism** is an economic system based on public ownership and government control of the economy and the distribution of goods and services for the benefit of the society as a whole. Early socialist thinkers, like England's Robert Owen and France's Henri De Saint-Simon, called attention to the injustice of laissez-faire capitalism, in which a relatively small number of people became wealthy at the expense of the masses of workers who were paid little for their labor and, as a result, like many farm workers today, lived in deplorable and unhealthy conditions. In the latter half of the nineteenth century, Karl Marx, one of the harshest critics of capitalism, predicted that these conflicts and inequities, which he believed were inherent in the system, would eventually lead to a working-class revolution that would do away with private ownership of the means of production. In its place, the workers themselves would decide how goods and services should be produced and distributed. Marx died before he could finish writing about how such a society would operate in practice, and it was left to later thinkers and political revolutionaries to create socialist systems.

Generally speaking, in socialist economies, a central committee decides what goods and services are to be produced, how they should be distributed, and at what price they should be sold. Neither profit nor competition factor into this decision making. Cuba and North Korea are the best examples of modern-day socialism. Prior to its breakup, the former Soviet Union and its satellite countries in Eastern Europe also had socialist economies. Today, however, the economies of Russia and the other nations of the former Soviet Union are moving in the direction of capitalism. This transition is not without problems. On the one hand, efforts to privatize industries and to allow market forces to regulate the supply of goods and services have created economic growth and made many individuals wealthy in those countries. On the other hand, however, these same processes have dislocated many workers, leaving them unemployed and living in poverty, forcing many into crime as a means of survival. China, which also had a highly developed socialist economy, is also moving to a market economy and has eased some of its controls, encouraging its people to buy their own homes and to acquire other private property.

Mixed Economies

As the name implies, there are societies that try to combine the elements of both capitalism and socialism. **Mixed economies,** also known as democratic socialism, are economic systems that incorporate both competitive markets and the institution of private property as well as state ownership of large corporations which are run for the benefit of all citizens. Sweden is the prime example of the mixed economy. Other Scandinavian countries, Holland, Germany, France, and Italy practice these economic principles but to a lesser degree. In a mixed economy, the government owns some of the largest industries and services such as transportation, health care, utilities, and the media. Countries with mixed economies often have high taxes which, in turn, are used to generate various social welfare programs such as health care, low-cost housing, child care, and retirement pensions for all citizens.

Assessing Capitalism and Socialism

Given the enormous economic and political changes that have taken place in the last ten years, the ideological debates about which system best serves the needs of people may be outmoded. As these economic systems evolve, new ways of assessing them will emerge. Nevertheless, a comparative examination of some of the differential outcomes in productivity and efficiency, income inequality, and civil rights that have commonly been observed between capitalism and socialism can be useful. Such an analysis helps us to see how closely intertwined these economic systems are with the political system of the societies in which they developed.

Productivity and Efficiency   One important measure of productivity is the gross national product (GNP), the value of all the goods and services produced for the market that year. Table 14.1 allows us to compare societies of different population sizes by looking at the per capita (per person) GNP. Clearly, the capitalist countries (and those with mixed economies) have outperformed socialist countries on this measure. However, the capitalist countries are also the most technologically advanced of the countries shown here. According to both official and unofficial reports of travelers, socialist countries are less efficient than capitalist countries. For example, consumer goods are often in short supply because central planners had other priorities, for example military buildups, or because workers were unable to fill their quotas due to outmoded machinery or inadequate supplies. Getting accurate data on socialist economies is often difficult because of governmental secrecy. For example, indications are that North Korea is currently experiencing enormous food shortages and that hundreds of thousands, perhaps millions, of its people are dying of starvation. Although the world community has offered help, North Korea has been reluctant to let outsiders in to appraise the extent of its needs.

Income Inequality   The most significant charge leveled against capitalism is that, by its nature, it creates and maintains a system of inequality. As we saw in Chapter 9, the hierarchical class system produced by capitalism consists of a relatively small number of wealthy and powerful people at the top and a large number of poorly paid people at the bottom. The system of capitalism, built as it is around making a profit, demands a flexible work force. When there is a great demand, workers will be needed; when demand falls, however, and profits contract, workers become expendable and people lose their jobs. Farm workers are a typical example. They

are in great demand during harvest time but are released without benefits after the crops are picked. Although the unemployment rates in Denmark, Japan, the Netherlands, Norway, and the United States averaged under 6 percent in 1997, other countries were not as fortunate: Spain had an unemployment rate of 20.8 percent, France was at 12.4 percent, and Canada had a rate of 9.2 percent (U.S. Bureau of the Census, 1998). Because the *unemployment rate* is officially defined as the percentage of the working-age population that is currently out of work but actively looking for a job, it underestimates the human dimensions of this problem. *Discouraged workers,* those who have given up any hope of finding a job, for whatever reason, are not counted among the officially unemployed. Additionally, when the economy slows, some workers may experience **underemployment,** working at jobs beneath their training and abilities or being forced to take only part-time work.

In contrast, unemployment is relatively unknown in socialist countries. Because the profit motive is not an issue, government-controlled companies will continue to employ workers even when they are not needed. With relatively little private ownership permitted, extreme variations in wealth are not common. Nevertheless, socialism has not eradicated all forms of economic advantages; many people do have significant economic advantages, but they are based on factors such as membership in the ruling party and geographical residence (Kerblay, 1983).

Capitalism has also been criticized for some of the ways in which people make their profits and become wealthy. Although the selling of stocks and bonds creates capital for businesses to invest, it can also create enormous wealth for people who do not produce any products or create any jobs (see the Sociology through Literature box). In fact, the emphasis on meeting stockholder's expectations has often resulted in company downsizing to improve the bottom line, which usually means dislocating hundreds or thousands of employees. This was especially the case in the late 1980s and early 1990s in the United States.

Civil Rights   The harshest criticism of socialist systems centers around violations of personal liberties. As we noted earlier, there is a close link

TABLE 14.1 ☉ **Per Capita GNP, by Countries, 1995**

Country	Constant (1995) Dollars
North Korea*	894
Cuba*	2,068
China*	2,303
Russia*	4,478
Canada	19,000
Sweden	24,730
France	26,290
United States	27,550
Denmark	32,540
Japan	41,160

*estimated

Source: Adapted from U.S. Bureau of the Census. 1998. *Statistical Abstract of the United States, 1998.* Washington, DC: U.S. Government Printing Office Table 1354, p. 835.

Sociology through Literature

Masters of the Universe

The term *masters of the universe* appears frequently in Tom Wolfe's *The Bonfire of the Vanities,* a tale about the downfall of a Wall Street bond trader, Sherman McCoy. The following selections provide insight into the relentless pursuit of wealth.

. . . The bond department of Pierce & Pierce was like an Air Force fighter squadron. Sherman knew it even if this young South American didn't. As the number one bond salesman, Sherman had no official rank. Nevertheless, he occupied a moral eminence. You were either capable of doing the job and willing to devote 100 percent to the job, or you got out. The eighty members of the department received a base salary, a safety net, of $120,000 a year each. This was regarded as a laughably small sum. The rest of their income came from commissions and profit-sharing. Sixty-five percent of the department's profits went to Pierce & Pierce. But 35 percent was split among the eighty bond salesmen and traders themselves. All for one and one for all, and lots for oneself! And therefore . . . no slackers allowed! no deadwood! no lightweights! no loafers! You headed straight for your desk, your telephone, and your computer terminal in the morning. The day didn't start with small talk and coffee and perusals of *The Wall Street Journal* and the financial pages of the *Times,* much less *The Racing Form.* You were expected to get on the telephone and start making money. If you left the office, even for lunch, you were expected to give your destination and a telephone number to one of the "sales assistants," who were really secretaries, so that you could be summoned immediately if a new issue of bonds came in (and had to be sold fast). If you went out for lunch, it better have something directly to do with selling bonds for Pierce & Pierce. Otherwise—sit here by the telephone and order in from the deli like the rest of the squadron.

*   *   *

. . . At forty-five seconds before the auction deadline of 1:00 p.m., George Connor, at a telephone in the middle of the bond trading room, read off his final scaled-in bids to a Pierce & Pierce functionary sitting at a telephone at the Federal Building, which was the physical site of the auction. The bids averaged $99.62643 per $100 worth of bonds. Within a few seconds after 1:00 p.m., Pierce & Pierce now owned, as planned, $6 billion worth of the twenty-year bond. The bond department had four hours in which to create a favorable market. Vic Scaasi led the charge on the bond trading desk, reselling the bonds mainly to the brokerage houses—by telephone. By 2:00 p.m., the roar in the bond trading room, fueled more by fear than greed, was unearthly. They all shouted and sweated and swore and devoured their electric doughnuts.

By 5:00 p.m. they had sold 40 percent—$2.4 billion—of the $6 billion at an average price of 99.75062 per $100 worth of bonds, for a profit of not two but four ticks! *Four ticks!* That was a profit of twelve and a half cents per one hundred dollars. *Four ticks!* To the eventual retail buyer of these bonds, whether an individual, a corporation or an institution, this spread was invisible. But—*four ticks!* To Pierce & Pierce it meant a profit of almost $3 million for an afternoon's work. And it wouldn't stop there. The market was holding firm and edging up. Within the next week they might easily make an additional $5 to $10 million on the 3.6 billion bonds remaining. *Four ticks!*

By five o'clock Sherman was soaring on adrenaline. He was part of the pulverizing might of Pierce & Pierce, Masters of the Universe. The audacity of it all was breathtaking. To risk $6 billion in one afternoon to make *two ticks*—six and a quarter cents per one hundred dollars—and then to make four ticks—*four ticks!*—the audacity!—the audacity! Was there any more exciting power on the face of the earth?

What insight does this novel give to the changing meaning of work in society? What are the implications of this type of work for individuals and the society at large?

Source: Excerpts from *The Bonfire of the Vanities* (pp. 61, 69–70) by Tom Wolfe. Copyright © 1987 by Tom Wolfe. Reprinted by permission of Farrar, Straus & Giroux, Inc.

---

between economic and political systems. There appears to be a relatively strong relationship between economic liberties, the freedom to pursue individual economic goals, and political freedoms, such as free elections and freedom of speech (Huntington, 1992/93). Because the goal of socialism is the benefit of the collective, the state sets goals and procedures that often act to limit individual liberties. Over the years, numerous stories of the imprisonment of political dissidents have come out of China, Cuba, and the countries of the former Soviet Union. One of the most visible indications of this was the 1989 televised images of Chinese troops firing on protestors in Bejing's Tiananmen Square.

The Underground Economy

Finally, it is important to recognize that some economic activity takes place outside these major economic systems in what has come to be called the **underground economy** or hidden economy, where work and income are not reported to the appropriate agencies overseeing the economy. The work itself may be legal except that it is not reported, such as someone working on construction and being paid in cash, or it may be illegal, such as selling drugs, illegal gambling, and selling on the black market. This latter activity seems to be increasing among many of the countries in the former Soviet Union as many people find themselves unemployed as their countries move to a market economy. Growth in the underground economy translates into lost tax revenues, which means less money is available for investment in the public sector, thus further contributing to a country's economic woes.

The Global Economy: Challenges and Constraints

Not only are we witnessing major changes in the economic systems of individual countries but also another transformation of major significance is well under way. Technological innovations in transportation and communication have closed the time and distance gaps between nations. As a result, workers today participate in a vast, integrated global economy, producing products in one part of the world that are consumed by workers in other parts of the world. Because production facilities can be moved easily from one location to another, workers around the world increasingly find themselves competing for the same jobs (Hodson & Sullivan, 1995). Additionally, the globalization of the economy will increasingly require many workers to learn the languages and cultures of other countries in which their companies do business in order to avoid misunderstandings (Weiss, 1994a, 1994b). International trade between nations existed in previous centuries, but what is different about today's global economy is that, to a large extent, it is dominated by multinational corporations rather than by nation states, as was true in the past.

Multinational Corporations

Multinational corporations (MNCs) are economic enterprises that have headquarters in one country and conduct business activities in one or more other countries. For example, Mitsubishi and Honda have their headquarters in Japan but manufacture and sell cars in the United States and around the world. Nike is headquartered in the United States, but its shoes are assembled and sewn in Indonesia and sold throughout the globe. The concept of multinational corporations has a long history. During the period of colonization, it was common for colonial powers to grant charters to trading companies that then had exclusive rights to trade with the colonies for goods and resources, often exploiting native populations in the process. These trading companies created the world economy. Like the trading companies that came before them, multinational corporations are once again transforming the world economy, but with a much greater concentration of economic power. By 1985, the 200 largest world corporations controlled over 80 percent of the assets of the Western world (Hodson & Sullivan, 1995). Today, approximately one-half of the world's total economic activity is conducted by only 500 multinational corporations. As Table 14.2 shows, these companies, headquartered in a small number of countries, control enormous revenues and make huge profits. The United States and Japan account for nearly three-fifths of these corporations. The extent and reach of today's MNCs have raised concerns among both social scientists and political leaders around the world. Chief among them are the creation of an international work force and the extensive power and control of MNCs, the focus of the next section.

TABLE 14.2 ☉ World's 500 Largest Corporations and Revenues, by Country, 1995

Country	Number of Companies	Revenues (in billions of dollars)	Profits (in billions of dollars)
Total*	500	$11,378	$323
Japan	141	3,985	30
United States	153	3,221	158
Germany	40	1,017	17
France	42	880	3
United Kingdom	32	516	38
Switzerland	16	345	18
South Korea	12	263	7
Italy	12	255	7
Netherlands	8	171	9
Britain/Netherlands	2	160	9
Spain	6	81	4
Canada	6	66	6
Belgium	5	56	2
Sweden	3	54	2
Brazil	4	54	−3
Australia	4	45	4

*Includes other countries not shown separately

Source: U.S. Bureau of the Census, 1997. *Statistical Abstract of the United States, 1997.* Washington, DC: U.S. Government Printing Office, Table 1367, p. 847.

International Workforce

One of the major outcomes of the modern expansion of multinational corporations is the creation of an international workforce as a result of the relocation of work. In their ongoing effort to find a source of cheap labor, multinationals export manufacturing jobs, and increasingly professional and high technology jobs, to countries where labor is cheaper. Today sixty countries, mostly located in Asia, now have Export Processing Zones, tax-free industrial areas where foreign companies can hire workers to assemble clothes, electronics, and other products at low wages. These new global assembly lines are composed primarily of women, who can be paid even less than their male counterparts. For example, in Taiwan, the Philippines, Sri Lanka, Mexico, and Malaysia, upward of 80 percent of these assembly line workers are female (Seager, 1997).

The movement of jobs from one area to another has serious ramifications for both the sending and the receiving countries. For the sending society, unemployment rates may increase, especially among semiskilled workers who worked in the manufacturing sector. Without additional education and training, they will be forced to work for lower wages in the expanding low-paid end of the service sector or perhaps become dependent on an already heavily burdened welfare system. The receiving society may initially benefit by a growth in jobs for its population, but there is often a high price to pay. Although families may benefit from an infusion of women's wages, they may also suffer some dislocation as a result of the reduced time women can spend in child care and other domestic services, especially when husbands and fathers can't or won't fill in the gap. Additionally, many of these new jobs are low-paying and not governed by health, safety, and environmental protection laws, thus threatening public health. The world was made aware of these possibilities in 1984, when a Union Carbide plant in Bhopal, India, released toxic chemicals into the air that killed thousands of people and left thousands more permanently injured. Despite the extensive damage it caused, the cost to Union Carbide was minimal. Since then, attempts have been made to improve working conditions in poorer countries, but progress has been slow.

One solution to these problems would be international work standards that reduce the gap between pay and working conditions from one society to another. Another would be the creation of a strong international worker movement. An example of this is the new cooperation emerging among unions from Mexico, the United States, and Canada. In 1993, North American union leaders opposed passage of the North American Free Trade Agreement. They feared that this agreement, designed to remove tariff barriers between the United States, Canada, and Mexico, would lead to the export of U.S. jobs across the border to Mexico, where labor costs are lower. They have now shifted tactics and are working with their Mexican counterparts to strengthen independent unions in Mexico. Union leaders believe that the improvement of wages and conditions in Mexico would also benefit workers north of the border by reducing the incentive for corporations to move factories south (Dillon, 1997). As of yet, the development of international work standards and an international worker movement remain in their infancy.

Economic Power and Control

As Table 14.2 revealed, multinationals have enormous wealth at their disposal and their presence in host societies is not without benefits. They create jobs; pay taxes; invest in the infrastructure in terms of roads, buildings, and new technology; and train the local work force. However, at the same time, they expropriate much of a host country's natural resources and often interfere in its internal affairs in order to protect their interests. For example, multinationals have been involved in attempts to destabilize countries in order to rid them of "unfriendly" leaders; they have paid bribes to get the concessions and contracts they wanted; and, whenever it suits them, they take their business elsewhere, leaving behind much economic and political chaos (Simon, 1996). Given that multinational corporations operate in many countries, no one country has the power to regulate them. Their immense size and wealth allow them to make decisions independent of the nations in which they operate (Hodson & Sullivan, 1995). The information in the Data Box shows how extensive this wealth can be. Now that we have examined some of the aspects of economic systems in general, we will focus our attention on issues surrounding work.

The Meaning of Work

A major theme in early sociological thought was the centrality of work and its impact on every facet of social life. Karl Marx, Max Weber, and Émile Durkheim all recognized that the organization and availability of work in large measure affects the social and economic well-being of individuals, neighborhoods, communities, and the society at large. Despite widespread agreement regarding the importance of work, the diversity of work experiences makes it difficult to define. Are Mark McGwire and Sammy Sosa working when they are swinging their bats, having fun playing the game of baseball they are said to love? Is the homeless person who scours neighborhoods for cans and other recyclables working? Is a student who is studying working? Is a parent working when she or he takes a child to the park? Obviously, all of these activities involve the expenditure of energy, but that, in and of itself, does not necessarily constitute work as it has been traditionally defined. The practice of many economists and labor statisticians who collect data on work in industrialized countries is to apply this concept only to activities that people do for pay. Thus, in these examples, only McGwire and Sosa work because they are the only ones to receive wages for their expenditure of effort.

Other scholars think that this definition is too narrow and exclusionary in that it ignores

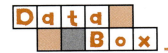

The Growth Leaders

Eight of the companies on *Industry Week's* list of 1,000 largest companies experienced revenue growth of over 100 percent between 1991 and 1996.

- Compaq Computer Corp. (453.8%)—Relying on a strong dealer network, the highly innovative Houston-based firm in 1994 surpassed IBM Corp. and Apple Computer Incorporated to become the world's leading PC maker. Its sales . . . soared from $3.27 billion in 1991 to $18.11 billion [in 1996].
- Microsoft Corp. (371.2%)—[Between 1991 and 1996], Bill Gates' Redmond, Washington-based company . . . introduced Windows NT for client/server networks . . . [and] established numerous partnerships . . . During that time frame, its revenues [grew] from $1.84 billion to $8.67 billion. [The company is currently under investigation for possible anticompetitive practices.]
- Intel Corp. (335.9%)— . . . The Santa Clara, Calif.-based chipmaker builds a new $2 billion factory every nine months or so . . . Intel's revenues [grew] from $4.78 billion to $20.85 billion.
- Lockheed Martin Corp. (173.9%)—The 1995 merger between Lockheed and Martin Marietta accounts for a big chunk of the firm's revenue growth—from $9.8 billion in 1991 to nearly $26.9 billion [in 1996].

- Glaxo Wellcome PLC (155.9%)—One of the world's largest drug manufacturers, the London-based company's . . . top-selling prescription medicines include Zantac (used for ulcers) and Retrovir (a widely prescribed treatment for AIDS patients). . . .[T]he firm intends to emphasize rapid expansion in such emerging markets as Eastern Europe and Latin America.
- Nokia Corporation (126.8%)—[This Helsinki-based firm] is one of the world's leading manufacturers of digital and analog cellular telecommunications systems . . . [It] has seen revenues climb from $3.73 billion in 1991 to $8.46 billion in 1996.
- L. M. Ericsson Telephone Co. ($121.8%)—[This Stockholm-based . . . firm . . . passed Motorola Inc. to become the largest vendor of digital mobile phones in—of all places—the U.S. market . . . Ericsson's revenues [grew] from $8.27 billion to $18.35 billion.
- Chrysler Corp. (118.0%)—[Between 1991 and 1996, Chrysler's] revenues . . . escalated from $28.1 billion to $61.4 billion . . . [The company] has abandoned earlier diversification efforts, [in 1996] selling most of its aerospace and defense units . . . [and] strengthening the company's focus on its core auto and truck businesses.

Source: Excerpted with permission from "The Growth Leaders" (1997, June 9). *IndustryWeek,* p. 45. Copyright, Penton Media, Inc., Cleveland, Ohio.

too many activities that people perform on a regular basis. Although none of the people in these examples easily fit the popular image of "a worker," nor do the sites of their activities invoke visions of conventional workplaces (Wharton, 1998), their activities do fit a broader definition of work preferred by many social scientists. For our purposes, we will define **work** as the activities that produce goods and services for one's own use or in exchange for pay or support. This definition has the advantage of encompassing three kinds of work: *paid or market work,* which generates an income; *coerced work,* which people are forced to do against their will and with little or no pay, as in the case of slaves or prison inmates; and *unpaid* or *nonmarket work,* which people do for themselves and others, including domestic work and volunteer work (Reskin & Padavic, 1994).

Applying the Sociological Imagination

Conduct a survey of your classmates, family, and friends asking them to respond to the following situation: "Imagine that you have won the state lottery and that you now have enough money that you will never have to work another day in your life. Will you work? Why or why not?" If not, what would you be doing instead of working? Analyze their responses to see what functions work plays in people's lives. Did the responses differ on the basis of age, gender, education, or race?

The Relationship between Work and Society

Work and society are related in a variety of ways. First, at the individual level, work shapes our identities, values, and beliefs. We saw how this happens in Chapter 6, when we examined work as one of the agencies of socialization. Second, work competes with other social institutions, such as school and family, for our time and energy. And as we saw in Chapter 12, individuals, especially those who are parents, today must increasingly struggle to balance the competing demands of work and family. Third, the distribution of workers (segregation and concentration) and how work is rewarded (earnings gap) are major sources of inequality in society. Finally, work settings provide an arena in which social interactions and group dynamics unfold. Several factors are important here: the changing nature of work, the growing diversity of the labor force, job satisfaction, and labor-management relationships.

The Changing Nature of Work

Economists use the terms *primary, secondary,* and *tertiary* to describe the economic sectors of a society's economy. The **primary sector** consists of activities that extract raw materials directly from the natural environment. Agriculture, fishing, forestry, mining, and animal husbandry are primary sector activities. In 1800, the United States was a nation of farmers; approximately 74 percent of employed persons sixteen years of age or older were either farm owners or farm laborers. Today, fewer than 3 percent of the U.S. labor force is so occupied. This sector, however, still dominates the economies of countries described by the World Bank (1995) as low-income countries, located primarily in Africa and Asia. In the

United States, farming has changed dramatically over the past several decades. Corporate agribusinesses have replaced family farms. And as we saw at the outset of this chapter, farm workers, even in a high-income country like the United States, receive low pay and few benefits.

The **secondary sector,** also known as the industrial sector, involves activities that transform natural resources into manufactured products. In the early 1800s, textile mills modeled after those in England began to appear in the New England states. The majority of the early mill workers were women and children. Then, as now, these workers were paid less than their male counterparts. Industrial development was given a major boost by the need for guns and tools during the Civil War. As factories turned to heavy industry, males came to be the employers' workers of choice. During World War II, when there was a shortage of male workers, female workers stepped in and built the planes, tanks, guns, and trucks that the country needed. After the war, regardless of their wishes, women were forced out of these high-paying jobs so that the returning veterans could have them back. Manufacturing jobs dominated the U.S. economy until 1960, when the tertiary sector began to expand at a rapid rate.

The **tertiary sector** is that part of the economy that provides services rather than goods. About 60 to 74 percent of employment in the developed and high-income countries now takes place in the tertiary sector (U.S. Bureau of the Census, 1997), as compared to about 22 percent in low-income countries (World Bank, 1995). This sector is broad, including low-paying work in the fast-food and retail industries as well as high-paying work in the fields of law, medicine, and technology. Currently, the ten fastest growing occupations in the United States are in the tertiary or service sector. They include jobs at both ends of the pay scale, but low-paying jobs are more evident: personal and home care aides, home health aides, systems analysts, computer engineers, physical and corrective therapy assistants and aides, electronic pagination systems workers, occupational therapy assistants and aides, physical therapists, residential counselors, and human service workers. And the majority of the fastest declining occupations are in the manufacturing or secondary sector (Bureau of the Census, 1997), thus making it increasingly difficult for unskilled and semiskilled workers to find jobs that pay sufficient wages to support a family.

Another major change taking place in the world of work in the United States and other developed countries is the rapid decline of the traditional full-time job with its attendant benefits and job security. At the same time, we are seeing a parallel increase in the number and types of jobs that are temporary, part-time, or subcontracted—from unskilled worker to college professors, computer scientists, doctors, and lawyers. Such work is called **contingency work,** a term that was coined in 1985 to call attention to the increasing proportion of people who had transitory and temporary relationships with their employers (Polivka & Nardone, 1989). Changing economic conditions and employer demands have fueled this trend. Employers argue that to be competitive in the global economy, they must cut their costs and have the flexibility to draw on a large pool of workers as needed.

This argument has been pressed most forcefully in European countries, where labor unions and legislation traditionally made it extremely difficult for companies to lay off workers for all but the most extreme reasons. Now that declining economic growth has resulted in the current high rates of unemployment in Europe, labor unions and governments have consented to increases in contingency work. For example, between 1983 and 1995, the percentage of temporary workers in Finland increased from 11.3 to 17.2 percent and in France from 3.3 to 12.6 percent. Similarly, part-time workers (less than thirty-five hours per week) rose from 9.6 to 16.0 percent in France and from 21.0 to 35.5 percent in the Netherlands. The proportion of part-time workers in the United States has been relatively stable at about 18 percent over the last decade (Andrews, 1997). However, there has been a significant increase in both temporary employment and subcontracted work in the United States (Rothman, 1998). Some workers find this a preferable arrangement because it meets their current career or family needs, but many other workers accept contingent work because they have no alternative (Rothman, 1998). In European countries, as here, there is concern that the expansion of contingency work is creating a two-tiered system—one of workers who have job security and promising futures and one composed of workers who have little hope of finding stable employment.

Diversity of the Labor Force Although the majority of today's workers are white, as people of color continue to increase in numbers due to higher birth rates and patterns of migration, there will be corresponding changes in the racial and ethnic composition of the labor force. These changes can be seen in Table 14.3, which shows the race and sex composition of the labor force in 1997 and projections for the year 2006. These numbers clearly show that women and people of color will make up the majority of new entrants into the labor force in the twenty-first century.

This trend has serious implications for employers and society as a whole. First, as we have seen in Chapter 11, the rapid increase in the proportion of females in the labor force has affected families. With the increase of single-parent and dual-earner families, child care has become a problem for many families. Thus, in the decades ahead, there will be more pressure on employers and the government to find creative ways for

TABLE 14.3 ○ Civilian Labor Force, by Race* and Sex, 1997 and Projections for 2006 (in millions)

Race	1997	2006	Percentage Change
White males	62.6	66.0	+ 5.0
White females	52.1	57.6	+10.5
Black males	7.4	8.0	+ 8.1
Black females	8.2	9.2	+12.1
Latinos†	8.3	10.2	+22.9
Latinas†	5.5	7.2	+30.9

*This does not include all racial groups in the civilian labor force.

†Persons of Latino origin may be of any race.

Source: Adapted from U.S. Bureau of the Census. 1998. *Statistical Abstract of the United States, 1998.* Washington, DC: U.S. Government Printing Office, Table 645, p. 403.

workers to balance the demands of work and family.

Second, although the passage of the Civil Rights Act of 1964 and other related legislation has contributed to the improvement of the economic position of women and people of color in the workplace, equality with white males is still a distant goal. Prejudice and discrimination in the workplace continue to create obstacles for women and people of color, thus limiting their opportunities and preventing society from benefiting from the full use of their talents.

Third, no one can predict the nature of the global economy in the future, but if present trends continue, it is likely that there will be what Randy Hodson and Teresa Sullivan (1995) have called an *innovative sector* and a *marginal sector*. In the first sector, technological and organizational innovations will lead to increased productivity. Jobs will be relatively secure, adequately paid, and provide a fair amount of autonomy for the workers. In contrast, the marginal sector will be characterized by a reduction in labor costs through lowered wages and benefits. Jobs will be insecure, wages will be low and working conditions will be poor. To succeed in the first sector will require increased worker education and participation unencumbered by racism, sexual harassment, and a gender gap in earnings. If the United States is to be a major player in the innovative sector in the next century, it will have to find solutions to some of the problems currently confronting its educational system.

Job Satisfaction   Given that work plays such a central role and occupies a significant amount of time in most people's lives, the question of whether or not people find satisfaction in their work has been an important topic of sociological research for most of this century. Job satisfaction is typically measured by a survey that asks the question, "All in all, how satisfied are you with your current job?" When the question is posed this way, the consistent finding is that the vast majority of Americans (80 to 85 percent) report general satisfaction with their jobs (Eichar et al., 1991).

Some analysts, however, caution that this broad question may overestimate levels of job satisfaction among some respondents. For example, workers who are trapped in unrewarding positions might attempt to minimize the problem by exaggerating the positive aspects of their jobs. Other respondents might be concerned that admitting dissatisfaction would reflect badly on them for making a poor job choice or for remaining in an unhappy work setting (Rothman, 1998). More detailed analysis shows that the level of job satisfaction depends on several factors: the nature of the job itself, the organizational environment in which a person works, and the worker's overall expectations and values.

In general, workers whose job responsibilities are diverse, challenging, and allow for some degree of autonomy experience less psychological stress on the job and report higher levels of job satisfaction than do workers who have more repetitive or routine type jobs (Kohn, 1990). Other factors found to be related to worker satisfaction are: adequate pay and benefits, opportunities for promotion, safe and healthy working conditions, participation in decision making, and peer interaction (Judge, 1993; Rothman, 1998; Russell and Rus, 1991). Nonetheless, work doesn't always provide satisfaction; at times, it is alienating.

Job Alienation   Karl Marx (1958) was one of the first writers to call attention to **alienation,** the breakdown of the natural connections between people and the products they produce, the process of their work, and other people, which leads to feelings of self-estrangement. Although Marx saw early capitalism as the cause of this alienation, the problems he identified can occur in any modern economic system, especially in situations in which work becomes monotonous and repetitious and workers feel powerless.

Traditional assembly-line work has been associated most closely with the experience of alienation. Here, workers toil for eight or more hours a day, performing a set task with little or no variation. Images of such repetitive work come easily to mind—putting a small part into a larger one, tightening bolt after bolt, and inspecting chicken after chicken. Workers have little or no control of the pace of the work or of how the task itself should be done, nor are they likely to see their activity as connected to a finished product. Hence, they derive no pleasure or satisfaction from their jobs and they experience feelings of powerlessness, meaninglessness, and self-estrangement. These workers often feel isolated from other workers. The noise level and pace may be such that it prohibits any significant interaction with others on the line, or company policy may forbid any social interaction on the line, when it is running (Seeman, 1959).

Workers are not completely passive in this process, however; many develop coping mechanisms (Roy, 1996). Rest and lunch periods and the occasional line breakdown, sometimes caused by worker's sabotage, become much anticipated respites. Some workers psychologically remove themselves from the tedium and boredom of their jobs by daydreaming; others use drugs.

Various other workers, especially in data entry and other information and service occupations, have work experiences similar to factory workers. Even physicians are complaining about their loss of autonomy and decision-making power as more and more hospitals and clinics are merged into large-scale, for-profit health-care corporations.

Recognizing the problem, some employers, concerned by the absentee rate and low productivity of their employees, have taken steps to reduce some of the alienating properties of assembly line work. A number of today's high technology assembly-lines, for example in the automobile industry, have been modified to give workers more control over the process itself by allowing them to shut down the line if they spot a problem. Training workers to perform a number of tasks and allowing them to rotate their activities have also improved worker satisfaction and morale in these plants. A good case in point is General Motors' Spring Hill, Tennessee, Saturn plant, where management introduced the "team" concept of building its cars. Team members participate in all aspects of building the car and thus see their work directly reflected in the finished product. In addition, time-clocks disappeared, an outdoor exercise course was installed, and a casual dress code for all employees, including the plant's CEO, was introduced to soften the hierarchical organization of work (Gwynne, 1990). Alienation is one of the factors that led many workers to join **labor unions,** organizations of workers seeking improved wages and working conditions through collective bargaining with their employers.

Unions and Labor-Management Relationships

The struggle of the farm workers in California's strawberry fields is only the latest in the centuries-old struggle between the propertied classes and workers. With the beginning of industrialization in the United States, workers joined together to represent their interests against those of the factory owners and managers. A few local craft unions were formed as early as the 1790s by skilled carpenters and printers in the cities of New York, Boston, and Philadelphia, but because these worker movements challenged the existing system, they were resisted. As early as 1806, when the Philadelphia Cordwainers (shoemakers) tried to organize, the court found them "guilty of a combination to raise wages." They were fined and ordered to disband (Foner, 1947). Over the next several decades, as other attempts to organize met a similar fate, workers tried other tactics, forming their own working-men's political parties and calling for free public education, reform of tax laws, higher wages, and a ten-hour work day. Although the workingmen's parties were short-lived, they did lead to some modest improvements in working conditions. For example, by 1860, the average work day dropped from twelve and a half hours to eleven and some skilled male workers even went on a ten-hour day (Foner, 1947).

After the Civil War, tensions between labor and management increased. When workers organized, resisted, and went on strike, there were armed clashes between the strikers and armed guards hired by management. Many workers were injured and killed. As businesses grew, they had tremendous power, and they used many tactics to keep unions out of their plants. Among them were *blacklists,* which barred fired union activists from gaining employment elsewhere; *yellow-dog contracts,* which workers had to sign promising not to join a union as a condition of employment; and *lockouts,* keeping workers from entering the plants until they agreed to management's terms. By the 1930s, however, antiunion attitudes on the part of the federal government and the public in general had begun to change. With approximately one-third of the labor force unemployed, something had to be done or capitalism itself would be threatened.

President Franklin Roosevelt promised the country a New Deal, including a new look at labor issues. The **National Labor Relations Act of 1935,** also know as the Wagner Act, recognized the right of workers to organize and bargain collectively through a union of their choice.

The Wagner Act gave a big boost to the union movement, and unions quickly increased their strength and numbers. By the end of World War II, approximately one-third of the nonfarm labor force were union members. However, union membership experienced a dramatic decline during the 1970s and 1980s, stabilizing somewhat in the 1990s. In 1997, a little over 6 million workers carried union cards, representing 14.1 percent of the labor force (U.S. Bureau of the Census, 1998). Although other highly developed countries have also witnessed a decline in union membership, it has not been nearly as dramatic as in the United States. For example, 80 percent of workers belong to unions in the Scandinavian countries, 40 percent of workers in Europe are union members, and approximately one-third of the Canadian and Japanese labor forces is unionized (Western, 1993, 1995).

A combination of factors are responsible for the decline in union membership in the United States. Chief among them were periodic recessions, which triggered massive layoffs in the highly unionized manufacturing sectors, especially in the automobile and steel industries. In an effort to prevent further loss of jobs, unions agreed to wage and benefits cuts, angering many rank-and-file members. Then, in 1981, President Ronald Reagan challenged the labor movement by ordering the striking members of the Professional Air Traffic Controllers Organization (PATCO) to return to work or lose their jobs. PATCO, with the support of the AFL-CIO, stood its ground but lost. Not only did Reagan fire and replace the strikers with nonunion substitutes but also he banned the fired workers from any further employment as air traffic controllers. This ban remained in effect until it was lifted during the Clinton Administration.

President Reagan's action proved to have a chilling effect on the the union movement in this country for many years. Employers, emboldened by his actions and the country's shift to a more conservative mood, engaged in increasingly sophisticated antiunion campaigns, which discouraged membership. Three other factors contributed to labor's problems. First, charges of misusing pension funds and other criminal activities were brought against officials of several unions, including the Teamsters Union, one of the nation's largest. Second, as we have discussed earlier, many jobs in the highly unionized sector of the economy have been transferred overseas in the cost-cutting moves of the global economy. The fast-growing segment of the economy is in the service sector,

Although the number of union members has declined dramatically since the 1950s, union members continue to demand fair treatment and adequate benefits. These United Parcel Service workers went on strike and won a new contract that improved their salaries and working conditions.

which until relatively recently was not a major target of union organizing. Also, the high worker turnover in this sector, which relies on temporary and part-time workers, makes organizing a worksite especially difficult. Finally, as strange as it may seem, the union's past successes contributed to its current decline. As the wages and benefits of union members increased, many of their children were able to go to college and enter professional and white-collar jobs, traditionally not union strongholds. In the past, when two or three generations of a family worked in the same plant, union members regenerated themselves. This is no longer the pattern today.

Even though the challenges are daunting, some analysts are predicting a resurgence in the union movement due to several factors. First, as the case of Karen Nussbaum illustrates (Chapter 11), union members, regardless of sex (or industry), earn more than their nonunion counterparts. As more workers become aware of this fact, they may want to unionize. Second, the job insecurity associated with the global economy may make union membership more attractive to workers who believe that their jobs may be the next to be exported abroad. Third, John Sweeney, the current president of the AFL-CIO, is keeping his campaign pledge to put considerable union resources into organizing, focusing heavily on the service sector. These efforts are being headed by energetic new leaders, such as Arturo Rodriguez of the United Farm Workers, whom we met at the outset of this chapter. Further, women make up a large segment of service workers, and in a recent survey, 42 percent of the women surveyed said they would vote for a union if they had a chance. Only 35 percent of the male respondents said they would do so (Kleiman, 1997). Finally, the union movement is adopting new strategies in an attempt to strengthen its bargaining power, such as having a presence at stockholder's meetings, using the Internet to reach out to members and the general public more quickly and effectively, and forging links with workers around the globe. There is some evidence that these global linkages are occurring, but in some unexpected segments of the working population (see the Cultural Snapshot box).

AGENT OF CHANGE: NELSON MANDELA

As pointed out in Chapter 10, a system of racial segregation and stratification, known as apartheid, existed in South Africa from its legal establishment in 1948 until its demise in 1994 with the election of Nelson Mandela to the presidency. Nelson Mandela, along with many other South Africans, both black and white, demonstrated that a system, however deeply entrenched, can be changed. Mandela was born in 1918 into the royal household of the Thembu tribe, where his father served as counselor to the rulers of the tribe. When his father refused an order to appear before a local white magistrate, he was stripped of his title, his land, his herd, and his livelihood. For a time, Mandela lived with his father in reduced circumstances in a small village, but after his father died, he was returned to the household of the Thembu ruler. After attending boarding school, Mandela was sent to the only college for blacks in South Africa, being groomed for success in the world of his fellow Africans. In 1941, he fled to Johannesburg to escape an arranged marriage and began studying law at one of the few firms willing to hire a black as a clerk. Mandela became a lawyer, but soon turned to political organizing as he became more and more aware of the injustices of the apartheid system. He joined the African National Congress (ANC) in 1944, and in 1949, he became one of that black-liberation group's leaders, engaging in increasingly militant resistance against the apartheid policies of the ruling National Party. Because of these activities, he was arrested and tried for treason, but he was acquitted in 1961. The following year, he was jailed

Cultural Snapshot

The Global Economy and Prostitution

On a recent morning in Rio de Janeiro, a group of working women gathered to discuss forming a union. Their concerns were like those of most working women, finding affordable day care, insurance, and health care and having money for retirement. They would also like to enjoy paid holidays like many other Brazilian workers. What makes this situation a bit unusual is that these women are some of the 1,500 women of Vila Mimosa, Rio's best-known brothel, and they want to unionize in order to win greater benefits from the state and their employers and to enjoy more respect as workers. According to Carmen Nascimento, health coordinator of the emerging Association of Residents, Owners, and Friends of Vila Minosa, "This is a profession, a job like any other. People do it for the same reasons they do any job, money" (quoted in Goering, 1998 p. 4). In Rio, the minimum monthly wage is approximately $120, and even low-paying jobs such as maids and other service workers are in short supply. Many women feel that working as a prostitute, or a sex worker as some prefer to be called, is about the only way they can pay their bills and support their families.

This desire to organize and to gain more respect is understandable when we examine the larger context within which it is occurring. Prostitution is on the increase in many countries, and accompanying this new growth are some changing attitudes. Analysts like Martha Mensendiek attribute its rise to numerous interconnected problems affecting women in developing countries. In Thailand, for example, women have long been responsible for the economic maintenance of the household. In the past, women in rural areas were able to sell food and other products to meet household needs. However, the rural economy has changed. No longer able to subsist on family farms, women have been forced to migrate in search of work. But work is difficult to find. Thus, many women end up selling their bodies to meet their families' needs. According to Mensendiek, a com-

mon attitude toward prostitutes in Thailand is that if a woman is fulfilling her traditional family obligations, her behavior is justified. Thus, prostitution is tolerated as an option for women and a coping mechanism for the rural household.

Similar developments are occurring in countries undergoing a move from one economic system to another. For example, in Saratov, Russia, a city of 1 million inhabitants, local officials are sponsoring legislation to open government brothels which would allow licensed prostitutes to work freely in a designated area. The prostitutes would have to be of age, pass regular health inspections, register their clients, and pay taxes, like other businesses. This action follows a major increase in prostitution and a rise in venereal diseases and crime in Saratov. This rise in prostitution also accompanied an ailing economy in which wages rarely top $40 a month. As a result, hundreds of local women—teachers, nurses, single mothers, and even schoolgirls—now work as prostitutes. One prostitute, echoing her Rio counterparts' view of prostitution as work, said, "If I could work as a nurse and be paid decently, then believe me, I wouldn't work as a prostitute" (Stanley, 1998, p. A1).

These are not isolated stories. They are being repeated in many countries experiencing dislocation in their economies, making it clear that the issue of prostitution is an international issue which cannot be divorced from issues of economic transformation. World leaders need to include prostitution on their agendas when talking about the impact of the global economy.

Source: Goering, L. 1998. "Brazil's Prostitutes Seek Better Benefits." *Chicago Tribune* (January 31):4; Mensendiek, M. 1997. "Women, Migration and Prostitution in Thailand." *International Social Work* (April):163–176; Rocks, D. 1998. "Czech Border Town Resents Being a Brothel for Tourists." *Chicago Tribune* (March 9):4; Stanley, A. 1998. "With Prostitution Booming, Legalization Tempts Russia." *New York Times* (March 3):A1.

again; this time, he was sentenced to five years of imprisonment.

In 1963, while still imprisoned, Mandela and several other men were tried for sabotage, treason, and violent conspiracy after police discovered quantities of arms and equipment in a raid on the ANC's military wing. On June 11, 1964, Mandela was sentenced to life imprisonment. He spent twenty-seven years behind bars. Some of the time, he was in solitary confinement; some of the time was spent doing hard labor; and some of the time, he went on hunger strikes. But all of the time, he attempted to communicate with other political prisoners and get messages to the outside world. Largely due to pressure from an international community increasingly critical of the South African system, President F. W. de Klerk finally released Mandela from prison on February 11, 1990. On March 2 of that year, Mandela was chosen deputy president of the ANC, and he assumed the presidency of the organization in July 1991. With a remarkable lack of bitterness and an ability to put the past behind, he and de Klerk fashioned a mechanism for tranforming South Africa's political system to a multiracial democracy. For their efforts, Mandela and de Klerk were awarded the Nobel Peace Prize in 1993. The future of South Africa is yet to be written. It will take time to undo the consequences of decades of racial discrimination. Yet, there is reason for optimism. Foreign investments are flowing back into the country and governmental initiatives to improve the housing, education, and economic development of the country's black population are slowly taking hold (Meer, 1990; Mandela, 1994).

Source: Information from Fatima Meer. 1990. *Higher than Hope: The Authorized Biography of Nelson Mandela.* New York: Harper and Row; Nelson Mandela. 1994. *Long Walk to Freedom.* New York: Little, Brown.

The Nature of Power and Authority

Earlier, we discussed how the union movement empowered workers to improve their wages and working conditions. On an international scale, Nelson Mandela and the African National Congress were able to enlist the support of enough people to put pressure on the government of South Africa to effect significant change. In both of these situations, participants on both sides of the issues were involved deeply in **politics,** the social processes through which individuals and groups acquire, exercise, maintain, or lose power. The exercise of power can take place on two levels. *Micropolitics* refers to the routine exercise of power in everyday lives. Human beings are political animals, and power struggles are a daily fact of life. Examples of micropolitics come easily to mind: parents expend considerably energy in getting reluctant children to clean their rooms and to be home on time; spouses struggle over which movie to see, what kind of car to buy, and who will take out the garbage; and professors work to enforce their classroom expectations. Our discussion will focus on the second level, *macropolitics,* or the exercise of power in large-scale groups or institutions. We will begin by examining the meaning of power.

As we saw in Chapter 9, sociologists, beginning with Max Weber (1968), have defined power as the ability to realize one's will despite resistance from others. The exercise of power can take two forms. On the one hand, legitimate power, or **authority,** is exercised over people with their consent. Although we complain every April 15 when our federal taxes are due, the vast majority of us pay them. We observe parking restrictions, marry at the legal age, send our children to school, pay the interest on our mortgages, and comply with many other constraints on our

After years of bitter struggle, South Africa's apartheid system was dismantled. President Nelson Mandela and Deputy President F. W. de Klerk greet crowds outside Parliament after the approval of South Africa's new constitution.

behavior because we believe the people or institutions making those demands on us have the right to do so. On the other hand, **coercion,** or illegitimate power, refers to the exercise of power through the use of force or the threat of force. For example, the person who has a gun and demands your money does not have the authority or the right to do so. Of course, that fact does not stop the mugger. However, if the police or other people happen on the scene, the mugger will not be able to sustain power for very long. This is true at the macro level as well. Governments that coerce their populations are vulnerable to acts of rebellion and are often shorter lived than governments based on legitimate authority.

Types of Authority

According to Max Weber, there are three distinct sources of authority, each varying according to a society's level of development. **Traditional authority** has its source in people's respect for long-established cultural patterns that are passed down from one generation to the next. Traditional authority is usually hereditary and often reinforced by a belief that the authority is bestowed by a higher power such as a god or other supernatural being. Tribal chieftains, feudal lords, kings, and queens all rule by virtue of customs and not because they are particularly competent, just, wise, or kind, though they may be

that in fact. Although traditional authority is most closely associated with small, homogeneous preindustrial societies, aspects of traditional authority are still present in modern-day societies. For example, fundamentalist groups use centuries-old religious books, like the Bible and the Koran, to support claims that it is divinely ordained that men should have authority over women (Rossides, 1990).

More complex and diverse societies rely on **rational-legal authority**—power that is legitimized by legally enacted rules and regulations that define the ruler's rights and duties. The authority is not vested in rulers but in the positions they hold. Every four years, the United States holds presidential elections, and, although the specific office holder may change, the authority of the office of president remains. People comply with these rational-legal authorities, not because it is customary to do so, but because it is required by the law or by the rules and regulations of the organization to which they belong. In this system, leaders can rule as long as they act within the boundaries of the law. In the twentieth century, two U.S. presidents were accused of abusing their presidential power. The House of Representatives impeached President Clinton, but after a trial, the Senate acquitted him of the charges. When President Nixon was accused of acting outside the law, he chose to resign his presidency rather than be forced out by an impeachment process.

Last, some individuals have **charismatic authority,** exercising power by virtue of exceptional personal qualities, or charisma. History is replete with charismatic leaders who helped to transform their nations—Mahatma Gandhi, whose nonviolent tactics helped to end British colonial rule in India; Martin Luther King, Jr., who applied Gandhi's nonviolent approach to the U.S. civil rights movement; Nelson Mandela, who helped to change the face of South Africa; and Cesar Chavez, founder of the United Farm Workers. Because charismatic authority resides in an individual, political systems or movements dependent on a charismatic leader are inherently unstable, weakening or collapsing when that leader leaves or dies. If the organization is to survive, it must go through a process of *routinization,* whereby followers switch their personal allegiance from a leader and commit themselves instead to the movement or the political system, thus replacing charismatic authority with rational-legal authority (Madsen & Snow, 1983). This was the situation that confronted the Southern Christian Leadership after the assassination of Martin Luther King, Jr., and was the challenge facing Arturo Rodriguez when he became president of the United Farm Workers after the sudden death of Cesar Chavez.

Although we have considered these three types of authority as if they were completely independent of one another, the reality is that they often overlap. U.S. presidents, for example, derive their power from laws, but some have been more successful than others because they also possessed charisma. Additionally, presidents are able to call on a variety of traditions from the past to strengthen their authority. In the next section, we turn our attention to the ways in which power is distributed in a society.

Models of Power and Authority

Considerable effort has gone into trying to assess who has power in the United States. Research on this topic is complicated by two critical factors. First, the the exercise of power is often hidden from public view. Decisions are frequently made behind closed doors in corporate or governmental offices or in restricted social clubs and on private golf courses. Second, traditional cultural beliefs about equality lead many to underestimate the extent and full impact of power relations in social life. Over time, two competing models of power have emerged—the power elite model and the pluralist model.

The Power Elite Model   The power elite model is closely associated with the theory of social conflict and in particular with the work of C. Wright Mills (1956). Mills argued that the United States is dominated by a **power elite,** a relatively small group of wealthy and well-connected individuals who routinely interact together, frequently intermarry, share a worldview, and work together to achieve a political agenda that serves their interests. Operating as CEOs and board members of major corporations, high-ranking officials in the federal government, and top military officers in the armed forces, this group is able to exert control over three major institutional areas—the economy, the government, and the military. They further strengthen their control by rotating in and out of these different institutional areas. Dwight Eisenhower, the highest ranking U.S. military officer and later president of the United States, fits this description well. Having been a member of the power elite, Eisenhower warned the country about the grave implications of the concentration of power in the "military-industrial complex" in his farewell address to the nation.

G. William Domhoff (1990) describes a U.S. ruling class made up of the richest 1 percent of the population. Because they have disproportionate representation in the key decision-making groups and institutions in the country, Domhoff argued, their interests will be well served, regardless of the impact on the general welfare. Running for national office, and increasingly for state offices as well, is becoming prohibitively expensive except for those who are politically and economically well connected. These people often have the support of Political Action Committees (PACs) and lobbyists for major corporations and other interest groups, who funnel millions of dollars into their campaign coffers (see Table 14.4).

While acknowledging the role the wealthy play in the political process, critics of the elitist model point out a need to be cautious about applying this elitist perspective uniformly across the board for several reasons. First, they argue

TABLE 14.4 ○ PAC Contributions to Congressional Campaigns, by Type of PAC, 1995–1996 (in millions of dollars)

Type of PAC	Democrats	Republicans	Incumbents	Challengers	Open
House of Representatives					
Corporate	16.2	36.8	45.8	1.9	5.2
Trade Association	16.8	28.4	35.5	3.8	5.9
Labor	37.3	2.7	22.0	11.8	6.0
Nonconnected	6.8	8.7	9.5	3.5	2.5
Senate					
Corporate	4.9	18.5	13.7	2.7	7.1
Trade Associations	4.1	10.3	7.7	1.7	5.1
Labor	7.0	0.7	2.4	1.5	3.8
Nonconnected	2.7	5.2	3.8	1.3	2.7

Source: Adapted from U.S. Bureau of the Census, *Statistical Abstract of the United States, 1998.* Washington, DC: U.S. Government Printing Office: Table 495, p. 302.

that there are political decisions that run counter to elite interests and instead favor the "common" interest or that benefit both (Chambliss & Zatz, 1994). Examples include consumer and environmental protection laws and improvements in the minimum wage, workers' compensation, and unemployment insurance and many others. Second, they argue that elites themselves often have divergent interests and are not as monolithic as the elitist model suggests. Finally, these critics point to the many interest groups that exist among nonelites that organize and press agendas favorable to their interests with varying degrees of success. Their behavior is more readily understood by the pluralist model.

The Pluralist Model   In contrast to Mills and Domhoff, other analysts describe a **pluralist model** whereby power is dispersed among many competing interest groups. The pluralists do not deny that power is unequally distributed, but they argue that, overall, power is widely dispersed throughout society in the form of multiple power centers in the United States. These

include churches, business associations, unions, community organizations, and countless other special interest groups, such as those based on race (the National Association for the Advancement of Colored People, the Urban League, the Southern Christian Leadership Association), gender (the American Association of University Women, the National Organization for Women, the Women's Political Caucus), age (the American Association of Retired Persons, the Gray Panthers), and sexual orientation (The Gay and Lesbian Alliance). This model is closely associated with functional theorists who argue that the diffusion of power among different interest groups functions to prevent any one group from gaining control of the government and using it to oppress other groups (Dahl, 1982). The ongoing presence and activities of competing interest groups force the government to be responsive to citizen needs.

In this model, the exercise of power involves several social processes. Power centers that are relatively weak may still be able to block the actions of other groups by acting as a veto group even if they can't achieve their own goals. For example, opposition by senior citizens forced Congress to rescind a plan that would require increases in Medicare premiums to cover long-term disability insurance. Given the existence of so many power centers, no one individual or group can get everything it wants. Rather, they must be willing to compromise and settle for achieving only part of their agendas. For example, when labor and management negotiate contracts, the general pattern is a give-and-take situation. Workers agree to certain management prerogatives in order to gain specific benefits and vice versa.

Despite the fact that various groups like these do make progress at times, the utility of the pluralist model to explain power relations in the United States is limited. First, power does not move easily from one sector to the next. It stays pretty well entrenched. A good example of this is the advantage that incumbents have in running for reelection against challengers. In every Congressional election between 1964 and 1994, upwards of 85 percent of the members of the House of Representatives won reelection (U.S. Bureau of the Census, 1997, p. 281). Table 14.4. shows that in the 1995–1996 election for House seats, PACs overwhelmingly gave financial support to incumbents and to those running for open seats and relatively little to challengers. Additionally, the table reveals the disproportionate resources of various groups. Both corporations and trade associations outspent labor by a considerable amount. Similar patterns held true for the Senate races as well.

There are other indications that the playing field is not as level as the pluralist model implies. For the most part, even when interest groups achieve some of their stated goals, they remain relatively powerless vis-à-vis the established power structure. Several examples clearly illustrate this point. Although women won the right to vote and can influence the outcome of elections, they still are not central players in determining who gets slated for those offices nor do they hold a proportionate representation in either elected or appointed positions in leadership roles. In South Africa, white Africaners still own and control the majority of the country's wealth. And, when the economy slows down, unions are forced to make concessions, some-

times giving back benefits that they had struggled so hard to win, such as we saw in the case of European job security earlier in this chapter. Similarly, special interest groups are not evenly matched. This was clearly evident in the initial year of the Clinton presidency when his health care proposals, strongly endorsed by many consumer groups, were defeated as a result of strong opposition by the insurance and medical industries. The National Rifle Association has resources far in excess of those enjoyed by hand gun control advocates, and, as a result, the NRA has enjoyed considerable success in preventing more stringent legislation regarding gun ownership in the United States. And, although the number of African American and Latina/o voters decided some of the 1998 election outcomes in the South and the Southwest, these groups remain underrepresented in elective and appointed offices at both the state and national levels.

Applying the Sociological Imagination

Compare and contrast the elite and pluralist models of power distribution in the United States. Then select one or two recent debates that have taken place in the United States, such as gun control, tax reform, environmental concerns, the tobacco trials, or welfare reform. Which model best addresses these issues? What outcomes are predicted by these models? Whose interests were best met after these issues were "resolved"?

The Disenfranchised

Both the elite and pluralist models of power neglect a small but significant part of the population. For our purposes here, we will call them the disenfranchised or powerless part of the U.S. citizenry—the homeless, the poor, and the mentally impaired. To a large extent, they exist outside the political system, having little if any control over their lives and insufficient resources to alter their circumstances. They are unlikely to vote, to contribute to a PAC, or to join an interest group, although as we saw in

Chapter 9, some, such as those organized by Mitch Snyder, do act in their collective interest. In general, however, if their needs do make it to a local, state, or national agenda, the way in which these needs get addressed may not always be in their best interests. For example, in the 1970s, the courts decided that it was a violation of people's rights to institutionalize them for "minor" mental impairments. The conventional wisdom was that many of these custodial patients could live on their own. Thus, they were released from mental hospitals and allowed to move freely in the larger community, initially saving tax dollars. However, without adequate living alternatives and rehabilitative programs, many of these individuals ended up on the streets, homeless.

New immigrants, especially those most unfamiliar with the language and political customs of their new country, are also frequently disenfranchised. However, as their numbers, visibility, and naturalization rates increase, they may come to see themselves as a distinct ethnic group and to demand recognition based on their significant presence in the population. For example, New York's Dominican community, in collaboration with other Latinas/os, led a successful campaign to redraw district lines in Washington Heights (District 10), thereby increasing their political strength (Pessar, 1995). The measure of any political system is how well it meets the needs of all its citizens, not just those with power. As we will see in the following section, some types of political systems perform better in this regard than do others.

Types of Political Systems

Political systems, like the economic systems we studied earlier, developed over time and within specific cultural contexts (Lenski, Nolan, & Lenski, 1995). In early hunting and gathering societies, political structures, as we think of them today, were nonexistent. Small in size and without any surpluses to speak of, these societies tended to be egalitarian in nature. Although individuals having special skills or knowledge assumed leadership roles when their expertise was needed, collective decision making was the gen-

eral norm. As societies settled in a given location and turned their attention to growing crops and herding livestock, surpluses began to accumulate and so, too, did inequalities in wealth and power. Hierarchies emerged; those with the greatest wealth could assume positions of power because they had the means to reward some people and to punish others by giving or withholding goods. As these powerful few governed, traditional authority took hold and they were able to pass this power to the next generation.

As communication and technology developed, these rulers were able to extend their power over larger territories, establishing geographical entities called *city-states.* Further developments in technology and communication made it easier to move from one area to another, and rulers of different city-states contested with each other for even more territory to control. By the twelfth century, a political unit called the *nation-state* had evolved which had recognizable geographical boundaries. However, the populations of many of these nation-states were racially, religiously, and ethnically heterogeneous as a result of periodic migrations and conquests. Throughout the following centuries, wars and political realignments altered many of these geographical boundaries, sometimes maintaining and at other times rearranging the mix of populations. Some of the current animosities and conflicts between the different groups in countries like Serbia and Ireland date back to centuries-old feuds.

Today, there are nearly 200 independent nation-states in the world. A cross-national comparison would reveal numerous variations in how each of these political systems function. Nevertheless, in general, the current world's political systems can be classified under four major types: democracy, monarchy, authoritarianism, and totalitarianism. Like our earlier discussion of economic systems, our descriptions of political systems are of ideal types, and they range along a continuum of how much power and political participation belong to the people living under those systems (Figure 14.2).

Democracy

Democracy is a form of government in which citizens are able to participate directly or indirectly

Democracies, constitutional monarchies	Authoritarianism, absolute monarchies	Totalitarianism
United States, France, England, Spain	Congo, Ethiopia, Saudi Arabia, Kuwait	North Korea, China

FIGURE 14.2 ⊙ **Political Continuum**

in their own governance and to elect their leaders. In a *direct democracy,* every eligible citizen would have the right to participate in every governmental decision. Although fifth-century B.C. Athens, Greece, and contemporary New England town meetings are often given as examples of direct democracy, modern conditions inhibit this form of democracy. Populous nations that not only have to conduct their internal affairs but also must manage complex international relationships with numerous other countries must often act quickly and must rely on trained experts for day-to-day fact finding and implementation of decisions. Thus, democracies today take the form of *representative democracy,* a political system in which citizens, through open and free elections, choose representatives who are expected to make decisions that convey the desires and interests of the majority of the people who have elected them to office. Long-lived and current representative democracies include the United States and France.

Monarchy

A political system in which power resides in one person or a single family and is passed from generation to generation through lines of inheritance is called a **monarchy.** Historically, monarchies were commonly found in agrarian societies and exemplified the role of traditional authority. Monarchies generally take one of two forms, depending on the degree of political control exercised by the monarch. In an *absolute monarchy,* the ruler claims a divine right to rule. Absolute monarchs exercise enormous control over their people and often act and are treated as if they are above the law. Saudi Arabia, Kuwait, and Jordan are examples of contemporary countries that exhibit many of the characteristics of an absolute monarchy.

Absolute monarchies flourished during the Middle Ages. Over time, they gave way to other forms of government or were transformed into *constitutional monarchies.* In this latter form, the monarch serves as a symbolic ruler or head of state whose major role is to perform ceremonial functions; the actual function of running the government is in the hands of elected officials whose authority is specified in a constitution. Sweden, Norway, Denmark, the Netherlands, Belgium, Spain, and Great Britain currently have constitutional monarchies. Although most of the contemporary European monarchs and their subjects appear to be quite comfortable with this role, the British public in recent years has openly criticized its royal family, especially Queen Elizabeth II and her eldest son and heir, Prince Charles, for being out of touch with the people. The criticism was especially harsh after the death in a car crash of Diana, Princess of Wales, in 1997. It is widely believed that the royal family's recent initiatives to reduce royal spending, pay certain taxes, devote more time to public charities, and appear more accessible are attempts to address the public longing for a more modern monarchy. In a move that was highly praised, the Queen told Parliament that she approves of plans to end the ages-old tradition of primogeniture whereby the eldest son succeeds to the throne, a practice that dates to the Bill of Rights of 1689 and the Act of Settlement of 1701 (Hoge, 1998). Elizabeth II became monarch only because her father, King George VI, had no sons. If this change is adopted, as seems likely, the monarch's eldest child, regardless of sex, can ascend to the throne.

Authoritarianism

Some political systems are characterized by **authoritarianism,** whereby authority is concentrated in the hands of rulers who severely restrict popular participation in government. Under authoritarian systems, people have few, if any, political rights and there is no way for ordinary citizens to remove rulers even when they prove to be incompetent or ruthless. Leaders come to assume power in one of four ways: (1) they inherit their position by virtue of birth, for example, in absolute monarchies; (2) they are chosen by the current leader to succeed upon his death or retirement, as "Poppa Doc" Duvalier's son did in Haiti; (3) a small, powerful clique selects a leader without concern for the public's desires; or (4) they are installed after an armed insurrection. When military officers seize power from the government, it is called a **military junta.** In the latter part of the twentieth century, military juntas have come to power in some African and South American countries. It is only recently that a military junta has given up power in Chile. On September 11, 1973, the armed forces, under the leadership of three generals and an admiral, stormed the presidential palace. President Salvador Allende was killed in the assault. Subsequently, General Augusto Pinochet was installed as president, and he ruled from 1974 to 1990.

Totalitarianism

The latest type of political structure to emerge on the world stage is **totalitarianism,** a form of government in which the state controls almost all aspects of people's lives. Although many versions of authoritarianism have existed throughout history, it wasn't until technology made surveillance of large population areas possible that governments could exert such total control over peoples lives. Under a totalitarian system, there is virtually no organized opposition party and information is tightly controlled by the state. Elections may and do take place, but the candidates are those selected by the ruling party. Any dissent is quickly suppressed by threats, intimidations, imprisonment, and even torture and death. Totalitarian states employ a secret police that uses spies and contacts to monitor the activities of its citizens both at home and abroad for any potential sign of dissent. Travel within and outside the country is strictly controlled, often with prohibitions on families traveling together outside the country to prevent defections. In the twentieth century, there have been, and continue to be, many blatant examples of the excesses of totalitarian regimes: Nazi Germany under Adolph Hitler, the Soviet Union under Joseph Stalin, the Republic of China under Mao Tse-Tung, and Iraq under Saddam Hussein.

Shifting Political Sands

Modern electronic communication and the move to a global economy are eroding the almost total control that totalitarian regimes were able to exercise in the past. First, short-wave radios, then television cameras, and now the fax and the Internet have meant that competing messages are being heard by increasing numbers of people living under all forms of political structures. At the same time, the international community can no longer remain ignorant of human rights violations in other places, regardless of how remote they are and what form of government exists there. Television coverage of the antigovernment protests and riots in Albania in 1997, the 1998 Serbian slaughter of Albanians in Kosovo, Serbia, and the 1997–1998 killing of hundreds of Indians in the Mexican state of Chiapas, reportedly by government forces, were watched by millions of viewers as these events unfolded. As a result, political systems are coming under increased international pressure to make changes in some of their internal practices, especially with regard to human rights abuses.

Today, to a greater or lesser degree, every nation has a stake in attracting foreign investment, selling its goods or services on world markets, and sharing in important new scientific developments. Thus, all societies, regardless of the form their governments take, and whether they like it or not, are no longer as free to disregard world opinion, to take independent action, or to treat their own populations any way they want as they may have been in the past. For example, in recent years, for all the posturing on both sides, Iraq's Saddam Hussein could not continue to persist in violating the United Nations' weapons inspection requirements imposed on Iraq after the 1991 Persian Gulf War, without some retaliation from countries like the United States and Great Britain. Neither could President Clinton make use of as much military force against Iraq as he desired. At least for that moment in time, the international community forced both sides to draw back, minimizing what could have been a major military conflict.

Militarism and the Military

Many people believed that with the demise of the Soviet Union and the end of the Cold War, the threat of war would diminish, the size of the military would shrink, and more and more standing armies would serve peaceful ends. Instead, conflicts, such as the one with Iraq, threaten to break out in many parts of the world. Indeed, in recent years, we have seen increases in the number of conventional wars (for instance, in the Persian Gulf and Bosnia), armed conflicts among civilians (for instance, in Somalia), and various military uprisings, particularly in Asian and African countries, with devastating results that live on long after the conflict is over, as evidenced by the number of landmines left behind (see the Sociological Reflection box). A major challenge in the twenty-first century will be how to reduce **militarism,** the societal focus on military ideals and an aggressive preparedness for war, which has characterized much of world history. Militarism seems to have increased in recent years as a result of the rise of powerful multinational corporations that want their overseas interests to be

Sociological Reflections

Campaign against Landmines

In 1997, the Nobel Committee awarded its prestigious Nobel Peace Price to the International Campaign to Ban Landmines and to the campaign's coordinator, Jody Williams, for their work for the banning and clearing of antipersonnel mines. It is estimated that there are currently more than 110 million mines scattered in sixty-four countries, mostly in the developing world, where deaths and injuries from mines as well as the costly efforts to clear them strain already-limited resources. Landmines are long-lived and difficult to detect. Thus, they remain a threat to civilian populations for decades after wars have ended and the troops have gone home. Over 2,000 people are injured or killed by mine explosions every month. The majority of these victims are civilians, often children at play. According to the World Federation of Public Health Associations, landmines in Cambodia have resulted in an amputee population of more than 30,000, and they have been called the third greatest public health hazard in the country. Seventy-five percent of landmine victims in Somalia are children. An area of approximately 1 million acres along the Zambia–Zimbabwe border has remained largely deserted because it was so heavily mined during their recent war. In Poland as late as 1977, thirty to forty people were being killed annually by mines laid during World War II, despite the fact that over 25 million mines had already been cleared.

Recently, representatives from over one hundred nations gathered in Ottawa to sign a treaty to ban the stockpiling, export, production, and use of antipersonnel landmines. The United States was noticeably absent, having rejected the treaty because it did not contain an exemption allowing the United States to keep using landmines to defend South Korea. Although the United States did not sign the treaty, it has pledged financial and personnel support for mine-clearing operations.

What do you think it must be like to live in a place where injuries and deaths from landmines are a frequent occurrence? Do you agree or disagree with the United States' decision not to sign the landmines treaty? Explain.

Source: Adapted by permission from World Federation of Public Health Associations. 1998. Landmines, http://www.apha.org/wfpha/landmines.html.

protected as well as of the proliferation of arms sales around the world. Thus, although the threat of a nuclear war between the superpowers has diminished, the world is now faced with the problem of monitoring arms races between developing nations such as Iran and Iraq and India and Pakistan.

Throughout this chapter, we have considered how current economic and political systems are changing in light of the challenges of a global economy. We will conclude this chapter by considering some of the changes taking place in a related institution, the military.

The Changing Face of Today's Military

Archaeologists excavating graves near the town of Pokrovka in Kazakhstan where ancient nomad cultures buried their dead discovered skeletons of women buried with swords and daggers. These skeletons raise questions about the likelihood that these women played an active role in warfare and in the political structure of their society (Wilford, 1997). Today, some women in Asmara, Eritrea, are struggling to readjust to the traditional and patriarchal society they left when they joined the rebel army and fought side by side with men to free their country from Ethiopian

rule in 1991. Their return to civilian life is difficult because in the Marxist-oriented Eritrean People's Liberation Front, they were treated as equals. Now, as civilians, these women are expected to conform to a more subservient role (McKinley, 1996). Despite these and other isolated stories about women's role in the military, it has been and remains, to a large extent, a heterosexual man's world. However, in recent decades, many countries, including the United States, have moved their military toward being more inclusive by recruiting women and altering their bans against homosexuals.

Women in the Military   In 1972, the year before Congress ended the draft for men, thereby creating a volunteer army, women made up only 1.2 percent of military personnel. In 1994, one out of eight military personnel (12 percent) was female. Like their male counterparts, women of color are overrepresented in the military. For example, although African Americans constitute 12.6 percent of the general population, they accounted for 48 percent of the women in enlisted ranks and 20 percent of female officers in 1992 (Kirk & Okazawa-Rey, 1998). Similar patterns exist for African American men and Latinos. Women enter military life for many of the same reasons

Women now make up 12 percent of the U.S. military. They enter the service for many of the same reasons as men do—better job opportunities, a sense of duty, and a chance at education, travel, and adventure. Increasingly, they are deployed in combat areas such as the Persian Gulf, Bosnia, and Kosovo.

men do—better job opportunities than in civilian life with better pay and benefits; a chance for education, travel, and adventure; patriotism; and a sense of duty. Although many women have made successful careers in the military, they continue to be subjected to a great deal of sexual harassment (see Chapter 11). Racism, too, remains a serious problem in the U.S. military.

Homosexuals in the Military   Historically, homosexuals were banned from serving in the U.S. military on the premise that their very presence would undermine its mission and the morale of other members, even though no scientific evidence has been found to support this belief (Dyer, 1990). This same argument was used to support earlier race segregation in the armed forces and to deny women full equality, including the right to combat training that leads to higher pay and promotions. In reality, lesbians and gays have always been a part of the armed forces. However, to take part they had to keep their sexual orientation secret. Anyone suspected of being homosexual was subject to being investigated, interrogated, and discharged from service, regardless of her or his service record and without benefit of judicial proceedings. Between 1980 and 1991, on average, some 1400 military personnel were discharged annually for this reason alone, at an estimated cost of $494 million dollars, not including the cost of investigation (Cammermeyer, 1994).

After taking office in January 1993, President Clinton tried to end this discrimination against homosexuals in the military, but in the face of fierce opposition from military leaders and from members of Congress, he was forced to accept a compromise policy of "Don't ask, don't tell." The year the policy went into effect saw a drop in the number of homosexuals being discharged from the service. However, since 1994, the numbers of such discharges have increased in each successive year. Some analysts argue that the policy may have created a backlash against homosexuals by focusing attention on them (Shenon, 1997). Other countries have been more successful in this regard than the United States. Denmark, Canada, Australia, Belgium, Finland, the Netherlands, and France allow lesbians and gays to serve in the military. Even in these countries, however, homosexual service personnel often encounter restrictions excluding them from the higher ranks and certain job classifications. The military's effectiveness in the future will depend on how well it addresses issues of sexism and homophobia.

Power and Politics in the Twenty-First Century

It may be that years from now, social scientists will look back on the latter part of the twentieth century and proclaim it a time of revolutionary change. In this chapter, we have seen how economic and political systems are being transformed by technological changes that have made a global economy possible. What these economic and political institutions will look like in fifty years is not yet clear, but they will certainly be affected by how well the international community deals with the following challenges—the growing economic inequality among and within nations, the growing power of multinational corporations, and the proliferation of sophisticated weapons of mass destruction.

Key Points to Remember

1. Throughout history, societies have created a variety of different ways to produce and distribute the goods and services needed for their survival. Two major economic systems have emerged and become dominant in the modern age: capitalism and socialism. In between, there are a number of mixed economies that share characteristics of both capitalism and socialism.

2. Capitalism is an economic system based on private ownership of property, competition in the production and distribution of goods and services, and the maximization of profits. In

contrast, socialism is an economic system based on public ownership and government control of the economy and the distribution of goods and services for the benefit of the society as a whole.

3. Over the years, both systems have undergone major changes. Government is playing more of a role in regulating capitalism today, and many socialist economies are moving in the direction of a market economy. Each system has strengths and weaknesses. Capitalist societies tend to be more efficient and productive, but they have high levels of inequality and the potential for high rates of unemployment. Socialist economies have low rates of unemployment, but they tend to be inefficient and place more limitations on the personal freedoms of their citizens.

4. Regardless of the type of economic system, multinational corporations are coming to have more power and control. One of the consequences of the growth in multinational corporations is the growth of an international work force. Work in industrialized countries is increasingly shifting to the tertiary or service sector, while work in the manufacturing or secondary sector is relocating to many developing countries. Much work in this sector is te-

dious and boring and leads to feelings of alienation. One way in which workers have fought alienation is to get more control over their work situations through the formation of labor unions.

5. Power is the ability to realize one's will despite resistance from others. The exercise of power can take two forms—legitimate power or authority and illegitimate power or coercion. There are three sources of authority: traditional, rational-legal, and charismatic; each varies according to a society's level of development.

6. Sociologists hold two views of the way power is distributed in the United States: the power elite model holds that a small, ruling elite exercises power, whereas the pluralist model sees power as more widely dispersed. The weight of the empirical evidence gives more support to the power elite model.

7. Political systems, like economic systems, developed over time and within specific cultural contexts. Today most countries of the world can be classified into one of four types: democracy, monarchy, authoritarianism, and totalitarianism.

8. Among the many challenges facing the world today is the proliferation of arms and the threat of conventional wars.

Key Terms

monopoly
socialism
mixed economies
underemployment
underground economy
multinational corporations
work
primary sector
secondary sector
tertiary sector

contingency work
alienation
labor unions
National Labor Relations Act
politics
authority
coercion
traditional authority
rational-legal authority

charismatic authority
power elite
pluralist model
democracy
monarchy
authoritarianism
military junta
totalitarianism
militarism

Key People

Cesar Chavez
Dolores Huerta

Adam Smith
Karl Marx

Nelson Mandela
Max Weber

Questions for Review and Discussion

1. Compare and contrast the strengths and weaknesses of capitalism, socialism, and mixed economies. In which system would you prefer to live and why? How has the development of a global economy affected these three types of systems? Has the global economy affected your life in any visible and concrete way? Explain.
2. How does the way in which we define the concept of work impact people's lives? Consider any job that you have held. Did you find it satisfying or alienating? Explain. What characteristics do you want to find in the work that you do? Explain.

3. What does the history of labor–management relationships in the United States reveal about how power is distributed in this country? Some people believe that unions were necessary in the past but that they are not needed today. Do you agree or disagree with that view? Explain. Do you favor an international labor movement or not? Explain.
4. Compare and contrast the modern types of political systems: democracy, monarchy, authoritarianism, and totalitarianism. What are the special challenges that face each of these types of systems today? Explain.

For Further Reading

Applebaum, E., and R. Batt. 1994. *The New American Workplace.* Ithaca, NY: ILR Press. This book describes how the workplace is changing due to technology and globalization.

Garson, Barbara. 1988. *The Electronic Sweatshop: How Computers Are Transforming the Office of the Future into the Factory of the Past.* New York: Penguin. The author presents a thought-provoking look at the "second industrial revolution," showing how computers have changed the modern workplace.

Rubin, B.A. 1996. *Shifts in the Social Contract: Understanding Change in American Society.* Thousand Oaks, CA: Pine Forge Press. The author analyzes how changes in the world economies led to changes in politics and how this affects our everyday lives.

Terkel, S. 1974. *Working.* New York: Pantheon. In this highly readable book, ordinary people talk about what they do all day and how they feel about what they do.

Sociology through Literature

Koestler, Arthur. 1941. *Darkness at Noon.* New York: MacMillian. The hero of this story is an aging revolutionary, imprisoned and psychologically tortured by the Party to which he has dedicated his life. Provides vivid insights into the excesses of totalitarian movements.

Internet Resources

http://www.aflcio.org/index.htm   The AFL-CIO Labor Web provides a master list of national boycotts sanctioned by the group as well as a glossary of the group's 78 affiliate unions.

http://www.cldc.howard.edu/~neca/   The Network of Educators on the Americas distributes classroom materials that exhibit a critical perspective on global issues.

http://www.labornet.org/jwj/   Jobs with Justice is a national labor, community, and religious coalition organized to fight for the rights of working people.

15

Health, Illness, and the Delivery of Health Care

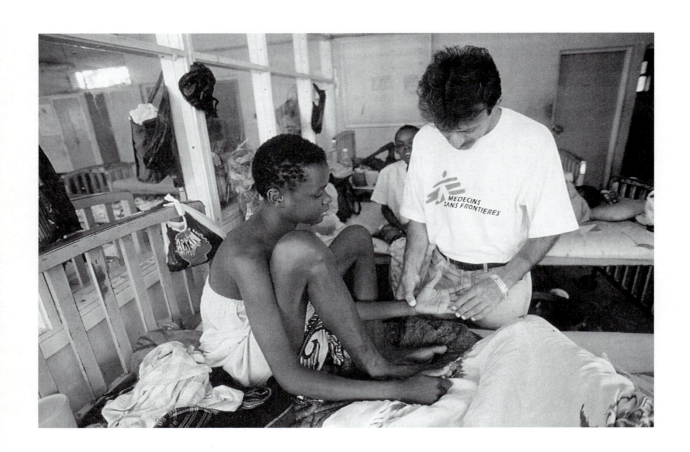

AGENT OF CHANGE: DOCTORS WITHOUT BORDERS

The World Health Report 1998 detailed major advances in health and health care around the globe. However, the report also found that despite increasing life expectancy, two-fifths of all deaths in the world can be considered premature in that more than 20 million people a year are dying before the age of fifty. Ten million of these deaths are of children under five years of age; 7.4 million others are of adults aged twenty to forty-nine. Most of these premature deaths occur in developing countries where food shortages and infectious diseases take a heavy toll. Many other deaths are the results of natural disasters and armed conflicts (World Health Organization).

Since 1971, a France-based group, Médecins sans Frontieres (Doctors without Borders), has organized teams of health care workers to provide medical relief to people in danger due to war, civil strife, epidemics, or natural disasters. This private, nonprofit, international humanitarian organization operates independently of all government, institutional, political, economic, and religious influences and depends on volunteer health professionals to fulfill its mission. Doctors without Borders (DwB) has offices in nineteen countries, including the United States, and sends 2,000 volunteers of more than forty-five nationalities to some eighty countries annually. These health care teams work with local officials of the United Nations' relief agencies to offer education in nutrition and health, help with water processing and sanitation, establish hospitals, train and supervise local staff, vaccinate children, provide surgery and maternity care, distribute drugs, and devise ways to provide shelter in refugee camps, besieged cities, isolated areas, and any-place where war, disease, or poverty threaten the health of populations.

DwB teams often travel on foot, by boat, or by helicopter to reach remote areas. For example, Kathy Mahoney of Wellesley, Massachusetts, and Molly Savitz of Santa Cruz, California, are working in the Javari River Valley of Brazil, near the borders of Peru and Colombia. Kathy and Molly, both nurse volunteers, navigate treacherous waterways, mountains, and jungles to reach villagers in need of health care. The population of this area has been decimated by malaria, a disease which was eradicated in the United States during the 1950s but which today still threatens 40 percent of the world's population. One out of every twenty African children dies of malaria; the most common age of death is four.

DwB also works in refugee camps and areas hurt by wars and natural disasters. For example, in June 1998, nutritional data collected by DwB teams in the Bahr El Ghazal and Western Upper Nile provinces indicated an extremely serious food shortage. This crisis was the result of a poor harvest, drought, and Sudan's ongoing civil war, which has caused massive population displacements. An estimated 1.5 million people had already died in the fighting and accompanying famine, and, according to DwB, another million people in southern Sudan were at risk of malnutrition and possible starvation. Hoping to prevent such a disaster, DwB teams opened eleven supplementary feeding centers in the Bahr El Ghazal and Western Upper Nile regions (Doctors without Borders).

When medical assistance is not enough to save lives, DwB speaks out against human rights abuses and violations of humanitarian law that its teams witness when providing aid. Team members testified about the horrors of ethnic cleansing taking place in the former Yugoslavia, which helped to alert people around the world and to galvanize resistance to such policies.

A cursory examination of the twentieth century reveals a pattern of social and economic advances that have brought extended life expectancy and better living standards to millions of people worldwide. As our discussion of Doctors without Borders makes clear, however, health and longevity are not equally distributed around the globe. Such inequity can no longer be tolerated if for no other reason than that advances in transportation have made it possible not only for people to move around the globe at dizzying speeds but also for germs to be freed from captivity in a localized area. Therefore, standards of health and health care must increasingly be internationalized.

Source: Information is from the following: (1) Adapted from World Health Organization. 1998. *The World Health Report 1998: Executive Summary,* http://www.who.org/whr/exsum98e.htm. (2) Doctors without Borders/Médecins sans Frontieres, http://www.dwb.org/index.htm; http://www.doctorswithoutborders.org.

Defining Concepts

Generally, when a baby is born, the parents tell family and friends, "It's a *healthy* baby girl," or "It's a *healthy* baby boy." Being born healthy and remaining so most of one's life is a valuable commodity. But what exactly do we mean when we say someone is healthy? For most of us, being healthy means being free of **disease,** a medically diagnosed illness. But, as you will see, health is not nearly so simplistic as this because not only does it have biological and physiological dimensions, but also it has psychological and sociocultural dimensions.

Sociologists recognize health as a biological or physiological condition, but they also view it as socially constructed. What gets defined as illness has as much to do with society and cultural definitions as it does with objective symptoms. Consequently, sociologists have adopted a World Health Organization definition of **health** as a state of complete physical, mental, and social well-being. Thus, to be *healthy* means more than simply being free of disease or injury; it also means experiencing a sense of well-being, an absence of distress or impaired capacity to carry out one's daily activities. If *health* refers to the positive sense of social, psychological, and emotional wellness, then **illness** is the opposite, the interference with health. Illness involves **healing**, the personal and institutional responses to perceived disease, injury, and illness. Sociologists focus on both these aspects of healing. However, most often, they examine the institutionalization of healing: health care and the health care delivery system in a society. *Health care* is any activity or response aimed at improving health.

As our definition of health implies, sociologists are interested primarily in the social and cultural factors that impact health. Sociocultural conditions and situations not only promote the possibility of illness and disability but also they enhance prospects for disease prevention and health maintenance. According to many experts in the field of health and illness, the greatest threats to an individual's health and physical well-being today stem largely from unhealthy lifestyles and health-risk behavior. Sociocultural factors also have an important impact on the ways in which societies organize their resources to cope with health hazards and deliver medical care to the population at large. Individuals and societies tend to respond to health problems in a manner consistent with their culture, norms, and values. Thus, health is not simply a matter of biology but involves a number of factors that are social, cultural, political, and economic in nature (Cockerham, 1998).

Many sociologists working in the field of medicine are *epidemiologists.* **Epidemiology** refers to the study of the origins and spread of diseases and bodily injuries within a given population. The major focus of the epidemiologist is not the individual but rather the health problems of large groups of people. As epidemiologists, sociologists and other medical scientists identify societal and cultural factors related to a particular health problem, study patterns and trends in the causes and distribution of it, and construct a chain of inferences that explains its existence. They do this by studying what all of the victims of a particular disease have in common beside the disease. Over time, the focus of epidemiologists has broadened to include an examination of de-

mographic characteristics such as race, class, gender, and age as well as the physical and social environment (such as employment status, stress, and exposure to toxic substances) in which people (and agents) exist (Weiss & Lonnquist, 1994).

Indicators of Health

There are many cultural and social factors that impact health and illness. Later, we will examine some of these factors up close. Right now, let's turn our attention to two commonly used social indicators of health and well-being: *life expectancy* and *infant mortality.*

Life expectancy rate refers to the average number of years that a person born in a given year can expect to live. Life expectancy increased more during the twentieth century than in all prior human history. However, as Table 15.1 illustrates, there is considerable variation in rates among types of countries as well as across specific countries. For example, whereas North Americans can expect to live, on average, seventy-six years, Africans have a life expectancy of only fifty-two years. In the United States, life expectancy has increased approximately twenty-nine years since 1900, when Americans could expect to live, on average, only forty-seven years. The average life expectancy in a country is significantly reduced by infant and early childhood mortality rates.

Infant mortality rate refers to the number of deaths of infants under the age of one year per 1,000 live births in a given year. As shown in Table 15.1, there is a dramatic difference in infant mortality between developed and developing countries. In 1998, nearly one of every ten children born in Africa died before her/his first birthday. Those children who survived their first year of life, as we have seen, could expect to live only about fifty-one more years. Their counterparts in every other country shown in the table are far more fortunate. Worldwide, 5.8 percent of all infants born in 1998 died before reaching their first birthdays. The percentage of infant deaths worldwide is expected to decrease by one half, to 2.9 percent by the year 2025. Improved nutrition, sanitation, medical care (including immunization against various diseases and the development of penicillin and various other antibiotics), medical intervention (such as that provided by

TABLE 15.1 ☉ Indicators of Health, by World Areas, 1998

	Life Expectancy at Birth (in years)			Infant Mortality Rate (per 1,000 live births)
	Total	Male	Female	
World	66	64	68	58
More Developed Countries	75	71	79	8
Less Developed Countries	63	62	65	64
Africa	52	50	53	91
North America	76	73	79	7
Latin America/Caribbean	69	66	72	36
Asia	65	64	67	57
Europe	73	68	77	10
Oceania	73	71	76	28

Source: Population Reference Bureau. 1998. *1998 World Population Data Sheet.* Washington, DC. Reprinted by permission.

DwB), as well as economic development have combined to increase the likelihood of children worldwide surviving the first year of life.

The Social Construction of Health and Illness

Our discussion of health and illness thus far emphasizes the connection between health and society. Just as humans give meaning to such experiences as birth, marriage, death, and social status, we also give meaning to illness, disease, and injury. And the meanings we give to these phenomena will likely suggest a cure. For example, if people in a particular society believe that all illness is spread in the air, they most likely will be unreceptive to strategies or cures designed to stop diseases transmitted through water. The Swazi of southeastern Africa are a case in point. The Swazi's social definition of diarrhea is based in their cultural belief that diseases are frequently carried in the air. They recognize three types of diarrhea, each with a specific method of healing. One of these types, *kukabula,* is believed to be caused by invisible

vapors to which a child may be deliberately or accidentally exposed. Healing is in the domain of traditional healers, who perform ceremonies or prescribe measures aimed at driving out evil spirits or "bad air." The Swazi cure for *kukabula* involves giving the child medicine and enemas to purify or drain out the bad air that is believed to be the cause of the illness. This set of beliefs and healing measures is in direct conflict with Western practices and beliefs, in which recognized healers are medical doctors. Western medicine considers dehydration to be one of the most serious symptoms of diarrhea. Thus, it is believed that an enema would aggravate rather than relieve the effects of diarrhea (Robbins, 1993).

It is often the case that health standards are used to enforce cultural norms. You will recall our discussion of female genital mutilation in Chapter 7. In some cultures that practice female genital mutilation, girls as young as one year old are "circumcised" in order to guarantee their later marriageability. This practice is tied to the cultural belief that women should be virgins when they marry; thus, circumcised females are considered to be healthy and desirable, whereas those who are not are viewed as unhealthy and undesirable. It is noteworthy that while the practice of removing the female external genitalia is defined as circumcision and thus considered a health practice in some cultures, in others this practice is viewed as genital mutilation and defined as a violent violation of females that leads to a wide variety of health problems and illnesses and can result in death.

What is considered healthy, wholesome, or an illness as well as the appropriate healing measures not only varies cross-culturally but also changes over time across and within cultures. For example, recent changes in the United States in terms of how we view and treat alcoholism and drug abuse highlight the social construction of illness and the importance of cultural definitions of health and illness. At one time in our history, people addicted to alcohol were viewed as unsavory characters with little or no will power or desire to stop drinking. In short, it was believed that drinking was a character or behavioral flaw—a bad habit, not a medical problem. Today, however, alcoholism has come to be defined as an illness, and some medical researchers have even suggested that it is hereditary. The Americans with Disabilities Act includes alcoholism, and many employers have special Employee Assistance Programs (EAPs) which help alcoholics cure their illness. Given that the social construction of health and illness is related to the cultural norms and political and economic arrangements in a society, how do particular ways of thinking about health and illness become dominant? Perhaps the most obvious and powerful force in defining what is and is not healthy and what is or is not an illness is the medical establishment.

The Medicalization of Health and Illness

As with health and illness, *medicine* reflects the culture and structure of a society. Some sort of **medicine**—a social institution established to diagnose, treat, and prevent illness and to promote health—exists in every society. Social scientists typically classify medicine as either traditional (based on cultural practices, traditions, and beliefs) or scientific. As our discussion of the Swazi illustrated, traditional medicine is commonly practiced in nonindustrialized societies, while scientific medicine is characteristic of industrialized societies. Whereas traditional med-

icine is often based on notions of witchcraft, evil spirits, and supernatural punishment as the cause of sickness, *scientific medicine* is based on the notion that some identifiable malfunction of the body underlies all sickness and the cure rests with medical treatment. Sociologists refer to this latter belief as **medicalization,** the process of defining a behavior or condition as an illness in need of medical treatment. However, this simple dichotomy is somewhat misleading in that in both nonindustrialized and industrialized societies, both traditional and scientific medicine are often practiced side by side. For example, in Swaziland, diseases are divided into two categories: (1) traditional, caused by sorcery or the withdrawal of spiritual protection by ancestors and (2) nontraditional, such as venereal diseases, cholera, and tuberculosis, introduced by Europeans. Traditional healers are sought for traditional diseases, while Western clinics and doctors are sought when the disease is thought to be European (Robbins, 1993). Likewise, in the United States and other industrial societies, scientific and traditional methods of medicine often coexist.

The social construction of medicine can also be seen in the fact that the medical establishment continuously constructs and reconstructs our definitions of sickness and health, and, in recent times, it has vastly expanded the boundaries of what is considered the domain of health care. This trend toward medicalization of various behaviors has been particularly apparent in the United States since World War II. Today, for example, obesity is often diagnosed as caused by a *compulsive eating disorder,* and those who eat too little are diagnosed as suffering from eating disorders such as *anorexia nervosa* or *bulimia.* Likewise, various behaviors such as drug and alcohol addiction and child abuse are now defined as diseases or medical problems, as are things such as the inability to sleep (*insomnia*) and snoring (a symptom of *sleep apnea*). Even some of life's normal, natural, and generally nonpathological events, such as birth, death, and sexuality, have come to be viewed as "medical problems." Although these behaviors can present serious problems, there is some question as to whether or not they are really medical problems (Conrad, 1997).

Some observers of the health scene in industrialized societies have suggested that the increasing medicalization of human behavior is more social and political than scientific. Health care, thus the practice of medicine, is a multi-billion dollar (profit-making) business in the United States. A wide variety of industries have developed to treat the growing list of behaviors defined as medical problems, for example, smoking clinics to cure the habit of smoking, Weight Watchers and other diet programs and clinics to treat obesity, and sleep clinics to treat a variety of sleep-related problems or complaints. In the past, these behaviors were individualized and viewed as the fault of the individual. Today, when they are defined as diseases, fault is removed from the individual and more people are encouraged to admit that they have a problem and to seek a remedy. Critics of the trend toward medicalization and the medical model argue that medical treatment is a form of social control and further, that such a model overlooks the social situation as the possible source of medical problems. With this understanding of the interrelationship between health, illness, healing, culture, and social structure, we now can turn our attention to some of the major sociological perspectives on health and illness.

Sociological Perspectives of Health and Illness

Medical sociology, the study of health, illness, and healing and their relationship to social factors as well as health care as it is institutionalized in a society, is an important subdiscipline of sociology. Medical sociologists apply the perspectives, conceptualizations, theories, and methodologies of sociology to any phenomena having to do with human health and disease. In this section, we will look briefly at four major theoretical frameworks within which medical sociologists operate: structural functionalist, conflict, feminist, and symbolic interactionist.

The Structural Functionalist Perspective

Talcott Parsons (1951) is credited with formulating the basic structural functionalist perspective on health, illness, and medicine. In his structural functionalist model of society, Parsons pre-sented an analysis of the function of medicine which contained the concept of the sick role. In general, he postulated that a healthy population is essential to the optimal functioning of society. Illness, then, is dysfunctional for society because it prevents people from performing their routine social roles and thus disrupts societal equilibrium. The "lure" of sickness—the attraction of escaping responsibilities—requires society to exercise some control over the sick person and the sick role so that disruption is kept to a minimum (Weiss & Lonnquist, 1994).

From this point of view, the institution of medicine serves an important social function in that it keeps members of society healthy so that they can perform the social roles necessary for a well-functioning society. However, people do get sick. When they do, they follow certain socially prescribed behaviors identified by Parsons as the **sick role,** a set of social expectations regarding how a sick person should act. Parsons identified four major characteristics of the sick role:

1. Sick people are excused from their usual responsibilities, such as reporting to work or school.
2. Sick people are considered worthy of sympathy from others, particularly if they did not do anything to cause their illness.
3. Sick people must show a sincere desire to get well.
4. Sick people must make every attempt possible to get well. This part of the sick role leads to the reciprocal healing role played by doctors.

As do patients, doctors follow certain socially prescribed behaviors, and these can be subsumed under the title **doctor role,** a set of social expectations regarding how a doctor should act. Parsons identified two major components of the doctor role:

1. Doctors evaluate people's claims of sickness, assessing whether they are really sick and, if so, determining the source of the illness.
2. Doctors prescribe medication and cure the sick so that they are able to resume their normal social roles.

These and various other social roles related to health and illness contribute to social order;

they serve the positive function of maintaining the general health of a society. In turn, the system of medical care helps to prevent illnesses from spreading and from disrupting family relations, economic production, and social activities. The system of medicine facilitates the improvement of the collective health of a society through medical inventions, such as vaccines and drugs that cure infectious diseases such as polio and tuberculosis. Functionalists have also observed how other social institutions such as religion can positively impact health and well-being (see the Sociological Reflections box). An examination of the sick and doctor roles demonstrates how social norms impinge on both health and illness. The utility of these concepts is that they describe a patterned set of expectations defining the norms and values appropriate to being sick, both for the sick person and others who interact with that person (Cockerham, 1998). Such an analysis also provides good insight into the doctor as the gatekeeper to the sick role and the person who ultimately decides what constitutes an illness, verifies a person's condition as an illness, and designates an ill person as recovered.

On the other hand, critics of Parsons's analysis of the sick role point out that it implies that people are only sick temporarily, that doctors can restore them to normal functioning fairly expeditiously, and that they will resume their usual social roles rather quickly. Although this may be true for some acute illnesses, it is not the case for those suffering chronic illnesses. Although some chronic illnesses can be controlled, they cannot be cured, and they often leave a person permanently unable to resume or perform normal social roles. Critics also argue that the sick role is more applicable to middle-class patients and middle-class values than it is to persons in lower socioeconomic groups. Not everyone can follow the sick role pathway. For example, low-income people generally have less freedom to curtail their normal responsibilities, especially their jobs, and thus have a more difficult time complying with the sick role model (Weiss & Lonquist, 1994). In addition, the Parsonsian analysis of health and medicine is often criticized for ignoring the negative consequences of social inequality for health and medicine. Most sick people do not want to be or to remain sick;

they want to get well. However, for many sick people, their access to medical care is limited by their financial status. These criticisms notwithstanding, many functionalist sociologists continue to use the Parsonsian model for a functional analysis of the relationship between illness and cultural expectations for the sick.

The Conflict Perspective

In contrast to a functionalist perspective of health and illness, a conflict perspective emphasizes the social, political, and economic forces that impact health and the health care delivery system. In the Marxian tradition, a conflict analysis would view health and medicine as commodities that can be bought and sold. Thus, such an analysis would direct our attention to the pursuit of private profit under capitalism and suggest that the profit motive has driven the cost of quality health care beyond the reach of the average U.S. citizen. Researcher Howard Waitzkin (1997) argues that this profit motive has driven corporations to oversell some technological advances, such as fetal monitoring, even though they have not significantly improved the health of the population at large.

Focusing attention on the unequal distribution of health and wellness as a result of unequal access to medical care, such an analysis would suggest that the unequal distribution of health and medical care in a society is a clear reflection of the larger social inequality in the society. For example, poor people in capitalist societies suffer from higher rates of most diseases than do the rich, and poor people are also far more likely to receive inadequate, less, or no medical care than are wealthier patients when admitted to hospitals (Kahn, Pearson, & Harrison, 1994). Because health and medicine are commodities, those with the greatest resources have not only the most access to care but also access to the best care available.

As with other topics of conflict analysis, the conflict perspective is viewed by critics as too narrowly focused on capitalist societies generally and on the United States specifically. Critics point out that the general state of health of people in the United States and other capitalist societies is far better than in many socialist countries. This is true, in part, because the

Is Religion Good for Your Health?

According to a substantial number of mental health professionals such as Sigmund Freud (1927), Albert Ellis (1988), and Wendell Watters (1992), to name just a few, the answer to the question, "Is religion good for your health?" is a resounding no. Their argument, based largely on their clinical experiences, is that religion is detrimental to sound mental and emotional health in that it fosters feelings of guilt, depression, and other mental disorders. Although less negative toward religion, their counterparts in the physical health sciences have tended to view religion as irrelevant to health or health care except when they find religious beliefs interfering with their ability to deliver medical treatment as, for example, when a Jehovah's Witness refuses a blood transfusion or when Christian Scientist parents won't authorize medical treatment for a child. Such negative or indifferent views of religion have led many health care practitioners to ignore what may be a powerful resource in the treatment of a wide variety of medical problems.

In recent years, researchers have subjected these views to empirical testing, asking what kind of effects, if any, religious beliefs and practices have on health (see, for example, Koenig, 1997). The majority of such studies to date point to a positive relationship between religion and mental and physical well-being. More specifically, a study of hospitalized patients who depended heavily on their religious faith to cope were found to be significantly less depressed than those who did not (Koenig, 1994). Numerous other studies found similar patterns. People who were religiously active reported higher feelings of self-esteem, lower rates of depression, better adaptation, and less frequent negative emotional states than did people who were not active (Krause, 1995; Idler & Kasl, 1992; O'Connor & Vallerand, 1990). Similar relationships were reported in a national sample of African Americans and in a study of three generations of Mexican Americans living in Texas (Levin, Chatters, & Taylor, 1995; Levin, Markides, & Ray, 1996). A wide array of studies found that religion seems to have a beneficial effect on physical health as well. For example, researchers have found that people who are religious have lower death rates following cardiac surgery and lower mortality in general than people who are not (Oxman, Freeman, & Manheimer, 1995; Zuckerman, Kasl, and Ostfeld, 1984).

After reviewing the scientific research conducted on the relationship between religion and health, physician and psychiatrist Harold Koenig (1997) suggested that at least three mechanisms operated to explain why religion might promote mental health. First, religious beliefs provide hope and a sense of control over one's life. Belief in a caring and forgiving god offers comfort to those who are lonely, anxious, discouraged, or feeling out of control. Past sins or mistakes can be forgiven

---

standard of living is higher and because a far greater number of people have access to health care in capitalist than in most socialist societies.

Feminist Perspectives

Feminist analyses pay particular attention to the effects of sexism on health and medicine and its consequences for the health and well-being of women. Many of these analyses also emphasize the intersections of health and wellness with various other inequalities, such as those related to race, class, and sexual orientation. Some feminist analyses, for example, focus on the differential treatment of women and men patients by doctors and other medical personnel and the detrimental effect this can have on women's longevity. For example, researchers have found that most doctors do not respond to female patients' symptoms of illnesses such as heart disease or HIV/AIDS as quickly as they respond to male patients' symptoms. With the diagnosis of HIV/AIDS, for instance, women, on average, tend to die sooner after the diagnosis than do men. According to a feminist analysis, this reflects the fact that HIV/AIDS in women is generally diagnosed later than it is in men. This is largely due to the fact that a lack of research on

and guilt lessened, thus easing psychological discomforts. Second, by actively participating in a religious community, people interact with others who have common interests and who can provide social support in times of stress or illness. Third, religious doctrines promote a healthy, balanced love of God, self, and others. Putting trust in a higher power and helping others can liberate a person's psyche from a debilitating concentration on one's own problems. Reaching out to others can have a positive effect on a person's mindset.

Koenig (1997) suggests that religiousness can affect physical health directly in two ways. First, religious teachings emphasize respect for one's physical body. Therefore, religious persons are more likely to seek earlier diagnosis for problems and to follow a prescribed course of treatment more scrupulously than those who are less religious. Second, many religions discourage behaviors and other activities that may adversely affect health, such as excess alcohol and drug use, smoking, and risky sexual behaviors. Evidence of the positive health effects of low-risk lifestyles and healthy diets have been found among religious groups like the Mormons and Seventh-Day Adventists, who have lower mortality from cancer and heart and other diseases than do members of the population at large.

Although the majority of studies point to a positive relationship between religion and mental and physical health, religion can also be used in destructive ways.

Paul Pruyser (1977) and Ronald Enroth (1994) have examined the negative ways in which some individuals and churches use and abuse religious beliefs and practices. For example, some individuals, usually those with low self-esteem, may take scriptural verses out of context and use them to justify their hatred, aggression, and prejudice toward those who are seen as deviant or in some way different from themselves. Charismatic religious leaders may demand total obedience from their followers, even to the point of self-destruction, as was the case with the followers of Jim Jones, David Koresh, and the Heaven's Gate leaders. That such behavior happens should not blind us to the fact that the vast majority of people use religious beliefs and practices in ways that contribute positively to their mental and physical health. Thus, health care workers may be well advised to consider establishing collaborative relationships with clergy and religious organizations in an ongoing effort to enhance the mental and physical health of the population.

Interview people that you know, especially those individuals who have been ill, about the role that religion plays in their lives. Does religion seem to help them cope with the difficult or stressful events in their lives? How might health care providers utilize the data on the relationship between religion and health?

women with HIV/AIDS meant that many symptoms specific to women were not included among the indicator diseases for HIV/AIDS (Schwartz & Scott, 1997).

Feminist researchers have also documented a history of negative and stereotypic attitudes among doctors and other health professionals toward poor women, women of color, elderly women, and lesbians. The health concerns of these women are often trivialized and sometimes even ignored. As a result, women in these groups often end up receiving less effective and less respectful medical care or no medical care at all (Nechas & Foley, 1994). Feminist perspec-

tives would also point out the heterosexist characteristic of health care. For example, research shows that doctors are often disapproving of lesbian and gay lifestyles and that such disapproval often negatively affects how they diagnose and treat lesbian and gay patients. As a result of such attitudes and behaviors, some lesbians and gays drop out of the medical care system and forgo medical care altogether. The majority, however, simply closet their sexual orientation even though doing so may mean that they will not receive the specific care that they may need. While recognizing that sexism and inequality exists in health care delivery and medicine, some critics argue that this problem will lessen as more women and people of color enter the medical profession (Franks & Clancey, 1993; Lurie et al., 1993).

The Symbolic Interactionist Perspective

A symbolic interaction perspective focuses our attention on the symbolic communication between doctor and patient, that is, on the meanings that they give to their social interactions. Symbolic interactionists concern themselves with any of the infinite number of episodes of interaction in which sick people and doctors or other health providers interpret social messages and base their responses on these interpretations. For example, research on doctor/patient relationships suggests that patients who view their doctors as friendly tend to rate them higher and express more satisfaction with them than do those patients who view their doctors as cold and bureaucratic (Twaddle & Kessler, 1987). Each element of the interaction between doctor and patient contributes to the social construction of not only the statuses of doctor and patient but also the doctor/patient relationship, one which is generally unequal and hierarchical, with the doctor assuming the more powerful and authoritative role. When doctors treat their patients with detachment and reinforce their power in the relationship, research shows that many of these patients feel intimidated and often describe their doctors as cold and uncaring. On the other hand, when doctors spend time talking and listening to their patients, developing a rapport with them, patients tend to view this behavior positively and they believe that the doctor is a good doctor.

Symbolic interactionism provides valuable insight into the nature and process of medicine and health care delivery. It helps us understand how particular behaviors and symptoms are defined as healthy or sick, who has the power to define illness, and how these definitions are often derived from nonmedical factors. However, the symbolic interactionist perspective is often criticized for paying too little attention to the objective reality of health and illness. People do get sick and suffer debilitating illnesses and pain whether or not they are medically diagnosed or socially labeled as ill. Symbolic interactionism is also criticized for ignoring how social inequality affects who and what gets defined as sick or well.

Race, Class, Gender, Sexual Orientation, and Disabilities

An examination of the health profiles of various groups within the United States shows that disability and death are not evenly distributed throughout the population. Some groups are far more likely to suffer certain disabilities and illnesses than are others. For example, men are twice as likely as women to die from coronary heart disease. However, although men have a greater overall risk, they are more likely than women to have a favorable prognosis if they survive the first serious heart attack (Cockerham, 1998). Although there are many factors that impact health and wellness, some of the most important are race, class, gender, sexual orientation, and disabilities. Researchers have found that each of these factors represent important differences between people that is correlated with health and life expectancy. In this section we will briefly look at each of these factors and assess their relationship to health and wellness from a sociological perspective.

Race and Health

As you learned in Chapters 9 and 10, a major dimension along which people in the United States are unequal is the dimension of race. A significant reflection of that inequality can be seen in the differences in the health and longevity of the various racial and ethnic groups in the United States. Higher infant mortality rates and an overall lower life expectancy among people of color compared with whites have been attributed to living in poverty, living in low-income neighborhoods or central cities with higher rates of violence, more environmental pollution, and a lack of preventive health care. In addition, various groups of color are much more likely to suffer or die from diseases such as HIV/AIDS and pneumonia than are whites. On the other hand, some groups, such as Native Americans and Latinas/os, are less likely than whites to die from diseases such as cancer and heart disease. However, this is due primarily to the fact that these groups have a much lower life expectancy than do whites. Research shows that the longer one lives, the greater one's chances of contracting a chronic illness such as cancer or heart disease (Cockerham, 1998). Although some people of color have made notable economic gains over the last several decades and the life expectancy has increased for all groups, recent studies show that health differences across race remain.

According to some health experts, the United States has a two-tiered health care system. Although limited education, violence, and addiction as well as the higher prevalence of several life-threatening illnesses such as cancer, heart disease, and hypertension help to explain some of the disparity in groups' health profiles, analysts of health systems have found increasing evidence that race, discrimination, and social and cultural factors influence the care that people receive and, consequently, their health. In addition, class or economic status is also a big source of the gap. However, even when researchers control for class and other social factors, race remains a big source of the health gap.

Government and academic research shows a widening gap between African Americans and others in the incidences of asthma, diabetes, major infectious diseases, and several forms of cancer. Of particular significance is the extremely high rate of death among African American males for heart disease, cancer, homicide, and HIV/AIDS (see Table 15.2). For example, the Centers for Disease Control and Prevention reports that from 1990 to 1995, the death rate for all women with breast cancer fell 10 percent, from 23.1 to 21 per 100,000. However, African American women's higher rate did not change from 27.5 per 100,000 during this same period. Additionally, African American men, alone among population groups, had rising rates of cancer. The death rate from cancer among African American men increased 62 percent, compared with 19 percent for all American men. Also, according to a report by the Center for Health Policy Research, when African Americans and whites are in the same situation, such

TABLE 15.2 ↻ Age-Adjusted Death Rates for Selected Causes of Death, for African American and White Women and Men, 1990*

	African American Females	African American Males	White Females	White Males
All causes	581.6	1,061.3	369.9	644.3
Heart disease	168.1	275.9	103.1	202.0
Cancer	137.2	248.1	111.2	160.3
Cerebrovascular diseases	42.7	56.1	23.8	27.7
Pulmonary disease	10.7	26.5	15.2	27.4
Pneumonia and influenza	13.7	28.7	10.6	17.5
Liver disease and cirrhosis	8.7	20.0	4.8	11.5
Diabetes	25.4	23.6	9.5	11.3
Accidents	20.4	62.4	17.6	46.4
Suicide	2.4	12.4	4.8	20.1
Homicide	13.0	68.7	2.8	8.9
AIDS	9.9	44.2	1.1	15.0

*Deaths per 100,000 resident population

Source: National Center for Health Statistics. 1993. In Cockerham, W.C. 1995. *Medical Sociology,* 6th ed. Englewood Cliffs, NJ: Prentice Hall, p. 49.

as being hospitalized for a heart attack, and have the same insurance, the chance that the African American patient will get advanced care is much less than it is for the white patient. The health care system appears to treat them differently. Although research shows a slight genetic predisposition among African Americans for some illnesses and diseases, the major disparities in health arise less from genetic differences among races than from attitudes toward the races and unequal health care (Kilborn, 1998).

Other groups of color also show poor health profiles when compared to whites. Recent studies show that, like African Americans, Latinas/os have a higher infant mortality rate, a shorter life expectancy, and higher rates of death from various diseases such as diabetes and tuberculosis. Latinas/os tend to suffer more fatal and disabling strokes, and Puerto Rican children have the highest rates of asthma. According to statistics from the Centers for Disease Control, while Asian Americans have a generally high level of health, tuberculosis rates are almost fifteen times higher than among whites and almost twice as high as among African Americans. Nonetheless, African Americans continue to have the highest death rates among all racial and ethnic groups in the U.S. (Braithwaite & Taylor, 1992; U.S. Department of Health and Human Services, 1996). Despite an exceptionally high incidence of diabetes, Native American health generally improved over the last half of the twentieth century. Native Americans have the lowest cancer rates of any group in the United States, and they have the lowest mortality rate from heart disease of all groups. However, on the other hand, they suffer high rates of alcoholism and alcohol-related diseases such as cirrhosis of the liver, venereal disease, hepatitis, and tuberculosis. They also have suicide rates that are twenty times greater than that of the general population (Cockerham, 1998).

Class and Health

In the United States and around the world, social class is one of the most significant and consistent predictors of a person's health and life expectancy. The poor are more susceptible to both communicable and chronic diseases and have a lower life expectancy and a higher infant

mortality rate than their middle- and upper-class counterparts. Diseases such as coronary heart disease which were once associated with an affluent lifestyle are now concentrated among the poor and working class. Research indicates that the lower classes experience more obesity, more smoking, more stress, higher levels of blood pressure, and less leisure-time exercise, all of which contribute to the incidence of heart disease. In addition, poor men who live in overcrowded urban neighborhoods have a much higher risk of dying from cancer than do other men. This is especially true for unemployed and underemployed men (Cockerham, 1998).

Race and ethnicity are closely linked with class. For example, a disproportionate percentage of people who are poor in the United States are members of racial and ethnic groups of color. Some research attributes the class gap in health and illness to several social factors associated with the lifestyles of the poor. For example, poor people tend to live more often in hazardous, toxic, and unhygienic environments than do those of the middle and upper classes (Shweder, 1997). Nutrition and diet are also significant factors. Poor people tend to have higher amounts of sugar, salt, and fat in their diets than do others, and many experience serious nutritional deficiencies because they don't have enough money for food. Stress and stress-related illness induced by poverty and racism are also more prevalent among the poor. For example, poor African Americans have a higher rate of stress-related diseases, such as high blood pressure, than do middle- and upper-class African Americans (Klag et al., 1991). Poor housing and sanitation and inadequate heating all contribute to the higher rate of illnesses such as whooping cough, pneumonia, and alcoholism.

Moreover, poor people's experience in obtaining adequate health services in the United States has been fraught with problems. First of all, researchers such as Anselm Strauss (1970) have pointed out that the U.S. medical system has not been designed to meet the needs of poor people. The lifestyles of the poor are not always considered by health care providers, nor is there always an open and understanding line of communication between poor patients and health care providers. To treat all patients the same based on some medical model of diseases and re-

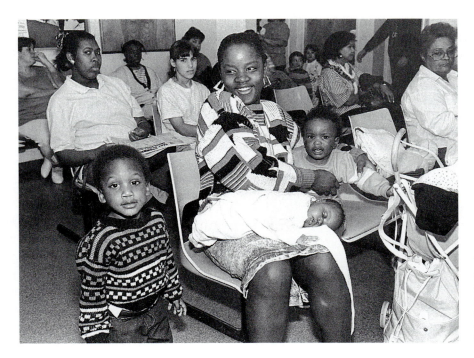

The majority of poor people either go without medical care or are forced to seek medical services in overcrowded storefront medical centers such as this one in the Bronx, New York.

covery is to ignore the differential life experiences of individuals and groups. Second, studies continue to show a significant relationship between poverty and a lack of access to quality medical care (for example, Kaplan, 1989). In sum, the most significant relationship between social class and health is the way in which social class affects the opportunities that a person has for a generally healthy life (Cockerham, 1998).

Gender and Health

According to some researchers, in the past, in many preindustrial societies, the life expectancy of women and men was virtually the same. However, there is today a definite gender gap in life expectancy that exists in most of the world, with women having superiority in life expectancy (Hart, 1991). Although life expectancy has increased for both women and men, women worldwide tend to live, on average, four years longer than men. The exception occurs in South Asian countries such as Bangladesh, India, Nepal, and Pakistan, where men outlive women. For example, in Pakistan, the life expectancy for

women is forty-nine years and for men it is fifty-one years (Cockerham, 1998). This gap is partially caused by factors such as the high rate of maternal mortality (for example, women dying during childbirth).

Some sociologists attribute the gender gap in health, particularly in the United States, to behavioral differences between the sexes. Conforming to traditional gender norms affects life expectancy, particularly male gender norms having to do with smoking, alcohol consumption, risk-taking behavior such as high-speed driving and violent sports, and being in hazardous situations both at work and during leisure. Researcher Lois Verbruge (1985) suggests that the distinguishing health feature between the sexes is not the types of health problems they experience but rather the "frequency of those problems and the pace of death" (p. 163). Women suffer from most of the same diseases as men. The difference is at what point in life they encounter those diseases. For example, coronary heart disease is the number-one cause of death for women after age sixty-six; however, it is the number-one cause of death in men after the age of thirty-nine.

The intersection of race and gender is clear when we consider the fact that African American males have higher death rates than any other group for most causes of death except pulmonary disease and suicide. It is noteworthy that since 1980, African American men are the only group of Americans actually to experience a decrease in life expectancy of two months, while every other group, including African American women, has experienced a gain from three to six years (Coleman, 1992).

This fact notwithstanding, women's health is inextricably linked to their status in society. It benefits from equality and suffers from discrimination. Today, the status and well-being of countless millions of women worldwide is extremely low. In many parts of the world, discrimination against women begins before they are born and remains with them as long as they live. Throughout human history, female babies have been unwanted in some societies and are at a disadvantage from the moment of birth. Today, girls and women continue to be denied the same rights and privileges as boys and men at home, at work, in the classroom, and in the health care delivery system. They suffer more from poverty and low social status as well as the many hazards associated with their reproductive role (World Health Report, 1998). Thus, although women live longer than men, they experience more illness and disabilities. Some researchers suggest that women are better able to endure sickness and survive than are men. They attribute this to the fact that women's most common health disorders are not usually as serious or as life threatening as those experienced by men. Other researchers, however, suggest that this is true because women tend to be more sensitive to their bodily discomforts and are much more willing than men to report their symptoms to others or to see a doctor, thus increasing their survival rate.

In any event, a down side of women's advantage in longevity is twofold. First, women seem to feel physically ill more often than men, and second, various studies have found that women suffer higher rates of depression and anxiety than do men. While there continues today to be a gender gap in health, we must keep in mind that U.S. women and men may be moving toward greater equality in mortality given that there is an increasing correspondence in the ways in which women and men live out their lives. In the past, the lives of women and men were more predictable in that the sexes typically behaved in ways distinct from one another. For example, men smoked in great numbers, but it was unfashionable for women to smoke. American women did not begin to smoke in large numbers until after World War II; their rates of lung cancer are now matching those of men (Cockerham, 1998).

Sexual Orientation and Health

Should people be denied access to quality health care because of their sexual orientation? Most Americans would answer no. However, the fact is that lesbians, gays, and bisexuals often encounter barriers to accessing health care primarily because of their sexual orientation.

In a survey conducted by the American Association of Physicians for Human Rights, 90 percent of the physicians reported seeing antigay bias in health care and another 67 percent reported knowing of lesbian or gay patients who had received substandard care because of their sexual orientation. Furthermore, some insurance companies "redline" lesbian and gay neighborhoods and refuse to cover certain employers, ostensibly to avoid enrolling people with HIV/AIDS (Human Rights Campaign Fund, 1994).

Research also indicates that lesbians may be at a greater risk for getting cancer than heterosexual women because:

1. Lesbians are less likely to seek health care because of the discomfort of "coming out" to health care providers.
2. Lesbians are less likely to visit a doctor for routine gynecological services such as birth control and prenatal care; lesbians are thus less likely to have cancers detected at earlier, more treatable, stages.
3. Lesbians are at higher risk of breast, cervical, and ovarian cancers because they are less likely to have children by age thirty, if at all.
4. Lesbians are affected more directly by women's lower earning power and do not have the benefit of a spouse's health insurance coverage ("What Specific," 1998).

Moreover, while many lesbian and gay teens are struggling with their sexual identities, the harsh realities of homophobia and heterosexism in health care has had some specific negative consequences for homosexual and bisexual teen health. For example, researchers have found that lesbian, gay, and bisexual adolescents are more likely to be at risk for suicide, victimization, high-risk sexual behaviors, and substance abuse. Recent research findings, for instance, indicate that these adolescents are at a four-times higher risk for suicide than their straight peers. Some researchers have concluded that combining the stresses of normal adolescence with the stresses of dealing with being lesbian, gay, or bisexual in a culture that is very often nonaccepting of homosexuality and bisexuality increases the health risks for these teens. Most people agree that educational efforts, prevention programs, and health services must be designed to address the needs of this population (Children's Hospital, Boston, 1997–1998; Gibson, 1989).

Disabilities and Health

Earlier, we discussed the social construction of health and illness. This same process can be applied to society's changing view of people with disabilities. For much of human history, people with disabilities were often perceived as "defective," "deviant," "dangerous," "sick," "evil," or in some way subhuman. All too frequently, people with disabilities were ignored, isolated, discriminated against, and, in some cases, even put to death (Albrecht, 1992). In the United States, compulsory sterilization laws were and are still being used to deny reproductive rights to those deemed physically or mentally unfit to parent. These punitive actions arise out of a number of misconceptions about disabilities. Despite the fact that fewer than 15 percent of persons with a disability today were born with it, many people incorrectly believe that the majority of disabilities are inherited. Most disabilities stem from accidents, diseases, war, and environments that are harmful to health, such as those that contain air and water pollutants, pesticides, and other toxic chemicals. Nevertheless, many people continue to believe that disabilities are contagious or that they are associated with

incompetence and low intelligence or that all people with disabilities are unhealthy or sick.

Some of these misconceptions can be traced to the medical community's tendency to define disability in terms of organically based impairments (Albrecht, 1992) despite the fact that many people with disabilities and mobility restrictions are able to lead productive and full lives that include working and raising a family, usually accomplished through creative adjustments to the challenges posed by their disabilities (Shaul, Dowling, & Laden, 1985). For this reason, some experts in the field, such as Joseph Shapiro (1993), refer to a **disability** as a physical or health condition that stigmatizes or causes discrimination. The advantage of this definition is that it calls attention to the fact that in many cases, discriminatory obstacles prove more limiting to people with disabilities than do the actual disabilities themselves. For example, a person in a wheelchair can be extremely mobile if there are automatic door openers, reachable elevator buttons, curbless street crossings, and building entrance ramps. It should also be noted that disabilities refer to mental as well as physical impairments or conditions that stigmatize or cause discrimination.

A strong disability rights movement emerged in the United States in the 1970s, challenging the negative images of and discrimination against people with disabilities and drawing public attention to the needs and concerns of this long-neglected segment of the U.S. population. Over 46 million Americans fifteen years old or older (23.5 percent of the population) are disabled in some way (U.S. Bureau of the Census, 1996), making them this country's largest minority group. Although anyone can sustain a disability, race, class, and gender are important factors. For example, whites have lower rates of disabilities, including more serious disabilities, than do African Americans, and persons with lower incomes have higher rates of disability than do those with higher incomes (Weitz, 1995). Further, only 52 percent of persons twenty-one to sixty-four years of age who have a disability are employed (U.S. Bureau of the Census, 1997). Many employers are reluctant to hire persons with disabilities for jobs, such as receptionist or salesperson, in which the public might be concerned more with their personal appearance than with their ability to perform the job. Problems such as these prompted Congress to pass and President George Bush to sign the **Americans with Disabilities Act** (ADA) in 1990, which prohibits discrimination against people with disabilities in the areas of employment, transportation, public accommodations, and telecommunications.

Health and Illness in Global Perspective

As social phenomena, health and illness vary from one society to another and, as we have seen, from one group to another even within the same society. From these variations, we can see how social factors affect health and illness. In this section, we will take a brief look at environmental pollution and the emergence and reemergence globally of the following infectious diseases: STDs, HIV/AIDS, and tuberculosis.

Environmental Pollution

According to some health authorities, one of the most fundamental challenges to health worldwide at the end of the twentieth century may be the same as it was four millennia ago: sanitation. The lack of adequate levels of sanitation presents an increasing challenge to the health of people, particularly those residing in developing countries. For example, in some places such as India, Cambodia, and many parts of Africa, water is a deadly menace to adults and children alike. In Thane, India, for instance, water comes from a pipe system that runs through the town. The pipes are cracked and run along a path that is filled with sewage—human feces along with rats. Most of the residents in this city are so poor that they cannot afford to buy fuel to boil water on a consistent basis. They therefore often choose to drink water that has not been boiled. According to health workers, even if the water was properly treated at its origin, sewage would nonetheless seep into the water and produce one of the most deadly illnesses in the world today: diarrhea. Diarrhea kills 3.1 million people each year, almost all of them children (Olshansky, Carnes, Rogers, & Smith, 1997).

A vast range of diseases and parasites infect people because of contaminated water and food and poor personal and domestic hygiene. Table 15.3 provides statistics and a brief description of four of the most common of these diseases and parasitic conditions. Even in developing countries, we cannot always be assured of safe drinking water. For example, in recent times, in both Sydney, Australia, and Milwaukee, Wisconsin, drinking water has been contaminated by various bacteria, resulting in many illnesses and some deaths. On a brighter note, some countries such as India have reduced diarrhea-related deaths by providing many villages with covered wells and sometimes with chlorinated water. Bolivia reduced diarrhea among children by showing poor people how to disinfect water and then keep it in their homes. And, although some communist countries do not have the best track record relative to improving the lives of their citizens, they have done well in promoting community health projects that emphasize sanitation, immunization, and basic health care. For example, Cuba has achieved a life expectancy of seventy-six years, which is roughly equivalent to that in the United States (Kristof, 1997b).

The Emergence and Reemergence of Infectious Diseases

As medical and public health institutions around the world work to eliminate known diseases, they are confronted with the emergence of "new" diseases, such as HIV/AIDS, and with the reemergence of diseases they thought were under control, such as malaria and tuberculosis. The World Health Organization defines an emerging disease as one that has been increasing for at least two decades or appears likely to increase in the near future. At least twenty-eight such emerging diseases have been identified since 1973, including a number of viruses such as Ebola, HIV, hepatitis E, and hepatitis C. Many of these diseases have no known cure or treatment, and health professionals have very narrow options for controlling their spread. These diseases are already having a profound impact on human health and longevity worldwide (Olshansky et al., 1997).

STDs   As we reported in Chapter 7, sexually transmitted diseases (STDs) are fairly common

TABLE 15.3 ⊙ Water: A Deadly Drink

A huge range of diseases and parasites infect people because of contaminated water and food, and poor personal and domestic hygiene. Millions die, most of them children. Here are some of the deadliest water-related disorders.

Disorder/ Estimated Deaths per Year	
Diarrhea 3,100,000	Diarrhea is itself not a disease but is a symptom of an underlying problem, usually the result of ingesting contaminated food or water. In children, diarrhea can cause severe, and potentially fatal, dehydration.
Schistosomiasis 200,000	A parasitic disease caused by any of three species of flukes called schistosomes and acquired from bathing in infested lakes and rivers. The infestation causes bleeding, ulceration, and fibrosis (scar tissue formation) in the bladder, intestinal walls and liver.
Trypanosomiasis 130,000	A disease caused by protozoan (single-celled) parasites known as trypanosomes. In Africa, trypanosomes are spread by the tsetse fly and cause sleeping sickness. After infection, the parasite multiplies and spreads to the bloodstream, lymph nodes, heart and, eventually, the brain.
Intestinal helminth infection 100,000	An infestation by any species of parasitic worm. Worms are acquired by eating contaminated meat, by contact with soil or water containing worm larvae or from soil contaminated by infected feces.

Source: "A Closer Look: Death by Water." In Nicholas D. Kristof (1997, January 9), "For Third World, Water Is Still a Deadly Drink." *New York Times,* p. A8. Data from the World Health Organization and the AMA's *Encyclopedia of Medicine.* Copyright © 1997 by The New York Times Company. Reprinted by permission.

in today's society. Worldwide, it is estimated that approximately 333 million people are stricken with curable STDs each year, and, in the United States, more than 13 million people acquire an STD each year, two-thirds of whom are persons under the age of twenty-five; 3 million are teenagers.

Chlamydia is currently the most common bacterial STD in the United States. In 1996, half a million cases of chlamydial infection were reported to the Centers for Disease Control. Reported rates for women (322 per 100,000 people) far exceeded those for men (60 per 100,000). Most people who have this disease do not know that they have it and thus are not being treated for it.

The most common viral STD is herpes. An estimated 45 million Americans are infected with herpes, and, as with people with chlamydia, many do not know they are infected. The rate of herpes infection is higher for women than for men, perhaps because the infection spreads more easily from men to women than from

women to men. Herpes can be severe and may cause a weakened immune system, such as that found in HIV/AIDS patients (Centers for Disease Control and Prevention, 1998; Division of STD Prevention, 1997; WHO, 1995).

The U.S. populations most vulnerable to STDs and their consequences include women and infants, adolescents and young adults, some groups of color, and populations in the southern United States. The health consequences of STDs can be most serious, particularly for women. For example, STDs can cause women to have chronic pelvic pain, become sterile, have an ectopic pregnancy, be unable to carry a fetus to term, or infect their babies during delivery. In fact, STDs, especially gonorrhea and chlamydia, are responsible for most involuntary childlessness in both low-income and industrialized countries. Chlamydia also raises the risk of pneumonia and syphilis, increases the probability that women will have low-birth-weight babies who, in turn, are vulnerable to a wide range of health problems themselves (Olshansky et al., 1997). The high prevalence of STDs among adolescents reflects multiple barriers to quality STD prevention services, including lack of insurance or other ability to pay, lack of transportation, discomfort with facilities and services designed for adults, and concerns about confidentiality (Division of STD Prevention, 1997).

Many people are largely ignorant of the dangers of STDs. This ignorance is dangerous: left untreated, many types of STDs can be lethal, as in the cases of advanced syphilis and HIV/AIDS. HIV/AIDS is, perhaps, the most deadly STD to date. It is a threat to women and men, the young and old, poor and rich, homosexual and heterosexual, and all across races and ethnicities around the world.

HIV/AIDS In the late 1970s, when smallpox was eradicated worldwide, health experts believed that infectious and parasitic diseases (IPDs) could at long last be conquered. However, the world was in for a rude awakening with the discovery of HIV/AIDS in the early 1980s. As we indicated in Chapter 7, AIDS is a deadly disease that destroys a person's immunity against infection, thereby leaving the individual defenseless against a variety of illnesses such as cancer, pneumonia, and a host of viruses. AIDS first appeared in large numbers in the United States among male homosexuals. In addition to homosexuals, the HIV/AIDS-exposure categories now include intravenous drug users, heterosexuals, children born to mothers with or at risk for HIV infection, hemophiliacs, and people who have been infected through blood transfusions. Contrary to popular misinformation about the transmission of HIV/AIDS, it is *not* spread through casual, everyday contact. A person cannot become infected with the virus unless bodily fluids pass from one person to another. HIV is transmitted in three major ways:

- Through having sex with someone infected with HIV
- Through sharing needles and syringes with someone who has HIV
- Through exposure (in the case of infants) to HIV before or during birth, or through breast feeding

The Prevalence of HIV/AIDS in the United States HIV/AIDS and the clinical complications that follow represent one of the most critical and devastating epidemics in U.S. history. The total number of infected persons in the United States is estimated to range from 650,000 to 900,000, equal to approximately one in one hundred Americans of all ages. Through the end of June 1998, a cumulative total of 665,357 persons with AIDS had been reported to the Centers for Disease Control and Prevention, of which 401,028 (60 percent) had died. A sociological portrait of who gets HIV/AIDS in the United States (shown in Table 15.4) reveals that 83 percent of adult AIDS cases are men; 55 percent are gay men; all diagnosed cases traced to intimate same-sex contact among homosexuals have been male; and the preponderance of AIDS victims are either males who have had intimate same-sex contacts or intravenous drug users who have shared a hypodermic needle (Centers for Disease Control, 1998). As these statistics reveal, in the United States, the rates of HIV/AIDS is highest in groups that are typically socially devalued by many in the larger population: gays and IV drug users. Given this fact, AIDS is often attributed to irresponsible behavior, and victims are therefore stigmatized and blamed for their illness and treated not only unsympathetically but sometimes with hostility and violence. However, as the rate of heterosexuals infected with AIDS has risen, the general public is much more aware that it does not occur just among gays and IV drug users. In fact, in many parts of the world, such as Asia and Africa, the overwhelming majority of those infected with HIV/AIDS are heterosexual and do not use IV drugs.

The intersections of sexual orientation, age, race, class, and gender are clearly revealed in various HIV/AIDS statistics. For example, the number of new HIV/AIDS cases among white homosexuals has declined in several major cities since 1990, while the rate of infection among homosexuals of color has increased significantly. In 1998, 45 percent of all reported AIDS cases were white people, 36 percent were African Americans, 18 percent were Latinas/os, and Asian Americans, Pacific Islanders, Native Americans, and Alaska Natives taken together accounted for just about 1 percent of people with

TABLE 15.4 ⊘ **Cumulative Percentage of Persons in U.S. with AIDS, by Gender, 1998**

	Males (83% of adult AIDS cases)	Females (16% of adult AIDS cases)	Totals
Men who have sex with men	49%	NA	49%
IV drug users	18	7%	25
Men who have sex with men who are IV drug users	6	NA	6
Heterosexuals	2	4	6
Heterosexuals who have sex with IV drug users	1	2	3
Hemophiliacs	0.7	0.03	0.73
Through blood transfusions	0.7	0.5	1.2
Undetermined	6	2	8

Note: Not shown in table: 8,280 (1 percent) of AIDS cases are children less than 13 years of age. The percentages in this table are based on persons reported with AIDS through June 30, 1998.

Source: Centers for Disease Control and Prevention. 1998. "HIV/AIDS Trends"; U.S. Bureau of the Census. *Statistical Abstract of the United States, 1998.* Washington, DC: U.S. Government Printing Office, Table 226.

AIDS (see Figure 15.1). Moreover, although African Americans constitute only 12 percent of the U.S. population, 54 percent of all children, 53 percent of all women, and 32 percent of all men with AIDS are African American. White women constitute 25 percent of cases, Latinas 21 percent, and Asian American and Native American women only 1 percent ("Black Clergy,"

FIGURE 15.1 ⊘ **AIDS Cases by Race or Ethnicity**

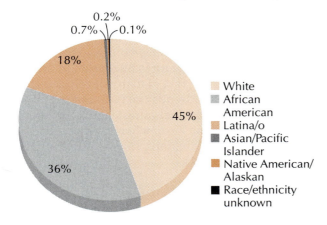

- White
- African American
- Latina/o
- Asian/Pacific Islander
- Native American/ Alaskan
- Race/ethnicity unknown

0.2%
0.7%
0.1%
18%
45%
36%

1993; Centers for Disease Control and Prevention, 1993).

Women and children are among the groups most severely impacted by AIDS. During the first decade of the AIDS epidemic, there were about 500,000 cases of AIDS in women and children, most of which went unrecognized. Today, one of every five new cases of AIDS is a woman, most of whom are at childbearing ages. As the rate of infected women increases, the rate of babies being born with AIDS also increases (Centers for Disease Control and Prevention, 1997; Tsai, 1998).

The good news is that the age-adjusted HIV/AIDS death rate is currently the lowest since 1987, when mortality data for the disease were first available. Age-adjusted death rates from HIV/AIDS in the United States declined an unprecedented 47 percent from 1996 to 1997, and HIV infection fell from eighth to fourteenth among the leading causes of death in the United States over the same period. For those aged twenty-five to forty-four (the age group hardest hit by HIV/AIDS), HIV/AIDS dropped from the leading cause of death in 1995 to the fifth-leading in 1997 (U.S. Department of Health and

Human Services, 1998). Although there is no cure for HIV/AIDS, it can be prevented or the risk for it greatly reduced through behavioral changes such as sexual abstinence, safe sexual practices (such as exclusive relationships and using latex condoms), avoiding high-risk behaviors (such as intravenous drug use or the sharing of needles between drug users), and the careful monitoring of transfusions of blood and other body fluids.

HIV/AIDS in Global Perspective HIV/AIDS constitutes a challenge to human health and well-being and to the resources of communities around the world. According to the Centers for Disease Control (1998), an estimated 33.4 million people worldwide are living with HIV/AIDS. Of these, 32.2 million are adults. About 13.8 million are women, and 1.2 million are children under the age of fifteen. An estimated 14 million people have died from AIDS since the epidemic began. Women worldwide are becoming increasingly affected by HIV. As Figure 15.2 shows, women represent anywhere from one-fifth to almost one-half of all cases of HIV/AIDS in most countries of the world. Worldwide, 43 percent of adults living with HIV/AIDS are women. Figure 15.2 also shows that more than 95 percent of all HIV-infected people now live in the developing world, which has likewise experienced 95 percent of all deaths from AIDS (Centers for Disease Control and Prevention, 1998). Approximately 70 percent of HIV-positive people live in Africa. However, over the last decade, health experts have noted a rapid increase in HIV infections in Asia, especially in Southeast Asian countries such as Thailand, Burma, and India. Although the number of HIV/AIDS cases in Asia is currently below the level of Africa, it is very likely that it will exceed Africa because of the lack of testing, diagnostic facilities, and change in social behavior (Tsai, 1998).

The relationship between health and society is reciprocal: just as society has an important impact on health, health can also have an important impact on society. For example, the HIV/AIDS epidemic has produced some of the most rapid and dramatic demographic effects of all IPDs in this century. HIV/AIDS has slowed population growth in sub-Saharan Africa and has the potential to cut by one-half the average life

AIDS is a disease that knows no national boundaries. To combat the escalating number of AIDS cases in Hanoi, this government poster warns against prostitution, drug use, and other activities leading to the spread of AIDS.

expectancy at birth in some African countries by the year 2010. In Zimbabwe, where an estimated 900,000 people are infected with HIV, some scientists have projected that AIDS may reduce this country's life expectancy at birth from its 1997 level of fifty-one years to thirty-three years by the year 2010. If, on the other hand, HIV/AIDS were eliminated, Zimbabwe's life expectancy would be expected to rise to 69.9 years in 2010, a level approaching that of many developed nations today. Similar trends can be found in many other parts of Africa, including Uganda, Nigeria, Kenya, and Burkina Faso, where the prevalence of HIV/AIDS is particularly high and rising (Olshansky et al., 1997).

The Reemergence of Tuberculosis The forces of demographic change are a significant part of the "environment" of the microbes that cause

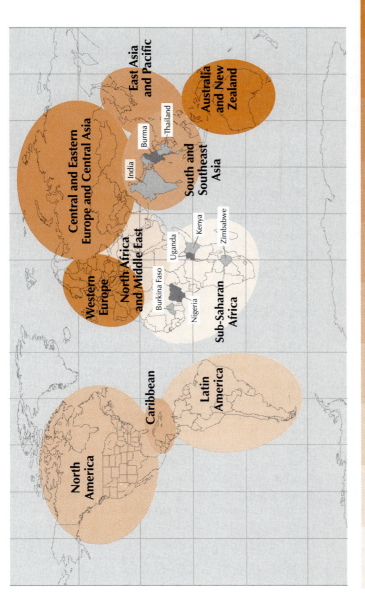

	Sub-Saharan Africa*	North Africa and Middle East	Latin America	North America	Caribbean	South and Southeast Asia†	East Asia and Pacific	Central and Eastern Europe and Central Asia	Western Europe	Australia and New Zealand
People living with HIV/AIDS	14,000,000	200,000	1,300,000	750,000	270,000	5,200,000	100,000	50,000	510,000	13,000
Percentage of women	50+%	20%	20%	20%	40+%	30+%	20%	20%	20%	20%
Deaths in 1996	783,700	10,800	70,900	61,300	14,500	143,700	1,200	1,000	21,000	1,000

* 70 percent of cases worldwide occur in Sub-Saharan Africa.
† Where HIV/AIDS is spreading most rapidly. This area accounts for about 20 percent of all infections.

FIGURE 15.2 ⊘ HIV/AIDS: A Global Perspective *Source:* Data from UNAIDS: The Joint United Nations Programme on HIV/AIDS (for the latest information, see http://www.unaids.org/highband/index.html).

infectious and parasitic diseases. Just as changes in the prevalence of IPDs can impact change in society, such as in mortality and fertility, likewise demographic trends can impact the spread of infectious diseases. For most of human history, the spread of various IPDs was limited, for example, by a number of factors including the number of people living in a particular area. However, demographic changes such as the increasing development of urban centers at the end of the eighteenth century contributed greatly to the spread of various IPDs. Today, the spread, or "reemergence," of some IPDs, such as tuberculosis, is linked to the increasing urbanization of the world. The number of people living in cities of 1 million or more people is expected to grow from 927 million in 1995 to 1.7 billion by 2015 (Olshansky et al., 1997).

Tuberculosis (TB) is one of the oldest and most widespread diseases to infect humans. It is an airborne disease that spreads from one individual to another through tiny water droplets released primarily when someone coughs or sneezes. Because the bacilli that cause TB can remain alive and airborne for days, the disease thrives in colder climates where people remain indoors with windows closed during the cold months. In its common pulmonary form, TB eventually damages the lungs, causing extreme fatigue, chest pains, fever, and other progressively debilitating symptoms. Without treatment, about half of the people infected with TB die within five years. Although effective antibiotics have been available to treat TB since the 1940s, new multidrug-resistant forms of tuberculosis have appeared, making it much harder to treat. Modern medical and agricultural practices, especially the overuse of antibiotics and pesticides, unwittingly promote the rise of drug-resistant strains of infectious diseases.

Complacency toward TB over the last three decades has led to the demise or elimination of control programs in many countries. The result has been a powerful reemergence of TB, currently estimated to kill 3 million people worldwide each year. In 1995, 9 million people contracted the disease, and it is still a major killer in developing countries. One-third of the increase in cases of TB since 1993 can be attributed to coinfection with HIV/AIDS. By the late 1980s, it was clear that, with increasing coinfections with HIV/AIDS and the spread of multidrug-resistant strains, the TB epidemic was growing worse, and in 1993, the World Health Assembly declared a global TB emergency. As in the past, the urban poor are especially vulnerable because they tend to live in crowded quarters and because they often have immune systems compromised by malnutrition (Olshansky et al., 1997; World Health Report, 1998).

Mental Health and Disorders in the United States

Sociologists are equally interested in the mental as well as the physical health, well-being, and illness of a society. As with physical health and illness, most people tend to think of mental health as an objective condition that can be measured in terms of the absence of illness. However, as with physical health, sociologists study mental health within a social construction framework. Let's take a brief look at mental health and illness in the United States. What is mental illness? Although some people use the terms interchangeably, many medical professionals distinguish between a *mental disorder,* a condition that makes it difficult or impossible for a person to cope with everyday life, and *mental illness,* a condition that requires extensive treatment with medication, psychotherapy, and sometimes hospitalization (Kendall, 1998). Sociologically speaking, how mental disorder or illness is defined and diagnosed and what and who gets defined as mentally ill each depends on a number of sociocultural, political, and demographic factors such as cultural norms, political climate, and ideologies as well as race, class, gender, age, and sexual orientation. For example, some conditions or behaviors such as homosexuality that were once considered to be mental illnesses are no longer defined as such. Similarly, some mental disorders are unique to specific cultures, and some conditions that are considered evidence of mental illness in some cultures are considered natural and normal behavior in others. In some East Asian countries such as Malaysia, some people exhibit a condition labeled *koro,* which is a morbid fear of their nipples and sexual organs receding into the body, causing their death. This disorder is not known outside these cultures. Researchers have even found that people in different cultures sometimes manifest very different symptoms in response to the same clinically defined mental disorder. For example, in some cultures, schizophrenics are loud and quite aggressive, whereas in other cultures, they have been found to be particularly quiet and withdrawn.

The social construction of mental disorders can also be seen in the differential attribution of mental disorders and illnesses across race, class, gender, sexual orientation, and age. For example, although there does not appear to be any significant differences in the diagnosis of mental disorders between African Americans and white Americans or women and men, there are some exceptions. Also, interestingly, studies of racism reveal a link between racism and the mental health of African Americans. For example, in their study of the effects of racism in the everyday lives of middle-class African Americans, Joe Feagin and Melvin Sikes (1994) found that repeated personal experiences of racism, discrimination, and hostility have a significant impact on the psychological well-being of most African Americans, regardless of social-class level. As we indicated in Chapter 10, racism impacts everyone, not just the victims of racism. Consistent with this point are the findings of a study by Joe Feagin and Hernan Vera (1995) which indicated that white Americans also pay a "mental cost" for the prevalence of racism, both their own and that of others in the society. Many social researchers today concur with Thomas Pettigrew's (1981) early suggestion that racism of all types constitutes a mentally unhealthy situation that limits people's ability to achieve to their fullest potential.

With the exception of anxiety and mood disorders, the highest rates of mental disorder/illness are found among the lower classes; as social class increases, mental disorders decrease (Williams, Takeuchi, & Adair, 1992). Social scientists typically use three possible explanations for the high incidence of mental disorders among the lower classes and the poor:

1. The *genetic* explanation suggests that members of the lower classes are genetically predisposed to mental disorders. This explanation has not been supported by research.
2. The *social stress* explanation suggests that as a result of a lack of resources and of living under difficult conditions, lower-class

Following the deinstitutionalization of the mentally ill, many poor people receive little or no treatment for their mental disorders. Consequently, many of them end up sleeping on the street in doorways as does this New York woman who has been homeless for a number of years.

3. The *social selection* explanation suggests that mentally ill people may drift downward in the class structure or that those who are mentally healthy among the lower classes tend to be upwardly mobile and thus leave the mentally ill in the lower classes (Cockerham, 1989).

However, some social scientists use a social structural explanation that centers on the ability of the socially powerful to label those with less power mentally ill.

In terms of gender, most studies focusing on the relationship between gender and mental disorder have not found any consistent differences between women and men in clinically diagnosed cases of mental illness, with the exception of mood and anxiety disorders. Studies indicate that women have higher rates of prolonged depression or elation and anxiety while men have higher rates of personality disorders. Tendencies toward depression and anxiety that are outside of the clinical definition of these disorders are also found much more frequently among women than among men. This has been found to be the case not only in the United States but also in countries around the world (Cockerham, 1998). Generally, these gender differences begin in puberty, and they increase as women and men reach adulthood and live out their unequal statuses. This observation provides support for feminist and other social researchers who suggest that gender differences in mental disorders are a function of gender role socialization that socializes girls/women to be passive and boys/men to be aggressive. Support for this position also comes from studies that show that women who work outside the home have fewer mental disorders than do women who remain at home and that women in high-income, high-status jobs have fewer mental disorders and greater levels of psychological well-being regardless of their marital status (Kendall, 1998).

Finally, as we pointed out earlier, as a result of the combined stresses of normal adolescence and the stresses of dealing with being lesbian, gay, or bisexual, gay teenagers are much more likely than their heterosexual counterparts to experience depression and isolation and to be suicidal. In a 1993 study, two-thirds of the lesbian, gay, and bisexual respondents reported that hiding their sexual orientation from teachers and others left them feeling overwhelmed to the point of being dysfunctional. Those who knew about their sexual orientation for longer periods of time had lost more friends and reported more mental problems ("What Specific," 1998). In the final analysis, there is still much more work to be done in the area of intersecting inequalities in the area of mental health, disorder, and illness. It may well be that additional factors such as religiosity, type of religion, geographic location, type of home environment, and type of work could add significantly to our knowledge of mental health and illness.

Death and Dying

We cannot talk about health and wellness without dealing with the last stage of life, dying and death. In 1997, of a global total of 52.2 million deaths, 17.3 million were due to infectious and parasitic diseases (tuberculosis, diarrhea, HIV/AIDS, and malaria), 15.3 million were due to circulatory diseases (coronary heart disease and cerebrovascular diseases), 6.2 million were due to cancer, 2.9 million were due to respiratory diseases, and 3.6 million were due to perinatal conditions. Figure 15.3 identifies the main causes of death by a country's level of development. Although death may occur at any stage of the life course, in developing societies, children are among the most vulnerable, whereas in modern industrial societies, death is most likely to occur in old age. Many of the diseases in developing countries are associated with extreme poverty. By contrast, many of the diseases in developed countries are associated with affluence and unhealthy lifestyles—little physical exercise combined with a diet high in fat and the use of tobacco and alcohol.

The Process of Dying

Dying is not a simple matter, and every society has its own rituals and ways of coping with dying and death. In many developing countries, death takes place at home among family and

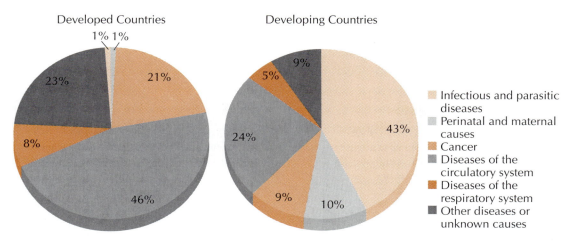

Developed Countries · Developing Countries

Infectious and parasitic diseases
Perinatal and maternal causes
Cancer
Diseases of the circulatory system
Diseases of the respiratory system
Other diseases or unknown causes

FIGURE 15.3 ☉ **Causes of Death, by Level of Development, 1997** *Source:* Data from World Health Organization. 1998. *World Health Report 1998: Executive Summary.* http://www.who.org/whr/1998/exsum98e.htm.

friends and is part of daily life events. Although this was true in the United States until relatively recently, the majority of people today die in hospitals and nursing homes, often isolated from their loved ones. At times, however, people lack even this minimal level of support (see Sociology through Literature box). Among the most critical need of the dying is simply to know that death is near, yet access to this information is not always available. Even though the medical community now advocates more openness with patients about their conditions, some doctors are still reluctant to tell patients they are dying. This reluctance on the part of doctors is compounded by the different views of various immigrant groups toward knowing about impending death. For example, a recent study of 800 elderly patients found that African American and white respondents were about twice as likely as Korean Americans and about one-and-one-half times as likely as Mexican Americans to agree that a patient should be told of a terminal prognosis (Mydans, 1995). A lack of information can prevent a person from attending to important tasks—getting insurance and financial paperwork in order, making decisions about medical treatment, arranging for distribution of personal property, making a will, informing family and friends about wishes regarding funeral arrangements, and saying good-bye. Consequently,

these death preparations are made hurriedly at the last minute or are left to the grief-stricken spouse or family to cope with during a period of enormous stress. Although anticipating and planning for our own death or that of a loved one is difficult, doing so in advance can make it more manageable for the survivors.

The Hospice Movement

In Chapter 8, we discussed some of the controversy surrounding "the right to die" movement and physician-assisted suicide. Many health care professionals believe that increasing the availability and affordability of hospices would eliminate the desire for physician-assisted suicide. A **hospice** is a physical environment within which dying patients are allowed to die with dignity as defined by the patients and their families. Thus, the patients structure the dying process to fit their needs rather than the needs of the medical staff or institution. This movement began in 1967 when British physician Cicely Saunders opened St. Christopher's Hospice in London. Her approach to dying patients was geared to making them comfortable and controlling their pain. Her philosophy and model of an interdisciplinary team composed of doctors, nurses, volunteers, and clergy who would communicate effectively, treat the symptoms of terminal disease, and offer

Sociology through Literature

A Summer Tragedy

The excerpt below tells the story of Jennie and Jeff Patton, an elderly black sharecropping couple who are in poor health. Their adult children are dead, and they have no financial or social resources to draw on. Dressed in their Sunday clothes, they drive their old car to the river:

Jennie waited a few seconds, then said, "You reckon we oughta do it, Jeff? You reckon we oughta go 'head an' do it, really?"

Jeff's voice choked; his eyes blurred. He was terrified to hear Jennie say the thing that had been in his mind all morning. She had egged him on when he had wanted more than anything in the world to wait, to reconsider, to think things over a little longer. Now she was getting cold feet. Actually there was no need of thinking the question through again. It would only end in making the same painful decision once more. Jeff knew that. There was no need of fooling around longer.

"We jes as well to do like we planned," he said. "They ain't nothin' else for us now—it's the bes' thing."

Jeff thought of the handicaps, the near impossibility, of making another crop with his leg bothering him more and more each week. Then there was always the chance that he would have another stroke, like the one that had made him lame. Another one might kill him. The least it could do would be to leave him helpless. Jeff gasped—Lord Jesus! He could not bear to think of being helpless, like a baby, on Jennie's hands. Frail, blind Jennie. The little pounding motor of the car worked harder and harder. The puff of steam from the cracked radiator became larger. Jeff realized theat they were climbing a little rise. A moment later the road turned abruptly and he looked down upon the face of the river. . . .

"Jennie, I can't do it. I can't." His voice broke pitifully.

She did not appear to be listening. All the grief had gone from her face. She sat erect, her unseeing eyes wide open, strained and frightful. Her glossy black skin had become dull. She seemed as thin, as sharp and bony, as a starved bird. Now, having suffered and endured the sadness of tearing herself away from beloved things, she showed no anguish. She was absorbed with her own thoughts, and she didn't even hear Jeff's voice shouting in her ear.

Jeff said nothing more. . . .

. . . Now he was old, worn out. Another paralytic stroke (like the one he had already suffered) would put him on his back for keeps. In that condition, with a frail blind woman to look after him, he would be worse off than if he were dead.

Suddenly Jeff's hands became steady. He actually felt brave. He slowed down the motor of the car and carefully pulled off the road. Below, the water of the stream boomed, a soft thunder in the deep channel. Jeff ran the car onto the clay slope, pointed it directly toward the stream and put his foot heavily on the accelerator. The little car leaped furiously down the steep incline toward the water. The movement was nearly as swift and direct as a fall. The two old black folks, sitting quietly side by side, showed no excitement. In another instant the car hit the water and dropped immediately out of sight. A little later it lodged in the mud of a shallow place. One wheel of the crushed and upturned little Ford became visible above the rushing water.

What problems did this couple face? Why did they think they had no other alternatives but to end their lives? This story was written in 1933. Do you think similar stories are unfolding today? Explain. What can be done to prevent such tragedies from occurring?

Source: Extract from "A Summer Tragedy" by Arna Bontemps. Copyright 1933 by Arna Bontemps. Reprinted by permission of Harold Ober Associates Incorporated. In E.P. Stoller and R.C. Gibson. 1997. *Worlds of Difference,* 2nd ed. Thousand Oaks, CA: Pine Forge Press, pp. 283–285.

support to patients as well as their families, was brought to the United States in the 1970s (Torrens, 1985). As hospices increased, many of them took on variant forms. Today, a hospice environment might be the patient's home or an institutionalized setting in a hospital or nursing home. The average length of stay in hospice is fifty-nine days and the average age of a hospice patient is just over seventy-one years old (Rhymes, 1995). Race, class, and family structure play a role in who uses hospice care. Typically, hospice patients are white, middle- or working-class, and from reasonably intact families (Levy, 1994).

Bereavement and Grief Work   Death and the dying process inevitably leave others behind who must cope with the loss of a loved one. A death occasions a series of responses and adjustments. First is the painful process of **bereavement,** the state of being deprived of a loved one by death. It is often associated with psychological symptoms (confusion; difficulty in concentrating; and intense feelings of loss, depression, and loneliness) as well as physiological symptoms (loss of appetite, an inability to sleep, and deteriorating health). Sociologist Helen Lopata (1973), in her now classic study of widows, illustrated the importance of doing **grief work,** confronting and acknowledging the emotions brought about by death. Resolving grief is not an automatic process. Rather, successful grief resolution involves four tasks: accepting the reality of loss, experiencing the pain of grief, adjusting to an environment in which the deceased is missing, and withdrawing emotional energy and reinvesting it in another relationship (Worden, 1982). The duration and intensity of these tasks as well as the degree of social support the bereaved receives depend, in large measure, on the manner and timing of a death, the person's age, and her or his relationship to the survivors.

Some individuals experience **disenfranchised grief**—circumstances in which a person experiences a sense of loss but does not have a socially recognized right, role, or capacity to grieve (Doka, 1989). All societies construct norms or "grieving rules" that tell us who, when, where, how, how long, and for whom people should grieve. For example, employment personnel policies tell us how much time, if any, we can take for the death of a loved one. Society chooses to recognize and sanction some relationships, primarily familial, but not others. When the relationship between the bereaved and deceased lacks recognizable kin ties, the depth of the relationship may not be understood, appreciated, or acknowledged by others. Yet the relationships between friends, roommates, neighbors, colleagues, and in-laws are often intimate and long-lasting. Homosexual, cohabiting, and extramarital relationships are often

disapproved of in and of themselves, and, thus, such a loss might engender little sympathy from others. Other losses, such as those due to miscarriages or abortions and even the death of a pet, may not be viewed as significant by others. Some people, for example, a child or a person with a mental disability, may erroneously be thought of as being incapable of grief. Despite the distinctiveness of each of these situations, they all share the problems associated with disenfranchised grief—they lack supports that facilitate mourning. Too often, people in these situations are not given the opportunity to talk about their loss or to receive the expressions of sympathy and material supports that help people through this difficult time. Consequently, their grief work may remain incomplete for a long period of time (Schwartz & Scott, 1997).

Contemporary Issues in Health Care

As we have seen, there are many issues in health care both in the United States and globally. In the United States, for example, some of the major issues today include a growing problem of physician *malpractice* and an increasing number of lawsuits brought by patients attempting to recover damages; the emergence of *defensive medicine,* which adds significantly to the cost of health care; the practice and debated benefit of *alternative medicine;* and health care reform, including insuring health care so that access to medical care is more equally distributed. Let's take a closer look at these issues.

Malpractice and Defensive Medicine

Historically, the social control of medical practice has presented significant problems for U.S. society. On the one hand, it has been argued that because doctors set the medical standards enforced by governmental regulating agencies and because the lay public is not qualified to judge medical performance, two of the most important forms of social control in an industrial society— bureaucratic supervision and evaluation by the recipients of services—are missing. It is further argued that this problem is solved, however, because doctors are members of a self-controlled community that provides a vital function for society's general good.

On the other hand, it is counterargued that individuals do, in fact, evaluate the technical performance of doctors whether or not they are qualified to do so. They do this by shopping around and choosing doctors whom they view as able to meet their expectations and needs. Some research shows that the choices that patients make act as a form of social control over professionals and can militate against the survival of a group as a profession or the career success of particular professionals. In addition, the notion that doctors are self-regulating is not entirely accurate. Research has found that while doctors have indeed developed a set of standards that define the limits of acceptable performance, they are basically restricted to the evaluation of work per se while accountability and critical evaluation of one another as professionals are discouraged in order to maintain group harmony (Conrad, 1997). Researcher Marcia Millman (1977) found, for example, that while many doctors are willing to criticize their colleagues' errors in small group discussions or behind their backs, they were not willing to criticize another doctor's errors at any official meeting because of a feeling of common group interests and a fear of reprisal.

Civil-rights based social movements such as the movements for racial, gender, and sexual preference equality sparked a movement for the rights of patients in the form of *malpractice litigation* (litigation for the purpose of compensating patients who have been preventably harmed as a result of the actions or inactions of a doctor and of discouraging such harms from occurring). Malpractice suits rose dramatically over the last half of the twentieth century, from a few hundred such suits in the early 1950s to more than 10,000 by the end of the 1980s, when claims began to decline somewhat. At the beginning of the 1990s, there were about thirteen claims per one hundred doctors.

The typical malpractice claims involve surgery, birth-related improper treatment, and failure to diagnose cancer. Nearly one-half of all medical malpractice suits result in some payment to the plaintiff, and this proportion has remained fairly stable over the last two decades.

Approximately one in every twenty doctors is successfully sued each year. Of the 6 percent of cases that actually go to court, 80 percent are won by the defendant doctor (Weiss & Lonnquist, 1994). A recent decline in malpractice litigation is attributable to a number of factors including:

1. Doctors have generally adopted improved standards to reduce patient injuries and have developed a better rapport with patients than in the past.
2. A number of states have set limits on the amount of money awarded in malpractice lawsuits.
3. A national data bank was established in 1989 to identify incompetent doctors and other licensed health practitioners.
4. Doctors have become more careful in dealing with patients (Conrad, 1997).

In this latter context, prompted by the increasing risk of law suits, many doctors practice **defensive medicine,** medical practices that include every imaginable test or procedure for patients, not for medical reasons but for the purpose of protecting doctors from the possibility of a malpractice suit in the case of a negative patient outcome. A growing concern has been focused on defensive medicine as a factor in the escalating cost of health care. Defensive medicine exacts huge costs in both fiscal and human terms. Although it is difficult to measure precisely the effect of malpractice on defensive medicine and the cost of health care, it is estimated that doctors and hospitals spent $25 billion on defensive medical practices in the early to mid-1990s. During this period, malpractice costs increased 48.6 percent, far outpacing the 16.6 percent increase in overall tort costs during the same period (Anderson, 1998). According to Peter Conrad (1997), the increasing number of malpractice suits can be viewed as an indication not of increasing poor medical practice but of the fact that such suits are about the only form of medical accountability presently available to patients.

Integrating Alternative Medicine

What do the terms *medical care* and *healing practices* mean to you? If you are like the majority of Americans, you associate these terms with orthodox or traditional medical doctors and services. However, the preeminence of scientific medicine in the United States notwithstanding, available data show that millions of people use *alternative healing practices,* those founded on therapeutic principles and practices that are inconsistent with the scientific medical model, such as prayer, home remedies, and alternative healers. For example, some of you probably believe in or have participated in faith healing or have witnessed such healing performed by television evangelists or your own minister. Pentecostals and other Christians believe that the *laying of hands* on a person, particularly in the area of the disease or injury, will cure it. Others in U.S. society make frequent visits to herbalists who prescribe and dispense various herbs and oils believed to be cures for certain physical as well as emotional maladies. An early classification of types of alternative healers is still useful:

- **Limited practitioners**—whose services are typically limited to specific parts of the human anatomy (for example, podiatry, optometry, dentistry, and psychology). Although they are considered "alternative healers," they are not outside of the mainstream of conventional medicine.
- **Marginal practitioners**—whose services cover the total range of bodily functions and disorders but who use methods and procedures that are unacceptable to conventional medicine (such as acupuncture, chiropractic, and the methods of ethnic folk healers such as *curanderos* and Native American healers).
- **Quasi-practitioners**—whose services are incidental to some other function, usually religious (spiritual healers). (Wardwell, 1979)

People choose alternative healing over traditional medicine for a number of reasons, including religious reasons and dissatisfaction with traditional medical care. However, researchers have found that many people integrate alternative and traditional healing. That is, they use alternative healing at the same time as they receive care from a medical doctor. For example, some patients use chiropractors for chronic back problems or naprapaths for colonic irrigation (colon cleansing) but continue to use a medical doctor for other problems, such as those requiring surgery. With a few exceptions, researchers have found very little difference in the use of alternative medicine by race, class, or gender. Although neither class nor gender is related to the use of a chiropractor, whites are slightly more likely than African Americans to do so. In addition, some researchers have found that African Americans are more likely than whites to pray about health problems and to use faith healing (Weiss & Lonnquist, 1994).

Reforming the Health Care System

Escalating costs and lack of access to health care in the United States have ignited a debate in Congress over ways to improve the health care system. Some critics have proposed establishing a national health care system modeled after the Canadian system, which guarantees all citizens equal access to health care through a national health service paid for and administered by the government. Under such a proposal, the federal government would guarantee health care for all citizens, regardless of employment status, and finance it with tax dollars. Coverage would be through a *single-payer plan* whereby the government would regulate health care fees and streamline administrative procedures, thus cutting costs. All bills would be submitted to the government for payment. Such efforts to reform the system during the early years of the Clinton Administration failed due in large part to the well-financed lobbying power of the insurance industry and the medical establishment. Opponents argued that a national health care system would be too costly and that patient–doctor relationships would be impeded by government regulation. Critics also questioned whether, in fact, such a system could remain as comprehensive as the current private pay system, which in its own way rations certain procedures and technologies to those who are insured or who can afford to pay for such services themselves.

Given the level of political partisanship in Congress and the lack of strong grass-roots support and political activism, it is unlikely that the United States will adopt the idea of a government-administered health care system any time soon.

Instead, piecemeal attempts at reform, such as recent efforts to extend health care coverage to the uninsured and to control escalating health care costs, are the most likely scenarios.

Insuring Health Care

The provision of health care in the United States has traditionally been based on a fee-for-service payment system in which health care providers are paid a specified amount by the patient for whatever services are rendered. Simply stated, people with adequate resources, including health insurance, receive good medical care and those without don't.

Health care expenditures in the United States are the highest in the industrialized world, yet the United States is last in terms of the percent of its population covered by public health insurance (Sivard, 1991). Comprehensive government-run national health programs exist in most of the industrialized countries. In contrast, access to the health care system in the United States is primarily through private insurance, with two major public exceptions—Medicare for the elderly and Medicaid for the poor. A little over 70 percent of the population is covered under private insurance, obtained primarily as a fringe benefit of their employment. However, as insurance costs have increased, employers have shifted more of the cost to their employees, especially the cost of insuring workers' families. Currently, over 16 percent of the population (over 43 million Americans) do not have health insurance, up from 13 percent in 1987. Those most likely to be uninsured are young adults between eighteen and thirty-four years of age, African Americans and Latinas/os who are unemployed, and the working poor (Pear, 1998).

Many jobs, especially part-time jobs and most minimum-wage jobs, do not include insurance benefits. Approximately 20 million more people are underinsured, that is, their level of benefits is not adequate to see them through any major accident or illness. People who lack insurance are extremely vulnerable on a number of fronts. For the most part, they receive little preventive care. Worried about costs, they often delay treatment until they are very sick, and then they most likely go to hospital emergency rooms, adding further strain to an already overburdened system. Although some reforms have made it technically possible for people to keep their insurance coverage after they have become unemployed or divorced, such reforms have not solved the problem of affordability, nor have they appreciably reduced the numbers of uninsured. In fact, they have added a new concern about privacy and health care.

Controlling Costs

The cost of medical care in the United States is among the highest in the world. The proportion of the gross domestic product (GDP) going to health care has risen from 9 percent in 1980 to 14 percent in 1995. In comparison, Canada, France, and Germany spent approximately 10 percent of their GDPs on health care; the Scandinavian countries spent under 8 percent. Health care is now the second-biggest item in the federal budget, consuming twenty cents of every dollar spent (Moody, 1998). Several interrelated factors account for such high expenditures in the United States:

1. Until recently, there was relatively little push for preventive medicine. Instead, emphasis was on dealing with the disease or accident after it occurred.
2. There is a constant push for new technology for diagnosis and treatment.
3. People are living longer and, therefore, have more years to consume medical care.

And as we have seen,

4. The practice of defensive medicine as well as a fee-for-service system often prompt unnecessary tests and procedures. For example, researchers have documented a substantial amount of unnecessary surgery in the United States.

Efforts to reduce these costs center on two fronts: the extension of managed care programs and prevention. **Managed care** refers to any system of cost containment that closely monitors and controls health care providers' decisions about medical procedures, diagnostic tests, and other services that should be provided to patients (Weitz, 1995).

Today, an increasing number of Americans belong to managed care plans, typically **health maintenance organizations (HMOs)**, medical coverage plans that provide medical services to subscribers at a fixed rate and that emphasize preventive medicine. In 1980, there were 235 plans with a total enrollment of 9.1 million people; by 1997, there were 651 plans with an enrollment of almost 67 million (U.S. Bureau of the Census, 1998). HMOs keep costs down primarily in two ways. One way is by emphasizing prevention through the provision of patient education programs focusing on exercise, nutrition, immunization, controlling stress, substance abuse avoidance, safe sex, domestic violence, and early detection. The other way is by offering prepaid health care plans. Doctors, or increasingly medical corporations, know in advance the annual fee they will be paid. Thus, they have an incentive to be efficient and avoid unnecessary procedures which will erode their profit. Hospitalization costs are included in the doctor's annual fee, which provides incentives for doctors to minimize hospital stays for patients. This has resulted in criticisms that some patients are being discharged too soon and that too many serious procedures are being performed on an outpatient basis.

The managed care industry has pressured doctors to take cuts in their incomes or to take on more paying or insured patients to maintain their current income, thus overburdening them and affecting their ability to treat patients effectively, according to doctors. Additionally, concern has been raised about the fact that with many of these medical practices, accountants, not a patient's personal physician, decide what type of care is allowed. Concerns over such practices have caused several state legislatures to pass laws mandating length of stays for certain procedures, for example, giving birth and mastectomies. Congress is also debating legislation dealing with a wide variety of patients' rights in this new climate of managed care.

Health, Illness, and Health Care in the Twenty-First Century

During the past century, tremendous advances have been made in the control and prevention of many diseases and in knowledge about the role nutrition and exercise play in maintaining health and wellness. According to the World Health Report (1998), in recent years, the food supply has increased faster than population growth, adult literacy rates have improved, life expectancy has increased while fertility rates have fallen, and, thanks in large part to the efforts of organizations like Doctors without Borders, more of the world's population have access to at least minimum health care and safer water and sanitation facilities. Nevertheless, continued improvements in the health and well-being of the world's population is not yet assured. Continued progress in this regard is likely to be tempered by several challenges that will confront both developing and developed nations in the decades ahead. Among these are the potential danger of a global spread of infectious diseases, changing demographics, and the prospect of health care rationing.

Globalization of Infectious Diseases

As we saw earlier in this chapter, infectious diseases remain a major problem in many developing countries, especially those nations that continue to be plagued with poverty and civil strife. Increasing globalization, as measured by expanding international travel and trade, especially in the exchange of produce and other foodstuffs, will intensify the likelihood that infectious diseases will spread beyond their current borders in the next century unless the international community allocates more resources for: (1) the inspection and regulation of worldwide trade; (2) improved programs of vaccination and sanitation, especially in poorer countries; (3) the training of local residents in prevention techniques; and (4) more rapid dissemination of new medical advances.

Changing Demographics

The twentieth century began with a world population of 1.6 billion. By 1960, the population had nearly doubled, increasing to 3 billion. It will be over 6 billion at century's end, having

TABLE 15.5 ◑ Percentage of World's Population by Selected Ages, 1998

Area	Age	
	<15	65+
World	32%	7%
More developed countries	19	14
Less developed countries	35	5
Africa	44	3
North America	21	13
Latin America/Caribbean	34	5
Asia	32	6
Europe	19	14
Oceania	27	10

Source: Population Reference Bureau. 1998. *1998 World Population Data Sheet.* Washington, DC. Reprinted by permission.

doubled again, but this time in only forty years. Ninety-eight percent of the world population growth today takes place in developing regions of the world, which have younger populations. Table 15.5 shows some of this variation by comparing the two ends of the age structure in different regions of the world. Currently, developed societies have the highest percentages of elderly. However, if current trends continue, by 2025, the number of the world's population sixty-five years of age and older will have increased from 390 million in 1997 to 800 million, an increase from 6.6 percent of the world's population to 10 percent. Two-thirds of the elderly will live in developing countries. During that same period of time, the proportion of young people under twenty years of age will have fallen from 40 percent to 32 percent of the total population (World Health Report, 1998). These demographic changes mean that there will be fewer working people to support those who can no longer work. The proportion of older people requiring support from working adults is expected to increase from 12.3 percent in 1995 to 17.2 percent in 2025. Thus,

like developed societies before them, developing societies will have to struggle with how to prevent and postpone disease and disability and to maintain the health and independence of their elderly populations.

As a society ages, health care needs shift and chronic conditions associated with the aging process, such as heart disease, cancer, and diabetes, increase. People over sixty-five now consume one-third of this country's health care expenditures—nearly $200 billion in Medicare payments alone each year. That figure will increase as the population continues to age (Moody, 1998). Although perhaps desirable, medical efforts to prolong life have become exceedingly expensive. As resources become strained, debate shifts to how best to allocate existing resources. In 1987, philosopher Daniel Callahan fueled the debate in his controversial book, *Setting Limits,* in which he proposed rationing health care, using age as a basic criterion.

The Rationing of Health Care

The rationing of health care, although not a public policy, does exist in the United States. It is based on one's ability to pay. Arguments for age-based rationing center around three factors. First, compared to other adults, the elderly are less productive in the economy. Second, the benefit and duration of survival derived from medical intervention would be less for the elderly than for their younger counterparts. Third, if we live long enough, we will all be elderly someday and, thus, at least theoretically, it will be everyone's time to move over and let younger people have their fair share. Opponents of age-based rationing cite moral objections and point to the fact that the elderly are not a homogeneous population and that chronological age by itself is a poor predictor of the impact of any medical treatment. Other critics argue that the solution to rising health care costs is not rationing but eliminating the waste, inefficiency, and fraud that exist in the existing system. For example, it is estimated that fraud and abuse account for 10 percent of current medical costs, or $90 billion a year (Moody, 1998).

The problem posed by rising health care costs combined with declining resources cannot be solved overnight, and consideration needs to be given to a variety of ways in which efficiency and cost saving can be achieved to maximize the quality of health care available for all citizens, regardless of age. Clearly, rationing raises many ethical questions for medical practitioners and society at large. As scientists continue to push the boundaries of medical knowledge, the need for ethical standards in the application of this knowledge will intensify.

Applying the Sociological Imagination

What is your position on health care rationing? Explain. Interview people you know about their willingness to ration health care. Explain any differences you might find. How might societies like the United States avoid the need to resort to health care rationing?

Key Points to Remember

1. Sociologists recognize health as a biological or physiological condition, but they also view it as socially constructed. Sociologists examining health and illness most often focus on the institutionalization of healing: health care and the health care delivery system in a society.

2. Standards of health reflect the values and norms of a society. Two commonly used indicators of health are life expectancy and infant mortality. These measures vary cross-culturally as well as within cultures. Some sort of medicine exists in every society. Sociologists studying health, illness, and healing apply the perspectives, theories, and methodologies of sociology: functionalism, conflict, feminist, and symbolic interactionism.

3. An examination of the health profiles of various groups within the United States reveal that mental and physical health as well as premature death are unequally distributed throughout the population. Some groups suffer certain illnesses and disabilities and die prematurely at rates far greater than others. Although there are many cultural and social factors that explain these differences, some of the most important are race, class, gender, sexual orientation, age, and disabilities. A disability is a physical or health condition that stigmatizes or causes discrimination. Today, the Americans with Disabilities Act prohibits discrimination against people with disabilities in the areas of employment, transportation, public accommodations, and telecommunications.

4. Some of the most fundamental challenges to health and wellness around the globe today are related to environmental pollution, the emergence and spread of HIV/AIDS and other STDs,

as well as the reemergence of various diseases such as tuberculosis.

5. Like physical illness, mental illness is socially constructed. What and who gets defined as mentally ill depends on a number of social, cultural, political, and demographic factors, as well as on factors such as race, class, gender, age, and sexual orientation.

6. People in developing countries are more likely to die of infectious diseases, whereas people in developed societies are more likely to die of cancer and diseases of the circulatory and respiratory systems. A hospice is a physical environment within which dying patients are allowed to die with dignity as defined by the patients and their families. Emphasis is on controlling pain and making the patient comfortable.

7. After the death of a loved one, survivors must do grief work, confronting and acknowledging the emotions brought about by death. Some individuals experience disenfranchised grief, circumstances in which they do not have a socially recognized right, role, or capacity to grieve.

8. Some of the major health care issues in U.S. society today include a growing problem of physician malpractice and malpractice lawsuits, the emergence of defensive medicine, and the practice of alternative medicine. The preeminence of scientific medicine in the United States notwithstanding, millions of Americans frequently and routinely use alternatives to medical doctors (from prayer to home remedies to alternative healers such as spiritual healers).

9. The escalating costs and lack of access to health care in the United States have ignited a debate over ways to reform the health care system. Over 43 million Americans are without health

insurance; another 20 million are underinsured. An increasing number of Americans belong to health maintenance organizations, which provide medical services to subscribers at a fixed rate and which emphasize preventive medicine.

10. Continued progress in health care worldwide will depend on how well the international community meets the challenges of increasing globalization, the aging of populations, limited health care funds, and calls for the rationing of health care.

Key Terms

disease
health
illness
healing
epidemiology
life expectancy rate
infant mortality rate
medicine

medicalization
medical sociology
sick role
doctor role
disability
Americans with Disabilities Act
hospice

bereavement
grief work
disenfranchised grief
defensive medicine
managed care
health maintenance organizations (HMOs)

Key People

Doctors without Borders

Talcott Parsons

Questions for Review and Discussion

1. What does it mean to say that health and illness are socially constructed? How does this constructed social reality affect how we relate to people who are said to be healthy or ill? What insight does this concept give us into the roles of doctors and their patients? How might these socially constructed roles engender problems in the delivery of adequate health care?

2. Reflect on your own experiences with health, illness, and the medical profession. Which theoretical perspective best explains your experiences? Do you think that your experiences would be different if you were a different gender, a member of a different class, race, or ethnic group or if your age and sexual orientation were different? Explain.

3. Compare and contrast indicators of health and well-being as well as death rates in developed and developing countries. What theories of stratification help to explain these discrepancies? Should countries like the United States be concerned about such discrepancies? Explain. What, if anything, should developed countries do to improve world health standards? Explain.

4. Some people have argued that the U.S. health care system is racist, sexist, and class biased. Do you agree or disagree with that assessment? Provide evidence to support your position. What could be done to improve the quality of health care for all people?

For Further Reading

Mechanic, David. 1994. *The Imperatives of Health Reform*. New Brunswick, NJ: Transaction. The author presents a critical analysis of the problems inherent in the U.S. health care system and offers concrete suggestions for reforming the system.

Nechas, E., and D. Foley. 1994. *Unequal Treatment*. New York: Simon and Schuster. An examination of how sexism in medical care impacts the health of women.

Shapiro, Joseph P. 1993. *No Pity: People with Disabilities Forging a New Civil Rights Movement*. New York: Times. The author presents insights into the motivations and political activism of people with disabilities and how they forged a social movement.

Williamson, J. B., and E. S. Shneidman. 1995. *Death: Current Perspectives* (4th ed.). Mountain View, CA: Mayfield. Essays written by psychologists, sociologists, thanatologists, historians, anthropologists, philosophers, and ethicists provide a unique insight into the multifaceted study of death and dying.

Sociology through Literature

Cook, Robin. 1998. *Toxin*. Putnam. The author, a doctor, writes a gripping novel about bacterial poisoning and corporate malevolence.

McMurtry, Larry. 1992. *Terms of Endearment*. Pocket. An insightful story of the intimate relationship between a mother and her daughter who is dying of cancer.

Internet Resources

http://www.old.ircam.fr/solidarites/sids/index-e.html A variety of information and resources on HIV/AIDS.

http://www.cdc.gov/nchswww/products/ppubs/pubd/netpubs.htm The National Center for Health Statistics Web site provides full-text versions of its reports, including *Monthly Vital Statistics Report* and *Vital Statistics of the United States*.

http://www.public.iastatee.edu/~sbilling/ada.html The Americans with Disabilities Act homepage provides information on the provisions of the act as well as links to other disability-related sites.

Social Action: By Whom?
Social Change:
For Whom?

Introduction

Throughout this textbook, we have emphasized the two constants of social life—stability and change. On the one hand, how individuals, groups, and whole societies interact remains largely unchanged. On the other hand, organizational structures, behaviors, and social constructions do change all the time. But although change is ubiquitous, it occurs at different rates, depending on conditions.

Some sociologists, such as Gary Marx and Douglas McAdam (1994), predict that existing social conditions will contribute to a period of heightened collective action and change. We share their view. We have therefore spotlighted, throughout this book, a number of people and groups whom we have identified as agents of change. Should we wish to be change agents ourselves, an understanding of the following principles can be a powerful tool:

- Change agents illustrate the functioning of the sociological imagination.
- The actions of change agents illustrate the process of social construction, that is, the idea that the social order is actively produced by human beings rather than merely a given that is passively accepted by societal members.
- Change agents demonstrate that, although extremely risky at times, social action can alter the social world.
- No entity is too large or too powerful to be susceptible to the behavior of individuals and groups working to effect change.
- Change is a normal fact of all of our social lives.

In this textbook, for emphasis, we chose agents of change who have high visibility because they are involved in issues of national or international significance. But millions of other people around the world are also actively working for change, albeit on a smaller scale—for example, the neighbor who campaigns for a stop sign on the corner of a busy street or the Little League player who covered up the name of the liquor store sponsor on her team shirt to protest what she perceives as the promotion of alcohol use among young athletes.

If you are interested in promoting social change, we encourage you. But you must ask yourself why, exactly, you want such change to occur; how you will accomplish it; and whom it will affect, both positively and negatively.

Social Action: By Whom?

People become involved in social action and react to social change in a variety of ways depending on their circumstances.

- **The promoter or creator role:** The most visible social actors are those who lead or participate openly in demonstrations, lobbying efforts, fund raising, speech making, and other public activities. Other change promoters take less visible or interactive roles, preferring to make contributions, write letters, or use e-mail to communicate support for their causes.
- **The resistor role:** As we discussed in Chapter 3, change generally does not occur without a struggle. People resist change for a wide range of reasons, including self-interest and simple inertia.
- **The passive role:** Some people desire to be left alone or to let things happen as they will. They may be satisfied with the status quo or indifferent to its functioning. Thus, when change occurs, they may ignore it and behave as they always have.
- **The adaptive role:** Other people may share such indifference to social change, but they adapt to it either without much thought and effort or out of a feeling of necessity rather than any strong enthusiasm for the change itself.

These roles are not mutually exclusive. Depending on the changes underway, people may play a number of these roles at the same time.

Social Change: For Whom?

Throughout this textbook, we have stressed the importance of social action that leads to meaningful social change. Many social change agents hope to extend what they perceive to be the benefits of their own, "modern" societies to people in other, more "traditional" societies. But such social change is not always welcomed, for good reason. Would-be change agents must use the sociological imagination to consider the possible ramifications of social change in different contexts.

A Macro Perspective: Traditional and Modern Societies

According to David Maybury-Lewis (1997), perhaps the most fundamental difference between modern and traditional societies lies in the relative importance of individuals within the society. The ideology of independence in modern society stresses the individual's economic independence at the expense of our interconnections in the social sphere. While traditional societies often denounce individualism as antisocial and maintain a focus on the obligations of kin and community to support and constrain the individual as a fundamental aspect of society, modern societies tend to believe in and glorify the rights and dignity of individuals as the most important aspect of society.

Other comparisons and contrasts between traditional and modern societies offered by Maybury-Lewis include:

- Traditional societies operate a moral economy, one permeated by personal and moral considerations. In such a system, unlike in modern societies, exchanges of goods in the market are not divorced from but are part of the personal relationships between those who exchange.
- In modern societies, there is a sense of disconnection that affects not only the rela-

tions between people but also the relations between people and their environment. Consequently, members of modern societies may be gradually making the planet uninhabitable for everyone. For example, fresh air and clean water are disappearing. In contrast, traditional societies have a strong sense of the interconnectedness of things on earth and beyond. In short, in traditional societies, it is believed that humans belong to the earth, whereas in modern society, the thinking is that the earth belongs to humans.

- Some sociologists have argued that modernization is a process of secularization that has not only undermined people's religious beliefs but also deprived them of their spirituality, their belief that human beings are part of something greater than themselves.

We do not want to leave the impression that all is wrong with modernization and all is right with traditionalism. To the contrary, as Maybury-Lewis (1997) points out, when the modern system works, it works well. However, when it does not work, it causes a lot of pain, violence, and destruction for individuals and whole societies.

Likewise, there are aspects of traditional society that allow human beings to live in harmony with nature and to have a less fragmented view of physical reality and the place of the individual within the larger scheme of things. But there are also aspects of traditional society that create, reinforce, and maintain ignorance, poverty, sickness, violence against women and girls, and strong internal systems of social stratification. Although social change in these aspects is needed, some sociologists advocate that such change should involve planned programs of intervention that take into account the ways in which traditional societies differ from their more modern counterparts and the relationship between changing social institutions and the environment.

A Micro Perspective: Individuals and Groups within Society

Thus far, we have focused our discussion on total societies, recognizing that change that is regarded as positive in one society may be perceived as detrimental in another society. The same is true at the micro level within societies. Throughout this textbook, we have examined the intersections of race, class, gender, and sexual orientation, and we have seen that social actions aimed at improving the economic, political, and social position of people of color, poor and working-class people, women, and lesbians and gays are often controversial and resisted by other segments of the population. Some people oppose a change because they believe it is unnecessary or undeserved or they fear that the change will somehow erode values they define as basic and/or diminish their own positions in society. Such reasoning is evidenced in the opposition of some members of U.S. society to the granting of domestic partnership benefits to lesbians and gays.

Further, although a given change may be intended to benefit all members of society, this is rarely achieved. For instance, the Clinton Administration set a goal of having all schools connected to the information superhighway by the beginning of the twenty-first century. To date, however, schools serving the most disadvantaged students lag far behind their more affluent counterparts in terms of the technological resources available to their students. Similarly, the North American Free Trade Agreement was touted as good for the whole country, yet many people living in U.S. communities located along the border with Mexico saw their jobs and local businesses wither as Mexican trucks loaded with "made-in-Mexico" products by-passed their communities. Thus, whenever we are evaluating change, we are well advised to keep in mind two key questions: Social change, by whom? And, social change, for whom?

Responding to Social Change: Convergence, Conflict, or . . .

Hardly a day goes by that we here in the United States do not read about or see examples of cultural diffusion and the spreading global economy. One day, it is the opening of a Disney World in Paris; another day brings images of the Chinese lining up to buy a McDonald's hamburger in the streets of Beijing, and on still another, we anxiously watch as the U.S. stock market moves downward in response to news of financial troubles in Asia or Latin America. Thanks to fax machines, satellite dishes, and the World Wide Web, cultural images and news of world events unfolding in distant places circle the globe in a matter of seconds, contributing to the perception that the world is fast shrinking into a global village.

The magnitude of cultural contact and cultural diffusion suggests the possibility of a future, homogeneous world culture (Featherstone, 1990, 1995). Yet, as our discussion of traditional and modern societies makes clear, there is still much that distinguishes and even divides nations and their peoples from one another. Globalism itself has sharpened these differences, creating fear and anger in some groups who believe their way of life is being threatened by changes over which they have little, if any, control.

The Future World Order

Although it is still too early to predict how the changes already underway as a result of new technology and political and economic transformations will affect the shape and look of the future, two distinct and opposing versions of a world order are already vying for dominance. The first involves a movement toward global convergence, and the second suggests increasing global conflict. Let's first examine these developing patterns and then raise questions about the possibilities of some as yet unidentified new model.

Global Convergence or Conflict   A global convergence ideally implies economic interdependence, some cultural diffusion, and a general acceptance of cultural diversity within an atmosphere of cooperation and peace. Such behavior implies a movement toward homogenization of societies and their socioeconomic structures. Global convergence is, no doubt, more palatable to people who live in dynamic societies in which change and progress are desired and considered normal. Members of these societies, already highly educated by the world's standards, stand to be the beneficiaries of such a system, whereas

the vast millions of illiterate and poor people are not likely to see their lives improve in the immediate future. To many people living in traditional societies, any global convergence represents an attack on age-old patterns of authority and customs. If you have never made a telephone call, the idea of instant global communication may be more frightening than exciting. If the women in your society cannot be seen unveiled, television images of even modestly dressed women may be deeply offensive. If your entire life and that of your ancestors has been governed by tribal or parental authority, the principles of free choice and expression may appear subversive and revolutionary (Longworth, 1998). This is especially the case when economic and political inequalities are exacerbated or sparked by globalization or when new technology suddenly presents alternatives and challenges to ancient belief systems.

Finding an Alternative World Order   The questions that the founders of sociology struggled with remain with us today. Sociologists continue to ask the questions posed in Chapter 1: How is social order possible? How can societies cope with ever-accelerating forces of social change? Because technology now makes mass destruction possible, finding answers to these two questions becomes more urgent than ever before, and in this context, additional questions arise. Can a satisfactory alternative to global convergence, with its emphasis on cultural uniformity, and global conflict be constructed? Can societies maintain their cultural uniqueness and still be economically integrated? The ultimate answers to these questions will depend heavily on how well the world's players understand and exercise control over the forces of change. There are some signs that such an alternative is already gestating. Many nations, even those that remain suspicious of one another, are engaging in a variety of cultural exchanges that highlight both the commonalities and the contrasts among human societies. Student and faculty study exchanges, traveling exhibits of national art and consumer goods, and touring dance, music, and theater groups can all build bridges of respect and understanding across different ethnic and cultural groups. The continuation and expansion of international bodies such as the United Nations, the World Health Organization, and the International Monetary Fund, acting together to relieve illiteracy, world hunger, disease, poverty, and injustice, are also a constructive force on the world's stage. The more citizens are willing to exert pressure on their nations' leaders to focus on resolving intra- and international problems and conflicts through diplomacy and negotiation rather than recrimination, dictatorship, or violence, the more progress will be achieved. This depends, in large measure, on people perceiving themselves as agents of social change.

Final Thoughts: Social Change and You

As we indicated in Chapter 3, when we think about social change, most of us typically think in terms of large-scale social movements such as the women's movement, civil rights movement, labor movement, lesbian and gay rights movement, right-to-life movement, pro-choice movement, consumer rights movement, and environmental justice movement. To be sure, these types of direct and mass collective actions are perhaps the most effective way to create and promote social and cultural change. However, as we have also stressed, not all social change comes about in this manner. Rather, each of us in our daily lives participates in the processes of social change. We have attempted to show how the strategies and achievements of individuals as well as of people acting collectively have historically been the impetus for social and cultural change.

As we conclude this textbook and pull together the major threads of social activism and social change, we invite you to think about how social change and social activism apply to you. On the face of it, you may think that neither applies to you. However, whether or not you consider yourself a social activist, what you *do* as well as what you *do not do* has an impact on the shape of society. Feminist scholar Virginia Cyrus (1993) makes this point with the following example: You may not consider yourself prejudiced, but when a friend tells you a racist joke, you might laugh so that you won't offend her. Your laughter, however, indicates your approval of the joke's racist assumptions, and without be-

ing aware of it, you have added one more stitch to the racist fabric of our society. On the other hand, had you not laughed but rather made a quiet comment that you don't care for that kind of joke, you would have begun to unravel at least one little thread of racism. Throughout this textbook, we have raised issues of social inequality and social justice. We have pointed out how racism, sexism, heterosexism, class elitism, and various other "isms" contribute to the pervasiveness of oppression and inequality in U.S. society. We have also tried to make it clear that *all* of us are impacted by the various "isms," and we have reported, where relevant, some of the emerging new research that provides continuing support for our position.

Although it may appear that some of the social issues or problems raised in this textbook are inevitable and unalterable, this is not necessarily the case. They can and are being changed daily, as you have seen in our discussions of agents of change. If you are not already consciously involved in social action for social change, you can become so now. In fact, you have already begun the process by reading and learning about a variety of sociopolitical and economic issues facing us as citizens of the United States and as members of the global village. You have learned how a variety of individuals and groups have actively engaged in actions to change their own lives and the social environment in which we live. This learning process is a key prerequisite for social action because we cannot begin to address an issue until we see and understand it (Cyrus, 1993). We end this book with the following step-by-step process[1] for those interested in taking action to effect social and cultural change.

- **Identify the problem.** Decide what it is specifically that you are interested in changing. The general issue of racism, for example, has many specific issues to consider: individual acts of racism in the workplace, school, and public places; institutional racism; and the myriad of issues that are closely linked to the existence of racism, such as poverty, high

---

[1]This process is based on a six-step process of creating social change presented by Virginia Cyrus (1993, p. 371–373).

school dropout rates, teen pregnancy, unemployment, and underemployment.

- **Identify the desired outcome.** Decide what specific change you would like to see. For example, your goal or desired outcome might be to find a way to motivate and encourage students of color who have been turned off by the present educational system to continue in school, learn as much as they possibly can, and go on to higher education.
- **Develop a set of strategies for realizing your goal.** This means that you should give serious and sometimes prolonged thought to methods that you can realistically implement to realize your desired outcome. Try brainstorming ways (programs, incentives, etc.) to motivate students of color to remain in school and go on to higher education.
- **Develop a plan for action.** Decide which strategy(ies) you will use and develop your plan of action: the resources you will need, your time frame, the people you need to work with you, and so on.
- **Implement the plan.** It is now time to put your plan into action. Consider beforehand the possible types of resistance you may encounter in order to develop methods to respond to or counteract resistance.
- **Evaluate your actions.** Assess the effectiveness of your actions for change, identifying those strategies that were successful and those that were not.

We do not intend to imply that these steps are easy to perform and that social change comes about easily. Each step requires commitment and an investment of time, energy, intellectual acumen, and access to economic and human resources. Although successful social action cannot be guaranteed, your chances of success will be enhanced by thorough research, careful thought and extensive planning, strong motivation and commitment, and lots of time.

Taking Action for Social Change

Throughout this textbook, we have attempted to show that each of us can do something to effect social change. This might be a good time to reflect on your own community, your university campus, or some idea or issue of concern to you and to identify some aspect of social/cultural life that you would like to see changed. If you decide to develop and implement an action plan, we would like to hear from you about your experience and your successes and failures. You can e-mail us at the following addresses: b-scott1@neiu.edu, m-schwartz@neiu.edu.

Glossary

absolute poverty A condition in which people do not have the means to secure the most basic necessities of life.

achieved status A position that is earned by individual effort.

acquaintance rape Rape involving a rapist who knows or who is familiar with the victim.

acquired immune deficiency syndrome (AIDS) A viral syndrome, or group of diseases, that destroys the body's immune system, thereby rendering the victim susceptible to all kinds of infections and diseases.

activity theory The view that the more active and involved older people are, the more likely they are to experience life satisfaction.

affirmative action Any special effort by an employer or a college admissions office to hire or admit more females or people historically defined as members of minority groups and/or to upgrade their positions.

Age Discrimination Employment Act Prohibited the use of age as a criterion for hiring, firing, and discriminatory treatment on the job.

age norms Expectations and guidelines about what people in a given life stage are allowed to do and to be as well as what they are required to do and to be.

ageism A term coined by Robert Butler (1975) to describe age stereotypes and the discriminatory treatment applied to the elderly.

agents of socialization Individuals and organizations responsible for transmitting the culture of a society.

alienation The breakdown of the natural connections between people and the products they produce, the process of their work, and other people, which leads to feelings of self-estrangement.

Americans with Disabilities Act Prohibits discrimination against people with disabilities in the areas of employment, transportation, public accommodations, and telecommunications.

anomie A condition of society in which the normative standards of conduct are weak or absent and social control becomes ineffective as a result of the loss of shared values and a sense of purpose in society.

anticipatory socialization Social learning that prepares us for the statuses and roles we are likely to assume in the future.

apartheid A system by which white supremacy is assured and separation between groups is legally maintained.

applied sociology Consists of research designed to focus knowledge on a particular issue or concern with some practical outcome in mind.

ascribed status A position that is assigned at birth and over which we have little or no control.

assimilation A broad term used to describe the process whereby racial and ethnic minority groups gradually adopt patterns of the majority group and become absorbed into the larger societal mainstream.

authoritarianism A political system whereby authority is concentrated in the hands of rulers who severely restrict popular participation in government.

authority Legitimate power.

aversive racism A modern form of prejudice that characterizes the racial attitudes of many whites holding egalitarian values who regard themselves as nonprejudiced but who nevertheless discriminate in subtle, rationalizable ways.

bereavement The state of being deprived of a loved one by death.

biphobia Prejudice, negative attitudes, and misconceptions related to bisexuals and their lifestyle.

bisexuals People who have sexual partners of both sexes either simultaneously or at different times.

bureaucracy A large-scale formal organization in which a complex division of labor based on expertise, hierarchical authority, and written rules is used to achieve maximum efficiency.

capitalism A privately owned system of production of goods and services that are sold to a wide range of consumers in which the owners try to maximize profits.

capitalists Owners of the factories and other scarce goods and services in society that produce wealth.

castes Rigid and static hereditary systems of rank, usually religiously dictated, that tend to be fixed and permanent.

cenogamy All of the women and men in a group are simultaneously married to one another.

charismatic authority Power held by virtue of exceptional personal qualities, or charisma.

church A large religious organization that is well established and well integrated into society; characterized by a formal, bureaucratic structure, including a professional clergy arranged in a hierarchy of authority.

civil religion The set of beliefs, rituals, and symbols that makes sacred the values of a society.

class Any group of people who occupy a similar economic position in society.

class consciousness An awareness of and identification with the interests of a particular social class, and an understanding of the ways in which society operates to produce class inequality.

class stratification The institutionalized system by which some groups have more economic resources and power than do others.

closed systems Stratification systems in which people are ranked on the basis of ascribed characteristics and mobility within the system is not possible.

coercion Illegitimate power.

collective behavior The relatively spontaneous and unstructured behavior engaged in by large numbers of people who are reacting to a common stimulus.

colonization A powerful country's establishment of control over a foreign country and its people.

communism A classless system in which the means of economic production are collectively owned and wealth and power are evenly distributed.

conjugal ties Marriage relations.

consanguine ties Blood ties.

content analysis The systematic examination of pre-collected data guided by some rationale in order to extract thematic patterns and draw conclusions about social life.

contingency work A term that was coined in 1985 to call attention to the increasing proportion of people who had transitory and temporary relationships with their employers.

corporate crime Illegal acts committed by company officials.

counterculture A subculture that exists within the context of a larger, more pronounced culture but whose norms and values are often diametrically opposed to, or at least clash with, those of the larger culture.

craze Exciting mass involvement that lasts for a relatively long period of time.

crime The violation of a law.

crowd A temporary gathering of individuals in close physical proximity who share a common focus or interest.

cult A dissident religion, organized into a tight community in great tension with the larger environment.

cultural assimilation A process whereby various cultural groups in a society become more similar to one another so that the differences that form the basis for prejudice and discrimination are minimized or eliminated.

cultural capital The general cultural background and social assets (including values, beliefs, attitudes, and competencies in language and culture) that are passed from one generation to another.

cultural diversity The wide range of differences across cultures.

cultural hegemony The domination of culture by elite groups.

cultural lag The unequal rate of change in different parts of society.

cultural pluralism A state in which various racial and ethnic groups maintain most or all of their cultural patterns but share some elements of the culture with the larger society.

cultural racism The conscious or unconscious conviction that white or European-American cultural practices and patterns are superior to those of other visible racial/ethnic groups.

cultural relativity The idea that culture is a unique way of adjusting to particular sets of circumstances and that there is therefore no one right or moral way to do things.

cultural universals Those elements or characteristics that can be found in every known culture.

culture All of the ways of knowing, acting, thinking, and feeling that humans acquire as members of societies; when taken together, these ways compose the total way of life of a particular group.

culture wars Ideological and/or political conflicts, often accompanied by hostility and sometimes violence, rooted in different cultural values.

defensive medicine Medical practices that include every imaginable test or procedure for patients, not for medical reasons but for the purpose of protecting doctors from the possibility of a malpractice suit in the case of a negative patient outcome.

democracy A form of government in which citizens are able to participate directly or indirectly in their own governance and to elect their leaders.

demographic trends Changes in birth, death, and migration rates.

denomination A religious organization, independent of the state, that is generally tolerant of religious diversity and that competes with other denominations for members.

dependent variable Any trait, quality, or characteristic thought to be influenced or affected by the independent variable.

desegregation The abolishment of legally sanctioned racial and ethnic separation in public and private facilities.

desocialization The "unlearning" of previous normative expectations and roles.

deviance The violation of cultural norms.

differential association The process of social interaction through which people learn deviance.

differentiation A pattern of social change whereby one part of society splits into two or more new parts.

diffusion The spread of culture traits from one society to another.

disability A physical or health condition that stigmatizes or causes discrimination.

discrimination The unfair actions or practices of an individual, group, or subpopulation of individuals that deny another individual, group, or subpopulation of individuals access to valued resources.

disease A medically diagnosed illness.

disenfranchised grief Circumstances in which a person experiences a sense of loss but does not have a socially recognized right, role, or capacity to grieve.

disengagement theory The view that as people age, they gradually withdraw from specific roles and activities and simultaneously are relieved of social responsibilities.

doctor role A set of social expectations regarding how a doctor should act.

dysfunctional social patterns Patterns that have negative effects that may hamper the achievement of group goals or reduce the capacity of the system to adapt and survive.

ecclesia A church that is formally allied with the state and is the "official" religion for the society.

education The transmission of the knowledge, skills, and cultural norms and values of members of a society.

egalitarian family A family structure whereby both partners share power, authority, and decision making equally.

ego The rational part of the self whose function is to mediate between the id and the superego, allowing the individual socially approved ways of satisfying the id.

elite deviance Wrongdoing by wealthy and powerful individuals and organizations.

empirical evidence Data that can be confirmed using one or more of the humans senses.

epidemiology The study of the origins and spread of diseases and bodily injuries within a given population.

estate system of stratification A system of inequality based on noble birth and ownership and/or control of land.

ethnic group A group within a larger society that shares (or is believed to share) a common cultural heritage that sets it off from the society's mainstream or modal culture.

ethnocentrism The judgment of other cultures using one's own culture as the standard; often based on the belief that one's own culture is the only right and good way of life.

extended or **multigenerational family** Consists of one or both of our parents, our siblings, if any, and other relatives, including grandparents, aunts, and uncles living in the same household.

fads Short-lived patterns of unexpected behavior, engaged in by only a segment of the population, most often adolescents and young adults.

family Any relatively stable group of people who are related to one another through blood, marriage, or adoption or who simply live together and who provide one another with economic and emotional support.

family of orientation The family into which a person is born or adopted and in which s/he is raised.

family of procreation The family created when we marry or have an intimate relationship with someone or bear or adopt children.

fashions The styles of appearance or behavior that are favored by a large number of people for a limited period of time.

felonies Serious offenses, such as murder, rape, assault, and robbery, which are punishable by heavy fines and/or imprisonment for a year or more.

feminization of poverty A trend whereby women are disproportionately represented among the poor.

fertility rate The number of births per 1,000 women in their childbearing years (fifteen to forty-four).

folkways Synonymous with *customs;* the norms that specify the ways things are or are not typically done.

forced assimilation The process whereby the majority group either prohibits or makes it difficult for a minority group to practice its language, religion, and other customs.

formal education Systematic and structured training in school.

formal organizations Groups whose activities are rationally designed to achieve specific goals.

functional social patterns Patterns that have positive effects that may help to maintain the social system in a balanced state and/or promote the achievement of group goals.

functionally illiterate Unable to use reading, speaking, writing, and computational skills in everyday life situations.

fundamentalism A religious orientation characterized by the belief in strict and unambiguous rules and by a literal and dogmatic acceptance of scripture exactly as written.

gatekeeping Determining who will enter what occupations.

gender The socially constructed cluster of behavioral patterns and personality traits that are associated with being female or male, or what we commonly call *femininity* and *masculinity.*

gender roles Society's behavioral expectations for its female and male members.

gender stratification The unequal distribution of a society's wealth, power, and privilege between females and males.

generalized other Mead's term for the widely accepted cultural norms and values that are used as references in evaluating ourselves.

genocide The extermination or wholesale killing of a racial or ethnic group.

global interdependence A state in which the lives of people around the world are intertwined closely and in which any one nation's problems increasingly cut across cultural and geographic boundaries.

grief work Confronting and acknowledging the emotions brought about by death.

group Two or more people who interact with each other in patterned ways, share common interests and goals, and experience a sense of identity and belonging.

groupthink A process in which group members ignore alternative solutions in order to maintain group consensus and harmony.

Hawthorne Effect Research subjects performing behaviors or answering questions in an untypical way because they want to be viewed in a favorable light.

healing The personal and institutional responses to perceived disease, injury, and illness.

health A state of complete physical, mental, and social well-being.

health maintenance organizations (HMOs) Medical coverage plans that provide medical services to subscribers at a fixed rate and that emphasize preventive medicine.

heterosexuality The preference for having intimate and sexual activities with a person of a sex different from one's own.

hidden curriculum The unwritten rules of accepted behavior and attitudes.

homophobia Strongly held negative attitudes and beliefs, irrational fears, and outright hatred of lesbians and gays and their lifestyle.

homosexuality The preference for having intimate and sexual activities with a person of the same sex.

hospice A physical environment within which dying patients are allowed to die with dignity as defined by the patients and their families.

human capital theory The economic theory that assumes that labor markets operate in a nondiscriminatory fashion, rewarding workers for their productivity.

human immunodeficiency virus (HIV) The virus believed to be the main cause of AIDS.

human sexuality The feelings, thoughts, and behaviors of humans who have learned a set of cues that evoke a sexual or erotic response.

hypothesis A statement about the relationship between two or more events or phenomena that can be tested to determine its validity.

id The infant's basic biological urges aimed at obtaining pleasure.

illness The interference with health.

in-group A group to which a person belongs and toward which a person directs positive feelings.

incest Sexual abuse of a child by a blood relative who is assumed to be a part of the child's family.

incest taboo A cultural norm prohibiting marriage or sexual relations between certain kin.

income The amount of money an individual or family earns from occupational wages or salaries and from investments.

independent variable Any trait, quality, or characteristic thought to be the cause of changes in other variables.

individual racism When individuals or groups self-defined as superior act against individuals whom they define as inferior.

industrialization The process by which whole societies were transformed from reliance on human and animal power and handmade products to reliance on machines and other advanced technology.

infant mortality The number of deaths of infants under the age of one year per 1,000 live births in a given year.

instincts Unlearned, biologically predetermined behavior patterns common to a particular species that occur whenever certain environmental conditions exist.

institutional racism Established laws, customs, and practices that systematically reflect and produce racial inequalities in a society, whether or not the individuals maintaining these practices have racist intentions.

intergenerational mobility Movement upward or downward in the stratification system as compared to one's parents.

intragenerational mobility Movement upward or downward in the stratification system over the life course.

invention The creation of new things, whether material, such as the telephone and the computer, or nonmaterial, such as women's suffrage and the theory of relativity.

juvenile delinquency Illegal or antisocial behavior on the part of a minor.

kinship Relationships resulting from blood, marriage, or adoption or among people who consider one another family.

labeling theory A symbolic interactionist theory that sees deviance as the product of others who react to a norm violator.

labor-force participation rate The percentage of workers in a particular group who are employed or who are actively seeking employment.

labor unions Organizations of workers seeking improved wages, benefits, and working conditions through collective bargaining with their employers.

language A system of symbols learned within a particular culture that convey ideas and enable people to think and communicate with one another.

latent functions Social patterns that are hidden or unrecognized, unexpected, and unintended.

laws Legally enacted norms; their violation is formally punished.

life chances The likelihood that individuals and groups will have access to important societal resources, positive experiences, and opportunities for long, healthy, and successful lives.

life expectancy rate The average number of years that a person born in a given year can expect to live.

linguistic-relativity hypothesis Holds that people who speak a particular language must necessarily interpret the world through the unique grammatical forms and categories that their language supplies.

looking-glass self The process by which one's self is formulated in response to one's perceptions of the reactions of others toward one.

majority group A category of people within a society who possess distinct physical or cultural characteristics and maintain superior power, authority, and resources.

managed care Any system of cost containment that closely monitors and controls health care providers' decisions about medical procedures, diagnostic tests, and other services that should be provided to patients.

manifest destiny A set of beliefs about white supremacy that rationalizes the exploitation of people defined as inferior on the basis that it is the God-ordained destiny of whites to direct inferior people's movement toward participation in modern political and technological life.

manifest functions Social patterns that are overt or obvious and intended.

marriage A union between people (whether widely or legally recognized or not) that unites partners sexually, socially, and economically; that is relatively consistent over time; and that accords each member certain agreed-upon rights.

marriage squeeze When one sex has a more limited pool of eligibles than does the other.

mass behavior Behavior that develops when people who are geographically dispersed but who have access to the same stimulus act in similar ways and influence one another indirectly.

mass hysteria A form of dispersed collective behavior by which people react emotionally to a real or perceived threat or danger.

master status The position, whether ascribed or achieved, that is perceived as dominant over all others we may hold.

matriarchal family A family in which the female (wife or mother) is the head of the family and exercises authority and decision-making power over her husband and children.

meaningful social action The motives that underlie human behavior, the ways in which people interpret and explain their own behavior and that of others, and the way that these actions and meanings affect the social order.

medical sociology The study of health, illness, and healing and their relationship to social factors as well as health care as it is institutionalized in a society.

medicalization The process of defining a behavior or condition as an illness in need of medical treatment.

medicine A social institution established to diagnose, treat, and prevent illness and to promote health.

meritocracy System of social stratification based on ability and achievement rather than social background.

migration The movement of people into or out of a geographic area.

militarism The societal focus on military ideals and an aggressive preparedness for war.

military junta When military officers seize power from the government.

minority group Any category of people having recognizable racial or ethnic traits that place it in a position of restricted power and inferior status so that its members suffer limited opportunities and rewards.

misdemeanors Less serious offenses, such as drunkenness and disturbing the peace, which are punishable by small fines and less than a year in prison.

mixed economies Economic systems that incorporate both competitive markets and the institution of private property as well as state ownership of large corporations which are run for the benefit of all citizens.

modified extended family A variety of relatives who live not necessarily in the same household but in very close proximity to one another (upstairs, next door, down the block, around the corner), interact on a frequent basis, and provide emotional and economic support to one another.

monarchy A political system in which power resides in one person or a single family and is passed from generation to generation through lines of inheritance.

monogamy One person married to one other person of the other sex.

monopoly A market controlled by a single business firm which can then dictate prices and set quality standards.

mores Rules for behavior that are embedded in our morality.

mortality rate The number of deaths per 1,000 members of the population.

multicultural education Teaching and learning about the equal human worth of distinctive groups of people acting in customary spheres of social life.

multiculturalism The notion that society is a combination of many different subcultures or groups, that each of these groups retains some of its customs and traditions, that these should be accepted as valid and valuable, and that all of these groups should coexist.

multinational corporations Economic enterprises that have headquarters in one country and conduct business activities in one or more other countries.

National Labor Relations Act of 1935 Also know as the Wagner Act, recognized the right of workers to organize and bargain collectively through a union of their choice.

no-fault divorce The dissolution of a marriage on the basis of irreconcilable differences.

norms The rules or standards and expectations that guide the behavior of members of a society.

nuclear family A mother, father, and siblings.

occupational concentration The overrepresentation of women in a limited number of occupations.

occupational segregation The tendency for women and men to be employed in different occupations.

old-age dependency ratio The ratio of elderly people to working-age adults.

Older Americans Act Established an Administration on Aging as part of the Department of Health, Education and Welfare (later the Department of Health and Human Services).

one-drop rule Defines as a black person anyone who has any trace of black heritage (at least a drop of black African blood) in her or his ancestral history.

open systems Stratification systems in which people are ranked on the basis of merit, talent, ability, or past performance and movement upward or downward in the system is possible.

operationalize To restate concepts in concrete, measurable terms.

organized crime Crime perpetrated by an illegal business operation.

out-group A group to which a person does not belong and about which a person may harbor negative feelings.

panic An irrational, collective flight from some real or perceived danger.

patriarchal family A family in which the male (husband or father) is the head of the family and exercises authority and decision-making power over his wife and children.

personality A relatively stable set of attitudes, values, and behaviors.

pluralism A pattern of racial/ethnic relations in which a variety of subcultures live side by side but maintain their respective cultures and lifestyles.

pluralist model A model whereby power is dispersed among many competing interest groups.

political crime Misconduct and crime committed within or against a political system.

politics The social processes through which individuals and groups acquire, exercise, maintain, or lose power.

polyandry One female has two or more husbands.

polygamy One person of one sex married to several people of the other sex.

polygyny One male has two or more wives.

positivism The belief that knowledge should be guided by facts rather than by imagination, intuition, speculation, or purely logical analysis; the use of observation, comparison, experimentation, and the historical method to gain the facts needed to analyze society.

power The ability to realize one's will, even against the resistance of others.

power elite A relatively small group of wealthy and well-connected individuals who routinely interact together, frequently intermarry, share a worldview, and work together to achieve a political agenda that serves their interests.

prejudice An attitude, generally negative, based on any categorical and unfounded overgeneralization about selected groups.

prestige The social esteem or social honor accorded to people by others.

primary deviance Violations that a person commits for the first time and without consciously thinking about them as deviant.

primary group A relatively small number of people who routinely interact on a face-to-face basis, have close emotional ties, and share an enduring sense of belonging.

primary sector Activities that extract raw materials directly from the natural environment.

primary socialization The acquisition of the basic skills, norms, values, and behavioral expectations of a culture as well as the development of the concept of self.

profane The ordinary aspects of everyday life.

proletariat Workers whose labor produces the products of capitalism.

pure sociology Refers to the notion that sociological research should be value neutral and that the motivation for research should be the desire for basic knowledge that will advance understanding of human society and behavior, not the values of a particular researcher.

qualitative analysis Analysis that focuses on specific or distinct qualities within data that show patterns of similarity or difference among research subjects. These similarities and differences are distinguishable in terms of quality and kind but not in terms of magnitude or numbers.

quantitative analysis A process in which data can be analyzed using numerical categories and statistical techniques.

racism An ideology of domination and a set of attitudes, ideas, and social, economic, and political practices by which one or more groups define themselves as superior and other groups as inferior and then systematically deny these groups the dignity, freedoms, opportunities, and rewards that the society has to offer.

rape Legally, a sexual assault in which a man uses his penis to vaginally penetrate a woman against her will by force or threat of force or when she is mentally or physically unable to give her consent.

rational-legal authority Power that is legitimized by legally enacted rules and regulations that define the ruler's rights and duties.

reference groups Groups that provide standards for judging our own attitudes, behaviors, and achievements.

relative poverty A fluid standard of deprivation by which people compare their lifestyles to others in the society or elsewhere.

reliability The ability of a measure to meet the test of replication, that is, repeated applications should produce the same results.

religion A unified system of beliefs and practices relative to sacred things.

resocialization Learning a new set of norms, attitudes, values, beliefs, and behaviors.

reverse socialization The process in which the supposed targets of socialization influence the supposed socializers.

rituals Specialized rites and ceremonies that, along with a set of rules, believers use to guide their daily behavior.

role A pattern of behavior that is expected of an individual who occupies a particular status.

role conflict Occurs when individuals occupy two or more statuses that involve contradictory expectations of what should be done at a given time.

role overload Occurs when the total number of statuses and role sets overwhelm all activity.

role performance The term used to describe the actual behavior of the person who occupies a given status.

role set The multiple roles connected to any one status.

role strain Occurs when a single status calls for incompatible role behaviors.

role taking Mentally putting ourselves in another person's shoes, thus seeing the world as that person does.

rumors Unverified forms of information transmitted informally from one person to another in a relatively rapid fashion.

sacred Those things that transcend the ordinary, are associated with the supernatural, and inspire awe, respect, worship, and even fear.

sample The selection of a number of individuals in such a way that they are representative of the larger group.

sanctions A form of control in which rewards and punishments are meted out to ensure the proper functioning of society.

scapegoat A racial, ethnic, or religious group in close proximity that is not capable of offering protracted resistance to the hostility or aggression of others.

scientific method A systematic, organized set of procedures that ensure accuracy, honesty, and consistency throughout the research process and, when taken together, produce the best possible results for the creation of empirical knowledge.

secondary deviance Deviation that results from social reaction.

secondary group Larger numbers of people, who interact on a limited, formal, and impersonal basis to accomplish a specific purpose or goal.

secondary sector Activities that transform natural resources into manufactured products.

secondary socialization The process by which we learn additional skills, values, attitudes, and behaviors and take on new statuses and roles.

sect A relatively dogmatic and homogeneous religious group that is considerably smaller in size and less well integrated into society than a church.

sectarian conflict Interreligious strife.

segregation The physical and social separation of racial/ethnic groups in a society.

self The conscious recognition of being a distinct individual.

self-fulfilling prophecies, The tendency of people to respond to and act on the basis of stereotypes, a predisposition that can lead to validation of false definitions.

serial monogamy Individuals may marry more than once, with each prior marriage ended by death, divorce, or annulment.

sex The biological characteristics that differentiate females from males.

sex ratio The number of males for every one hundred females.

sexual assault Any behaviors, either physical or verbal, intended to coerce an individual into sexual activity against her or his will.

sexual evolution A gradual process of development and growth toward a new system of sexual ethics.

sexual harassment Any sexual conduct that makes the workplace environment so hostile or abusive to the victims that they find it difficult to perform their jobs.

sexual identity An individual's awareness of herself or himself as female or male, knowledge of her or his body and bodily functions, images of femininity and masculinity, and sexual preferences and sexual history.

sexual orientation The pattern of sexual and emotional attraction toward a person of one's own or another gender.

sexual revolution A radical change throughout society in sexual behaviors and attitudes.

sexual scripts A society's guidelines or blueprints for defining and engaging in sexual behaviors.

sexually transmitted diseases (STDs) Diseases acquired primarily through sexual contact.

sick role A set of social expectations regarding how a sick person should act.

significant others Key people who are important in children's lives and whose views have the most influence on their development of self, such as mothers, fathers, and siblings.

social change A process through which patterns of social behavior, social relationships, social institutions, and systems of stratification are altered, modified, or transformed over time.

social control Systematic practices developed within a culture to encourage conformity to norms and to discourage deviation.

social facts Norms or collective practices that include all of the ways of acting, thinking, and feeling that exist outside of individuals but exercise control over their behavior.

social gerontology The study of the impact of sociocultural conditions on the process and consequences of aging.

social institutions Relatively stable clusters of values, norms, social statuses, roles, groups, and organizations that meet basic social needs.

social mobility The movement (or lack of movement) by individuals and households from one social position to another in the stratification system.

social movement Any collection of people who organize together to achieve or prevent some social or political change.

social network Web of social relationships that connect us directly or indirectly to other organizations, groups, or individuals.

social policy A plan or course of action adopted by a political body, business, or other organization designed to influence and determine decisions, actions, or other matters of concern.

social stratification An institutionalized form of inequality in which categories of people are ranked in a graded hierarchy on the basis of arbitrary criteria, which then serves to create and perpetuate unequal access to rewards, resources, privileges, and life chances in a society.

social structure Relatively permanent patterns of interaction and relationships found within a society.

socialism An economic system based on public ownership and government control of the economy with the distribution of goods and services for the benefit of society as a whole.

socialization The process of social interaction by which individuals acquire the knowledge, skills, norms, and values of their society and by which they develop their human potential and social identity.

socioeconomic status One's social location in the stratification system as defined by one's level of education, occupation, and financial resources.

sociological imagination The ability to see how individual experiences are connected to the larger society.

sociology The systematic study of human social behavior, groups, and societies and how these change over time.

statistical discrimination The practice of treating individuals on the basis of beliefs about groups.

status A position in the social structure.

status inconsistency A situation in which a person occupies two or more statuses of different rank or prestige.

status set Multiple statuses that a person holds at the same time.

stereotype An exaggerated belief about the appearance, behavior, or other characteristics of a group of people, an assumption that all people in a group share certain characteristics.

stigma An attribute that discredits people.

structural mobility Movement upward or downward in the social class hierarchy as a result of changes in the structure of society.

structured inequality A recurrent pattern of differential access to goods and services and the things that count in a society.

subculture A smaller culture that exists within the context of a larger, more pronounced culture, sharing most of the larger cultural norms and values while simultaneously holding norms, values, and beliefs that differ from it in some important or even fundamental ways.

superego The conscience.

symbol Anything that meaningfully represents something to human beings.

symbolic racism The denial of the presence of racial inequality in society and the opposition to any social policy that would enable disadvantaged groups to escape their disadvantaged position in U.S. society.

taboos Norms that are considered so basic to a society that to violate them would be to weaken the moral fiber and integrity of the society.

technology The application of knowledge for practical ends.

tertiary sector The part of the economy that provides services rather than goods.

theoretical paradigm A definition of reality; an abstract model for selecting crucial concepts and forms of evidence.

theory A statement (or set of statements) that explains how or why facts are related.

Thomas Theorem "If [humans] define situations as real, they are real in their consequences. "

Title IX A federal law that prohibits discrimination on the basis of sex or gender in all federally assisted education programs in all institutions, public and private, that receive monies from the federal government.

total fertility rate The total number of births the average woman will have given current birth rates.

total institutions "Places of residence and work where a large number of like-situated individuals, cut off from the wider society for an appreciable period of time, together lead an enclosed, formal, administered round of life."

totalitarianism A form of government in which the state controls almost all aspects of people's lives.

tracking system Sorting students into different educational programs (such as college preparatory,

vocational education, or remedial programs) on the basis of real or perceived abilities.

traditional authority Power based on people's respect for long-established cultural patterns that are passed down from one generation to the next.

transgendered People who dress and otherwise present themselves as the other sex but have not undergone sex-change surgery.

transsexuals People who have undergone plastic surgery in order to change their genitalia to match their gender identities.

underemployment Working at jobs beneath one's training and abilities or being forced to take only part-time work.

underground economy The hidden economy where work and income are not reported to the appropriate agencies overseeing the economy.

unobtrusive techniques Methods that allow researchers to collect data without disturbing the social situation or the actors within it.

urban legend A contemporary, orally transmitted, unsubstantiated story that is widely circulated and believed.

urbanization The process by which masses of people moved from rural to urban areas and the increase in urban influence over all areas of culture and society.

validity The extent to which a research instrument accurately measures the variable it claims to measure.

values Collective ideas and criteria used by members of a society to evaluate objects, ideas, acts, feelings, or events concerning their relative desirability, merit, correctness, and appropriateness.

variables Any traits, qualities, or characteristics that can take on different values in different individual cases.

vertical mobility Movement upward or downward in the stratification system.

victimless crimes Illegal acts engaged in for the most part by consenting adults.

wealth The total value of money and other assets that individuals or families own, less all outstanding debts.

white-collar crime Crime committed by persons of respectability and high status in the course of their occupations.

work The activities that produce goods and services for one's own use or in exchange for pay or support.

References

Aday, R. H., Rice, C., and Evans, E. 1991. "Intergenerational Partners Project: A Model Linking Elementary Students with Senior Center Volunteers." *Gerontologist* 21, 2:263–266.

Adelson, J. 1996. "Sex among the Americans." In S. J. Bunting (ed.), *Human Sexuality 96/97.* Guilford, CT: Dushkin, pp. 41–45.

Adler, P. A., and Adler, P. 1997. *Constructions of Deviance: Social Power, Context, and Interaction* (2nd ed.). Belmont, CA: Wadsworth.

Adorno, T., Frenkel-Brunswick, E., Levinson, D., and Sanford, R. 1950. *The Authoritarian Personality.* New York: Harper and Row.

Aguero, J. E., Bloch, L., and Byrne, D. 1984. "The Relationship among Sexual Beliefs, Attitudes, Experiences and Homophobia." *Journal of Homosexuality* 11:95–107.

Aguirre, A., Jr., and Turner, J. H. 1998. *American Ethnicity: The Dynamics and Consequences of Discrimination.* Boston: McGraw-Hill.

Aguirre, B. E., Quarantelli, E. L., and Mendoza, J. L. 1988. "The Collective Behavior of Fads: The Characteristics, Effects, and Career of Streaking." *American Sociological Review* 53:569–584.

Ahlander, N. R., and Bahr, K. S. 1995. "Beyond Drudgery, Power, and Equity: Toward an Expanded Discourse on the Moral Dimensions of Housework in Families." *Journal of Marriage and the Family* (February):54–68.

Albanese, J. 1989. *Organized Crime in America* (2nd ed.). Cincinnati: Anderson.

Albrecht, G. L. 1992. *The Disability Business: Rehabilitation in America.* Newbury Park, CA: Sage.

Allport, G., and Postman, L. 1947. *The Psychology of Rumor.* New York: Holt.

American Association of University Women Educational Foundation. 1998. *Separated by Sex: A Critical Look at Single-Sex Education for Girls.* New York: Marlowe.

American Medical Association. 1995–1997. "Facts About Sexual Assault." [Online]. Available: http://www.ama-assn.or . . . ases/assault/facts.html [1999, January 30].

Amnesty International. 1998. http://www.amnesty.org/news/1998/P1000498.htm.

Andersen, M. 1997. *Thinking about Women: Sociological Perspectives on Sex and Gender* (4th ed.). Needham Heights, MA: Allyn & Bacon.

Andersen, M. L., and Collins, P. H. 1995. *Race, Class, and Gender: An Anthology* (2nd ed.). Belmont, CA: Wadsworth.

Anderson, R. 1998. "Healthcare Liability Alliance." (Online). Available: http://www.hcla.org/html/incla861498. htm [1999, July 12].

Andrews, E. L. 1997. "Only Employment for Man in Europe Is Part-Time Work." *New York Times* (September 1):A1.

Angell, M., and Kassifer, J. P. 1994. "Alcohol and Other Drugs: Toward a More Rational and Consistent Policy." *New England Journal of Medicine* 331:537–539.

Applebome, P. 1995. "For the Ultimate Safe School, Official Eyes Turn to Dallas." *New York Times* (September 20):A1, B8.

Armor, D. 1989. "After Busing: Education and Choice." *The Public Interest* 95: pp. 24–37.

Asante, M. K. 1993. *Malcolm X as Cultural Hero and Other Afrocentric Essays.* Trenton, NJ: Africa World Press.

Asch, S. 1952. *Social Psychology.* Englewood Cliffs, NJ: Prentice-Hall.

Associated Press. 1997a. "Oh, Baby: Bundle of Joy Costs More Than $8,000 a Year." *Chicago Tribune* (December 25):17.

Associated Press. 1997b. "Covenant Marriage Option Would Make Divorcing Hard." *Chicago Tribune* (June 20):4.

Associated Press. 1998a. "Romance Turning into a Tragedy." *Chicago Tribune* (February 20):sec 1, p. 6.

Associated Press. 1998b. "More Japanese Give Approval of Childless Marriages, Divorce." *News-Press* (January 4):10A.

Atchley, R. C. 1997. *Social Forces and Aging* (8th ed.). Belmont, CA: Wadsorth.

Babbie, E. 1992. *The Practice of Social Research* (6th ed.). Belmont, CA: Wadsworth.

Ballantine, J. H. 1993. *The Sociology of Education: A Systematic Analysis* (3rd ed.). Englewood Cliffs, NJ: Prentice Hall.

Baltzell, E. D. 1994. *Judgment and Sensibility: Religion and Stratification.* New Brunswick, NJ: Transaction.

Banfield, E. C. 1974. *The Unheavenly City Revisited.* Boston: Little, Brown.

Bannister, S. 1991. "The Criminalization of Women Fighting Back against Male Abuse." *Humanity and Society* 15, 4:400–416.

Bannister, S. 1992. "Women and Violence." Lecture presented at North Park College, Chicago, IL.

Barnett, R. C., and Rivers, C. 1996. *She Works? He Works: How Two-Income Families Are Happier, Healthier, and Better-Off.* San Francisco: HarperCollins.

Basow, S. 1992. *Gender Stereotypes and Roles* (3rd ed.). Belmont, CA: Wadsworth.

Becker, H. 1963. *Outsiders: Studies in the Sociology of Deviance.* New York: Free Press.

Beeghley, L. 1996. *The Structure of Social Stratification in the United States.* Boston: Allyn & Bacon.

Beirne, P., and Messerschmidt, J. 1995. *Criminology* (2nd ed.). San Diego: Harcourt Brace Jovanovich.

Bellah, R. N. 1970. *Beyond Belief.* New York: Harper.

Bendavid, N. 1998. "Gates' Defense: It's About Ideas." *Chicago Tribune* (March 4):1.

Benjamin, L. 1991. *The Black Elite: Facing the Color Line in the Twilight of the Twentieth Century.* Chicago, IL: Nelson-Hall.

Bennett, W. 1988. *American Education: Making It Work.* Washington, DC: U.S. Government Printing Office.

Benokraitis, N. V. 1993. *Marriages and Families: Changes, Choices, and Constraints.* Englewood Cliffs, NJ: Prentice-Hall.

Benokraitis, N. V., and Feagin, J. R. 1986. *Modern Sexism.* Englewood Cliffs, NJ: Prentice Hall.

Berger, P. 1963. *Invitation to Sociology: A Humanistic Perspective.* New York: Anchor.

Berger, P. L. and Luckmann, T. 1963. *The Social Construction of Reality.* New York: Doubleday.

Bernard, J. 1972,1982. *The Future of Marriage.* New York: Bantam.

Bernard, J. 1984. "The Good-Provider Role: Its Rise and Fall." In P. Voydanoff (ed.), *Work and Family: Changing Roles of Men and Women.* Palo Alto, CA: Mayfield, pp. 43–60.

Best, J., and Horiuchi, G. T.. 1996. "The Razor Blade in the Apple: The Social Construction of Urban Legends." In J. W. Heeren and M. Mason (eds.), *Sociology: Windows on Society* (4th ed.). Los Angeles: Roxbury.

Betz, N., and Fitzgerald, L. 1987. *The Career Psychology of Women.* New York: Academic Press.

Betzold, M. 1997. "The Selling of Dr. Death." *The New Republic* 216:22–28.

Bianchi, S. M., and Spain, D. 1996. "Women, Work, and Family in America." *Population Bulletin* 51, 3 (December). Washington, DC: Population Reference Bureau.

Billingsley, A. 1968. *Black Families in White America.* Englewood Cliffs, NJ: Prentice Hall.

"Black Clergy Gather to Fight AIDS." 1995. *Christian Century* (October 20):1009.

Blackwood, E. 1984. "Sexuality and Gender in Certain Native American Tribes: The Case of Cross-Gender Females." *Signs* 10:27–42.

Blackwood, E. 1986. "Breaking the Mirror: The Construction of Lesbianism and the Anthropological Discourse on Homosexuality." In Evelyn Blackwood (ed.), *The Many Faces of Homosexuality: Anthropological Approaches to Homosexual Behavior.* New York: Harington Park, pp. 1–17.

Blau, P., and Duncan, O. D. 1967. *The American Occupational Structure.* New York: Wiley.

Blumenstyk, G. 1998. "Western Governors U. Takes Shape as a New Model for Higher Education." *Chronicle of Higher Education* (February 6):A21.

Blumer, H. 1951. "Collective Behavior." In A. M. Lee (ed.), *Principles of Sociology.* New York: Barnes and Noble, pp. 165–222.

Blumer, H. 1969. "Collective Behavior." In A. M. Lee (ed.), *Principles of Sociology* (3rd ed.). New York: Barnes and Noble, pp. 65–121.

Blumstein, P., and Schwartz, P. 1983. *American Couples: Money, Work, Sex.* New York: Morrow.

Bose, C. E. 1985. *Jobs and Gender: A Study of Occupational Prestige.* New York: Praeger.

The Boston Women's Health Book Collective. 1992. *The New Our Bodies, Ourselves: A Book by and for Women.* New York: Simon and Schuster Inc.

Bound, J., Duncan, G., Laren, D., and Oleinick, L. 1991. "Poverty Dynamics in Widowhood." *Journal of Gerontology* 46,3 (May):S115–24.

Bourdieu, P. 1984. *Distinction: A Social Critique of the Judgment of Taste.* Richard Nice (Trans.). Cambridge, MA: Harvard University Press.

Bourdieu, P., and Passeron, J. 1990. *Reproduction in Education, Society and Culture.* Newbury Park, CA: Sage.

Braithwaite, R., & Taylor, S. (Eds.) 1992. *Health Issues in the Black Community.* San Francisco: Jossey-Bass.

Braun, D. 1997. *The Rich Get Richer: The Rise of Income Inequality in the United States and the World.* Chicago: Nelson-Hall.

Brazelton, T. B. 1990. *The Earliest Relationship: Parents, Infants, and the Drama of Early Attachment.* Reading, MA: Addison-Wesley.

Bread for the World Institute. 1998. [Online]. Available: http://www.bread.org/html [November 8].

Brettell, C. B., and Sargent, C. F. (Eds.). 1997. *Gender in Cross-Cultural Perspective.* Upper Saddle River, NJ: Prentice Hall.

Brewster, K., Billy, J., and Grady, W. R. 1993. "Social Context and Adolescent Behavior: The Impact of Community on the Transition to Sexual Activity." *Social Forces* 71:713–740.

Brooke, J. 1998a. "Gay Man Dies from Attack, Fanning Outrage and Debate." *New York Times* (October 12):A1, A17.

Brooke, J. 1998b. "Sex-Change Industry a Boon to Small City." *New York Times* (November 8):A14.

Brookhiser, R. 1991. *The Way of the WASP.* New York: Free Press.

Brooks, A. P., and South, J. 1995. "School choice Plans Worry Resegregation Critics." *Austin American-Statesman* (April 9):A1, A18.

Brotman, B. 1996. "Women Gallup Away from Having a Woman Boss." *Chicago Tribune* (April 7):Sec. 13, 1.

Brunvand, J. H. 1981. *The Vanishing Hitchhiker: American Urban Legends and Their Meanings.* New York: Norton.

Brunvand, J. H. 1989. *Curses! Broiled Again! The Hottest Urban Legends Going.* New York: Norton.

Brush, L. D. 1990. "Violent Acts and Injurious Outcomes in Married Couples: Methodological Issues in the National Survey of Families and Households." *Gender and Society* 4, 1:56.

Bullard, R. D. 1997. "Dismantling Environmental Racism in the Policy Arena: The Role of Collaborative Social Research." In P. Nyden et al., *Building Community: Social Science in Action.* Thousand Oaks, CA: Pine Forge Press, pp. 67–73.

Bullough, V. L. 1976. *Sexual Variance in Society and History.* New York: Wiley.

Bullough, V. L., and Bullough, B. 1993. *Cross-Dressing, Sex and Gender.* Philadelphia: University of Pennsylvania Press.

Bunker, B. B., Subek, J. M., Vanderslice, V. J., and Rice, R. W. 1992. "Quality of Life in Dual-Career Families: Commuting versus Single-Residence Couples." *Journal of Marriage and the Family* 54:399–407.

Butler, R. 1975. *Why Survive? Being Old in America.* New York: Harper and Row.

Bynum, J. E., and Thompson, W. E. 1996. *Juvenile Delinquency: A Sociological Approach* (3rd. ed). Boston: Allyn & Bacon.

Calderone, M. S., and Johnson, E. W. 1989. *Family Book about Sexuality* (rev. ed.). New York: Harper & Row.

Cameron, B. 1993. "Gee, You Don't Seem Like an Indian from the Reservation." In V. Cyrus, *Experiencing Race, Class, and Gender in the United States.* Mountain View, CA: Mayfield.

Cammermeyer, M. 1994. *Serving in Silence: The Story of Margarethe Cammermeyer.* New York: Penguin.

Cantril, H. 1940/1982. *The Invasion from Mars: A Study in the Psychology of Panic.* Princeton, NJ: Princeton University Press.

Carley, K. 1991. "A Theory of Group Stability." *American Sociological Review* 56, 3:331–354.

Carmichael, S., and Hamilton, C. V. 1967. *Black Power: The Politics of Liberation in America.* New York: Vintage Books/Random House.

"Car Phone Use Raises Risk of Accident, Study Asserts." 1997. *Chicago Tribune* (February 13):3.

Carter, R. T. 1997. "Is White a Race? Expressions of White Racial Identity." In M. Fine et al., (eds.), *Off White: Readings on Race, Power and Society.* New York: Routledge, pp. 198–209.

Casper, L. M., McLanahan, S. S., and Garfinkel, I. 1994. "The Gender Gap: What We Can Learn from Other Countries." *American Sociological Review* 59:594–605.

CBS News, *60 Minutes.* 1997. "Strive." (May 4).

Center Against Sexual Abuse: Education, Prevention and Treatment. (1999). "Sexual Assault Statistics." [Online]. Available: http://www.syspac.com/~casa/stats.html [1999, January 30].

Centers for Disease Control and Prevention. 1993. *HIV/AIDS Surveillance Report.* 5 (No. 2): 1–23.

Centers for Disease Control and Prevention. 1997. *HIV/AIDS Surveillance Report.* 9 (No. 2): 1–43.

Centers for Disease Control and Prevention. 1998. *HIV/AIDS Surveillance Report.* 10 (No. 1): 1–40.

Chafetz, J. S. 1988. *Feminist Sociology: An Overview of Contemporary Theories.* Itasca, IL: F. E. Peacock.

Chagnon, N. 1992. *Yanamamo: The Fierce People* (4th ed.). Fort Worth: Harcourt Brace Jovanovich.

Chalfant, H. P., Beckley, R. E., and Palmer, C. E. 1994. *Religion in Contemporary Society.* Itasca, IL: F. E. Peacock.

Chambliss, W. J., and Zatz, M.. 1994. *Making Law: Law, State, and Structural Contradiction.* Bloomington: Indiana University Press.

Charon, J. M. 1995. *Ten Questions: A Sociological Perspective.* Belmont, CA: Wadsworth.

Chatzky, J. S. 1992. "A Brief History of Stock Fads." *Forbes* (September 14):253–268.

Cherlin, A. 1992. *Marriage, Divorce, Remarriage.* Cambridge, MA: Harvard University Press.

Cherlin, A., and Furstenberg, Jr., F. F. 1991. "Longitudinal Studies of Effects of Divorce on Children in Great Britain and the United States." *Science* 252:1386–1389.

Chesney-Lind, M., and Rodriquez, N. 1993. "Women Under Lock and Key." *Prison Journal* 63:47–65.

"Childless by Choice." 1998. *Working Woman* (March):18.

Children's Defense Fund. 1992. *Vanishing Dreams: The Economic Plight of America's Young Families.* Washington, DC: Author.

Children's Defense Fund. 1996. *The State of America's Children Yearbook.* Washington, DC: Author.

Children's Hospital, Boston. 1997–1998. "Homosexual and Bisexual Teens More Likely to Take Health Risks." [Online]. Available: http://www.childrensho . . . archive/1998/may4.html [1999, March 4].

Choo, K. 1998. "As for Equality, That's for the Rest of the World." *Chicago Tribune* (August 2):sec. 13, 1.

Chow, Ngan-Ling, E., Wilkerson, D., and Zinn, M. Baca (Eds.). 1996. *Race, Class, and Gender: Common Bonds, Different Voices.* Thousand Oaks, CA: Sage.

Christian, S. E. 1997. "It's Not Always Grand Parenting a 2nd Time." *Chicago Tribune* (October 4):1.

Clark, K. 1965. *Dark Ghetto.* New York: Harper and Row.

Clark, N., and Liebig, P. S. 1996. "The Politics of Physician-Assisted Death: California's Proposition 161 and Attitudes of the Elderly." *Politics and the Life Sciences* (September):273–280.

Cleckley, H. 1976. *The Mark of Sanity.* St. Louis: Mosby.

Clements, M. 1994. "Sex in America Today." *Parade Magazine* (August 7):4–6.

Clinard, M. B., and Meier, R. F. 1995. *Sociology of Deviant Behavior* (9th ed.). New York: Harcourt Brace & Company.

Cloward, R. A., and Ohlin, L. E. 1960. *Delinquency and Opportunity: A Theory of Delinquent Gangs.* New York: Free Press.

Cockerham, W. C. 1989. *Sociology of Mental Disorders.* (2nd ed.) Englewood Cliffs, NJ: Prentice Hall.

Cockerham, W. C. 1998. *Medical Sociology* (7th ed.). Englewood Cliffs, NJ: Prentice Hall.

Cole, S. 1997. "Maria, A Portuguese Fisherwoman." In C. Brettell and C. Sargent (eds.), *Gender in Cross-*

Cultural Perspective. Upper Saddle River, NJ: Prentice Hall, pp. 318–321.

Coleman, D. 1992. "Black Scientists Study the 'Pose' of the Inner City." *The New York Times* (April 21):C1, C7.

Coleman, M., and Ganong, L. H. 1990. "Remarriage and Stepfamily Research in the 1980s: Increased Interest in an Old Family Form." *Journal of Marriage and the Family* 52:925–940.

Coles, R., and Stokes, G. 1985. *Sex and the American Teenager.* New York: Harper and Row.

Collins, P. H. 1989. "The Social Construction of Black Feminist Thought." *Signs* 14:745–773.

Collins, P. H. 1991. *Black Feminist Thought: Knowledge, Consciousness, and the Politics of Empowerment.* New York: Routledge.

Coltrane, S. 1995. "Stability and Change in Chicano Men's Family Lives." In M. Killel and M. Messner (eds.). *Men's Lives* (3d ed.). Boston: Allyn and Bacon, pp. 469–484.

Congregational United Church of Christ. 1998. "About the Mitch Snyder Awards." [Online]. Available: http://www.firstchurchcambridge.org/shelter_mitch.html [November 21].

Conner, K. 1992. *Aging America: Issues Facing an Aging Society.* Englewood Cliffs, NJ: Prentice Hall.

Conrad, P. 1997. *The Sociology of Health and Illness: Critical Perspectives.* New York: St. Martin's.

Cooley, C. H. 1902. *Human Nature and the Social Order.* New York: Scribner.

Cooley, C. H. 1964. *Human Nature and Social Order.* New York: Schocken (original publication 1902).

Coontz, S. 1995. "The Way We Weren't: The Myth and Reality of the 'Traditional' Family." In R. Schaefer and R. Lamm (eds.), *Sociology: Annual Editions.* Guilford, CT: Dushkin/McGraw-Hill, pp. 70–73.

Coontz, S. 1998. "The Way We Never Were: American Families and the Nostalgia Trap." In S. Ferguson (ed.), *Shifting the Center: Understanding Contemporary Families.* Mountain View, CA: Mayfield, pp. 50–62.

Corsaro, W. A., and Eder, D. 1990. "Children's Peer Cultures." *Annual Review of Sociology* 16:197–220.

Cortese, A. J. P. 1990. *Ethnic Ethics: The Restructuring of Moral Theory.* Albany: State University of New York Press.

Cose, E. 1995. *A Man's World.* New York: HarperCollins.

Coser, L. 1956. *The Functions of Social Conflict.* New York: Free Press.

Coser, L. A. (Ed.). 1963. *Sociology through Literature.* Englewood Cliffs, NJ: Prentice-Hall, Inc.

"Couple Break Law Naming Their Little Devil." 1994. *Chicago Tribune* (February 2):8.

Cox, O. 1948. *Caste, Class and Race.* New York: Monthly Review Press.

Crown, J., and Heatherington, L. 1989. "The Costs of Winning? The Role of Gender in Moral Reasoning and Judgments about Competitive Athletic Encounters." *Journal of Sport and Exercise Psychology* 11, 3:281–89.

Crystal, Graef. 1995. "Growing the Pay Gap." *Los Angeles Times* (July 23):D2.

Cullen, J. B., and Novick, S. M. 1979. "The Davis-Moore Theory of Stratification: A Further Examination and Extension." *American Journal of Sociology* 84:1414–1437.

Cumming, E. C., and Henry, W. E. 1961. *Growing Old: The Process of Disengagement.* New York: Basic Books.

Curtis, J. E., Grabb, E. G., and Baer, D. 1992. "Voluntary Association Membership in Fifteen Countries: A Comparative Analysis." *American Sociological Review* 57, 2:139–152.

Curtiss, S. 1977. *Genie: A Psycholinguistic Study of a Modern-Day "Wild Child."* New York: Academic Press.

Cyrus, V. 1993. *Experiencing Race, Class, and Gender in the United States.* Mountain View, CA: Mayfield.

Cyrus, V. 1997. *Experiencing Race, Class, and Gender in the United States.* Mountain View, CA: Mayfield Publishing Company.

Dahl, R. A. 1982. *Dilemmas of Pluralist Democracy: Autonomy vs. Control.* New Haven, CT: Yale University Press.

Dahrendorf, R. 1959. *Class and Class Conflict in Industrial Society.* Stanford, CA: Stanford University Press.

Dale, R. 1977. "Implications of the Rediscovery of the Hidden Curriculum of the Sociology of Teaching." In Dennis Gleeson (ed.), *Identity and Structure: Issues in the Sociology of Education.* Driffield, England: Nafferton Books.

Darrett, B., and Rutman, A. H. 1979. "Now Wives and Sons-in-Law: Parental Death in Seventeenth-Century Virginia Country." In T. W. Tote and D. L. Ammerman (eds.), *The Chesapeake in the Seventeenth Century.* Chapel Hill: University of North Carolina.

Davidson, J. 1996. "Menace to Society." *Rolling Stone* (February 22):38–9.

Davies, J. C. 1962. "Towards a Theory of Revolution." *American Sociological Review* 27:5–19.

Davis, J. A., and Smith, T. 1984. *General Social Surveys, 1972–1984: Cumulative Data.* New Haven: Yale University Press/Roper Center.

Davis, J. A., and Smith, T. 1991. *General Social Surveys, 1972–1991.* Chicago: University of Chicago Press.

Davis, K. 1940. "Extreme Social Isolation of a Child." *American Journal of Sociology* (January):554–564.

Davis, K. 1947. "Final Note on a Case of Extreme Isolation." *American Journal of Sociology* (March):432–437.

Davis, K., and Moore, W. 1945. "Some Principles of Stratification." *American Sociological Review* 10:242–249.

Dean, A., Kolody, B., and Wood, P. 1990. "Effects of Social Support from Various Sources on Depression in Elderly Persons." *Journal of Health and Social Behavior* 31:48–161.

Deardorff, J. 1998. "Experts in Teen Intervention Tell Tipoffs to Trouble." *Chicago Tribune* (May 24):sec. 1, p. 16.

de la Garza, R. O. 1993. "Researchers Must Heed New Realities When They Study Latinos in the U.S." *The Chronicle of Higher Education* (June):B1, B2.

DeLamaster, J. 1987. "Gender Differences in Sexual Scenarios." In K. Kelly (ed.), *Females, Males and Sexuality.* Albany: State University of New York Press, pp. 127–139.

Delgado, R., and Stefancic, J. 1997. *Critical White Studies: Looking behind the Mirror*. Philadelphia: Temple University Press.

Deloria, V. 1995. *Red Earth, White Lies*. New York: Scribner's.

D'Emilio, J. 1997. "Capitalism and Gay Identity." In R. N. Lancaster and M. di Leonardo (eds.), *The Gender Sexuality Reader*. New York: Routledge, pp. 169–178.

Demo, D. H., and Acock. A. C. 1993. "Family Diversity and the Division of Domestic Labor: How Much Have Things Really Changed?" *Family Relations* 42:323–331.

Democratic Presidential Platform. 1996.

DePalma, A. 1997. "Father's Killing of Canadian Girl: Mercy or Murder." *New York Times* (December 1): p. A3.

"Descendant of Slave, White Planter Challenges Racial Label." 1982. *Chicago Sun-Times* (September 14):24.

DeSpelder, L. A., and Strickland, A. L. 1996. *The Last Dance: Encountering Death and Dying* (4th ed.). Mountain View, CA: Mayfield.

DeStefano, L., and Colasanto, D. 1990. "Unlike 1975, Most Americans Think Men Have It Better." *Gallup Poll Monthly* (February):29.

de Tocqueville, A. 1969. *Democracy in America*. Ed. J. P. Mayer. Garden City, NY: Anchor Books (original publication 1835).

Diamond, M. 1993. "Homosexuality and Bisexuality in Different Populations." *Archives of Sexual Behavior* 22:291–310.

di Leonardo, M. 1997. "The Female World of Cards and Holidays: Women, Families, and the Work of Kinship." In C. Brettell and C. Sargent (eds.), *Gender in Cross-Cultural Perspective*. Upper Saddle River, NJ: Prentice Hall, pp. 322–331.

Dillon, S. 1997. "After 4 Years of Nafta, Labor Is Forging Cross-Border Ties." *New York Times* (December 20):A1.

Disch, E. 1997. *Reconstructing Gender: A Multicultural Anthology*. Mountain View, CA: Mayfield.

Divine, R., Breen, T., Fredrickson, and Williams R. H. 1991. *America: Past and Present* (3rd ed.). Glenview, IL: HarperCollins.

Division of STD Prevention, U.S. Department of Health and Human Services, Public Health Service. September, 1997. *Sexually Transmitted Disease Surveillance*. Atlanta: Centers for Disease Control and Prevention.

Doctors without Borders: http://www.dwb.org/index.htm.

Dodge, K. 1990. "Development of Psychopathology in Children of Depressed Mothers." *Developmental Psychology* (January):3–6.

Doka, K. (Ed.). 1989. *Disenfranchised Grief: Recognizing Hidden Sorrow*. Lexington, MA: Lexington.

Dollard, J., Miller, N. E., Dobb, L. W., Mowrer, O. H., and Sears, R. 1939. *Frustration and Aggression*. New Haven, CT: Yale University Press.

Domhoff, G. W. 1974. *The Bohemian Grove and Other Retreats*. New York: Harper and Row.

Domhoff, G. W. 1990. *The Power Elite and the State: How Policy is Made in America*. New York: Aldine de Gruyter.

Doob, C. B. 1996. *Racism: An American Cauldron*. New York: HarperCollins.

Dovidio, J. 1997. "Aversive Racism and the Need for Affirmative Action." *The Chronicle of Higher Education* (July 25):A60.

Doyle, J. A., and Paludi, M. A. 1995. *Sex and Gender: The Human Experience*. Boston: McGraw-Hill.

Doyle, J. A., and Paludi, M. A. 1998. *Sex & Gender: The Human Experience* (4th ed.). Boston: McGraw-Hill.

Duke, B. 1986. *The Japanese School: Lessons for Industrial America*. New York: Praeger.

Duncan, D. F. 1990. "Prevalence of Sexual Assault Victimization among Heterosexual and Gay/Lesbian University Students." *Psychological Reports* 66(1):65–67.

Duneier, M. 1992. *Slim's Table: Race, Respectability, and Masculinity*. Chicago: University of Chicago Press.

Dunn, J., and Plomin, R. 1990. *Separate Lives: Why Siblings Are So Different*. New York: Basic Books.

Durkheim, E. 1947. *The Elementary Forms of Religious Life*. Glencoe, IL: Free Press (original publication 1912).

Durkheim, E, 1964. *The Division of Labor in Society*. New York: Free Press (original publication 1895).

Dyer, K. (Ed.). 1990. *Gays in Uniform: The Pentagon's Secret Reports*. Boston: Alyson.

Dyson, M. E. 1991. "2 Live Crew's Rap: Sex, Race and Class." *The Christian Century*, vol. 108 (January 2–9), pp. 7–8.

Dyson, M. E. 1993. "Be Like Mike? Michael Jordan and the Pedagogy of Desire." In Michael Eric Dyson, *Reflecting Black: African American Cultural Criticism*. Minneapolis: University of Minnesota Press, pp. 64–75.

Eckersley, R. 1996. "The West's Deepening Cultural Crisis." In Harold A. Widdison (ed.), *Social Problems Annual Editions*. Guilford, CT: Dushkin, pp. 227–230.

Eichar, D. M., Norland, S., Brady, E. M., and Fortinsky, R. 1991. "The Job Satisfaction of Older Workers." *Journal of Organizational Behaviour* 12:609–620.

Ellis, A. 1988. "Is Religiosity Pathological?" *Free Inquiry* 18:27–32.

Elmer-Dewitt, P. 1994. "Now for the Truth about Americans and SEX." *Time* (October 17):62–70.

England, P. 1997. "The Sex Gap in Pay." In D. Dunn (ed.), *Workplace/Women's Place*. Los Angeles: Roxbury, pp. 74–87.

Enroth, R. 1994. *Recovering from Churches that Abuse*. Grand Rapids, MI: Zondervan.

Erikson, E. 1975. *Life History and Historical Moment*. New York: Norton.

Erman, M. D., and Lundman, R. J. (eds.). 1996. *Corporate and Governmental Deviance: Problems of Organizational Behavior in Contemporary Society* (5th ed.) New York: Oxford University Press.

Esbensen, F., and Huizinga, D. 1993. "Gangs, Drugs, and Delinquency in a Survey of Urban Youth." *Criminology* 31, 4:565–89.

Etzioni, A. 1975. *A Comparative Analysis of Complex Organizations* (revised and enlarged ed.). Glencoe, IL: Free Press.

Fain, T. C., and Anderson, D. L. 1987. "Sexual Harassment: Organizational Context and Diffuse Status." *Sex Roles* 5/6:291–311.

Faison, S. 1995. "In China, Rapid Social Change Brings a Surge in the Divorce Rate." *New York Times* (August 22):A1.

Farber, S. 1981. *Identical Twins Reared Apart*. New York: Basic Books.

Farley, J. 1995. *Majority-Minority Relations* (3d ed.). Englewood Cliffs, NJ: Prentice-Hall.

Faruqi, A. 1996. "Edit Hits Afghan Orphans Hard." *Chicago Tribune* (October 15):sec. 1:3.

Feagin, J. R. 1991. "The Continuing Significance of Race: Antiblack Discrimination in Public Places." *American Sociological Review* 56 (February):101–116.

Feagin, J. R., and Feagin, C. B. 1996. *Racial and Ethnic Relations*. (5th ed.). Englewood Cliffs, NJ: Prentice-Hall.

Feagin, J. R., and Sikes, M. 1994. *Living with Racism: The Black Middle-Class Experience*. Boston: Beacon.

Feagin, J. R., and Vera, H. 1995. *White Racism: The Basics*. New York: Routledge.

Featherstone, M. (Ed.). 1990. *Global Culture: Nationalism, Globalization and Modernity*. Newbury Park, CA: Sage.

Featherstone, M. 1995. *Undoing Culture*. London: Sage.

Felson, R., and Zielinski, M. 1989. "Children's Self-Esteem and Parental Support." *Journal of Marriage and the Family* (August):727–735.

Fernea, E. 1997. *The Arab World: Forty Years of Change*. Anchor Books edition. New York: Anchor Books.

Ferrante, J. 1992. *Sociology: A Global Perspective*. Belmont, CA: Wadsworth.

Ferrante, J. 1998. *Sociology: A Global Perspective* (3rd ed.). Belmont, CA: Wadsworth.

Ferraro, K. J. 1989. "Policing Woman Battering." *Social Problems* (36):61–74.

Finkelhor, D., and Yllo, K. 1985. *License to Rape: Sexual Abuse of Wives*. New York: Holt, Rinehart, & Winston.

Foner, P. S. 1947. *History of the Labor Movement in the United States: From Colonial Times to the Founding of the American Federation of Labor*. New York: International Publishers.

Ford, C. S., and Beach, F. A. 1951. *Patterns of Sexual Behavior*. New York: Harper & Row.

Ford, R. L. 1988. *Work, Organization, and Power*. Boston: Allyn and Bacon.

Fowler, R. B., and Hertzke, A. D. 1995. *Religion and Politics in America*. Boulder, CO: Westview.

Frankenberg, R. 1993. *White Women, Race Matters: The Social Construction of Whiteness*. Minneapolis: University of Minnesota Press.

Franks, P., & Clancy, C. 1993. "Physician Gender Bias in Clinical Decision-Making: Screening for Cancer in Primary Care." *Medical Care* 31:213–218.

Freud, S. 1927. *Future of an Illusion*. London: Hogarth.

Freud, S. 1947. *The Ego and the Id* (4th ed.). J. Riviere (trans.). London: Lt. V. Woolf at the Hogarth Press and the Institute of Psychoanalysis.

Fromm, E. 1970. *The Art of Loving*. New York: Bantam.

Furstenberg, F. 1988. "Good Dads–Bad Dads: Two Faces of Fatherhood." In Andrew Cherlin (ed.), *The Changing American Family and Public Policy*. Washington DC: Urban Institute, pp. 193–217.

Gaertner, S. L., and Banker, B. S. 1997. "Does White Racism Necessarily Mean Antiblackness? Aversive Racism and Prowhiteness." In M. Fine, L. Weis, L. Powell, and L. Wong (eds.), *Off White: Readings on Race, Power, and Society*. New York: Routledge, pp. 167–186.

Gagnon, J. H., and Simon, W. 1973. *Sexual Conduct: The Social Sources of Human Sexuality*. Chicago: Aldine.

Gagnon, J. H., and Simon, W. 1987. "The Sexual Scripting of Oral-Genital Contacts." *Archives of Sexual Behavior* 16:1–25.

Gallagher, C. A. 1997. "White Racial Formation: Into the Twenty-First Century." In R. Delgado and J. Stefancic (eds.), *Critical White Studies: Looking behind the Mirror*. Philadelphia: Temple University Press, pp. 6–11.

Gamson, W. 1990. *The Strategy of Social Protest* (2nd ed.). Belmont, CA: Wadsworth.

Gans, H. 1995. *The War against the Poor: The Underclass and Antipoverty Policy*. New York: Basic.

Garfinkel, H. 1956. "Conditions of Successful Degradation Ceremonies." *American Journal of Sociology* (March):420–424.

Garfinkel, H. 1967. *Studies in Ethnomethodology*. Englewood Cliffs, NJ: Prentice-Hall.

Garfinkel, H. 1988. "Evidence for Locally Produced, Naturally Accountable Phenomena of Order, Logic, Reason, Meaning, Method, etc. In and As of the Essential Quiddity of Immortal Ordinary Society (I of IV): An Announcement of Studies." *Sociological Theory* 6:103–109.

Geiss, S. K., and O'Leary, K. D. 1981. "Therapists' Ratings of Frequency and Severity of Marital Problems: Implications for Research." *Journal of Marital and Family Therapy* 7:515–520

Gerlach, M. L. 1992. *The Social Organization of Japanese Business*. Berkeley and Los Angeles: University of California Press.

Gibbs, N. 1991. "When Is It Rape?" *Time* (June 3), pp. 48–55.

Gibbs, N. 1993. "How Should We Teach Our Children about SEX?" *Time* (May 24):60–66.

Gibson, P. 1989. "Gay Male and Lesbian Youth Suicide." Report of the Secretary's Task Force on Youth Suicide. Washington, DC: U.S. Department of Health and Human Services.

Gilbert, D., and Kahl, J. 1998. *The American Class Structure: A New Synthesis*. Homewood, IL: Dorsey.

Gilbert, S. 1997. "Youth Study Elevates Family's Role." *New York Times* (September 10):C10.

Gill, R. T., Glazer, N., and Thernstrom, S. A. 1992. *Our Changing Population*. Englewood Cliffs, NJ: Prentice Hall.

Gilligan, C. 1982. *In a Different Voice: Psychological Theory and Women's Development*. Cambridge, MA: Harvard University Press.

Gilligan, C. 1990. "Teaching Shakespeare's Sister: Notes from the Underground of Female Adolescence." In C. Gilligan, N. P. Lyons, and T. J. Hanmer (eds.), *Making Connections*. Cambridge, MA: Harvard University Press, pp. 6–29.

Gittins, D. 1998. "The Family in Question: What Is the Family? Is It Universal?" In Susan J. Ferguson (ed.), *Shifting the Center: Understanding Contemporary Families*. Mountain View, CA: Mayfield, pp. 1–11.

Glazer, N., and Moynihan, D. P. 1975. "Introduction." In N. Glazer and D. P. Moynihan (eds.), *Ethnicity: Theory and Experience.* Cambridge, MA: Harvard University Press, pp. 1–26.

Glenn, N. D., and Supancic, M. 1984. "The Social and Demographic Correlates of Divorce and Separation in the United States: An Update and Reconsideration." *Journal of Marriage and the Family* 46:563–575.

Glick, H. 1992. *The Right to Die: Policy Innovation and Its Consequences.* New York: Columbia University Press.

Glueck, S., and Glueck, E. 1950. *Unraveling Juvenile Delinquency.* New York: Commonwealth Fund.

Godson, R., and Olson, W. J. 1997. "International Organized Crime." In L. M. Salinger (ed.), *Deviant Behavior 97/98.* Guilford, CT: Dushkin, pp. 120–131.

Godwin, D. D., and Scanzoni, J. 1989. "Couple Consensus during Marital Joint Decision-Making: A Context, Process, Outcome Model." *Journal of Marriage and the Family* 51:943–956.

Goffman, E. 1959. *The Presentation of Self in Everyday Life.* Garden City, NY: Anchor.

Goffman, E. 1961. *Asylums: Essays on the Social Situation of Mental Patients and Other Inmates.* Garden City, NY: Anchor Books.

Goffman, E. 1963. *Stigma: Notes on the Management of Spoiled Identity.* Englewood Cliffs, NJ: Prentice-Hall.

Goldberg, C. 1997. "Study Casts Doubts on Wisdom of Mandatory Terms for Drugs." *New York Times* (November 25):A11.

Goldstein, M. C. 1971. "Stratification, Polyandry, and Family Structure in Central Tibet." *Southwest Journal of Anthropology* 27:65–74.

Gollin, A. 1980. "Comments on Johnson's 'On the Prevalence of Rape in the United States.' " *Sex Roles* 6, 346–349.

Good Morning America. 1998. ABC Television. (May 7).

Goodman, S., and Brumley, E. 1990. "Schizophrenic and Depressed Mothers: Relational Deficits in Parenting." *Developmental Psychology* (January):31–39.

Goodstein, L. (with M. Connelly). 1998. "Teen-Age Poll Finds Support For Tradition." *New York Times* (April 30):A1.

Gordon. M. 1964. *Assimilation in American Life.* New York: Oxford University Press.

Goring, C. 1913. *The English Convict.* London: His Majesty's Stationery Office.

Gottfredson, M. R., and Hirschi, T. 1990. *A General Theory of Crime.* Stanford, CA: Stanford University Press.

Gove, W. 1995. "Is Sociology the Integrative Discipline in the Study of Human Behavior?" *Social Forces* 73, 4:1197.

Gracey, H. 1999. "Learning the Student Role: Kindergarten as Academic Boot Camp." In James Henslin (ed.), *Down to Earth Sociology.* New York: Free Press, pp. 418–430.

Greene, B. 1994. "Lesbian Women of Color: Triple Jeopardy." In L. Comas-Diaz and B. Greene (eds.), *Women of Color: Integrating Ethnic and Gender Identities in Psychotherapy.* New York: Guilford Press, pp. 389–427.

Greenhouse, S. 1996. "Child-Labor Abuses Draw Youthful Protests." *New York Times* (December 15):A10.

Grossman, H., and Grossman, S. H. 1994. *Gender Issues in Education.* Boston: Allyn and Bacon.

Gwynne, S. C. 1990. "The Right Stuff." *Time* (October 29):74–84.

Haddad, Y. Y. 1985. "Islam, Women and Revolution in Twentieth-Century Arab Thought." In Y. Y. Haddad and E. B. Findley (eds.), *Women, Religion and Social Change.* Albany: State University of New York Press, pp. 275–306.

Haizlip, S. T. 1994. *the sweeter the juice: A Family Memoir in Black and White.* New York: Touchstone.

Hale-Benson, J. 1986. *Black Children: Their Roots, Culture, and Learning Styles* (rev. ed.). Provo, UT: Brigham Young University Press.

Hall, D. R., and Zhao, J. 1995. "Cohabitation and Divorce in Canada: Testing the Selectivity Hypothesis." *Journal of Marriage and the Family* 57 (May):421–27.

Hall, P. M. (Ed.). 1997. *Race, Ethnicity, and Multiculturalism: Policy and Practice.* New York: Garland.

Hamburg, D. A. 1992. *Today's Children: Creating a Future for a Generation in Crisis.* New York: Time Books.

Hamburg, G. V. 1998. "A Quest for Justice." *Chicago Tribune* (May 24) 13:3.

Harris, D. 1996. "How Does Your Pay Stack Up?" *Working Women* (February):23–25.

Hart, N. 1991. "The Social and Economic Environment and Human Health." In W. Holland, R. Detels, and G. Knox (eds.), *Oxford Textbook of Public Health.* Oxford, UK: Oxford University Press, pp. 151–180.

Hatfield, E., and Rapson, R. L. 1996. *Love and Sex: Cross-Cultural Perspectives.* Needham Heights, MA: Allyn & Bacon.

Haub, C., and Cornelius, D. 1997. *1997 World Population Data Sheet.* Washington, DC: Population Reference Bureau.

Hauser, P., and Schnore, L. (Eds). 1965. *The Study of Urbanization.* New York: Wiley.

Hayghe, H. V., and Bianchi, S. M. 1994. "Married Mothers' Work Patterns: The Job-Family Compromise." *Monthly Labor Review* (June):24–30.

Hearn, J., and Parkin, W. 1995. *"Sex" at "Work": The Power and Paradox of Organization Sexuality.* New York: St. Martin's Press.

Heaton, T. B. 1990. "Marital Stability throughout the Childrearing Years." *Demography* (February):55–63.

Henslin, J. M. 1997. "On Becoming Male: Reflections of a Sociologist on Childhood and Early Socialization." In J. M. Henslin (ed.), *Down to Earth Sociology* (9th ed.). New York: Free Press, pp. 130–140.

Herring, C., and Collins, S. 1995. "Retreat from Equal Opportunity? The Case of Affirmative Action." In M. P. Smith and J. R. Feagin (eds.), *The Bubbling Cauldron: Race, Ethnicity and the Urban Crisis.* Minneapolis, MN: University of Minnesota Press.

Herrnstein, R., and Murray, C. 1994. *The Bell Curve: Intelligence and Class Structure in American Life.* New York: Free Press.

Hersh, P. 1998. "Playing by the Rules." *Chicago Tribune* (June 14):Sec. 13, p. 1.

Hess, B. 1990. "Beyond Dichotomy: Drawing Distinctions and Embracing Differences." *Sociological Forum* 5, 1:75–93.

Hess, B. B., Markson, W., & Stein, P. J. 1996. *Sociology.* Boston: Allyn & Bacon.

Hetherington, E. M., and Clingempeel, W. G. (in collaboration with E. R. Anderson et al.). 1992. *Coping with Marital Transitions.* Chicago: University of Chicago Press, for the Society for Research in Child Development.

Higgenbotham, E., and Weber, L. 1992. "Moving with Kin and Community: Upward Social Mobility for Black and White Women." *Gender and Society* (September): pp. 416–440.

Hobbs, F. V. B. 1996. *65+ in the United States.* Washington, DC: U.S. Bureau of the Census.

Hochschild, A. 1989. *The Second Shift: Working Parents and the Revolution at Home.* New York: Viking.

Hodson, R., and Sullivan, T. A. 1995. *The Social Organization of Work* (2nd ed.). Belmont, CA: Wadsworth.

Hoge, W. 1998. "Equal Rights to English Throne: Firstborn Would Be First in Line." *New York Times* (February 28):A1.

Holden, C. 1996. "Small Refugees Suffer the Effects of Early Neglect." *Science* 27, 5290:1076–1077.

Holden, V. S., Holden, W., and Davis, G. 1997. "The Sports Team Controversy: A Study in Community and Race Relations." In S. Biagi and M. Kern-Foxworth, *Facing Difference: Race, Gender, and Mass Media.* Thousand Oaks, CA: Pine Forge.

Holland, B. 1996. "Anti-Rap Campaign to be Directed at 5 Major Record Labels." *Billboard* 108 (June 8):8.

Holson, L. M. 1998. "There's a Steady Rush to the Corporate Altar." *New York Times* (March 4):C1.

Hosokawa, W. K. 1969. *Nesei: The Quiet Americans.* New York: Morrow.

Hostetler, J. A. 1981. *Amish Society.* Baltimore: John Hopkins University Press.

Human Rights Campaign Fund. 1994. "Helms and Allies to Attack Non-Discrimination Clause in Health Reform Bill." [Online]. Available: http://grd.rdrop.com/q . . . lth.care.bill-08.08.94 [1999, March 5].

Humphreys, L. 1970a. "Tearoom Trade." *Transaction* (January):10–25.

Humphreys, L. 1970b. *Tearoom Trade: Impersonal Sex in Public Places.* Chicago: Aldine.

Humphreys, L. 1975. *Tearoom Trade: Impersonal Sex in Public Places* (enlarged ed.). Chicago: Aldine.

Hundley, T. 1997. "Always Poor, Albanians Going for Broke in Scam." *Chicago Trubune* (February 3):1.

Hunter, J. 1991. *Culture Wars: The Struggle to Define America.* New York: Basic Books.

Huntington, S. P. 1992/1993. "What Cost Freedom? Democracy and/or Economic Reform." *Harvard International Review* (Winter):8–13.

Hyde, J. S. 1984. "Children's Understanding of Sexist Language." *Developmental Psychology* 20, 4:697–706.

Iannaccone, L. R. 1994. "Why Strict Churches Are Strong." *American Journal of Sociology* (March):1180–1211.

Idler, E. L. and Kasl, S. V. 1992. "Religion, Disability, Depression, and the Timing of Death." *American Journal of Sociology* 97:1052–1079.

Ihinger-Tallman, M. and Pasley, K. 1994. "Building Bridges, Reflections on Theory, Research, and Practice." In K. Pasley and M. Ihinger-Tallman (eds.),

Stepparenting: Issues in Theory, Research and Practice. Westport, CT: Greenwood, pp. 239–250.

Impoco, J. 1995. "Separating Church and School." *U.S. News and World Report* (April 24):30.

International Anti-Euthanasia Task Force. 1997. [Online]. Available: http://www.iaetf.org/whatnow.htm.

International Labor Organization. 1993. *Condition of Work Digest: Preventing Stress at Work.* New York: Author.

International Labor Organization. 1995. "Women Work More, But Are Still Paid Less." (August 25). Press Release.

Jackson, D. Z. 1998. "Skimming the Surface: Media's Irresponsible Welfare Coverage." *New York Times* (May 5):15.

Jacobs, W. R. 1985. *Dispossessing the American Indian: Indians and Whites on the Colonial Frontier.* Norman, OK: University of Oklahoma Press.

Jagarowsky, P. A., and Bane, N. J. 1990. *Neighborhood Poverty: Basic Questions Discussion Paper Series H-90-3.* John F. Kennedy School of Government. Cambridge, MA: Harvard University Press.

James, D. 1989. "City Limits on Racial Equality." *American Sociological Review* 54:963–985.

James, F. 1997. "International Cyber-Swat Teams Planned to Fight Computer Crimes." *Chicago Tribune* (December 11):10.

Janis, I. L. 1972. *Victims of Groupthink.* Boston: Houghton Mifflin.

Janis, I. L. 1982. *Groupthink: Psychological Studies of Policy Decisions and Fiascoes.* Boston: Houghton Mifflin.

Janszen, K. 1981. "Meat of Life." In Ian Robertson (ed.), *The Social World.* New York: Worth, pp. 366–371.

Janus, S. S., and Janus, C. L. 1993. *The Janus Report on Sexual Behavior.* New York: John Wiley & Sons.

Jaret, C. 1995. *Contemporary Racial and Ethnic Relations.* New York: HarperCollins.

John, D., Shelton, B. A., and Luschen, K. 1995. "Race, Ethnicity, Gender, and Perceptions of Fairness." *Journal of Family Issues* (May):357–379.

Johnson, M. P. 1995. "Patriarchal Terrorism and Common Couple Violence: Two Forms of Violence Against Women." *Journal of Marriage and the Family* 57: 283–294.

Jones, M. D. 1997. "Darkness Made Visible: Law, Metaphor, and the Racial Self." In R. Delgado and J. Stefancic (eds.), *Critical White Studies: Looking behind the Mirror.* Philadelphia: Temple University Press, pp. 65–78.

Judge, T. A. 1993. "Validity of the Dimensions of the Pay Satisfaction Questionnaire: Evidence of Differential Prediction." *Personnel Psychology* 46:331–355.

Juergensmeyer, M. 1993. *The New Cold War? Religious Nationalism Confronts the Secular State.* Berkeley: University of California Press.

Kagan, J., Resnick, J. S., and Snidman, N. 1988. "Biological Bases of Childhood Shyness." *Science* (April 1):167–71.

Kahn, K., Pearson, M., and Harrison, E. 1994. "Health Care for Black and Poor Hospitalized Medicare Patients." *Journal of the American Medical Association* 271: 1169–1174.

Kanamine, L. 1992. "Amid Crushing Poverty, Glimmers of Hope." *USA Today* (November 30):A7.

Kanter, R. M. 1977. *Men and Women of the Corporation.* New York: Basic Books.

Kantrowitz, B., and Wingert, P. "A New Era of Segregation." *Newsweek* (December 27):44.

Kapferer, J. 1992. "How Rumors Are Born." *Society* (July/August):53–60.

Kaplan, H. B. 1989. "Health, Disease, and the Social Structure." In H. Freeman and S. Levine (eds.). *Handbook of Medical Sociology.* Englewood Cliffs, NJ: Prentice Hall, pp. 46–68.

Karmen, A. 1994. "Defining Deviancy Down: How Senator Moynihan's Misleading Prase about Criminal Justice Is Rapidly Being Incorporated into Popular Culture." *Journal of Criminal Justice and Popular Culture* (October 15):99–127.

Keith, V. M., and Finlay, B. 1988. "The Impact of Parental Divorce on Children's Educational Attainment, Marital Timing, and Likelihood of Divorce." *Journal of Marriage and the Family* 50:797–809.

Kelley, P. 1995. *Developing Healthy Stepfamilies: Twenty Families Tell Their Stories.* New York: Haworth.

Kelly, G. F. 1994. *Sexuality Today: The Human Experience* (4th ed.). Guilford, CT: Dushkin.

Kemp, A. A. 1990. "Estimating Sex Discrimination in Professional Occupations with the *Dictionary of Occupational Titles.*" *Sociological Spectrum* 10, 3:387–411.

Kendall, D. 1997. *Race, Class, and Gender in a Diverse Society.* Boston: Allyn and Bacon.

Kendall, D. 1998. *Social Problems in a Diverse Society.* Boston: Allyn & Bacon.

Kerblay, B. 1983. *Modern Soviet Society.* New York: Pantheon.

Kerbo, H. R. 1993. *Social Stratification and Inequality.* New York: McGraw-Hill.

Kilborn, P. T. 1998. "Health Gap Grows, with Black Americans Trailing Whites, Studies Say." *New York Times* (January 26):A16.

Kim, E. 1993. "Home Is Where the Ham Is: Korean American Perspective on the Los Angeles Upheavals." In Robert Gooding-Williams (ed.), *Reading Rodney King: Reading Urban Uprising.* New York: Routledge, pp. 215–235.

Kimmel, M. 1990. *Revolution: A Sociological Interpretation.* Philadelphia: Temple University Press.

Kinder, D. R., and Sears, D. O. 1981. "Symbolic Racism versus Racial Threats to the Good Life." *Journal of Personality and Social Psychology* 40:414–431.

Kinsey, A., Pomeroy, W., and Martin, C. 1948. *Sexual Behavior in the Human Male.* Philadelphia: Saunders.

Kinsey, A., Pomeroy, W., Martin, C., and Gebhard, P. 1953. *Sexual Behavior in the Human Female.* Philadelphia: Saunders.

Kirk, G., and Okazawa-Rey, M. 1998. *Women's Lives: Multicultural Perspectives.* Mountain View, CA: Mayfield.

Kitt, J. F. 1984. *Rites of Passage: Adolescence in America, 1790 to the Present.* New York: Basic Books.

Klag, M., Whelton, P. K., Coresh, J., Grim, C. E., and Kuller, L. H. 1991. "The Association of Skin Color with Blood Pressure in U.S. Blacks with Low Socioeconomic Status." *Journal of the American Medical Association* 265:599–640.

Klare, M. T. 1997. "Redefining Security: The New Global Schisms." In Robert M. Jackson (ed.), *Annual Editions: Global Issues 97/98.* Guilford, CT: Dushkin/McGraw-Hill, pp. 25–30.

Kleiman, C. 1991. "Then and Now, Sexual Harassment Widespread." *Chicago Tribune* (December 9):sec. 4, 3.

Kleiman, C. 1997. "Voice of Unions Now Has the Pitch of Women Workers." *Chicago Tribune* (May 6):sec. 3, p. 3.

Kluckholm, C. 1999. "Mirror for Man: The Relation of Anthropology to Modern Life." In Kurt Finsterbusch (ed.), *Sources: Notable Selections in Sociology.* Guilford, CT: Dushkin/McGraw-Hill, pp. 15–20.

Kluegel, J. R. 1990. "Trends in Whites' Explanation of the Black–White Gap in Socioeconomic Status, 1977–1989." *American Sociological Review* 55:512–525.

Knapp, P. 1994. *One World—Many Worlds: Contemporary Sociological Theory.* New York: Harper-Collins.

Knoke, D. 1990. *Political Networks: The Structural Perspective.* New York: Cambridge University Press.

Koenig, H. G. 1994. *Aging and God.* Binghamton, NY: Haworth.

Koenig, H. G. 1997. *Is Religion Good for Your Health? The Effects of Religion on Physical and Mental Health.* New York: Haworth Pastoral Press.

Kohlberg, L. 1969. "Stages and Sequence: The Cognitive-Developmental Approach to Socialization." In D. A. Goslin (ed.), *Handbook of Socialization Theory and Research.* Chicago: Rand McNally, pp. 347–480.

Kohlberg, L. 1981. *The Philosophy of Moral Development: Moral Stages and the Idea of Justice.* Vol. 1: *Essays on Moral Development.* San Francisco: Harper and Row.

Kohn, A. 1988. "You Know What They Say . . ." *Psychology Today* (April):36–41.

Kohn, M. L. 1959. "Social Class and Parental Values." *American Journal of Sociology* 64:337–351.

Kohn, M. L. 1977. *Social Competence, Symptoms and Underachievement in Childhood: A Longitudinal Perspective.* Washington, DC: Winston.

Kohn, M. L. 1990. *Social Structure and Self-Direction.* Cambridge, MA: Basil Blackwell.

Kohn, M. L., Naoi, A., Schoenbach, C., Schooler, C., and Slomczynski, K. M. 1990. "Position in the Class Structure and Psychologocial Functioning in the United States, Japan, and Poland." *American Journal of Sociology* 95:964–1008.

Kohn, M. L., and Schooler, C. 1969. "Class, Occupation, and Orientation." *American Sociological Review* 34:659–678.

Kolata, G. 1993. "Family Aid to Elderly Is Very Strong, Study Shows." *New York Times* (May 3):A16.

Kottak, C. 1994. *Cultural Anthropology.* (6th ed). New York: McGraw-Hill.

Kozol, J. 1991. *Savage Inequalities.* New York: Crown.

Kramer, L. (Ed.). 1991. *The Sociology of Gender: A Text-Reader.* New York: St. Martin's.

Kraus, L. A., Davis, M. H., Bazzini, D., Church, M., and Kirchman, C. M. 1993. "Personal and Social Influences on Loneliness: The Mediating Effect of Social Provisions." *Social Psychology Quarterly* 56, 1:37–53.

Krause, N. 1995. "Religiosity and Self-Esteem among Older Adults." *Journal of Gerontology* 50: P236–246.

Kristof, N. 1995a. "Japan Confronting Gruesome War Atrocity." *New York Times* (March 17):A1, A4.

Kristof, N. 1995b. "Japan's Schools: Safe, Clean, Not Much Fun." *New York Times* (July 18):A1, A4.

Kristof, N. 1995c. "Japanese Outcasts Better Off Than in Past but Still Outcast." *New York Times* (November 30):A1.

Kristof, N. 1996. "Aging World, New Wrinkles." *New York Times* (February 27):C1, C3.

Kristof, N. 1997a. "Japanese Parents Wonder Who Will Look after Them." *The Globe and Mail* (August 14):A10.

Kristof, N. 1997b. "For Third World, Water Is Still a Deadly Drink." *New York Times* (January 9):A1, A6.

Kristof, N. 1998. "Casanovas, Beware! It's Risky for Non-Koreans." *The New York Times* (February 2):A4

Kuhn, T. 1962. *The Structure of Scientific Revolutions.* Chicago: University of Chicago Press.

Kurdek, L. 1988. "Correlates of Negative Attitudes toward Homosexuals in Heterosexual College Students." *Sex Roles* 18:727–738.

Lacayo, R. 1998. "The Jonesboro Shootings: Toward the Root of the Evil." *Time Magazine* (April 6): pp. 38–39.

Lapham, S. 1995. "Census Bureau Finds Significant Differences Among Immigrant Groups." In John A. Kromkowski (ed.), *Race and Ethnic Relations.* Guilford, CT: Dushkin, pp. 55–59.

Lauer, R. H. 1991. *Perspectives on Social Change* (4th ed.). Boston: Allyn and Bacon.

Laumann, E. O., Gagnon, J. H., Michael, R. T., and Michaels, S. 1994. *The Social Organization of Sexuality: Sexual Practices in the United States.* Chicago: University of Chicago Press.

Lawrence, J. 1997. "Political Battlegrounds of the Future." *USA Today.* (August 8), p. 6A.

Laws, J. L., and Schwartz, P. 1977. *Sexual Scripts.* Washington, DC: Dryden Press.

Le Bon, G. 1960. *The Crowd: A Study of the Popular Mind.* New York: Viking (original publication 1895).

Lee, S. M. 1998. *Population Bulletin: Asian Americans: Diverse and Growing* 53, no. 2. Washington, DC: Population Reference Bureau.

Lee, S. M., and Yamanaka, K. 1990. "Patterns of Asian American Intermarriage and Marital Assimilation." *Journal of Comparative Family Studies,* 21, 2 (Summer): pp. 287–305.

Lehrer, E. L., and Chiswick, C. U. 1993. "Religion as a Determinant of Marital Stability." *Demography* (August):385–404.

Lemert, C. (Ed.). 1993. *Social Theory: The Multicultural and Classic Readings.* San Francisco: Westview.

Lemert, E. 1951. *Social Pathology.* New York: McGraw Hill.

Lengermann, P. M., and Brantley, J. N. 1988. "Feminist Theory." In G. Ritzer (ed.), *Sociological Theory.* New York: Knopf, pp. 400–443.

Lengermann, P. M., and Niebrugge-Brantley, J. 1996. "Contemporary Feminist Theory." In G. Ritzer (ed.), *Modern Sociological Theory* (4th ed.). New York: McGraw-Hill, pp. 299–350.

Lennon, M. C., and Rosenfield, S. 1994. "Relative Fairness and the Division of Housework: The Importance of Options.' *American Journal of Sociology* (September):506–531.

Lenski, G. 1966. *Power and Privilege.* New York: McGraw-Hill.

Lenski, G., Nolan, P., and Lenski, J. 1995. *Human Societies: An Introduction to Macrosociology* (7th ed.). New York: McGraw-Hill.

Leo, J. 1995. "The Modern Primitives." *US News and World Report* (July 31):16.

Leonard, J. S. 1991. "The Federal Anti-Bias Effort." In E. P. Hoffman (ed.), *Essays on the Economics of Discrimination.* Kalamazoo, MI: W.E. Upjohn Institute for Employment Research, pp. 85–113.

Lev, M. A. 1998. "Japan Worries as Women Turn from Marriage." *Chicago Tribune* (March 30):1, 9.

Levin, J. S., Chatters, L. M., and Taylor, R. J. 1995. "Religious Effects on Health Status and Life Satisfaction Among Black Americans." *Journal of Gerontology* 50B:S154–163.

Levin, J. S., Markides, K. S., and Ray, L. A. 1996. "Religious Attendance and Psychological Well-Being in Mexican Americans: A Panel Analysis of Three-Generation Data." *The Gerontologist* 36 (August): 454–63.

Levinson, D. J. 1978. *The Seasons of a Man's Life.* New York: Knopf.

Levinson, D. 1981. "Physical Punishment of Children and Wife Beating in Cross-Cultural Perspective." *Child Abuse and Neglect* 5,4:93–96.

Levy, J. A. 1994. "The Hospice in the Context of an Aging Society." In H. D. Schwartz (ed.), *Dominant Issues in Medical Sociology* (3rd ed.). New York: McGraw-Hill, pp. 351–361.

Lewin, T. 1995. "In Home Schooling, a New Type of Student." *New York Times* (November 29):B8.

Lewin, T. 1998a. "American Colleges Begin to Ask, Where Have All the Men Gone?" *New York Times* (December 6):1, 28.

Lewin, T. 1998b. "All Girl-Schools Questioned as a Way to Attain Equity." *New York Times* (March 12):A12.

Lewin, T. 1998c. "Men Assuming Bigger Share at Home, New Survey Shows." *New York Times* (April 15):A16.

Lewis, O. 1966. "The Culture of Poverty." *Scientific American* 215 (October):19–25.

Libby, R. 1990. "Review of Sex and Morality in the U.S." *SIECUS Report* 18(5):14–15.

Lim, L. L. 1996. *More and Better Jobs for Women: An Action Guide.* Geneva: International Labor Organization.

Lin, N., and Xie, W. 1988. "Occupational Prestige in Urban China." *American Journal of Sociology* 93:793–833.

Lindsey, L. 1994. *Gender Roles: A Sociological Perspective* (2nd ed.). Englewood Cliffs, NJ: Prentice Hall.

Lindsey, L. L. 1997. *Gender Roles: A Sociological Perspective* (3rd ed.). Upper Saddle River, NJ: Prentice Hall.

Linton, R. 1937. "One Hundred Percent American." *The American Mercury* (April):427–429.

Lips, H. M. 1993. *Sex and Gender: An Introduction.* Mountain View, CA: Mayfield.

Litt, R. S. 1997. Statement Presented to the Subcommittee on Social Security, Senate Ways and Means Committee.

United States Senate. Washington, DC (May 6):2. http://www.usdoj.gov/criminal/cybercrime/sensocsctes.htm.

Lofland, J. 1985. *Protest: Studies of Collective Behavior and Social Movements*. New Brunswick, NJ: Transaction.

Lohr, S. 1998. "Rivals Say Unfair Practices Smother Competition." *New York Times* (March 4): A1.

Longworth, R. C. 1998. "America's Embrace Feels, to Some, Like a Fatal Squeeze." *Chicago Tribune* (August 30):sec. 2, p. 1.

Lopata, H. Z. 1973. *Widowhood in an American City*. Cambridge, MA: Schenkman.

Lott, B. 1994. *Women's Lives: Themes and Variations in Gender Learning* (2nd ed.). Pacific Grove, CA: Brooks/Cole.

Lowery, C. D., and Marszalek, J. F. (Eds.). 1992. *Encyclopedia of African American Civil Rights: From Emancipation to the Present*. New York: Greenwood.

Lund, K. 1990. "A Feminist Perspective and Divorce Therapy for Women." *Journal of Divorce* 13,3:57–67.

Lurie, N., Slater, J., McGovern, P., Ekstrum, J., Quam, L., & Margolis, K. 1993. "Preventive Care for Women: Does the Sex of the Physician Make a Difference?" *New England Journal of Medicine* 329:478–482.

MacDonald, K., and Park, R. D. 1986. "Parent-Child Physical Play: The Effects of Sex and Age on Children and Parents." *Sex Roles* 15:367–378.

MacFarquhar, N. 1996. "With Mixed Feelings, Iran Tiptoes to Internet." *New York Times* (October 8):A4.

MacKinnon, C. 1983. "Feminism, Marxism, Method, and the State: Toward Feminist Jurisprudence." *Signs* (Summer):635–658.

Madsen, D., and Snow, P. G.. 1983. "The Dispersion of Charisma." *Comparative Political Systems* 16:337–362.

"Maggie Kuhn, One of the Founders of Gray Panthers." 1995. *Chicago Tribune* (April 23):6.

Maines, J. 1993. "Long-Distance Romances." *American Demographics* (May):47.

Majors, R. 1995. "Cool Pose: The Proud Signature of Black Survival." In M. S. Kimmel and M. A. Messner (eds.), *Men's Lives*. Boston: Allyn and Bacon, pp. 82–85.

Malinowski, B. 1929. *The Sexual Life of Savages in Northwestern Melanesia*. New York: Harvest.

Mandela, N. 1994. *Long Walk to Freedom*. New York: Little, Brown.

Manning, P. 1992. *Erving Goffman and Modern Sociology*. Stanford, CA: Stanford University Press.

Marger, M. N. 1985. *Race and Ethnic Relations: American and Global Perspectives*. Belmont, CA: Wadsworth.

Marger, M. N. 1994. *Race and Ethnic Relations: American and Global Perspectives* (3rd ed.). Belmont, CA: Wadsworth.

Marriott, S. S. 1994. "Violence and Its Impact on Women." *Vital Sign* 10(2):6.

Marsiglio, W., and Scanzoni, J. 1995. *Families and Friendships: Applying the Sociological Imagination*. New York: HarperCollins.

Marshall, D. 1971. "Sexual Behavior on Mangaia." In Donald Marshall and Robert Suggs (eds.), *Human Sexual Behavior*. New York: Basic Books.

Martin, J. R. 1997. "A Philosophy of Education for the Year 2000." In Fred Schultz (ed.), *Education: Annual Editions 97/98*. Guilford, CT: Dushkin/McGraw-Hill, pp. 261–264.

Martin, M. K., and Voorhies, B. 1975. *Female of the Species*. New York: Columbia University Press.

Martin, T. C., and Bumpass, L. L. 1989. "Recent Trends in Marital Disruption." *Demography* 26:37–52.

Martineau, H. 1837. *Society in America*. Paris: Bandry's European Library.

Martineau, H. 1838. *How to Observe Manners and Morals*. London: C. Knight.

Martinez, G. A. 1997. "Mexican-Americans and Whiteness." In R. Delgado and J. Stefancic (eds.), *Critical White Studies: Looking behind the Mirror*. Philadelphia: Temple University Press, pp. 210–213.

Marx, G. T., and McAdam, D. 1994. *Collective Behavior and Social Movements: Process and Structure*. Englewood Cliffs, NJ: Prentice Hall.

Marx, K. 1958. *The Economic and Philosophic Manuscripts of 1844*. M. Milligan (trans). Moscow: International Publishers (original publication 1844).

Marx, K. 1964. *Karl Marx: Selected Writings in Sociology and Social Philosophy*. T. B. Bottomore (trans.). New York: McGraw Hill.

Marx, K. 1967. *Capital*. (Edited by Frederick Engels.) Unabridged. Samuel Moore and Edward Aveling (trans.). Vol. I. (original publication 1867).

Masters, W. H., and Johnson, V. E. 1966. *Human Sexual Response*. Boston: Little, Brown.

Masters, W. H., and Johnson, V. E. 1970. *Human Sexual Inadequacy*. Boston: Little, Brown.

Maugh, T. 1990. "Sex: American Style Trend to the Traditional." *Los Angeles Times* (February 18):A1,A22.

Mauldin, T. A., and Meeks, C. B. 1990. "Sex Differences in Children's Time Use." *Sex Roles* 22, 9/10:537–554.

Maybury-Lewis, D. 1997. "Tribal Wisdom." In Richard T. Schaefer and Robert P. Lamm (eds.), *Annual Editions to Accompany Sociology, Sixth Edition*. Guilford, CT: Dushkin/McGraw-Hill, pp. 1–5.

Maynard, R. A. (Ed.). 1997. *Kids Having Kids: Economic Costs and Social Consequences of Teen Pregnancy*. Washington, DC: The Urban Institute Press.

McAdam, D., McCarthy, J. D., and Zald, M. N. 1988. "Social Movements." In N. J. Smelser (ed.), *Handbook of Sociology*. Newbury Park, CA: Sage, pp. 695–737.

McAdoo, J. L., and McAdoo, J. B. 1995. "The African-American Father's Roles within the Family." In M. S. Kimmel and M. A. Messner (eds.), *Men's Lives* (3rd ed.). Boston: Allyn and Bacon, pp. 485–494.

McArdle, T. 1994. "Do Kids Learn More at Home?" *Investor's Business Daily* (March 14):1,2.

McAuliffe, D. 1996. "For Many Indian Tribes, the Buffalo Are Back." *Washington Post National Weekly Edition*, 13 (March 24), pp. 8–9.

McClary, S. 1990. "Living to Tell: Madonna's Resurrection of the Fleshy." *Genders* (Spring):2.

McClelland, K., and Auster, C. 1990. "Public Platitudes and Hidden Tensions: Racial Climates at Predominantly White Liberal Arts Colleges." *Journal of Higher Education* 61:607–642.

McIntosh, P. 1998. "White Privilege and Male Privilege: A Personal Account of Coming to See Correspondences through Work in Women's Studies." In M. Anderson and P. H. Collins (eds.), *Race, Class, and Gender*. Belmont, CA: Wadsworth, pp. 94–105.

McIntyre, L. D., and Pernell, E. 1985. "The Impact of Race on Teacher Recommendations for Special Education Placement." *Journal of Multicultural Counseling and Development* 13:112–120.

McKinley, J. C. Jr., 1996. "In Peace, Warrior Women Rank Low." *The New York Times* (May 4):4.

McLanahan, S. 1994. "The Consequences of Single Motherhood." *The American Prospect* (Summer):48–58.

McLanahan, S., and Sandefur, G. 1994. *Growing Up with a Single Parent: What Hurts, What Helps*. Cambridge, MA: Harvard University Press.

McPhail, C. 1991. *The Myth of the Maddening Crowd*. New York: Aldine.

McQuire, M. B. 1992. *Religion: The Social Context* (3rd ed.). Belmont, CA: Wadsworth.

Mead, G. H. 1934. *Mind, Self, and Society*. Chicago: University of Chicago.

Mead, G. H. 1962. *Mind, Self and Society*. Ed. Charles W. Morris. Chicago: University of Chicago Press (original publication 1934).

Mead, M. 1963. *Sex and Temperament in Three Primitive Societies*. New York: Morrow (original publication 1935).

Medved, M. 1992. *Hollywood vs. America: Popular Culture and the War on Traditional Values*. New York: HarperCollins.

Meer, F. 1990. *Higher than Hope: The Authorized Biography of Nelson Mandela*. New York: Harper and Row.

Mental Health Issue of the Month. (1999). "Sexual Assault —What You Need to Know." [Online]. Available: http://www.clarke.edu/ . . . es/sexual_assault_.html [1999, January 30].

Merton, R. 1957. *Social Theory and Social Structure* (2nd ed.). New York: Free Press.

Merton, R. 1968. *Social Theory and Social Structure* (enlarged ed.). Glencoe, IL: Free Press (original publication 1949).

Meyers, H. F. 1991. "His Statues Topple, His Shadow Persists: Marx Can't Be Ignored," *Wall Street Journal* (November 25): A1, 10.

Michels, R. 1966. *Political Parties*. New York: Free Press (original publication 1911).

Mickelson, R. A., and Smith, S. S. 1997. "Education and the Struggle Against Race, Class, and Gender Inequality." In Estelle Disch (ed.), *Reconstructing Gender: A Multicultural Anthology*. Mountain View, CA: Mayfield, pp. 303–317.

Milgram, S. 1974. *Obedience to Authority*. New York: Harper & Row.

Millman, M. 1977. *The Unkindest Cut*. New York: Morrow.

Mills, C. W. 1956. *The Power Elite*. New York: Oxford University Press.

Mills, C. W. 1959. *The Sociological Imagination*. New York: Oxford University Press.

Mindel, C. H., Habenstein, R. W., and Wright, R., Jr. (Eds.). 1988. *Ethnic Families in America: Patterns and Variations*. New York: Elsevier.

Mintz, S., and Kellogg, S. 1988. *Domestic Revolution: A Social History of American Family Life*. New York: Free Press.

Moen, P., Dempster-McClain, D., and Williams, R. 1989. "Social Integration and Longevity: An Event-History Analysis of Women's Roles and Resilience." *American Sociological Review* 54:635–647.

Mohr, N. 1997. "A Time with a Future." In E. P. Stoller and R. C. Gibson. *Worlds of Differences*. Thousand Oaks, CA: Pine Forge Press, pp. 306–314.

Molotsky, I. 1988. "New and Old School Chief Differ on Issues and Styles." *New York Times* (September 22), p. A22.

Money, J. 1991. "Semen-Conversion Theory vs. Semen-Investment Theory, Antisexualism, and the Return of Freud's Seduction Theory." *Journal of Psychology and Human Sexuality* 4(4):31–45.

Moody, H. R. 1998. *Aging: Concepts and Controversies* (2nd ed.). Thousand Oaks, CA: Pine Forge Press..

Moore, K. A., Morrison, D. R., and Greene, A. D. 1997. "Effects on the Children Born to Adolescent Mothers." In R. A. Maynard (ed.), *Kids Having Kids: Economic Costs and Social Consequences of Teen Pregnancy*. Washington, DC: The Urban Institute Press, pp. 146–180.

Moore, R. B. 1993. "Racism in the English Language." In V. Cyrus (ed.), *Experiencing Race, Class, and Gender in the United States*. Mountain View, CA: Mayfield, pp. 152–159.

Moorhead, G., Ference, R., and Neck, C. 1991. "Group Decision Fiascoes Continue: Space Shuttle *Challenger* and a Revised Groupthink Framework." *Human Relations* 44:539–550.

Morgan, L. 1990. "The Multiple Consequences of Divorce: A Decade Review." *Journal of Marriage and the Family* 52:913–924.

Morgan, L. H. 1877. *Ancient Society*. Chicago: H. Kerr.

Moynihan, D. P. 1993. "Defining Deviancy Down." *The American Scholar* 62, 1:17–30.

Munson, B. 1997. "Common Themes and Questions about the Use of 'Indian' Logos." [Online]. Available: http://www.lwchildren.org/barb/html [1998, April 8].

Murdock, G. 1949. *Social Structure*. New York: Macmillan.

Murray, C. 1984. *Losing Ground: American Social Policy, 1950–1980*. New York: Basic Books.

Musto, D. F. 1997. "Opium, Cocaine and Marijuana in American History." In L. M. Salinger (ed.), *Deviant Behavior 97/98*. Guilford, CT: Dushkin, pp. 152–157.

Mydans, S. 1995. "Should Dying Patients Be Told? Ethnic Pitfall Is Found." *New York Times* (September 13):A13.

Myers, D. G. 1993. *The Pursuit of Happiness*. New York: Avon.

Nakao, K., and Treas, J. 1990. "Occupational Prestige in the United States Revisited: Twenty-Five Years of Stability and Change." Paper presented at the annual meetings of the American Sociological Association.

Nakonezny, P. A., Shull, R. D., and Rodgers, J. L. 1995. "The Effect of No-Fault Divorce Laws on the Divorce Rate across the 50 States and Its Relation to Income,

Education, and Religiosity." *Journal of Marriage and the Family* (May):477–488.

Nanda, S. 1990. *Neither Man nor Woman: The Hijras of India.* Belmont, CA: Wadsworth.

Naoi, A., and Schooler, C. 1985. "Occupational Conditions and Psychological Functioning in Japan." *American Journal of Sociology* 90:729–52.

Nash, M. 1962. "Race and the Ideology of Race." *Current Anthropology* (June):285–288.

National Center for Health Statistics. 1993. *Morbidity and Mortality Weekly Report* 23, 20. Washington, DC: U.S. Government Printing Office.

National Center for Health Statistics. 1996. "Births, Marriages, Divorces, and Deaths, November, 1995." *Monthly Vital Statistics Report* (May):11.

National Coalition Against Domestic Violence. 1996. [Online]. Available: http://www.medpatients . . . %20Resources/NCADV.html.

Neal, A. G., Groad, H. T., and Wicks, J. W. 1989. "Attitudes about Having Children: A Study of 600 Couples in the Early Years of Marriage." *Journal of Marriage and the Family* 59:313–328.

Nechas, E., and Foley, D. 1994. *Unequal Treatment.* New York: Simon & Schuster.

Neikirk, W. 1998. "Clinton Asks $21 Billion for Child-Care Package." *Chicago Tribune* (January 8):1.

Nemeth, C. J. 1985. "Dissent, Group Process, and Creativity: The Contribution of Minority Influence." *Advances in Group Processes* 2:57–75.

Newman, D. M. 1995. *Sociology: Exploring the Architecture of Everyday Life.* Thousand Oaks, CA: Pine Forge Press.

Niebuhr, G. 1998. "Laws Aside, Some in Clergy Quietly Bless Gay 'Marriage.' " *New York Times* (April 17): A1.

Norman, M. 1998. "Feminists Nurture a More Tolerant Christianity." *New York Times* (April 11):A13.

Norton, A. J., and Miller, L. F. 1992. "Marriage, Divorce, and Remarriage in the 1990s." U.S. Bureau of the Census, *Current Population Reports,* P23–180. Washington, DC: U.S. Government Printing Office.

Nyden, P., Figert, A., Shibley, M., & Burrows, D. 1997. *Building Community: Social Science in Action.* Thousand Oaks, CA: Pine Forge.

Oakes, J. 1985. *Keeping Track: How Schools Structure Inequality.* New Haven: Yale University Press.

Oberschall, A. 1973. *Social Conflict and Social Movements.* Englewood Cliffs, NJ: Prentice Hall.

O'Connor, B. P., and Vallerand, R. J. 1990. "Religious Motivation in the Elderly. A French-Canadian Replication and an Extension." *Journal of Social Psychology* 130:53–59.

O'Dea, T., and Aviada, J. O'D. 1983. *Sociology of Religion* (2nd ed.). Englewood Cliffs, NJ: Prentice Hall.

Ogburn, W. 1922. *Social Change.* New York: Huebsch.

Ohio Right to Life. 1995. [Online]. Available: http://www.infinet.com/~life/euth/amaltr.htm.

Oliver, D. 1955. *Solomon Island Society.* Cambridge, MA: Harvard University Press.

Olshansky, S. J., Carnes, B., Rogers, R. G., and Smith, L. 1997. "Infectious Diseases—New and Ancient Threats to World Health." *Population Bulletin* (July): Vol. 52, No. 2, pp. 1–52.

Omi, M., and Winant, H. 1986. *Racial Formation in the United States: From the 1960s to the 1980s.* New York: Routledge.

Orfield, G., Eaton, S. E., and the Harvard Project on School Desegregation. 1996. *Dismantling Desegregation: The Quiet Reversal of Brown v. Board of Education.* New York: New Press.

Ouellette, L. 1993. "The Information Lockout." *Utne Reader* (September–October):24–25.

Oxman, T. E., Freeman, D. H., and Manheimer, E. D. 1995. "Lack of Social Participation or Religious Strength and Comfort as Risk Factors for Death after Cardiac Surgery in the Elderly." *Psychosomatic Medicine* 57:5–15.

Packer, A. J. 1997. "Everything Your Kids Want to Know about Sex and Aren't Afraid to Ask." In S. J. Bunting (ed.), *Human Sexuality: Annual Editions.* Guilford, CT: Dushkin/McGraw-Hill, pp. 163–165.

Page, C. 1997. "Happily Ever After? Fix Marriages Before They Start." *Chicago Tribune* (August 20):19.

Page, C. 1998. "Armed Teachers and Other Suburban School Reforms, or . . ." *Chicago Tribune* (May 24):sec. 1, p. 21.

Pagelow, M. 1988. "Marital Rape." In V. B. Van Hasseit, R. L. Morrison, A. S. Bellack, and M. Hersen (eds.), *Handbook of Family Violence.* New York: Plenum, pp. 207–232.

Paludi, M. A. 1996. *Sexual Harassment on College Campuses: Abusing the Ivory Power.* Albany: State University of New York Press.

Papanek, H. 1973. "Men, Women, and Work: Reflections on the Two-Person Career." *American Journal of Sociology* (January):852–872.

Parenti, M. 1995. *Democracy for the Few* (6th ed.). New York: St. Martin's Press.

Parenti, M. 1998. "The Super Rich." *Z Magazine.* [Online]. Available: http://www.lbbs.org/zm . . . icles/Parentimar98.html [February 14].

Parillo, V. N. 1994. *Strangers to These Shores: Race and Ethnic Relations in the United States.* New York: MacMillan.

Parkinson, C. N. 1957. *Parkinson's Law and Other Studies in Administration.* New York: Ballantine.

Parsons, T. 1951. *The Social System.* Glencoe, IL: Free Press.

Parsons, T. 1964. *The Social System* (Free Press paperback edition). New York: Free Press.

Parsons, T., and Shils, E. (Eds.). 1951. *Toward a General Theory of Social Action.* Cambridge, MA: Harvard University Press.

Pear, R. 1995. "No Cash for Unwed Mothers, G.O.P. Affirms." *New York Times* (January 21):9.

Pear, R. 1998. "Americans Lacking Health Insurance Put at 16 Percent." *The New York Times* (September 26): A1.

Pearlin, L. I., and Kohn, M. L. 1966. "Social Class, Occupation, and Parental Values: A Cross-National Study." *American Sociological Review* 31:466–479.

Peart, K. N. 1993. "Converts to the Faith." *Scholastic Update* (October 22):16–18.

"Pentagon Survey Finds Sexual Harassment Rife." 1996. *Willmington News Journal* (June 16):11A.

Perry-Jenkins, M., and Crouter, A. C. 1990. "Men's Provider Role Attitudes: Implications for Household Work and Marital Satisfaction." *Journal of Family Issues* 11:136–156.

Pessar, P. R. 1995. *A Visa for A Dream: Dominicans in the United States.* Boston: Allyn and Bacon.

Peter, L. J., and Hull, R. 1969. *The Peter Principle: Why Things Always Go Wrong.* New York: William Morrow.

Peterson, G. W., and Rollins, B. C. 1987. "Parent–Child Socialization." In M. B. Sussman and S. K. Steinmetz (eds.), *Handbook of Marriage and the Family.* NY: Plenum.

Peterson, R. R. 1996. "A Re-Evaluation of the Economic Consequences of Divorce." *American Sociological Review* 61:528–536.

Pettigrew, T. 1981. "The Mental Health Impact." In B. Bowser and R. Hunt (eds.), *Impacts of Racism on White Americans.* Beverly Hills, CA: Sage, p. 117.

Pettigrew, T. F. 1985. "New Black–White Patterns: How Best to Conceptualize Them." In R. H. Turner and J. F. Short (eds.), *Annual Review of Sociology* (vol. 2). Palo Alto, CA: Annual Review, pp. 329–346.

Piaget, J. 1954. *The Construction of Reality in the Child.* New York: Basic Books.

Pillard, R. C. 1990. "The Kinsey Scale: Is it Familial?" In D. P McWhirter et al. (eds.), *Homosexuality/Heterosexuality: Concepts of Sexual Orientation.* New York: Oxford University Press, pp. 88–100.

Piper, A. 1997. "Passing for White, Passing for Black." In R. Delgado and J. Stefancic (eds.), *Critical White Studies: Looking behind the Mirror.* Philadelphia: Temple University Press, pp. 425–431.

Pitts, M. B. 1994. "Where the Boys Are." *USA Weekend* (February 4–6):6.

Plotkin, M. J. 1994. *Tales of a Shaman's Apprentice.* New York: Penguin.

Polivka, A. E., and Nardone, T. 1989. "On the Definition of Contingent Work. *Monthly Labor Review* 112:9–16

Pomerleau, A., Bolduc, D., Makuit, G., and Cossette, L. 1990. "Pink or Blue: Environmental Stereotypes in the First Two Years of Life." *Sex Roles* 22, 5/6:359–367.

Population Reference Bureau. 1997. *1997 World Population Data Sheet.* Washington, DC: Author.

Porter, J. 1971. *Black Child, White Child.* Cambridge, MA: Harvard University Press.

Pratt, M. W., Pancer, M., and Hunsberger, B. 1990. "Reasoning about the Self and Relationships in Maturity: An Integrative Complexity Analysis of Individual Differences." *Journal of Personality and Social Psychology* 59, 3:575–581.

Prior, M. 1997. "Matrifocality, Power, and Gender Relations in Jamaica." In C. Brettell and C. Sargent (eds.), *Gender in Cross-Cultural Perspective.* Upper Saddle River, NJ: Prentice Hall, pp. 310–318.

Pruyser, P. 1977. "The Seamy Side of Current Religious Beliefs." *Bulletin of the Menninger Clinic* 41:329–348.

Puente, T. 1998. "On the Record." *Chicago Tribune* (February 22):sec. 2, p. 3.

Purcell, P., and Stewart, L. 1990. "Dick and Jane in 1989." *Sex Roles* 22:177–185.

Putnam, R. D. 1996. "The Strange Disappearance of Civic America." *The American Prospect* (Winter):34–48.

Pyke, K. D. 1994. "Women's Employment as Gift or Burden?" *Gender and Society* 8:73–91.

Quinney, R. 1980. *Class, State, and Crime* (2nd ed.). New York: Longman.

Radbill, S. 1930. "A History of Child Abuse and Infanticide." In C. H. Kempe and R. Helfer (eds.), *The Battered Child.* Chicago: University of Chicago Press, pp. 3–20.

Raffalli, M. 1994. "Why So Few Women Physicists?" *New York Times Supplement* (January): sec. 4A, pp. 26–28.

Raine, A. 1993. *The Psychopathology of Crime: Criminal Behavior as a Clinical Disorder.* New York: Academic Press.

Rathus, S. A., Nevid, J. S., and Fichner-Rathus, L. 1997. *Human Sexuality in a World of Diversity* (3rd ed.). Boston: Allyn & Bacon.

Reckless, W. 1967. *The Crime Problem.* New York: Meredith.

Reecer, M. 1996. "Children without Childhoods." *American Educator,* Special Reprint (Summer):2–9.

Reiman, J. 1998. *The Rich Get Richer and the Poor Get Prison: Ideology, Class, and Criminal Justice.* Boston: Allyn & Bacon.

Reinharz, S. 1993. *A Contextualized Chronology of Women's Sociological Work* (2nd ed). Waltham, MA: Brandeis University Women's Studies Program Working Papers Series (September).

Reiss, I. L. 1990. *An End to Shame: Shaping our Next Sexual Revolution.* Buffalo: Prometheus.

Renzetti, C. M. and Curran, D. J. 1992. *Women, Men and Society: The Sociology of Gender* (2nd ed.). Boston: Allyn & Bacon.

Renzetti, C. M., and Curran, D. J. 1998. *Living Sociology.* Boston: Allyn & Bacon.

Reskin, B., and Padavic, I. 1994. *Women and Men at Work.* Thousand Oaks, CA: Pine Forge Press.

Reynolds, L. 1997. "Sex Harassment Claims Surge." *HR Focus* (March): 8.

Reynolds, R., Rizzo, J., and Gonzales, M. 1987. "The Cost of Medical Professional Liability." *JAMA* 258:2543–2547.

Rheingold, H. L. 1969. "The Social and Socializing Infant." In D. H. Goslin (ed.), *Handbook of Socialization Theory and Research.* Chicago: Rand McNally, pp. 779–790.

Rhymes, J. A. 1995. "Hospice Care—Too Little, Too Late? *Journal of the American Geriatrics Society* 43, 5:553–562.

Rich, A. 1980. "Compulsory Heterosexuality and Lesbian Existence." *Signs* 5:631–660.

Ridgeway, C., and Walker, H. A. 1995. "Status Structures." In K. S. Cook, G. A. Fine, and J. S. House (eds.), *Sociological Perspectives on Social Psychology.* Boston: Allyn & Bacon.

Riessman, C. K. 1990. *Divorce Talk: Women and Men Make Sense of Personal Relationships.* New Brunswick, NJ: Rutgers University Press.

Ritzer, G. 1996. *Modern Sociological Theory.* New York: McGraw-Hill.

Ritzer, G. 1998. *The McDonaldization Thesis: Explorations and Extensions.* Newbury Park, CA: Sage.

Rivers, C., and Barnett, R. 1997. "Marriage at Odds with Men Solely in Charge." *Chicago Tribune* (October 6): sec. 1, p. 10.

Robbins, R. H. 1993. *Cultural Anthropology: A Problem-Based Approach*. Itasca, IL: F. E. Peacock.

Robinson, I., Ziss, K., Ganza, B., and Katz, S. 1991. "Twenty Years of the Sexual Revolution, 1965–1985: An Update" *Journal of Marriage and the Family* (February):216–220.

Roethlisberger, F. J., and Dickson, W. J. (with Wright, H. A.). 1961. *Management and the Worker*. Cambridge, MA: Harvard University Press (original publication 1939).

Rose, P. I. 1997. *They and We: Racial and Ethnic Relations in the United States*. New York: McGraw-Hill.

Rosenthal, R., and Jacobson, L. 1973. "The Pygmalion Effect Lives." *Psychology Today* 56–63.

Rosow, I. 1974. *Socialization to Old Age*. Berkeley: University of California Press.

Ross, C. 1987. "The Division of Labor at Home." *Social Forces* 65:816–833.

Rossi, P. H. 1989. *Down and Out in America: The Origins of Homelessness*. Chicago: University of Chicago Press.

Rossides, D. W. 1990. *Comparative Societies: Social Types and Their Interrelationships*. Englewood Cliffs, NJ: Prentice Hall.

Rossides, D. W. 1997. *Social Stratification: The Interplay of Class, Race, and Gender*. Upper Saddle River, NJ: Prentice-Hall.

Rothman, R. A. 1998. *Working: Sociological Perspectives* (2nd ed.). Upper Saddle River, New Jersey: Prentice Hall.

Roy, D. 1996. "Banana Time: Job Satisfaction and Informal Interaction." In C. J. Auster, *The Sociology of Work: Concepts and Cases*. Thousand Oaks, CA: Pine Forge Press, pp. 230–239.

Ruane, J., and Cerulo, K. 1997. *Second Thoughts: Seeing Conventional Wisdom through the Sociological Eye*. Thousand Oaks, CA: Pine Forge Press.

Rubin, L. B. 1990. *Erotic Wars: What Happened to the Sexual Revolution?* New York: HarperCollins.

Rubin, L. B. 1994. *Families on the Fault Line: America's Working Class Speaks about the Family, the Economy, Race, and Ethnicity*. New York: HarperCollins.

Rubinstein, R. P. 1994. *Dress Codes: Meanings and Messages in American Society*. Boulder, CO: Westview.

Rudwick, E. 1974. "W. E. B. Du Bois as Sociologist." In J. E. Blackwell and M. Janowitz (eds.), *Black Sociologists: Historical and Contemporary Perspectives*. Chicago: University of Chicago Press, pp. 25–55.

Russel, C. 1995. "Find the Missing Men." *American Demographics* (May):8.

Russell, D. 1982. *Rape in Marriage*. Riverside, NJ: Macmillan.

Russell, D. 1990. *Rape in Marriage* (rev. ed.). Bloomington, IN: Indiana University Press.

Russell, R., and Rus, V. (Eds.). 1991. *International Handbook of Participation in Organizations, Vol. 2, Ownership and Participation*. Oxford: Oxford University Press.

Ryan, T. 1993. "Indian Crusader Seeks to Halt Child Slavery." *Far Eastern Economic Review* (July 8):62.

Ryan, W. 1976. *Blaming the Victim* (rev. ed.). New York: Vintage.

Rymer, R. 1993. *Genie: An Abused Child's Flight from Silence*. New York: HarperCollins.

Sacks, O. 1989. *Seeing Voices: A Journey into the World of the Deaf*. Los Angeles: University of California Press.

Sadker, M., and Sadker, D. 1994a. *Failing at Fairness: How America's Schools Cheat Girls*. New York: Schribner's.

Sadker, M., and Sadker, D. 1994b. "What Schools Must Tell Girls: You're Smart, You Can Do It." *USA Weekend* (February 4–6):4–6.

Sagarin, E. 1975. *Deviants and Deviance*. New York: Praeger.

Salinger, L. M. (Ed.). 1997. *Deviant Behavior 1997/1998*. Guilford, CT: Dushkin.

Salopek, P. 1997. "Basically, We Are All the Same." *Chicago Tribune* (April 27): sec. 1, pp. 10–11.

Saltzman, J. 1996. "Why Ordinary Americans Like Daytime Talk Shows." *USA Today* (November):63.

Saluter, A. F. 1994. "Marital Status and Living Arrangements: March 1993." U.S. Bureau of the Census, *Current Population Reports*, Series P20–478. Washington, DC: U.S. Government Printing Office.

Sanday, P. 1981. *Female Power and Male Dominance: On the Sexual Origins of Inequality*. New York: Cambridge University Press.

Sapir, E. 1929. "The Status of Linguistics as a Science," *Language* 5:207–214.

Sapiro, V. 1994. *Women in American Society*. Palo Alto, CA: Mayfield.

Savells, J. 1997. "Social Change among the Amish." In J. M. Henslin (ed.), *Down to Earth Sociology: Introductory Readings* (9th ed.). New York: Free Press, pp. 474–482.

Sayle, M. 1982. "A Textbook Case of Aggression." *Far Eastern Economic Review* (August 20): pp. 36–38.

Scarce, R. 1993. "Confidential Sources." *The Progressive* 57 (October):38.

Scarce, R. 1994. "(No) Trial (But) Tribulations." *Journal of Contemporary Ethnography* (July):123–149.

Schaefer, R. T., and Lamm, R. P. 1998. *Sociology*. New York: McGraw-Hill.

Schaffer, J. 1996. "Report Sees Growing Gap Between Rich and Poor Nations." [Online]. Available: http://www.mtholyoke.e . . . ad/intrel/incomgap.html [November 8].

Schnarch, B. 1992. "Neither Man nor Woman: Berdache—A Case for Non-Dichotomous Gender Construction." *Anthropologica* 34(1): 105–121.

Schneider, L., and Silverman, A. 1997. *Global Sociology*. Boston: McGraw-Hill.

Schultz, D. P. 1964. *Panic Behavior*. New York: Random House.

Schultz, F. 1993. "Morality and Values in Education." In *Education: Annual Editions 97/98*. Guilford, CT: Dushkin, pp. 94–95.

Schultz, F. (Ed.). 1995. *Multicultural Education: Annual Editions 95/96*. Guilford, CT: Dushkin.

Schwartz, M. A., and Scott, B. M. 1997. *Marriages and Families: Diversity and Change*. Upper Saddle River, NJ: Prentice Hall.

Schwirian, K. P., and Mesch, G. S. 1993. "Embattled Neighborhoods: The Political Ecology of Neighborhood Change." In Ray Hutchison (ed.), *Research in Urban Sociology: Urban Society in Transition* 3:83–110.

Sciolino, E. 1996. "The Many Faces of Islamic Law." *The New York Times* (October 13):4.

Scott, B. M. 1988. "The Making of a Middle-Class Black Woman: A Socialization for Success." Ph.D. dis., Northwestern University. Evanston, IL.

Scott, K., and Schau, C. 1985. "Sex Equity and Sex Bias in Instructional Materials." In S. Klein (ed.), *Handbook for Achieving Sex Equity through Education.* Baltimore, MD: Johns Hopkins University Press, pp. 216–260.

Seager, J. (Ed.). 1997. *The State of the Women in the World Atlas* (2nd ed.). London: Penguin Reference.

Seeman, M. 1959. "On the Meaning of Alienation." *American Sociological Review* (December):783–791.

SERAPH Security Consulting and Training. 1997. "New Justice Department Report Shows Decreases Across the U.S. in Violent Crime Except Sexual Assault." [Online]. Available: http://www.seraph.net/news3.html [1999, January 30].

Seter, J. I. 1994. "U.S. Concerns: Bride Burnings, Infanticide." *U.S. News & World Report* (February 14):14.

Sewell, W. H., Jr. 1992. "A Theory of Structure: Duality, Agency, and Transformation." *American Journal of Sociology* 98:1–29.

Shapiro, B. 1995. "Corliss and Maggie." *The Nation* 260, 21 (May 29): 744.

Shapiro, J. 1993. *No Pity: People with Disabilities Forging a New Civil Rights Movement.* New York: Time.

Shaul, S., Dowling, P. J. U., and Laden, B. F. 1985. "Like Other Women: Perspectives of Mothers with Physical Disabilities." In M. J. Deegan and N. A. Brooks (eds.), *Women and Disability: The Double Handicap.* New Brunswick, NJ: Transaction, pp. 133–142.

Sheldon, W. H., Hartl, E. M., and McDermott, E. 1949. *Varieties of Delinquent Youth.* New York: Harper.

Shenon, P. 1997. "New Study Faults Pentagon's Gay Policy." *New York Times* (February 26):A8.

Sherif, M. 1936. *The Psychology of Social Norms.* New York: HarperCollins.

Shoop, R. J., and Edwards, D. L. 1994. *How to Stop Sexual Harassment in our Schools.* Boston: Allyn and Bacon.

Shweder, R. A. 1997. "It's Called Poor Health for a Reason." *New York Times* (March 9):E5.

Sidel, R. 1996. *Keeping Women and Children Last: America's War on the Poor.* New York: Penguin.

Sidel, R. 1997. "Conflict Within the Ivory Tower." In Estelle Disch (ed.), *Reconstructing Gender: A Multicultural Anthology.* Mountain View, CA: Mayfield, pp. 324–334.

Simmel, G. 1950. *The Sociology of Georg Simmel.* Ed. and Trans Kurt Wolff. Glencoe, IL: Free Press (original publication 1908).

Simon, D. R. 1996. *Elite Deviance* (5th ed.). Boston: Allyn & Bacon.

Simons, M. 1993. "France Jails Woman For Daughters' Circumcisions." *New York Times* (January 11).

Sivard, R. L. 1991. *World Military and Social Expenditures: 1991.* Washington, DC: World Priorities.

Skolnick, A., and Rosencrantz, S. 1994. "The New Crusade for the Old Family." *The American Prospect* (Summer):59–65.

Slomczynski, K. M., Miller, J., and Kohn, M. L. 1981. "Stratification, Work, and Values: A Polish–United States Comparison." *American Sociological Review* 46, 6:720–744.

Small, G. W., Propper, M. W., and Randolph, E. T. 1991. "Mass Hysteria among Student Performers: Social Relationship as a Symptom Predictor." *American Journal of Psychiatry* (September):1200–1205.

Smelser, N. J. 1963. *The Theory of Collective Behavior.* New York: Free Press.

Smelser, N. J. 1966. "The Modernization of Social Relations." In M. Weiner (ed.), *Modernization.* New York: Basic Books, pp. 110–121.

Smelser, N. J. 1981. *Sociology.* Englewood Cliffs, NJ: Prentice Hall.

Smith, E., Udry, R., and Morris, N. 1985. "Pubertal Development and Friends: A Biosocial Explanation of Adolescent Sexual Behavior." *Journal of Health and Social Behavior* 26:183–192.

Smith, T. W. 1990. "A Report: The Sexual Revolution?" *Public Opinion Quarterly* 54(3):415–435.

Snarey, J. R. 1985. "Cross-Cultural Universality of Social-Moral Development: A Critical Review of Kohlbergian Research." *Psychological Bulletin* (March): 202–320.

Sniderman, P. M., and Piazza, T. 1996. "The Scar of Race." In J. Arthur and A. Shapiro (eds.), *Class, Color, Identity: The New Politics of Race.* Boulder, CO: Westview, pp. 44–64.

Snipp, M. 1992. "Sociological Perspectives on American Indians." *Annual Review of Sociology* 18:351–371.

Snow, D. A., and Anderson, L. 1993. *Down on Their Luck: A Case Study of Homeless Street People.* Berkeley: University of California Press.

Snow, D. A., and Benford, R. D. 1988. "Ideology, Frame Resonance, and Participant Mobilization." *International Social Movement Research* 1:197–217.

Sochting, I., Skoe, E. E., and Marcia, J. E. 1994. "Care-Oriented Moral Reasoning and Prosocial Behavior: A Question of Gender or Sex-Role Orientation." *Sex Roles* 31, 3/4:131–147.

South, S., and Felson, R. 1990. "The Racial Patterning of Rape." *Social Forces.* 69(1):71–93.

Spain, D., and Bianchi, S. M. 1996. *Balancing Act: Motherhood, Marriage, and Employment.* New York: Russell Sage Foundation.

Spengler, O. 1926–1928. *The Decline of the West.* 2 Vols. Charles E. Atkinson (Trans.). New York: Alfred A. Knopf. (Original publication 1919–1922).

Spitz, R. 1945. "Hospitalism." *Psychoanalytic Study of the Child* 1:53–72.

Spitz, R. 1946. "Hospitalism: A Follow-Up Report." *Psychoanalytic Study of the Child* 2:113–117.

Spitzer, S. 1980. "Toward a Marxian Theory of Deviance." In D. H. Kelly (ed.), *Criminal Behavior: Readings in Criminology.* New York: St. Martin's Press, pp. 175–192.

Stack, C. 1986. "The Culture of Gender: Women and Men of Color." *Signs* 11, 2:321–324.

Stack, C. 1997. "Domestic Networks: 'Those You Count On.'" In C. Brettell and C. Sargent (eds.), *Gender in*

Cross-Cultural Perspective. Upper Saddle River, NJ: Prentice Hall, pp. 301–310.

Stahl, S., and Lebedun, M. 1974. "Mystery Gas: An Analysis of Mass Hysteria." *Journal of Health and Social Behavior* (March):44–50.

Stainton, M. C. 1985. "The Fetus: A Growing Member of the Family." *Family Relations* 34:321–326.

Stampp, K. 1956. *The Peculiar Institution.* New York: Alfred A. Knopf.

Stanko, B., and Miller, G. J. 1996. "Sexual Harassment and Government Accountants: Anecdotal Evidence from the Profession." *Public Personnel Management* 25 (Summer):219–35.

Stark, R., and Bainbridge, W. 1985. *The Future of Religion: Secularization, Revival, and Cult Formation.* Berkeley, CA: University of California Press.

The State of World Population 1997 Report. 1997. "Rights for Sexual Reproductive Health." In *The Right to Choose: Reproductive Rights and Reproductive Health.* [Online]. Available: http://home.ptd.net/~n . . . 997-right-to-choose.html [1997, November 11].

Steinberg, S. 1981. *The Ethnic Myth.* Boston: Beacon Press.

Stevenson, H., Lee, S., and Stigler, J. 1986. "Mathematics Achievement of Chinese, Japanese, and American Children." *Science* 231:693–699.

Stiller, N. J., and Forrest, L. 1990. "An Extension of Gilligan and Lyon's Investigation of Morality: Gender Differences in College Students." *Journal of College Student Development* 31, 1:54–63.

Stolberg, S. 1998. "U.S. Awakes to Epidemic of Sexual Diseases and Funds No Safety Net." *New York Times.* (March 9):A1, A14.

Stoller, E. P., and Gibson, R. C. 1997. *Worlds of Difference: Inequality in the Aging Experience.* Thousand Oaks, CA: Pine Forge Press.

Stouffer, S. A., Suchman, E. A., DeVinney, L. C., Starr, S. A., and Williams, R. M. 1949. *The American Soldier: Adjustment during Army Life,* Vol. 1. Princeton, NJ: Princeton University Press.

Strauss, A. (Ed.). 1970. *Where Medicine Fails.* Chicago: Aldine.

Strong, B., DeVault, C., and Sayad, B. 1996. *Core Concepts in Human Sexuality.* Mountain View, CA: Mayfield.

"Study: Blacks Seen to Portray Poverty." 1997. *Chicago Tribune.* (August 19):6.

Sue, D., Sue, D. W., and Sue, D. M. 1983. "Psychological Development of Chinese-American Children." In G. Powell (ed.), *The Psychological Development of Minority Group Children.* New York: Brunner/Mazel, pp. 159–166.

Sullivan, T. J. 1992. *Applied Sociology: Research and Critical Thinking.* New York: Macmillan.

Sumner, W. G. 1960. *Folkways.* New York: New American Library (original publication 1906).

Sutherland, E. H. 1939. *Principles of Criminology* (4th ed.). Philadelphia: Lippincott.

Sutherland, E. H. 1949. *White Collar Crime.* New York: Dryden.

Sutherland, E. H., and Cressey, D. R. 1978. *Criminology* (10th ed.). Philadelphia: Lippincott.

Swarns, R. L. 1998. "Mothers Poised for Workfare Face Acute Lack of Day Care." *New York Times* (April 14):A1.

Sweet, J. A., and Bumpass, L. L.. 1987. *American Families and Households.* New York: Russell Sage Foundation.

TAASA Program Facts. 1997. "Facts About Sexual Assault." [Online]. Available: http://www.taasa.org/facts.html [1999, January 30].

Takaki, R. T. 1998. "A Different Mirror." In M. Andersen and P. H. Collins (eds.), *Race, Class, Gender.* Belmont, CA: Wadsworth, pp. 52–65.

Takezawa, Y. I. 1995. *Breaking the Silence: Redress and Japanese American Ethnicity.* Ithaca, NY: Cornell University Press.

Tarrow, S. G. 1994. *Power in Movement: Social Movements, Collective Action, and Politics.* Cambridge, England: Cambridge University Press.

Task Force on Aging Research. 1995. *The Threshold of Discovery: Future Directions for Research on Aging.* Washington, DC: U.S. Government Printing Office.

Taubman Center for State and Local Government. 1998. *The Resegregation of American Schools.* Cambridge, MA: John F. Kennedy School of Government, Harvard University.

Tavris, C. 1993. *The Mismeasure of Women.* New York: Touchstone.

Teitelbaum, M. S., and Russell, S. S. 1994. "Fertility, International Migration, and Development." In R. Casson (ed.), *Population and Development: Old Debates, New Conclusions.* Washington, DC: Overseas Development Council, pp. 229–249.

Tennenbaum, D. J. (1977). "Personality and Criminality." *Journal of Criminal Justice* 5:1–9.

"Textbook Sexism." 1992. *Chicago Tribune* (July 12):sec. 6, p. 1.

Thomas, M. 1993. "Race, Class, and Personal Income: An Empirical Test of the Declining Significance of Race Thesis, 1968–1988." *Social Problems* 40:328–342.

Thomas, M., Herring, C., and Horton, H. 1994. "Discrimination Over the Life Course: A Synthetic Cohort Analysis of Earning Differences Between Black and White Males, 1940–1990." *Social Forces* 72:45–76.

Thompson, K. 1994. *Sociology* (Study Guide). New York: McGraw Hill.

Thompson, L., and Walker, A. J. 1989. "Women and Men in Marriage, Work, and Parenthood." *Journal of Marriage and the Family* 51:845–872.

Thompson, L., and Walker, A. J. 1991. "Gender in Families." In A. Booth (ed.), *Contemporary Families: Looking Forward, Looking Back.* Minneapolis: National Council on Family Relations, pp. 275–296.

Thompson, W., and Hickey, J. 1996. *Society in Focus.* New York: HarperCollins.

Thornton, A., and Freedman, D. 1983. "The Changing American Family." *Population Bulletin 38.* Washington, DC: Population Reference Bureau.

Tilly, C. 1978. *From Mobilization to Revolution.* Reading, MA: Addison-Wesley.

Tipton, S. M. 1982. *Getting Saved from the Sixties: Moral Meaning in Conversion and Cultural Change.* Berkeley: University of California Press.

Torrens, P. R. *Hospice Programs and Public Policy.* Chicago: American Hospital Publishing.

Tower, C. 1989. *Understanding Child Abuse and Neglect.* Boston: Allyn & Bacon.

Townsend, A., and Luthar, H. K. 1995. "How Do the Men Feel?" *HRMagazine* (May):92–94.

Toynbee, A. 1946. *A Study of History.* New York: Oxford University Press.

"Transgendered Economist Publishes First Book as a Woman." 1997. *Chronicle of Higher Education* (May 2):A15.

Troeltsch, E. 1931. *The Social Teaching of the Christian Churches.* New York: Macmillan.

Tsai, S. 1998. "World Health Organization AIDS." [Online]. http://apollo.gse.uci.edu/chsmun/WHO.HTML [1998, August 8].

Tumin, M. 1953. "Some Principles of Stratification: A Critical Analysis." *American Sociological Review* 18:378–394.

Turner, P. A. 1993. *I Heard It through the Grapevine: Rumor in African-American Culture.* Berkeley: University of California Press.

Turner, R. H. 1994. "Race Riots Past and Present: A Cultural-Collective Behavior Approach." *Symbolic Interaction* 17:309.

Turner, R. H., and Killian, L. M. 1987. *Collective Behavior* (3rd ed.). Englewood Cliffs, NJ: Prentice Hall.

Turner, R., and Killian, L. 1993. *Collective Behavior* (5th ed.). Englewood Cliffs, NJ: Prentice Hall.

Twaddle, A., and Kessler, R. 1987. *A Sociology of Health* (2nd ed.). New York: Macmillan.

U.S. Bureau of the Census. 1975. *Historical Statistics of the United States: Colonial Times to 1970* (Bicentennial ed., part 1). Washington, DC: U.S. Government Printing Office.

U.S. Bureau of the Census. 1992. *Statistical Abstract of the United States, 1992.* Washington, DC: U.S. Government Printing Office.

U.S. Bureau of the Census. 1994. *Statistical Abstract of the United States, 1994.* Washington, DC: U.S. Government Printing Office.

U.S. Bureau of the Census. 1995. *Statistical Abstract of the United States, 1995.* Washington, DC: Government Printing Office.

U.S. Bureau of the Census. 1996. *Statistical Abstract of the United States, 1996.* Washington, DC: Government Printing Office.

U.S. Bureau of the Census. 1997. *Statistical Abstract of the United States, 1997.* Washington, DC: Government Printing Office.

U.S. Bureau of the Census. 1998. *Statistical Abstract of the United States, 1998.* Washington, DC.: U.S. Government Printing Office.

U.S. Department of Education, National Center for Education Statistics. 1992. *The Condition of Education.* Washington, DC: U.S. Government Printing Office.

U.S. Department of Education. 1993. *Adult Literacy in America.* Washington, DC: National Center for Education Studies.

U.S. Department of Education. 1997. *1994 Elementary and Secondary School Civil Rights Compliance Report.* Washington, DC: U.S. Department of Education.

U.S. Department of Health and Human Services. 1996. "Health, United States, 1996." [Online]. Available: http://www.cac.gov/nchswww/data/hus96.Paf [1999, March 5].

U.S. Department of Health and Human Services. 1998. "AIDS Falls from Top Ten Causes of Death; Teen Births, Infant Mortality, Homicide all Decline." [Online]. Available: http://www.cac.gov/nch . . . ws/98news/aidsmort.html [October 7].

U.S. Department of Justice, Bureau of Justice Statistics. 1999. *A National Crime Victimization Survey Report.* [Online]. Available: http://www.ojp.usdoj.gov/bjs/pub/asci/CV97.txt.

U.S. Department of Justice, Federal Bureau of Investigation. 1996. *Crimes in the United States, 1995.* Washington, DC: Government Printing Office.

United Farm Workers homepage, http://www.ufw.org/98.htm.

United Nations Development Program. 1991. *Human Development Report.* New York: Oxford University Press.

"UPS Manager Awarded Millions for Harassment." 1998. *New York Times* (February 13):A16.

Valocchi, S. 1993. "External Resources and the Unemployed Councils of the 1930s: Evaluating Six Propositions from Social Movement Theory." *Sociological Forum* 8:451–470.

van der Gaag, N. 1997. "Women: Still Something to Shout About." In Robert M. Jackson (ed.), *Annual Editions: Global Issues 97/98.* Guilford, CN: Dushkin/McGraw-Hill, pp. 254–256.

Veblen, T. 1922. *The Instinct of Workmanship.* New York: Huebsch.

Verbruge, L. 1985. "Gender and Health: An Update on Hypotheses and Evidence." *Journal of Health and Social Behavior* 26:156–182.

Verhovek, S. H. 1999. "Record for Women in Washington Legislature." *New York Times* (Feb. 4):A14.

Virshup, A. 1997. "Surfing Tidal Wave." *The Washington Post Magazine: A Special Issue About Education* (February 2):1–12; 24–30.

Vogt, A. 1997. "Even in Virtual Reality, It Is Still a Man's World." *Chicago Tribune* (August 24):sec. 13, 1.

Waitzkin, H. 1997. "A Marxian Interpretation of the Growth and Development of Coronary Care Technology." In P. Conrad (ed.), *The Sociology of Health and Illness.* New York: St. Martin's, pp. 247–259.

Wallace, R., and Wolf, A. 1991. *Contemporary Sociological Theory.* Englewood Cliffs, NJ: Prentice Hall.

Wallace, R. L. 1983. *Those Who Have Vanished: An Introduction to Prehistory.* Homewood, IL: Dorsey.

Wallechinsky, D. 1997. "How One Woman Became the Voice of Her People." *Parade* (January 19):4.

Wallerstein, I. 1974. *The Modern World System: Capitalist Agriculture and the Origins of the European World-Economy in the Sixteenth Century.* New York: Academic Press.

Wallerstein, I. 1984. *The Politics of the World-Economy: The States, the Movements, and the Civilizations.* Cambridge, England: Cambridge University Press.

Wallerstein, I. 1990. "Culture as the Ideological Battleground of the Modern World-System." In M. Featherstone (ed.), *Global Culture: Nationalism, Globalization, and Modernity.* London: Sage, pp. 31–55.

Wanner, R. A., and Lewis, L. S. 1978. "The Functional Theory of Stratification: A Test of Some Structural Hypotheses." *Sociological Quarterly* 19:414–428.

Wardwell, W. 1979. "Limited, Marginal, and Quasi-Practitioners." In H. E. Freeman, S. Levine, and L. Reeder (eds.), *Handbook of Medical Sociology* (2nd ed.). Englewood Cliffs, NJ: Prentice Hall, pp. 250–273.

Watters, W. W. 1992. *Deadly Doctrine: Health, Illness, and Christian God-Talk.* Amherst, NY: Prometheus.

Weber, M. 1922. *The Sociology of Religion.* Boston: Beacon.

Weber, M. 1968. *Economy and Society: An Outline of Interpretive Sociology.* G. Roth and G. Wittich (Trans.). New York: Bedminster Press. (original publication 1922).

Weber, M. 1976. *The Protestant Ethic and the Spirit of Capitalism.* Talcott Parsons (Trans). New York: Scribner (original publication 1904–1905).

Weikel, D. 1995. "War on Crack Targets Minorities over Whites." *Los Angeles Times* (May 21):Al.

Weinberg, D. H. 1998. "Income and Poverty 1997." Press Briefing on 1997 Income and Poverty Estimates. Washington, DC: U.S. Census Bureau, Housing and Household Economic Statistics Division.

Weiner, A. 1988. *The Trobrianders of Papua, New Guinea.* New York: Rinehart and Winston.

Weiss, G. L., and Lonnquist, L. E. 1994. *The Sociology of Health, Healing, and Illness.* Englewood Cliffs, NJ: Prentice-Hall.

Weiss, S. 1994a. "Negotiating with 'Romans'—Part 1." *Sloan Management Review* 35,2:51–61.

Weiss, S. 1994b. "Negotiating with 'Romans'—Part 2." *Sloan Management Review* 35, 2:85–99.

Weitz, R. 1995. *A Sociology of Health, Illness, and Health Care.* Belmont, CA: Wadsworth.

Weldon, M. 1998. "Districts Ban Morrison, Angelou Books." *Chicago Tribune* (January 25):13, 3.

Welter, B. 1978. "The Cult of True Womanhood: 1820–1860." In M. Gordon (ed.), *The American Family in Social-Historical Perspective.* New York: St. Martin's Press, pp. 313–333.

Werbe, P. 1998. "Rich Get Much Richer: More Wealth for the Forbes 400." [Online]. Available: http://www. goodfelloweb.com/werbe/forbes400.html [December 3].

Western, B. 1993. "Postwar Unionization in Eighteen Advanced Capitalist Countries." *American Sociological Review* (April):266–282.

Western, B. 1995. "A Comparative Study of Working-Class Disorganization: Union Decline in Eighteen Advanced Capitalist Countries." *American Sociological Review* (April):179–201.

Westside Crisis Pregnancy Center. 1997. "The Media and Adolescent Sexual Activity." [Online]. Available: http://www.w-cpc.org/sexuality/media.html [1999, January 28].

Wharton, A. (Ed.). 1998. *Working in America: Continuity, Conflict, and Change.* Mountain View, CA: Mayfield.

"What Specific Health Concerns Do Lesbians, Gay Men, Bisexuals, and Transgendered People Face?" 1998. Georgetown University Student Affairs: Health Education Services. [Online]. Available: http://www. georgetown. . . ./healthed/glbhealt.html [1999, March 5].

Whatley, M. H. 1994. "Keeping Adolescents in the Picture: Construction of Adolescent Sexuality in Textbook Images and Popular Films." In J. M. Irvine (ed.), *Sexual Cultures and the Construction of Adolescent Identities.* Philadelphia: Temple University Press, pp. 183–205.

White, A. J. 1991. "Dyad/Triad." In P. Bell-Scott, B. Guy-Sheftall, J. Royster, J. Sims-Wood, M. DeCosta-Willis, and L. Fultz (eds.), *Double Stitch: Black Women Write about Mothers and Daughters.* Boston: Beacon, pp. 188–195.

Whitehead, B. D. 1997. *The Divorce Culture.* New York: Alfred Knopf.

Whitney, J. 1995. "When Talk Gets Too Cheap." *U.S. News & World Report* 18 (June 12): 57–8.

Whorf, B. 1956. *Language, Thought, and Reality.* New York: Wiley.

Wickham, T. 1997. "AFL-CIO to Push for Equal Breaks for Working Women." *The Flint Journal* (September 4) [Online]. Available: http://fl.mlive.com/business/ 4women$.03.htm.

Wilber, R. 1997. "Searching for Terms." In Fred Schultz (ed.), *Education: Annual Editions 97/98.* Guilford, CT: Dushkin/McGraw-Hill, pp. 265–272.

Wilford, J. N. 1997. "Ancient Graves of Armed Women Hint at Amazons." *New York Times* (February 25):B7.

Williams, C. 1992. "The Glass Escalator: Hidden Advantages for Men in the 'Female' Professions." *Social Problems* (August):253–267.

Williams, D., Takeuchi, D., and Adair, R. 1992. "Socioeconomic Status and Psychiatric Disorders Among Blacks and Whites." *Social Forces* 71:179–195.

Williams, R. M. 1970. *American Society: A Sociological Interpretation* (3rd ed.). New York: Knopf.

Williams, W. I. 1986. *The Spirit and the Flesh: Sexual Diversity in American Indian Culture.* Boston: Beacon.

Willie, C. V. 1989. *Caste and Class Controversy on Race and Poverty.* New York: General Hall.

Wilson, E., and Ng, S. H. 1988. "Sex Bias in Visual Images Evoked by Generics: A New Zealand Study." *Sex Roles* 18:159–168.

Wilson, E. O. 1978. *On Human Nature.* Cambridge, MA: Harvard University Press.

Wilson, W. 1988. "Rape as Entertainment." *Psychological Reports* 63(2):607–610.

Wilson, W. J. 1978. *The Declining Significance of Race: Blacks and Changing American Institutions.* Chicago: University of Chicago Press.

Wilson, W. J. 1987. *The Truly Disadvantaged: The Inner City, The Underclass, and Public Policy.* Chicago: University of Chicago Press.

Wilson, W. J. 1996. *When Work Disappears: The World of the New Urban Poor*. New York: Alfred A. Knopf.

Wineberg, H. 1994. "Marital Reconciliation in the United States: Which Couples Are Successful?" *Journal of Marriage and the Family* (February):80–88.

Witt, L. 1994. "Woman Warrior." *Mother Jones* (September/October): p. 15, http://medusa.prod.oclc.org:3051/F . . . tml/fs-fulltext.htm%22:fstxtr.htm.

Woodard, C. 1997. "Student Protests over Elections in Bulgaria and Yugoslavia End in Victory." *The Chronicle of Higher Education* (February 14):A45.

"Women Politicos War on Musical 'Garbage.'" 1993. *Jet* (September 6):59.

Worden, J. W. 1982. *Grief Counseling and Grief Therapy: A Handbook for the Mental Health Practitioner*. NY: Springer-Verlag.

The World Bank. 1995. *World Development Report 1995: Workers in an Integrating World*. New York: Oxford University Press.

World Health Organization. 1995. Cited in "Rise in STDs Concerns Group." *Newsday* (September 12):B27.

World Health Organization. 1997. "UN Agencies Call for End to Female Genital Mutilation." Press Release WHO/29. [Online]. Available: http://www.who.ch/press/1997/pr97-29.html [1997, November 11].

World Health Organization. 1998. "Executive Summary: Life in the 21st Century—A Vision For All." *1998 World Health Report*. [Online]. Available: http://www.who.org/whr/1998/exsum98e.htm.

Wright, E. O. 1985. *Classes*. London: Verso.

Wright, E. O. 1989a. "A General Framework for the Analysis of Class Structure." In E. O. Wright et al., *The Debate on Classes*. London: Verso, pp. 3–46.

Wright, E. O. 1989b. "Rethinking, Once Again, the Concept of Class Structure." In E. O. Wright et al., *The Debate on Classes*. London: Verso, pp. 269–348.

Wright, E. O. 1996. "Marxism after Communism." In S. P. Turner (ed.), *Social Theory and Sociology: The Classics and Beyond*. Cambridge, MA: Blackwell, pp. 121–145.

Wronski, R. 1995. "Experts Sing Praises of Prayer." *Chicago Tribune* (December 6):14.

Wurtele, S., Melzer, A., and Kast, L. 1992. "Preschoolers Knowledge of and Ability to Learn Genital Terminology." *Journal of Sex Education and Therapy* 18(2):115–122.

Yacker, N., and Weinberg, S. L. 1990. "Care and Justice Moral Orientation: A Scale for its Assessment." *Journal of Personality Assessment* 55,1/2:18–27.

Yanagisako, S. J. 1977. "Women-Centered Kin Networks in Urban Bilateral Kinship." *American Ethnologist* 2:207–226.

Zack, N. 1998 *Thinking about Race*. Belmont, CA: Wadsworth.

Zastrow, C. 1995. *Social Problems: Issues and Solutions* (4th ed.). Chicago: Nelson-Hall.

Zborowski, M. 1952. "Cultural Components in Responses to Pain." *Journal of Social Issues* 8:16–30.

Zeitlin, I. M. 1994. *Ideology and the Development of Sociological Theory* (5th ed.). Englewood Cliffs, NJ: Prentice Hall.

Zimbardo, P. 1972. "Pathology of Imprisonment." *Society* (April) 9:4–8.

Ziv, L., and Claire, M. 1997. "The Tragedy of Female Circumcision." In S. J. Bunting (ed.), *Human Sexuality: Annual Editions*. Guilford, CT: Dushkin/McGraw-Hill, pp. 9–12.

Zuckerman, D. M., Kasl, S. V., and Ostfeld, A. M. 1984. "Psychosocial Predictors of Mortality among the Elderly Poor. The Role of Religion, Well-Being, and Social Contacts." *American Journal of Epidemiology* 119:410–423.

Zurcher, L. A., Jr. 1996. "Navy Boot Camp: Role Assimilation in a Total Institution." In J. W. and M. Mason (eds.), *Sociology Windows on Society* (4th ed.). Los Angeles, CA: Roxbury, pp. 56–61.

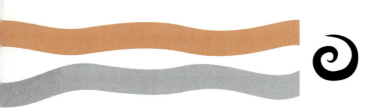

Name Index

Clinton, W. J., 64, 117, 189, 250, 298, 304, 364, 394, 420, 424, 430, 433, 465, 475
Cloward, R. A., 217
Cockerham, W. C., 439, 443, 446, 447, 448, 449, 450, 460
Cole, S., 346
Coleman, D., 450
Coleman, M., 363
Coles, R., 177
Collins, P. H., 12, 145, 280
Collins, S., 298
Coltrane, S., 356
Comte, A., 12, 17, 35
Connelly, M., 158n
Conrad, P., 441, 464
Cooley, C. H., 40, 121, 122, 142, 145–146
Coontz, S., 337, 339
Corsaro, W. A., 146
Cortese, A. J. P., 144
Cosby, W., 290
Cose, E., 357
Coser, L. A., 9, 123, 215
Cox, O., 279–280
Cressey, D. R., 214
Crouter, A. C., 356
Crown, J., 144
Crystal, G., 240
Cullen, J. B., 239
Curran, D. J., 193, 265
Curtis, J. E., 128
Curtiss, S., 142
Cyrus, V., 24, 25, 477

Dahl, R. A., 426
Dahrendorf, R., 65
Dale, R., 385
Darrett, B., 361
Darrow, C., 222–223, 371
Darwin, C., 12–13
Dasi, G., 117, 119
Davidson, J., 90
Davies, J. C., 79
Davis, G., 51
Davis, J. A., 185
Davis, K., 141, 238, 240
Dean, A., 124
Deardorff, J., 393
Degeneres, E., 186
de Klerk, F. W., 423, 424
de la Garza, R. O., 56
DeLamaster, J., 177
Delany, B., 324
Delany, S., 324
Delgado, R., 266
Deloria, V., 288
D'Emilio, J., 187
Demo, D. H., 355
DePalma, A., 202
De Saint-Simon, H., 408–409
DeSpelder, L. A., 201
Deukmejian, G., 406
Diamond, M., 184
Diana, Princess of Wales, 150, 429
Dickson, W. J., 133
di Leonardo, M., 346
Dillon, S., 414

Disch, E., 383
Divine, R., 103
Dobrzynski, J. H., 305n
Dodge, K., 142
Doka, K., 463
Dole, R., 89
Dollard, J., 278
Domhoff, G. W., 124, 425
Domingue, S., 394n
Doob, C. B., 271, 274, 283
Dovidio, J., 274
Dowling, P. J. U., 451
Doyle, J. A., 193
Du Bois, W. E. B., 18–20
Duke, B., 386
Duncan, D. F., 180
Duncan, O. D., 251
Duneier, M., 6
Dunn, J., 147
Durkheim, E., 14–15, 21, 35, 215, 220, 372, 373, 414
Dyer, K., 433
Dyson, M., 106

Eckersley, R., 109
Eder, D., 146
Eichar, D. M., 418
Eisenhower, D. W., 425
Elizabeth II, Queen of England, 429
Ellis, A., 444
Elmer-Dewitt, P., 173
English, D., 5
Enroth, R., 445
Erikson, E., 157
Ermann, M. D., 209
Esbensen, F., 217
Etzioni, A., 128

Faison, S., 359
Farber, S., 141
Farley, J., 282, 296
Faruqi, A., 82
Faubus, O., 82
Feagin, C. B., 296
Feagin, J. R., 132, 191, 273, 277, 296, 459
Featherstone, M., 476
Felner, J., 406n
Felson, R., 146, 180
Fernea, E., 96
Ferrante, J., 25, 285
Ferraro, K. J., 49
Finkelhor, D., 191
Finlay, B., 359
Foner, P. S., 419
Ford, C. S., 185
Ford, R. L., 407
Forrest, L., 144
Fowler, R. B., 376n, 380
Frankenberg, R., 45–46, 47, 51, 152
Franks, P., 446
Franks, R., 222
Freedman, D., 353
Freeman, D. H., 444
Freud, S., 142–143, 177, 444
Friere, P., 369
Fromm, E., 156
Furstenberg, F. F., Jr., 339, 360

Gaertner, S. L., 274
Gagnon, J. H., 177
Galilei, G., 8
Gallagher, C. A., 270
Gamson, W., 78
Gandhi, M. K., 75, 232, 425
Ganong, L. H., 363
Gans, H., 255
Garfinkel, H., 41–42, 160
Garvey, M., 20
Gates, W., 232, 244, 408, 415
Geiss, S. K., 359
George VI, King of England, 429
Gerlach, M. L., 408
Gerritsen, T., 53, 54
Gibbs, N., 191
Gibson, P., 451
Gibson, R. C., 140, 158, 340n, 462n
Gilbert, D., 247, 248, 249
Gilbert, S., 157
Gilens, M., 150
Gill, R. T., 339
Gilligan, C., 144–145, 157
Gittens, D., 337
Glazer, N., 271, 339
Glenn, N. D., 359
Glick, H., 201
Glueck, E., 214
Glueck, S., 214
Godson, R., 209, 222
Godwin, D. D., 355
Goering, L., 422
Goffman, E., 40–41, 129, 160, 204
Goldberg, C., 221
Golden, R., 369–370, 375
Goldstein, M. C., 341
Gollin, A., 173, 190
Gonzales, M., 464
Goodman, S., 142
Goodstein, L., 157, 158n
Gordon, M., 280
Gorham, J., 244n
Goring, C., 213
Gottfredson, M. R., 217
Gove, W., 7
Gracey, H., 398
Greene, B., 157
Greenhouse, S., 4n, 5
Groad, H. T., 352
Gwynne, S. C., 419

Habenstein, R. W., 355
Haddad, Y. Y., 375
Haizlip, S. T., 270
Hale-Benson, J., 148
Hall, D. R., 7
Hall, P. M., 268
Hamburg, D. A., 357
Hamburg, G. V., 370
Hamilton, C. V., 273
Harmston, J., 342
Harrison, E., 443
Hart, N., 449
Haslam, N., 345n
Hatch, O., 408
Hatfield, E., 171, 172, 183, 185
Hayghe, H. V., 356
Hayman, J., 264n

Subject Index

International Labor Organization, 4, 318
International Monetary Fund, 476
International organized crime, 222–223
Internet, gaining information through, 161–162
Internment, 292
Interpretive (social constructionist) perspective, on human sexuality, 176–177
Interracial marriages, 351–352
Interviews, 52
Intestinal helminth infection, 453
Intimate relationships, developing, 350–352. See also Families; Marriage
Intragenerational mobility, 251
Invention, and social change, 67
Invitation to Sociology, An (Berger), 5
Ireland, human sexuality in, 170
Iron law of oligarchy, 132
Islam (Muslims), 321, 377
Isolated children, socialization of, 141–142

Japan
    courtship in, 351
    discrimination in, 119–120
    elderly in, 353
Japanese Americans
    internment of, 292
    as percentage of Asian Americans, 291
    race relations with, 291–292
J-curve theory of social movements, 79
Jews, 377
    American, 296
    discrimination against, 123, 266
    prejudice and, 272
    race relations with, 296
    sexuality among, 172
Job alienation, 418–419
Job satisfaction, 418
Joe Camel, 125
Judaism, 377. See also Jews
Junta, 430
Justice, U.S. Department of, 207n, 210, 408
Juvenile delinquency, 210

Kapital, Das (Marx), 13
Khasis of Meghalaya, 345
Kinship, 344–346. See also Families
Knowledge, 96
Korean Americans
    African Americans and, 292–293
    as percentage of Asian Americans, 291
    race relations and, 292–293
Kukabula, 440
Ku Klux Klan, 263–264, 265, 289, 290

Labeling theory of deviance, 218–219
Labor, division of, 130, 355–356. See also Work
Labor, U.S. Department of, 304, 320n

Labor force
    children in, 3–4, 157
    diversity of, 417–418
    international, 413–414
    job alienation in, 418–419
    job satisfaction in, 418
    women in, 253, 256, 303–304, 305–306, 307–313, 353–357
Labor-force participation rate, 307–308
Labor-management relationships, 419–421
Labor relations, law on, 420
Labor Statistics, U.S. Bureau of, 304
Labor unions
    agricultural workers and, 404, 405–406
    labor-management relationships and, 419–421
    women and, 303–304, 422
Laissez-faire capitalism, 407, 409
Landmines, 431
Language, 92–93
Latchkey kids, 157
Latent functions, 36
Latinas/os
    causes of death in, 448
    comparative well-being in United States, 288
    education of, 386, 387, 389, 390, 395
    elderly, 327
    ethnic origins of, 293
    health insurance coverage for, 330
    locations of, 293
    in politics, 428
    poverty among, 252, 253
    race relations with, 293–294
    research and, 56
    sexual behavior of, 174
Laws, 94–95
    on affordable housing, 228
    on age discrimination, 322, 327–328
    on child abuse, 363
    on civil rights, 289, 418
    on compensation for internment, 292
    on disabilities, 441, 452
    on education, 396
    on hate crimes, 187
    on immigration, 291
    on labor relations, 420
    on land ownership by aliens, 292
    on monopolies, 407
    on product safety, 407
    on vocational rehabilitation, 80
    on voting rights, 264
    on welfare reform, 364
Laying of hands, 465
Learning, sexual. See Sexual learning
Lesbian(s), 174, 175, 184–187
Lesbian families, 338
Liberals, fair-weather, 276
Liberation theology, 369–370
Liberty, as value, 98
Life chances, 233–234
Life course, 155–160
Life expectancy, 358, 439, 440

Life on the Color Line (Williams), 153
Linguistic-relativity hypothesis, 93
Literacy, 313, 400
Literature
    Amistad (Pesci), 284
    "Between the Funerals" (Tracy), 340
    Bonfire of the Vanities (Wolfe), 411
    Compulsion (Levin), 222–223
    Harvest (Gerritsen), 54
    Having Our Say (Delany and Delany), 324
    The House on Mango Street (Cisneros), 249, 250
    Inherit the Wind (Lawrence and Lee), 371
    Life on the Color Line (Williams), 153
    Pigs in Heaven (Kingsolver), 118
    Redburn (Melville), 9–10
    reviewing, in research process, 46
    "A Summer Tragedy" (Bontemps), 462
    The War of the Worlds (Wells), 73–74
    Your Blues Ain't Like Mine (Campbell), 192
Lockheed Martin Corp., 415
Lockouts, 419
Longevity, 324, 326, 327, 450. See also Aging; Elderly
Looking-glass self, 145–146
Losing Ground: American Social Policy, 1950–1980 (Murray), 364

Macropolitics, 423
Magazines. See Print media
Majority group, 271–272
Malpractice, 463–464
Managed care, 466–467
Mangaian culture, 170
Manifest destiny, 283
Manifest functions, 36
Marginal sector, 418
Marital rape, 189–190, 191
Marital status, of elderly, 327
Marriage
    cenogamy, 342
    child care in, 356–357
    commuter, 354
    contrasting views of, 336–337
    courtship and, 350–352
    death of spouse in, 362
    decision making in, 355
    defined, 337–338
    divorce and, 357–360
    dual-earner couples in, 354–355
    future concerns of, 363–364
    group, 342
    interethnic, 340
    interracial, 351–352
    parenting decision in, 352–353
    polyandry, 341
    polygamy, 341, 342–343
    polygyny, 341–343
    remarriage, 362–363
    satisfaction in, 357
    social, 338
    theories of, 346–350

Racial cleansing, 285–286
Racial formation, 268, 269
Racial socialization, 151–154
Racism, 265–280
    aversive, 274
    cultural, 271
    defined, 265
    environmental, 31–32, 39–40
    individual, 273
    institutional, 273–274
    prejudice and, 273–274
    social action and, 477–478
    symbolic, 274
    in U.S. military, 433
    values and, 98
    violence and, 263–264, 265, 290,
        291
Racist ideology, 265–266
Random sample, 47
Rape, 189–193
    acquaintance, 189–190
    of children, 191, 193
    defined, 189
    marital, 189–190, 191
    mass, 318–319
    sexual scripts and, 179
    statistics on, 190
    as weapon of war, 318–319
Rationalization, 130
Rational-legal authority, 424
Rational proof, 8
Real culture, 99
Rebellion, 216–217
Reconstituted families, 338
Redburn (Melville), 9
Reference groups, 123–124
Reform
    educational, 395–397
    of health care system, 465–467
    of welfare system, 364
Reform movements, 79–80
Relative deprivation theory, 78–79
Relative poverty, 252
Relativistic fallacy, 102
Reliability, of research, 46
Religion, 369–382
    capitalism and, 15
    caste system and, 230–231,
        232–233, 374
    churches and, 372, 377–378
    civil, 378
    cults and, 380
    defined, 372
    education and, 370–372
    focus of, 8
    forms of organization in, 376–380
    fundamentalist revivals, 381–382
    future concerns in, 381–382
    gender and, 376
    health and, 444–445
    liberation theology and, 369–370
    meaning of, 372
    polygamy and, 342–343
    sects and, 378–380
    as social institution, 133
    sociological perspectives on,
        372–376
    statistics on, 377

    symbols of, 379
    technology and, 381
    in United States, 380–381
    women and, 369–370, 375, 376
Religious movements, 81–82
Religious nationalism, 382
Relocation camps, 292
Remarriage, 362–363
Reparations, 298
Representative democracy, 429
Reproduction. See Parenting
Reputational approach, 246
Research, 44–52
    activist, 57
    conclusions in, 51–52
    data analysis in, 51–52
    data collection in, 46–51
    diversity and, 56–57
    ethics in, 48, 52–56, 127
    field, 48–50, 52
    literature review in, 46
    problem definition in, 45–46
    reliability of, 46
    research design in, 46–48
    scientific method in, 44–52
    technology and, 56
    theory and, 32–33, 44
    trends in, 57
    validity of, 46
Research design, 46–48
Resegregation, 395–396
Reservations, for Native Americans,
    286–287
Residential segregation, 282
Resistance movements, 80–81
Resocialization, 151, 160, 161
Resource mobilization theory, 78
Responsibility
    for household labor, 355–356
    sexual, 193–194
Retreatism, 216, 217
Reverse discrimination, 276, 298
Reverse socialization, 150–151
Revolution, 66, 80
Rights. See Civil rights; Human rights
Riot, 75
Rising expectations, 79
Rite of passage, 33
Ritual(s)
    defined, 372
    initiation, 161
    rites of passage, 33
Ritualism
    bureaucratic, 131
    deviance and, 216
Roe v. Wade decision, 77
Role, 117–121
    doctor, 442
    gender, 307
    sick, 442
Role conflict, 120
Role exit, 120
Role expectations, 117, 119–120
Role overload, 120
Role performance, 120
Role set, 117
Role strain, 120
Role taking, 146–147

Routinization, 425
Rules and regulations, 130
Rumors, 71–72

Sacred, 372
Samaritans: The Mitch Snyder Story
    (TV movie), 228
Sample, in research, 47
Sanctions, 95, 220
Sandwich generation, 159
Sapir-Whorf hypothesis, 93
Satanic Verses, The (Rushdie), 8
Scapegoat, 278
Schistosomiasis, 453
Schools
    as agent of socialization, 148,
        383–384
    alternative, 398
    assimilation and, 384
    change and innovation and, 385
    choice in, 397
    desegregation of, 395–396
    hidden curriculum in, 148, 385
    home, 398
    per pupil expenditures in, 390–391
    restructuring of, 397–399
    violence in, 392–394
    voucher system for, 397
Science, as value, 98
Scientific medicine, 441
Scientific method, 44–52
Secondary deviance, 219
Secondary groups, 122
Secondary sector, 416
Secondary socialization, 156
Sect, religious, 378–380
Sectarian conflict, 374
Segregation
    defined, 282
    desegregation and, 395–396
    hypersegregation, 282
    occupational, 308–309
    race and ethnic relations and,
        281–282, 298
    resegregation and, 395–396
    residential, 282
Self
    defined, 140
    looking-glass, 145–146
    social, 145–147
Self-esteem, and gender, 157
Self-fulfilling prophecies, 150
Sensorimotor stage of cognitive devel-
    opment, 143
Sentencing, creative, 221
Separation by Sex: A Critical Look at
    Single-Sex Education for Girls,
    399
Serial monogamy, 341
Setting Limits (Callahan), 468
Sex, vs. gender, 306–307
Sex-change surgery, 188
Sex drive, 177
Sex ratio, 327
Sex-typed materials, in classroom,
    314–315
Sexual assault, 189–193
Sexual evolution, 173

(continued from page ii)

p. 49, Ovie Carter; p. 60, Anat Givon/Sygma; p. 68, Mimi Forsyth/Monkmeyer; p. 88, AP/Wide World Photos; p. 97, Corbis/Bettmann; p. 108, Paul Conklin/Monkmeyer; p. 112, Aliana/The Gamma Liaison Network; p. 123, Corbis/Bettmann-UPI; p. 129, Andrew Lichtenstein/The Image Works; p. 138, José Adorno/Courtesy of Strive; p. 145, Will Faller, p. 157, Brian Smith; p. 166, M. Grant/UN Photo 185 291; p. 174, Lee Snider/The Image Works; p. 186, Rommel Pecson/Impact Visuals; p. 198, AP/Wide World Photos; p. 206, AP/Wide World Photos; p. 213, Marilyn Humphries/Impact Visuals; p. 226, Corbis/Bettmann; p. 241, Fredrik Bodin/Stock, Boston; p. 254, Dave LaBelle/The Image Works; p. 262, Walter P. Reuther Library/Wayne State University; p. 281, J. Sohm/The Image Works; p. 289, Piet van Lier/Impact Visuals; p. 302, AFL-CIO File Photo; p. 312, Robert Harbison; p. 326, AP/Wide World Photos; p. 334, Leo Sorel; p. 348, Nancy Sheehan/Index Stock Imagery; p. 360, Will Hart; p. 368, Courtesy of Renny Golden; p. 384, Will Hart; p. 396, Will Faller; p. 404, Corbis/Bettmann-UPI; p. 420, Erik Lesser/Gamma Liaison; p. 424, Reuters/Pool/Archive Photos; p. 432, Tom Stoddart/Katz/Woodfin Camp & Associates; p. 436, Anne Nosten/Gamma Liaison; p. 449, Mel Rosenthal/The Image Works; p. 456, AP/Wide World Photos; p. 459, Ann Marie Rousseau/The Image Works; p. 472, AP/Wide World Photos.

Color Inserts

Front Insert: p. 1: top left, Catherine Karnow/Woodfin Camp & Associates; top right, Bob Daemmrich/The Image Works; middle left, Tom McCarthy/Index Stock Imagery; bottom left, Steven Rubin/The Image Works, bottom right, Will Hart; p. 2: top left, Reuters/Mike Fisher/Archive Photos; top right, Reuters/HO/Archive Photos; bottom left, Reuters/Str/Archive Photos; bottom right, Tim Reese/The Image Works; p. 3: top, Corbis/Richard T. Nowitz; middle, Bernard Wolf/Monkmeyer; bottom left, A. Ramey/Woodfin Camp & Associates; bottom right, Steven Rubin/The Image Works; p. 4: top left, AP/World Wide Photos; top right, Ed Lallo/Index Stock Imagery; bottom left, Janice Fullman/Index Stock Imagery; bottom right, L. Mulvehill/The Image Works.

Back Insert: p. 1: top left, A. Ramey/PhotoEdit; middle left, D. Harse/The Image Works; bottom left, John Coletti/Index Stock Imagery; right, Emil Muench/Photo Researchers; p. 2: top, Rick Winsor/Woodfin Camp & Associates; middle, Robert Harbison; bottom, Robert Harbison; p. 3: top, Reuters/Lou Dematteis/Archive Photos; bottom, Larry Downing/Woodfin Camp & Associates; p. 4: top, M. Farrell/The Image Works, middle, AP/Wide World Photos; bottom, AP/Wide World Photos.